T0235289

Lecture Notes in Computer Science　　9127

Commenced Publication in 1973
Founding and Former Series Editors:
Gerhard Goos, Juris Hartmanis, and Jan van Leeuwen

More information about this series at http://www.springer.com/series/7412

Rasmus R. Paulsen · Kim S. Pedersen (Eds.)

Image Analysis

19th Scandinavian Conference, SCIA 2015
Copenhagen, Denmark, June 15–17, 2015
Proceedings

 Springer

Editors
Rasmus R. Paulsen
Technical University of Denmark
Lyngby
Denmark

Kim S. Pedersen
University of Copenhagen
Copenhagen
Denmark

ISSN 0302-9743 ISSN 1611-3349 (electronic)
Lecture Notes in Computer Science
ISBN 978-3-319-19664-0 ISBN 978-3-319-19665-7 (eBook)
DOI 10.1007/978-3-319-19665-7

Library of Congress Control Number: 2015939817

LNCS Sublibrary: SL6 – Image Processing, Computer Vision, Pattern Recognition, and Graphics

Springer Cham Heidelberg New York Dordrecht London

Printed on acid-free paper

Springer International Publishing AG Switzerland is part of Springer Science+Business Media (www.springer.com)

Preface

The 19th Scandinavian Conference on Image Analysis was held at the IT University of Copenhagen in Denmark during June 15-17, 2015. The SCIA conference series has been an ongoing biannual event for more than 30 years and over the years it has nurtured a world-class regional research and development area within the four participating Nordic countries. It is a regional meeting of the International Association for Pattern Recognition (IAPR).

We would like to thank all authors who submitted works to this year's SCIA, the invited speakers, and our Program Committee.

In total 67 papers were submitted to SCIA 2015 and were reviewed by members of the Program Committee and additional reviewers. Each paper was reviewed by at least two independent reviewers followed by a meta-review by the Program Committee. Finally, 26 papers were chosen for oral presentation and 19 papers for poster presentation. The topics of the accepted papers range from novel applications of vision systems, pattern recognition, machine learning, feature extraction, segmentation, 3D vision, to medical and biomedical image analysis. The papers originate from all the Scandinavian countries and several other European countries.

It is our sincere hope that the participants had an enjoyable and fruitful experience, both scientifically and socially, in Copenhagen.

June 2015   Rasmus R. Paulsen
                                                                                        Kim Steenstrup Pedersen

Organization

SCIA 2015 was organized by the Pattern Recognition Society of Denmark (DSAGM) in cooperation with IAPR (International Association for Pattern Recognition).

General Chairs

Rasmus Larsen	DTU Compute, Denmark
Mads Nielsen	University of Copenhagen, Denmark
Dan Witzner Hansen	IT University of Copenhagen, Denmark

Program Chairs

Rasmus R. Paulsen	DTU Compute, Denmark
Kim Steenstrup Pedersen	University of Copenhagen, Denmark

Organizing Comittee

Ulla Jensen	DTU Compute, Denmark
Susan Nasirumbi Ipsen	University of Copenhagen, Denmark
Hanne Kvalheim	CAP Partner, Copenhagen, Denmark

IAPR Invited Speakers

Tim Cootes	University of Manchester, UK
Dorin Comaniciu	Siemens Corporate Technology, Princeton, USA

Invited Speakers

Carolina Wählby	Uppsala University, Sweden
Robert Jenssen	University of Tromsø, Norway
Thomas B. Moeslund	Aalborg University, Denmark
Kalle Åström	Lund University, Sweden
Christoph Busch	Gjøvik University College, Norway

Program Committee

Adrien Bartoli	ISIT – CENTI – Faculté de Médecine, France
Christoph Busch	Gjøvik University College, Norway
Michael Felsberg	Linkoping University, Sweden
Luc Florack	Eindhoven University of Technology, The Netherlands
Jon Yngve Hardeberg	Gjøvik University College, Norway
Janne Heikkilä	University of Oulu, Finland
Anders Heyden	Lund University, Sweden
Christian Igel	University of Copenhagen, Denmark
Sarang Joshi	University of Utah, USA
Norbert Krüger	University of Southern Denmark, Denmark
Joni Kämäräinen	Tampere University of Technology, Finland
Marco Loog	Delft University of Technology, The Netherlands
Diana Mateus	Technical University of Munich, Germany
Thomas Moeslund	Aalborg University, Denmark
Nassir Navab	Technical University of Munich, Germany
Erkki Oja	Aalto University, Finland
Daniel Rueckert	Imperial College London, UK
Julia Schnabel	University of Oxford, UK
Joachim Weickert	Saarland University, Germany

Additional Reviewers

A. Berge	H. Pan
A. Buch	H. Aanæs
A. Bærentzen	I. Austvoll
A. Dahl	I. Nystrom
A. Feragen	I.-M. Sintorn
A. Hadid	J. Fagertun
A. Kaarna	J. Kannala
A. Solberg	J. Levine
A.-B. Salberg	J. Laaksonen
C. Trinderup	J. Roning
D. Kraft	J. Sporring
E. Alpaydin	J. Sullivan
E. Bengtsson	J. Thielemann
E. Rahtu	J. Tohka
F. Imai	J. Weickert
F. Lauze	K. Chen
G. Einarsson	K. Nasrollahi
H. Huttunen	K. Skretting
H. Kalviainen	L. Clemmensen
H. Martin Kjer	L. Eikvil

L. Hansen   N.C. Overgaard
L. Lensu   O. Camara
L. Zollei   R. Jenssen
L. Østergaard   R. Lenz
M. de Bruijne   S. Brandt
M. Ganz   S. Darkner
M. González Ballester   S. Keller
M. Hauta-Kasari   S. Olsen
M. Koskela   T. Eerola
M. Lyksborg   T. Haavardsholm
M. Mirmehdi   T. Kinnunen
M. Olsen   V. Viitaniemi
M. Pedersen   X. Chen
M. Sjöberg   Z. Yang
N. Strokina   Ö. Smedby

Sponsors and Sponsoring Institutions

We gratefully thank our sponsors for making this event a success.

Contents

Motion Tracking

Pattern Recognition

Biomedical Image Analysis

Pattern Recognition and Computational Imaging

3D Vision and Pattern Recognition

Posters

Feature Extraction and Segmentation

Texture Removal Preserving Edges by Diffusion

Baptiste Magnier$^{(\boxtimes)}$, Philippe Montesinos, and Daniel Diep

LGI2P de l'Ecole des Mines d'ALES, Parc Scientifique G.Besse, 30035 Nîmes, France
{baptiste.magnier,philippe.montesinos,daniel.diep}@mines-ales.fr

Abstract. This article is devoted to a new method for removing texture in images through an image region classification technique using a smoothing rotating filter followed by a diffusion process designed to preserve object contours. This approach lies in associating a descriptor, capable of classifying each pixel as a texture pixel, a homogenous region pixel or an edge pixel, with an anisotropic edge detector serving to define two directions of the edges introduced into an anisotropic diffusion algorithm. Due to the presence of the image region descriptor, the anisotropic diffusion is able to accurately control diffusion near the edges and corner points and moreover remove textured regions. Our results and evaluations based on image segmentation and classical edge detection, which correctly extract objects within the image, compared with anisotropic diffusion methods and nonlinear filters, enable validating our approach.

Keywords: Anisotropic diffusion · Half gaussian kernels

1 Introduction

Texture removal is fundamental for image segmentation [1] [2] [3] [4] or cartoon generation [5]. Filtering techniques cannot be adapted in the presence of strong texture [6]. Though efficient for removing impulse noise in images, the median filter, the α-trimmed means filter [7], the Kuwahara filter [8] and all their generalizations are still unable to remove heavy texture while preserving edges in the image and moreover wind up eroding corners (Fig. 1).

In [5], the authors have developed an approach for both removing textures and preserving edges. The algorithm is able to determine whether a pixel belongs to a textured region via a local total variation of the image around this point. If the pixel belongs to a textured region, then the local total variation is strong. This approach depends on the scale parameter, namely the standard deviation of the Gaussian σ convolved with the original image, which proves to be efficient at removing thin textures in images. However, a low value of parameter σ will maintain a strong texture, whereas a high parameter value will remove small objects and blur edges.

In image restoration, the Partial Differential Equation (PDE) is often used to regularize images in instances where image boundaries control a diffusion process [9] [10]. Over homogenous regions, the diffusion is isotropic; at edge points on the other hand, diffusion is either altered by the gradient magnitude in the contour

© Springer International Publishing Switzerland 2015
R.R. Paulsen and K.S. Pedersen (Eds.): SCIA 2015, LNCS 9127, pp. 3–15, 2015.
DOI: 10.1007/978-3-319-19665-7_1

(a) Original image,   (b) Median filter,   (c) α-trimmed means   (d) Kuwahara filter,
411×384   5×5   filter, 3×3   2 iterations

Fig. 1. Nonlinear filters are not efficient for texture removal

direction or else inhibited [11]. For the diffusion scheme developed by Perona-Malik [12], control is performed with finite differences, making it possible to preserve many contours of small objects or small structures. The *Mean Curvature Motion (MCM)* method consists of solely diffusing in the contour direction [13], even within homogeneous regions. According to some diffusion approaches, Gaussian filtering is used for gradient estimation, thus improving the robustness of diffusion control over noise [11] [14] [15] [16]. Nevertheless, these methods are often introduced to enhance small structures but not necessarily to restore images containing considerable noise, therefore resulting in greater texture yet without the ability to remove texture while preserving the accuracy of edges.

In this paper, we have combined two techniques stemming from our previous work [3] [17]. We will begin by describing the rotating filter and its texture detection capabilities before presenting an anisotropic edge detector that defines two contour directions for an edge crossing a pixel. As a final step, we will introduce an anisotropic diffusion method to accurately control diffusion near the edges and corner points while proceeding with an isotropic diffusion inside the textured regions. More specifically, our detector yields two distinct directions on edges or corners, with this information enabling anisotropic diffusion in the detected directions.

2   Texture Detection

In order to detect whether a pixel belongs to a textured region, a homogeneous region or an edge, we apply a smoothing rotating filter and then analyze the resulting signal. For each pixel of the original image, a rotating half smoothing filter produces a signal s, which is a function of both a rotation angle θ and the underlying signal. Smoothing with rotating filters ensures that the image is smoothed with a bank of rotated anisotropic half Gaussian kernels:

$$G_{(\mu,\lambda)}(x,y,\theta) = C \cdot I_\theta * H(-y) \cdot e^{-\left(\frac{x^2}{2\lambda^2} + \frac{y^2}{2\mu^2}\right)} \qquad (1)$$

where I_θ corresponds to a rotated image of orientation θ (the image is oriented instead of the filter so as to decrease algorithmic complexity and to allow use of a recursive Gaussian filter [3]), C is a normalization coefficient [2], (x,y) are pixel coordinates, and (μ,λ) are the standard deviations of the Gaussian filter

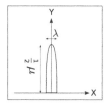  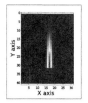

(a) Smoothing filter   (b) Rotating filters (c) Discretized filter

Fig. 2. A half smoothing rotating filter

(as illustrated in Fig. 2). Since only the causal part of the filter is actually needed, we simply "cut" the smoothing kernel in half; this operation corresponds to the Heaviside function H, and its implementation is rather straightforward. Like in [3], the image is oriented instead of the filter due to concern over increased algorithmic complexity while allowing for use of a recursive Gaussian filter [2]. Application of the rotating half-filter at a single point of a gray level image in a 360 scan provides each pixel with a characterizing signal $s(\theta)$, which is a single function of the orientation angle θ. From these pixel signals, we are now able to extract the descriptors that will discriminate edges and regions [17].

For all pixels lying in a homogeneous region, $s(\theta)$ will remain constant. On the contrary, in a textured region, $s(\theta)$ will be stochastic. If a pixel lies at the border between several different homogenous regions, $s(\theta)$ will contain several flat areas. If the pixel lies between a homogenous region and a textured region, $s(\theta)$ will contain only one flat area. However, if the textured region is not too accentuated, $s(\theta)$ will only consist of a flat signal as a result of the smoothing filter, and moreover the region will be considered as a homogenous region. This protocol enables classifying pixels located between two textured regions.

The main purpose behind analyzing a 360 scan signal is to detect significant flat areas, which correspond to homogeneous regions of the image. After smoothing, i.e. $s_M(\theta) = (s(\theta-\Delta\theta)+s(\theta)+s(\theta+\Delta\theta))/3$, the derivative $s_\theta(\theta)$ is calculated and flat areas are detected as intervals: $s_\theta(\theta) = s_M(\theta - \Delta\theta) - s_M(\theta + \Delta\theta)$, so:

$$s_\theta(\theta) = (s(\theta - 2\,\Delta\theta) + s(\theta - \Delta\theta) + s(\theta + \Delta\theta) + s(\theta + 2\,\Delta\theta))/3. \qquad (2)$$

A flat area is considered to be detected when the largest angular sector lies between $30°$ and $360°$.

The texture suppression method consists of both an anisotropic diffusion at edges, corner points and points between two textured regions, so as to preserve borders between regions, and an isotropic diffusion inside homogenous and textured regions. The black regions shown in Fig. 4(c) can be viewed as a rough edge detection and indicate regions where flat areas have been detected in Fig. 4(a). The original image will therefore be smoothed anisotropically in the black regions of Fig. 4(c) and isotropically in white regions; so it is interesting to apply a dilatation operator and then attenuate with of the black regions or remove some isolated black pixels. The curvatures of signal $s(\theta)$ (i.e. the second derivative of $s(\theta)$, similar to Eq. 2) serve to define two directions used for anisotropic diffusion in [17], though these diffusion directions are not accurate and may have a blurring effect on edges. We will use herein the diffusion directions computed from an anisotropic edge detector that has defined two directions, thus yielding a much more accurate diffusion.

3   Edge Detection Using Half Gaussian Kernels

Steerable filters [18] or anisotropic edge detectors [19] perform well in detecting large linear structures. Near the corners however, the gradient magnitude decreases as edge information within the scope of the filter also decreases. Consequently, the robustness to noise relative to small objects declines substantially.

A simple solution to avoiding this effect is to consider paths that cross each pixel in several directions. The idea developed in [3] is to "cut" the derivative kernel (with smoothing) into two parts: the first part along an initial direction, and the second part along a second direction. At each pixel (x, y), a derivation filter is applied to obtain a derivative information $\mathcal{Q}(x, y, \theta)$:

$$\mathcal{Q}(x, y, \theta) = I_\theta * C_1 \cdot H(-y) \cdot x \cdot e^{-\left(\frac{x^2}{2\lambda^2} + \frac{y^2}{2\mu^2}\right)} \tag{3}$$

where C_1 represents a normalization coefficient [2]. $\mathcal{Q}(x, y, \theta)$ denotes the slope of a line derived from a pixel in the direction perpendicular to θ (as diagrammed in Fig. 3).

To obtain a gradient magnitude measure $\|\nabla I\|$ on each pixel P, we first compute the global extrema of the $\mathcal{Q}(x, y, \theta)$ function with θ_1 and θ_2 (some examples are presented in Fig. 4(b)). Two of these extrema can then be combined to obtain $\|\nabla I\|$:

$$\begin{cases} \|\nabla I\| = \max_{\theta \in [0,360[} \mathcal{Q}(x, y, \theta) - \min_{\theta \in [0,360[} \mathcal{Q}(x, y, \theta) \\ \theta_1 = \arg\max_{\theta \in [0,360[}(\mathcal{Q}(x, y, \theta)) \\ \theta_2 = \arg\min_{\theta \in [0,360[}(\mathcal{Q}(x, y, \theta)) \end{cases} \tag{4}$$

Once $\|\nabla I\|$, θ_1 and θ_2 have been obtained, they are entered into our diffusion scheme. Due to the rotating filter lengths, this approach maintains its robustness

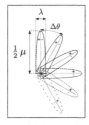

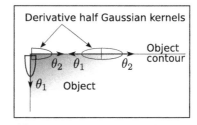

(a) Rotated derivation filter

(b) Half Anisotropic Gaussian kernels at linear portions of contours and at corners.

Fig. 3. Oriented half kernel enables extracting two edge directions (θ_1, θ_2)

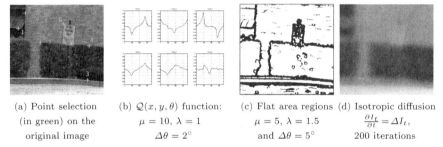

(a) Point selection (in green) on the original image	(b) $\mathcal{Q}(x, y, \theta)$ function: $\mu = 10, \lambda = 1$ $\Delta\theta = 2°$	(c) Flat area regions $\mu = 5, \lambda = 1.5$ and $\Delta\theta = 5°$	(d) Isotropic diffusion $\frac{\partial I_t}{\partial t} = \Delta I_t,$ 200 iterations

Fig. 4. Points selection and associated $\mathcal{Q}(x, y, \theta)$

to noise and computes two accurate diffusion orientations in the edge directions (illustrated in Fig. 3(b)). The authors in [20], evaluated the edge detection used in this method as a function of noise level and in [10] is shown how to restore images in function of $\|\nabla I\|$ and (θ_1, θ_2) directions.

4 Anisotropic Diffusion in Two Edges Directions

Unlike several diffusion schemes [12] [11] [14] [15] [16], our control function does not depend on the image gradient but rather on a pre-established classification map of the initial image. As stated in Section 2, this classification lacks sharp distinction between region and edges. Tensor diffusion schemes preserve edges [14] [15] [16]; however, in order to remove texture while preserving contours, the standard deviation of the Gaussian σ must be high. Yet this solution will blur edges and over-smooth corners. Moreover, in [11] [14] [15] [16], only one direction is considered at the edges. To minimize these effects, let's consider the two directions (θ_1, θ_2) provided by Eq. 4 of the anisotropic edge detector only where flat areas have been detected (as illustrated in Fig. 4(c)).

The diffusion process can thus be described by the following newly equation:

$$\frac{\partial I_t}{\partial t} = F_A(I_0) \cdot \Delta I_t + (1 - F_A(I_0)) \cdot \frac{\partial^2 I_t}{\partial\theta_1\partial\theta_2}, \tag{5}$$

- t is the diffusion time,
- I_0 is the original image,
- I_t is the diffused image at time t,
- F_A represents those regions where flat areas have been detected (illustrated in Fig. 5(a)):
  - $\to$ $F_A = 0$ in contour regions, thus: $\frac{\partial I_t}{\partial t} = \frac{\partial^2 I_t}{\partial\theta_1\partial\theta_2}$
  - $\to$ $F_A = 1$ in textured or homogeneous regions, thus: $\frac{\partial I_t}{\partial t} = \Delta I_t$, corresponding to the heat equation [21], an example can be seen in Fig. 4(d).

The authors in [22] have developed a diffusion method based on the same pixel classification. Inside edge regions, a function of both the gradient magnitude derived by half Gaussian kernels (Eq. 4) and the angle between the two

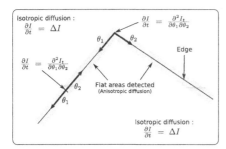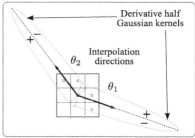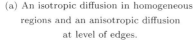

(a) An isotropic diffusion in homogeneous regions and an anisotropic diffusion at level of edges.

(b) Interpolations directions are estimated by the derivatives half Gaussian kernels and the diffusion computed by interpolations is calculated in the two directions (θ_1, θ_2) on a 3×3 mask.

Fig. 5. Diagram of our diffusion scheme

diffusion directions (θ_1, θ_2) drives the diffusion process. This technique combines isotropic and anisotropic diffusion, while preserving the edges and corners of various objects in highly noisy images. Nonetheless, as shown in Fig. 8(h), textures are preserved inside contour regions given that they may contain a high gradient value, thereby inhibiting the diffusion process (unlike Eq. 4).

A discretization of the diffusion process $\frac{\partial I_t}{\partial t} = \frac{\partial^2 I_t}{\partial \theta_1 \partial \theta_2}$ leads to the difference between the derivative in the θ_1 direction and the derivative in the θ_2 direction, respectively, at the pixel level. As diagrammed in Fig. 5(b), at the time t, the diffused pixel results from interpolations in both the θ_1 and θ_2 orientations on a 3×3 mask.

5   Quantitative Comparison of Region Detection

In order to carry out some quantitative results, we have conducted a number of tests of texture suppression using several approaches. The reference image contains only 5 known regions and these 5 regions are substituted by 5 different textures grey-level images, as illustrated in Fig. 6. As soon as the reference image is synthetic, it is straightforward to compare the processed images to ground truth. The original image being composed of 5 distinct regions, we compared each true region to the regions issued from a texture suppression method followed with a region segmentation algorithm [4]. This quantitative comparison is led with several approaches for the texture suppression: Perona-Malik [12], Alvarez et al. [11], Bilateral filter [6], texture filter of Buades et al. [5], anisotropic diffusion scheme based on derivatives half Gaussian kernels of Magnier et al. [10] and our proposed method. Note that in Fig. 7, we compare the region segmentation of the different texture suppression schemes with the region segmentation on the original image. As for our general applications, we used our texture detector with $\mu=5$, $\lambda=1.5$ and $\Delta\theta=5°$ for flat area detection. The parameters used in an anisotropic edge detector to compute $\mu=5$, $\lambda=1.5$ and $\Delta\theta=2°$. λ represents the width the filter for the contour extraction (see Fig. 3), we use the same standard deviation parameter for each method using a Gaussian filter i.e. $\sigma = 1$ for [11], [6], [5], and [10]. This pairwise comparison resulted into a 2×2 contingency table, or confusion matrix, which reports the number true positives, true negatives, false positives, and false negatives. False positive in this case means that the region segmentation scheme results in several regions for a considered known region on the 5 distinct regions and false negatives represent regions segmented growing outside a considered true region.

Fig. 7 represents false positive/negative pixels on the region segmented images. Compared to other approaches, our method creates less false positive pixels and in general less false negatives (excepted for image 4, the segmentation region scheme creates two regions inside 3 distinct regions instead only one for

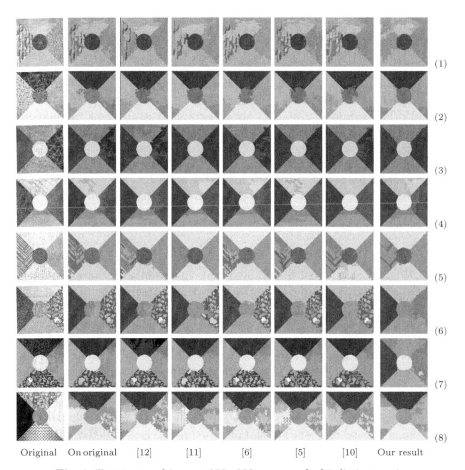

Original   On original   [12]   [11]   [6]   [5]   [10]   Our result

Fig. 6. Test textured images 200×200 composed of 5 distinct regions

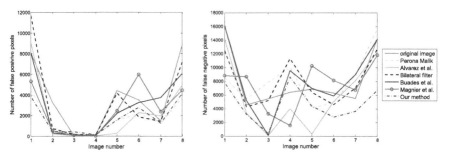

Fig. 7. Errors evaluation using several diffusion schemes on images in Fig. 6

each, thus creating pic in the graph). As illustrated in Fig. 6, note also that how our method is able to remove efficiency the high texture in images (6) and (7).

6   Experimental Results

In the image displayed in Fig. 8(a), the aim is to smooth the various textures present (wall, bushes) while preserving all objects (windows, panel, sidewalk). We introduced our detector with μ=5, λ=1.5 and $\Delta\theta$=5° for flat area detection (Fig. 4(c)). The parameters used in an anisotropic edge detector to compute (θ_1, θ_2) are μ=5, λ=1.5 and $\Delta\theta$=2° (λ represents the width of the derivation filter, it must not be too thin in order to obtain robust edges directions in presence of strong textures). The result of our anisotropic diffusion is shown in Fig. 8(l) after 25 iterations. Note that a number of objects are perfectly visible and corners are sharp, whereas texture regions are smoothed and some have even merged, preserving edges between all of them.

We can now compare our results with several approaches, as well as with the well-known bilateral filters [6] and image regularization approaches using PDEs. For most of these methods, the texture has not been completely removed from the wall (Fig. 8(b), (c), (d), (e), (f) and (g)). In the majority of cases, bush boundaries (Fig. 8(b), (c), (d), (e) and (f)) or panel corners (Fig. 8(e), (g) and (k)) have not been properly preserved. Tensorial approaches add a fiber effect to the texture provided the standard deviation of the Gaussian σ is small enough. Substitute σ leeds the diffusion to blur edges (e.g. $\sigma = 4$ in Fig. 8(j)).

To show the efficiency of our texture removal method (Fig. 9(d)), we compared edge detection [24] on the original image and on the image obtained after diffusion. Edge detection on our diffused image (Fig. 8(p)) is less noisy than on the original. Moreover, edges of bushes, panels and windows appear clearly, whereas the contours of bushes and the wall have not been completely detected on the original image. Also, the method proposed in [17] fails to detect the top of the panel, and the approach in [16] blurs the edges of bushes (see bush on the left on Fig. 8(n) and (o)). We have also shown the efficiency of our texture removal approach using the region segmentation of Monga [4] as a post-processing step. Fig. 8(t) illustrates that our texture suppression allows a segmentation of bushes,

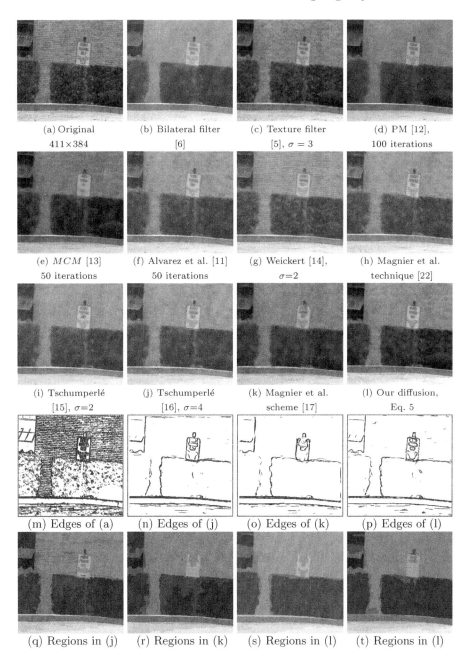

(a) Original
411×384

(b) Bilateral filter
[6]

(c) Texture filter
[5], $\sigma = 3$

(d) PM [12],
100 iterations

(e) MCM [13]
50 iterations

(f) Alvarez et al. [11]
50 iterations

(g) Weickert [14],
$\sigma=2$

(h) Magnier et al.
technique [22]

(i) Tschumperlé
[15], $\sigma=2$

(j) Tschumperlé
[16], $\sigma=4$

(k) Magnier et al.
scheme [17]

(l) Our diffusion,
Eq. 5

(m) Edges of (a)

(n) Edges of (j)

(o) Edges of (k)

(p) Edges of (l)

(q) Regions in (j)

(r) Regions in (k)

(s) Regions in (l)

(t) Regions in (l)

Fig. 8. Texture diffusion using several methods then evaluation with edge detection (Prewitt kernels [24]) and region segmentation

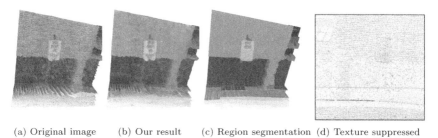

(a) Original image   (b) Our result   (c) Region segmentation (d) Texture suppressed

Fig. 9. Image surface of the original image, our result region segmentation of our result (see Fig. 8) and texture suppressed with our method

the panel, the sidewalk and so on, contrary to Fig. 8(q), (r) and (s). Moreover, Fig. 9 indicates the efficiency of our method in depicting the image surface before and after our regularization scheme, during which regions become entirely flat so as to preserve sharp edges, close to the region segmentation of our result (Fig. 9 (c)).

In the second result presented in Fig. 10, the aim here is to remove the t-shirt texture as the acquisition noise in the original image. The first step is to compute flat areas from each color channels of the colored image. To proceed, we apply the flat area detection technique to each channel [23]. For each pixel, if we detect at least one flat area for a given channel, then the diffusion will be anisotropic. Otherwise, if no flat area has been detected in any channel, then the diffusion will be isotropic. Thus, as shown in [22], before synthesizing the regularized color image, we diffuse each image channel using the diffusion scheme presented in Eq. 4. We introduced our texture detector with μ=5, λ=1.5 and $\Delta\theta$=5° for flat area detection. The parameters used in an anisotropic edge detector to compute (θ_1, θ_2) are μ=5, λ=1.5 and $\Delta\theta$=2°.

Our result presented in Fig. 10(f) was compared with several methods and evaluated with edge detection of Canny (σ=1) merged on the original image in order to move forward the contour preservation and the texture removal. Thereby, as shown here, the bilateral filter removes correctly the noise but preserves the t-shirt texture. Tensorial method [16] does not removes t-shirt stripes and blurs edges because the standard deviation of the Gaussian filter used for this method is too large (σ=3). The texture filter [5] blurs edges and is not capable to remove the noise on the image top. Finally, we have compared our method with the Magnier et al. approach [17] extended in color [23] which suppress correctly the texture, but, as it is pointed with the edge detector, these technique blurs edges. On the contrary, our method eliminates both the texture of the t-shirt, the acquisition noise preserving sharped precise edges.

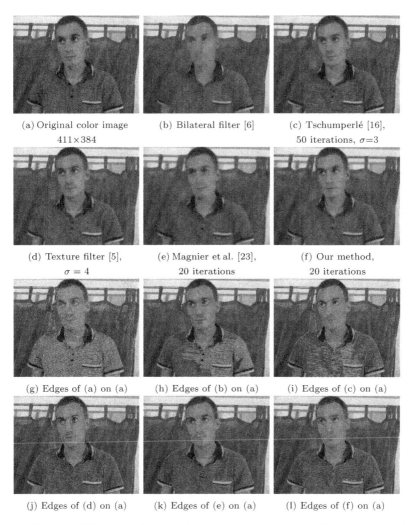

Fig. 10. Texture diffusion and evaluation with edge detection (Canny edge detector using the first derivative of the Gaussian filter with $\sigma = 1$)

7 Conclusion

This paper is dedicated to defining a new method for removing texture in images by means of pixel classification using a smoothing rotating filter. Our classification method appears to be very promising since we have been able to correctly classify texture regions, homogenous regions and edge regions for various image types. Two-direction anisotropic diffusion provided by an edge detector using derivative half smoothing kernels maintains sharp edges and the corners of different objects. Comparing our results with existing algorithms and region segmentation on our results serves to validate our method. Next on our work program agenda is to enhance this method to treat medical images which are corrupted by a heavy noise.

References

1. Canny, F.: A computational approach to edge detection. TPAMI **8**(6), 679–698 (1986)
2. Deriche, R.: Recursively implementing the gaussian and its derivatives. In: IEEE ICIP, pp. 263–267 (1992)
3. Montesinos, P., Magnier, B.: A new perceptual edge detector in color images. In: Blanc-Talon, J., Bone, D., Philips, W., Popescu, D., Scheunders, P. (eds.) ACIVS 2010, Part I. LNCS, vol. 6474, pp. 209–220. Springer, Heidelberg (2010)
4. Monga, O.: An optimal region growing algorithm for image segmentation. Int. J. on Pattern Recognition and Art. Intel. **1**(3), 351–376 (1987)
5. Buades, A., Le, T., Morel, J., Vese, L.: Fast cartoon+ texture image filters. IEEE TIP **19**(8), 1978–1986 (2010)
6. Tomasi, C., Manduchi, R.: Bilateral filtering for gray and color images. In: ICCV, pp. 839–846 (1998)
7. Bednar, J., Watt, T.: Alpha-trimmed means and their relationship to median filters. IEEE TASSP **32**(1), 145–153 (1984)
8. Kuwahara, M., Hachimura, K., Eiho, S., Kinoshita, M.: Processing of RI-angiocardiographic images. Digital Proc. of Biomedical Images, 187–203 (1976)
9. Aubert, G., Kornprobst, P.: Mathematical problems in image processing: partial differential equations and the calculus of variations, 2nd edn, vol. 147. Springer-Verlag (2006)
10. Magnier, B., Montesinos, P.: Evolution of image regularization with PDEs toward a new anisotropic smoothing based on half kernels. IS&T/SPIE Electronic Imaging, pp. 86 550M–86 550M (2013)
11. Alvarez, L., Lions, P.-L., Morel, J.-M.: Image selective smoothing and edge detection by nonlinear diffusion. ii. SIAM J. Numer. Anal. **29**(3), 845–866 (1992)
12. Perona, P., Malik, J.: Scale-space and edge detection using anisotropic diffusion. Trans. on Pattern Recognition and Machine Intelligence **12**, 629–639 (1990)
13. Catté, F., Dibos, F., Koepfler, G.: A morphological scheme for mean curvature motion and applications to anisotropic diffusion and motion of level sets. SIAM J. Numer. Anal. **32**, 1895–1909 (1995)
14. Weickert, J.: Anisotropic diffusion in image processing. Teubner-Verlag, Stuttgart, Germany (1998)
15. Tschumperlé, D., Deriche, R.: Vector-valued image regularization with PDEs: a common framework for different applications. In: TPAMI, pp. 506–517 (2005)
16. Tschumperlé, D.: Fast anisotropic smoothing of multi-valued images using curvature-preserving PDEs. IJCV **68**(1), 65–82 (2006)
17. Magnier, B., Montesinos, P., Diep, D.: Texture removal by pixel classification using a rotating filter. In: IEEE ICASSP, pp. 1097–1100 (2011)
18. Freeman, W.T., Adelson, E.H.: The design and use of steerable filters. TPAMI **13**, 891–906 (1991)
19. Perona, P.: Steerable-scalable kernels for edge detection and junction analysis. IMAVIS **10**(10), 663–672 (1992)

20. Magnier, B., Montesinos, P., Diep, D.: Fast anisotropic edge detection using gamma correction in color images. In: IEEE 7th ISPA, pp. 212–217 (2011)
21. Koenderink, J.: The structure of images. Biological cybernetics **50**(5), 363–370 (1984)
22. Magnier, B., Montesinos, P., Diep, D.: Perceptual color image smoothing via a new region-based PDE scheme. ELCVIA **12**(1), 17–32 (2013)
23. Magnier, B., Montesinos, P., Diep, D.: Texture removal in color images by anisotropic diffusion. In: VISAPP, pp. 40–50 (2011)
24. Prewitt, J.M.S.: Object enhancement and extraction. Picture Processing and Psychopictorics, Lipkin, B., Rosenfeld, A. (eds.) Academic Press, New York (1970)

Oriented Shape Index Histograms
for Cell Classification

Anders Boesen Lindbo Larsen[✉], Anders Bjorholm Dahl, and Rasmus Larsen

Department of Applied Mathematics and Computer Science,
Technical University of Denmark, Kongens Lyngby, Denmark
{abll,abda,rlar}@dtu.dk

Abstract. We propose a novel extension to the shape index histogram feature descriptor where the orientation of the second-order curvature is included in the histograms. The orientation of the shape index is reminiscent but not equal to gradient orientation which is widely used for feature description. We evaluate our new feature descriptor using a public dataset consisting of HEp-2 cell images from indirect immunoflourescence lighting. Our results show that we can improve classification performance significantly when including the shape index orientation. Notably, we show that shape index orientation outperforms the gradient orientation on the dataset.

1 Introduction

When characterising texture-like structures in images, it is often desirable to be invariant towards orientations of the image structure at larger scales [2,7,11,12]. However, in cases where one can assume or estimate an orientation in the image, it becomes relevant to describe the texture relative to this orientation to better characterise the structure.

The problem we wish to solve is classification of HEp-2 cell images captured using indirect immunoflourescence lighting. This is a quintessential task in medical image analysis where good performance of an automated system can save manual labour hours and speed up the diagnosis process [4,5]. A common approach is to regard the problem as an instance of texture classification because the staining patterns of the cells exhibit texture characteristics. Furthermore, for cell images, a local coordinate system can be contrived pixel-wise by letting the origin be the cell centre, the first axis be the vector from the origin to the pixel, and the second axis be orthogonal to the first axis in either the clockwise or counter-clockwise direction. This yields a fidicual orientation for every pixel that we can use for describing local texture orientation.

In this paper we explore the possibility of capturing texture orientation in combination with *shape index histograms* (SIHs) [7,13]. The shape index is a second-order curvature measure derived from the eigenvalues of the local image Hessian [6]. With the shape index, rotation invariance is achieved by construction because the eigenvectors (the *principal directions*) are discarded. We extend the work on shape index histograms by reincorporating the orientation in the feature description. We call our extension *oriented shape index histograms* (OSIHs).

© Springer International Publishing Switzerland 2015
R.R. Paulsen and K.S. Pedersen (Eds.): SCIA 2015, LNCS 9127, pp. 16–25, 2015.
DOI: 10.1007/978-3-319-19665-7_2

1.1   Related Work

Feature description using SIHs has recently shown good performance for medical image analysis [7] and for analysing galaxy images [13]. SIHs have shown superior performance compared with popular texture descriptors and came ind 2nd 0.11% below the 1st place at the ICIP 2013 competition on cell classification[1] [7].

The construction of SIHs is comparable to most histogram-based feature descriptors that typically rely on first-order image structure, *e.g.* SIFT [10], DAISY [15] and HOG [3]. The histogram approach to feature description has had enormous success because it offers good discriminability and robustness. For SIFT, DAISY and HOG, the robustness is towards local translations and rotation. For SIHs as used in [7,13], the histogram description achieves robustness from the smoothing of adjacent second-order curvatures captured in the histogram bins. For histograms over shape index orientation, the histogram approach allow for robustness towards rotation; again from the bin smoothing.

When constructing histograms over multiple features with potential correlations we have a choice between 1) creating a joint histogram, or 2) concatenating the marginal histograms. The authors of the basic image features descriptor [2] opt for the latter and show good results using a multi-scale joint histogram for texture description. While the joint histogram should allow for a more discriminative description, it quickly becomes high-dimensional which may be impractical. This is a likely explanation for why joint histograms are rarely seen in the feature description literature. In this paper, we wish to experiment with both approaches.

We note that second-order orientation of the shape index should not be confused with the first-order orientation of the gradient. The gradient orientation is the direction with the steepest increase in image intensity whereas the shape index orientation is the angle along which the second-order curvature is strongest. To the best of our knowledge, the orientation of the second-order curvature has not been used for feature description before.

1.2   Contributions

- We formulate the shape index orientation and show how eigenvectors of the local image Hessian capture second-order orientation. We also formulate a strength measure of the second-order curvature to be used for weighting histogram contributions.
- We develop OSIHs as an extension of SIHs by including the shape index orientation.
- We evaluate our new feature descriptor and show that it improves classification performance on the ICIP 2013 dataset compared to plain SIHs and gradient orientation histograms.

---

[1] Dataset available at http://nerone.diiie.unisa.it/contest-icip-2013

2   Oriented Shape Index Histograms

In this section we formulate our new feature descriptor. The shape index is an image geometry measure originally proposed by Koenderink and van Doorn [6]. It is based on the scale-space framework as presented in [9]. Note that we have made our implementation of OSIHs available online[2] .

2.1   Differential Image Structure

We formulate our oriented shape index histograms using the Gaussian scale-space framework where the differential structure of a 2-dimensional image $I(\boldsymbol{x})$: $\Omega \to R$, $\Omega \subseteq R^2$ is defined by

$$L_{x^n y^m}(\boldsymbol{x}; \sigma) = \sigma^{n+m} \frac{\partial^{n+m}}{\partial x^n \partial y^m} (G * I)(\boldsymbol{x}; \sigma) \quad . \tag{1}$$

$*$ denotes convolution, G is a Gaussian kernel, σ is the width of the Gaussian kernel, n and m indicate the differentiation order along the x and y axis respectively. For notational convenience we omit the arguments and substitute $L_{x^n y^m}(\boldsymbol{x}; \sigma)$ with simply $L_{x^n y^m}$. Thus, $L_{x^n y^m}$ is implicitly assumed to be computed at some scale σ and location $\boldsymbol{x}$.

2.2   The Shape Index

The shape index is derived from the Hessian matrix $\nabla^2 L$ that captures the second-order curvature at scale σ,

$$\nabla^2 L(\boldsymbol{x}; \sigma) = \begin{bmatrix} L_{x^2} & L_{xy} \\ L_{xy} & L_{y^2} \end{bmatrix} \quad . \tag{2}$$

The Hessian matrix is square and symmetric allowing us to compute the pair of real eigenvalues κ_1 and κ_2 capturing the *principal curvatures*. The shape index $s \in \left] \frac{-\pi}{2}, \frac{\pi}{2} \right[$ is defined as

$$s(\boldsymbol{x}; \sigma) = \arctan \left(\frac{\kappa_1 + \kappa_2}{\kappa_1 - \kappa_2} \right) \quad . \tag{3}$$

The shape index has the attractive property that it maps all second-order shapes onto a continuous interval providing a smooth and intuitive transition between the shapes, see Figure 1. In addition to the shape index a measure of *curvedness* c is defined,

$$c(\boldsymbol{x}; \sigma) = \sqrt{\kappa_1^2 + \kappa_2^2} \quad . \tag{4}$$

The curvedness indicates the strength of the shape described by the shape index such that we differentiate between flat and indistinct vs. large and prominent shapes. See Figure 1 for examples.

---

[2] Implementation available at http://compute.dtu.dk/~abll.

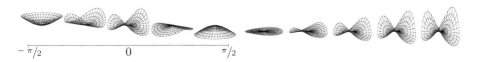

$-\pi/2$ 0 $\pi/2$

Fig. 1. Left: Second-order curvatures along the shape index interval $]-\pi/2, \pi/2[$. Right: The saddle shape $s = 0$ with increasing curvedness.

2.3   Shape Index Orientation

The orientation of the shape index is described by the eigenvectors of $\nabla^2 L$. The eigenvectors are the *principal directions* along which the curvature is minimal and maximal respectively. Because $\nabla^2 L$ is symmetric, the eigenvectors are orthogonal. Therefore, we can rely on a single eigenvector $\boldsymbol{v} = (v_1, v_2)$ to capture the shape index orientation $\theta \in]-\pi/2, \pi/2[$:

$$\theta(\boldsymbol{x}; \sigma) = \arctan\left(\frac{v_2}{v_1}\right) \tag{5}$$

The angle is unsigned (0–180°) because the shape index curvature is symmetric around $\boldsymbol{v}$. As an example, we show the shape index orientation θ for a test image in Figure 2. We see that the saddle points in the checkerboard patterns have orthogonal directions. For the rings we see that θ changes smoothly and is periodic in $]-\pi/2, \pi/2[$. Note that θ is unstable at the centre of the small dots. This is because the shape index curvature has no dominant orientation for a blob structure where $\kappa_1 = \kappa_2$.

Along with the shape index orientation we introduce a measure of its strength,

$$m = \kappa_1 - \kappa_2 \quad . \tag{6}$$

The shape index orientation magnitude m is computed from the difference between the eigenvalues. If m is small it means that the principal curvatures along the principal directions are similar and the second-order shape is radially symmetric with no orientation. In Figure 2, we show an example of the second-order orientation magnitude. We see that its response is different from the gradient magnitude (introduced later in Section 2.5) as it gives weight only where second-order structure has orientation.

2.4   Histogram Construction

The ordinary SIH is constructed by choosing a set of n_s bin centres $b_{s1}, \ldots, b_{sn_s}$ equidistantly distributed along the shape index interval $]-\pi/2, \pi/2[$. The shape index bin contribution C_s at location $\boldsymbol{x}$ is computed from

$$C_s(\boldsymbol{x}; \sigma, b_s, \beta_s) = \exp\left(-\frac{(b_s - s)^2}{2\beta_s^2}\right) \quad , \tag{7}$$

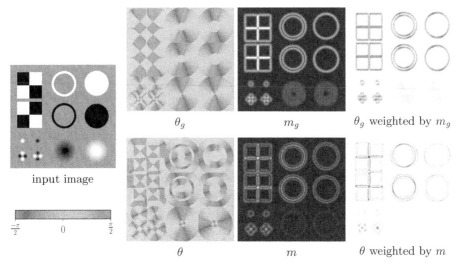

input image

$\frac{-\pi}{2}$ 0 $\frac{\pi}{2}$

θ_g m_g θ_g weighted by m_g

θ m θ weighted by m

Fig. 2. A toy example to illustrate the shape index orientation and its difference with the gradient orientation. Top row: Gradient orientations (unsigned). Bottom row: Shape index orientations. The abrupt transitions to grey in the left column is caused by limited floating point precision. In the right column we perform alpha-blending using the magnitudes emphasise the orientations with high magnitudes.

where a Gaussian window of width β_s is used for smooth binning in the *tonal* range (the shape index range). The total bin contributions from all image locations is computed from

$$B_s(\sigma, b_s, \beta_s) = \sum_{\boldsymbol{x}} C_s c \quad . \tag{8}$$

Note that we use the curvedness as weight for each bin contribution in order to increase the influence of prominent shapes in the image. The shape index histogram is then constructed as the vector of total bin contributions for all bin centres:

$$H_s(\sigma, \beta_s) = [B_s(\sigma, b_{s1}, \beta_s), \ldots, B_s(\sigma, b_{sn_s}, \beta_s)] \tag{9}$$

In the same way as above we can construct a histogram over shape index orientations by choosing a set of n_θ bin centres $b_{\theta 1}, \ldots, b_{\theta n_\theta}$ distributed along the orientation interval $]-\pi/2, \pi/2[$ and calculate the bin contribution, the total bin contributions and the histogram from:

$$C_\theta(\boldsymbol{x}; \sigma, b_\theta, \beta_\theta) = \exp\left(\frac{1}{\beta_\theta}\cos(b_\theta - o)\right) \tag{10}$$

$$B_\theta(\sigma, b_s, \beta_\theta) = \sum_{\boldsymbol{x}} C_\theta m \tag{11}$$

$$H_\theta(\sigma, \beta_\theta) = [B_\theta(\sigma, b_{\theta 1}, \beta_\theta), \ldots, B_\theta(\sigma, b_{\theta n_\theta}, \beta_\theta)] \tag{12}$$

Again, we choose a β_θ as smoothing parameter for the tonal range. Note that we have changed the smoothing from a normal distribution to the circular normal distribution to accommodate for the periodic behaviour of θ.

To construct a joint histogram over the shape index and its orientation we calculate the contributions to a bin centred at shape index b_s and orientation b_θ from

$$B_{s\theta}(\sigma, b_s, b_\theta, \beta_s, \beta_\theta) = \sum_x C_s c C_\theta m \tag{13}$$

We can then construct the joint oriented shape index histogram $H_{s\theta}$ from the combination of all $B_{s\theta}$:

$$H_{s\theta}(\sigma, \beta_s, \beta_\theta) = \begin{bmatrix} B_{s\theta}(\sigma, b_{s1}, b_{\theta 1}, \beta_s, \beta_\theta) & \cdots & B_{s\theta}(\sigma, b_{sn_s}, b_{\theta 1}, \beta_s, \beta_\theta) \\ \vdots & \ddots & \vdots \\ B_{s\theta}(\sigma, b_{s1}, b_{\theta n_\theta}, \beta_s, \beta_\theta) & \cdots & B_{s\theta}(\sigma, b_{sn_s}, b_{\theta n_\theta}, \beta_s, \beta_\theta) \end{bmatrix} \tag{14}$$

At this point, we can perform multi-scale feature description by concatenating histograms at different scales. Following [2], we propose selecting n_σ different scales such that

$$\sigma_i = \sigma_{\text{base}} \cdot \sigma_{\text{ratio}}^i \quad , \quad i = 1, \ldots, n_\sigma \quad . \tag{15}$$

σ_{base} is the smallest shape index scale and σ_{ratio} is the ratio between σ_i and σ_{i+1}. As a final step we normalise the histogram vectors in order to make the description robust to image contrast variations. We have experimented with different normalisation schemes (L_1, L_2 and RootSIFT [1]) without observing significant differences in discriminative performance. We choose L_1 normalisation.

2.5   Gradient Orientation Histograms

For completeness, we also list the gradient orientation histogram which will be used in our experiments. The gradient orientation θ_g and its magnitude m_g are computed from

$$\theta_g(x; \sigma) = \arctan2(L_y, L_x) \quad , \quad m_g = \sqrt{L_x^2 + L_y^2} \tag{16}$$

Similar to the shape index orientation we can construct a histogram by choosing a set of n_g bin centres $b_{g1}, \ldots, b_{gn_g}$ distributed along the gradient orientation interval $]-\pi, \pi[$ and the histogram from:

$$C_g(x; \sigma, b_g, \beta_g) = \exp\left(\frac{1}{\beta_g} \cos\left(\frac{b_g - \theta_g}{2}\right)\right) \tag{17}$$

$$B_g(\sigma, b_s, \beta_g) = \sum_x C_g m_g \tag{18}$$

$$H_g(\sigma, \beta_g) = [B_g(\sigma, b_{g1}, \beta_g), \ldots, B_g(\sigma, b_{gn_g}, \beta_g)] \tag{19}$$

3   Experiments

We evaluate the oriented shape index histograms on the dataset from the *Competition on Cell Classification by Fluorescent Image Analysis* at ICIP 2013 [4]. The dataset consists of 13.596 indirect immunoflourescence images of HEp-2 cells. The cell images come from 83 patients and the task is to classify the cells into 6 classes according to their fluorescence staining pattern. See Fig. 3 for examples.

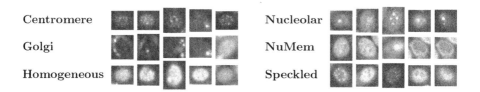

Fig. 3. Examples of the 6 different staining pattern classes in the ICIP 2013 dataset

We assess classification performance from a leave-one-patient-out cross-validation study across all 83 patients in the dataset. Because the patients have different numbers of cells, we measure performance as the weighted average over classification accuracies for the 83 patients where the weights are the number of cells per patient. We employ a standard pipeline consisting of feature extraction and classification. As classifier, we use an RBF kernel SVM with a fixed $C = 1$ and $\gamma_{\text{RBF}} = 1/N$ where N is the dimensionality of the feature vector. Multiclass support is achieved with a one vs. one comparison scheme. We argue that this fixed classifier configuration is suitable for our comparison since the focus of this paper is on feature description and because our (non-shown) experiments indicate that only very small performance improvements can be achieved from adjusting these parameters.

We consider a variety of different feature descriptors in our experiments. In an attempt avoid bias in the comparison, we optimise the parameters for each texture measure using Bayesian optimisation with the framework provided in [14]. For each texture measure, we let the framework perform around 150 function evaluations before selecting the optimal configuration. To avert selecting an accidentally good parameter setting among the 150 parameter configurations that overfits to the dataset, we perform the Bayesian optimisation using cross-validation on 40 randomly selected patients.

In the following, we list the feature descriptor variants that we use for our experiments and their optimised parameters. For all experiments we have set $n_s = 18$, $n_\theta = 16$, $n_{\theta_g} = 16$, $n_\sigma = 5$ when applicable. When calculating the shape index orientation, we use the vector from the cell centre (the centre of the image) to the location of the shape index orientation as fiducial orientation.

- SIH – The shape index histogram H_s with dim. $n_\sigma n_s = 90$ and $\sigma_{\text{base}} = 1.8$, $\sigma_{\text{ratio}} = 1.5$, $\beta_s = 0.33$.

- SIH+GOH – The concatenation of shape index histograms H_s and gradient orientation histograms (GOHs) H_{θ_g} with dim. $n_\sigma(n_s + n_{\theta_g}) = 170$ and $\sigma_{\text{base}} = 1.0$, $\sigma_{\text{ratio}} = 1.8$, $\beta_s = 0.16$, $\beta_{\theta_g} = 0.21$.
- OSIH – The concatenation of H_s and H_θ with dim. $n_\sigma(n_s + n_\theta) = 170$ and $\sigma_{\text{base}} = 1.2$, $\sigma_{\text{ratio}} = 1.6$, $\beta_s = 0.19$, $\beta_\theta = 0.26$,.
- JOSIH – The joint oriented shape index histogram $H_{s\theta}$ with dim. $n_\sigma n_s n_\theta = 1440$ and $\sigma_{\text{base}} = 1.2$, $\sigma_{\text{ratio}} = 1.7$, $\beta_s = 0.19$, $\beta_\theta = 0.25$.
- GOH+OSIH – The concatenation of H_s, H_θ and H_{θ_g} with dim. $n_\sigma(n_s + n_\theta + n_{\theta_g}) = 250$ and $\sigma_{\text{base}} = 1.1$, $\sigma_{\text{ratio}} = 1.8$, $\beta_s = 0.17$, $\beta_s = 0.22$, $\beta_\theta = 0.27$, $\beta_{\theta_g} = 0.21$.

The performance of the descriptors are shown in Figure 4. The significance of the differences in performance is difficult to asses from the boxplots alone and therefore we provide significance levels[3] when comparing descriptor by their performances in the following.

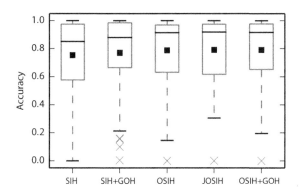

Fig. 4. Comparison of feature descriptors. The boxplot statistics are gathered from the cross-validation across 83 patients. The boxplot is generated using weighted percentiles with the weights being equal to the number of cells per patient. The black square indicates the weighted average accuracy. For the 5 feature descriptors the weighted average accuracies are 0.7530, 0.7696, 0.7878 0.7906, 0.7902.

We see that plain SIH achieves a weighted average accuracy of 0.7530. By adding gradient orientation (SIH+GOH) the accuracy increases to 0.7696 which is significant at a 0.018 confidence level. By adding shape index orientations

---

[3] Our hypothesis test for determining if descriptor A has greater performance than descriptor B is based on bootstrapping. We generate 10,000 bootstrap samples. Each sample is obtained by drawing 83 patients with replacement and computing $\mu_{\text{diff}} = \mu_A - \mu_B$ where μ_A is descriptor A's weighted mean performance on the drawn patients. That is, our bootstrap estimator is the difference between the two weighted mean performances. We wish to test $H_0 : \mu_A \leq \mu_B$ versus $H_1 : \mu_A > \mu_B$. We report the significance level as the bootstrap estimated p-value.

(OSIH) the accuracy increases to 0.7878 which is significant at a 0.004 confidence level. However, going from OSIH to either JOSIH or OSIH+GOH offer only very small improvements significant at 0.318 and 0.359 confidence levels respectively. When comparing SIH+GOH to OSIH the discriminative ability of the shape index orientation over the gradient orientation is significant on a 0.0651 confidence level.

4   Discussion

As we have seen from our experiments, the orientation of second-order curvature improves the discriminative ability of SIHs for the task of cell classification. We find it noteworthy the performance improvements of OSIH are significant from the improvements of GOH. This leads us to conclude that the orientation of the shape index and the gradient capture different image structures. We have also investigated if joint histograms yield better feature description. However, we have shown that this is barely the case on our dataset - especially considering the cost of a much higher feature vector dimensionality. We speculate that this result might be caused by the dataset that contains small images (approximately 80×80 pixels). If the images are too small, we might not be able to collect sufficient statistics for the large joint histograms to become representative. This would favour marginal histograms.

A limitation of OSIHs is that we require an orientation to be given in the image. This cannot be assumed in all situations; *e.g.* for general texture classification we are only given an image. We imagine that one in those cases can detect a dominant orientation and extract OSIHs relative to this orientation. This approach is reminiscent of SIFT where dominant orientations are estimated from peaks in a local gradient orientation histogram. We consider this direction future work.

The purpose of this paper has been to investigate the effectiveness of second-order orientation for texture description. We could have applied other common techniques to improve classification performance (e.g. spatial decomposition [7,8] or bag-of-visual-words [16]). However, this would have muddled our message that second-order orientation is indeed useful and competitive with first-order orientation; at least for the dataset considered in this paper.

5   Conclusion

In this work we introduce the orientation of second-order image structure for feature description. We extend shape index histogram description by including the shape index orientation and evaluate our methods on the task of cell image classification. On the ICIP 2013 dataset, we are able to increase classification accuracy with around 3.5 percentage points (a relative error reduction of 14%) by including the shape index orientation. This exceeds the performance gains achieved by using classic gradient orientations indicating that second-order orientation captures useful image structure.

References

1. Arandjelovic, R., Zisserman, A.: Three things everyone should know to improve object retrieval. In: 2012 IEEE Conference on Computer Vision and Pattern Recognition (CVPR), pp. 2911–2918 (2012)
2. Crosier, M., Griffin, L.: Using basic image features for texture classification. International Journal of Computer Vision 88(3), 447–460 (2010)
3. Dalal, N., Triggs, B.: Histograms of oriented gradients for human detection. In: IEEE Computer Society Conference on Computer Vision and Pattern Recognition. CVPR 2005, vol. 1, pp. 886–893 (2005)
4. Foggia, P., Percannella, G., Soda, P., Vento, M.: Benchmarking HEp-2 cells classification methods. IEEE Transactions on Medical Imaging PP(99), 1–1 (2013)
5. Foggia, P., Percannella, G., Saggese, A., Vento, M.: Pattern recognition in stained HEp-2 cells: Where are we now? Pattern Recognition 47(7), 2305–2314 (2014)
6. Koenderink, J.J., van Doorn, A.J.: Surface shape and curvature scales. Image and Vision Computing 10(8), 557–564 (1992)
7. Larsen, A.B.L., Vestergaard, J.S., Larsen, R.: HEp-2 cell classification using shape index histograms with donut-shaped spatial pooling. IEEE Transactions on Medical Imaging 33(7), 1573–1580 (2014)
8. Lazebnik, S., Schmid, C., Ponce, J.: A sparse texture representation using local affine regions. IEEE Transactions on Pattern Analysis and Machine Intelligence 27(8), 1265–1278 (2005)
9. Lindeberg, T.: Scale-space theory in computer vision. Springer (1993)
10. Lowe, D.G.: Distinctive image features from scale-invariant keypoints. International Journal of Computer Vision 60, 91–110 (2004)
11. Nosaka, R., Ohkawa, Y., Fukui, K.: Feature extraction based on co-occurrence of adjacent local binary patterns. In: Ho, Y.-S. (ed.) PSIVT 2011, Part II. LNCS, vol. 7088, pp. 82–91. Springer, Heidelberg (2011)
12. Ojala, T., Pietikainen, M., Maenpaa, T.: Multiresolution gray-scale and rotation invariant texture classification with local binary patterns. IEEE Transactions on Pattern Analysis and Machine Intelligence 24(7), 971–987 (2002)
13. Pedersen, K., Stensbo-Smidt, K., Zirm, A., Igel, C.: Shape index descriptors applied to texture-based galaxy analysis. In: 2013 IEEE International Conference on Computer Vision (ICCV), pp. 2440–2447 (December 2013)
14. Snoek, J., Larochelle, H., Adams, R.P.: Practical bayesian optimization of machine learning algorithms. In: Pereira, F., Burges, C., Bottou, L., Weinberger, K. (eds.) Advances in Neural Information Processing Systems, vol. 25, pp. 2951–2959. Curran Associates, Inc. (2012)
15. Tola, E., Lepetit, V., Fua, P.: Daisy: An efficient dense descriptor applied to wide-baseline stereo. IEEE Transactions on Pattern Analysis and Machine Intelligence 32(5), 815–830 (2010)
16. Wiliem, A., Sanderson, C., Wong, Y., Hobson, P., Minchin, R.F., Lovell, B.C.: Automatic classification of human epithelial type 2 cell indirect immunofluorescence images using cell pyramid matching. Pattern Recognition (2013)

Dictionary Based Image Segmentation

Anders Bjorholm Dahl$^{(\boxtimes)}$ and Vedrana Andersen Dahl

Department of Applied Mathematics and Computer Science,
Technical University of Denmark, Lyngby, Denmark
{abda,vand}@dtu.dk

Abstract. We propose a method for weakly supervised segmentation of natural images, which may contain both textured or non-textured regions. Our texture representation is based on a dictionary of image patches. To divide an image into separated regions with similar texture we use an implicit level sets representation of the curve, which makes our method topologically adaptive. In addition, we suggest a multi-label version of the method. Finally, we improve upon a similar texture representation, by formulating the computation of a texture probability in terms of a matrix multiplication. This results in an efficient implementation of our segmentation method. We experimentally validated our approach on a number of natural as well as composed images.

1   Introduction

Typically, image segmentation is based on obtaining regions with boundaries in between. This involves modeling of both the image data and the segment boundaries. Approaches ensuring boundary smoothness include modeling the connection between image elements using e.g. Markov random fields [18] which has been efficiently solved using st-cut [1,27]. Modeling the boundary using an explicitly represented deformable curve is another approach that originates from the snakes model [17].

Deformable curves may also be represented using level sets [5], with a number of methods suggesting to use a global information obtained from the curve to guide the segmentation, e.g. Chan and Vese [8] and Yezzi Jr et al. [34]. These methods do not rely on a well defined intensity gradient between regions, but still assume that regions are distinguished by their grey level.

In some cases, however, the average gray level is similar between regions and only textures differ. Textures must therefore be handled differently than intensity and color. The typical approach is to use a texture characterization, mapping the image to a texture descriptor space for segmentation in a similar manner to the intensity method. Here the assumption is that descriptors within textures are similar while they differ between textures.

Such an approach was suggested by Chan and Vese [8] using texture orientation, which has been extended in e.g. Rousson et al. [28] using the structure tensor. Here they estimate the probability of different regions based on estimates of the joint probability of the elements of the structure tensor to evolve the level

© Springer International Publishing Switzerland 2015
R.R. Paulsen and K.S. Pedersen (Eds.): SCIA 2015, LNCS 9127, pp. 26–37, 2015.
DOI: 10.1007/978-3-319-19665-7_3

set. The structure tensor is, however, estimated at a certain scale and in images with textures at different scale the segmentation might fail. To overcome this problem a local texture scale estimate based on total variation was proposed [3,4], where the scale estimate is used for obtaining an improved structure tensor characterization and hereby an improved segmentation. In Brox et al. [2] they use diffusion based on the structure tensor to obtain improved segmentation.

Many other texture descriptors characterizing the local image structure that allow for discriminating between textures have been suggested. These include local fractal features [32], gradient histograms [11,29], local binary patterns [25], textons [22], and more. Often images contain texture on different scale that can be deformed or rotated versions of the same texture. Typically, this is handled in by designing descriptors invariant to such properties.

A related approach for image segmentation is based on sparse dictionaries of image patches [12,19]. Coding the image using sparse dictionaries has shown impressive results for image processing problems like denoising or inpainting. The idea for segmentation is to utilize the strong reconstructive properties of sparse coding by building a dictionary for each texture class. High segmentation performance is obtained by utilizing that the texture class used for learning the dictionary can be reconstructed well whereas other texture classes cannot. Methods focusing on optimal reconstruction have been suggested [26,30], and improved performance has been obtained by also optimizing for discrimination [20,21]. Recently Gao et al. [13] suggested to use sparse dictionaries together with an active contour for segmentation. The algorithm learns the sparse dictionaries from rough user input in the image that must be segmented, and they show accurate segmentations of natural images.

Our texture representation is based on a dictionary of image patches similar to our earlier work [9], where the dictionary is obtained from the image that we want to segment. This approach does not assume any characteristics of the texture, instead we consider texture being information obtained from the image at a given scale. In this broad sense, a texture may also be intensity or color. As such, this dictionary based texture representation is different and in some ways simpler than both texture descriptors and sparse coding. The method [9] uses snakes to divide an image into a object and background. In contrast, in this work we evolve a curve using a level sets representation. By doing so, we obtain topological adaptivity, where disjoint regions with similar texture can be segmented to have the same label. In addition, our novel method can segment an image into an arbitrary number of textures, instead of the two in the formulation from [9]. Finally, we provide an improved texture encoding based on matrix multiplication, resulting in a efficient implementation of the method.

2   Method

Our algorithm is strongly motivated by a region based segmentation method, called active contours without edges, which was originally proposed by Chan and Vese [6] (see also [34] for a related approach) and has led to a number of extensions [7,33] and various numerical implementations [14,16,31]. Our segmentation uses the same fundamental principle but we utilize a dictionary-based texture representation. In the description of our method, we will briefly go through the basic elements of active contours without edges in order to clarify the connection to our model. When explaining our texture representation, we start by considering two labels and then generalize to a multi-label segmentation.

Region Based Curve evolution. Early deformable models [5,17,23] are based on finding edges in the image, which provides only local support and is unsuitable for noisy or textured images. Region based approaches [6,8], on the other hand, utilize the global information obtained from the curve to guide the segmentation.

For example, consider an image $I : \Omega \subset \mathbb{R}^2 \to \mathbb{R}$ containing an object and a background characterized by two different intensities. A curve initialized in the image, and represented by a zero level set of a function $\phi : \Omega \to \mathbb{R}$, leads to labeling of pixels as either *inside* or *outside*. The mean label intensities m_{in} and m_{out} are calculated given this labeling, and here we assume that *inside* contains more of the object, while *outside* contains more of the background. Now the curve is evolved to segment the image. The curve shrinks where pixel intensities are close to m_{out}, while the curve expands where pixel intensities are close to m_{in}. The value $(m_{\mathrm{in}} + m_{\mathrm{out}})/2$ defines a threshold between shrinking and expanding. This two-step proces is repeated. As the curve evolves, mean label intensities are recalculated to more accurately discriminate the intensities of the object and the background, and the curve eventually segments out the object.

Such an evolution of a zero level set is given by

$$\frac{\partial \phi}{\partial t} = \delta_\epsilon(\phi) \left[(m_{\mathrm{out}} - m_{\mathrm{in}})(2I - m_{\mathrm{out}} - m_{\mathrm{in}}) + b\kappa \right] , \tag{1}$$

where $\kappa = \nabla \cdot \left(\frac{\nabla \phi}{|\nabla \phi|} \right)$ is a curvature of the level set curve and the term weighted with b is minimizing the length of the curve. To extend the evolution to all level sets, and depending on the implementation of the level sets, a regularization of the delta function $\delta_\epsilon(\phi)$, may be replaced with $|\nabla \phi|$, or left out [14].

Texture Dictionary. The central part of our method is a dictionary based texture representation, with overlapping image patches being assigned to dictionary elements just as in [9,10]. In this section we will show how this dictionary assignment defines a transformation from an arbitrary labeling of the image into a related probability image. If parts of the image are labeled as *inside* or *outside* this transformation will result in pixel-wise probability of belonging to *inside* or *outside*. The probabilities are computed based on the textures present in the two labels. Having a probability image, we can evolve the curve so that it shrinks where probability for inside is smaller and expands where probability for inside is larger. Just as with region based image segmentation, we can iterate this two-step process, by recomputing probabilities and evolving the curve.

To construct the dictionary we extract a certain number of $M \times M$ patches from an image, collect pixel intensities in patch-vectors of length $m = M^2$, and cluster the patches in n clusters using the k-means algorithm with Euclidian distance. It is the cluster centers that define our dictionary. Figure 1 shows a small image and a small dictionary computed from the image. In this case, the first dictionary element represents the background, elements 2–8 represent the textured object, while elements 9-16 represent transitions from the object to the background. In general, to make sure that the nature of the textures present in an image is captured by the dictionary, we need a large number, typically a few hundred, of dictionary elements, which results in a significant redundancy. Having a texture dictionary we can assign overlapping image patches to the closest dictionary element, again using Euclidian distance. This assignment, also shown in Figure 1 is crucial for our method, because it defines a binary relation between image pixels and dictionary pixels.

Notice the following important property of this construction. Each image patch is assigned to a single dictionary element, but since image patches are overlapping, every image pixel relates to $m = M^2$ dictionary pixels. (Image pixels in a margin of width $M - 1$ relate to less than m dictionary pixels.) In other words, an assignment of a certain image patch to a certain dictionary element makes m pixels from the image patch relate to m pixels from the dictionary element. This binary relation between image pixels and dictionary pixels may be represented using a sparse binary matrix $\mathbf{B}$ with $|\Omega|$ rows and nm columns, where $|\Omega|$ is a total number of image pixels and nm is a total number of dictionary pixels. Note that the matrix $\mathbf{B}$ captures the texture information of the image by simultaneously encoding two things: a dictionary assignment of each image patch and a spatial relationship between the patches. Notice also that for calculating the matrix $\mathbf{B}$ we only need an assignment image.

In case of having an RGB image as an input, we would collect intensities from all three color channels when constructing the dictionary. Once the assignment of image patches to dictionary elements is completed, all computations are the same for any number of color channels.

Label to Probability Transformation.   Having an assignment image (i.e. being able to calculate $\mathbf{B}$) we can define the transformation from a label image to a probability image. A label image is an arbitrary partitioning of Ω in discrete labels, see Figure 1. In case of *inside* or *outside* segmentation, it is sufficient to consider only one label, e.g. *inside*. For this one label, a label image is a binary map $L_{in} : \Omega \rightarrow \{0,1\}$. Each patch from an image I has a corresponding (i.e. extracted from the same position in the image space) label patch from L_{in}. In turn, each dictionary element has a number of image patches assigned to it. This allows us to compute labels of dictionary elements. A label of a dictionary element is computed as a pixel-wise average of the label patches corresponding to image patches that are assigned to the dictionary element in question. Due to averaging, dictionary labels are no longer binary. Figure 1 shows how dictionary labels capture the texture information, e.g. the labels of the dictionary elements representing the transition from the texture to the background show this transition.

Dictionary labels can be computed efficiently by arranging the pixels of the label image in a binary vector $\mathbf{l}_{in}$ and multiplying with $\mathbf{B}$ which is normalized

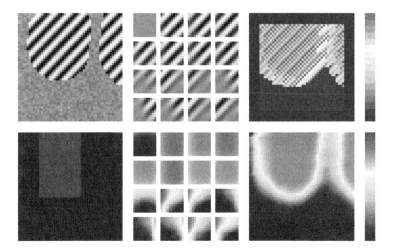

Fig. 1. Elements of the dictionary based texture representation. For a better illustration, both the image and the dictionary are small. Top left: input image. Top middle: dictionary consisting of 16 dictionary elements, ordered in rows. Top right: assignment of the image patches to the dictionary elements, shown as a color of the central patch pixel. The colorbar (far right) runs from darkest blue color representing 0 to red representing 16. Bottom left: An initial labeling of the image. Bottom middle: A dictionary labeling shown in the same order as dictionary elements. Bottom right: A probability image. The colorbar (far right) for the dictionary labeling and the probability image runs from 0 to 1.

so that all its rows sum to 1. The resulting vector

$$\mathbf{d}_{\mathrm{in}} = \mathrm{diag}(\mathbf{B1})^{-1}\mathbf{B}\,\mathbf{l}_{\mathrm{in}} \tag{2}$$

contains a pixel-wise frequency of dictionary elements belonging to *inside*. Here, **1** is a column vector of ones. To obtain dictionary labels, elements of $\mathbf{d}_{\mathrm{in}}$ need to be re-arranged according to the size of the dictionary.

Labels $\mathbf{d}_{\mathrm{in}}$ and $\mathbf{d}_{\mathrm{out}} = 1 - \mathbf{d}_{\mathrm{in}}$ are biased due to the ratio of the area inside $|\Omega_{\mathrm{in}}|$ and area outside $|\Omega_{\mathrm{out}}| = |\Omega| - |\Omega_{\mathrm{in}}|$. For example, had the initial labeling covered just a small part of the textured object, the frequency of *inside* label would be small also for the dictionary elements representing texture. To alleviate this we define a pixel-wise normalization function

$$\tilde{d}_{\mathrm{in}} = \frac{1}{Z}\frac{d_{\mathrm{in}}}{|\Omega_{\mathrm{in}}|}, \quad Z = \frac{d_{\mathrm{in}}}{|\Omega_{\mathrm{in}}|} + \frac{d_{\mathrm{out}}}{|\Omega_{\mathrm{out}}|}, \tag{3}$$

which operates on each element of $\mathbf{d}_{\mathrm{in}}$.

The next transformation involves computing pixel-wise image probabilities from the dictionary labels. This is again performed by averaging. Each dictionary label is placed in the image space at the positions of image patches that are assigned to the dictionary element in question. Due to the patch overlap, up to m values need to be averaged to compute a pixel probability.

The efficient computation is performed by multiplying

$$\mathbf{p}_{\text{in}} = \text{diag}(\mathbf{B}^{\text{T}}\mathbf{1})^{-1}\mathbf{B}^{\text{T}}\,\tilde{\mathbf{d}}_{\text{in}} \,. \tag{4}$$

Rearranging elements of $\mathbf{p}_{\text{in}}$ into an image grid results in the probability image $P_{\text{in}} : \Omega \to [0,1]$. Note that P_{in} is different from L_{in} because image patches from both inside and outside may be assigned to the same dictionary element. The binary values from L_{in} will therefore diffuse according to the texture information encoded in $\mathbf{B}$. We will utilize this diffusion to drive the curve evolution.

Our way of obtaining a probability image is closely related to the method described in [9]. However, our approach is more efficient. In [9] a sequences of patch averaging is performed every time a probability image needs to be computed. Here we notice that the relation between dictionary and image is unchanged, and that computing probability image includes two linear transformations. This allows us to precompute the matrix $\mathbf{B}$, significantly speeding up the computation of a probability image. Note that $\mathbf{B}$ is a binary and sparse matrix, so storing this large matrix may be done space efficiently.

Multiple Labels. To handle multiple labels, and not just *inside* or *outside*, we create a layered label image with layers L_1 to L_K. Each layer is a binary indicator of a label, and layers sum to one in each pixel. The transformation (2) is applied to each layer, resulting in dictionary labels $\mathbf{d}_1$ to $\mathbf{d}_K$. Area normalization is now performed pixel-wise for all layers

$$(\tilde{d}_1, \tilde{d}_2, \dots, \tilde{d}_K) = \frac{1}{Z}\left(\frac{d_1}{|\Omega_1|}, \frac{d_2}{|\Omega_2|}, \dots, \frac{d_K}{|\Omega_K|}\right), \quad Z = \sum_{k=1}^{K}\frac{d_k}{|\Omega_k|} \,. \tag{5}$$

After area normalization the transformation (4) is applied to each $\tilde{\mathbf{d}}_k$, resulting in K probability images, P_1 to P_K, which sum to one in each pixel, but are no longer binary.

Curve Evolution. We can now define a curve evolution for texture segmentation. Again we initially consider segmentation into *inside* and *outside*. A closed curve represented as a zero level set of a function $\phi : \Omega \to \mathbb{R}$ defines a label image L_{in} which attains value one where ϕ is negative and zero otherwise. The label image is transformed into probability image P_{in} as described above. Curve points at locations with large P_{in} should move outwards, curve points with large $P_{\text{out}} = 1 - P_{\text{in}}$ should move inwards, and the curve should converge in a band where $P_{\text{in}} = P_{\text{out}}$. To obtain the desired behaviour we define a curve evolution as

$$\frac{\partial \phi}{\partial t} = \frac{1}{2} - P_{\text{in}} + b\kappa|\nabla \phi| \,, \tag{6}$$

with a curve length minimization term as in (1). Notice that $0.5 - P_{\text{in}} = 0.5(P_{\text{out}} - P_{\text{in}})$.

To segment multiple labels we represent each of the K labels with a single level set function ϕ_k, $k = 1, \dots, K$. Using such an approach a care has to be taken to avoid vacuum and overlap [35]. Indeed, if we generalized to multiple labels by evolving each level set ϕ_k using (6) and a corresponding probability image P_k, a vacuum would occur. This is because probabilities sum to one in each pixels, and situation might occur where none of the label probabilities P_k are larger than 0.5 in some places, leading to all level set curves shrinking, and causing vacuum. Therefore we perform a following pixel-wise transformation of probabilities for all labels

$$(\tilde{p}_1, \tilde{p}_2, \ldots, \tilde{p}_K) = \left(\frac{p_1}{p_1 + \max_{j \neq 1}(p_j)}, \frac{p_2}{p_2 + \max_{j \neq 2}(p_j)}, \ldots, \frac{p_K}{p_K + \max_{j \neq K}(p_j)} \right). \quad (7)$$

Basically, we normalize the probability p_k not by using the sum of all $p_j, j = 1, \ldots, K$, but only considering the most probable of other labels. Resulting probabilities $(\tilde{p}_1, \tilde{p}_2, \ldots, \tilde{p}_K)$ have the property that the two largest values sum to 1, therefore avoiding vacuum (as at least one value is larger or equal to 0.5) and avoiding overlap (as only one value may be larger than 0.5). Notice also that the transformation defined by (7) reduces to an identity for $K = 2$.

The resulting level set evolution for a multi-label segmentation is

$$\frac{\partial \phi_k}{\partial t} = \frac{1}{2} - \tilde{P}_k + b\kappa |\nabla \phi_k|, \quad k = 1, \ldots, K. \quad (8)$$

Our relative probabilities $\tilde{P}_k$ do not guarantee elimination of vacuum and overlap. However, based on experiments we concluded that the level set curves align well.

Algorithm. Our deformable model for the dictionary based image segmentation is initialized with an image I, an initial curve ϕ^0 (or, in the case of multiple labels curves ϕ_k^0, but we will from now leave out the subscript k) and a few parameters defining the dictionary: patch size m, dictionary size n and normalization flag. Normalization flag indicates whether the image patches have been normalized to unit length. In a preprocessing step, the dictionary is constructed, overlapping image patches are assigned to the dictionary patches, and a sparse binary matrix **B** is constructed.

After preprocessing, a curve is iteratively evolved. In each evolution step a (multi-layered) label image L is obtained by thresholding ϕ. The label image is transformed to a dictionary labels using (2), area normalization is performed as in (5), and result is transformed back to the image using (4). In the case of a multi-label segmentation the resulting probability images are transformed using (7). Finally, the curve is updated by (6) or (8) in a multi-label case, withe

$$\phi^{t+1} = \phi^t + \Delta t \frac{\partial \phi}{\partial t} \quad (9)$$

until convergence. This leaves us with the resulting segmentation $\hat{\phi}$ and the resulting probability images $\hat{P}$.

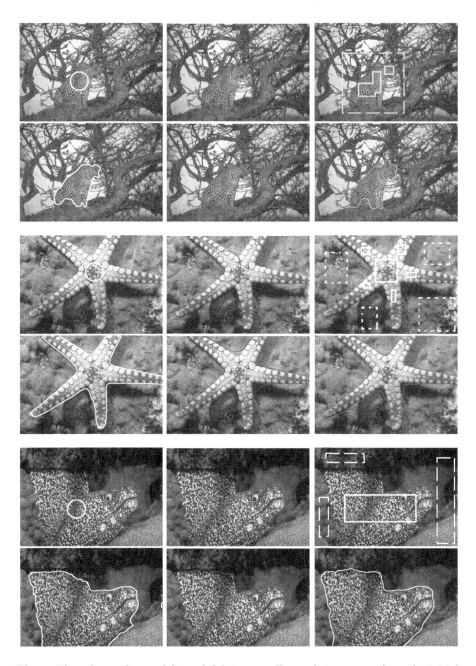

Fig. 2. Three leopard, star fish, and fish images. For each image we show the initialization at the top row and segmentation result at the bottom. Left – the proposed method. Middle – dictionary snakes [9]. Right – sparse texture active contours [13].

Fig. 3. Zebras and lions images. For each image we show the initialization at the top row and segmentation result at the bottom. Left – the proposed method. Middle – dictionary snakes [9]. Right – sparse texture active contours [13].

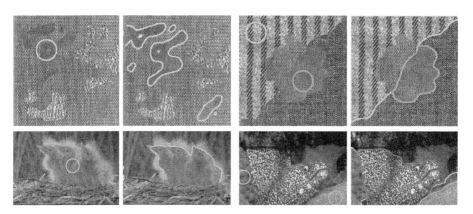

Fig. 4. Two composite and two natural images with three-label and four-label segmentation. For each image we show the initialization to the left and the segmentation to the right. One label (the background) is not shown by the curve, as it is the region not covered by other labels.

Implementation Details. Without the term minimizing the curve length, our iterative algorithm converges very fast, since the large time steps can be taken. On the other hand, the regularization by the length of the curve imposes a stringent time step restriction. This issue is addressed in [14–16] where fast approximations are obtained by replacing or supplementing the curve evolution with smoothing. Our current implementation is therefor as follows. When evolving the curve using a forward Euler step we use a large time step, ignoring the stability restrictions. This might introduce numerical errors, which we damp by smoothing the level set function with a Gaussian kernel.

3   Results

To demonstrate the strengths of our algorithm, we show results on the images from the Berkley segmentation dataset [24], such that we can make a direct comparison with related scientific work. We use the same parameters for all results shown in this section. Our dictionary is build from clustering 20000 randomly sampled image patches of size 3×3 pixels into 1000 clusters. The parameter b from (6) is set to 1.5 and the smoothing is performed by a Gaussian kernel with a standard deviation of 1.5.

Figures 2 and 3 show our inside-outside segmentation results compared to a number of images presented in [9] and [13]. The advantages of our method compared to [9] are topological adaptivity and a higher accuracy due to easier curve regularization. Compared to [13], our method accepts a much simpler initialization than the elaborated marking of both the object and the background.

Neither [9] or [13] support multiple labels, so for a multi-label case we bring only our results in Figure 4.

4   Discussion and Conclusion

Our texture representation with image patches clustered in a relatively large number of clusters might seem redundant. Indeed, some dictionary elements might be very similar. Therefore, a small variation in an image patch may result in a change in an assignment. This is, however, not an issue as long as similar dictionary elements have similar labels.

The experiments show a good discriminative properties of our texture representation, especially when we consider the simplicity and the general nature of the approach. Likewise, our segmentation results are encouraging compared to related work, especially considering the limited user input for initialization.

Acknowledgments. The authors acknowledge the financial support from CINEMA: the allianCe for ImagiNg of Energy MAterials (grant no. 1305-00032B) and NEXIM project (grant no. 11-116226), both funded by the Danish Council for Strategic Research.

References

1. Boykov, Y., Kolmogorov, V.: An experimental comparison of min-cut/max-flow algorithms for energy minimization in vision. TPAMI **26**(9), 1124–1137 (2004)
2. Brox, T., Rousson, M., Deriche, R., Weickert, J.: Colour, texture, and motion in level set based segmentation and tracking. Image and Vision Computing **28**(3), 376–390 (2010)
3. Brox, T., Weickert, J.: A tv flow based local scale measure for texture discrimination. In: Pajdla, T., Matas, J.G. (eds.) ECCV 2004. LNCS, vol. 3022, pp. 578–590. Springer, Heidelberg (2004)
4. Brox, T., Weickert, J.: A tv flow based local scale estimate and its application to texture discrimination. Journal of Visual Communication and Image Representation **17**(5), 1053–1073 (2006)
5. Caselles, V., Catté, F., Coll, T., Dibos, F.: A geometric model for active contours in image processing. Numerische mathematik **66**(1), 1–31 (1993)
6. Chan, T., Vese, L.A.: An active contour model without edges. In: Nielsen, M., Johansen, P., Fogh Olsen, O., Weickert, J. (eds.) Scale-Space 1999. LNCS, vol. 1682, pp. 141–151. Springer, Heidelberg (1999)
7. Chan, T.F., Sandberg, B.Y., Vese, L.A.: Active contours without edges for vector-valued images. Journal of Visual Communication and Image Representation **11**(2), 130–141 (2000)
8. Chan, T.F., Vese, L.A.: Active contours without edges. TIP **10**(2), 266–277 (2001)
9. Dahl, A.B., Dahl, V.A.: Dictionary snakes. In: ICPR (2014)
10. Dahl, A.L., Larsen, R.: Learning dictionaries of discriminative image patches. In: BMVC (2011)
11. Dalal, N., Triggs, B.: Histograms of oriented gradients for human detection. In: CVPR, vol. 1, pp. 886–893. IEEE (2005)
12. Elad, M.: Sparse and redundant representations: from theory to applications in signal and image processing. Springer (2010)
13. Gao, Y., Bouix, S., Shenton, M., Tannenbaum, A.: Sparse texture active contour. TIP (2013)
14. Gibou, F., Fedkiw, R.: A fast hybrid k-means level set algorithm for segmentation. In: 4th Annual Hawaii International Conference on Statistics and Mathematics, pp. 281–291. Hawaii, USA (2005)
15. Goldenberg, R., Kimmel, R., Rivlin, E., Rudzsky, M.: Fast geodesic active contours. TIP **10**(10), 1467–1475 (2001)
16. He, L., Osher, S.J.: Solving the chan-vese model by a multiphase level set algorithm based on the topological derivative. In: Sgallari, F., Murli, A., Paragios, N. (eds.) SSVM 2007. LNCS, vol. 4485, pp. 777–788. Springer, Heidelberg (2007)
17. Kass, M., Witkin, A., Terzopoulos, D.: Snakes: Active contour models. IJCV **1**(4), 321–331 (1988)
18. Li, S.Z.: Markov random field modeling in computer vision. Springer-Verlag New York, Inc. (1995)
19. Mairal, J., Bach, F., Ponce, J.: Task-driven dictionary learning. TPAMI **34**(4), 791–804 (2012)
20. Mairal, J., Bach, F., Ponce, J., Sapiro, G., Zisserman, A.: Discriminative learned dictionaries for local image analysis. In: CVPR, pp. 1–8. IEEE (2008a)
21. Mairal, J., Bach, F., Ponce, J., Sapiro, G., Zisserman, A.: Supervised dictionary learning (2008b). arXiv preprint arXiv:0809.3083

22. Malik, J., Belongie, S., Leung, T., Shi, J.: Contour and texture analysis for image segmentation. IJCV **43**(1), 7–27 (2001)
23. Malladi, R., Sethian, J.A., Vemuri, B.C.: Shape modeling with front propagation: A level set approach. TPAMI **17**(2), 158–175 (1995)
24. Martin, D., Fowlkes, C., Tal, D., Malik, J.: A database of human segmented natural images and its application to evaluating segmentation algorithms and measuring ecological statistics. In: ICCV, vol. 2, pp. 416–423. IEEE (2001)
25. Ojala, T., Pietikainen, M., Maenpaa, T.: Multiresolution gray-scale and rotation invariant texture classification with local binary patterns. TPAMI **24**(7), 971–987 (2002)
26. Peyré, G.: Sparse modeling of textures. Journal of Mathematical Imaging and Vision **34**(1), 17–31 (2009)
27. Rother, C., Kolmogorov, V., Blake, A.: "grabcut": Interactive foreground extraction using iterated graph cuts. ACM Trans. Graph. **23**(3), 309–314 (2004)
28. Rousson, M., Brox, T., Deriche, R.: Active unsupervised texture segmentation on a diffusion based feature space. In: CVPR, vol. 2, p. II-699. IEEE (2003)
29. Santner, J., Unger, M., Pock, T., Leistner, C., Saffari, A., Bischof, H.: Interactive texture segmentation using random forests and total variation. In: BMVC, pp. 1–12. Citeseer (2009)
30. Skretting, K., Husøy, J.H.: Texture classification using sparse frame-based representations. EURASIP journal on applied signal processing **2006**, 102 (2006)
31. Song, B., Chan, T.: A fast algorithm for level set based optimization. UCLA Cam Report **2**(68) (2002)
32. Varma, M., Garg, R.: Locally invariant fractal features for statistical texture classification. In: ICCV, pp. 1–8. IEEE (2007)
33. Vese, L.A., Chan, T.F.: A multiphase level set framework for image segmentation using the mumford and shah model. IJCV **50**(3), 271–293 (2002)
34. Yezzi Jr, A., Tsai, A., Willsky, A.: A statistical approach to snakes for bimodal and trimodal imagery. In: ICCV, vol. 2, pp. 898–903. IEEE (1999)
35. Zhao, H.K., Chan, T., Merriman, B., Osher, S.: A variational level set approach to multiphase motion. Journal of computational physics **127**(1), 179–195 (1996)

Faces and Gestures

A Framework for Articulated Hand Pose Estimation and Evaluation

Gernot Riegler[✉], David Ferstl[✉], Matthias Rüther[✉],
and Horst Bischof[✉]

Institute for Computer Graphics and Vision, Graz University of Technology,
Inffeldgasse 16, 8010 Graz, Austria
{riegler,ferstl,ruether,bischof}@icg.tugraz.at.com

Abstract. We present in this paper a framework for articulated hand pose estimation and evaluation. Within this framework we implemented recently published methods for hand segmentation and inference of hand postures. We further propose a new approach for the segmentation and extend existing convolutional network based inference methods. Additionally, we created a new dataset that consists of a synthetically generated training set and accurately annotated test sequences captured with two different consumer depth cameras. The evaluation shows that we can improve with our methods the state-of-the-art. To foster further research, we will make all sources and the complete dataset used in this work publicly available.

Keywords: Pose estimation · Random forest · Convolutional networks · Segmentation · Synthetic data

1 Introduction

The availability of affordable depth sensors in the consumer market, especially beginning with the first Microsoft Kinect, provided new ways for human computer interaction. This hardware combined with data-driven methods [10,22,23] enabled the estimation of human body pose in real-time which is now used for example in video games. The latest depth sensors, especially those based on the time-of-flight principle, have a smaller package size than ever. They can be integrated into notebooks, tablets, or bundled with a virtual reality headset, which allows new and interesting possibilities for natural interactions by hand gestures and movements.

Although the pose estimation of an articulated hand shares similarities with body pose estimation, it remains a challenging problem. First of all, a human hand has many degrees of freedom. This implies also the possibilities for a high degree of self occlusions. For instance, only a few joints are visible in the depth map of a fist gesture. Further, depending on the viewpoint, one hand pose can be mapped to significantly different depth maps. An additional difficulty is inherited from the sensors themselves. The output of a consumer depth sensor is typically of low resolution and contains noise of different distributions.

© Springer International Publishing Switzerland 2015
R.R. Paulsen and K.S. Pedersen (Eds.): SCIA 2015, LNCS 9127, pp. 41–52, 2015.
DOI: 10.1007/978-3-319-19665-7_4

Current methods for articulated hand pose estimation can be roughly divided into two areas. Model based tracking methods such as [1,11,16,20] try to fit a known hand-model to the depth data and track it over time. Whereas discriminative approaches like [14,24–26] try to learn a mapping from the visual input of the depth sensor to a pose vector. However, a comparison between different methods remained difficult in the past, because of the lack of available datasets and source codes. Only recently, Tang *et al.* [24] and Tompson *et al.* [26] independently published datasets of varying quality.

In this work we provide a common framework for hand pose estimation. This includes interchangeable methods for hand segmentation, preprocessing, model training and inference. We re-implemented several published methods and introduce also extensions, especially for methods based on convolutional networks. Further, we propose a mean-shift method for hand segmentation that gives a very good trade-off between speed and accuracy. To overcome the limitations of existing datasets, we created a new one that contains more than $4 \cdot 10^5$ annotated training images, rendered from a realistic human model. To evaluate the different methods, we additionally annotated test sequences captured with two different depth sensors. To foster further research of articulated hand pose estimation, we will make the source code of the complete framework and the datasets publicly available at our project page: http://rvlab.icg.tugraz.at/pose.

2   Related Work

Pose estimation and the related gesture recognition of a human hand has due to its importance for human computer interaction a long history in the computer vision community. Mitra and Acharya [17] give a good overview of gesture recognition. Erol *et al.* [7] focus specifically on hand pose estimation, where the authors divide the approaches based on the data input, color images and depth maps, and between model based tracking methods and discriminative methods.

With the availability of affordable depth sensors in the consumer market, the interest in pose estimation from depth maps has increased. In the seminal work of Shotton *et al.* [22], the authors utilize a random decision forest for body pose estimation from depth data. They predict for each pixel a class probability, if it belongs to the background, or to one of the 38 defined body parts. In the same spirit, Girshick *et al.* [10] and Sun *et al.* [23] refine the random forest framework with joint regression methods and incorporating dependency relationships between output variables, respectively.

Earlier methods to estimate the articulated hand pose rely on model based tracking. Oikonomidis *et al.* [20] fit a hand model with 26 degrees of freedom to the data with particle swarm optimization. Similar, De La Gorce *et al.* [11] use a detailed hand mesh with simulated texture and lightning to fit and track a model to a monocular image stream. To handle occlusions, Balan *et al.* [1] detect finger tips as salient points and assign them to the hand jointly with the pose estimation. Further, they include edge and optical flow clues in their objective function. Melax *et al.* [16] propose a tracker based simulation of a hand model to fit the depth data in terms of a 3D error function. They spawn multiple simulations and constrain the hand model to improve the overall accuracy.

Following the success in body pose estimation, discriminative methods have recently become popular for articulated hand pose estimation. Keskin *et al.* [14] propose to cluster the training data based on their shape with a random decision forest and train for each cluster an expert similar to [22]. In [25], Tang *et al.* train a semi-supervised random forest to combine on synthetic data in combination with sparsely labeled real depth data. The structure of the hand in a random forest framework is exploited by Tang *et al.* [24]. The authors treat the joint localization as a structured coarse to fine search by conditioning the trees on the previous estimations and a latent tree model.

In contrast to random forest based methods, approaches that rely on convolutional networks have become popular since the enormous success in object classification [15]. Hand segmentation with a convolutional network is described by Neverova *et al.* [18]. They combine synthetic and real depth data to conduct a pixel-wise prediction of 20 different hand parts. In the work of Tompson *et al.* [26] the authors train a convolutional network to predict joint locations in a coarse 2D heat-map. The depth of the joint is obtained by the depth value at the 2D joint location. An additional inverse kinematic model is utilized to refine the results.

All of the above mentioned methods use their own datasets for training and evaluation. Unfortunately, most of the authors did not publish their datasets, making a fair comparison complicated. Only very recently Tang *et al.* [24] and Tompson *et al.* [26] independently released their images along with annotations. However, these datasets have their drawbacks. The annotations provided by Tang *et al.* are located on the bone centers, rather than on the joint locations of a human hand skeleton. This prohibits refinement and regularization techniques that rely on this skeletal information. Further, the annotations were obtained by the tracking method of [16] and only little effort was put into refining the estimates. The dataset of Tompson *et al.* has a higher annotation accuracy, but lacks in variability of the training data. Only a sequence of a single user was recorded for training. The test set consists of two persons, whereby one is the same as in the training sequence.

Our synthetic dataset that is used for training provides a high annotation accuracy in terms of joint locations. To ensure a high variability in the dataset we use several size and shape variations of the animated hand. Because the training set is synthetically generated, the test sequences are guaranteed to be completely independent to the test sequences. Further, we provide test sequences captured with two different depth sensors to evaluate all methods within our framework.

3   Framework

In this section we describe the general framework we utilize for articulated hand pose estimation. We summarize the existing methods implemented in our framework and propose a new method for hand segmentation and extensions to infer the joint locations. An overview of the framework is visualized in Figure 1.

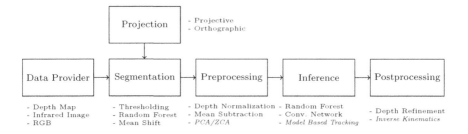

Fig. 1. Framework Overview: The main building blocks of our hand pose estimation pipeline. The data provider loads depth maps and optional infrared images from a specified dataset, or from a camera stream. The projection is an abstraction of the camera parameters and maps the pixels of a depth map from the 2D image space to 3D world coordinates and vice versa. In the next step, the hand gets segmented from the background. The segmentation results are then preprocessed including depth normalization and mean subtraction. Finally, the joint locations are predicted in an inference step and postprocessing is conducted to refine the results.

Data Provider. The data provider abstracts the access to the various sources of data. This allows the evaluation of a single method on different datasets. Further, the data provider can encapsulate a camera stream to qualitatively test a method on new data. The type of data itself depends on the depth sensor. For a typical time-of-flight sensor the data consists of a depth map and an infrared image. However, it could also include a color image, or any combination of it.

Projection. The focus of this work is on hand pose estimation from depth data. This implies that we can project the points from the 2D image space to a metric 3D space and vice versa given the camera projection model. For the remainder of this work we will stick to the following convention: We denote a coordinate in the 2D image space with associated depth d as $\mathbf{u} = (u, v, d)^T$. Given a projection ϕ the 2D point is related to a 3D world coordinate $\mathbf{x} = (x, y, z)$ by $\phi(\mathbf{u}) = \mathbf{x}$. Conversely, given a 3D point we get the corresponding image coordinate with a depth value by $\phi'(\mathbf{x}) = \mathbf{u}$. The projection model ϕ highly depends on the camera. It can be a projective model, or an orthographic one. Further, the camera intrinsics need to be known, for example from a camera calibration procedure. For more details we refer to [12].

Segmentation. Most of the existing methods need a hand detection or segmentation prior to the inference. The result of this step is either one, or possibly more detection results represented as bounding boxes, or as pixel-wise segmentation masks. Currently, we have implemented two existing approaches and we additionally propose a new mean-shift based approach.

The most simple hand segmentation is given by depth thresholding. Based on the common assumption that the hand is the nearest object to the sensor, one defines all pixels as belonging to a hand where the depth d is in the interval $[d_{\text{nearest}}, d_{\text{nearest}} + t_t]$, where t_t is a user defined threshold. One can easily see, that the parameter t_t is very critical and that the segmentation, depending on the arm posture, will include many pixels of other body parts and the background.

The second existing approach implemented in our framework is derived from [22] and used for example in [26] for hand segmentation. We train a random forest that assigns each pixel a probability if it belongs to a hand or the background. Following the work of [22], we sample split functions in the training phase of the form

$$D\left(u + d^{-1}\Delta u, v + d^{-1}\Delta v\right) - D(u, v) \geq t_d \tag{1}$$

where (u, v) is the current pixel location with associated depth d, $(\Delta u, \Delta v)$ is a random offset vector sampled from a log-space, t_d is a sampled threshold and D is the depth map. We further apply a median filter and a morphological closing to remove outliers from the segmentation result.

The two segmentation methods described above work in the 2D image space. We propose a new simple technique that is fast and directly works with the points in 3D. Given the set of 3D points $\{x_i\}_{i=1}^N$ and a starting point $\mathbf{x}^{(0)}$, for example the nearest point to the sensor, we apply a mean shift segmentation [5] to find the hand center by iterating

$$\mathbf{x}^{(t+1)} = \sum_i k\left(\left\|\frac{\mathbf{x}_i - \mathbf{x}^{(t)}}{h}\right\|\right) \mathbf{x}_i \left(\sum_i k\left(\left\|\frac{\mathbf{x}_i - \mathbf{x}^{(t)}}{h}\right\|\right)\right)^{-1} \tag{2}$$

until convergence or a maximum number of iterations. With an appropriate kernel profile $k(\cdot)$, the bandwidth parameter h can be related to the circumference of a common hand. A point x_i is considered as belonging to a hand, if $k(\cdot)$ is greater than ϵ.

Preprocessing. Convolutional networks, need an input of a predefined size. Therefore, we resize the segmented hand to an uniform patch size $p_w \times p_h$. However, this is also beneficial for other methods, because it decreases the variability between depth sensors that have different resolutions. We improve this robustness further, by enforcing a zero mean and a unit standard deviation of the depth values in each patch.

Convolutional network based methods have a better training convergence by decorrelating the data. For this purpose, we subtract the mean of all training samples from the data. Optionally, we could perform a Zero Component Analysis [4].

Inference. Given the segmented and preprocessed patch, we want to infer the hand posture that is defined by the set of joint locations. At the moment, we have implemented a random forest method and different approaches based on convolutional networks. All methods have in common that they determine the location in the 2D image space (u, v) with an associated depth value d, $\mathbf{u} = (u, v, d)$.

The first method is a simple regression forest similar to [9]. Given the segmented and preprocessed hand patches P_i as input, the samples are separated by split functions of the form

$$P_i(u_1, v_1) - P_i(u_2, v_2) \geq t_p \tag{3}$$

where (u_i, v_i) get sampled from the interval $[0, p_w) \times [0, p_h)$. In each leaf node we store the mean joint locations of the training samples that reach this node. At test time, the estimated joint locations are then given by the mean of the independent tree predictions.

The second type of methods that we have implemented are based on convolutional networks. One existing approach to compute predictions for (u, v) is to regress the locations of each joint in a discrete heat-map of size $h_w \times h_h$ as proposed in [26]. This has the drawback that the depth of each joint has to be determined in an additional postprocessing step. Hence, we extend this approach by adding for each joint an additional 1D discrete heat-map of size h_d to also infer the depth. A full 3D heat-map for each joint would not be feasible, because of the huge amount of parameters that have to be computed.

Instead of regressing a heat-map for the joint locations, we propose to regress the values directly. This has the benefit that we do not have to discretize the space of valid locations and further it reduces the amount of parameters in the convolutional network. In this way we can directly regress the depth values and along with the 2D joint locations.

An addition to this model relies on the assumption that the set of joint locations lies on a lower dimensional sub-space. Therefore, we can regress the values of the lower dimensional sub-space and reducing the number of parameters we have to estimate. One way to compute a mapping to a lower dimensional space is by applying a Principal Component Analysis (PCA) on the set of joint locations given by the training data [19]. This maps the joint space to a linear sub-space. However, we can implement a non-linear mapping directly in the convolutional network with an auto-encoder [13] and learn the sub-space jointly with the network itself. This is achieved by introducing a fully-connected layer of N neurons between fully-connected layers of M neurons, given $N \ll M$ [13].

Postprocessing. The postprocessing step serves two purposes. First, for methods that do not directly infer the depth of a joint, we try to estimate it from the depth map itself by choosing the depth value at the estimated 2D joint location. The second purpose is the refinement of the estimation result. For the heat-map estimates we obtain sub-pixel accuracy by fitting a 2D Gaussian distribution [26] to the heat-map. For the future we also plan to implement different kinds of inverse kinematic models, as for example proposed in [25], or [26].

4   Dataset

This section describes the proposed dataset that consists of a synthetically generated training set and three test sequences captured by two different consumer depth sensors. With this approach we can cover a wide range of hand shapes and also many hand postures in the training set, ensuring a high variability. Further, we minimize with this approach the cumbersome manual annotation of the data and therefore increase the accuracy of the annotations. The test sets are recorded with two different depth sensors. This has the benefit that we can evaluate the generalization-abilities of the different methods.

An important decision for the annotation is the placement of the points that define the hand skeleton. We defined those points in a way that they closely resemble the anatomy of a human hand. Therefore, we place them directly at the real joints of the hand and additionally on the finger tips. A 2D sketch of this is shown in Figure 2(a). A major advantage of this placement is that the distance between the single points stay almost constant in 3D.

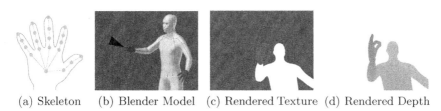

(a) Skeleton   (b) Blender Model   (c) Rendered Texture   (d) Rendered Depth

Fig. 2. Hand Skeleton and Blender Data: (a) A sketch of the hand skeleton that we use for the annotation. It closely resembles the anatomy of a real human hand so that the distances in 3D stay almost constant. (b) A textured MakeHuman mesh in Blender with the complete skeleton. The black pyramid visualizes the camera. (c) The rendered textures can be used to train segmentation algorithms. (d) The corresponding rendered depth map of the Blender scene.

The whole synthetic training data is rendered in Blender [3]. We utilize therefore a high quality mesh of a complete human body that is created with Make-Human [2]. For the model visualized in Blender see Figure 2(b). By using a complete human body model over a hand model alone, it is possible to generate more realistic images. We also texture the model by coloring the hand in red. In this way, we also create training data for segmentation algorithms. The output of a Blender rendering is the segmentation mask of the hand, a depth map that is perfectly pixel-aligned to the segmentation mask, and the joint annotations. For an example see Figures 2(c) and 2(d). After the rendering we add a Gaussian noise with a zero mean and a standard deviation of $\sigma = 3$ to the depth maps to simulate some of the sensor noise.

To achieve a high variability in the training set, we alter the model in two ways. First, we change the size of the hand and the fingers to simulate the diversity of different people. Second, we model a wide range of hand gestures and arm postures. This set is further increased by interpolating between random pairs of the modeled poses. In total, we rendered over 4×10^5 depth maps with associated hand segmentation masks and annotations with this setup.

For the test set we recorded three sequences with 400 frames each. We employ as depth sensors the Creative GestureCam [6] and the PMD Pico [21]. Both

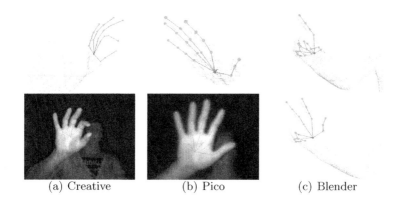

(a) Creative   (b) Pico   (c) Blender

Fig. 3. Annotations: (a) and (b) depict sample annotations in the 3D point cloud and the 2D infrared image. In comparison, (b) shows the annotation and the point cloud of the synthetic generated data.

sensors use the time-of-flight principle to compute dense depth measurements. Additionally to the depth maps, the sensors provide infrared images. We annotated the data with the aid of those infrared images and the 3D point clouds associated with the depth maps. Samples of the annotations from the test sequences in comparison to the synthetically generated data is shown in Figure 3.

5 Evaluation

In this section, we evaluate the above described methods on our proposed dataset. We compare the different approaches to segment the hand from the background in Section 5.1. The evaluation of the pose estimation is afterwards described in Section 5.2.

5.1 Hand Segmentation

To evaluate the performance of the hand segmentation we use the intersection-over-union metric as it is commonly used in object localization [8]:

$$r = \mathrm{area}\,(B_{\mathrm{es}} \cap B_{\mathrm{gt}}) \cdot \mathrm{area}\,(B_{\mathrm{es}} \cup B_{\mathrm{gt}})^{-1} \ . \tag{4}$$

B_{es} is the estimated hand localization and defined as the rectangle that encloses the hand segmentation. Similarly, we define B_{gt} as the rectangle with minimum area that encloses the 2D ground-truth joint locations. The value r is in the interval of $[0, 1]$ and higher values correspondent to better hand segmentations.

We evaluate the random forest based hand segmentation as explained in [26] and our proposed mean-shift based approach. The parameters for the random forest are chosen as in [26], with four trees, a maximal tree depth of 25 and 10.000 sampled split-functions per node. The random forest is trained on a subset of 20% of the training images. For the mean-shift based approach we use a exponential kernel profile $k(x) = \exp(-x)$ and set the bandwidth parameter to $h = 13.5$. As baseline, we also include a simple depth thresholding. In this case, the segmentation contains all pixels with depth value d in the interval $[d_{\text{nearest}}, d_{\text{nearest}} + t_t]$ and $t_t = 300$mm.

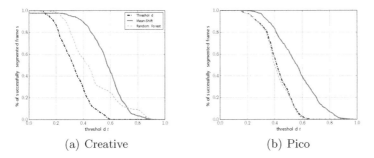

(a) Creative   (b) Pico

Fig. 4. Segmentation Results: The plots depict the percentage of frames where the intersection-over-union r is greater than a threshold t. The first test sequence was recorded with the Creative GestureCam (a) and the second one with a PMD Pico (b).

We evaluated those three methods on a test sequence captured by a Creative GestureCam and on one captured by a PMD Pico. In Figure 4 we plot the percentage of frames with a intersection-over-union value r greater than an increasing threshold t. We can see that the proposed mean-shift based approach delivers the best segmentations in terms of fitting the ground-truth 2D joint locations the tightest. Our method also generalizes better over different camera models. The random forest method and the thresholding include many pixels of the arm and other body parts. However, the mean-shift approach fails in some cases to find the hand, in contrast to the random forest and the thresholding method. This is especially the case, if the hand is not the nearest object to the depth sensor. Another advantage of the mean-shift segmentation is the speed as it runs a magnitude faster than the random forest based method.

5.2 Pose Estimation

In this section we evaluate the above described methods for inference on two of our three test sequences[1]. We use for all experiments the proposed mean-shift approach to segment the hand from the background, with the previously stated parameters. However, instead of initializing the algorithm with the pixel with the smallest depth value, we set $\mathbf{x}^{(0)}$ to the ground truth location of the palm to ensure a successful hand segmentation. After scaling the segmented hand to a patch size of 96×96, we normalize the depth within each patch to zero mean and a unit standard deviation. Further, we subtract the mean over the training set from each patch.

---

[1] Results on additional test sequences can be found on our project page.

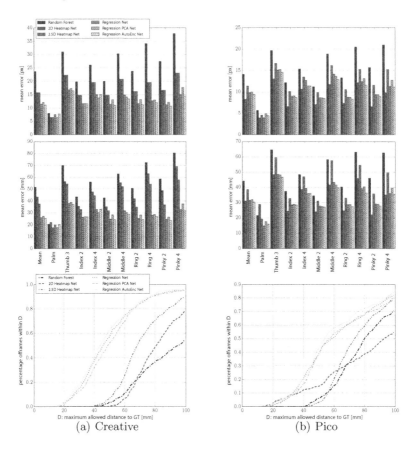

Fig. 5. Quantitative Evaluation: The graphs show the inference result in 2D and 3D for three test sequences. (a) was captured with a Creative GestureCam, whereas (b) was captured with a PMD Pico. In the first row, we plot the mean estimation results in 2D. The second row shows the same in 3D. Finally, we show in the last row the percentage of frames where all joints are within a distance of D.

The first method is the regression forest, where we trained 8 trees with a maximal depth of 25. For each node we sample 10^4 split functions and optimize them with a random sub-set of $5 \cdot 10^3$ training patches. In the leaf node we store the mean of the regression vectors that reaches this node and at inference, we compute the mean over all tree results to get the final estimate. For the convolutional network based methods we utilize the same multi-resolution architecture as in [26]. Only the fully connected layers differ for these networks. As activation functions we use a ReLU in the hidden layers, and a linear one in the output layer. To improve generalization, we apply dropout with a probability of 0.5 in the fully-connected layers. The first network is similar to the one in [26], except that we have 20 output heat-maps of size 18×18 instead of 14. In the second network we add for each joint a 1D heat-map of size 25 to infer also a depth value from the network. We replace the heat-maps with standard regression in the third network architecture and have two fully-connected layers with 4096 neurons each, so we get an output structure of $4096 \times 4096 \times 60$ neurons. Finally, we evaluate the network methods that are based on the sub-space assumption described above. In the first variant, we approximate a PCA with an auto-encode of the form $4096 \times 4096 \times 20 \times 60$, where we utilize also linear units in the layer before the last. Finally, we use a non-linear auto-encoder in the output layers of the form $4096 \times 4096 \times 20 \times 4096 \times 60$. This projects the pose space to a non-linear sub-space as described in [13].

The results are depicted in Figure 5. We show in the first row the 2D mean error in pixels. Similarly, the second row compares the mean error of the 3D estimates in mm. In the last row, we visualize the percentage of frames where all 3D joint estimates are within an increasing distance D to the ground-truth.

We can observe that the convolutional network methods outperform the regression forest. Our proposed extension to the heat-map to infer also the depth is beneficial. In 2D the accuracy stays identical, however in 3D we get an improvement of the results. Interesting is the fact that the regression based networks perform even better. While the PCA based network achieves nearly no gain of performance, we can see that the non-linear auto-encoder further boosts the results, validating the sub-space assumption.

6   Conclusion

We presented in this a paper a framework for articulated hand pose estimation that includes state-of-the art segmentation and inference methods. Further, we proposed a new method for segmenting the hand from the background and improving existing inference approaches. To overcome common problems with current benchmarks for hand pose estimation, we created a new dataset that consists of a synthetically generated training set that covers a large space of possible postures. Additionally, we accurately annotated three test sequences obtained by two consumer depth sensors. In the evaluations we showed the benefits of our proposed methods. To foster further research in the community we make all sources and the dataset publicly available. In the future, we plan to add test sequences from more depth sensors, as for example the Microsoft Kinect One[TM] and implementing further segmentation and inference methods within our framework.

Acknowledgments. This work was supported by the Austrian Research Promotion Agency (FFG) under the *FIT-IT Bridge* program, project #838513 (TOFUSION).

References

1. Ballan, L., Taneja, A., Gall, J., Van Gool, L., Pollefeys, M.: Motion capture of hands in action using discriminative salient points. In: Fitzgibbon, A., Lazebnik, S., Perona, P., Sato, Y., Schmid, C. (eds.) ECCV 2012, Part VI. LNCS, vol. 7577, pp. 640–653. Springer, Heidelberg (2012)

2. Bastioni, M., Re, S., Misra, S.: Ideas and methods for modeling 3D human figures: the principal algorithms used by makehuman and their implementation in a new approach to parametric modeling. In: COMPUTE (2008)
3. Blender Online Community: Blender - A 3D Modelling and Rendering Package. Blender Foundation (2015). http://www.blender.org
4. Coates, A., Ng, A.Y.: Selecting receptive fields in deep networks. In: NIPS (2011)
5. Comaniciu, D., Meer, P.: Mean Shift: A Robust Approach Toward Feature Space Analysis. TPAMI **24**(5), 603–619 (2002)
6. Creative Technology Inc., Singapore.: Creative Interactive Gesture Camera
7. Erol, A., Bebis, G., Nicolescu, M., Boyle, R.D., Twombly, X.: Vision-Based Hand Pose Estimation: A Review. CVIU **108**(1–2), 52–73 (2007)
8. Everingham, M., Eslami, S., Van Gool, L., Williams, C., Winn, J., Zisserman, A.: The Pascal Visual Object Classes Challenge: A Retrospective. IJCV, 1–39 (2014)
9. Gall, J., Yao, A., Razavi, N., Gool, L.J.V., Lempitsky, V.: Hough Forests for Object Detection, Tracking, and Action Recognition. TPAMI **33**(11), 2188–2202 (2011)
10. Girshick, R.B., Shotton, J., Kohli, P., Criminisi, A., Fitzgibbon, A.W.: Efficient regression of general-activity human poses from depth images. In: ICCV (2011)
11. de Gorce, M.L., Fleet, D.J., Paragios, N.: Model-Based 3D Hand Pose Estimation from Monocular Video. TPAMI **33**(9), 1793–1805 (2011)
12. Hartley, R., Zisserman, A.: Multiple View Geometry in Computer Vision. Cambridge University Press. 2 edn. (2003)
13. Hinton, G.E., Salakhutdinov, R.R.: Reducing the Dimensionality of Data with Neural Networks. Science **313**(5786), 504–507 (2006)
14. Keskin, C., Kıraç, F., Kara, Y.E., Akarun, L.: Hand pose estimation and hand shape classification using multi-layered randomized decision forests. In: Fitzgibbon, A., Lazebnik, S., Perona, P., Sato, Y., Schmid, C. (eds.) ECCV 2012, Part VI. LNCS, vol. 7577, pp. 852–863. Springer, Heidelberg (2012)
15. Krizhevsky, A., Sutskever, I., Hinton, G.E.: ImageNet classification with deep convolutional neural networks. In: NIPS (2012)
16. Melax, S., Keselman, L., Orsten, S.: Dynamics based 3d skeletal hand tracking. In: I3D (2013)
17. Mitra, S., Acharya, T.: Gesture Recognition: A Survey. SMC **37**(3), 311–324 (2007)
18. Neverova, N., Wolf, C., Taylor, G.W., Nebout, F.: Hand segmentation with structured convolutional learning. In: Cremers, D., Reid, I., Saito, H., Yang, M.-H. (eds.) ACCV 2014. LNCS, vol. 9005, pp. 687–702. Springer, Heidelberg (2015)
19. Oberweger, M., Wohlhart, P., Lepetit, V.: Hands deep in deep learning for hand pose estimation. In: CVWW (2015)
20. Oikonomidis, I., Kyriazis, N., Argyros, A.: Full DoF tracking of a hand interacting with an object by modeling occlusions and physical constraints. In: ICCV (2011)
21. PMD Technologies. Germany.: Camboard Pico
22. Shotton, J., Sharp, T., Kipman, A., Fitzgibbon, A., Finocchio, M., Blake, A., Cook, M., Moore, R.: Real-time human pose recognition in parts from single depth images. In: CVPR (2011)
23. Sun, M., Kohli, P., Shotton, J.: Conditional regression forests for human pose estimation. In: CVPR (2012)
24. Tang, D., Chang, H.J., Tejani, A., Kim, T.K.: Latent regression forest: structured estimation of 3D articulated hand posture. In: CVPR (2014)
25. Tang, D., Yu, T.H., Kim, T.K.: Real-time articulated hand pose estimation using semi-supervised transductive regression forests. In: ICCV (2013)
26. Tompson, J., Stein, M., Lecun, Y., Perlin, K.: Real-Time Continuous Pose Recovery of Human Hands Using Convolutional Networks. TOG **33**(5), 169 (2014)

Exploring Compression Impact on Face Detection Using Haar-like Features

Peter Elmer, Artur Lupp, Stefan Sprenger, René Thaler, and Andreas Uhl[(⊠)]

Department of Computer Sciences, University of Salzburg,
Jakob Haringerstr. 2, 5020 Salzburg, Austria
`andreas.uhl@sbg.ac.at`

Abstract. The main goal in our experimental study was to explore the impact of image compression on face detection using Haar-like features. In our setup we used the JPEG, JPEG2000 and JPEG XR compression standards to compress images from selected databases at given compression ratios. We performed the face detection using OpenCV on the reference images from the database as well as on the compressed images. After the detection process we compared the detected areas between the reference and the compressed image gaining the average coverage, false positive and false negative areas. Experimental results comparing JPEG, JPEG2000 and JPEG XR are showing that the average coverage of the detected face area differ between 79,58% in the worst and 99,61% in the best case. The false negative (not covered) areas range between 0,33% and 19,75% and false positive (fallout) areas between 0,38% and 9,45%. We conclude that the JPEG compression standard is performing worse than JPEG2000 and JPEG XR while both latter providing quite equal and good results.

1 Introduction

While the research in the field of face recognition is blooming, face detection receives much less attention. Nevertheless face detection, widely used for interactive user interfaces or as a feature in cameras, is the very first and necessary stage for many automated and semi-automated face recognition systems. Given that, the tasks of detecting faces for recognition are becoming required more frequently - e.g. in security systems at airports for preventing acts of terrorism. In order to detect a face it is necessary to differentiate between the background and the desired area where the face is. The huge quantities of visual data collected and stored makes the application of lossy image compression algorithms ubiqitous. The impact of these algorithms on pattern recognition tasks like face detection is often neither well investigated nor well understood.

Image compression algorithms are classically either optimised with respect to human perception (e.g. the JPEG default quantisation (Q-)table) or with respect to rate-distortion criteria (e.g. Tier-2 coding in JPEG 2000 or design of a specific Q-table for JPEG). For applications in pattern recognition, optimisation with respect to these criteria is not necessarily the optimal solution. For example, in

© Springer International Publishing Switzerland 2015
R.R. Paulsen and K.S. Pedersen (Eds.): SCIA 2015, LNCS 9127, pp. 53–64, 2015.
DOI: 10.1007/978-3-319-19665-7_5

[17] the JPEG Q-table is tuned for application in the pattern recognition context by emphasising middle and high frequencies and discarding low frequencies (the standard JPEG Q-table is rotated by 180 degrees). JPEG Q-table optimisation has already been considered in face recognition [16] which leads to superior recognition performance as compared to the standard matrix. A further example is the optimisation of JPEG 2000 Part 2 wavelet packet decomposition structures with respect to optimising iris recognition accuracy[26] which provides better results compared to rate-distortion optimised wavelet packet structures. These observations raise the question and severe doubt if compression algorithms exhibiting better rate-distortion performance are indeed better in a specific pattern recognition context.

With respect to standardization of image compression in biometrics, the ISO/IEC IS 19794 represents the most relevant standard, recommending JPEG 2000 exclusively for lossy compression. Also, the ANSI/NIST-ITL 1-2011 standard on "Data Format for the Interchange of Fingerprint, Facial & Other Biometric Information" (former ANSI/NIST-ITL 1-2007) supports only JPEG 2000 for applications tolerating lossy compression. Apart from standardization, a variety of independent studies dealing with compression and the respective impact on biometric recognition performance exist: E.g., iris compression [11], fingerprint compression [12,13] and 3D face recognition [14]. Also for face image compression and its impact on face recognition performance a significant corpus of research exists [15], considering e.g. the impact of JPEG [16], JPEG 2000 [18,25], SPIHT [19], and H.264 [20]. However, systematic investigations on the effect of lossy compression on **face detection** robustness and accuracy have remained elusive. The only work in this direction is restricted to JPEG [21] and also considers tracking and recognition. Most work on face detection and compression deals with face detection techniques in the compressed domain, i.e. detecting faces analysing the bitstream only without the necessity for full decoding (e.g. from JPEG and MPEG [22,23], H.264 [24], and wavelet-based data).

In the seminal work of Viola and Jones [5,6] they describe a way for rapid object detection using simple distinctive features. Haar-like features have scalar values representing the differences between two rectangular regions in average intensities. Using these features faces are distinguished from the background and the desired area where the face gets detected. Due to the simple set of classifiers used the general error rate is quite high. For better detection rates, an extension of these Haar-like features, i.e. a specially trained cascade set introduced by Lienhart and Maydt [8] can be used. The OpenCV [9] Library offers this feature set for face object detection.

In this work, we use OpenCV Viola-Jones face detection with the Haar Cascade File created by Lienhart and three widely used ISO still image coding standards: JPEG, JPEG2000 and JPEG XR. The main aim is to investigate the robustness of face detection to the three types of compression and to answer the question if face detection robustness matches to measured image quality in terms of PSNR. In our study three different sets of images were converted using 10 different compression ratios with each compression standard. After the compression, face detection was applied on the reference images from the image sets and the compressed images. Then we compare the detected areas between the reference images from the data sets and the compressed ones showing the average, false negative and false positive coverage. Experimental results achieved with this method show that JPEG is performing poor with low bitrate pictures and high compression ratios whereas JPEG2000 and JPEG XR show consistent performance. In the following sections, we first describe the compression standards we used. Thereafter the data sets, employed software and setup used in our experiments are described followed by results and a conclusion.

2   Compression Standards

2.1   JPEG

JPEG (Joint Photographic Experts Group ISO/IEC IS 10918-1)[10], despite its age, is still one of the most used standards in digital imaging technology. The JPEG compression divides the image data into blocks of 8x8 pixels. To each of these blocks a discrete cosine transform (DCT) is applied. Depending on the quality factor, quantization is applied on the coefficients of the DCT. Then the data is compressed using Huffman encoding. Due to the quantization reconstruction errors occur and are distributed over an entire 8 x 8 pixels block, leading to blocking artifacts.

(a) Face detection applied on JPEG images. The left image is the reference image. The image on the right is compressed with a compression ratio of 2. As mentioned, the area where the face is detected differs a little bit from the reference image. [Image is Part of LFW Database]

(b) This image was compressed with ratio of 100. Due its high compression leading to blocking artifacts, the detection of a face was not possible. [Image is Part of LFW Database]

Fig. 1. JPEG Compression

These artifacts have an impact on the face detection rate. See [Figure 1a] for an example of face detection applied on a JPEG image. The lower the quality factor the higher the compression leading to more blocking artifacts which can abstract an image with faces to a point where the face detection is inaccurate or simply not possible at all. See [Figure 1b] for an example of face detection applied on a JPEG image.

2.2 JPEG2000

JPEG2000 was created as well by the JPEG committee (ISO/IEC IS 15444-1) with the intention of superseding the DCT based approach used in the JPEG compression standard with a wavelet based method. The JPEG2000 compression standard is highly flexible offering a superior compression performance than JPEG, a multiple resolution representation and the possibility to either use a lossless or lossy compression. During compression in JPEG2000 the image is, like in JPEG, optionally partitioned into rectangular non overlapping blocks (tiles). The tiles can be compressed independently as they were entirely distinct images. Wavelet transform, quantization and entropy coding are applied independently in these blocks. Splitting the image into tiles reduces memory requirements and since they are reconstructed independently it is possible to decode specific parts of the image instead of the whole image. This however is required only for large images and induces artifacts.

(a) As in [Figure 1a], these pictures show the reference image (left) and the same image compressed with the compression ratio of 2 (right). There are just minor differences in the detected areas.

(b) Image with a compression ratio of 100. If we Compare [Figure 2b] with [Figure 1b], there are significant less blocking artifacts using JPEG2000.

Fig. 2. Face detection applied on JPEG2000 compressed image [Image is Part of LFW Database]

Coding of coefficient subsets ("code-blocks") results in a code stream after being coded by the arithmetic coding stage which is called Tier-1. Tier-1 coding produces a code steam containing first the data with the greatest distortion reductions achieved through a fractional bit-plane coder. The last stage of coding is the reorganization of the code stream. This process codes the auxiliary data which is needed to identify the content of the quality layers into the code stream. The auxiliary data is stored in the packet header of the code blocks. This header contains the information for the code block whether or not the block contributes to the quality layer, the number of the encoding passes, length of the encoded data, and the number of the magnitude bit planes. This allows features like quality and resolution progressiveness. It is to note that the superior compression as well as the high flexibility of this standard have to be paid with restrictions in terms of computational performance since run-time can be increased by a factor of 10 as compared to JPEG. As visible in [Figure 2b] there are (of course) much less blocking artifacts compared to JPEG compressed images [Figure 1b], while pictures compressed with low compression ratios are quite similar to the original [Figure 2a].

2.3 JPEG XR

JPEG XR is the most recent still image coding standard from the JPEG committee (ISO/IEC IS 29199-2), published in early 2009, we used to evaluate the compression impact on. Primarily targeting extended range imagery initially, JPEG XR finally managed in getting high image quality almost equivalent to JPEG2000. The advantages compared to JPEG2000 are on one hand primary the lower complexity allowing us to archive almost identical quality during compression while needing lower computational resources as well as storage capacity, on the other hand also providing high dynamic range support. As JPEG2000, JPEG XR is offering better lossy compression ratios in comparison to JPEG for encoding an image with identical quality, the possibility to compress lossless, support for more color accuracy and transparency map support and meta data support. It is one of the most recent still image coding standards available. Due to its lower complexity compared to JPEG2000 we wanted to evaluate if there is also a difference in terms of face detection. In the work of Horvat, Stögner and Uhl, JPEG XR was analyzed on Iris Recognition Systems [7] and they concluded that JPEG XR performed better than JPEG2000.

Fig. 3. Face detection applied on images compressed JPEG XR. From left to right the compression ratios are: 1 (reference image), 2 and 100. Image quality is almost identical to JPEG2000. [Image is Part of LFW DB]

3   Experimental Setup and Results

This section describes our datasets, the software and setups we used. At the end
of this section we will provide the results of our experiments.

3.1   Used Databases

Labeled Faces in the Wild[1]. The Labeled Faces in the Wild Database set
contains more than 13000 images of faces collected from the web. We randomly
selected 431 of these .jpg images with the average quality factor of 75. Most of
these images show motives of people during events or speeches. The resolution
of the images differ, starting from 233 x 409 and going up to 410 x 450 pixels.
This data set of images contains motives with more than one face. Due to that
fact there is a high possibility that small faces will not be detected at high
compression ratios. See [Figure 2b] for an example.

BIOID Face Database[2]. This dataset consists of 1521 grey level images
with a resolution of 284 x 386 pixels recorded under natural conditions so that
the test set is featuring a large variety of illumination, background as well as
face sizes. The images are labeled "BioID_xxxx.pgm" where the characters xxxx
are replaced by the index of the current image (with leading zeros).

Bao Face Database[3]. The Bao Face Database consists of 221 .jpg images
with mostly people from Asia. The resolution differs, starting from 250 x 205
and going up to 1836 x 1190 pixels. Some images were altered or cropped. The
images are labeled "x.jpg" where x is a number between 1 and 221. As this
set of images contains a lot of group picture motives it is very likely that with
increasing compression ratios face detection will miss faces. Therefore the false
negative areas will tend upwards as compression ratio is increasing.

   Please note that with these datasets, we are able to assess eventual influence
of double compression. Since the BIOID dataset comes in uncompressed grey
level format, similar behaviour to one of the other two datasets confirms that no
double compression effects are observed. In the plots we will refer to the datasets
with abbrevations: "LFW DB" for Labeled Faces in the Wild, "BIOID DB" for
BIOID Face Database and "BaoDB" for the Bao Face Database

3.2   Setup

The images from the data sets where compressed with JPEG, JPEG2000 and
JPEG XR. We implemented the standard libraries and converted the images
with given compression ratios. The Software we used in our setup to convert
the image data was ImageMagick with default settings. To obtain a specific
compression ratio, a divide-and-conquer algorithm was used to determine the
quality parameter for the specific compression ratios. We took a reference image
out of the dataset and obtained its size. Then we applied the compression on

this file and checked if the compressed file size is the target file size we wanted to have. The target file size depends on the compression ratio. With a compression ratio of 50 the target file size should be 1/50 of the original file size. To obtain the desired file size for our images, we changed the quality parameters for the compression. Our compression ratios were 1, 2, 5, 10, 12.5, 16.67, 25, 33.33, 50, 100 for this experiment. In the beginning the ratios are very small, that is to evaluate eventual double compression effects.

After the image compression, we performed face detection using the OpenCV library with the Haar Cascade File (haarcascade_frontalface_alt.xml[4]) created by Lienhart. During the face detection the reference image was used first. We gained the desired areas as y and x coordinates where x ranges from 0 to the maximal width and y ranges from 0 to the maximal height of the image. Each detected face has four parameters. These parameters are the four corners of the detected face area. We used these parameters to compare them with the ones achieved during the face detection of the compressed images. While comparing the areas of the reference image with the areas of the compressed images we gained three values. The first one is the average coverage of the areas. The more of the reference area where the face was detected in the original was covered in the compressed image, the higher this value gets (denoted as "**cov**" in the plots). The second value describes the false negative areas that where covered in the reference but not on the compressed image (denoted as "**notc**" in the plots). The third value describes the false positive areas that where covered in the compressed image but not in the reference image (denoted as "**morc**" in the plots). These values were saved for each picture in a database. With this data we could compute the average coverage, average false positive and average false negative for our images. For each dataset we gained three different plots [See Figures 5 to 7 for Bao Face Database, 8 to 10 for BIOID Database and 11 to 13 for Labeled Faces in the Wild] for each compression standard used. Each of these plots [Figures 5 to 13] is showing the average coverage, average false positive and average false negative for the specific compression ratio.

3.3   Results

First, we display the average rate-distortion performance of the three compression standards on the considered datasets. In [Figure 4a and 4b] we observe the classical and expected behaviour: Especially for high compression ratios, JPEG performance gets very poor, while JPEG2000 and JPEG XR are close with slight advantages for JPEG2000. For enabling a fair comparison, the same Haar Cascade file [4] was used during all face detection experiments. The following plots show the coverage using the y-axis value on the left side where a higher value is better. The false negative areas (notc) and the false positive areas (morc) are using the right y-axis where a lower value is better. The x-axis is showing the used compression ratio. Looking at [Figures 5 to 7], JPEG is performing very poor because the images in the Bao Face Database are patchy and already pre compressed in JPEG. Comparing the results from the images compressed using JPEG2000 [Figure 6] and JPEG XR [Figure 7] we can see that the results are

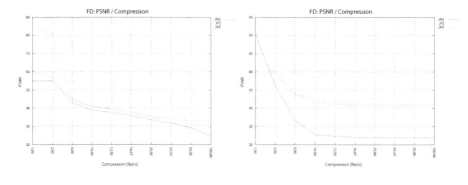

(a) BIOID Database   (b) Bao Database

Fig. 4. PSNR / Compression Ratio

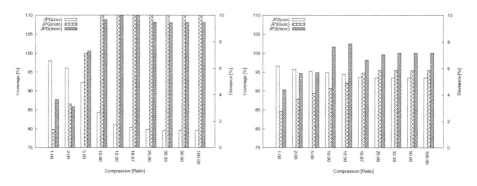

Fig. 5. BaoDB - JPEG. At compression ratio 100, avg cov: 79.58, FN: 19.75, FP: 9.45

Fig. 6. BaoDB - JPEG2000. At compression ratio 100, avg cov: 93.50, FN: 5.86, FP: 7.15

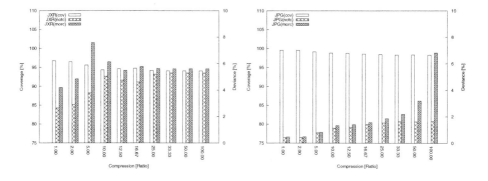

Fig. 7. BaoDB - JPEG XR. At compression ratio 100, avg cov: 94.06 FN: 5.29, FP: 5.61

Fig. 8. BIOID DB - JPEG. At compression ratio 100, avg cov: 98.31, FN: 1.63, FP: 6.81

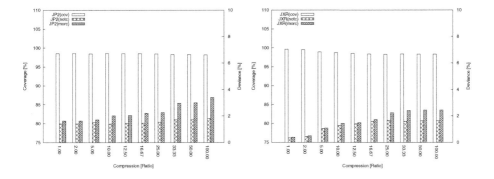

Fig. 9. BIOID DB - JPEG2000. At compression ratio 100, avg cov: 98.14, FN: 1.80, FP: 3.42

Fig. 10. BIOID DB - JPEG XR. At compression ratio 100, avg cov: 98.30, FN: 1.64, FP: 2.44

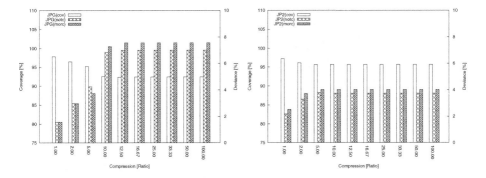

Fig. 11. LFW DB - JPEG. At compression ratio 100, avg cov: 92.42, FN: 7.01, FP: 7.57

Fig. 12. LFW DB - JPEG2000. At compression ratio 100, avg cov: 95.68, FN: 3.74, FP: 4.01

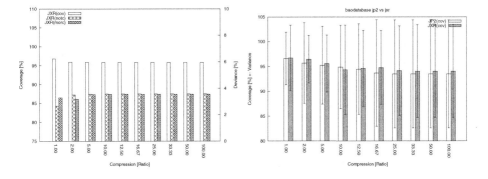

Fig. 13. LFW DB - JPEG XR. At compression ratio 100, avg cov: 95.87, FN: 3.57, FP: 3.54

Fig. 14. Bao DB - JPEG XR & JPEG2000, Coverage with standard deviations

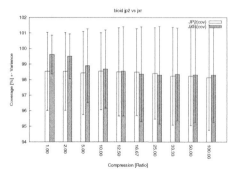 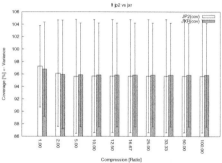

Fig. 15. BIOID DB - JPEG XR & JPEG2000, Coverage with standard deviations

Fig. 16. LFW DB - JPEG XR & JPEG2000, Coverage with standard deviations

quite alike but JPEG XR is performing better if we look at the numbers. At compression ratio 100, images compressed using JPEG2000 [Figure 6] have an average coverage of 93.50, false negative 5.86 and false positive 7.15. Detecting faces on images compressed with JPEG XR [Figure 7] is slightly better. The average coverage is 94.06, false negative 5.29 and false positive 5.16. This set of images shows the highest false positive and false negative values we achieved in our experiments. This is most likely due the group picture motives in the images. With higher compression and emerging blocking artifacts faces especially small ones will not be detected. [Figures 8 to 10] show us the results for the BIOID Database. As all the images provided by the data set have the same aspect ratio and only one face to detect, the over all performance is good for all compression standards used. It also seems, that there is no difference if the detected images are color or gray scale images. Looking at [Figure 8] which shows us the results of the face detection using JPEG, we can see a slightly higher area with false positives at compression ratio 100. If looking at [Figure 9] using JPEG2000 and [Figure 10] using JPEG XR compression, JPEG XR performs better. The BIOID data set achieves the best results with a good over all coverage, low false positives and false negatives. That is because each of the images in this data set shows one frontal face only. The Labeled faces in the Wild Database (JPEG pre-compressed as well), shows a quite similar trend as the rest of the datasets, see [Figures 11 to 13], JPEG2000 [Figure 12] and JPEG XR [Figure 13] achieving better results compared to JPEG [Figure 11]. The results of the images compressed using JPEG XR [Figure 13] are slightly better than JPEG2000 [Figure 12]. Despite the differences between the three data sets there are similarities when analyzing the results. The Bao Face Database as well as the Faces in the Wild Database have higher false negatives and false positives compared to the BIOID Database due images with more faces on them.

4   Conclusion

Our experiment demonstrates that in the context of face detection using sets of Haar-like features, JPEG XR and JPEG2000 are superior to JPEG, especially when the images are compressed at high ratios. Due to the significant lower computational demand and slightly better results in face detection JPEG XR is a good alternative to JPEG2000 in all considered settings. In order to focus on the differences between JPEG XR and JPEG2000 we show +- one standard deviation in addition to the mean values [Figures 14 to 16] which confirm the former observation. Concerning the relation between PSNR and detection accuracy we have found that JPEG is correctly predicted to be the worst algorithm by its PSNR values, however, the slight advantages of JPEG XR over JPEG 2000 are not correctly predicted by PSNR, in contrary [Figure 4]. It has also turned out that a slight JPEG precompression does not influence the performance and the ranking of the three compression algorithms when considering the similarity of the results obtained on pre-compressed and not pre-compressed datasets.

References

1. Huang, G.B., Ramesh, M., Berg, T., Learned-Miller, E.: Labeled Faces in the Wild: A Database for Studying Face Recognition in Unconstrained Environments, pp. 07–49. University of Massachusetts, Amherst (2007)
2. Jesorsky, O., Kirchberg, K.J., Frischholz, R.W.: Robust face detection using the hausdorff distance. In: Bigun, J., Smeraldi, F. (eds.) AVBPA 2001. LNCS, vol. 2091, pp. 90–95. Springer, Heidelberg (2001)
3. Frischholz, R.: Bao face database at the face detection homepage. http://www. facedetection.com (last accessed September 26, 2014)
4. Stump-based 20x20 gentle adaboost frontal face detector, Created by Rainer Lienhart. https://github.com/Itseez/opencv/blob/master/data/haarcascades/ haarcascade_frontalface_alt.xml (last accessed September 23, 2014)
5. Viola, P., Jones, M.: Rapid object detection using a boosted cascade of simple features. In: Proceedings of the 2001 IEEE Computer Society Conference on Computer Vision and Pattern Recognition. CVPR 2001, vol. 1, pp. I-511–I-518 (2001)
6. Viola, P., Jones, M.J.: Robust Real-Time Face Detection. International Journal of Computer Vision **57**(2), 137–154 (2004)
7. Horvath, K., Stögner, H., Uhl, A.: Effects of JPEG XR compression settings on iris recognition systems. In: Real, P., Diaz-Pernil, D., Molina-Abril, H., Berciano, A., Kropatsch, W. (eds.) CAIP 2011, Part II. LNCS, vol. 6855, pp. 73–80. Springer, Heidelberg (2011)
8. Lienhart, R., Maydt, J.: An extended set of Haar-like features for rapid object detection. In: Proceedings of the 2002 International Conference on Image Processing, vol. 1, pp. I-900–I-903 (2002)
9. Bradski, G.: The OpenCV Library. Dr. Dobb's Journal of Software Tools (2000). http://drdobbs.com/opensource/184404319
10. Wallace, G.K.: The JPEG still picture compression standard. IEEE Transactions on Consumer Electronics **38**(1), 18–34 (1992)
11. Rakshit, S., Monro, D.M.: An Evaluation of Image Sampling and Compression for Human Iris Recognition. IEEE Transactions on Information Forensics and Security **2**(3), 605–612 (2007)

12. Figueroa-Villanueva, M.A., Ratha, N.K., Bolle, R.M.: A comparative performance analysis of JPEG2000 vs. WSQ for fingerprint compression. In: Kittler, J., Nixon, M.S. (eds.) AVBPA 2003. LNCS, vol. 2688, pp. 385–392. Springer, Heidelberg (2003)

13. Kidd, R.C.: Comparison of wavelet scalar quantization and JPEG for fingerprint image compression. Journal of Electronic Imaging $4(1)$, 31–39 (1995)

14. Granai, L., Tena, J.R., Hamouz, M., Kittler, J.: Influence of compression on 3D face recognition. Pattern Recognition Letters, $30(8)$, 745–750

15. Delac, K., Grgic, S., Grgic, M.: Image compression in face recognition - a literature survey. In: Recent Advances in Face Recognition, pp. 236–250. I-Tech (2008)

16. Jeong, G.-M., Kim, C., Ahn, H.-S., Ahn, B.-J.: JPEG Quantization Table Design for Face Images and Its Application to Face Recognition. IEICE Transactions on Fundamentals of Electronics, Communications and Computer Science **E69–A**(11), 2990–2993 (2006)

17. Chen, M., Zhang, S., Karim, M.A.: Modification of standard image compression methods for correlation-based pattern recognition. Optical Engineering **43**(8), 1723–1730 (2004)

18. Delac, K., Grgic, S., Grgic, M.: Face recognition in JPEG and JPEG2000 compressed domain. Image and Vision Computing **27**, 1108–1120 (2009)

19. Kamasack, M., Sankur, B.: Face recognition under lossy compression. In: Proceedings of the International Conference on Pattern Recognition and Information Processing, PRIP 1999, pp. 27–32 (1999)

20. Klare, B., Burge, M.: Assessment of H.264 video compression on automated face recognition performance in surveillance and mobile video scenarios. In: Proceedings of SPIE, Biometric Technology for Human Identification VII, vol. 7667, p. 76670X (2010)

21. Korshunov, P., Ooi, W.T.: Video quality for face detection, recognition, and tracking. ACM Transactions on Multimedia Computing, Communications, and Applications (TOMM), **7**(3), article 14 (2011)

22. Luo, H., Eleftheriadis, A.: On face detection in the compressed domain. In: Proceedings of the ACM International Conference on Multimedia, pp. 285–294 (2000)

23. Fonseca, P., Nesvadha, J.: Face detection in the compressed domain. In: Proceedings of the IEEE International Conference on Image Processing, ICIP 2004, pp. 2015–2018 (2004)

24. Zhuang, S.-S., Lai, S.-H.: Face detection directly from h.264 compressed video with convolutional neural network. In: Proceedings of the IEEE International Conference on Image Processing, ICIP 2009, pp. 2485–2488 (2009)

25. Quinn, G.W., Grother, P.J.: Performance of Face Recognition Algorithms on Compressed Images. NIST Interagency Report 7830, Information Technology Laboratory, The National Institute of Standards and Technology (2011)

26. Hämmerle-Uhl, J., Karnutsch, M., Uhl, A.: Evolutionary optimisation of JPEG2000 part 2 wavelet packet structures for polar iris image compression. In: Ruiz-Shulcloper, J., Sanniti di Baja, G. (eds.) CIARP 2013, Part I. LNCS, vol. 8258, pp. 391–398. Springer, Heidelberg (2013)

Computer Vision for Head Pose Estimation: Review of a Competition

Heikki Huttunen[1]([✉]), Ke Chen[1], Abhishek Thakur[2], Artus Krohn-Grimberghe[2], Oguzhan Gencoglu[1], Xingyang Ni[1], Mohammed Al-Musawi[1], Lei Xu[1], and Hendrik Jacob van Veen[3]

[1] Tampere University of Technology, Tampere, Finland
heikki.huttunen@tut.fi
[2] University of Paderborn, Paderborn, Germany
[3] Zorgon, Utrecht, The Netherlands

Abstract. This paper studies the prediction of head pose from still images, and summarizes the outcome of a recently organized competition, where the task was to predict the yaw and pitch angles of an image dataset with 2790 samples with known angles. The competition received 292 entries from 52 participants, the best ones clearly exceeding the state-of-the-art accuracy. In this paper, we present the key methodologies behind selected top methods, summarize their prediction accuracy and compare with the current state of the art.

Keywords: Head pose estimation · Computer vision · Competition

1 Introduction

Head pose estimation [5,6,9–11,15] attempts to predict the viewing direction of human head given a facial image. More specifically, the output of a head pose estimator consists of the yaw and pitch angles in 2D space and optionally the roll angle in 3D space. The estimation of head orientation is difficult due to variations in illumination, sparsity of data and ambiguity of labels.

On one hand, collecting data for head pose estimation is difficult although there exists large facial databases such as *Labeled Faces in the Wild* [12] and *Youtube Faces Dataset* [22]. However, it is almost impossible to manually annotate these collected images with an exact head orientation. The available solution adopted by the public benchmarking datasets is to ask the participants to look at a set of markers that are located in predefined direction in the measurement room (*e.g.*, 93 direction marks of Pointing'04 dataset [8]). Therefore, the data of the benchmark sets is sparse, both in terms of subjects and angles. For example, there are only 30 images for each head pose angle acquired from 15 subjects in the Pointing'04 dataset. The data are then further divided into training and testing set, which makes the data for training even more sparse.

On the other hand, the annotated labels obtained with the pose direction markers are noisy because they in fact define the direction of *gaze* instead of the

© Springer International Publishing Switzerland 2015
R.R. Paulsen and K.S. Pedersen (Eds.): SCIA 2015, LNCS 9127, pp. 65–75, 2015.
DOI: 10.1007/978-3-319-19665-7_6

head pose direction. In other words, even the within-subject head pose direction can have a large variation while looking at the same marker. As a result, the images with the same label can actually have different true poses.

In addition to the ambiguity caused by the varying appearance of different persons, the mentioned two challenges lead to a complicated observation-label relation, which requires a model that is truly robust. Considering the labels for head pose estimation as sparse discrete integers, such a problem can be formulated into the following three types of frameworks: 1) regression-based approaches [3,5,10,19]; 2) classification-based approaches [6,11]; and 3) hybrid of the two [9]. In this paper we mostly concentrate on the classification approach, but will first briefly review the principles behind all approaches.

In *regression* frameworks for head pose estimation, a regression mapping is learned from low-level image features to continuous scalar-valued label space. Reference [5] introduced a two-layer regression framework in a coarse-to-fine fashion, which first approximately determines the range of predicted labels and then learns a regression function to discover the exact label values. Alternatively, regression forests have shown superior efficiency in head pose estimation [3] compared to other regression methods. After the introduction of the tree-based approach [3], alternating regression forests were proposed [19] to incorporate the global loss across all trees during training instead of independently growing trees in the original random forests. Recently, a K-clusters regression forest was proposed with a more flexible multi-branch splitting algorithm instead of the standard binary function, thus integrating the locality in randomized label subspace into the whole regression framework [10].

When using the *classification* approach, the labels are treated as independent class labels [11], which discards the ordered dependency across labels. Geng *et al.* [6] introduced the concept of soft labeling to capture the correlation of adjacent labels around true pose and also model the noise in the labels. Guo *et al.* [9] investigated both advantages and disadvantages of regression based and classification based algorithms, and then introduced a hybrid approach by adding an extra classification step to locally adjust the regression prediction.

In this paper we consider a large variety of prediction methods crowdsourced from the research community in a form of a competition. The *TUT Head Pose Estimation Challenge* was organized in the Kaggle.com competition hosting platform[1] during the Fall 2014, and attracted altogether 292 submissions from 52 teams around the world. In the sequel we describe selected methods of the top participants and compare them with recently proposed state-of-the-art methods.

Apart from the learning based approach considered in this paper, there has been increasing interest in geometry-based approaches that fit a geometric face model into the measurements using algorithms such as Iterative Closest Point (ICP). State of the art methods in this field typically use a 3D sensor with applications in the transportation and driver monitoring [17,21]. The model based approach and the depth measurements can reach significant accuracy gain in comparison to plain 2D data. Nevertheless, plain RGB cameras are extremely

---

[1] https://inclass.kaggle.com/c/tut-head-pose-estimation-challenge/

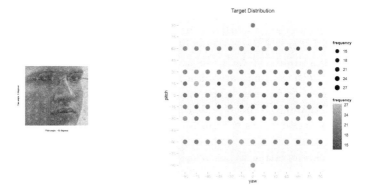

Fig. 1. Left: An example image with green lines illustrating the HOG features. Right: All combinations of yaw and pitch angles in the training set. The size and color of each point represents the number of images in each category.

widespread and purely data driven methods have surpassed human accuracy in many areas [20], so we will limit our attention to this line of research. We also hope that the manuscript will serve other researchers in the field as a collection of benchmark methods. All data together with the ground truth and benchmark code are publicly available at the supplementary site of this paper[2].

2   Material and Methods

The material used in the experiments is derived from the widely used Pointing'04 dataset [8]. The original data was collected by requesting test subjects to look at markers located at different viewing directions in the measurement room, and an example of the original images is shown in Figure 1 (left). The locations of the total of 93 angles (markers) are then the basis of the annotations. The 93 directions are the product of 13 different pitch angles and 9 different yaw angles, as illustrated in Figure 1 (right). The dataset in our experiments is slightly modified by a tight cropping and resizing the head area from the original 384×288 resolution to images of size 150×150 pixels, thus forcing the methods to estimate the angles based on relative location of face features instead of the absolute location. The database consists of pictures of 15 subjects, each looking at the 93 angles twice. In total this results in $15 \times 93 \times 2 = 2790$ samples.

The cropped and resized images were transformed to feature vectors using dense Histogram of Oriented Gradient (HOG) features as defined by Felzenszwalb *et al.* [4] with a 9×9 grid. The HOG features are the most common feature set for head pose estimation representing the state of the art in the field [6,10]. The Felzenszwalb variant differs from the original HOG features [2] in that it uses both directed and undirected histogram bins as well as additional

---

[2] http://sites.google.com/TUT-head-pose/

energy features. In our case, the image was split to 9×9 blocks, and the HOG features with 9 undirected bins, 18 directed bins and 4 energy features were calculated to result in a feature vector of dimension $9 \times 9 \times (9 + 18 + 4) = 2511$.

For the competition, the data was split to three parts: The training set with 1953 randomly selected images, validation set with 279 and test set with 558 samples. In other words, the proportions of the three subsets are 70 %, 10% and 20% of all samples. The role of separate validation and test sets is that the competition participants can probe the accuracy of their algorithm on the validation set, while the final standings are determined based on the test set. This discourages overfitting to the test set and results in better generalization.

In the following, we will consider two criteria for prediction accuracy. The main accuracy metric is the Mean Absolute Error (MAE) defined as MAE = $\frac{1}{2N} \sum_{n=1}^{N} \left(|\hat{\theta}_n - \theta_n| + |\hat{\phi}_n - \phi_n| \right)$, where θ_n and ϕ_n denote the true yaw and pitch angles of the n'th sample and $\hat{\theta}_n$ and $\hat{\phi}_n$ their estimates, respectively. For classification based methods, we will also consider the mean accuracy, *i.e.*, the proportion of cases when the two angles are predicted exactly correct.

2.1   State of the Art

This section reviews two recent algorithms for head pose estimation, which were proposed in 2014 top conferences: Multivariate Label Distribution (MLD) [6] and K-clusters Regression Forests (KRF) [10]. As mentioned in the introductory section, MLD and KRF methods represent the state of the art among classification and regression based approaches, respectively.

K-clusters Regression Forests. Based on the standard random forests for regression a *K-cluster Regression Forest* was recently proposed [10] by introducing more flexible node split algorithm instead of binary split. The splitting rule of K-cluster Regression Forests at each node consists of three steps: 1) Cluster the training samples into multiple groups according to the distribution of the label space; 2) Learn the decision function to distinguish the samples in the same cluster from others as a classification problem; 3) Split the data using the predicted cluster label by the trained classifier.

As a result, the novel splitting scheme gives more freedom of choosing partitioning rule and increases the accuracy in comparison to a standard regression forest. It is worth noting that the size of clusters can be determined by either adaptive selection or cross-validation. In the experiments, we adopt the adaptive K-clusters Regression Forests (AKRF) with the same parameters as in [10] as the baseline state-of-the-art regression method for comparing the results generated by the participants of the competition.

Multivariate Label Distribution. Multivariate Label Distribution (MLD) is a recently proposed classification method [6] aimed at capturing the correlation between neighboring poses in the label space. Based on standard Label Distribution Learning (LDL), Multivariate Label Distribution is extended to model the two-dimensional output of head pose estimation (i.e., yaw and pitch angles of head viewing direction), which can mitigate the data sparsity and imbalancedness. By mining the correlation across labels, MLD can intuitively be treated as multi-label learning with correlated labels.

2.2   Top Methods of the TUT Head Pose Estimation Challenge

The TUT Head Pose Estimation Challenge was organized in Fall 2014, and provided the participants readily calculated HOG feature vectors together with the ground truth yaw and pitch angles for the 1953 training samples. The participants were requested to predict the corresponding angles for the validation and test sets. The participating teams were allowed to submit the predicted angles four times each day for assessment. The Kaggle.com platform automatically calculates the accuracy of both subsets but reveals only the validation set accuracy (called public leaderboard score), while the test set accuracy (called private leaderboard score) is visible to organizers only until the end of the competition.

The top scoring participants all use a classification based approach. The exact methods that can be divided into three broad categories: 1) Support Vector Machines (SVM), 2) Neural Networks, and 3) Ensemble methods.

Support Vector Machines. The support vector machine is a widely used classifier due to its maximum margin property, which separates the classes with a largest possible distance between them [18]. Typically the SVM is used together with the kernel trick that implicitly maps the data into a high dimensional kernel space, but also the linear kernel is widely used, especially with large data sets.

The basic linear two-class SVM has later been extended to nonlinear decision boundaries via the kernel trick (substituting each dot product by a higher order mapping), and to multiclass classification problems via the one-vs-all (each class is compared against the rest) and one-vs-one (each pair of classes is compared) heuristics. Probably the most famous implementation is the LIBSVM [1], which was also used by the participating methods described below. The LIBSVM implementation is also the optimization engine of many machine learning packages, including the *Scikit-learn* [16] also used by some of the teams.

There were two SVM-based submissions to the TUT Head Pose Estimation Challenge ending up as 2nd (team *Abhishek*) and 4th best (team *Aurora*) in the final results (Table 2). Team *Abhishek* standardizes the features by removing the mean and scaling to unit variance. Without standardization, a feature with large variance may dominate the objective function. The team uses the SVM with Radial Basis Function (RBF) kernel defined as $K(\mathbf{x}, \mathbf{x}') = \exp\left(-\gamma \|\mathbf{x} - \mathbf{x}'\|^2\right)$, with $\gamma \in \mathbb{R}$ a free parameter selected by cross-validation. The method also separates the yaw and pitch angles and trains a separate SVM model for each. So, for both pitch and yaw, a prediction for a given test sample is always among the angles found in the training set. The separation of the full 93 class problem into two problems with 13 and 9 classes simplifies the estimation and may be particularly helpful with the SVM, whose extension to multiclass problems is non-trivial.

Team *Abhishek* fine-tunes the SVM model parameters using an extensive grid-search on a parameter grid consisting of different values of penalty and gamma parameters. The grid search was performed on a 5-fold Cross Validation set and optimized the Mean Absolute Error (MAE) which was set as the evaluation metric for the task. Interestingly, the optimal parameters for both the pitch and yaw model are the same with $C = 10$ and $\gamma = 0.0$.

Team *Aurora* was another team whose solution relies on the SVM. The method is a straightforward application of a single SVM classifier to the data with the original 93 class encoding. The score is however, significantly improves by averaging the predictions of an ensemble of SVM classifiers obtained by randomly subsampling the data. More specifically, random samples of 80% of the training data are used to train a large number of models. Each of these is used for prediction and the resulting predicted angles are then combined together. The team experimented with different fusion strategies, and ended up taking the median of the SVM predictions as the most accurate method.

Neural Networks. Artificial neural networks (ANN) are powerful, nonlinear models that can learn complex relationships between variables. They have been studied already for over six decades and have been shown to be successful in various machine learning problems including image recognition [13] and optical character recognition [14]. Due to their nature, the ANN treats the multi-label encoding of the classes in a straightforward manner and does not require any multi-category heuristics like inherently binary classifiers such as the SVM.

Team *ogencoglu* uses ANN in the TUT Head Pose Estimation Challenge placing in the third best position. The method first standardizes the features to zero mean and unit variance, and treats the data as a single estimation problem simultaneously for both angles. However, the encoding of the classes is nontrivial: Instead of the straightforward 93-class encoding, the multi-label target vector is obtained by concatenating the yaw and pitch into 22-element indicator vectors (first 13 elements indicate the yaw angle, and the remaining 9 elements indicate the pitch angle). The target always contains exactly two nonzero elements (one among the first 13 and one among the 9 last ones). The final classification for yaw angle is completed by selecting the angle that gives the maximum output probability among the first 13 outputs. Similarly, classification of pitch angle is performed by examining the remaining 9 elements of the output vector.

The neural network topology consists of 2 hidden layers having 200 and 70 neural units respectively with sigmoid activation functions. The output is a softmax layer of size 22. The neural network is trained with the backpropagation algorithm with minibatch stochastic gradient descent optimization to minimize the negative log-likelihood. The batch size and learning rate are selected to be 50 and 0.01 respectively. The training is run for total of 750 iterations. The solution

Table 1. Effect of stacking the classifiers. The first three rows tabulate the public (validation) and private (test) MAE of straightforward use of a 500-tree random forest, 5-nearest neighbor and logistic regression classifiers, respectively. The bottom row shows the decreased MAE when augmenting the original features with the outputs of the first three classifiers.

Model	Public MAE	Private MAE
500-tree random forest	6.156	6.546
5-nearest neighbor	6.828	7.460
Logistic regression	6.694	6.949
Extremely randomized trees (with stacking)	**4.772**	**4.718**

is implemented using pylearn2 [7] library on an NVIDIA graphics processing unit (GPU) for faster computations.

Ensemble Methods and Stacked Generalization. Stacked Generalization was proposed already in 1992 as a tool for improved generalization using a pool of classifiers. The seminal paper by Wolpert [23] has inspired later work on averaging the predictions of a collection of classifiers in various ways. The basic principle is to train a pool of first level classifiers and feed their outputs to a second layer predictor, possibly together with the original features.

In the TUT Head Pose Estimation Challenge, team *Triskelion* used the stacked generalization framework ending up on the 6th place. The first layer of classifiers consists of a pool of logistic regression, random forest and nearest neighbor classifiers. The predicted class membership probabilities of the three are appended to the 2511-dimensional feature vector as three additional higher level features. Note that the three classifiers are first trained on the training set, after which their outputs are calculated for the training, validation and test sets. At first sight one could imagine that the augmented features are highly overfitted to the training set, but practice has shown this not to be the case. As the final second layer predictor, an extremely randomized trees classifier is trained on the training data with augmented features. The problem is encoded as a multi-class classification task. In other words, separate models are trained for yaw and pitch angles. Table 1 shows the effect of stacking in terms of Public MAE and Private MAE for the individual models and the stacked ensemble. One can see that adding the three high-level features decreases the error about 30 %.

3   Results

The TUT Head Pose Estimation Challenge was open for submissions approximately one month. During that period, altogether 292 entries were submitted by 52 players in 37 teams. As a baseline, the competitors were given the result of a ridge regression model, whose MAE score for the test set equals 9.06. The MAE can be lowered in a straightforward manner to approximately 6.0 using, *e.g.*, random forest classifier with enough trees. In this section we concentrate the top-6 teams, whose entries clearly outperform this level.

The results of the six top performing teams for the test data (private MAE score) are summarized at the top of Table 2. The columns of the table correspond to the MAE of the pitch and yaw angles separately, and the third column is the average of the two. The three rightmost columns show the classification accuracy of the methods, for pitch and yaw angles and their average, respectively. More specifically, the accuracy refers to the proportion of cases where the angle was predicted exactly as annotated. Note that this measure is not reliable with regression based methods, as the exact prediction seldom occurs in a continuous-valued output (same applies to averaged output of a classifier). Nevertheless, we include this accuracy criterion as it gives valuable insight as to why a particular method works well.

From the table, one can clearly see that the differences between the top performing teams is relatively small. In terms of the pitch angle, the SVM based approaches (teams *Abhishek* and *Aurora*) seem to dominate, while the yaw angle is most accurately predicted by the neural network (team *ogencoglu*).

In addition to the prediction errors of individual submissions, the table also shows the accuracy of committee predictors. More specifically, the rows *TOP-6-mean* and *TOP-6-median* are the scores of combining the TOP-6 teams by averaging and taking the median of the 6 predictions, respectively. Table 2 shows that averaging the predictions does not improve the prediction accuracy compared to individual submissions. Instead, the median of individual submissions clearly improves the accuracy compared to any individual submission.

The two bottom rows of the table show the accuracy of two recent reference methods for this data. The KRF method [10] is a recent regression tree based method, and MLD [6] is a classifier method, both developed for the same feature extraction approach as with our data. However, one can clearly see that the methods of the competitors clearly outperform the state of the art.

4   Discussion

In this paper we summarized a collection of well performing methods for head pose estimation from still images. Moreover, the approach illustrates the importance of collaboration between different players in developing accurate solutions to real world problems. In the case of the TUT Head Pose Estimation Challenge, the competition was originally opened as an exercise for the participants of a graduate level course, but soon gathered submissions from an international audience. The discussion on the competition forum was quite lively, discussing various approaches and proposing novel ideas.

The paper describes a collection of community machine learning methods for head pose estimation. Data driven machine learning is becoming more and more mainstream as the advances in software and hardware allows easier adoption of

Table 2. Competition results. All numbers denote the Mean Absolute Error between the true and predicted yaw and pitch angles for the test set (20 % of all data). The best score in each column is highlighted in boldface font.

Method	Pitch MAE	Yaw MAE	Overall MAE	Pitch Accuracy	Yaw Accuracy	Overall Accuracy
Team f623	3.47	5.30	4.38	**0.81**	0.66	0.54
Team Abhishek	3.55	5.30	4.42	0.80	0.67	0.53
Team ogencoglu	4.17	**4.78**	4.48	0.79	**0.71**	**0.55**
Team Aurora	3.84	5.54	4.69	0.79	0.66	0.52
Team RainStorm	3.92	5.24	4.58	0.80	0.69	0.54
Team Triskelion	4.23	5.31	4.77	0.73	0.60	0.43
TOP-6-mean	3.76	5.17	4.46	0.60	0.44	0.26
TOP-6-median	**3.35**	5.04	**4.20**	0.80	0.64	0.51
KRF [10]	5.33	6.03	5.68	0.29	0.17	0.05
MLD [6]	4.49	5.43	4.96	0.76	0.65	0.48

recent methods. The paper gives a partial answer on how well a generic data driven machine learning methods implemented by non-experts in the field (of head pose estimation) compare against tailored state of the art methods.

The results of the top-scoring teams are clearly exceeding the state of the art. One should bear in mind that the submissions are somewhat optimized against this particular dataset and its HOG representation. Although the test data was hidden from the participants until the end, the results probably are slightly optimistic and favourable for the participating teams, because the data split was random and not a more systematic "leave-one-person-out" type of split. On the other hand, the competitors were not given the origin of the dataset, so they were not aware of the exact feature extraction procedure.

With thorough optimization the performance of the comparison methods could probably be improved because the image size and feature extraction parameters of the two are different from the test data (and from each other). Nevertheless, the top competitors used *general* machine learning tools without domain specific knowledge (the approach of a non-academic pattern recognition engineer implementing a real application) and proved that they can reach the accuracy of highly sophisticated *tailored* algorithms.

The number of submissions to the competition was relatively large, and gained worldwide attention. The feedback from the students of the course was also positive proving the significance of gamification as a tool for motivating students to put forth their best effort and to combine research aspects with classroom education.

References

1. Chang, C.C., Lin, C.J.: LIBSVM: a library for support vector machines. ACM Trans. on Intell. Syst. and Technology **2**(3), 27 (2011)
2. Dalal, N., Triggs, B.: Histograms of oriented gradients for human detection. In: IEEE Conf. Comp. Vis. and Patt. Recogn., vol. 1, pp. 886–893 (2005)
3. Fanelli, G., Gall, J., Van Gool, L.: Real time head pose estimation with random regression forests. In: IEEE Conf. Comp. Vis. and Patt. Recogn., pp. 617–624 (2011)
4. Felzenszwalb, P.F., Girshick, R.B., McAllester, D., Ramanan, D.: Object detection with discriminatively trained part-based models. IEEE Trans. Pattern Anal. Machine Intell. **32**(9), 1627–1645 (2010)
5. Foytik, J., Asari, V.K.: A two-layer framework for piecewise linear manifold-based head pose estimation. Int. J. of computer vision, 270–287 (2013)
6. Geng, X., Xia, Y.: Head pose estimation based on multivariate label distribution. In: IEEE Conf. Comp. Vis. and Patt. Recogn., pp. 1837–1842, June 2014
7. Goodfellow, I.J., Warde-Farley, D., Lamblin, P., Dumoulin, V., Mirza, M., Pascanu, R., Bergstra, J., Bastien, F., Bengio, Y.: Pylearn2: a machine learning research library. arXiv preprint arXiv:1308.4214 (2013)
8. Gourier, N., Hall, D., Crowley, J.L.: Estimating face orientation from robust detection of salient facial structures. In: FG Net Workshop on Visual Observation of Deictic Gestures. FGnet (IST-2000-26434), Cambridge, UK, pp. 1–9 (2004)
9. Guo, G., Fu, Y., Dyer, C., Huang, T.: Head pose estimation: Classification or regression? In: Int. Conf. Pattern Recognition, pp. 1–4, December 2008
10. Hara, K., Chellappa, R.: Growing regression forests by classification: applications to object pose estimation. In: Fleet, D., Pajdla, T., Schiele, B., Tuytelaars, T. (eds.) ECCV 2014, Part II. LNCS, vol. 8690, pp. 552–567. Springer, Heidelberg (2014)
11. Huang, C., Ding, X., Fang, C.: Head pose estimation based on random forests for multiclass classification. In: Int. Conf. Pattern Recognition, pp. 934–937 (2010)
12. Huang, G.B., Ramesh, M., Berg, T., Learned-Miller, E.: Labeled faces in the wild: A database for studying face recognition in unconstrained environments. Tech. Rep. 07–49, University of Massachusetts, Amherst, October 2007
13. Krizhevsky, A., Sutskever, I., Hinton, G.E.: Imagenet classification with deep convolutional neural networks. In: Adv. in Neural Inf. Proc. Syst., pp. 1097–1105 (2012)
14. LeCun, Y., Bottou, L., Bengio, Y., Haffner, P.: Gradient-based learning applied to document recognition. Proc. IEEE **86**(11), 2278–2324 (1998)
15. Murphy-Chutorian, E., Trivedi, M.M.: Head pose estimation in computer vision: A survey. IEEE Trans. Pattern Anal. Machine Intell., 607–626 (2009)
16. Pedregosa, F., Varoquaux, G., Gramfort, A., Michel, V., Thirion, B., Grisel, O., Blondel, M., Prettenhofer, P., Weiss, R., Dubourg, V., Vanderplas, J., Passos, A., Cournapeau, D., Brucher, M., Perrot, M., Duchesnay, E.: Scikit-learn: Machine learning in Python. J. Machine Learning Res. **12**, 2825–2830 (2011)
17. Pelaez, C., Garcia, G., de la Escalera, A., Armingol, J.: Driver monitoring based on low-cost 3-d sensors. IEEE Trans. on Intelligent Transportation Syst. **15**(4), 1855–1860 (2014)
18. Scholkopf, B., Smola, A.J.: Learning with kernels: support vector machines, regularization, optimization, and beyond. MIT press (2001)

19. Schulter, S., Leistner, C., Wohlhart, P., Roth, P.M., Bischof, H.: Alternating regression forests for object detection and pose estimation. In: IEEE Conf. Computer Vision, pp. 417–424 (2013)
20. Taigman, Y., Yang, M., Ranzato, M., Wolf, L.: Deepface: closing the gap to human-level performance in face verification. In: IEEE Int. Conf. Computer Vision, pp. 1701–1708 (2014)
21. Tulyakov, S., Vieriu, R.L., Semeniuta, S., Sebe, N.: Robust real-time extreme head pose estimation. In: Int. Conf. Pattern Recogn., pp. 2263–2268, Aug 2014
22. Wolf, L., Hassner, T., Maoz, I.: Face recognition in unconstrained videos with matched background similarity. In: IEEE Int. Conf. Computer Vision, pp. 529–534 (2011)
23. Wolpert, D.H.: Stacked generalization. Neural Networks **5**(2), 241–259 (1992)

Matching, Registration
and Recognition

3D Point Representation For Pose Estimation: Accelerated SIFT vs ORB

K.K.S. Bhat[✉], Juho Kannala, and Janne Heikkilä

Center for Machine Vision Research, University of Oulu, Oulu, Finland
{sbhatkid,jkannala,jth}@ee.oulu.fi

Abstract. Many novel *local image descriptors* (Random Ferns, ORB etc) are being proposed each year with claims of being as good as or superior to SIFT for representing point features. In this context we design a simple experimental framework to compare the performances of different descriptors for realtime recognition of 3D points in a given environment. We use this framework to show that robust descriptors like SIFT perform far better when compared to fast binary descriptors like ORB if matching process uses *approximate nearest-neighbor search* (ANNS) for acceleration. Such an analysis can be very useful for making appropriate choice from vast number of descriptors available in the literature. We further apply machine learning techniques to obtain better approximation of SIFT descriptor matching than ANNS. Though we could not improve its performance, our in-depth analysis of its root cause provides useful insights for guiding future exploration in this topic.

Keywords: 3D point recognition · Augmented Reality · Interest Points

1   Introduction and Background

Estimating pose (position and orientation) of a camera in a given image is at the heart of many applications in Augmented Reality and Visual Robot Navigation. Over the past few years *interest point* or *keypoint* based 3D point recognition has facilitated substantial progress in vision based camera pose estimation. 3D point recognition provides the necessary input for well known PnP (Perspective n-Point) framework [13,15,29] for computing pose. Many high dimensional robust keypoint descriptors [3,18] have been developed in order to identify 3D points in images under the challenge of variation in camera viewpoint. SIFT descriptors are consistently proven to be one of the best candidates for point matching [8,19]. While they have been successfully applied on problems involving computation of camera pose [4,25], their cost of computation and matching prevents their use in applications which require real-time speed on video frames.

For achieving real-time speed on video frames, many keypoint recognition approaches which employ simple binary decisions based on raw pixel comparisons are being proposed. In [14] sequence of binary decisions based on comparing random pair of pixels around interest points (extremas of Laplacian of Gaussian

ⓒ Springer International Publishing Switzerland 2015
R.R. Paulsen and K.S. Pedersen (Eds.): SCIA 2015, LNCS 9127, pp. 79–91, 2015.
DOI: 10.1007/978-3-319-19665-7_7

filter) are used to identify the keypoints. Random Ferns framework [22] uses similar pixel comparisons, but the sequence of decisions are converted to binary coding which is indexed directly to attribute values for faster recognition. In [27] boosting is used to arrive at the optimal binary coding scheme for an image patch around a keypoint. In [24] depth values from Kinect sensors are also used along with the color information while learning the sequence of binary decisions.

Despite claims of significant success in each new approach, the effort to produce new methods to match the performance of SIFT seems to be still continuing. The reason may lie in the failure of those approaches to stand up to their claims in independent evaluations. For example, in [17] , it is shown that SIFT descriptors perform better than random ferns in terms of ability and accuracy of matching. Evaluation in [11] claims that SIFT outperforms many popular binary descriptors like BRIEF [6], BRISK [16], ORB [23].In this context we feel that it is immensely necessary to perform careful evaluation for a newly designed descriptor before claiming improvement over SIFT. Moreover, it is preferable if the evaluation framework can be applied on images of any environment and not limited to datasets which either have dense depth information [30] or put limitations on the geometric variations [1].

1.1   Contribution and Overview

In order to make a fair evaluation, we feel that it is necessary to match SIFT descriptors with operations having similar computational complexity as that of the type of descriptor with which it is being compared. We use approximate nearest neighbor search (ANNS) to accelerate SIFT based matching and compare its accuracy with that of ORB binary descriptor [23]. The choice of ORB is justified by the fact that ORB, like SIFT, has invariant property w.r.t. rotation and it is shown to be better compared to other binary descriptors in the presence of scale and rotation change [12]. We design an evaluation framework which needs only a sparse set of 3D points and camera positions in a set of images of the environment. This information can be obtained for any environment by simply running Structure from Motion (SfM) [28] on a set of images. The results from this experiment motivates us to explore further in the direction of improving techniques for matching SIFT descriptors rather than trying to design new binary descriptors. We train axis-parallel decision trees (APDT, decision trees which use only one attribute of the feature vector in a node to take decision) to learn SIFT based matching. We exploit the fact that SIFT descriptors are integer valued and perform exhaustive search to obtain optimal decision threshold at each node of the tree. We find that ANNS still performs slightly better than APDTs. Next we employ Canonical Correlation Analysis (CCA) [26] and train oblique decision trees whose decision boundaries need not strictly align to the axes of the SIFT descriptor space. Though we do not succeed in obtaining improvement over ANNS by using oblique decision trees for SIFT based matching, the insight obtained through these experiments which are detailed in this paper are useful for future exploration in this topic.

This paper is organized as follows. In section 2, we present the decision tree framework we used for accelerating SIFT based matching. The three types of different decision trees we use in our experiments are described in subsections 2.2, 2.3 and 2.4 respectively. Our evaluation framework and the results we obtained through experiments are presented in section 3. Finally, we mention concluding remarks and future work in section 4.

2   Decision Trees for Fast SIFT Descriptor Matching

Let $\mathbb{Q} = \{Q_1, Q_2, ..., Q_N\}$ be a sparse set of 3D points in the target environment. Let $S = \{f_i\}$ bet a set of SIFT vectors extracted from images of the environment. We use decision tree to identify 3D points using SIFT vectors extracted from images. For training decision tree we need class labels $C = \{c_i\}$ where each label c_i is associated with $f_i \in S$. For the task of 3D point recognition, labels are such that $c_i = k$ if f_i corresponds to 3D point Q_k, otherwise $c_i = 0$. For a vector f, we use the superscript f^j to denote the value of jth attribute. We can obtain $\mathbb{Q}, S, C$ by performing Structure from Motion (SfM) [28] on a set of images of the environment (as described with experimental setup in section 3.1). Rest of this section is as follows. First, we provide a brief description of general framework for training axis-parallel decision tree (APDT) in section 2.1. For APDT, the decision at each node is based on one of the attribute values of the descriptor vector. Two subsequent subsections present the methods we use for random and exhaustive search for optimal decision boundaries for APDT. In section 2.4 we present the method we used to learn *oblique* decision trees through *Canonical Correlation Analysis* [26]. Oblique decision trees use linear combination of values of multiple attributes of descriptor vector for decision at each node.

2.1   Training APDT

Decision trees are built recursively during training. Each tree node (starting with root node which receives all the training samples) decides whether the given set of training samples (S,C) should be split or not based on an entropy measure. The tree building procedure we employ at every tree node is described in Algorithm 1. If the samples need to be split, then an optimal combination of attribute t_S and threshold θ_S is computed. The training samples f with $f^{t_S} \leq \theta_S$ are directed towards left node. The rest are directed towards right node. If the samples need not be split, then a leaf node is created which stores the dominant label c_S and pointers to all the samples provided to it. We use *Information Gain* (IG) based measure [7] to choose optimal values θ_S and t_S. Optimal decision parameters maximize the IG. When a set S is split into S_L and S_R, IG of this division (denoted by $G(S)$) is defined as

$$G(S) = H(S) - \sum_{i \in \{LR\}} \frac{|S_i|}{|S|} H(S_i) \qquad (1)$$

Algorithm 1. Tree(S,C) : Basic tree growing algorithm

Description: This algorithm is recursively applied to build APDT from a set $S = \{f_i\}$ of SIFT descriptor training vectors with corresponding labels $C = \{c_i\}$. In each recursion, an information entropy value based on the class distribution of S is computed to decide whether the samples in S need to be split or not. If S need not be split, then a leaf node is created containing all the samples in S. Otherwise a decision node is created which splits S into two subsets by applying a threshold θ_S on one of the attributes t_S. The optimal value for the pair (t_S, θ_S) is selected so as to increase the IG (as defined in equation 1).

1: **if** SamplesNeedToBeSplit(S,C) **then**
2:     Create a decision node with attribute t_S and threshold θ_S which optimally splits S into two groups S_l and S_r with labels C_l and C_r respectively. (For details see section 2.1)
3:     Add the nodes Tree(S_l,C_l) and Tree(S_r,C_r) respectively as the left and right children of the decision node. Next level of recursion is applied on these two child-nodes.
4: **else**
5:     Create a leaf node storing the dominant label c_S and pointers to elements of S.
6: **end if**

where $H(S)$ is the information entropy of a set S defined as

$$H(S) = -\sum_{c \in C} p(c) \log p(c) \qquad (2)$$

We stop growing a tree node (and declare it as a leaf node) when the number of training samples available to it is less than N_{min} or when the entropy of the samples given to the node is less than H_{min}. As in [20], we set $N_{min} = 2$ and $H_{min} = 0$, that is, the training algorithm keeps on splitting the samples until all the samples in a subset belong to the same 3D point.

2.2   Random Search for Optimal Decision Parameters

In general, it is difficult to compute the best value for the decision parameters since SIFT vectors have 128 attributes and the number of different values that a descriptor attribute can have is very large. Hence, at each node, the IG measure is evaluated only on a small set of random pair of values (t_S, θ_S) and the best value among them is chosen. Multiple decision trees are learned with such strategy. During testing the outcome of those multiple trees are aggregated to obtain the final class label for a test sample. Aggregation is performed during testing through weighted voting scheme (More details in section 3.3). In our implementation we try 500 random decision values for each node. First, we randomly select 500 attributes between 1 to 128. For each random attribute, we choose a random threshold value between minimum and maximum value attained for the attribute by the samples used to train the node. We train 10 such trees during training.

Algorithm 2. FindBestThreshForAttribute(S,C,t)
Description: Finds threshold value for attribute t which optimally splits S for a given entropy measure

---

1: Find unique set of values (in the increasing order) $A = \{a_1, a_2, ..., a_k\}$ the samples in S take for attribute t.
2: Compute mid-values $B = \{b_i = \frac{a_i + a_{i+1}}{2}\}$.
3: Compute gap-values $g_i = a_{i+1} - a_i$
4: **for all** $i \in \{1, 2, ..., k-1\}$ **do**
5:     Compute $S_l = \{f \in S : f^t \le b_i\}$ and $S_r = \{f \in S : f^t > b_i\}$
6:     $G_i \leftarrow$ IG (equation 1) due to splitting S in to S_l and S_r using threshold b_i
7: **end for**
8: Return the b_i and g_i corresponding to the highest G_i.

2.3 Exhaustive Search for Optimal Decision Parameters on SIFT Training Vectors

The attributes of SIFT descriptors take integer values between 0 to 255 (provided they are not normalized to unit length). Hence, each attribute can partition S in at most 254 different ways. This enables us to perform exhaustive search for optimal attribute-threshold values. The procedure for performing this exhaustive search for a given attribute t on the set of training samples S with labels C is explained in Algorithm 2. We perform this search on each attribute of S to compute the optimal decision value.

It is easy to notice in Algorithm 2 that any threshold value in an interval $[a_i, a_{i+1})$ will split S in the same way and hence lead to same value for IG (equation 1). Hence, we need to try only one threshold value for each interval in order to search for best IG. For each interval we use mid-value for threshold $b_i = \frac{a_i + a_{i+1}}{2}$ in order to maximize the margin between left and right samples. For threshold value b_i, the IG (G_i) is computed and the best threshold value b_j with highest IG is chosen. The algorithm also returns gap between left and right samples which is $g_j = a_{j+1} - a_j$. This algorithm is executed on all the attributes and the attribute threshold pair leading to highest IG is chosen. If there are multiple such decision parameters, then, we choose the one which gives maximum gap g_j.

2.4 Training Oblique Decision Tree Through Canonical Cross Correlation (CCA)

Given two matrices $X = [x_1, x_2, ..., x_n] \in \mathbb{R}^{n \times d}$ and $Y = [y_1, y_2, ..., y_n] \in \mathbb{R}^{n \times k}$, CCA [26] computes two projection vectors $w_x \in \mathbb{R}^d$ and $w_y \in \mathbb{R}^k$ such that the correlation coefficient

$$\rho = \frac{w_x^T X Y^T w_y}{\sqrt{(w_x^T X X^T w_x)(w_y^T Y Y^T w_y)}} \tag{3}$$

is maximized. If X contains training SIFT vectors as its columns and Y contains corresponding class labels as its columns in *1-of-k* binary coding scheme, (i.e., in i^{th} column of Y the jth element is 1 if the SIFT vector x_i is associated with 3D point Q_j, otherwise it is zero) then the projection vector w_x can be used to obtain oblique decision at each node as follows. If X is the set of sample vectors provided to a tree node during training, we compute its w_x (which maximizes equation 3). For a threshold value θ, the training vectors satisfying $w_x^T x_i \leq \theta$ are directed towards left node and the rest are directed towards right node. Optimal value for θ is chosen based on the IG of the split. In our experiments we have used the regularized version of the CCA (rCCA) which solves the generalized eigenvalue problem

$$XY^T(YY^T + \lambda_y I)^{-1}YX^T w_x = \eta(XX^T + \lambda_x I)w_x \qquad (4)$$

in order to compute w_x [26]. We set $\lambda_y = 0, \lambda_x = 0.1$.

In [9] CCA is used to reduce the dimension of the input data and then Random Ferns [22] are trained to perform classification instead of decision trees. In such a framework, each class label needs $F \times 2^{d'}$ number of double values to be stored during the classification process, where F is the number of ferns and d' is the reduced dimension of the vector space. For the parameter values used in the experiments of [9] this amounts to a memory storage requirement of more than 10MB per 3D point. This is very costly since SfM on a small target environment (eg. a single office room) may produce thousands of 3D points. In contrast the decision trees need only 128 double values (128 is the dimension of the SIFT vector) at each node. In our experiments the tree contained nearly $100k$ nodes which requires less than 100MB memory in total.

3   Experiments

In this section, we present the experimental setup for evaluating 3D point recognition accuracy for pose estimation (Sec. 3.1), list the software libraries used in our experiments (Sec. 3.2) and, then, present experimental results and discussion based on those results (Sec. 3.3).

3.1   Evaluating Accuracy

For evaluating the accuracy of keypoint recognition methods for camera pose estimation we need the following information:
1. Camera positions corresponding to the images
2. 3D coordinates of at least some of the keypoints in the images

This information can be obtained by performing SfM [28] on the set of given images as follows. Keypoint descriptors extracted from the images can be matched to obtain point-to-point correspondences between each pair of images. Using these 2D matches, SfM computes the camera position in each image and the 3D coordinates of the points corresponding to matched image locations. The keypoint descriptors associated with the 2D matches of a 3D point can be labeled with the ID of the 3D point. The descriptor vectors not associated with any 3D point can be labeled as 0. Thus we obtain information (1) and (2) mentioned above.

Sometimes camera positions are given along with images (as in the case of 7Scenes dataset[24] we use). For such cases we can establish correspondence between the keypoint descriptors and 3D points through triangulation as follows:

1. Extract keypoint descriptors from each image
2. Obtain point-to-point matches between each pair of images by matching the descriptors extracted from those images
3. Discard those point-to-point matches which do not comply with epipolar constraints based on the fundamental matrix between a pair of images
4. The matched descriptors are tracked across images to obtain clusters
5. For each cluster obtain the 3D coordinates by performing triangulation [2] using the given camera positions
6. Label each descriptor vector associated with a 3D point using the ID of the 3D point. Otherwise the label is 0

Once we have the camera positions and labeled keypoint descriptors for a given set of images we can evaluate the accuracy of a 3D point identification method through reprojection error. We divide the set of images into Train and Test sets. The keypoint descriptors from the Train image set are used as samples for training. During testing the keypoint descriptors from test images are assigned one of the class labels. If a test descriptor is associated with a 3D point, then, we can measure its reprojection error in pixels using camera pose of the test image. In our experiments the matches which have less than 8 pixel error of reprojection are treated as *good* matches and those having higher error than that are considered as *bad* matches.

3.2   Libraries for ANNS, CCA and ORB

For performing ANNS on SIFT we use Balanced Box Decomposition (BBD) structure based library [21]. BBD is also a tree structure built using training set of vectors where each node is associated with a region in the descriptor vector space. It has many interesting properties like (i) the cardinality and geometric size of the region associated with a node reduce exponentially as one descends the tree, (ii) reasonable bound based on the tolerance ϵ on the distance ratio of the retrieved nearest neighbor (NN) to the actual NN while performing approximate search. For CCA, we use the code provided along with [26]. For computing ORB keypoints and descriptors we use OpenCV [5] library.

3.3   Results

In our experiments we use sequence 1 and 2 of the office sequences in 7Scenes dataset [24]. Both sequences contain 1000 images each. We subsample them by selecting 1 in every 8 images. We use the descriptors (SIFT and ORB) from 125 images of seq 1 for training and those from the other 125 images in seq 2 for

Table 1. APDT based classification on SIFT descriptors and hamming distance based classification on ORB descriptors. For descripton of columns please see section 3.3. Average time per image for Exh-Tree T-250 is 2 milliseconds, Random Tree with Maj vote takes 20 milliseconds, Random Tree with threshold and inv-dist vote takes 25 milliseconds. ORB descriptors take nearly 3 seconds per image (BruteForce matching in OpenCV [5]). Exh-Tree T-250 clearly outshines ORB in accuracy and speed.

	Exh-Tree	Exh-Tree T-200	Exh-Tree T-250	Rand-10 Maj	Rand-10 T-250	Rand-10 Inv-Dist Vote	ORB
Good	12.59	10.7	11.79	6.70	27.99	10.73	10.35
Bad	35.52	1.4	3.50	1.39	5.80	1.71	15.86

testing. There are around 90k and 80k SIFT descriptors in Train and Test set respectively. There are around 110k ORB descriptors each in Test and Train set.

Results with APDT and ORB. Results are shown in table 1, 2 and 3. Each column in these tables corresponds to a particular type of classification. There are two rows in each table showing the accuracy values. The 'Good' and 'Bad' rows indicate the % of matches that are good and bad respectively based on the reprojection error. The rest of the test vectors either matched with those training vectors which are not associated with any 3D point or did not match any training vector at all.

Table 1 shows the accuracy for APDT and ORB. Columns 2 to 7 show results of using different decision trees trained using SIFT training vectors. The last column shows the result of using hamming distance threshold based classification of ORB descriptors (we use the threshold 30). Exh-Tree in column 2, 3 and 4 indicates single decision tree trained using exhaustive search for optimal decision parameters. Column 2 (Exh-Tree) shows the result of assigning the class label of leaf node training samples to each test vector to which it reaches during classification. It contains only 12.59% good matches and 35.52% bad matches which is very large. In order to reduce bad matches we computed the distance between the test vector and the training samples at the leaf node and discarded those having distance higher than a particular threshold. Column 3 and 4 shows the result of Exh-Tree for distance threshold 200 and 250 respectively. We can see that thresholding at leaf reduces the bad matches significantly. But in order to perform thresholding at leaf we have to store all the training vectors even at run time. The time required for performing computation is 2 milliseconds which indicates that this method can be applied even in a larger environment to obtain real-time performance.

Next three columns (5, 6 and 7) show the results of classification by aggregating the outcome of 10 trained trees using random search for optimal decision parameters. Column 4 uses majority vote, column 5 applies a threshold on the distance to the NN among all the leaf samples of 10 trees and column 6 uses a voting mechanism in which each leaf sample's vote is weighed by inverse of its distance from the test vector. We can see that the only case having significantly

Table 2. ENN Classification using SIFT descriptors. Average time needed to compute the first neighbor is 7 seconds/image. Please refer to subsection "Results with ANNS" below for details.

	NN	R-of-NN				T-on-NN				
		0.6	0.7	0.8	0.9	100	150	200	250	300
Good	37.07	1.54	3.58	7.73	16.48	8.73	19.72	28.76	34.44	36.76
Bad	21.35	0.03	0.08	0.24	1.35	0.40	2.07	5.65	11.47	18.24

Table 3. ANN Classification using SIFT descriptors. Average time needed to compute the first neighbor is 2 milliseconds/image when approximation tolerance is set to 40. Please refer to subsection "Results with ANNS" below for details.

	NN	R-of-NN				T-on-NN				
		0.6	0.7	0.8	0.9	100	150	200	250	300
Good	19.35	5.49	7.73	10.53	14.22	5.76	11.79	15.79	17.96	18.97
Bad	36.70	0.24	0.85	2.98	10.10	0.28	1.50	4.58	9.76	17.72

higher good matches from Exh-Tree T-200 is column 6 (Rand-10 T-250). But the computational cost increases for it by a factor of 10 (20 milliseconds). Hence, using a single trained tree with exhaustive search by exploiting the integral value property of SIFT descriptors helps in achieving faster computation of matches.

The last column corresponding to ORB has 10.35% good matches and 15.86% bad matches. Such high % of incorrect matches is not suitable for pose estimation. We computed pose for each test image using the matches provided by Exh-Tree T-200. We use the algorithm [15] to compute pose with 1000 RANSAC [10] trials in order to reject outliers. After obtaining the pose, those images whose position is within 5cm and orientation is within 5° from the ground truth are declared to be correct (same as in [24]). We found that 92% of the camera positions obtained by our method are correct. This is better than that reported in [24] (86.8% when frame-to-frame tracking is used and 79.1% otherwise) which also uses depth information provided by the Kinect sensor along with the color image. This clearly indicates that it is better to use robust descriptors like SIFT with fast matching method rather than using binary descriptors for identifying 3D points for pose estimation.

Another thing we observe is that matching SIFT vectors through decision trees is much faster to matching ORB without any acceleration strategies. If approximate matching approaches are used for ORB for acceleration, it will only deteriorate the accuracy further from what is already considered very poor.

Results with ANNS. Table 2 and 3 show results of Exact Nearest Neighbor (ENN) and Approximate Nearest Neighbor (ANN) based classification respectively on SIFT descriptor vectors. The three column titles are described below:

- NN corresponds to NN classification (test vector is associated with the label of the closest training vector).
- R-of-NN corresponds to classification based on threshold on ratio of distances to two closest NNs belonging to different class labels. We compute 5 closest NNs for a test vector. If all the 5 training vectors belong to the same class, then the test vector is assigned to that class. Otherwise, we compute the ratio of distance of the NN and to the second NN belonging to a different class than the NN. If this ratio is less than a particular threshold, then, we assign the test vector to the class label of the NN. Otherwise, we discard it.
- T-on-NN classifies a test vector by applying a threshold on the distance.

The different threshold values applied on each case are indicated in the second row of these tables. From table 2, it is clear that ENN based classification provides better results than decision trees. For example T-on-NN with threshold 150 provides 19.72%, 2.07% good and bad matches which can be considered better than the results provided by Exh-Tree in columns 2, 3, 4 of table 1. But, ENN classification requires 7 seconds to finish computation where as Exh-Tree needs only 2 milliseconds. In order to accelerate NN matching we increased the tolerance value ϵ of ANNS to 40 at which the computation finished in 2 milliseconds per image. The results are shown in table 3. Though the approximation has reduced the accuracy of nearest neighbor matching it is still slightly better than decision trees. For example, T-on-NN with threshold 150 in table 3 gives 11.79%, 1.50% good and bad matches. Despite reduced accuracy it is still better than columns 2, 3, 4 of table 1.

Results with Oblique Decision Tree Based on CCA: We also experimented with oblique decision tree in order to improve the accuracy further. Due to the increased flexibility in decision boundaries we hoped to obtain better results. But, with oblique decision tree trained using CCA the results on test data only got much worse compared to APDT. In order to analyze the results we scaled down the problem to 4-class classification by selecting samples from only 4 clusters. We performed training and testing for one node on this reduced dataset using APDT and oblique decision trees. Fig. 1 shows typical decision boundaries and, the values of training and test samples on which decision threshold is applied. There are two subfigures each corresponding to axis-parallel (Fig. 1.a) and oblique tree (Fig. 1.b) respectively. The scalar values corresponding to the training and test samples used at the node of the respective decision trees are plotted along the x-axis. Each '+' mark indicates this scalar value. Its color (green, red, blue and magenta) indicates its class label. The training and test samples are shown at y=1 and y=-1 respectively. The vertical red line indicates the threshold value.

First, let us consider the distribution of training samples in Fig. 1.a and 1.b. APDT divides the training samples magenta and blue to left. The red and green training samples are spread at the right of the vertical line. Oblique decision tree divides red, green training samples to left and the rest to the right. In addition, we can see that Oblique decision tree packs the training samples tightly based

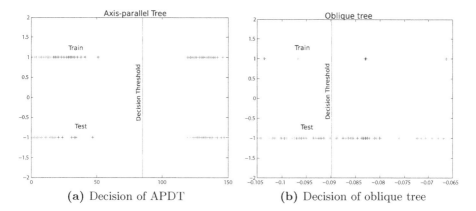

(a) Decision of APDT   (b) Decision of oblique tree

Fig. 1. Along x-axis these two figures show the attribute values of training and test samples used for decision making. Each '+' mark represents the attribute value of a sample. The samples to the left of the red vertical line are directed towards left and vice-versa. Its color (green, red, blue and magenta) indicates its class label. The training and test samples are displayed at y=1 and y=-1 respectively. By comparing the decision boundaries of test and train samples we can say (b) is a clear case of overfitting.

on the class label. All the training samples belonging to a class have almost same projected value and well separated from others. As one would expect, this indicates that oblique decision tree fits better to the provided training samples.

When we observe the distribution of test samples it reveals the reason for poor accuracy of oblique decision tree. APDT is more consistent with its behavior during training when compared to Oblique decision tree. For Oblique decision tree the test samples are scattered close to the decision boundary and some of them are even misclassified. It seems to be the case of overfitting. This problem cannot be mitigated by using more training samples because even if we increase the training samples the tree nodes at the lower level will receive only a small portion of it. Hence the same problem will appear at the lower levels. Perhaps a combination of using more flexible oblique decision tree nodes at the top level and APDT at lower level may improve the results.

4   Conclusion and Future Work

Our experiments show that we can obtain real-time performance for 3D point recognition with SIFT descriptors if we use ANNS based matching. The accuracy we obtain with such a method is better than binary descriptor based matching even when color and depth information are used. However, we could not improve this performance with SIFT even by using oblique decision trees. This was due to overfitting at lower levels which obtain very few training samples. We would like to mitigate this problem by using oblique decision trees at the top level nodes (which get large number of training samples) and APDT at lower level. It may also turn out that only NN based matching suits SIFT descriptors and hence using oblique decision trees at top level may also produce misclassification. In that case we would like to use BBD at the top level. BBD structure exponentially reduces the size of the region in the feature space associated with a node as we descend down. This will be similar to applying ANN classification at the top level. Then, APDTs can be used within the bounded regions at the lower levels.

References

1. Affine Covariant Regions data from Visual Geometry Group, Oxford University. http://www.robots.ox.ac.uk/~vgg/research/affine/
2. Matlab functions for multiple view geometry. http://www.robots.ox.ac.uk/~vgg/hzbook/code/
3. Bay, H., Ess, A., Tuytelaars, T., Van Gool, L.: Speeded-up robust features (SURF). Computer Vision and Image Understanding **110**(3), 346–359 (2008)
4. Bhat. S., Berger, M.O., Sur, F.: Visual words for 3D reconstruction and pose computation. 3DIMPVT 2011 (2011)
5. Bradski, G.: The OpenCV Library. Dr. Dobb's Journal of Software Tools (2000)
6. Calonder, M., Lepetit, V., Ozuysal, M., Trzcinski, T., Strecha, C., Fua, P.: BRIEF: Computing a Local Binary Descriptor Very Fast. PAMI 2012 (2012)
7. Criminisi, A., Shotton, J.: Decision Forests for Computer Vision and Medical Image Analysis. Springer Publishing Company, Incorporated (2013)
8. Dahl, A.L., Aanæs, H., Pedersen, K.S.: Finding the best feature detector-descriptor combination. In: 3DIMPVT 2011 (2011)
9. Donoser, M., Schmalstieg, D.: Discriminative feature-to-point matching in image-based localization. In: CVPR 2014 (2014)
10. Fischler, M.A., Bolles, R.C.: Random sample consensus: a paradigm for model fitting with applications to image analysis and automated cartography. Communications of the ACM **24**(6), 381–395 (1981)
11. Hartmann, J., Klussendorff, J., Maehle, E.: A comparison of feature descriptors for visual slam. In: European Conference on Mobile Robots 2013 (2013)
12. Heinly, J., Dunn, E., Frahm, J.-M.: Comparative evaluation of binary features. In: Fitzgibbon, A., Lazebnik, S., Perona, P., Sato, Y., Schmid, C. (eds.) Computer Vision-ECCV 2012. LNCS, vol. 2012, pp. 759–773. Springer, Heidelberg (2012)
13. Hesch, J., Roumeliotis, S.: A direct least-squares (dls) method for pnp. In: ICCV 2011 (2011)
14. Lepetit, V., Fua, P.: Keypoint Recognition using Randomized Trees. IEEE Transactions on Pattern Analysis and Machine Intelligence (PAMI) (2006)
15. Lepetit, V., Moreno-Noguer, F., Fua, P.: EPnP: An Accurate $O(n)$ Solution to the PnP Problem. IJCV 2009 (2009). http://cvlab.epfl.ch/software/EPnP/
16. Leutenegger, S., Chli, M., Siegwart, R.: Brisk: Binary robust invariant scalable keypoints. In: ICCV 2011 (2011)
17. Lieberknecht, S., Benhimane, S., Meier, P., Navab, N.: A dataset and evaluation methodology for template-based tracking algorithms. In: ISMAR (2009)
18. Lowe, D.G.: Distinctive image features from scale-invariant keypoints. IJCV 2004 (2004)

19. Mikolajczyk, K., Schmid, C.: A performance evaluation of local descriptors. IEEE Transactions on Pattern Analysis and Machine Intelligence **27**(10), 1615–1630 (2005)
20. Moosmann, F., Nowak, E., Jurie, F.: Randomized clustering forests for image classification. PAMI 2008 (2008)
21. Mount, D.M., Arya, S.: ANN: A library for approximate nearest neighbor searching. http://www.cs.umd.edu/~mount/ANN
22. Ozuysal, M., Calonder, M., Lepetit, V., Fua, P.: Fast Keypoint Recognition using Random Ferns. PAMI 2012 (2012)
23. Rublee, E., Rabaud, V., Konolige, K., Bradski, G.: Orb: An efficient alternative to sift or surf. ICCV 2011 (2011)
24. Shotton, J., Glocker, B., Zach, C., Izadi, S., Criminisi, A., Fitzgibbon, A.: Scene coordinate regression forests for camera relocalization in rgb-d images. CVPR 2013 (2013)
25. Snavely, N., Seitz, S.M., Szeliski, R.: Photo tourism: exploring photo collections in 3d. ACM Trans. Graph. 2006 (2006)
26. Sun, L., Ji, S., Ye, J.: Canonical correlation analysis for multilabel classification: A least-squares formulation, extensions, and analysis. PAMI 2011 (2011). http://www.public.asu.edu/~jye02/Software/CCA/index.html
27. Trzcinski, V.L.T., Christoudias, M., Fua, P.: Boosting Binary Keypoint Descriptors. Computer Vision and Pattern Recognition 2013 (2013)
28. Wu, C.: Towards linear-time incremental structure from motion. In: 3DV 2013 (2013)
29. Zheng, Y., Kuang, Y., Sugimoto, S., Astrom, K., Okutomi, M.: Revisiting the pnp problem: a fast, general and optimal solution. In: ICCV 2013 (2013)
30. Zhou, Q.-Y., Koltun, V.: Dense scene reconstruction with points of interest. ACM Trans. Graph. 2013 (2013). http://www.stanford.edu/~qianyizh/projects/scenedata.html

Überatlas: Robust Speed-Up of Feature-Based Registration and Multi-Atlas Segmentation

Jennifer Alvén$^{(\boxtimes)}$, Alexander Norlén, Olof Enqvist, and Fredrik Kahl

Department of Signals and Systems,
Chalmers University of Technology, Gothenburg, Sweden
`alven@chalmers.se`

Abstract. Registration is a key component in multi-atlas approaches to medical image segmentation. Current state of the art uses intensity-based registration methods, but such methods tend to be slow, which sets practical limitations on the size of the atlas set. In this paper, a novel feature-based registration method for affine registration is presented. The algorithm constructs an abstract representation of the entire atlas set, an überatlas, through clustering of features that are similar and detected consistently through the atlas set. This is done offline. At runtime only the feature clusters are matched to the target image, simultaneously yielding robust correspondences to all atlases in the atlas set from which the affine transformations can be estimated efficiently. The method is evaluated on 20 CT images of the heart and 30 MR images of the brain with corresponding gold standards. Our approach succeeds in producing better and more robust segmentation results compared to two baseline methods, one intensity-based and one feature-based, and significantly reduces the running times.

Keywords: Feature-based registration · Pericardium segmentation · Brain segmentation · Multi-atlas segmentation

1   Introduction

Segmentation is one of the most fundamental problems in medical image analysis and may be used in order to locate tumors, measure tissue volumes, for the study of anatomical structures, surgery planning, virtual surgery simulation, intra-surgery navigation etc. [22]. The value of automatic segmentation is huge, since manual delineation is time-consuming and sensitive to the skill of the expert. It is important that the segmentation algorithm is robust and fast in order to be useful in clinical care. Moreover, the segmentation algorithm should produce results comparable to those by a skilled expert.

One segmentation method that has become popular in recent years is multi-atlas segmentation [5,12,15,21,26] as it produces state-of-the-art results. Multi-atlas segmentation relies on a set of atlases (images with corresponding manual delineations), which are separately registered to an unlabeled target image.

© Springer International Publishing Switzerland 2015
R.R. Paulsen and K.S. Pedersen (Eds.): SCIA 2015, LNCS 9127, pp. 92–102, 2015.
DOI: 10.1007/978-3-319-19665-7_8

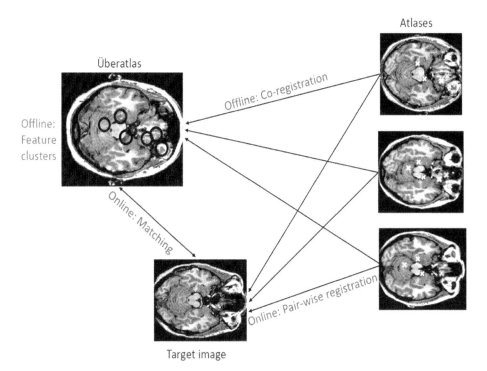

Fig. 1. A schematic drawing of the proposed framework. Offline: The atlases are co-registered to a reference atlas where the features are clustered both according to descriptor distance and spatial distance to make sure that the features in the cluster describe the same anatomical structure and to exclude outliers. Online: Robust matching between the target image and the überatlas is performed, directly gives feature correspondences between the target and all of the atlases. Using these correspondences all the atlases are robustly and efficiently registered to the target image.

Labels are transferred from the atlas images to the target image and fused by a voting scheme. In contrast to segmentation based on shape models, for example, active shapes [6], the solution is not constrained to be in the subspace spanned by the shape model. While being robust to non-satisfactory registrations multi-atlas segmentation has the disadvantage of being dependent on multiple image registrations which in general take a lot of time to compute and consequently limits the practical size of the atlas set.

In principle, there are two different approaches to image registration, feature-based and intensity-based registration, see the surveys [14,25]. Intensity-based methods are capable of producing very accurate registrations, but are often slow and sensitive to initialization. On the other hand, feature-based methods are fast, but risk failing due to the difficulty in establishing correct point-to-point correspondences between the images.

In this paper, a novel feature-based registration method is presented that combines the information of the entire atlas set and efficiently finds robust transformations between a target image and *all the images* in the atlas set. The general idea is to cluster the feature points in the atlas set, both according to descriptor distances and according to spatial distances after a careful co-registration of the atlases, into what will be referred to as an überatlas. The construction of the überatlas is done offline. At runtime, one only needs to register the überatlas to the target image, and correspondences to all images in the atlas set are automatically obtained. As the überatlas only contains the best fitted feature points for matching from the co-registration phase, the approach has the potential not only to improve speed, but also to reduce the amount of classification errors and improve the segmentation. Figure 1 shows a schematic drawing of the proposed solution.

2   Related Work

The work that is most closely related to ours is the standard multi-atlas approach, where registrations are computed between all the atlases and the target image independently, see [12,15]. Typically, the images are first registered using an affine transformation. If needed, this is followed by a refined nonrigid registration. In this paper, we focus on the first step of estimating an affine transformation. We experimentally compare to two such standard baselines, one using intensity-based registration and one using features. The intensity-based method performs image registration with the popular software package `Niftyreg`, meaning that an affine transformation is estimated via a block-matching strategy, proposed and implemented by Ourselin et al. [19,20]. The feature-based method is based on standard RANSAC optimization [9] which is further described in the sections below.

Dey et al. [7] proposed to first co-register a set of atlases of the heart using a nonrigid intensity based method and then, at runtime, to only register one of the atlases to a target image and letting the other atlases vote indirectly. To some extent this is contrary to the idea of multi-atlas segmentation as it relies on obtaining a single very accurate registration at run time. Gill et al. [10] proposed to create a mean atlas including feature points of a set of atlases of the lung, and use this mean atlas to initialize an active shape model.

Hence, the concept of using a mean atlas is not new, but we are not aware of any work using an intermediate representation for efficiently estimating all the transformations between atlases and target images. Our main contributions are the development of such a representation, which we refer to as an überatlas, and to experimentally demonstrate that we obtain comparable accuracy with respect to the two baselines while significantly reducing runtimes.

3   Proposed Solution

In order to perform a multi-atlas segmentation, one needs to register the atlases to a target image as accurately as possible. As previously mentioned, a common way of doing this is to estimate an affine transformation followed by a nonrigid transformation. In this paper, we focus on the affine estimation step.

The underlying idea of our approach is to construct an intermediate representation of the atlas images which can be used to perform the most time-consuming part of the process, namely the robust matching, that is, obtaining correct feature correspondences between the atlases and the target images. The überatlas is constructed in such a way that if a feature correspondence between the überatlas and the target image has been identified, one can immediately derive in which atlas images this particular feature correspondence was originally present, see Figure 1. Once good correspondences are obtained to all the atlases, one can quickly compute an affine transformation for each atlas individually.

First, we will describe how to construct the überatlas from the atlas set (Section 3.1). Note that this is an offline process done only once, so speed is less important than for the online steps. Then, we will describe how to register the überatlas to a new, unlabeled target image (Section 3.2), which is a process done online.

3.1 Überatlas Construction

The purpose of the überatlas is to gather information about corresponding feature points in all atlases, as well as an approximate way of describing all the feature points. To compute sparse features we use the code by Svärm et al. [24]. This code uses the method of SIFT for feature detection [17] and a descriptor similar to that of SURF proposed by Bay et al. [2].

Constructing an überatlas is done in two steps: co-registration and feature clustering.

Co-registration of atlases. In this step, a nonrigid transformation $\hat{T}_{i,\hat{i}}$ is estimated between each atlas, i, and the *reference atlas* $\hat{i}$, that has been chosen at random. An initial estimate of $\hat{T}_{i,\hat{i}}$, was given by affine feature-based registration. We used truncated l_2 as a loss function with a truncation threshold of 20 mm and optimized it using RANSAC [9] with one million iterations.

For the nonrigid registration, each atlas image, $\mathcal{I}_i$, is concatenated with its corresponding labeling, $\mathcal{L}_i$ into a two-channel 3D image. The labeling is weighted with a factor α_i to determine its impact on the solution. For our experiments α was set to the intensity span of the image. Finally, the actual registration is performed with NiftyReg using normalized mutual information, due to its capability of dealing with multi-channel images. For all other parameters we used the default values.

Feature clustering. A feature point f is uniquely determined by the index of the atlas from which it is extracted, i, the coordinates of the feature point in the coordinate frame of the atlas, x, and the corresponding descriptor, d, i.e., $f = (i, x, d)$. Using the transformations, $\hat{T}_{i,\hat{i}}$, obtained by co-registration, all feature points are transformed into a common coordinate system. The transformed coordinates are in other words the coordinates of a feature detected in any atlas, transformed accurately into the coordinate system of the reference atlas.

In order to construct the feature clusters, $\mathcal{F} = \{\boldsymbol{f}_k : k \in \mathcal{K}\}$ where $\mathcal{K}$ is the set of the feature indices in a cluster, agglomerative clustering is used [27]. A distance matrix based on the distances between all descriptors is constructed and sorted. When clustering M atlases, the $3 \times M$ smallest distances to each of the feature descriptors are taken into account and the remaining distances are considered infinitely large. The set of clusters is initialized with one cluster for every feature point (a cluster with size 1) and the clustering proceeds by merging pairs of clusters.

For merging clusters, a variant of single linkage is used, i.e., the shortest distance between two clusters is considered. However, these clusters are only merged if no features in the two clusters come from the same image and if all features in the two clusters are spatially consistent. More precisely feature k from image i is spatially consistent with feature l from image j if their coordinates satisfy,

$$\left| \hat{\boldsymbol{T}}_{i,\hat{i}} \circ \boldsymbol{x}_k - \hat{\boldsymbol{T}}_{j,\hat{i}} \circ \boldsymbol{x}_l \right| < \epsilon_s. \tag{1}$$

In practice, the spatial threshold, ϵ_s, was set to 10. Finally, we only keep clusters that contain at least 3 features.

These criteria make sure that the features in the clusters with high certainty describe the same anatomical feature. Further, it tells us that this anatomical feature is often detected by the feature detector meaning that we can expect to find the feature in a new image as well. Finally, it cleans the überatlas of features that are not found consistently between the atlases. These are features that most likely are outliers, noise, misplaced features or features describing uncertain anatomical regions.

An *überatlas* is a set of non-overlapping feature clusters with a corresponding descriptor, i.e.,

$$\{(\mathcal{F}_u, \hat{\boldsymbol{d}}_u) : u \in \mathcal{U}\} \tag{2}$$

where $\mathcal{U}$ is the set of feature cluster indices and $\hat{\boldsymbol{d}}_u$ is calculated as the mean of the feature descriptors included in the cluster $\mathcal{F}_u$.

3.2   Überatlas Registration

Registration using the überatlas is done in two steps. First the features of the target image are matched to the feature clusters in the überatlas in a robust manner. Then each atlas is registered efficiently to the target image using iteratively reweighted least squares (IRLS).

Matching.   Given a new target image, feature points are detected and descriptors are computed as explained in Section 3.1. For each cluster the cluster descriptor is matched to its nearest neighbor of the feature descriptors in the target image. The distance between the descriptors is measured using the Euclidean norm.

A match between a feature $\boldsymbol{f}_t$ in the target image and a cluster $\mathcal{F}_u$ in the überatlas simultaneously establishes correspondences to all features present in the cluster and therefore also to the atlases from which these features were extracted.

In order to eliminate outliers, a restriction on the distance between the descriptors of the correspondences is introduced. A correspondence between $\boldsymbol{f}_t$ and a feature in an atlas $\boldsymbol{f}_s$ found through matching to the cluster $\mathcal{F}_u$ is considered an inlier if the following criterion is fulfilled

$$\frac{\|\boldsymbol{d}_t - \boldsymbol{d}_s\|}{\boldsymbol{D}_u} < \epsilon_d, \tag{3}$$

where ϵ_d is a parameter and $\boldsymbol{D}_u$ is the maximum distance between the descriptors within the cluster $\mathcal{F}_u$, i.e.,

$$\boldsymbol{D}_u = \max\{\|\boldsymbol{d}_i - \boldsymbol{d}_j\| : \boldsymbol{f}_i, \boldsymbol{f}_j \in \mathcal{F}_u\}. \tag{4}$$

This can be viewed as a generalization of Lowe's ratio criterion for feature matching (see [17]), to the case of cluster matching. In practice, we used $\epsilon_d = 1$.

Finally, RANSAC is used in order to remove matches that are not consistent with an affine transformation between the überatlas and the target image. The coordinates of the clusters are set to the mean of the transformed feature coordinates. Also, the affine transformation is used as an initialization to the estimation of the affine transformation between the atlases and the target image, described below.

Affine transformation. As described in Section 1, the problem of using feature-based registration is the great amount of outliers produced. Even though the amount of outliers is reduced thanks to the construction of the überatlas, the problem is not entirely eliminated. Normally this is dealt with using RANSAC with a high number of iterations, but überatlas-based matching produces fewer outliers, so we can use a faster method for estimating the affine transformation, namely iteratively reweighted least squares (IRLS), see Chartrand and Yin [4].

Often truncated l_2-norm is viewed as an appropriate loss function in the presence of outliers, see Blake et al. [3]. However, we have found that using the truncated l_1-norm instead, reduces the sensitivity to the choice of outlier threshold and enables larger thresholds without losing robustness. The reason is that the l_2-norm is suitable mainly when the noise is Gaussian. This is a good assumption for the measurement errors of inliers but works poorly for the outliers. When increasing the value of the outlier threshold, we include more outliers making the the assumption of normally distributed residuals unsuitable. Truncated l_1-norm is less sensitive.

Given a set of N local correspondences, where the coordinates of the correspondences are given by $\{(\boldsymbol{x}_n, \boldsymbol{y}_n) : n = 1, \ldots, N\}$, the affine transformation is estimated via IRLS. The following minimization problem is solved iteratively with the l_2-norm as a loss function,

$$(\hat{\boldsymbol{A}}_i, \hat{\boldsymbol{t}}_i) = \underset{\boldsymbol{A}, \boldsymbol{t}}{\operatorname{argmin}} \sum_{n=1}^{N} \omega_{i,n} |\boldsymbol{A}\boldsymbol{y}_n + \boldsymbol{t} - \boldsymbol{x}_n|^2, \tag{5}$$

where i is the iteration number and the weight $\omega_{i,n}$ is a function of the errors in the previous iteration. In order to avoid dividing with zero, a regularization, $|\delta| \ll 1$, is introduced. For details on IRLS, see, e.g., Aftab and Hartley [1]. In the end, the weights are given by

$$\omega_{i,n} = \begin{cases} 1/\max\{|r_{i-1,n}|, |\delta|\}, & |r_{i-1,n}| < \epsilon, \\ 0, & |r_{i-1,n}| \geq \epsilon, \end{cases} \tag{6}$$

where the residuals are given by $r_{i,n} = \hat{A}_i y_n + \hat{t}_i - x_n$.

For the experiments, we used IRLS with 10 iterations, initialized by a composition of the transformation estimated by RANSAC described in the previous section and the known affine transformation between the atlas and the überatlas that was obtained in the offline co-registration. Results for truncation levels of both 10 and 50 mm are presented in the next section.

4   Experiments

The experimental evaluation was carried out on two different data sets and for two different settings, the first being pairwise affine registration and the second one, multi-atlas segmentation. To make full use of the data, the experiments were performed in a leave-one-out fashion, i.e., an überatlas was constructed using all but one image and then tested on that image.

4.1   Data Sets

The first data set consists of 20 CT images of the heart. For these images delineations of the pericardium were obtained using a gold standard approach. More precisely, the delineations were drawn for every 10th slice in all three viewing directions by an expert involved in the SCAPIS project [13]. These 2D delineations were then interpolated into a complete 3D delineation that was finally approved by the expert.

The second data set consists of 30 MR images of the brain of young adults and delineation of 83 regions of the brain, which are manually drawn according to the protocol in Hammers et al. [11]. The data set is available online on http://www.brain-development.org. The images of the brains were upsampled with a factor 2.

4.2   Pairwise Affine Registration

In this evaluation we consider the quality of the pairwise affine registrations obtained from a new target image to the individual atlas images as described in Section 3.2. Comparisons are given to two baseline methods: The first is affine intensity-based registration using `NiftyReg` with default values. The second one is standard feature-based registration, feature points were extracted by a feature detection and description program implemented by Svärm et al. [24]. The program was run with default values and without rotation invariance. The affine registration was performed with 10000-iteration RANSAC. As for the outlier threshold, ϵ, both 10 and 50 mm were evaluated.

Comparisons are done with respect to runtime and the dice index [8], which is a similarity measure between 0 and 1. The results for the heart images and brain images are given in Tables 1 and 2. Clearly, the überatlas registration produces larger values of the dice index than the compared methods and significantly reduces running times.

Table 1. Dice index and runtimes of the pair-wise affine registrations of the hearts. For the feature-based baseline and the überatlas registration, the runtimes include feature detection, matching and affine transformation. The feature-based baseline method and the überatlas registration was tested with two different values of the outlier threshold ϵ.

Method	$\epsilon = 10$ mm	$\epsilon = 50$ mm	Runtime
Intensity	0.754 ± 0.130	0.754 ± 0.130	1054 s
Features	0.870 ± 0.057	0.811 ± 0.084	11.7 s
Überatlas	0.874 ± 0.072	0.888 ± 0.038	2.7 s

Table 2. Dice index and runtimes of the pair-wise affine registrations of the brains. For the feature-based baseline and the überatlas registration, the runtimes include feature detection, matching and affine transformation. The feature-based baseline method and the überatlas registration was tested with two different values of the outlier threshold ϵ.

Method	$\epsilon = 10$ mm	$\epsilon = 50$ mm	Runtime
Intensity	0.637 ± 0.024	0.637 ± 0.024	63 s
Features	0.640 ± 0.023	0.630 ± 0.026	7.1 s
Überatlas	0.643 ± 0.022	0.638 ± 0.024	1.0 s

4.3   Multi-Atlas Segmentation

For multi-atlas segmentation three different setups were tested:

(II) Affine intensity-based registration + nonrigid intensity-based registration
(UI) Affine überatlas registration + nonrigid intensity-based registration
(UU) Affine überatlas registration + nonrigid feature-based registration

Implementation Details. The intensity-based nonrigid registration was based on the free-form deformation proposed by Rueckert et al. [23], and implemented by Modat et al. [18]. The affine transformation was used as an initialization for the nonrigid transformation. The program was run with default values. The feature-based nonrigid registration was based on a point-based free-form deformation implemented by D. Kroon based on a proposition of Lee et al. [16]. The correspondences marked as inliers according to the outlier threshold were used as input. The nonrigid feature-based transformation was run with default values, apart from the number of grid refinements that was set to 5.

Experimental results. Dice index and runtimes of the multi-atlas based segmentations are given in Tables 3 and 4 for heart and brain images, respectively. Clearly, the überatlas registration produces comparable values of the dice index for the compared methods and significantly reduces the runtimes. Considering the brain images, the multi-atlas based segmentation results are on par with the intensity-based multi-atlas approach by Heckemann et al. [12] which is current state of the art. They use the same brain data set and obtain a mean dice index equal to 0.8173. Furthermore, assuming a multi-atlas consisting of 100 images, the intensity-based multi-atlas segmentation would take 4.5 hours compared to our method that would take only 1.9 minutes. A multi-atlas segmentation with the feature-based baseline would take 13 minutes.

Table 3. Dice index and runtimes of the multi-atlas based segmentations of the hearts. For the affine überatlas registration, the runtimes include feature detection, matching and affine transformation. Abbreviations: AFF = affine registration, NR = nonrigid registration, II = intensity AFF + intensity NR, UI = überatlas AFF + intensity NR, UU = überatlas AFF + überatlas NR.

Method	Dice index	Runtime AFF	Runtime NR	Runtime total
II	0.933 ± 0.049	20026 s	36955 s	56981 s
UI	0.969 ± 0.033	52 s	36955 s	37007 s
UU	0.951 ± 0.019	52 s	121 s	173 s

Table 4. Dice index and runtimes of the multi-atlas based segmentations of the brains. For the affine überatlas registration, the runtimes include feature detection, matching and affine transformation. Abbreviations: AFF = affine registration, NR = nonrigid registration, II = intensity AFF + intensity NR, UI = überatlas AFF + intensity NR, UU = überatlas AFF + überatlas NR.

Method	Dice index	Runtime AFF	Runtime N-R	Runtime total
II	0.805 ± 0.010	1827 s	2900 s	4727 s
UI	0.806 ± 0.010	30 s	2900 s	2930 s
UU	0.769 ± 0.013	30 s	23 s	53 s

5   Conclusion

Our proposed überatlas registration framework, is a novel, feature-based method that uses co-registration of atlases and clustering of feature points as a preprocessing step in order to speed up the computations of the image registrations needed in multi-atlas segmentation, but also to reduce the amount of outliers. The robust estimation of the affine transformations are done with the truncated l_1-norm as loss function. The registration method is faster than the two methods used as a comparison. For instance, computing pair-wise affine registrations of the heart takes 2.7 seconds on average compared to 11.7 and 1054 seconds, respectively.

The experimental results show that the developed affine registration algorithm is more robust to outliers making it both less sensitive to parameter selection and allows for a higher truncation threshold. The need for tuning parameters is therefore decreased but this factor is especially valuable when an affine transformation describes the actual transformation between the images poorly.

The proposed method succeeds to produce better segmentation results with respect to the dice index and has a lower standard deviation, both compared to the intensity and the feature based baseline. It produces comparable multi-atlas segmentation results to the current state of the art. Fine-tuning of the algorithm (such as choosing reference atlas in a more structured way and optimizing parameters) could yield even better results.

References

1. Aftab, K., Hartley, R.: Convergence of iteratively re-weighted least squares to robust M-estimators. In: IEEE Winter Conference on Applications of Computer Vision (2015)
2. Bay, H., Tuytelaars, T., Van Gool, L.: SURF: Speeded up robust features. Computer Vision and Image Understanding **110**(3), 346–359 (2008)
3. Blake, A., Zisserman, A.: Visual reconstruction, p. 225. MIT Press (1987)
4. Chartrand, R., Yin, W.: Iteratively reweighted algorithms for compressive sensing. In: IEEE International Conference on Acoustics, Speech and Signal Processing, pp. 3869–3872 (2008)
5. Chen, A., Niermann, K.J., Deeley, M.A., Dawant, B.M.: Evaluation of multiple-atlas-based strategies for segmentation of the thyroid gland in head and neck CT images for IMRT. Physics in Medicine and Biology **57**(1), 93–111 (2012)
6. Cootes, T.F., Taylor, C.J., Cooper, D.H., Graham, J.: Active shape models - Their training and application. Computer Vision and Image Understanding **61**(1), 38–59 (1995)
7. Dey, D., Ramesh, A., Slomka, P.J., Nakazato, R., Cheng, V.Y., Germano, G., Bermana, D.S.: Automated algorithm for atlas-based segmentation of the heart and pericardium from non-contrast CT. In: Proceedings of SPIE (2010)
8. Dice, L.R.: Measures of the amount of ecologic association between species. Ecology **26**(3), 297–302 (1945)
9. Fischler, M.A., Bolles, R.C.: Random sample consensus: a paradigm for model fitting with applications to image analysis and automated cartography. Communications of the ACM **24**(6), 381–395 (1981)
10. Gill, G., Toews, M., Beichel, R.R.: Robust initialization of active shape models for lung segmentation in CT scans: A feature-based atlas approach. International Journal of Biomedical Imaging, 479154 (2014)

11. Hammers, A., Allom, R., Koepp, M.J., Free, S.L., Myers, R., Lemieux, L., Mitchell, T.N., Brooks, D.J., Duncan, J.S.: Three dimensional maximum probability atlas of the human brain, with particular reference to the temporal lobe. Human Brain Mapping 19(4), 224–247 (2003)
12. Heckemann, R.A., Keihaninejad, S., Aljabar, P., Rueckert, D., Hajnal, J.V., Hammers, A.: Improving intersubject image registration using tissue-class information benefits robustness and accuracy of multi-atlas based anatomical segmentation. NeuroImage 51(1), 221–227 (2010)
13. Hjärt och Lungfonden: SCAPIS - en världsunik nationell kunskapskälla (2014). http://www.hjart-lungfonden.se/scapis. (accessed September 30, 2014)
14. Khalifa, F., Beache, G.M., Gimel'farb, G., Suri, J.S., El-Baz, A.S.: State-of-the-art medical image registration methodologies: a survey. In: Multi modality state-of-the-art medical image segmentation and registration methodologies, pp. 235–280. Springer Science+Business Media (2011)
15. Kirisli, H. A., Schaap, M., Klein, S., Neefjes, L.A., Weustink, A.C., van Walsum, T., Niessen, W.J.: Fully automatic cardiac segmentation from 3D CTA data: a multi-atlas based approach. In: Proceedings of SPIE (2010)
16. Lee, S., Wolberg, G., Shin, S.Y.: Scattered data interpolation with multilevel B-splines. IEEE Transaction on Visualization and Computer Graphics 3(3), 228–244 (1997)
17. Lowe, D.G.: Object recognition from local scale-invariant features. In: Proceedings of International Conference on Computer Vision, vol. 2, pp. 1150–1157 (1999)
18. Modat, M., Ridgway, G.R., Taylor, Z.A., Lehmann, M., Barnes, J., Hawkes, D.J., Fox, N.C., Ourselin, S.: Fast free-form deformation using graphics processing units. Computer Methods and Programs in Biomedicine 98(3), 278–284 (2009)
19. Ourselin, S., Roche, A., Subsol, G., Pennec, X., Ayache, N.: Reconstructing a 3D structure from serial histological sections. Image and Vision Computing 19(1), 25–31 (2001)
20. Ourselin, S., Stefanescu, R., Pennec, X.: Robust registration of multi-modal images: towards real-time clinical applications. In: Dohi, T., Kikinis, R. (eds.) MICCAI 2002, Part II. LNCS, vol. 2489, pp. 140–147. Springer, Heidelberg (2002)
21. Panda S., Asman A.J., Khare S-P., Thompson L., Mawn L.A., Smith S.A., Landman B.A.: Evaluation of multi-atlas label fusion for in vivo MRI orbital segmentation. Journal of Medical Imaging 1(2) (2014)
22. Pham, D.L., Xu, C., Prince, J.L.: Current methods in medical image segmentation. Annual Review of Biomedical Engineering 2, 315–337 (2000)
23. Rueckert, D., Sonod, L.I., Hayes, C., Hill, D.L.G., Leach, M.O., Hawkes, D.J.: Non-rigid registration using free-form deformations: Application to breast MR images. IEEE Transactions on Medical Imaging 18(8), 712–721 (1999)
24. Svärm, L., Enqvist, O., Kahl, F., Oskarsson, M.: Improving robustness for inter-subject medical image registration using a feature-based approach. International Symposium on Biomedical Imaging (2015)
25. Sotiras, A., Davatzikos, C., Paragios, N.: Deformable medical image registration: A survey. IEEE Transactions on Medical Imaging 32(7) (2013)
26. Wang, H., Suh, J.W., Das, S.R., Pluta, J., Craige, C., Yushkevich, P.A.: Multi-atlas segmentation with joint label fusion. IEEE Transactions on Pattern Analysis and Machine Intelligence (2012)
27. Xu, R.: Survey of clustering algorithms. IEEE Transactions on Neural Networks 16(3), 645–678 (2005)

Classification of Alzheimer's Disease from MRI Using Sulcal Morphology

Simon Kragh Andersen, Christian Elmholt Jakobsen,
Claus Hougaard Pedersen, Anders Munk Rasmussen,
Maciej Plocharski$^{(\boxtimes)}$, and Lasse Riis Østergaard

Department of Health Science and Technology, Aalborg University,
Aalborg, Denmark
mpl@hst.aau.dk

Abstract. Alzheimer's disease (AD), an age-related progressive neu-rodegenerative disorder, is the most common cause of dementia. It is characterised by abnormal neuroanatomical changes in the brain, some of which can be difficult to distinguish from the alterations caused by normal aging. Sulcal morphology is affected by AD atrophy, indicates significant differences between cognitively normal (CN) and AD subjects, and proves to be a potential AD biomarker. 210 subjects (100 CN, 110 AD) were acquired from the ADNI database. 120 sulci were extracted per subject using BrainVISA sulcal identification pipeline. Mean curvature, surface area and volume were calculated for each sulcus, parameterized by a 3D mesh, and used as AD/CN classification features. 184 subjects were correctly classified (AD=98, CN=86), producing an accuracy of 88%, sensitivity of 89%, specificity of 86%, based on 33 features. Results indicate that sulcal morphology, when based on specific features, could be a valuable AD biomarker.

Keywords: AD · MRI · Sulcal morphology · Classification · Support vector machine · BrainVISA

1 Introduction

Dementia is a descriptive term indicating an observable decline in cognitive abilities. It is estimated that 35.6 million people were living with dementia in 2010, and this number is expected to almost double every 20 years as a result of the worldwide ageing population [1]. Alzheimer's disease (AD) is the most frequent neurodegenerative disease, the most common cause of dementia, and

Data used in preparation of this article were obtained from the Alzheimer's Disease Neuroimaging Initiative (ADNI) database (adni.loni.usc.edu). As such, the investigators within the ADNI contributed to the design and implementation of ADNI and/or provided data but did not participate in analysis or writing of this report. A complete listing of ADNI investigators can be found at: http://adni.loni.usc.edu/wp-content/uploads/how_to_apply/ADNI_Acknowledgement_List.pdf.

R.R. Paulsen and K.S. Pedersen (Eds.): SCIA 2015, LNCS 9127, pp. 103–113, 2015.
DOI: 10.1007/978-3-319-19665-7_9

is usually diagnosed in people over 65 years of age, but the early-onset AD can occur much earlier [2]. AD is an irreversible and progressive disorder, estimated to affect 60-65% of dementia patients [3]. By 2050 the expected prevalence of AD will have increased to 106.8 millions, from 30 millions in 2010 [4]. AD projection models suggest that primary prevention may successfully delay the onset of AD and as a result reduce the future prevalence of the disease.

Human brain morphology, the study of its form and shape, is considered a potential biomarker for diagnosis and prognosis of neurological diseases. Cortical thickness, surface area and its mean curvature, sulcal depth and width, have been applied to distinguish AD from CN [5,6]. Sulci are important macroscopic surface landmarks of the cerebral cortex (illustrated on Figure 1) which allow distinguishing between different functional areas of the brain. Their morphology has recently been utilized as means of investigating the structural brain changes, supplementing or replacing the measurements of cortical thickness, or approaches involving voxel-based methods. Sulcal surface and length as potential biomarkers have been investigated for Autism Spectrum Disorder [7], and they are also speculated to be in correlation with morphological changes in the cortex in schizophrenia, where sulcal abnormalities in language-related areas may be the underlying cause of hallucinations [8]. The atrophic changes in the brain are reflected in a loss of gray matter [9] and believed to first affect the entorhinal cortex and the hippocampus [10]. Sulcal widening, depth, and overall cortex atrophy have been linked with the progression of AD. The AD-related brain atrophy results in narrowing of cerebral gyri and widening of sulci. The widening of cortical sulci has been measured as a neuroimaging marker of brain atrophy, either age- or disease-related [6,11]. It is correlated with cognitive functions in the elderly, i.e. poorer cognitive performance was associated with a wider sulcal span [12].

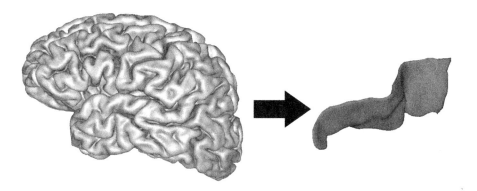

Fig. 1. Illustration of an extracted sulcal mesh by BrainVISA 4.4.0

Sulcal widening also showed the highest sensitivity in revealing differences between CN and AD [5]. Significant changes in sulcal depth have also been found in normal aging [11], as well as in AD and mild cognitive impairment patients, where a relationship between sulcal shape and volumetric changes was investigated. Im et al., 2008 [5] found a significantly lower sulcal mean curvature in AD subjects than in normal controls, and a significant difference in sulcal depth between CN and AD. Another study used similarity maps to examine correlation of mean cortical thickness between region of interest (ROI) [13]. Multi-kernel support vector machine (SVM) was used to classify regional mean cortical thickness, hippocampal volume, regional cortical volumes and a combination of those in CN and AD subjects, with a classification accuracy of 92.35%, and an area of 0.9744 under the receiver operating characteristic (ROC) curve [13].

The purpose of this cross-sectional study was to investigate the sulcal morphology (mean curvature, surface area, volume) as biomarkers complementing the structural changes seen in MRI, which would provide a successful classification of AD. The contribution of this paper is that the pipeline successfully extracted, calculated and selected a feature combination of sulcal mean curvature, surface area, and volume for AD/CN classification using SVM, while earlier studies focused on individual analysis of sulcal length, depth, or width.

2   Methods

Data

Data used in this project was obtained from the ADNI database. The ADNI database was launched in 2003 by the National Institute on Aging (NIA), the National Institute of Biomedical Imaging and Bioengineering (NIBIB), the Food and Drug Administration (FDA), private pharmaceutical companies and non-profit organizations, as a $60 million, 5-year public- private partnership. The primary goal of ADNI has been to test whether serial magnetic resonance imaging (MRI), positron emission tomography (PET), other biological markers, and clinical and neuropsychological assessment can be combined to measure the progression of mild cognitive impairment (MCI) and early AD. Determination of sensitive and specific markers of very early AD progression is intended to aid researchers and clinicians to develop new treatments and monitor their effectiveness, as well as lessen the time and cost of clinical trials.

210 1.5T pre-processed[1] T1-weighted magnetization-prepared rapid gradient echo (MP-RAGE) scans [CN (n=100), and AD (n=110)] were acquired from ADNI. The CN group was defined in the database as 'ADNI1 Screening', which consists of healthy controls, with no signs of depression, mild cognitive impairment nor dementia; while the AD group as 'ADNI1/GO Month 24', with AD subjects scanned 24 months after AD diagnosis. The criteria for CN were as follows: Mini-Mental State Examination (MMSE) score: 24-30, Clinical Dementia Rating (CDR) of 0, non–depressed, non MCI, and not demented. The criteria for AD were: MMSE score below 26, CDR of 0.5, and meet the National Institute of

---

[1] Image corrections are detailed at http://adni.loni.usc.edu/methods/mri-analysis/mri-pre-processing

Neurological and Communicative Disorders and Stroke-Alzheimer's Disease and Related Disorders Association criteria for probable AD. The demographics distribution for each group are represented in Table 1. T1-weighted MR scans were

Table 1. Demographics distribution of the subjects

Group	N (females)	Age ± sd	MMSE ± sd	CDR ± sd
AD	110 (52)	77.7±7.4	18.7±6.0	1.3±0.6
CN	100 (49)	75.8±5.3	29.1±1.1	0.0±0.0

processed in BrainVISA 4.4.0 Morphologist 2013 pipeline to extract sulci. Surface area, mean curvature, and volume were calculated. Exclusion criteria were applied to ensure the quality of the data. Figure 2 illustrates a simplified method pipeline. Selection of features was performed by means of forward selection and

Fig. 2. A simplified pipeline for the AD/CN classification based on sulcal morphology

backward elimination in order to ensure that only the best selected features and feature combinations produce the highest classification results. Each iteration was investigated and evaluated on accuracy in a k-fold (k=10) cross-validation SVM classifier. BrainVISA 4.4.0 Morphologist 2013 pipeline was used to extract all sulci labeled in the BrainVISA Sulci Atlas v. 2011 (n=60) for both left and right hemisphere. The mesh files, converted from a NIfTI to a polygon file format (.ply), were analyzed in MATLAB R2014b. The meshes created by BrainVISA are converted from consist of two main components: a vector of three-dimensional vertices, connected by edges, and a vector of polygons, or mesh faces, where each polygon is defined by the three vertices it links. The overall surface of the mesh consists of the mesh faces.

Sulcal Extraction and Feature Selection

BrainVISA extracted 60 sulci from the left hemisphere and 60 from the right (120 sulci total) for each subject. The total number of all extracted sulci from 210 subjects was 25200. In principle, every sulcus had to be extracted twice from each subject: once from the left hemisphere, once from the right; and this extraction was attempted on all 210 subjects. However, BrainVISA was not able to successfully extract some of the sulci for a number of subjects, either due to lower quality MRI data, or due to an error in sulcal identification and labeling. The following exclusion criterion was selected to avoid a situation where a certain sulcus would be extracted only in a small number. If the number of successful extractions for a given sulcus was below 95% of a total number of expected successful extractions from all 210 subjects, that specific sulcus was removed from the pooled data, both the left and right side. In this process, 48 sulci were removed. For each sulcus, three features were calculated: sulcal surface area, mean curvature, and volume, resulting a total of 216 features per subject: 108 from the left hemisphere and 108 from the right. Additionally, the ratios of the remaining features were created (n=108) (e.g. the ratio of a sulcus volume between the left and right hemisphere).

Surface Area: Heron's formula [14] was used to calculate the surface area of each triangle in the mesh. The total surface area was obtained by summing all thee triangles in the extracted sulcus.

Mean Curvature: The mean principal curvature of each sulcus was calculated by splitting the sulcus into parts consisting of one vertex, and the vertices connected via the face-matrix in two links or less. This part was then rotated into a normalized plane, and fitted to the function in Equation (1).

$$f(x,y) = \alpha_1 x^2 + \alpha_2 y^2 + \alpha_3 xy + \alpha_4 x + \alpha_5 y + \alpha_6 \tag{1}$$

α_1, α_2 and α_3 were used to create the Hessian matrix, from where the eigenvectors and eigenvalues were calculated. This was performed for every vertex in the sulcus. The mean of the eigenvalues was used as the mean curvature for the sulcus.

Volume: The volume for each sulcus in all subjects was calculated using Delaunay triangulation to split the sulcus into tetrahedrons. The volume for each tetrahedron was calculated by Equation (2). The total sulcal volume was defined as the total sum of all the tetrahedrons.

$$V = \frac{|(\boldsymbol{a} - \boldsymbol{d}) \cdot ((\boldsymbol{b} - \boldsymbol{d}) \times (\boldsymbol{c} - \boldsymbol{d}))|}{6} \tag{2}$$

$\boldsymbol{a}$, $\boldsymbol{b}$ and $\boldsymbol{c}$ are the coordinates for the base of the tetrahedron and $\boldsymbol{d}$ for the apex. All tetrahedrons with a circumsphere radius larger than a selected threshold (r=2) were removed.

The feature extraction and selection pipeline decreased the number of features from the initial 360 (surface area, mean curvature, and volume for 120 sulci per subject) to 324. The process of extracting and selecting features is illustrated on Figure 3. The next step involved selecting the features that best distinguish AD from CN by means of forward selection and backward elimination. During each iteration, 10-fold cross-validation was applied to evaluate the performance of the features, where the data was randomly partitioned into k=10 subgroups of equal size. A single subgroup was removed from the rest of the data, and

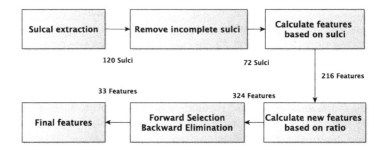

Fig. 3. Overview of the specific method pipeline, from feature extraction to obtaining final features

used as the validation data for testing the classification performance, while the remaining subgroups were used as training data. This cross-validation process was repeated k=10 times, where each subgroup was used exactly once. If the classification performance, based on a balancing index (below 0.40) [15] and the highest accuracy, performed better than the previous run, the feature was added to the feature set. This was repeated until adding additional features would not improve the outcome of the classifier. The highest classification accuracy was obtained with a set of 33 features.

Results

The two subject groups consisted of 110 AD and 100 CN subjects. The initial 324 features were used in a forward selection and backward elimination methods. A MATLAB SVM with a linear kernel was employed to evaluate the selected features with the following parameters: a standardized predictor matrix was used to train the classifier, and the prior probabilities for the two classes were uniform. Each iteration was evaluated based on a balancing index combined with accuracy in a 10-fold cross-validation SVM classifier. In Table 2 the sulci are sorted after feature type. The best feature combination consists of features related to surface area. Eleven features were based on sulcal surface area, and six were of the surface area ratio between the sulci in the left and the right hemisphere, resulting in a total of 17 surface area features. Eleven related to the sulcal curvature, out of which four were the ratio between the left and right hemisphere. Only five features were based on sulcal volume alone, not combined with the ratio between left and right hemisphere. The best classification result was obtained on 33 features, listed in Table 2, which shows in what order the features were selected and which were the most discriminating. 184 subjects were classified correctly (AD=98, CN=86), resulting with a sensitivity of 89%, specificity of 86% and accuracy of 88%. The receiver operating characteristic curve (ROC) and area under curve (AUC) were used to illustrate and evaluate the performance of the discrete classifier. The curve illustrates the true positive

Table 2. The 33 selected features, their means and standard deviations, sorted in what order they were selected and which were the most discriminating

Feat. no.	Sulcus:	Feature:	AD ± SD	CN ± SD
1	Superior temporal sulcus right	surface area	2520.75±581.07	2904.11±571.32
2	Calloso-marginal posterior fissure left	surface area	1144.14±381.26	1339.94±337.08
3	Posterior inferior temporal sulcus left	surface area	667.71±318.68	858.14±394.69
4	Calloso-marginal posterior fissure	surface area ratio	1.21±0.68	1.14±0.42
5	Central sulcus left	volume	1239.16±220.20	1215.34±207.26
6	Superior postcentral intraparietal sup. left	volume	471.79±202.23	540.54±233.63
7	Posterior intra-lingual sulcus left	volume	131.01±89.27	119.91±83.06
8	Olfactory sulcus right	surface area	513.06±132.77	566.39±152.23
9	Calloso-marginal posterior fissure right	curvature	0.13±0.04	0.11±0.05
10	Cuneal sulcus left	curvature	0.21±0.07	0.25±0.40
11	Rhinal sulcus right	surface area	290.27±225.70	292.93±186.07
12	Ascending ramus of the lateral fissure	surface area ratio	1.62±2.01	1.55±2.39
13	Posterior occipito-temporal lateral sulcus	curvature ratio	1.06±0.50	1.19±1.01
14	Posterior terminal ascending branch of superior temporal sulcus	curvature ratio	1.45±1.20	1.31±0.83
15	Anterior intralingual sulcus right	surface area	227.12±140.37	216.72±125.18
16	Rhinal sulcus right	curvature	0.22±0.13	0.21±0.07
17	Marginal frontal sulcus	surface area ratio	1.42±1.60	1.15±0.87
18	Olfactory sulcus right	volume	227.47±62.61	257.83±73.86
19	Anterior inferior temporal sulcus right	surface area	600.47±270.84	676.03±219.91
20	Central sulcus	surface area ratio	1.05±0.19	1.03±0.18
21	Internal frontal sulcus	surface area ratio	1.29±0.86	1.47±1.17
22	Polar frontal sulcus left	curvature	0.31±0.30	0.27±0.13
23	Posterior lateral fissure left	curvature	0.06±0.02	0.06±0.02
24	Polar temporal sulcus right	curvature	0.20±0.08	0.19±0.06
25	Posterior inferior temporal sulcus	curvature ratio	1.40±0.76	1.21±0.67
26	Intermediate precentral sulcus	surface area ratio	0.98±0.68	0.92±0.63
27	Posterior lateral fissure left	surface area	3093.19±563.32	3180.43±559.75
28	Collateral fissure right	surface area	1198.95±529.62	1396.36±463.40
29	Polar temporal sulcus right	surface area	326.65±164.55	371.70±137.46
30	Rhinal sulcus	curvature ratio	1.19±1.39	0.95±0.59
31	Superior frontal sulcus left	surface area	1768.61±648.59	1852.34±660.76
32	Superior precentral sulcus right	volume	191.85±107.98	221.87±117.69
33	Parieto-occipital fissure right	curvature	0.08±0.04	0.08±0.04

rate against the false positive rate (Figure 4). The ROC-AUC with the selected feature combination were 84%, based on 33 features (Table 2) from 24 sulci (Figure 5).

Discussion

The main objective of this paper was to investigate the sulcal morphology (mean curvature, surface area, volume) to evaluate the pattern recognition classification ability to distinguish between CN and AD subjects. Previous studies based solely on sulcal morphology have not, to the best of our knowledge, been able to achieve the same levels of specificity and sensitivity. Our results show that sulcal morphology, when based on specific features, could be used as a valuable biomarker. The contribution of this study is that it successfully investigated a classifier combination of sulcal mean curvature, surface area and volume, while

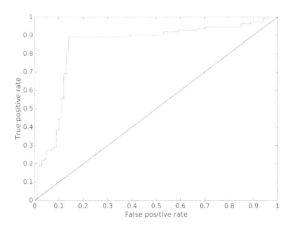

Fig. 4. ROC-curve for the AD/CN classification. The diagonal representing the random guess.

earlier studies focused on individual analysis of sulcal length, depth or width. The SVM classification of this study was based on a total of 33 features from 24 sulci (Figure 5). Several other classification methods have been proposed in literature to automatically distinguish between AD/MCI and cognitively normal controls [16,17]; a majority of them are multimodal. A study by [18], which combined three modalities of biomarkers (MRI, FDG-PET, and CSF), achieved a classification accuracy of 93.2%, 93% sensitivity, and 93.3% specificity, when combining all three modalities. However, a lower accuracy of 86.5% was achieved with the best individual modality, PET. With MRI alone, the specificity obtained was 86.3%, sensitivity 86% and accuracy 86.2%. Our study achieved a specificity of 89%, sensitivity of 86% and accuracy of 87% based on sulcal morphology from T1-weighted MRI, which therefore demonstrates promising results in the classification of AD and CN subjects.

The significance of our results facilitates further sulcal morphology studies in a combination with other biomarkers in order to improve early AD diagnosis. Most of sulcal morphology research on AD investigates very specific sulci, such as the central sulcus [19,20], or a combination of a few major, large sulci, since they are present in all individuals, they are relatively easy to identify and extract, and are located on different cerebral lobes [5,6]. Our approach involved the initial extraction of all cortical sulci. The subsequent feature extraction and selection excluded some sulci, which were incompletely extracted. Nonetheless, a large set of cortical sulci was studied (Figure 5). They varied in size and shape, and were located on different cerebral lobes, thus allowing us to investigate potential changes in sulcal morphology across the entire brain. The SVM classification in our study was based on 33 features (Table 2) from 24 sulci. The extracted sulci, which showed morphologic changes, were from the areas that are proved to be affected by AD atrophy. The Collateral fissure is located near the hippocampal

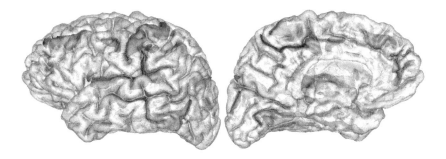

Fig. 5. The sagittal view of the selected 24 sulci

region where AD atrophy has been indicated [21,22]. Seven sulci (collateral fissure, rhinal sulcus, posterior inferior temporal sulcus, polar temporal sulcus, superior temporal sulcus, anterior inferior temporal sulcus, and the anterior terminal ascending branch of the superior temporal sulcus) are located in the medial temporal lobe, where AD atrophy also has been found [23–25]. The Callosomarginal posterior fissure and superior postcentral intraparietal superior sulcus are located in the parietal lobe, where morphological changes in AD have also been observed [22,24,26].

There are some potential limitations that should be addressed. BrainVISA toolbox is a commonly used sulcal identification and extraction pipeline. While the software is very efficient in automatically labeling and extracting the sulci, it is often advisable to address the data quality issue of the program. The majority of studies visually inspect the sulci after extraction to remove errors. This proves to be impossible with an immense set of subjects (n = 210) and sulci per subject (n = 120), since the initial extraction procedure resulted in a total of 25200 individual sulci. To asses the pipeline's performance and evaluate the quality of sulcal extraction, we performed an additional examination of a small subset of sulci (n=62) from 31 CN and 31 AD subjects. In this dataset, some of the extracted sulci (n=10) contained missing fragments, possibly due to lower quality of some MRI data, or an error in sulcal identification and labelling. It must be mentioned that this may have an impact on the calculated features. However, while it is possible that BrainVISA pipeline introduces a bias to the data, it still provides high classification results.

References

1. Prince, M., Bryce, R., Albanese, E., et al.: The global prevalence of dementia: a systematic review and metaanalysis. Alzheimer's & Dementia **9**(1), 63–75 (2013)
2. Uzun, S., Kozumplik, O., Folnegović-Šmalc, V.: Alzheimer's dementia: current data review. Collegium antropologicum **35**(4), 1333–1337 (2011)
3. Sonkusare, S.K., Kaul, C.L., Ramarao, P.: Dementia of Alzheimer's disease and other neurodegenerative disorders-memantine, a new hope. Pharmacological Research **51**(1), 1–17 (2005)

4. Brookmeyer, R., Johnson, E., Ziegler-Graham, K., Arrighi, H.M.: Forecasting the global burden of Alzheimer's disease. Alzheimer's & dementia **3**(3), 186–191 (2007)
5. Im, K., Lee, J.-M., Seo, S.W., et al.: Sulcal morphology changes and their relationship with cortical thickness and gyral white matter volume in mild cognitive impairment and alzheimer's disease. Neuroimage **43**(1), 103–113 (2008)
6. Liu, T., Sachdev, P.S., Lipnicki, D.M., et al.: Longitudinal changes in sulcal morphology associated with late-life aging and mci. NeuroImage **74**, 337–342 (2013)
7. Shokouhi, M., Williams, J.H.G., Waiter, G.D., Condon, B.: Changes in the sulcal size associated with autism spectrum disorder revealed by sulcal morphometry. Autism Research **5**(4), 245–252 (2012)
8. Cachia, A., Paillère-Martinot, M.-L., Galinowski, A., et al.: Cortical folding abnormalities in schizophrenia patients with resistant auditory hallucinations. Neuroimage **39**(3), 927–935 (2008)
9. Thompson, P.M., Hayashi, K.M., De Zubicaray, G., et al.: Dynamics of gray matter loss in Alzheimer's disease. The Journal of Neuroscience **23**(3), 994–1005 (2003)
10. Braak, H., Braak, E.: Neuropathological stageing of Alzheimer-related changes. Acta Neuropathologica **82**(4), 239–259 (1991)
11. Kochunov, P., Thompson, P.M., Coyle, T.R., et al.: Relationship among neuroimaging indices of cerebral health during normal aging. Human Brain Mapping **29**(1), 36–45 (2008)
12. Liu, T., Wen, W., Zhu, W., et al.: The relationship between cortical sulcal variability and cognitive performance in the elderly. Neuroimage **56**(3), 865–873 (2011)
13. Shen, D., Wee, C.-Y., Yap, P.-T.: Prediction of Alzheimer's disease and mild cognitive impairment using cortical morphological patterns. Wiley Periodicals Inc. (2012)
14. Stanojevic, M.: Proof of the hero's formula according to R. Boscovich. Mathematical Communications **2**, 83–88
15. Garde, A., Voss, A., Caminal, P., Benito, S., Giraldo, B.F.: Svm-based feature selection to optimize sensitivity-specificity balance applied to weaning. Computers in Biology and Medicine **43**(5), 533–540 (2013)
16. Davatzikos, C., Fan, Y., Wu, X., Shen, D., Resnick, S.M.: Detection of prodromal Alzheimer's disease via pattern classification of magnetic resonance imaging. Neurobiology of Aging **29**(4), 514–523 (2008)
17. Misra, C., Fan, Y., Davatzikos, C.: Baseline and longitudinal patterns of brain atrophy in MCI patients, and their use in prediction of short-term conversion to AD: results from ADNI. Neuroimage **44**(4), 1415–1422 (2009)
18. Zhang, D., Wang, Y., Zhou, L., Yuan, H., Shen, D.: Multimodal classification of Alzheimer's disease and mild cognitive impairment. Neuroimage **55**(3), 856–867 (2011)
19. Li, S., Xia, M., Fang, P., et al.: Age-related changes in the surface morphology of the central sulcus. Neuroimage **58**(2), 381–390 (2011)
20. McKay, D.R., Kochunov, P., Cykowski, M.D., et al.: Sulcal depth-position profile is a genetically mediated neuroscientific trait: description and characterization in the central sulcus. The Journal of Neuroscience **33**(39), 15618–15625 (2013)
21. Morra J.H., Tu, Z., Apostolova, L.G., et al.: Automated mapping of hippocampal atrophy in 1-year repeat mri data from 490 subjects with Alzheimer's disease, mild cognitive impairment, and elderly controls
22. Farias, S.T., Jagust, W.J.: Neuroimaging in non-alzheimer dementias. Clinical Neuroscience Research **3**, 383–395 (2004)

23. Ishii, K., Kawachi, T., Sasaki, H., et al.: Voxel-based morphometric comparison between early- and late-onset mild alzheimer's disease and assessment of diagnostic performance of z score images

24. Frisoni, G.B., Pievani, M., Testa, C., et al.: The topography of grey matter involvement in early and late onset Alzheimer's disease

25. Hamelin, L., de Souza, L.C., Corlier, F., et al.: Improved accuracy of the diagnosis of early Alzheimer's disease using combined measures of hippocampal volume and sulcal morphology (p4. 016). Neurology **82**(10 Supplement), P4–016 (2014)

26. Sabuncu, M.R., Desikan, R.S., Sepulcre, J., et al.: The dynamics of cortical and hippocampal atrophy in Alzheimer disease

Motion Tracking

Coloring Channel Representations
for Visual Tracking

Martin Danelljan$^{(\boxtimes)}$, Gustav Häger, Fahad Shahbaz Khan,
and Michael Felsberg

Computer Vision Laboratory, Linköping University, Linköping, Sweden
`martin.danelljan@liu.se`

Abstract. Visual object tracking is a classical, but still open research problem in computer vision, with many real world applications. The problem is challenging due to several factors, such as illumination variation, occlusions, camera motion and appearance changes. Such problems can be alleviated by constructing robust, discriminative and computationally efficient visual features. Recently, biologically-inspired channel representations [9] have shown to provide promising results in many applications ranging from autonomous driving to visual tracking.

This paper investigates the problem of coloring channel representations for visual tracking. We evaluate two strategies, channel concatenation and channel product, to construct channel coded color representations. The proposed channel coded color representations are generic and can be used beyond tracking.

Experiments are performed on 41 challenging benchmark videos. Our experiments clearly suggest that a careful selection of color feature together with an optimal fusion strategy, significantly outperforms the standard luminance based channel representation. Finally, we show promising results compared to state-of-the-art tracking methods in the literature.

Keywords: Visual tracking · Channel coding · Color names

1 Introduction

Visual tracking is the problem of estimating the trajectory of a target in an image sequence. It has a vast number of real world applications, including robotics [5] and surveillance [30]. In generic visual tracking nothing is known about the target except its initial location. It is one of the most challenging computer vision problems due to factors such as illumination variation, occlusions and fast motion. Many of the challenges encountered in visual tracking can be alleviated by the usage of robust and discriminative features. This paper therefore aims at investigating feature representations and fusion strategies for visual tracking.

In recent years, channel coded feature representations [9] have been successfully used in many computer vision applications, including visual tracking [8], autonomous driving [11], image diffusion [16] and real-time object

© Springer International Publishing Switzerland 2015
R.R. Paulsen and K.S. Pedersen (Eds.): SCIA 2015, LNCS 9127, pp. 117–129, 2015.
DOI: 10.1007/978-3-319-19665-7_10

gray channel ———— RGB-channel ———— CN + gray channel

Fig. 1. Comparison of the standard luminance based channel representation (blue) with color augmentation on two sequences (*coke* and *woman*). The straightforward channel representation of RGB (green) fails to improve the performance. The proposed color names extension of the luminance based channel representation (red) significantly improves the performance.

recognition [10]. The biologically inspired channel representation [13], is a technique for representing data. A set of feature values is represented by a number of channel coefficients, which essentially correspond to a soft histogram. In the visual tracking application, the EDFT method [8] employs a channel representation based appearance model. However, it only models the luminance distribution over the target template, while ignoring all color information. In this paper, we therefore extend channel representations to incorporate color information.

Channel coded color representations can be constructed using two standard strategies. In both cases, channel coding is first performed on each color space dimension (e.g. R, G and B) independently. In the *channel concatenation* strategy, the channel coefficients for each dimension are concatenated into a final representation. As an alternative, the final representation can be constructed by taking the outer product of the individual channel coefficients, called *channel products*. Typically, a large number of color channels are required to obtain a more discriminative feature representation. However, such high dimensional representations lead to an increased computational cost, and thereby restricting its applicability to real-time tracking.

When incorporating color information into visual tracking, two main research problems have to be addressed. The first issue is the selection of color representation to be used. Ideally, a color feature should possess a certain degree of photometric invariance while maintaining a high discriminative power. The second problem is how to fuse color and intensity information into a single representation. Recently, Danelljan et al. [6] evaluated several color features for visual tracking. In their evaluation, the color names representation [33] was shown to provide superior performance compared to other color features. However, the work of [6] only investigates what color feature to use, while employing raw pixel gray scale values to represent luminance information. Inspired by the success of channel coded luminance information, we investigate how to augment these representations with color information. Additionally, we extend the evaluation performed by [6] with channel coded color features. We show that our proposed feature representation outperforms the best color-intensity combination of [6].

Contributions: In this paper, we investigate how to incorporate color information into channel representations for visual tracking. Both channel concatenation and channel product coding strategies are evaluated on six different color spaces. Additionally, we investigate combining color names and channel coded luminance representations. The evaluated channel coded color representations are generic and can be used beyond visual tracking.

Experiments are performed on 41 challenging videos including all the color sequences from the online benchmark dataset [34]. Our experiments show that fusion of color names and channel coded luminance information outperforms the combination of color names and raw gray scale values [6]. By selecting the best feature (color names and channel coded luminance) and the optimal fusion strategy (concatenation), we achieve a significant gain of 5.4% in median distance precision compared to the standard channel concatenation using RGB. Finally, our approach is also shown to outperform state-of-the-art trackers in both quantitative and qualitative evaluations. Figure 1 shows the comparison of channel coded color representations with the standard channel coded luminance.

2   Related Work

Generic visual trackers can be categorized into generative [2,24,25,31] and discriminative [6,7,14,17,35] methods. The generative trackers search for image regions most similar to a generative appearance model. On the other hand, the discriminative approaches use machine learning techniques to differentiate the target from the background. Recently, the discriminative correlation filter [3] based trackers have received much research attention thanks to their accuracy, simplicity and speed. These approches utilize the circulant structure induced by correlation to efficiently train a regularized least squares regressor (ridge regression). Most of the computations required for learning and detection are performed using the Fast Fourier transform (FFT), which is the key for its low computational cost. Henriques et al. [17] further introduced kernels into this framework to allow non-linear classification boundaries. The work of Danelljan et al. [6] proposed a consistent learning approach for increased robustness.

Most of the research effort into generic visual tracking has focused on the learning aspect of appearance modeling, while relatively little work has been done on the problem of constructing robust and discriminative features. Most state-of-the-art methods rely on solely image intensity information [7,8,14,17,20,31,35], while others employ simple color space transformations [27–29]. On the contrary, feature representations have been thoroughly investigated in the related fields of object recognition and action recognition [21,22]. Recently, Danelljan et al. [6]

introduced the Adaptive Color Tracker (ACT), which learns an adaptive color representation based on Color Names [33]. However, this approach still employs a standard grayscale channel for capturing image intensity information.

Channel representations have been used in a large variety of applications [8,10,11,16]. The Distribution Field Tracker (DFT) [31] utilizes a feature representation similar to channel coding to capture the image intensity statistics of the target. The Enhanced DFT (EDFT) [8] employs channel coding instead of distribution fields and a more robust metric for computation of the objective function. The work of [12,19] investigate how to fuse color and channel coded luminance information. However, a comprehensive evaluation of color and channel coded luminance fusion is yet to be investigated for the task of tracking.

3   Tracking Framework

In this work, we use the discriminative correlation filter (DCF) based tracking framework proposed by Danelljan et al. [6], called the Adaptive Color Tracker (ACT). It has been shown to provide superior results on benchmark tracking datasets. The method works by learning a kernelized least squared classifier from several samples of the target appearance. The classifier is then applied to locate the target in the new frame.

To update the classifier at frame n, a template f_n centered around the target is first extracted. The template is of a fixed size of $M \times N$ pixels and contains a D-dimensional feature vector at each pixel location within the template. The features are preprocessed by a normalization step and a windowing operation. The classifier coefficients are updated in each frame through the recursive formula

$$\hat{u}_n = (1 - \gamma)\hat{u}_{n-1} + \gamma \hat{y}_n \hat{a}_n \tag{1a}$$
$$\hat{v}_n = (1 - \gamma)\hat{v}_{n-1} + \gamma \hat{a}_n (\hat{a}_n + \lambda). \tag{1b}$$

Here, a_n is the kernelized autocorrelation of the template f_n, and y_n is a Gaussian label function. The discrete Fourier transform (DFT) is denoted by a hat. The constants γ and λ are learning and regularization weights respectively. A target template t_n is also updated as: $t_n = (1 - \gamma)t_{n-1} + \gamma f_n$.

The classifier is applied to an image template g_n by first computing its kernelized cross-correlation b_n with the learned target template t_{n-1} from the previous frame. The classification scores s_n are obtained by evaluating

$$s_n = \mathscr{F}^{-1} \left\{ \frac{\hat{u}_{n-1}\hat{b}_n}{\hat{v}_{n-1}} \right\}. \tag{2}$$

Here, $\mathscr{F}^{-1}$ denotes the inverse DFT. Henriques et al. [17] showed that the kernelized correlations a_n and b_n can be computed efficiently for radial basis function kernels, using the FFT. For more details, we refer to [6].

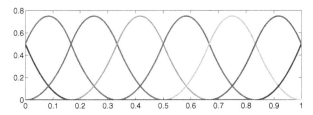

Fig. 2. A graphichal visualization of the binning functions employed in our channel representations. Here the configuration is shown for $n = 8$ channels.

4 Channel Representation

Channel representation [9] is a biologically inspired approach for representing data [13]. It is closely related to soft histograms and is used in many computer vision applications, including visual tracking [8]. A scalar value x is represented in terms of its channel coefficients $\{c_k\}_1^n$. The k:th coefficient c_k is computed by evaluating a kernel function K located at the k:th channel center $\tilde{x}_k$ using: $c_k = K(x - \tilde{x}_k)$. Common choices for the kernel function K include Gaussian, $\cos^2$ and B-spline functions. The coefficients $\{c_k\}_1^n$ can be interpreted as a soft histogram of the data, where the bins are centered at $\{\tilde{x}_k\}_1^n$ and the binning function K weights the contribution of x to each bin.

In this paper, we construct the channel representation using regularly spaced second order B-spline kernel functions. We set $K_w(x) = B(x/w)$, where w is the spacing between the channel centers and the second order B-spline is given by:

$$
B(x) = \begin{cases} \frac{3}{4} - x^2 & , \ |x| \leq \frac{1}{2} \\ \frac{1}{2}\left(|x| - \frac{3}{2}\right)^2 & , \ \frac{1}{2} \leq |x| \leq \frac{3}{2} \\ 0 & , \ |x| \geq \frac{3}{2} \end{cases} \tag{3}
$$

All color and luminance features used in this work only take values within a bounded interval, e.g. the red component of an RGB image pixel. It can therefore be assumed that $x \in [0, 1]$ by simply translating and re-scaling the feature appropriately. The range $[0, 1]$ is covered by n channels, which are centered at

$$
\tilde{x}_k = wk - \frac{3w}{2} \ , \ k = 1, \ldots, n. \tag{4}
$$

The spacing is set to $w = \frac{1}{n-2}$. With this configuration the channel coefficients always sum up to one, and thus have a direct probabilistic interpretation. The used channel configuration is visualized in figure 2 for $n = 8$ channels.

Channel representations can be extended to multi-dimensional features $\mathbf{x} = (x_1, \ldots, x_m)$ (e.g. the RGB value of a pixel) using either *channel concatenation* or *channel products*. In the former case, the final representation is obtained as the collection of channel coefficients for each scalar component x_j. The number of coefficients in the channel concatenation is $n = n_1 + \ldots + n_m$, where n_j denotes the number of channels used for representing x_j.

The channel product representation considers m-dimensional channels $c_{\mathbf{k}} = \hat{K}(\mathbf{x} - \tilde{\mathbf{x}}_{\mathbf{k}})$. For a separable kernel $\hat{K}(\mathbf{x}) = K_1(x_1) \cdots K_m(x_m)$, the final representation is obtained as the outer product of the individual channel coefficients

$$c_{\mathbf{k}} = c_{k_1, \ldots, k_m} = \prod_{j=1}^{m} c_{k_j}^{(j)}. \tag{5}$$

Here, $\{c_1^{(j)}, \ldots, c_{n_j}^{(j)}\}$ is the channel representation of x_j. The number of coefficients in the channel product representation is hence $n = n_1 \cdot \ldots \cdot n_m$.

5   Channel Coded Color Representations

In this paper, we investigate different channel coded color representations for visual tracking. We evaluate the two strategies mentioned in section 4 to construct channel coded color representations. Six color spaces are used for our evaluation: **RGB**, **Opp**, **C**, **HSV**, **YCbCr** and **LAB**. The opponent (Opp) color space is an orthonormal transformation of the RGB cube aligning the third dimension with the diagonal $O_3 = 3^{-\frac{1}{2}} \cdot (R + G + B)$. The image intensity is thus captured by O_3 while O_1 and O_2 are its color opponent dimensions. The C space further adds photometric invariance to Opp space by dividing O_1 and O_2 with the intensity dimension O_3. The HSV representation instead maps the RGB cube to a cylinder, providing the hue angle H, saturation S and value V components. The YCbCr space contains a luminance component Y and the two chroma components Cb and Cr. LAB is a perceptually uniform color space, which contains the lightness dimension L and the two color opponent dimensions A and B.

We evaluate the channel concatenation and product representations for each of the six aforementioned color spaces. In both cases, we use the channel configuration described in section 4 to code the individual color space dimensions.

The channel coded color representations are compared with Color Names (CN) [33], which achieved the best results among the evaluated color features in [6]. The CN representation is inspired by linguistics. An RGB value is mapped to probabilities for the 11 basic color names in the English language: black, blue, brown, grey, green, orange, pink, purple, red, white and yellow. This mapping was automatically learned from images retrieved by Google image search.

Color names have successfully been applied in object recognition [22], action recognition [21] and image stitching [26] to capture color information. On the other hand, channel coded intensity features have been used in visual tracking [8,31] to capture the image intensity statistics. The EDFT tracker [8] employs channel coded grayscale values with the same channel configuration as described in section 4. Inspired by their success, we propose to combine the two features into a single representation. Given an image template, color names and channel coded luminance are computed at each pixel. The two representations are then concatenated into a single feature vector.

Table 1. The median Distance Precision (DP) (%), Overlap Precision (OP) (%) and Center Location Error (CLE) (in pixels) results using different features on 41 videos. The best two results shown in red and blue fonts. In all cases, the channel concatenation using color names significantly improves the performance compared to luminance based channels and color names alone.

	IC	CN [6]	RGB-c	RGB-p	LAB-c	LAB-p	YCbCr-c	YCbCr-p	HSV-c	HSV-p	Opp-c	Opp-p	C-c	C-p	IC+CN
DP	77.1	81.4	71.7	71.2	71.1	62.1	79.8	57.3	75.6	73.4	74.1	56.7	81.5	60.1	83.1
OP	53.3	51	52.3	49.2	46.1	42	47.5	40.5	53.3	52.2	43.9	44.4	58.6	41.5	59
CLE	19.1	13.8	17.8	17.2	19.1	24.3	17.3	26.1	15.5	20.4	16.6	31.2	14.9	25.2	13.7

6 Experiments

We perform a comprehensive evaluation of the color representations for visual tracking described in section 5. The best performing representation is then compared to several state-of-the-art tracking methods.

6.1 Evaluation Methodology and Dataset

The results are evaluated using the standard benchmark protocol suggested by Wu et al. [34]. We present the results using three standard evaluation metrics, namely center location error (CLE), distance precision (DP) and overlap precision (OP). CLE is computed as the euclidean distance between the ground truth bounding box and the tracked bounding box centers. The average CLE value is then used for each sequence. Distance precision is the percentage of frames where the CLE is below a threshold. We present the DP value at 20 pixels, following [34], [17]. Overlap precision is the percentage of frames where the intersection-over-union overlap between the ground truth and tracked bounding boxes is greater than a threshold. We present numeric values of OP at the threshold 0.5, which corresponds to the PASCAL evaluation metric.

The results are also presented as precision plot and success plots [34]. In the plots, the average DP and OP is plotted over a range of thresholds. The mean DP value over all sequences is included in the legend of the precision plot, while the area under curve (AUC) is shown in the legend of the success plot.

We use the same dataset as employed in the evaluation performed by Danelljan et al. [6]. It consists of all the 35 color sequences from the benchmark dataset [34] and 6 additional color videos. All methods are thus evaluated on 41 videos.

6.2 Experiment 1: Channel Coded Color Representations

Here we present results of augmenting channel representations with color information. All features are evaluated in the DCF-based tracker proposed by [6] with the suggested parameters. However, no adaptive dimensionality reduction is performed. For the six color spaces mentioned in section 5, we use 16 channels per dimension for the channel concatenation and 4 channels per dimension for the channel product representation. The feature dimensionality is thus 48 and

Table 2. Quantitative comparison of our approach with 15 state-of-the-art trackers on 41 videos. The results are presented in median Distance Precision (DP) (%), Overlap Precision (OP) (%), Center Location Error (CLE) (in pixels) and frames per second (FPS). The two best results are shown in red and blue. In all cases, our approach significantly outperforms the best reported tracker (Struck) in the literature.

	CT	TLD	DFT	EDFT	ASLA	L1APG	CSK	SCM	LOT	CPF	CXT	Frag	Struck	LSST	LSHT	Ours
DP	20.8	45.4	41.4	49	42.2	28.9	54.5	34.1	37.1	37.1	39.5	38.7	*71.3*	23.4	55.9	**83.1**
OP	13.3	36.7	34.3	44.8	42.2	26.3	37.7	33.6	31.1	33.1	33.2	36.8	*53.8*	19.5	40.4	**59**
CLE	78.4	54.4	47.9	53.5	56.8	62.9	50.3	54.3	60.9	41.1	43.8	70.8	*19.6*	78.4	32.3	**13.7**
FPS	*68.9*	20.7	9.11	19.7	0.946	1.03	151	0.0862	0.467	55.5	11.3	3.34	10.4	3.57	12.5	**36.6**

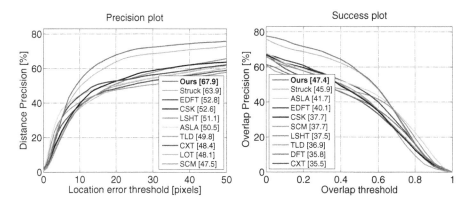

Fig. 3. Precision and success plots for comparison with state-of-the-art trackers. Only the top 10 trackers are displayed for clarity. Our approach outperforms the second best tracker (Struck) in both mean distance and overlap precision.

64 for the concatenation and product representations respectively. We denote the concatenation representation by adding a "c" to the color space name, e.g. RGB-c. Similarly, RGB-p denotes the channel product representation of RGB.

The channel coded color spaces are compared with the color names (CN) feature and the standard luminance based channel representation (IC). As in [8], we use 16 channels for the IC representation. For the IC+CN combination approach presented in section 5, we use 16 intensity channels combined with the 11 color names. For a fair comparison, we append the usual grayscale component (obtained by Matlab's `rgb2gray`) to all evaluated feature representations, including the channel representations. We further perform the appropriate normalization steps [6] to reduce the windowing effect within the DCF framework.

Table 1 shows a comparison of the evaluated feature representations. The standard luminance based channel representation achieves a median DP of 77.1%. The channel concatenation and product representations using the C color space achieve a median DP of 81.5% and 60.1% respectively. In all cases, the concatenation strategy provides improved results compared to the channel product representation. The CN approach of [6], employing color names and an intensity component, provides a median DP of 81.4%. Our channel concatenation using

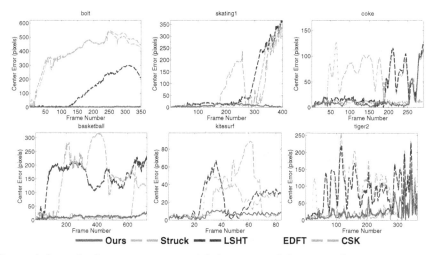

Fig. 4. A frame-by-frame comparison with four state-of-the-art trackers on six example videos. The results are shown in terms of center location error in pixels for each frame. Our approach provides favorable performance compared to the existing trackers.

color names provides an improvement of 1.7% in median DP compared to [6]. Similarly, our channel concatenation using color names also provides the best results in median OP and CLE. Based on this analysis, we select the channel-color names combination (IC+CN) as our proposed representation for tracking.

6.3 Experiment 2: State of the Art Comparison

We compare our proposed feature representation with 15 state of the art trackers: CT [35], TLD [20], DFT [31], EDFT [8], ASLA [18], L1APG [2], CSK [17], SCM [36], LOT [28], CPF [29], CXT [7], Frag [1], Struck [14], LSHT [15] and LSST [32]. Table 2 shows the comparison of our tracker with the state-of-the-art tracking methods using median DP, OP and CLE. The two best results are presented in red and blue fonts. The CSK tracker [17] achieves a median DP of 54.5%. The EDFT method [8] based on channel coded luminance provides a median DP of 49.0%. Among the existing tracking approaches, Struck [14] provides a median DP of 71.3%. Our approach significantly outperforms Struck by 11.8% in median DP. Similarly, our tracker achieves the best performance by providing a gain of 5.2% and 5.9 pixels in median OP and CLE respectively compared to Struck.

Figure 3 shows the results using precision and success plots, containing mean distance and overlap precision. The mean results are calculated over all the 41 videos. The values in the legends of precision and success plots are the mean DP at 20 pixels and the AUC respectively. Among the existing trackers, Struck provides the best results with mean DP of 63.9% in the precision plot. Our approach outperforms Struck by 5.6% in mean DP. Similarly, our approach also provides superior performance compared to existing methods in success plot.

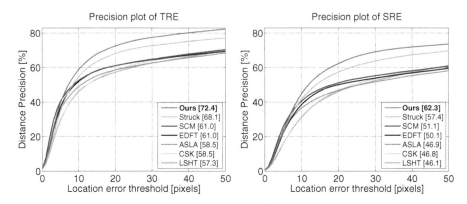

Fig. 5. Precision plots to compare the robustness of our approach with respect to initialization. The performance is validated using temporal and spatial robustness (TRE and SRE). Our method achieves superior performance compared to existing trackers.

Figure 4 shows a frame-by-frame comparison of our tracker with existing tracking methods in terms of center-pixel error. Our tracking method provides favorable performance compared to existing trackers on the six example videos.

Robustness to Initialization: We follow the protocol suggested by Wu et al. [34] to validate the robustness of our approach with respect to initialization. The performance is evaluated using two different strategies: temporal robustness (TRE) and spatial robustness (SRE). In the case of TRE, the trackers are initialized at different frames. In the case of SRE, the trackers are instead initialized at different locations in the first frame of the sequence. As in [34], twelve different initializations are performed for SRE whereas each video is segmented into 20 partitions for TRE. Figure 5 shows the results for both TRE and SRE. For clarity, we only compare with the top six trackers in our evaluation. In both cases, our approach provides promising results compared to existing methods.

Attribute-Based Comparisons: Here, we investigate the factors that can affect the performance of a visual tracker. The videos in the benchmark dataset [34] are annotated with 11 attributes: illumination variation, occlusion, deformation, scale variation, motion blur, fast motion, in-plane rotation, out-of-plane rotation, out-of-view, low resolution and background clutter. We show a comparison of our tracker with existing methods on 35 videos annotated with these 11 attributes.

Figure 6 shows the precision plots of six different attributes: in-plane rotation, motion blur, fast motion, illumination variation, occlusion and out-of-plane rotation. For clarity, we only show the results for the top 10 trackers in each attribute plot. Our approach performs favorably compared to existing methods. A significant improvement in performance is achieved in case of in-plane rotation, motion blur, illumination variation and out-of-plane rotation. This is due to the robustness and complementary properties of our feature representation. In the presence

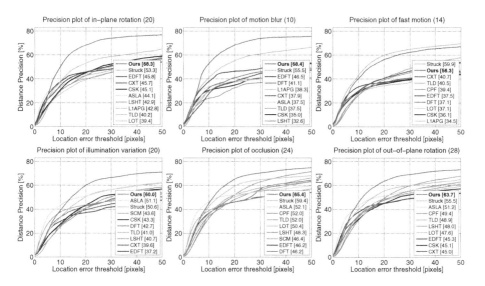

Fig. 6. Attribute-based comparison with the state-of-the-art trackers. The results are shown for in-plane rotation, motion blur, fast motion, illumination variation, occlusion and out-of-plane rotation. The number of videos for an attribute is mentioned in each title. Our approach provides favorable results compared to the existing methods.

of fast motion, Struck provides the best results. This is attributed to the local search strategy employed in the baseline DCF-based tracking algorithm.

7 Conclusions

In recent years, luminance based channel representations have shown to provide promising results in many vision applications. In this work, we investigate the problem of augmenting channel representations with color information. Our results clearly suggest that channel conatenation using color names significantly improves the performance of conventional channel coded luminance features. Our quantitative and attribute-based qualitative evaluations demonstrate promising results compared to existing methods.

Recently, efficient tracking methods with scale estimation capability have shown promising results in the VOT 2014 challenge [23]. Currently, our approach has no explicit scale estimation component. Future work involves investigating how to incorporate our feature representation into efficient scale adaptive trackers, e.g. the Discriminative Scale Space Tracker [4].

Acknowledgments. This work has been supported by SSF through a grant for the project CUAS, by VR through a grant for the projects ETT and EMC^2, by EU's Horizon 2020 Program through a grant for the project CENTAURO, through the Strategic Area for ICT research ELLIIT, and CADICS.

References

1. Adam, A., Rivlin, E., Shimshoni: Robust fragments-based tracking using the integral histogram. In: CVPR (2006)
2. Bao, C., Wu, Y., Ling, H., Ji, H.: Real time robust l1 tracker using accelerated proximal gradient approach. In: CVPR (2012)
3. Bolme, D.S., Beveridge, J.R., Draper, B.A., Lui, Y.M.: Visual object tracking using adaptive correlation filters. In: CVPR (2010)
4. Danelljan, M., Häger, G., Khan, F.S., Felsberg, M.: Accurate scale estimation for robust visual tracking. In: BMVC (2014)
5. Danelljan, M., et al.: A low-level active vision framework for collaborative unmanned aircraft systems. In: Agapito, L., Bronstein, M.M., Rother, C. (eds.) ECCV 2014 Workshops. LNCS, vol. 8925, pp. 223–237. Springer, Heidelberg (2015)
6. Danelljan, M., Khan, F.S., Felsberg, M., van de Weijer, J.: Adaptive color attributes for real-time visual tracking. In: CVPR (2014)
7. Dinh, T.B., Vo, N., Medioni, G.: Context tracker: exploring supporters and distracters in unconstrained environments. In: CVPR (2011)
8. Felsberg, M.: Enhanced distribution field tracking using channel representations. In: ICCV Workshop (2013)
9. Felsberg, M., Forssen, P.E., Scharr, H.: Channel smoothing: efficient robust smoothing of low-level signal features. PAMI **28**(2), 209–222 (2006)
10. Felsberg, M., Hedborg, J.: Real-time visual recognition of objects and scenes using P-channel matching. In: Ersbøll, B.K., Pedersen, K.S. (eds.) SCIA 2007. LNCS, vol. 4522, pp. 908–917. Springer, Heidelberg (2007)
11. Öfjäll, K., Felsberg, M.: Biologically inspired online learning of visual autonomous driving. In: BMVC (2014)
12. Forssen, P.E., Granlund, G., Wiklund, J.: Channel representation of colour images. Tech. rep., Linköping University (2002)
13. Granlund, G.H.: An associative perception-action structure using a localized space variant information representation. In: Sommer, G., Zeevi, Y.Y. (eds.) AFPAC 2000. LNCS, vol. 1888, pp. 48–68. Springer, Heidelberg (2000)
14. Hare, S., Saffari, A., Torr, P.: Struck: Structured output tracking with kernels. In: ICCV (2011)
15. He, S., Yang, Q., Lau, R., Wang, J., Yang, M.H.: Visual tracking via locality sensitive histograms. In: CVPR (2013)
16. Heinemann, C., Åström, F., Baravdish, G., Krajsek, K., Felsberg, M., Scharr, H.: Using channel representations in regularization terms: a case study on image diffusion. In: VISAPP (2014)
17. Henriques, J.F., Caseiro, R., Martins, P., Batista, J.: Exploiting the circulant structure of tracking-by-detection with kernels. In: Fitzgibbon, A., Lazebnik, S., Perona, P., Sato, Y., Schmid, C. (eds.) ECCV 2012, Part IV. LNCS, vol. 7575, pp. 702–715. Springer, Heidelberg (2012)
18. Jia, X., Lu, H., Yang, M.H.: Visual tracking via adaptive structural local sparse appearance model. In: CVPR (2012)
19. Jonsson, E.: Channel-Coded Feature Maps for Computer Vision and Machine Learning. Linköping Studies in Science and Technology. Dissertations No. 1160, Linköping University, Sweden (2008)
20. Kalal, Z., Matas, J., Mikolajczyk, K.: P-n learning: bootstrapping binary classifiers by structural constraints. In: CVPR (2010)

21. Khan, F.S., Anwer, R.M., van de Weijer, J., Bagdanov, A., Lopez, A., Felsberg, M.: Coloring action recognition in still images. IJCV **105**(3), 205–221 (2013)
22. Khan, F.S., van de Weijer, J., Vanrell, M.: Modulating shape features by color attention for object recognition. IJCV **98**(1), 49–64 (2012)
23. Kristan, M., et al.: The visual object tracking VOT2014 challenge results. In: Agapito, L., Bronstein, M.M., Rother, C. (eds.) ECCV 2014 Workshops. LNCS, vol. 8926, pp. 191–217. Springer, Heidelberg (2015)
24. Kwon, J., Lee, K.M.: Tracking by sampling trackers. In: ICCV (2011)
25. Liu, B., Huang, J., Yang, L., Kulikowski, C.: Robust tracking using local sparse appearance model and k-selection. In: CVPR (2011)
26. Meneghetti, G., Danelljan, M., Felsberg, M., Nordberg, K.: Image alignment for panorama stitching in sparsely structured environments. In: SCIA (2015)
27. Nummiaro, K., Koller-Meier, E., Gool, L.J.V.: An adaptive color-based particle filter. IVC **21**(1), 99–110 (2003)
28. Oron, S., Hillel, A., Levi, Avidan, S.: Locally orderless tracking. In: CVPR (2012)
29. Pérez, P., Hue, C., Vermaak, J., Gangnet, M.: Color-based probabilistic tracking. In: Heyden, A., Sparr, G., Nielsen, M., Johansen, P. (eds.) ECCV 2002, Part I. LNCS, vol. 2350, pp. 661–675. Springer, Heidelberg (2002)
30. Prokaj, J., Medioni, G.: Persistent tracking for wide area aerial surveillance. In: CVPR (2014)
31. Sevilla-Lara, L., Miller, E.: Distribution fields for tracking. In: CVPR (2012)
32. Wang, D., Lu, H., Yang, M.H.: Least soft-threshold squares tracking. In: CVPR (2013)
33. van de Weijer, J., Schmid, C., Verbeek, J.J., Larlus, D.: Learning color names for real-world applications. TIP **18**(7), 1512–1524 (2009)
34. Wu, Y., Lim, J., Yang, M.H.: Online object tracking: a benchmark. In: CVPR (2013)
35. Zhang, K., Zhang, L., Yang, M.-H.: Real-time compressive tracking. In: Fitzgibbon, A., Lazebnik, S., Perona, P., Sato, Y., Schmid, C. (eds.) ECCV 2012, Part III. LNCS, vol. 7574, pp. 864–877. Springer, Heidelberg (2012)
36. Zhong, W., Lu, H., Yang, M.H.: Robust object tracking via sparsity-based collaborative model. In: CVPR (2012)

High-Speed Hand Tracking for Studying Human-Computer Interaction

Toni Kuronen[1](✉), Tuomas Eerola[1], Lasse Lensu[1], Jari Takatalo[2],
Jukka Häkkinen[2], and Heikki Kälviäinen[1]

[1] Machine Vision and Pattern Recognition Laboratory (MVPR),
School of Engineering Science, Lappeenranta University of Technology (LUT),
P.O. Box 20, FI-53851 Lappeenranta, Finland
{toni.kuronen,tuomas.eerola,lasse.lensu,heikki.kalviainen}@lut.fi
http://www2.it.lut.fi/mvpr/
[2] Visual Cognition Research Group, Institute of Behavioural Sciences,
University of Helsinki, P.O. Box 9, FI-00014 Helsinki, Finland
{jari.takatalo,jukka.hakkinen}@helsinki.fi
http://www.helsinki.fi/psychology/groups/visualcognition/

Abstract. Understanding how a human behaves while performing human-computer interaction tasks is essential in order to develop better user interfaces. In the case of touch and gesture based interfaces, the main interest is in the characterization of hand movements. The recent developments in imaging technology and computing hardware have made it attractive to exploit high-speed imaging for tracking the hand more accurately both in space and time. However, the tracking algorithm development has been focused on optimizing the robustness and computation speed instead of spatial accuracy, making most of them, as such, insufficient for the accurate measurements of hand movements. In this paper, state-of-the-art tracking algorithms are compared based on their suitability for the finger tracking during human-computer interaction task. Furthermore, various trajectory filtering techniques are evaluated to improve the accuracy and to obtain appropriate hand movement measurements. The experimental results showed that Kernelized Correlation Filters and Spatio-Temporal Context Learning tracking were the best tracking methods obtaining reasonable accuracy and high processing speed while Local Regression filtering and Unscented Kalman Smoother were the most suitable filtering techniques.

Keywords: Hand tracking · High-speed video · Hand trajectories · Filtering · Human-computer interaction

1 Introduction

The motivation for this work comes from the human-computer interaction (HCI) research, and the need to accurately record hand and finger movements of test subjects in various HCI tasks. During the recent years, this has become particularly important due to the rapid development of touch display technology

© Springer International Publishing Switzerland 2015
R.R. Paulsen and K.S. Pedersen (Eds.): SCIA 2015, LNCS 9127, pp. 130–141, 2015.
DOI: 10.1007/978-3-319-19665-7_11

and amount of commercially available touchscreens in smartphones, tablets and other table-top and hand-held devices, as well as, the emergence of different gesture based interfaces. Recording the hand movements can be performed by using hand tracking or general object tracking which has been studied since the 1990s and is an active research area also today [4], [13], [15], [24], [25]. Despite the significant effort, however, the problem of hand tracking cannot be considered solved [9]. From a technical perspective, different robust approaches for hand tracking exist, such as data gloves with electro-mechanical or magnetic sensors that can measure the hand and finger location with high accuracy. However, such devices affect the natural hand motion, are expensive, and hence, cannot be considered a good solution when pursuing natural HCI. As a consequence, there is a need for image-based solutions that provide unobtrusive way to study and track human movement and enable natural interaction between technology.

To accurately record fast phenomena such as reaction times and to robustly track rapid hand movements, high frame rates are needed in imaging. To produce videos with good quality, the high-speed imaging requires more light when compared to imaging with conventional frame rates. Therefore, gray-scale high-speed imaging is in common use making the use of hand tracking methods relying specifically on color information unsuitable. This motivates to apply general object trackers for the problem. In [9], various general object trackers were compared for hand tracking with a primary focus on gray-scale high-speed videos. It was found out that by avoiding the most difficult environments and posture changes, the state-of-the-art trackers are capable of reliable hand and finger tracking.

The main problem in using the existing object tracking methods in accurate measurement of hand and finger movements is that they are developed for applications where high (sub-pixel) accuracy is unnecessary. Instead, the research has focused on developing more computationally efficient and robust methods, i.e., losing the target is considered a much more severe problem than a spatial shift of the tracking window. While these are justified choices in most tracking applications, this is not the case in the hand trajectory measurement in high speed videos where small hand movement between the frames and a controlled environment help to maintain higher robustness, but high accuracy is needed. Even small errors in spatial locations can cause high errors when computing the speed and acceleration. Therefore, the existing tracking algorithms are as such insufficient for the accurate measurements of hand movements and further processing of hand trajectories is required.

In this paper, the work started in [9] is continued by further evaluating an extended set of tracking algorithms to find the best methods for accurate hand movement measurements. Moreover, the earlier work is extended by processing tracked hand trajectories with various filtering techniques. The different methods are evaluated using novel annotated data consisting of high-speed gray-scale videos of a human performing HCI tasks using a touch user interface.

Since the trackers specific for hand tracking rely on color information, the focus of this study is on the state-of-the-art general object trackers. Based on a literature review and preliminary tracking tests, 12 trackers were selected for further study [14]. These methods are summarized in Table 1.

Table 1. Trackers selected for the experiments

Method	Abbreviation	Implementation
Real-time Compressive Tracking [27]	CT	MATLAB+MEX[1]
Fast Compressive Tracking [28]	FCT	MATLAB+MEX[2]
High-Speed Tracking with Kernelized Correlation Filters [8]	KCF	MATLAB+MEX[3]
Hough-based Tracking of Non-Rigid Objects [5]	HT	C++[4]
Incremental Learning for Robust Visual Tracking [19]	IVT	MATLAB+MEX[5]
Robust Object Tracking with Online Multiple Instance Learning [1]	MIL	MATLAB[6]
Tracking Learning Detection [12]	TLD	MATLAB+MEX[7]
Robust Object Tracking via Sparsity-based Collaborative Model [29]	RSCM	MATLAB+MEX[8]
Fast Tracking via Spatio-Temporal Context Learning [26]	STC	MATLAB[9]
Structured Output Tracking with Kernels [6]	struck	C++[10]
Single and Multiple Object Tracking Using Log-Euclidean Riemannian Subspace and Block-Division Appearance Model [10]	LRS	MATLAB+MEX[11]
Online Object Tracking with Sparse Prototypes [21]	SRPCA	MATLAB[12]

Real-time Compressive Tracking (CT) [27] is a tracking-by-detection method that uses a sparse random matrix to project high-dimensional image features to low-dimensional (compressed) features. The basic idea is to acquire positive samples near the current target location and negative samples far away from the target object at each frame, and use these samples to update the classifier. Then, the location for the next frame is predicted by getting samples from around the last known location and choosing the sample that gets the best classification

---

[1] http://www4.comp.polyu.edu.hk/~cslzhang/CT/CT.htm
[2] http://www4.comp.polyu.edu.hk/~cslzhang/FCT/FCT.htm
[3] http://www.isr.uc.pt/~henriques/circulant/
[4] http://lrs.icg.tugraz.at/research/houghtrack/
[5] http://www.cs.toronto.edu/~dross/ivt/
[6] http://whluo.net/matlab-code-for-mil-tracker/
[7] http://personal.ee.surrey.ac.uk/Personal/Z.Kalal/tld.html
[8] https://github.com/gnebehay/SCM
[9] http://www4.comp.polyu.edu.hk/~cslzhang/STC/STC.htm
[10] http://www.samhare.net/research/struck/code
[11] http://www.iis.ee.ic.ac.uk/~whluo/code.html
[12] http://faculty.ucmerced.edu/mhyang/project/tip13_prototype/TIP12-SP.htm

score. Fast Compressive Tracker (FCT) [28] is an improvement of CT. The speed of the tracker is improved by using a sparse-to-dense search method. First, the object search is done by using a sparse sliding window followed by detection using a dense sliding window for better accuracy.

HoughTrack (HT)[5] is a tracking-by-detection method which is based on the generalized Hough transform. In the method, a Hough-based detector is constantly trained with the current object appearance. Unlike the other selected algorithms, in addition to bounding box tracking, HT outputs also segmented tracking results which is used to limit the amount of background noise supplied to the online learning module.

Incremental learning for robust visual tracking (IVT) [19] learns a low-dimensional subspace representation of the target object and tracks it using a particle filter. Online object tracking with sparse prototypes (SRPCA)[21] is a particle filter based tracking method that utilizes sparse prototypes consisting of PCA basis vectors modeling the object appearance. The main difference to IVT is trivial templates that are applied to handle partial occlusions.

High-Speed Tracking with Kernelized Correlation Filters (KCF) [8] is an improved version of the kernelized correlation filters introduced in [7]. By over-sampling sliding windows, the resulting data matrix can be simplified, the size of the data reduced, and the computation made faster. This can be achieved by taking advantage of Fast Fourier Transform (FFT).

Tracking with online multiple instance learning (MIL) [1] is a tracking-by-detection method that applies the multiple instance learning approach to tracking to account ambiguities in the training data. In the multiple instance learning, positive and negative training examples are presented as sets, and labels are provided for the sets instead of individual instances. By using this approach, updates of the classifier with incorrectly labeled training examples may be avoided and thus, more robust tracking achieved.

Tracking-learning-detection (TLD) [12] is a framework aiming to long-term target tracking by decomposing the task into tracking, learning, and detection sub-tasks. The tracker is tracking the object during the frames whereas the detector localizes all the appearances observed earlier and reinitializes the tracker if required. The final tracker estimate is a combination of the tracker and detector bounding boxes. The third sub-task, learning, tries to estimate the errors of the detector and update it to avoid those in the following frames.

Robust Object Tracking via Sparsity-based Collaborative Model (RSCM) by Zhong et al. [29] contains a sparsity-based discriminative classifier (SDC) and a sparsity-based generative model (SGM). SDC introduces an effective method to compute the confidence value that assigns more weight to the foreground by extracting sparse and determinative features that distinguish the foreground and background better. SGM is a histogram-based method that takes the spatial information of each patch into consideration with an occlusion handling scheme.

Fast Tracking via Spatio-Temporal Context Learning (STC) [26] algorithm works by learning a spatial context model between the target and its surrounding background. The learned model is used to update the spatio-temporal context model for the following frame. The tracking task is formulated by convolution as a computing task of a confidence map, and the best object location can be estimated by maximizing the confidence map.

The main idea of Structured Output Tracking with Kernels (struck) [6] is to create positive samples from areas containing the object, and negative samples of the background further away from the object. It uses a confidence map and obtains the best location by maximizing a location likelihood function of an object.

Tracker based on Riemannian subspace learning (LRS)[10] is an incrementally learning tracking algorithm that focuses on appearance modeling using a subspace-based approach. The key component in LRS is the log-Euclidean block-division appearance model that aims to adapt to the changes in the objects appearance. In the incremental log-Euclidean Riemannian subspace learning algorithm, covariance matrices of image features are mapped into a vector space with the log-Euclidean Riemannian metric. The log-Euclidean block-division appearance model captures both local and global spatial layout information about the object's appearances. Particle filtering based Bayesian state inference is utilized as the core tracking technique.

2   Trajectory Filtering

In an ideal case, the motion between the frames should be at least one pixel in order to be quantifiable for the trackers. That is not always the case with high-speed videos and can create challenges for the trackers and trajectory analysis. Therefore, filtering of the trajectory data is necessary to obtain accurate velocity and acceleration measurements. Fig. 1 shows an example result of filtering the tracking data.

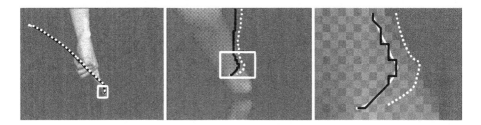

Fig. 1. Raw tracking data (black), the ground truth (dotted white) and filtered tracking data (white)

The following 8 filtering methods were considered in this work: Moving Average (MA) [20], Kalman Filter (KF) [22,23], Extended KF (EKF) [17], Unscented KF (UKF) [11], Local Regression (LOESS) [3], Locally Weighted Scatterplot Smoothing (LOWESS) [3], Savitzky-Golay (S-G) [18], and Total Variation Denoising (TVD) [2] .

MA filter operates by averaging subsets of input data points to produce a sequence of averages. A Kalman filter is an optimal recursive data processing algorithm. EKF is the nonlinear version of the Kalman filter and has been considered as the de-facto standard in nonlinear state estimation. In UKF, unscented transformation is used to calculate the statistics of a random variable which undergoes a nonlinear transformation. It is designed on the principle that it is easier to approximate a probability distribution than an arbitrary nonlinear function. In KF, the predictor predicts parameter values based on the current measurements. The filter estimates parameter values by using the previous and current measurements. The smoothing algorithm estimates the parameter values by using the previous, current, and future measurements: that is, all available data can be used for filtering [23]. Future measurements can be used because the Kalman smoother proceeds backward in time. This also means that the Kalman filter needs to be run before running the smoother.

LOESS and LOWESS were originally developed to enhance visual information on scatterplots by computing and plotting smoothed points by using locally weighted regression. LOESS and LOWESS are methods to estimate the regression surface through a smoothing procedure. S-G is a smoothing filter, also called the polynomial smoothing or least-squares smoothing filter. S-G smoothing reduces noise while maintaining the shape and height of peaks. Total variation (TV) of a signal measures the changes in the signal between signal values. TVD output is obtained by minimizing a TV-based cost function. It was developed to preserve sharp edges in the underlying signal.

3   Experiments

3.1   Data

Data was collected during a HCI experiment where test subjects were advised to perform intentional single finger pointing actions from trigger-box toward a colored target on a touchscreen. The target on the touchscreen was one of 13 objects which formed a circle on the screen, were of different sizes, and lay on different parallaxes. Hand movements were recorded with a Mega Speed MS50K high-speed camera equipped with Nikon Nikkor AF-S 14-24mm F2.8G objective fixed to a 14mm focal length. The camera was positioned on the right side of the test setup, and the distance to the screen was approximately 1.5 meters. The lighting was arranged using an overhead light panel 85 cm above the table surface and 58 cm in depth. The test subject was sitting at the distance of 65 cm from the touch screen and a trigger-box was placed 40 cm away from it.

Dataset contained 11 high-speed videos with 800×600 resolution recorded at 500 fps. Sample frames from the dataset can be seen in Fig. 2. These images illustrate the different end-points of the trajectories. The start-point for all the sequences was the same. The ground truth was annotated manually. Annotations were done for every 5th frame and then interpolated using spline interpolation to get the ground truths for every frame.

Fig. 2. The sample images are from the dataset used in the experiments. Those were all taken from the end point of respective videos. The ground-truth bounding-box can be seen as a white rectangle in the images.

3.2   Results

The tracking experiments were carried out using the original implementations of the authors except in the case of MIL; for that, the implementation by Luo [16] was used. Search area parameters of the trackers were tuned for the video data used, if it was possible with the implementation. For the other parameters, the default values proposed by the original authors were used. The tracking methods were run 10 times for each video and the results were averaged to minimize random factors in tracking. Table 2 shows the results of the trackers for the dataset. The tracking rate of 100% with threshold of 32 pixels center location error was achieved by three of the trackers, KCF being the best one in overall results with the smallest average center location error of 4.65. Also, struck, and STC achieved high accuracy. Length of the videos in total was 10798 frames and individual videos were between 544 and 1407 frames long.

Table 2. Tracking results for Dataset: percentage of correctly tracked frames (TR%) and average center location errors (Err.), and the processing speed (fps). Also, the range of the values from the results are shown. The best results are shown in bold.

Method	TR%	TR% range	Err.	Err. range	fps	fps range
CT	79.43%	0-100%	18.43	3.5-76	99.97	63-121
FCT	17.14%	0-73%	58.74	16-92	118.73	72-150
HT	97.12%	36-100%	15.29	3.1-226	4.65	4-4.9
IVT	74.50%	15-100%	86.75	2.0-448	63.38	51-70
KCF	**100%**	-	**4.65**	1.4-7.4	979.97	728-1236
LRS	20.51%	2-47%	291.32	76-540	8.79	7.8-9.4
MIL	93.82%	24-100%	11.35	2.8-138	0.55	0.4-0.6
RSCM	86.81%	40-100%	18.84	2.2-126	2.50	2.0-2.8
SRPCA	83.64%	24-100%	72.38	1.7-366	10.52	8.3-12.5
STC	**100%**	-	5.13	2.3-6.9	**1291.03**	1156-1330
struck	**100%**	-	4.72	1.6-6.5	118.62	99-153
TLD	68.48%	16-100%	43.55	4.4-139	16.46	8.8-24

When working with high-speed videos, the importance of processing speed is emphasized. The experiments were carried out using a desktop computer with an Intel i5-4570 CPU and 8 GB of memory. The fps measure used in the experiments was calculated without including the image loading times in the calculations to get the raw frame processing speed. The highest fps was measured for STC which showed the best average performance and for KCF which had the peak performance of over 1200 fps. Both achieved processing speeds well over the frame rate of the videos. However, it should be noted that due to the different programming environments (MATLAB, C, etc.) and levels of performance optimization, these results should be considered merely suggestive.

KCF was selected for the further study since it correctly tracked all the frames, had one of the smallest average center location error, was able to process the high-speed videos in real-time. Moreover, earlier tracking experiments [14] have shown that KCF is more robust than STC on diverse video content.

Table 3 summarizes the trajectory filtering results. The results were calculated by averaging the results from all dataset trajectories tracked with KCF tracker. The window size and method parameters were optimized separately for each filtering method. Filtering with Unscented Kalman Smoother (UKS) and TVD are included for comparison. UKS was selected to represent Kalman smoother algorithms since Extended Kalman Smoother and UKS produced similar results. Velocity and acceleration curves for trajectories obtained using Kalman filtering were computed using the Kalman filtering motion model. For the trajectories obtained using other filtering methods, velocity and acceleration curves were computed based on Euclidean distances between trajectory points in consecutive frames.

Table 3. Minimal mean and standard deviations of Position Errors (PE), Velocity Errors (VE), and Acceleration Errors (AE) with different filtering methods. In parentheses is the filtering window size which gave the best result for the filter. The best results are shown in bold.

Error	Moving Average	LOWESS	LOESS	Savitzky-Golay	TVD	UKS	unfiltered
Mean PE	4.6057 (3)	4.6057 (4)	**4.6029** (34)	4.6030 (25)	4.6474	4.6033	4.6099
Mean VE	0.0440 (17)	0.0419 (18)	**0.0415** (34)	0.0428 (31)	0.2052	0.0421	0.2085
Mean AE	0.0137 (83)	**0.0118** (23)	0.0119 (53)	0.0137 (97)	0.3026	0.0125	0.3074
std PE	1.3496 (5)	1.3495 (8)	**1.3459** (38)	1.3461 (29)	1.3860	1.3468	1.3917
std VE	0.0544 (15)	0.0522 (18)	**0.517** (34)	0.0532 (27)	0.2599	0.0526	0.2641
std AE	0.0210 (95)	0.0185 (23)	**0.0185** (39)	0.0206 (85)	0.4599	0.0190	0.4652

From the results shown in Fig. 3, it is obvious that different window sizes were optimal for each derivative of the position. The velocity and acceleration curves needed larger window sizes to get better results than the position. LOESS filtering was the least sensitive to window size with optimal filtering results from the window size range of 34 to 53. The problem with a large window size is that the estimated position starts to drift off from the true position which is very clear in case of moving average and LOWESS filtering.

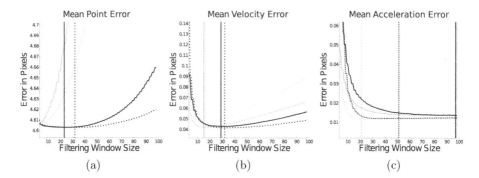

Fig. 3. Filtering the effect of the window size on the means of (a) point error; (b) velocity error and (c) acceleration errors. The location of minimum error for each of the methods is indicated with the vertical line. Moving average is shown in grey, LOWESS in dotted grey, LOESS in dotted black, and Savitzky-Golay in black.

An example of how filtering affects the tracking data is shown in Fig. 4. In Fig. 4(a) no filtering is applied to tracking data before calculating velocity and acceleration values. Fig. 4(b) shows the result when position data after tracking is filtered with LOESS filtering with a span of 40 frames, and the velocity and acceleration values are calculated from that filtered data. In Fig. 4(c), also the velocity data is filtered after position data filtering with the same LOESS filtering method. From these results, it is clearly visible that filtering is needed to achieve appropriate velocity and acceleration curves from the tracked hand movement data.

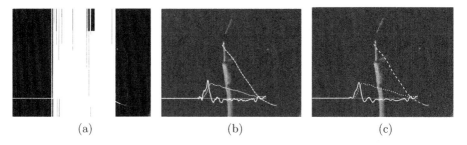

Fig. 4. Tracking data and velocity and acceleration curves computed from it using: (a) Raw data; (b) Position data filtered with LOESS (span of 40); (c) Position and velocity data filtered with LOESS (span of 40). Trajectory is shown in dashed, velocity in dotted, and acceleration in continuous.

4 Conclusion

In this paper, hand tracking in high-speed videos during HCI tasks, and post-processing of the tracked hand trajectories were studied. The results showed that objects in high-speed video feeds with almost black background can be tracked in real-time with two of the tested trackers. For this research, this meant reaching speeds of over 970 (KCF) and over 1290 (STC) fps on average for the test video sequences which were recorded at 500 frames per second. Thus, the trackers satisfied real-time needs. Even though the performance evaluation for the trackers in this setup did not include the image-loading times, 2.3 milliseconds on average per image with MATLAB, the results are still impressive.

Filtering helps to find smooth acceleration curves to allow us see clearly where the moments of maximum and minimal acceleration are. With appropriate filtering, the velocity and acceleration features of the trajectories got closer to the ground truth. Two filtering methods, LOESS and UKS, produced the most consistent results for all the tests. Selecting one method as the winner raised the question, which one is simpler to use, and that happened to be LOESS. To conclude, with filtering and smoothing the hand-tracking data, it is possible to get to the underlying characteristics of the real movement sequence.

Smoothing the trajectories produced by the trackers gave good results for the derivatives of the position, but sub-pixel accuracy for video sequences which require high precision could be alternative way. By having more accurate positions of the object, one would not need to smooth the trajectories and more accurate results also for the velocities and accelerations of the moving object would be generated. The videos used in this work did not have large scale changes, but adapting to the scale changes on sub-pixel level could help to make the tracking process even more accurate. Also, ground-truth annotation process proved to be a hard undertaking. Clearly visible and accurate marker in test subject's finger would have helped the ground-truth annotation process.

The results provide observations about the suitability of tracking methods for high-speed hand tracking and about how filtering can be applied to produce more appropriate velocity and acceleration curves calculated from the tracking data.

Acknowledgments. The research was carried out in the COPEX project (No. 264429) funded by the Academy of Finland.

References

1. Babenko, B., Yang, M.H., Belongie, S.: Robust object tracking with online multiple instance learning. IEEE Transactions on Pattern Analysis and Machine Intelligence **33**(8), 1619–1632 (2011)
2. Chambolle, A.: An Algorithm for Total Variation Minimization and Applications. Journal of Mathematical Imaging and Vision **20**(1–2), 89–97 (2004)
3. Cleveland, W.S.: Robust Locally Weighted Regression and Smoothing Scatterplots. Journal of the American Statistical Association **74**(368), 829–836 (1979)

4. Erol, A., Bebis, G., Nicolescu, M., Boyle, R.D., Twombly, X.: Vision-based hand pose estimation: A review. Computer Vision and Image Understanding **108**(1–2), 52–73 (2007). special Issue on Vision for Human-Computer Interaction
5. Godec, M., Roth, P.M., Bischof, H.: Hough-based tracking of non-rigid objects. Computer Vision and Image Understanding **117**(10), 1245–1256 (2012)
6. Hare, S., Saffari, A., Torr, P.H.S.: Struck: structured output tracking with kernels. In: IEEE International Conference on Computer Vision (ICCV), pp. 263–270 (2011)
7. Henriques, J.F., Caseiro, R., Martins, P., Batista, J.: Exploiting the circulant structure of tracking-by-detection with kernels. In: Fitzgibbon, A., Lazebnik, S., Perona, P., Sato, Y., Schmid, C. (eds.) ECCV 2012, Part IV. LNCS, vol. 7575, pp. 702–715. Springer, Heidelberg (2012)
8. Henriques, J.F., Caseiro, R., Martins, P., Batista, J.: High-Speed Tracking with Kernelized Correlation Filters. IEEE Transactions on Pattern Analysis and Machine Intelligence **37**(3), 583–596 (2015)
9. Hiltunen, V., Eerola, T., Lensu, L., Kälviäinen, H.: Comparison of general object trackers for hand tracking in high-speed videos. In: International Conference on Pattern Recognition (ICPR), pp. 2215–2220 (2014)
10. Hu, W., Li, X., Luo, W., Zhang, X., Maybank, S., Zhang, Z.: Single and multiple object tracking using log-Euclidean Riemannian subspace and block-division appearance model. IEEE Transactions on Pattern Analysis and Machine Intelligence **34**(12), 2420–2440 (2012)
11. Julier, S.J., Uhlmann, J.K.: A new extension of the kalman filter to nonlinear systems. In: Proceedings of The International Society for Optics and Photonics (SPIE) AeroSense: International Symposium on Aerospace/Defense Sensing, Simulations and Controls (1997)
12. Kalal, Z., Mikolajczyk, K., Matas, J.: Tracking-learning-detection. IEEE Transactions on Pattern Analysis and Machine Intelligence **34**(7), 1409–1422 (2012)
13. Kristan, M., Pflugfelder, R., Leonardis, A., Matas, J., et al.: The visual object tracking VOT2014 challenge results. In: Agapito, L., Bronstein, M.M., Rother, C. (eds.) ECCV 2014 Workshops. LNCS, vol. 8926, pp. 191–217. Springer, Heidelberg (2015)
14. Kuronen, T.: Post-Processing and Analysis of Tracked Hand Trajectories. Master's thesis, Lappeenranta University of Technology (2014)
15. Li, X., Hu, W., Shen, C., Zhang, Z., Dick, A., Hengel, A.V.D.: A Survey of Appearance Models in Visual Object Tracking. ACM Transactions on Intelligent Systems and Technology (TIST) **4**(4), 58:1–58:48 (2013)
16. Luo, W.: Matlab code for Multiple Instance Learning (MIL) Tracker. http://whluo. net/matlab-code-for-mil-tracker/. (accessed: August, 2013)
17. Montemerlo, M., Thrun, S.: Simultaneous localization and mapping with unknown data association using FastSLAM. In: IEEE International Conference on Robotics and Automation (ICRA), vol. 2, pp. 1985–1991 (2003)
18. Orfanidis, S.J.: Introduction to Signal Processing. Prentice Hall international editions, Prentice Hall (1996–2009)
19. Ross, D.A., Lim, J., Lin, R.S., Yang, M.H.: Incremental Learning for Robust Visual Tracking. International Journal of Computer Vision **77**(1–3), 125–141 (2008)
20. Smith, S.W.: The Scientist and Engineer's Guide to Digital Signal Processing. California Technical Publishing (1997)
21. Wang, D., Lu, H., Yang, M.H.: Online Object Tracking With Sparse Prototypes. IEEE Transactions on Image Processing **22**(1), 314–325 (2013)

22. Welch, G., Bishop, G.: An Introduction to the Kalman Filter. Tech. rep. Department of Computer Science, University of North Carolina (1995)
23. Welch, G., Bishop, G.: An Introduction to the kalman filter: SIGGRAPH 2001 course 8. In: Computer Graphics, Annual Conference on Computer Graphics & Interactive Techniques, pp. 12–17 (2001)
24. Wu, Y., Lim, J., Yang, M.H.: Object Tracking Benchmark. IEEE Transactions on Pattern Analysis and Machine Intelligence (2015)
25. Yilmaz, A., Javed, O., Shah, M.: Object Tracking: A Survey. ACM Computing Surveys **38**(4) (2006)
26. Zhang, K., Zhang, L., Liu, Q., Zhang, D., Yang, M.-H.: Fast visual tracking via dense spatio-temporal context learning. In: Fleet, D., Pajdla, T., Schiele, B., Tuytelaars, T. (eds.) ECCV 2014, Part V. LNCS, vol. 8693, pp. 127–141. Springer, Heidelberg (2014)
27. Zhang, K., Zhang, L., Yang, M.-H.: Real-time compressive tracking. In: Fitzgibbon, A., Lazebnik, S., Perona, P., Sato, Y., Schmid, C. (eds.) ECCV 2012, Part III. LNCS, vol. 7574, pp. 864–877. Springer, Heidelberg (2012)
28. Zhang, K., Zhang, L., Yang, M.H.: Fast Compressive Tracking. IEEE Transactions on Pattern Analysis and Machine Intelligence **36**(10), 2002–2015 (2014)
29. Zhong, W., Lu, H., Yang, M.H.: Robust Object Tracking via Sparse Collaborative Appearance Model. IEEE Transactions on Image Processing **23**(5), 2356–2368 (2014)

Correction of Motion Artifacts
for Real-Time Structured Light

Jakob Wilm[1,2]([✉]), Oline V. Olesen[1,2], Rasmus R. Paulsen[1],
and Rasmus Larsen[1]

[1] Department of Applied Mathematics and Computer Science,
Technical University of Denmark, Richard Petersens Plads, Building 324,
DK-2800 Kgs. Lyngby, Denmark
jakw@dtu.dk
http://compute.dtu.dk/
[2] Department of Clinical Physiology, Nuclear Medicine and PET, Rigshospitalet,
Copenhagen University Hospital, University of Copenhagen, Copenhagen, Denmark

Abstract. While the problem of motion is often mentioned in conjunction with structured light imaging, few solutions have thus far been proposed. A method is demonstrated to correct for object or camera motion during structured light 3D scene acquisition. The method is based on the combination of a suitable pattern strategy with fast phase correlation image registration. The effectiveness of this approach is demonstrated on motion corrupted data of a real-time structured light system, and it is shown that it improves the quality of surface reconstructions visually and quantitively.

Keywords: 3D vision · Structured light · Motion correction · Registration

1 Introduction

Structured light techniques are very popular for 3D scene capture, and a large variety of variants have been proposed. See [5] for an overview. The general idea is to aid in the detection of stereo correspondences by active projection of light onto the scene, followed by triangulation, to yield a surface reconstruction.

In time-multiplexed or multi-pattern structured light [13], a sequence of patterns is projected to generate one surface reconstruction, which encodes scene points, thereby disambiguating the matching process. The flexible nature of of structured light allows to choose a trade-off between number of patterns and accuracy, and to optimise for the radiometric properties of the scene.

With advances in light projection technology and computing power, it is today possible to perform structured light surface scanning with multiple patterns in real time. This enables accurate object tracking, dynamic deformation studies, fast object digitisation and many other applications. A general limitation with any multi-pattern method however is the underlying assumption of no motion between the patterns of a single sequence. A violation of this assumption

© Springer International Publishing Switzerland 2015
R.R. Paulsen and K.S. Pedersen (Eds.): SCIA 2015, LNCS 9127, pp. 142–151, 2015.
DOI: 10.1007/978-3-319-19665-7_12

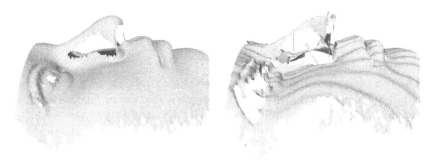

Fig. 1. Reconstructions of a phantom head using our structured light setup, showing the effects of motion during time-multiplexing. Left: static scene. Right: slight movement during acquisition.

often leads to large artifacts in the reconstructed surface. Such artifacts are shown as an example in figure 1.

By abandoning time multiplexing, single-shot structured light can be realised [14][6]. In the case of Microsoft Kinect 1, a static pseudorandom pattern is used. With single-shot techniques, the motion problem is avoided, but the reconstruction quality is also not very high or lateral resolution is lowered. Multiplexing by means of wavelength is also possible, i.e. by placing different patterns in the red, green and blue channels of the projection. This is not as robust to surface reflectance properties and spectral bleeding/crosstalk may occur. A review of single-shoot methods is provided in [20].

Time multiplexing remains the most robust technique, and is used in many commercial products, mainly for industrial inspection and reverse engineering. The chosen pattern strategy is important for the performance of the system, and two classes of methods remain very popular: binary Gray-coding and phase shifting profilometry (PSP). The former tends to be robust, but generally requires relatively many patterns, worsening the effects of motion. PSP can encode the scene unambiguously with only three patterns of a single sinusoid phase, shifted by 0 deg, 120 deg and 240 deg respectively. Depth resolution can be improved by using more shifts, or multiple phases, which gives a limited ambiguity that can be resolved using a phase-unwrapping algorithm.

In the presented method, we use the modified "2+1" phase shifting method of Zhang and Yau [19], which according to the authors reduces the effects of motion, and perform fast image registration on the acquired camera frames, to correct for the synchronisation error, and vastly improve the quality of scene reconstructions. By employing phase-based image registration, the motion correction is efficient enough to run in real-time in our 20 Hz surface scanning pipeline.

2   Previous Work

Employing more than three patterns in phase shifting profilometry allows for sanity checking, and masking corrupted output [9]. This is at the expense of additional patterns in the sequence, generally making it slower (but more accurate), but it is questionable to what degree the unmasked output can be trusted.

In [7], a motion corrected real-time method is presented, for one-dimensional known motion.

The consequences of motion can be alleviated to some extend by running at high frequencies. Zhang et al. have presented structured light with dithered binary sinusoid patterns running at 1000 Hz reconstructions per second [15]. Their method requires strong projector lighting and high-speed cameras due to the short integration time of any single camera frame, and involves quality trade-offs making it unsuitable for many applications.

Liu et al. [10] propose motion corrected light with binary patterns and estimation of a global velocity vector based on the reconstructions, while Lu et al. show the theoretical feasibility of motion correction by means of image alignment [11].

3   Structured Light and PSP

We use direct codification structured light, i.e. using a single camera-projector pair as described in [16]. Projector pixel coordinates are denoted (u_p, v_p), while camera pixel coordinates are (u_c, v_c). Employing a vertical baseline, the standard 3-step PSP algorithm encodes the projected images as

$$I_n^p(u_p, v_p) = \frac{1}{2} + \frac{1}{2} \cos\left(2\pi \left(\frac{u_p}{N_p} - \frac{n}{3}\right)\right),$$

where n indicates the pattern index, $n \in 1 \ldots 3$ and N_p the number of projector columns. The camera captures the n'th pattern as

$$I_n^c(u_c, v_c) = A^c + B^c \cos\left(2\pi \left(\frac{u_p}{N_p} - \frac{n}{3}\right)\right).$$

Note the dependency on the projectors horizontal coordinate, u_p. A^c is the scene intensity including ambient contributions, while B^c is the modulation by projector light. A^c can be considered the magnitude of the Fourier DC component, while B^c is the magnitude at the principle frequency, and $\frac{u_p}{N_p}$ its normalised phase. In order to create correspondences, $\frac{u_p}{N_p}$ is extracted with the Fourier transform and scaled by N_p.

Our camera and projector pair are calibrated according to the method described in [18]. Corresponding sets of u_p, u_c, v_c-coordinates are used to triangulate object surface points as shown in figure 2. We denote one collection of projected patterns a pattern sequence, and the corresponding camera frames a frame set.

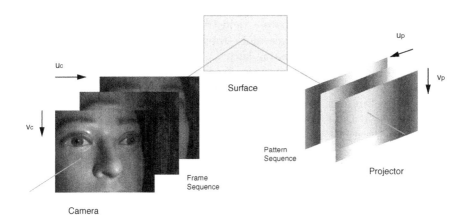

Fig. 2. Principle of structured light 3d scanning shown with the 3-step PSP pattern strategy. For each image point, the corresponding projector column coordinate, u_p, is extracted, which allows for triangulation of points on the object surface.

The "2+1" phase shifting method is a slight modification of the 3-step method, in which one of the patterns is a constant lit image:

$$I_1^p(u_p, v_p) = \frac{1}{2} + \frac{1}{2}\cos\left(2\pi\frac{u_p}{N_p}\right) \qquad (1)$$

$$I_2^p(u_p, v_p) = \frac{1}{2} + \frac{1}{2}\cos\left(2\pi\frac{u_p}{N_p} - \frac{\pi}{2}\right) \qquad (2)$$

$$I_3^p(u_p, v_p) = \frac{1}{2} \qquad (3)$$

From the corresponding camera frame set, the horizontal projector coordinate can be extracted from camera frames as

$$u_p = \frac{N_p}{2\pi}\, \mathrm{atan2}\left(I_2^c - I_3^c, I_1^c - I_3^c\right),$$

while intensity information is extracted simply as $A^c = I_3^c$.

The availability of these direct intensity frames, which are not corrupted by inter-frame motion, allows us to estimate the motion, and perform a correction. Specifically, we register intensity frames between frame sets, to estimate in 2D a global motion trend, $s = [\Delta x, \Delta y]$. All frames of a set are then corrected by interpolating from the motion trend. This removes most of motion induced artifacts from single object sources that undergo rigid motion.

4   Phase Correlation

In order estimate inter-frame motion, intensity frames are registered to each other. While the image deformation is most accurately described by a dense warp field, any estimation method for such would be computationally prohibitive in a real-time context. We therefore utilise phase correlation, also called the Fourier-Mellin method, which can estimate a rigid transformation very quickly. It is a long well known method that is very noise-robust and particularly efficient [8][3], lending itself to real-time processing such as video stabilisation [4]. We use it here to register images of two successive frame sets, in order to correct for the misalignment of frames and the resulting artifacts in the 3D reconstruction.

In many applications, such as pose tracking, the tracked object is considered to undergo rigid 6 DOF motion between frames. In such scenarios, fast phase correlation registration can account for most of the misalignment, and reduce artifacts considerably.

With two images, f_1, f_2, of dimensions $N_x \times N_y$ the phase correlation technique first applies a spatial discrete Fourier transform to both images. The determination of translational shift is based on the Fourier shift theorem.

Assuming only a circular translational shift, the images are given as

$$f_2(x, y) = f_1(\mathrm{mod}(x - \Delta x, \ N_x), \mathrm{mod}(y - \Delta y, \ N_y)),$$

and their respective Fourier spectra are related by

$$\mathcal{F}_2(u, v) = \ \mathrm{e}^{-2\pi i(u\Delta x/N_x + v\Delta y/N_y)}\mathcal{F}_1(u, v),$$

with (u, v) denoting frequency components.

The normalised cross-power spectrum is given by

$$P = \frac{\mathcal{F}_1 \odot \mathcal{F}_2^*}{\|\mathcal{F}_1 \odot \mathcal{F}_2^*\|} = \ \mathrm{e}^{2\pi i(u\Delta x/N_x + v\Delta y/N_y)},$$

with $\mathcal{F}^*$ denoting the complex conjugate, and $\odot$ the elementwise/Hadamard product. The cross correlation of f_1 and f_2 is now calculated as the inverse Fourier transform of P, and the shift estimated as its peak position

$$s = \arg\max_{x,y} \mathcal{F}^{-1}(P).$$

Since the discrete Fourier shift theorem holds only for circular shifts, a window function is used on the Fourier transforms. In fact, this is usually necessary, as the edges on tiled input images provide strong high-frequency features in Fourier domain.

To obtain the peak position with sub-pixel precision, the centroid of the cross-correlation peak is computed by also including values from a small neighbourhood around s.

It is also possible to recover scale and rotation parameters between images in an analogue way by converting magnitude spectra to the log-polar domain before computing the cross-power spectrum [3].

5   Experimental Setup

Our structured light setup consists of a single camera-projector pair. The camera integration time is a multiple of the projector refresh period for truthful gray-value reproduction, and a hardware trigger signal ensures accurate synchronisation of camera and projector. The projector update frequency is 120 Hz, and the camera integration time 8.333 ms. Due to trigger latency, we are able to capture every other projector image, resulting in $60\,\mathrm{s}^{-1}$ camera frames and 20 Hz surface reconstructions per second using the 2+1 phase shifting method.

With two consecutive frame sets $I_t^c = I_{1,t}^c, I_{2,t}^c, I_{3,t}^c$ and $I_{t+1}^c = I_{1,t+1}^c, I_{2,t+1}^c, I_{3,t+1}^c$ at times t and $t + 1$ respectively, we perform phase correlation based registration between the flat intensity frames $I_{3,t+1}^c$ and $I_{3,t}^c$. This shift, s, serves as the global motion estimate at that time point. Before reconstructing a surface from frame set I_{t+1}^c, its frames are corrected to:

$$I_{1,t}^c\left(\boldsymbol{x} - \frac{2}{3}\boldsymbol{s}\right) \quad I_{2,t}^c\left(\boldsymbol{x} - \frac{1}{3}\boldsymbol{s}\right) \quad I_{3,t}^c\left(\boldsymbol{x}\right)$$

As noted above, phase correlation in the log-polar domain allows for determination of global scale and rotation. However, in most cases of small-scale misalignment caused by camera or object movement, a translation registration is adequate and preferred by us due to the lower computational demands.

We carry out experiments by scanning a phantom head that is moving in a controlled manner. It is mounted on a stepper motor that rotates back and forth on a 36 deg arc at a constant speed of 11, 4 deg /s at a distance of approximately 20 cm to the camera. In our camera, this results in per-coordinate pixel shifts of up to 5 px between to consecutive frames. This scenario is modelled after our head-tracking approach used for medical imaging motion correction [12].

To quantify the quality of our motion corrected structured light approach, we perform a tracking experiment on the phantom head. The head is held stationary to capture an uncorrupted reference scene. The motor is then started, and the object surface is scanned and registered to the reference by means of the iterative closest point algorithm. We use the point-to-plane error metric [2], as it generally converges best on this kind of data [17]. Correspondences are found by means of back-projecting data into the camera frame [1]. The so-obtained tracking data is used to evaluate the quality of the reconstructed object surface by means of the root-mean-square (RMS) error of the alignment to the reference surface. Partial overlap of surfaces is handled by removing those point correspondences that match to the border of the reference point cloud.

6   Results

The alignment of image frames I_1^c and I_3^c during the motor controlled motion scene is shown in figure 3. It is seen, that the global shift was estimated correctly (see e.g. edge of iris, corners of the eye), and a large amount of misalignment between the images is accounted for.

The effect of motion correction on the resulting surface reconstruction is shown in figure 4.

The correction shows reduction of artifacts and distortion, especially around the nose area.

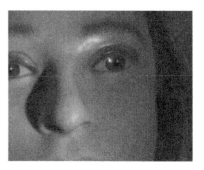

Fig. 3. Registration of camera frames I_1^c (green colour channel) and I_3^c (magenta colour channel) belonging to the same frame sequence. Left: before registration. Right: after registration. The misalignment is most easily seen at the edge of the iris and corners of the eye.

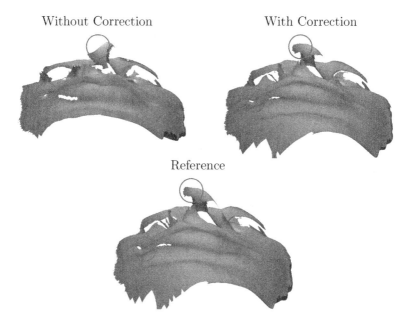

Fig. 4. Results of performing phase correlation based motion correction on an object moving at constant speed. Two aliased regions are highlighted in red circles. Top left: without correction. Top right: with correction. Bottom: stationary reference scan, e.g. no motion.

Using the rotating phantom head described, we use phase correlation to estimate the translational shift between intensity frames over time. This is shown in figure 5 with the raw shifts, and their cumulative sums. From these plots,

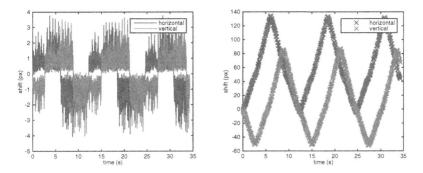

Fig. 5. Left: Translational shift estimates in horizontal (blue) and vertical (red) directions. Right: The cumulative sum of shift estimates.

it becomes apparent that phase correlation faithfully and reproducibly captures the global object movement over time.

RMS errors for the moving scene are shown in figure 6.

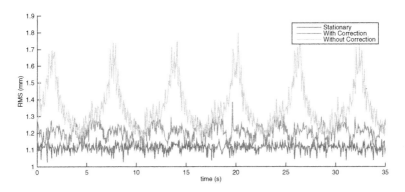

Fig. 6. RMS error of surface alignment to stationary scene at $t = 0$ using ICP. Variation in the stationary case is due to image noise. It is seen that motion corrected frame sets result in markedly lower RMS. In the uncorrected case, RMS peaks when the object is farthest from stationary situation. Mean RMS over time: stationary (1.12 mm), with correction (1.20 mm), without correction (1.34 mm).

The static scene trace is influenced solely by image noise in the camera frames. With corrected motion, the error increases by approximately 7% (time-averaged RMS), while in the uncorrected case, the increase in error is over 19%. It is noted that the increase in RMS is mainly due to large artifacts in high-frequency regions of the camera frame. It is seen that our motion correction approach effectively decreases these artifacts, and lowers the RMS alignment error.

The average processing time for the alignment of two camera intensity frames $(300 \times 200\,\text{px})$ was around $5\,\text{ms}$.

7   Conclusion and Discussion

We have proposed a fast alignment strategy to reduce motion artifacts in time-multiplexed structured light. While the method is limited to recovering a global translational shift, this was shown to explain a large amount of the misalignment, and hence reduce artifacts in the resulting surface reconstructions. The used method was used for its robustness and computational efficiency. With its fixed-time performance, the phase correlation technique is suitable for real-time processing, as done in our implementation.

The limitation of this method is that it only accurately explains single object translational movement. With offline-processing, a large variety of video stabilisation techniques can be combined with the 2+1 phase shifting method. These include, but are not limited to subframe correlation methods, feature-based parametric image registration and optical flow based methods.

For many situations in which structured light is used for tracking or object digitisation, our method promises to significantly improve reconstruction results.

References

1. Blais, G., Levine, M.D.: Registering multiview range data to create 3D computer objects. IEEE PAMI **17**(8), 820–824 (1995)
2. Chen, Y., Medioni, G.: Object Modeling by Registration of Multiple Range Images. Image and vision computing (1992)
3. De Castro, E., Morandi, C.: Registration of translated and rotated images using finite fourier transforms. IEEE PAMI **9**(5), 700–703 (1987)
4. Erturk, S.: Digital image stabilization with sub-image phase correlation based global motion estimation. IEEE Transactions on Consumer Electronics **49** (2003)
5. Geng, J.: Structured-light 3D surface imaging: a tutorial. Advances in Optics and Photonics **160**(2), 128–160 (2011)
6. Guan, C., Hassebrook, L., Lau, D.: Composite structured light pattern for three-dimensional video. Optics express **11**(5), 406–417 (2003)
7. Ishii, I., Koike, T., Takaki, T.: Fast 3D shape measurement using structured light projection for a one-directionally moving object. In: IECON 2011, pp. 135–140 (2011)
8. Kuglin, C.D., Hines, D.C.: The phase correlation image alignment method. In: IEEE International Conference on Cybernetics and Society, pp. 163–165 (1975)
9. Lau, D., Liu, K., Hassebrook, L.G.: Real-time three-dimensional shape measurement of moving objects without edge errors by time-synchronized structured illumination. Optics letters **35**(14), 2487–2489 (2010)
10. Liu, Y., Gao, H., Gu, Q., Aoyama, T., Takaki, T., Ishii, I.: A fast 3-d shape measurement method for moving object. In: Int. Conf. Progress in Informatics and Computing (PIC), pp. 219–223 (2014)
11. Lu, L., Xi, J., Yu, Y., Guo, Q.: New approach to improve the accuracy of 3-D shape measurement of moving object using phase shifting profilometry. Optics Express **21**(25), 30610–30622 (2013)

12. Olesen, O.V., Paulsen, R.R., Hjgaard, L., Roed, B., Larsen, R.: Motion tracking for medical imaging: a nonvisible structured light tracking approach. IEEE Transactions on Medical Imaging **31**(1), 79–87 (2012)
13. Posdamer, J.L., Altschuler, M.D.: Surface measurement by space-encoded projected beam systems. Computer Graphics and Image Processing **18**(1), 1–17 (1982)
14. Sakashita, K., Yagi, Y., Sagawa, R., Furukawaa, R., Kawasaki, H.: A system for capturing textured 3D shapes based on one-shot grid pattern with multi-band camera and infrared projector. In: Proc. 3DIMPVT, pp. 49–56 (2011)
15. Wang, Y., Laughner, J.I., Efimov, I.R., Zhang, S.: 3D absolute shape measurement of live rabbit hearts with a superfast two-frequency phase-shifting technique. Optics express **21**(5), 6631–6636 (2013)
16. Wilm, J., Olesen, O.V., Larsen, R.: SLStudio : open-source framework for real-time structured light. In: Proc IPTA 2014, pp. 1–4. IEEE Xplore (2014)
17. Wilm, J., Olesen, O.V., Paulsen, R.R., Højgaard, L., Roed, B., Larsen, R.: Real time surface registration for PET motion tracking. In: Heyden, A., Kahl, F. (eds.) SCIA 2011. LNCS, vol. 6688, pp. 166–175. Springer, Heidelberg (2011)
18. Wilm, J., Olesen, O.V., Larsen, R.: Accurate and Simple Calibration of DLP Projector Systems. SPIE Photonics West 2014, 897–909 (2014)
19. Zhang, S., Yau, S.T.: High-speed three-dimensional shape measurement system using a modified two-plus-one phase-shifting algorithm. Optical Engineering **46**, 1–6 (2007)
20. Zhang, Z.H.: Review of single-shot 3D shape measurement by phase calculation-based fringe projection techniques. Optics and Lasers in Engineering **50**(8), 1097–1106 (2012)

Brain Image Motion Correction: Impact of Incorrect Calibration and Noisy Tracking

Rasmus R. Jensen$^{(\boxtimes)}$, Claus Benjaminsen, Rasmus Larsen,
and Oline V. Olesen

DTU Compute, Technical University of Denmark, Richard Petersens Plads,
Building 321, DK-2800 Kgs. Lyngby, Denmark
{raje,clabe,rlar,ovol}@dtu.dk
http://www.compute.dtu.dk

Abstract. The application of motion tracking is wide, including: industrial production lines, motion interaction in gaming, computer-aided
surgery and motion correction in medical brain imaging. Several devices
for motion tracking exist using a variety of different methodologies. In
order to use such devices a geometric calibration with the coordinate
system in which the motion has to be used is often required. While most
devices report a measuring accuracy and precision, reporting a calibration accuracy is not always straight forward. We set out to do a quantitative measure of the impact of both calibration offset and tracking noise in
medical brain imaging. The data are generated from a phantom mounted
on a rotary stage and have been collected using a Siemens High Resolution Research Tomograph for positron emission tomography. During
acquisition the phantom was tracked with our latest tracking prototype.
The combined data set form a good basis for a quantitative analysis of
calibration accuracy and tracking precision on motion corrected medical
images and scanner resolution.

Keywords: Motion correction · Motion tracking · Calibration · PET ·
Medical imaging

1 Introduction

Motion tracking is used in a wide range of settings. Examples are found in
industrial production lines [4], gaming with user-motion interaction, computer-
aided surgery [6,21] and motion correction in medical brain imaging [1,7,12,
13,17,19]. The tracked motions are often obtained using secondary devices and
multiple solutions exist. These solutions are based on a variety of methodologies
e.g. optical systems [11,21], magnetic spatial measurement systems [6,18,20],
radio-frequency [5,17], videometric systems with one or multiple cameras [1,3,
12,19], accelerometers and gyroscopes [9], and structured light systems [8,13].
The tracking device has to be geometrically calibrated with the unit that uses
the information for motion control or motion compensation. The tracked motion
has to be transformed into the application coordinate system such as that of

© Springer International Publishing Switzerland 2015
R.R. Paulsen and K.S. Pedersen (Eds.): SCIA 2015, LNCS 9127, pp. 152–161, 2015.
DOI: 10.1007/978-3-319-19665-7_13

Fig. 1. Left: The rotating PET phantom with indication of the positions of the rods. Right: The phantom inside the Siemens HRRT scanner with the Tracoline 2.0 pointing at the face of the phantom from the far end of the bore (the dark shadow in the back).

the production line or the medical scanner. In the following the transformation, which brings the tracked motion into the coordinate system of its application will be referred to as the calibration. The required tracking accuracy and precision are often specified, while the accuracy of the calibration is overlooked. This is despite the fact that both tracking and calibration are essential for the performance of the device.

Within the field of medical brain imaging, the coordinate system of the tracking devices are calibrated to the medical scanner matching the image volume to features registered by the tracking devices. Direct point correspondence is possible if the tracking features can be identified in the image volume as for example done within magnetic resonance imaging [22] and positron emission tomography (PET) [2,14]. In these cases the tracking devices register markers that are also identified in the image volumes. Pairing image data and tracking data of the markers and optimizing a point-to-point matching the calibration transformation is obtained. With a markerless tracking device based on surface scanning the calibration can be determined directly by aligning the surface of the subject in the scanner volume [13]. In this work we quantitatively evaluate the impact of the calibration accuracy and tracking precision on image data from a Siemens High Resolution Research Tomograph (HRRT) [10]. The collected PET data are of a phantom with two line sources mounted on a rotary stage for accurate and precise angular movements. The motion of the phantom was recorded with our latest tracking prototype, Tracoline 2.0 [15]. Figure 1 shows the phantom setup in the scanner with our tracking system mounted in the far end of the narrow bore.

2 Method

We want to analyze the impact of inaccurate calibration and changes in precision of the tracking on motion correction applied in medical brain imaging. With an external tracking device motion correction of scanner data is in general given as

$$
\underbrace{\begin{bmatrix} x \\ y \\ z \\ 1 \end{bmatrix}}_{\text{corrected}} = \mathbf{A}_{\text{tcs2dcs}} \cdot \mathbf{A}_{\text{corrector}}^{-1}(t_0) \cdot \mathbf{A}_{\text{corrector}}(t) \cdot \mathbf{A}_{\text{tcs2dcs}}^{-1} \cdot \underbrace{\begin{bmatrix} x \\ y \\ z \\ 1 \end{bmatrix}}_{\text{uncorrected}} \tag{1}
$$

where $\mathbf{A}_{\text{tcs2dcs}}$ is the result of a geometric calibration and a transformation from the tracking coordinate system (tcs) to the device coordinate system (dcs). Only for image based tracking does tcs and dcs coincide. The tracking device provides the correcting transformation $\mathbf{A}_{\text{corrector}}(t)$, which transforms the current position of the subject back to the reference position of the tracking device. To correct to a certain position in time $\mathbf{A}_{\text{corrector}}^{-1}(t_0)$ is added, allowing for correction to a given time t_0. The desired t_0 often differs from the start of the tracking device.

2.1   Calibration Uncertainty Simulation

In order to analyze the effect of incorrect geometric calibration, we introduce an offset in the transformation

$$
\mathbf{A}_\epsilon = \begin{bmatrix} \mathbf{R}_\epsilon & \mathbf{t}_\epsilon \\ \mathbf{0} & 1 \end{bmatrix} \tag{2}
$$

and apply this to the calibration transformation in (1) as follows

$$
\mathbf{A}_{\text{tcs2dcs}}^* = \mathbf{A}_\epsilon \cdot \mathbf{A}_{\text{tcs2dcs}} \tag{3}
$$

where the offset in translation is given by $\mathbf{t}_\epsilon = [\epsilon_x, \epsilon_y, \epsilon_z]^\top$ and offset in angles $[\epsilon_{rx}, \epsilon_{ry}, \epsilon_{rz}]$ are applied to the rotation matrix as

$$
\mathbf{R}_\epsilon = \begin{bmatrix} \cos\epsilon_{rz} & -\sin\epsilon_{rz} & 0 \\ \sin\epsilon_{rz} & \cos\epsilon_{rz} & 0 \\ 0 & 0 & 1 \end{bmatrix}_{rz} \begin{bmatrix} \cos\epsilon_{ry} & 0 & \sin\epsilon_{ry} \\ 0 & 1 & 0 \\ -\sin\epsilon_{ry} & 0 & \cos\epsilon_{ry} \end{bmatrix}_{ry} \begin{bmatrix} 1 & 0 & 0 \\ 0 & \cos\epsilon_{rx} & -\sin\epsilon_{rx} \\ 0 & \sin\epsilon_{rx} & \cos\epsilon_{rx} \end{bmatrix}_{rx} \tag{4}
$$

Since the calibration of a device is generally not an ongoing process, we will look at different fixed values of offset. As translation and rotation are not comparable measures, the analysis is done exclusively with offset in translation or in rotation. Such offset in calibration will result in decreasing accuracy of the applied motion correction. This inaccuracy will increase for larger motions, while no correction is applied in (1) for $\mathbf{A}_{\text{corrector}}(t) = \mathbf{I}$ as everything then factors out. The latter is regardless of calibration.

2.2   Tracking Precision Simulation

In order to evaluate motion correction under the effect of changes in tracking precision we apply noise to the tracking in (1)

$$
\mathbf{A}_{\text{corrector}}(t)^* = \mathbf{T}_{\text{ref}}^{-1} \cdot \mathbf{A}_\epsilon(t) \cdot \mathbf{T}_{\text{ref}} \cdot \mathbf{A}_{\text{corrector}}(t) \tag{5}
$$

We use $\mathbf{A}_\epsilon(t)$ as in (2) but with Gaussian noise, $\epsilon(t) = \mathcal{N}(0, \sigma^2)$. The coordinate system of the tracker can be arbitrarily chosen. Therefore, we apply the noise in a coordinate system, with origin in the mean of the tracking markers. For a markerless system, this is just the mean of the reference surface. The translation matrix $\mathbf{T}_{\text{ref}}$ moves origo to the mean of the reference. This translation can be done regardless of the device and makes the results of the analysis comparable for different devices as the translation will bring origo close to the subject in all cases. As with the analysis of geometric calibration, we analyze the effect of changes in translation and rotation separately.

2.3 Resolution Estimation

As a measure of performance of the motion correction of the data presented in Sec. 3, we use the full width half maximum (FWHM) of the cross section of one rod of the phantom. The rod is aligned with the principal image axes and the FWHM is measured along both axes of slices intersecting the rod. We assume the line profile of the rod cross section can be described as a Gaussian function with standard deviation σ and mean μ. The FWHM is then given as

$$\text{FWHM} = 2\sqrt{2\ln 2}\ \sigma \qquad (6)$$

Errors in geometric calibration and tracking as well as the performed motion will impact the image frames of the rod in all directions. Therefore, the reported FWHM is the average along the length of the rod and also across the two dimensions of image slices intersecting the rod.

3 Data

A unique data set of a motion controlled PET phantom has been obtained [10]. The PET phantom was moved precisely into angular positions, while data were obtained on the Siemens HRRT scanner. The phantom consists of a low attenuation air filled mannequin head in which the positron emitting rods of Ge/Ga-68 with 3.4 MBq are inserted (Fig. 1). The left hand-side in Fig. 1 shows the orientation of the rods, which are neither parallel to each other nor to the principal image axes. The active diameter of the rods is 2.28 mm.

The mannequin head was mounted onto a rotary stage (NR360S/M, Thorlabs) with an accuracy of 0.083^o and a repeatability of 0.003^o. The phantom was programmed to stay in a fixed position for 20 s at 11 angular positions between $\pm 25^o$ in steps of 5°.

During PET acquisition the motion of the phantom was tracked with our latest tracking prototype [15]. This system is markerless and the motion is found by continuously surface scanning the subject and registering each scan to a reference surface. The resulting angular movement of the phantom is shown in Fig. 2. Compared to the 11 different reference angular positions, we found the maximum mean error at a position to be 0.098^o with a standard deviation (SD)

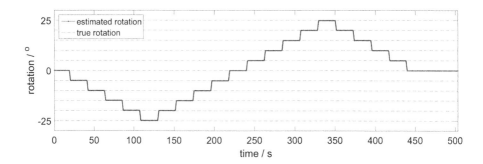

Fig. 2. The rotation of the rotary stage and the resulting tracking from our system. Compared to the programming of the rotary stage the tracking has an angular accuracy of $0.098°$ and a precision of (SD) of $0.031°$. Thorlabs reports $0.083°$ accuracy and a repeatability of (SD) $0.003°$ for the rotary stage (NR360S/M).

of $0.031°$. The accuracy is very close to that of the rotary stage (difference of $0.015°$), while the SD is a factor of 10 higher but still very small. Considering this, the tracking data can be used as a reference and by adding noise for analysis of precision. The PET data has been reconstructed using the multiple acquisition frames (MAF) method [16] with a voxelsize of 1.22 mm. The framing is based on the programmed motion of the stage. This results in 21 frames from the stationary positions (Fig. 2), while the frames with motion have been discarded. As a reference, a data set was also acquired in which the phantom remained motionless. The data sets provide a very good foundation for analysis of the impact of poor calibration and noise in tracking on motion correction. The calibration was done as an alignment between a reference surface scan from the tracking system and a point cloud extracted from a transmission volume.

4   Results and Discussion

The 21 PET frames with stepwise motion were repositioned according to (1) using spline interpolation. The simulated motion of the phantom is highly representative of the clinical situation, where sidewise rotations are typical. Further, the location of the rods is representative for the location of the brain. The diameter of the rod (2.28 mm) is in the order of the scanner resolution ($\sim$2 mm) across the PET field of view. Therefore the resolution of the scanner is comparable to the FWHM measured as in Sec. 2.3. The uncorrected frame with motion is shown in Fig. 3.a, while Fig. 3.d shows the corrected frame with a FWHM of 2.12 mm. The uncorrected reference with no motion is shown in Fig. 3.g and has a FWHM of 2.07 mm, which is only 0.05 mm lower than the corrected frame. This indicates a very accurate motion correction of the ruined uncorrected frame with motion.

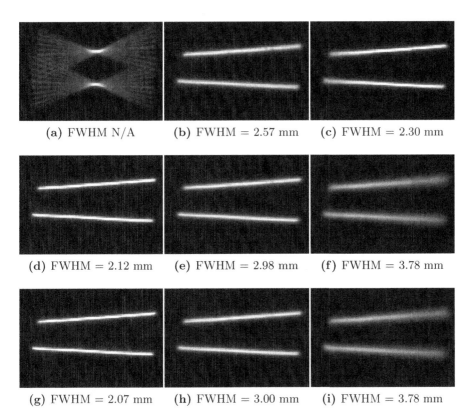

(a) FWHM N/A   (b) FWHM = 2.57 mm   (c) FWHM = 2.30 mm

(d) FWHM = 2.12 mm   (e) FWHM = 2.98 mm   (f) FWHM = 3.78 mm

(g) FWHM = 2.07 mm   (h) FWHM = 3.00 mm   (i) FWHM = 3.78 mm

Fig. 3. PET scans summed along the y-axis (100 mm x 140 mm region). The PET scans are corrected with different offset in the geometric calibration and noise in tracking. Uncorrected motion (a). Calibration offset: -4 mm on y (b) and $4°$ on rx (c). Motion corrected (d). Tracking noise in motion correction: 1 mm SD (e) and $1°$ SD (i). Reference with no motion (g). Reference corrected with Tracking noise: 1 mm SD (h) and $1°$ SD (i)

4.1   Geometric Calibration

The motion correction was done with different offset in calibration as described in Fig. 2.1. Figure 4.a shows the measured FWHM of 3 simulations for offset of ±4 mm in the translations $\epsilon_x, \epsilon_y, \epsilon_z$. The figure shows that even for offset in the range of the voxelsize (1.22 mm) and scanner resolution ($\sim$2 mm) there is a significant impact on the FWHM. The measured FWHM for offset in rotations $\pm4°$ in $\epsilon_{rx}, \epsilon_{ry}, \epsilon_{rz}$ is shown in Fig. 4.b. For offset greater than ±1 mm and $\pm1°$ the FWHM increases rapidly. Associated PET images for offset of 4 mm in y and $-4°$ in rx are shown in Fig. 3.b and 3.c. Within the specified range in offset the FWHM grows from 2.12 to 2.57 mm for translations and 2.4 mm for rotations. The is an increase of up to 21% and considering the resulting PET images, this means that detailed brain structures cannot be distinguished to the same extent

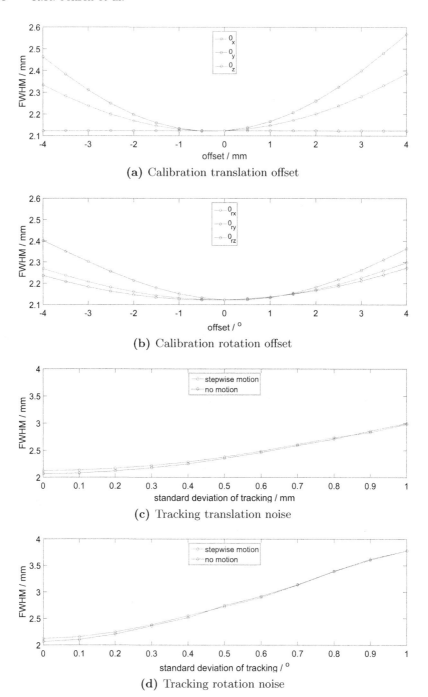

(a) Calibration translation offset

(b) Calibration rotation offset

(c) Tracking translation noise

(d) Tracking rotation noise

Fig. 4. Figures (a) and (b) show the impact of offset in geometric calibration in both translation and rotation. FWHM of the active rods show great increase even for small changes in offset. Figures (c) and (d) show the impact of noise in the tracking.

and small structures such as tumors are delineated significantly larger than they are. Since the rotation of the stage is perpendicular to the z-axis of the scanner, offset on this axis show very little impact (Fig. 4.a). The results are correlated with the performed motion as expected. The overall results show the importance of good geometric calibration between tracking system and scanner.

4.2 Tracking Precision

For the analysis of tracking noise, we again motion correct the 21 PET frames, now adding noise according to Sec. 2.2. For this analysis we have added Gaussian noise to all three translations and to all three rotations separately. Since we only have 21 PET frames, we repeated the motion correction of each frame 100 times for SD of up to 1 mm for translations and 1 (^{o}) rotations. To show the degradation on a frame with no motion, we did the same for a reference scan with no motion.

Figure 4.d and 4.c show a rapidly increasing FWHM as the standard deviation grows. The path of the curves are parabolic as for the calibration simulation, however with increased amplitude especially for the rotation. The impact is similar for both the stepwise motion corrected (red) and the no motion (green). Thus applying motion correction with incorrect tracking to motionless subjects will increase the resolution. The maximal FWHM for the translation simulation is 3.00 mm at 1 mm SD (Fig. 3.e) and 3.78 mm for the rotation simulation at 1 ^{o} SD (Fig. 3.f).

5 Conclusion

The impact of inaccurate tracking and incorrect calibration on motion corrected PET data was investigated. The tracking precision and calibration accuracy were simulated and the resulting effect on the PET images were evaluated quantitatively. The FHWM of the PET phantom was used as an evaluation measure. This provides a measure for changes in scanner resolution.

We found that errors of the calibration had a significant impact of the FWHM even for small rotations and translations offsets in the order of the voxelsize (1.22 mm). The FWHM was increased with up to 21% from 2.12 mm to 2.57 mm for a misalignment of 4 mm.

The impact of the tracking precision was even more important. The FWHM increased with 78% to 3.78 mm when adding noise to the rotation of the tracking with SD of 1°. The simulated errors of the calibration and the tracking are not directly comparable. However, variation in precision of the tracking in the tenths of a millimeter/degree has similar impact on the resolution as calibration errors in the millimeters/degrees range.

The results show a significant improvement on the frame with motion even with offset in calibration and noise in tracking, while the reference is heavily degraded. This indicates that there is a threshold for the benefit of motion correction, which is a relation between the quality of the tracking system and the amount of motion.

References

1. Aksoy, M., Forman, C., Straka, M., Skare, S., Holdsworth, S., Hornegger, J., Bammer, R.: Real-time optical motion correction for diffusion tensor imaging. Magnetic Resonance in Medicine **66**(2), 366–378 (2011)
2. Bühler, P., Just, U., Will, E., Kotzerke, J., van den Hoff, J.: An accurate method for correction of head movement in PET. IEEE Transactions on Medical Imaging **23**, 1176–1185 (2004)
3. Cai, Q., Aggarwal, J.K.: Tracking human motion using multiple cameras. Proceedings of the 13th International Pattern Recognition **3**, 68–72 (1996)
4. Chaumette, F., Rives, P., Espiau, B.: Positioning of a robot with respect to an object, tracking it and estimating its velocity by visual servoing. In: Proceedings of the 1991 IEEE International Conference on Robotics and Automation, 1991, pp. 2248–2253. IEEE (1991)
5. Darrow, R.D., Dumoulin, C.L., Souza, S.P.: Tracking system to monitor the position and orientation of a device using multiplexed magnetic resonance detection, US Patent 5,318,025, June 7, 1994
6. Fried, M.P., Kleefield, J., Gopal, H., Reardon, E., Ho, B.T., Kuhn, F.A.: Image-guided endoscopic surgery: Results of accuracy and performance in a multicenter clinical study using an electromagnetic tracking system. The Laryngoscope **107**(5), 594–601 (1997)
7. Fulton, R., Meikle, S., Eberl, S., Pfeiffer, J., Constable, C., Fulham, M.: Correction for head movements in positron emission tomography using an optical motion-tracking system. IEEE Transactions on Nuclear Science **49**, 116–123 (2002)
8. Geng, Z.: Method and system for three-dimensional imaging using light pattern having multiple sub-patterns US Patent 6,700,669, Mar 2, 2004
9. Horton, M., Newton, A.: Method and apparatus for determining position and orientation of a moveable object using accelerometers. US Patent 5,615,132, Mar 25, 1997
10. Jensen, R.R., Olesen, O.V., Benjaminsen, C., Højgaard, L., Larsen, R.: Markerless PET motion correction: tracking in narrow gantries through optical fibers. In: IEEE Nuclear Science Symposium Conference Record, pp. M10–M24 (2014)
11. Lopresti, B.J., Russo, A., Jones, W.F., Fisher, T., Crouch, D.G., Altenburger, D.E., Townsend, D.W.: Implementation and performance of an optical motion tracking system for high resolution brain PET imaging. IEEE Transactions on Nuclear Science **46**(6), 2059–2067 (1999)
12. Maclaren, J., Armstrong, B.S., Barrows, R.T., Danishad, K., Ernst, T., Foster, C.L., Gumus, K., Herbst, M., Kadashevich, I.Y., Kusik, T.P., et al.: Measurement and correction of microscopic head motion during magnetic resonance imaging of the brain. PLOS one **7**(11), e48088 (2012)
13. Olesen, O.V., Sullvian, J.M., Morris, E.D., Mulnix, T., Paulsen, R.R., Højgaard, L., Roed, B., Larsen, R.: List-mode PET motion correction using markerless head tracking: proof-of-concept in human studies. IEEE Transactions on Medical Imaging **32**, 200–209 (2013)
14. Olesen, O.V., Svarer, C., Sibomana, M., Keller, S., Holm, S., Jensen, J., Andersen, F., Højgaard, L.: A movable phantom design for quantitative evaluation of motion correction studies on high resolution PET scanners. IEEE Transactions on Nuclear Science **57**(3), 1116–1124 (2010)
15. Olesen, O.V., Wilm, J., van der Kouwe, A., Jensen, R.R., Larsen, R., Wald, L.L.: An MRI compatible surface scanner. In: Joint Annual Meeting ISMRM-ESMRMB and SMRT 23rd Annual Meeting Conference Record, p. 1303 (2014)

16. Picard, Y., Thompson, C.J.: Motion correction of PET images using multiple acquisition frames. IEEE Transactions on Medical Imaging **16**(2), 137–144 (1997)
17. Qin, L., van Gelderen, P., Derbyshire, J.A., Jin, F., Lee, J., de Zwart, J.A., Tao, Y., Duyn, J.H.: Prospective head-movement correction for high-resolution mri using an in-bore optical tracking system. Magnetic Resonance in Medicine **62**(4), 924–934 (2009)
18. Raab, F.H., Blood, E.B., Steiner, T.O., Jones, H.R.: Magnetic position and orientation tracking system. IEEE Transactions on Aerospace and Electronic Systems **5**(5), 709–718 (1979)
19. Schulz, J., Siegert, T., Reimer, E., Labadie, C., Maclaren, J., Herbst, M., Zaitsev, M., Turner, R.: An embedded optical tracking system for motion-corrected magnetic resonance imaging at 7T. Magnetic Resonance Materials in Physics, Biology and Medicine **25**(6), 443–453 (2012)
20. Seiler, P., Blattmann, H., Kirsch, S., Muench, R., Schilling, C.: A novel tracking technique for the continuous precise measurement of tumour positions in conformal radiotherapy. Physics in medicine and biology **45**(9), N103 (2000)
21. Watzinger, F., Birkfellner, W., Wanschitz, F., Millesi, W., Schopper, C., Sinko, K., Huber, K., Bergmann, H., Ewers, R.: Positioning of dental implants using computer-aided navigation and an optical tracking system: case report and presentation of a new method. Journal of Cranio-Maxillofacial Surgery **27**(2), 77–81 (1999)
22. Zaitsev, M., Dold, C., Sakas, G., Hennig, J., Speck, O.: Magnetic resonance imaging of freely moving objects: prospective real-time motion correction using an external optical motion tracking system. Neuroimage **31**(3), 1038–1050 (2006)

Pattern Recognition

Heartbeat Signal from Facial Video
for Biometric Recognition

Mohammad A. Haque$^{(\boxtimes)}$, Kamal Nasrollahi, and Thomas B. Moeslund

Visual Analysis of People Laboratory, Aalborg University, Aalborg, Denmark
{mah,kn,tbm}@create.aau.dk

Abstract. Different biometric traits such as face appearance and heartbeat signal from Electrocardiogram (ECG)/Phonocardiogram (PCG) are widely used in the human identity recognition. Recent advances in facial video based measurement of cardio-physiological parameters such as heartbeat rate, respiratory rate, and blood volume pressure provide the possibility of extracting heartbeat signal from facial video instead of using obtrusive ECG or PCG sensors in the body. This paper proposes the Heartbeat Signal from Facial Video (HSFV) as a new biometric trait for human identity recognition, for the first time to the best of our knowledge. Feature extraction from the HSFV is accomplished by employing Radon transform on a waterfall model of the replicated HSFV. The pairwise Minkowski distances are obtained from the Radon image as the features. The authentication is accomplished by a decision tree based supervised approach. The potential of the proposed HSFV biometric for human identification is demonstrated on a public database.

Keywords: Biometric · Identification · Radon transform · Heartbeat · Facial video

1 Introduction

Biometrics provides a way of identifying a person using his/her physiological and/or behavioral features. Among different biometric traits iris image, fingerprint, voice, hand-written signature, facial image, hand geometry, hand vein patterns, and retinal pattern are well-known for human authentication [1]. However, most of these biometric traits exhibit disadvantages in regards to accuracy, spoofing and/or unobtrusiveness. For example, fingerprint and hand-written signature can be forged [2], voice can be altered or imitated, and still picture can be used in absence of the person [3]. Thus, scientific community always searches for new biometric traits. When blood is pumped by the human heart, some electrical and acoustic changes occur in and around the heart in the body, which is known as heartbeat signal [4]. Heartbeat signal can be obtained by Electrocardiogram (ECG) using electrical changes and Phonocardiogram (PCG) using acoustic changes. Both ECG and PCG heartbeat signals have already been utilized for biometrics recognition in the literature. ECG based authentication was first introduced by Biel et al. [5]. They proposed the extraction of a set of temporal and amplitude features using industrial ECG equipment (SIEMENS ECG),

© Springer International Publishing Switzerland 2015
R.R. Paulsen and K.S. Pedersen (Eds.): SCIA 2015, LNCS 9127, pp. 165–174, 2015.
DOI: 10.1007/978-3-319-19665-7_14

reduced the dimensionality of features by analyzing the correlation matrix, and authenticated subjects by a multivariate analysis. This method subsequently drew attention and a number of methods were proposed in this area. For example, Venkatesh et al. proposed ECG based authentication by using appearance based features from the ECG wave [6]. They used Dynamic Time Wrapping (DTW) and Fisher's Linear Discriminant Analysis (FLDA) along with K-Nearest Neighbor (KNN) classifier for the authentication. Chetana et al. employed Radon transformation on the cascaded ECG wave and extracted a feature vector by applying standard Euclidean distance on the transformed Radon image [7]. Similar to [5], geometrical and/or statistical features from ECG wave (collected from ECG QRS complex) were also used in [8]–[10]. Noureddine et al. employed the Discrete Wavelet Transformation (DWT) to extract features from ECG wave and used a Random Forest approach for authentication [11]. A review of the important ECG-based authentication approaches can be obtained from [12]. The common drawback of all of the above ECG based methods is the requirement of using obtrusive (touch-based) ECG sensor.

The PCG based heartbeat biometric (i.e. heart sound biometric) was first introduced by Beritelli et al [13]. They use the z-chirp transformation (CZT) for feature extraction and Euclidian distance matching for identification. Puha et al. [14] proposed another system by analyzing cepstral coefficients in the frequency domain for feature extraction and employing a Gaussian Mixture Model (GMM) for identification. Subsequently, different methods were proposed, such as a wavelet based method in [15] and marginal spectral analysis based method in [16]. A review of the important PCG-based method can be found in [17]. Similar to the ECG-based methods, the common drawback of PCG-based methods for authentication is also the requirement of using obtrusive PCG sensor for the acquisition of ECG signal from a subject.

A recent study showed that circulation of blood through blood-vessels causes periodic change to facial skin color [18]. Takano et al. first utilized this fact in order to generate heartbeat signal from a facial video [19]. A number of other methods also utilized heartbeat signal obtained from facial video for measuring different physiological parameters such as heartbeat rate (HR) [20], respiratory rate and blood pressure [21], and muscle fatigue [20]. This paper introduces Heartbeat Signal from Facial Video (HSFV) for biometric recognition. The proposed system uses a simple webcam for video acquisition, and employs signal processing methods for tracing changes in the color of facial images that are caused by the heart pulses. The proposed biometric does not require any obtrusive sensor. It is universal and permanent, obviously because every living human being has an active heart. It can be more secure than its traditional counterparts as it is difficult to be artificially generated. This paper proposes a method for employing this new biometric for person's identity recognition by employing a set of signal processing methods with a decision tree based classifier. The rest of this paper is organized as follows. Section 2 describes the proposed biometric system and Section 3 presents the experimental results. Section 4 concludes the paper and discusses the possible future directions.

2   The HSFV Based Biometric Identification System

The block diagram of the proposed HSFV biometric for human identification is shown in Fig. 1. The steps are discussed in the following subsections.

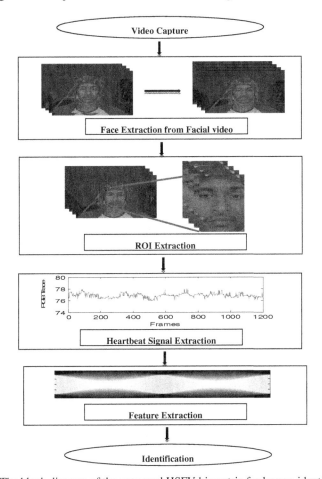

Fig. 1. The block diagram of the proposed HSFV biometric for human identification

2.1   Facial Video Acquisition and Face Detection

The proposed HSFV biometric first requires capturing facial video using a RGB camera, which was thoroughly investigated in the literature [21]–[23]. As recent methods of facial video based heartbeat signal analysis utilized simple webcam for video capturing, we select a webcam based video capturing procedure. After video capturing, the face is detected in each video frame by the face detection algorithm of [22].

2.2   ROI Detection and Heartbeat Signal Extraction

The heartbeat signal is extracted from the facial video by tracing color changes in RGB channels in the consecutive video frames using the method explained in [21]. This is accomplished by obtaining a Region of Interest (ROI) from the face by selecting 60% width of the face area detected by the automatic face detection method. The average of the red, green and blue components of the whole ROI is recorded as the RGB traces of that frame. Statistical mean of these three RGB traces of each frame is calculated and recoded for each frame of the video to obtain the heartbeat signal. The signal looks noisy and imprecise compared to the heartbeat signal obtained by ECG. This is due to the effect of external lighting, voluntary head-motion, and the act of blood as a damper to the heart pumping pressure to be transferred from the middle of the chest (where the heart is located) to the face. Thus, we employ a denoising filter by detecting the peak in the extracted heart signal and discarding the outlying RGB traces. The effect of the denoising operation on a noisy heartbeat signal obtained from RGB traces is depicted in Fig. 2. The signal is then transferred to the next module.

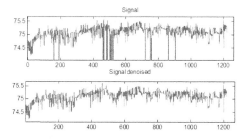

Fig. 2. A heartbeat signal containing outliers (top) and its corresponding signal obtained after employing a denoising filter (bottom)

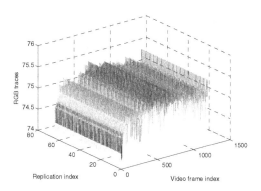

Fig. 3. Waterfall diagram obtained from an extracted heartbeat signal of a given video

2.3   Feature Extraction

We have extracted our features from radon images, as these images are shown in the ECG based system of [7] to produce proper results. To generate such images we need a waterfall diagram which can be generated by replicating the heartbeat signal obtained from a facial video. The number of the replication equals to the number of the frames in the video. Fig. 3 depicts an example of a waterfall diagram obtained from the heartbeat signal of Fig. 2. From the figure, it can be seen that the heartbeat signal is replicated and concatenated in the second dimension of the signal in order to generate the waterfall diagram for a 20 seconds long video captured in a 60 frames per second setting. The diagram acts as an input to a transformation module.

The features used in the proposed system are obtained by applying a method called Radon transform [24] to the generated waterfall diagram. Radon transform is an integral transform computing projections of an image matrix along specified directions and widely used to reconstruct images from medical CT scan. A projection of a two-dimensional image is a set of line integrals. Assume $f(x, y)$ is a two-dimensional image expressing image intensity in the (x, y) coordinates. The Radon transform (R) of the image, $R(\theta)[f(x, y)]$, can be defined as follows:

$$R(\theta)[f(x,y)] = \int_{-\infty}^{\infty} f(\dot{x} \cos\theta - \dot{y} \sin\theta, \dot{x} \sin\theta - \dot{y} \cos\theta)\, d\dot{y} \qquad (1)$$

where θ is the angle formed by the distance vector of a line from the line integral with the relevant axis in the Radon space, and

$$\begin{bmatrix} \dot{x} \\ \dot{y} \end{bmatrix} = \begin{bmatrix} \cos\theta & \sin\theta \\ -\sin\theta & \cos\theta \end{bmatrix} \begin{bmatrix} x \\ y \end{bmatrix} \qquad (2)$$

When we apply Radon transform on the waterfall diagram of HSFV a two-dimensional Radon image is obtained, which contains the Radon coefficients for each angle (θ) given in an experimental setting. An example Radon image obtained by employing Radon transform on the waterfall diagram of Fig. 3 is shown in Fig. 4.

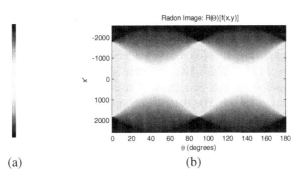

(a)   (b)

Fig. 4. Radon image obtained from the waterfall diagram of HSFV: (a) without magnification, and (b) with magnification

In order to extract features for authentication, we employ a pairwise distance method between every possible pairs of pixels in the transformed image. We use the well-known distance metric of Minkowski to measure the pairwise distance for a $m \times n$-pixels of the Radon image R by:

$$d_{st} = \sqrt[p]{\sum_{i=1}^{n} |R_{si} - R_{ti}|^p} \qquad (3)$$

where R_s and R_t are the row vectors representing each of the $m(1 \times n)$ row vectors of R, and p is a scalar parameter with $p = 2$. The matrix obtained by employing the pairwise distance method produces the feature vector for authentication.

2.4   Identification

We utilize the decision tree based method of [25] for the identification. This is a flowchart-like structure including three types of components: i) Internal node- represents a test on a feature, ii) Branch- represents the outcome of the test, and iii) Leaf node- represents a class label coming as a decision after comparing all the features in the internal nodes. Before using the tree (the testing phase), it needs to be trained. At the training phase, the feature vectors of the training data are utilized to split nodes and setup the decision tree. At the testing phase, the feature vector of a testing data passes through the tests in the nodes and finally gets a group label, where a group stands for a subject to be recognized. The training/testing split of the data is explained in the experimental results.

3   Experimental Results and Discussions

3.1   Experimental Environment

The proposed system has been implemented in MATLAB 2013a. To test the performance of the system we've used the publicly available database of MAHNOB-HCI. This database has been collected by Soleymani et al. [26] and contains facial videos captured by a simple video camera (similar to a webcam) connected to a PC. The database includes data in two categories: 'Emotion Elicitation Experiment (EEE)' and 'Implicit Tagging Experiment (ITE)'. Among these, the video clips from EEE are frontal face video data and suitable for our experiment [20], [27]. Thus, we select the EEE video clips from MAHNOB-HCI database as the captured facial videos for our biometric identification system. Snapshots of some video clips from MAHNOB-HCI database are shown in Fig. 5. The database composes of 3810 facial videos from 30 subjects. However, not all of these videos are suitable for our experiment because of short duration, file missing, and occluded face (forehead) in some videos. Thus, we selected 351 videos suitable for our experiment. These videos are captured from 18 subjects (16-20 videos for each subject). We used the first 20 seconds of each video for testing and 80 percent of the total data for training in a single-fold experiment.

Fig. 5. Snapshots of some facial video clips from MAHNOB-HCI EEE database [26]

3.2   Performance Evaluation

After developing the decision tree from the training data, we generated the authentication results from the testing data. The features of each test subject obtained from the HSFV were compared in the decision tree to find the best match from the training set. The authentication results of 18 subjects (denoted with the prefix 'S-') from the experimental database are shown in a confusion matrix (row matrix) at Table 1. The true positive detections are shown in the first diagonal of the matrix, false positive detections are in the columns, and false negative detections are in the rows. From the results it is observed that a good number of true positive identifications were achieved for most of the subjects.

Table 1. Confusion matrix for identification of 351 samples of 18 subjects using HSFV

Subjects	S1	S2	S3	S4	S5	S6	S7	S8	S9	S10	S11	S12	S13	S14	S15	S16	S17	S18
S1	16	2	0	0	0	1	0	0	0	0	0	0	1	0	0	0	0	0
S2	0	17	0	0	0	1	0	0	0	0	1	0	1	0	0	0	0	0
S3	1	1	16	0	0	0	0	1	0	0	0	0	0	0	1	0	0	0
S4	0	0	0	18	0	0	0	1	0	0	0	0	0	0	1	0	0	0
S5	0	0	0	0	19	0	1	0	0	0	0	0	0	0	0	0	0	0
S6	4	1	0	0	0	15	0	0	0	0	0	0	0	0	0	0	0	0
S7	0	0	0	0	0	0	18	0	0	0	0	0	0	2	0	0	0	0
S8	1	0	0	0	0	0	0	10	0	0	1	0	1	0	2	1	0	0
S9	0	0	0	0	0	0	0	0	20	0	0	0	0	0	0	0	0	0
S10	0	0	0	0	0	0	0	0	0	18	0	1	0	1	0	0	0	0
S11	2	2	0	0	0	1	0	1	0	0	13	0	0	0	0	0	0	0
S12	0	0	0	0	0	0	2	0	0	0	0	16	0	0	0	0	0	0
S13	1	2	0	0	0	0	1	2	0	0	0	0	12	0	2	0	0	0
S14	0	0	0	0	0	0	0	0	0	3	0	0	0	17	0	0	0	0
S15	0	1	2	0	0	0	0	1	0	0	0	0	1	0	15	0	0	0
S16	3	2	0	0	0	0	0	0	0	0	1	0	2	0	1	11	0	0
S17	0	0	0	0	0	0	3	0	0	0	0	0	0	0	0	0	16	0
S18	0	0	0	0	0	0	0	0	0	0	0	0	0	0	0	0	3	16

The performance of the proposed HSFV biometric was evaluated by the parameters defined by Jain et al. in [28], which are False Positive Identification Rate (FPIR) and False Negative Identification Rate (FNIR). The FPIR refers to the probability of a test sample falsely identified as a subject. If TP = True Positive, TN = True Negative, FP = False Positive, and FN = False Negative identifications among N number of trials in an experiment, then the FPIR is defined as:

$$FPIR = \frac{1}{N}\sum_{n=1}^{N}\frac{FP}{TP+TN+FP+FN} \qquad (4)$$

The FNIR is the probability of a test sample falsely identified as different subject:

$$FNIR = \frac{1}{N}\sum_{n=1}^{N}\frac{FN}{TP+TN+FP+FN} \qquad (5)$$

From FNIR we can calculate another metric called True Positive Identification Rate (TPIR) that represents the overall identification performance as:

$$TPIR = 1 - FNIR \qquad (6)$$

Besides the aforementioned metrics, we also calculated the system performance over four other metrics from [29]: precision, recall, sensitivity and accuracy. Precision and recall present the ratio of correctly identified positive samples with total number of identification and total number of positive samples in the experiment, respectively:

$$Precision = \frac{1}{N}\sum_{n=1}^{N}\frac{TP}{TP+FP} \tag{7}$$

$$Recall = \frac{1}{N}\sum_{n=1}^{N}\frac{TP}{TP+FN} \tag{8}$$

Specificity presents the ratio of correctly identified negative samples with total number of negative samples and sensitivity presents the ratio of correctly identified positive and negative samples with total number of positive and negative samples:

$$Specificity = \frac{1}{N}\sum_{n=1}^{N}\frac{TN}{TN+FP} \tag{9}$$

$$Sensitivity = \frac{1}{N}\sum_{n=1}^{N}\frac{TP+TN}{TP+TN+FP+FN} \tag{10}$$

Table 2 summarized the overall system performance in the standard terms mentioned above. From the results it is observed that the proposed HSFV biometric can effectively identify the subjects with a high accuracy.

Table 2. Performance of the proposed HSFV biometric based authentication system

Parameters	Results
FPIR	1.28%
FNIR	1.30%
TPIR	98.70%
Precision rate	80.86%
Recall rate	80.63%
Specificity	98.63%
Sensitivity	97.42%

One significant point can be noted from the results that the TPIR and precision rate have a big difference in values. This is because the true positive and true negative trials and successes are significantly different in numbers and the system achieved high rate of true negative authentication as indicated by specificity and sensitivity metrics. This implies that the proposed biometric, though is of high potential may need improvement in both the feature extraction and the matching score calculation.

To the best of our knowledge, this paper is the first to use HSFV as a biometric, thus, there is not any other similar systems in the literature to compare the proposed system against. Though touch based ECG [12] and PCG [14] biometrics obtained more than 90% accuracy on some local databases, we think their direct comparison against our system is biased towards their favor, as they use obtrusive touch-based sensors, which provide precise measurement of heartbeat signals, while we, using our touch-free sensor (webcam), get only estimations of those heartbeat signals that are obtained by touch based sensors. This means that it makes sense if our touch-free system, at least in this initial step of its development, does not outperform those touch-based systems.

4   Conclusions and Future Directions

This paper proposed heartbeat signal measured from facial video as a new biometric trait for person authentication for the first time. Feature extraction from the HSFV was accomplished by employing Radon transform on a waterfall model of the replicated HSFV. The pairwise Minkowski distances were obtained from the Radon image as the features. The authentication was accomplished by a decision tree based supervised approach. The proposed biometric along with its authentication system demonstrated its potential in biometric recognition. However, a number of issues need to be studied and addressed before utilizing this biometric in practical systems. For example, it is necessary to determine the effective length of a video viable to be captured for authentication in a practical scenario. Fusing face and HSFV together may produce interesting results by handling the face spoofing. Processing time, feature optimization to reduce the difference between precision and acceptance rate, and investigating different metrics for calculating the matching score are also necessary to be investigated. These could be future directions for extending the current work.

References

1. Jain, A.K., Ross, A.: Introduction to biometrics. In: Jain, A.K., Flynn, P., Ross, A.A. (eds.) Handbook of Biometrics, pp. 1–22. Springer, US (2008)
2. Hegde, C., Manu, S., Deepa Shenoy, P., Venugopal, K.R., Patnaik, L.M.: Secure authentication using image processing and visual cryptography for banking applications. In: 16th International Conference on Advanced Computing and Communications. ADCOM 2008, pp. 65–72 (2008)
3. Nixon, K.A., Aimale, V., Rowe, R.K.: Spoof detection schemes. In: Jain, A.K., Flynn, P., Ross, A.A. (eds.) Handbook of Biometrics, pp. 403–423. Springer, US (2008)
4. Phibbs, B.: The Human Heart: A Basic Guide to Heart Disease. Lippincott Williams & Wilkins (2007)
5. Biel, L., Pettersson, O., Philipson, L., Wide, P.: ECG analysis: a new approach in human identification. IEEE Trans. Instrum. Meas. **50**(3), 808–812 (2001)
6. Venkatesh, N., Jayaraman, S.: Human electrocardiogram for biometrics using DTW and FLDA. In: 2010 20th International Conference on Pattern Recognition (ICPR), pp. 3838–3841 (2010)
7. Hegde, C., Prabhu, H.R., Sagar, D.S., Shenoy, P.D., Venugopal, K.R., Patnaik, L.M.: Heartbeat biometrics for human authentication. Signal Image Video Process. **5**(4), 485–493 (2011)
8. Singh, Y.N.: Evaluation of Electrocardiogram for Biometric Authentication. J. Inf. Secur. **03**(01), 39–48 (2012)
9. Tan, W.C., Yeap, H.M., Chee, K.J., Ramli, D.A.: Towards real time implementation of sparse representation classifier (SRC) based heartbeat biometric system. In: Mastorakis, N., Mladenov, V. (eds.) Computational Problems in Engineering. Springer International Publishing, pp. 189–202 (2014)

10. Hegde, C., Prabhu, H., Sagar, D.S., Deepa Shenoy, P., Venugopal, K.R., Patnaik, L.M.: Statistical analysis for human authentication using ECG waves. In: Dua, S., Sahni, S., Goyal, D.P. (eds.) ICISTM 2011. CCIS, vol. 141, pp. 287–298. Springer, Heidelberg (2011)

11. Belgacem, N., Nait-Ali, A., Fournier, R., Bereksi-Reguig, F.: ECG Based Human Authentication Using Wavelets and Random Forests. Int. J. Cryptogr. Inf. Secur. 2(3), 1–11 (2012)

12. Nawal, M., Purohit, G.N.: ECG Based Human Authentication: A Review. Int. J. Emerg. Eng. Res. Technol. 2(3), 178–185 (2014)

13. Beritelli, F., Serrano, S.: Biometric Identification Based on Frequency Analysis of Cardiac Sounds. IEEE Trans. Inf. Forensics Secur. 2(3), 596–604 (2007)

14. Phua, K., Chen, J., Dat, T.H., Shue, L.: Heart sound as a biometric. Pattern Recognit. 41(3), 906–919 (2008)

15. Fatemian, S.Z., Agrafioti, F., Hatzinakos, D.: HeartID: cardiac biometric recognition. In: 2010 Fourth IEEE International Conference on Biometrics: Theory Applications and Systems (BTAS), pp. 1–5 (2010)

16. Zhao, Z., Shen, Q., Ren, F.: Heart Sound Biometric System Based on Marginal Spectrum Analysis. Sensors 13(2), 2530–2551 (2013)

17. Beritelli, F., Spadaccini, A.: Human Identity Verification based on Heart Sounds: Recent Advances and Future Directions. ArXiv11054058 Cs Stat (May 2011)

18. Wu, H.-Y., Rubinstein, M., Shih, E., Guttag, J., Durand, F., Freeman, W.: Eulerian Video Magnification for Revealing Subtle Changes in the World. ACM Trans Graph 31(4), 65: 1–65:8 (2012)

19. Takano, C., Ohta, Y.: Heart rate measurement based on a time-lapse image. Med. Eng. Phys. 29(8), 853–857 (2007)

20. Haque, M.A., Irani, R., Nasrollahi, K., Moeslund, T.B.: Physiological Parameters Measurement from Facial Video. IEEE Trans. Image Process. (September 2014) (Submitted)

21. Poh, M.-Z., McDuff, D.J., Picard, R.W.: Advancements in Noncontact, Multiparameter Physiological Measurements Using a Webcam. IEEE Trans. Biomed. Eng. 58(1), 7–11 (2011)

22. Haque, M.A., Nasrollahi, K., Moeslund, T.B.: Real-time acquisition of high quality face sequences from an active pan-tilt-zoom camera. In: 10th IEEE International Conference on Advanced Video and Signal Based Surveillance (AVSS), pp. 443–448 (2013)

23. Haque, M.A., Nasrollahi, K., Moeslund, T.B.: Constructing facial expression log from video sequences using face quality assessment. In: 9th International Conference on Computer Vision Theory and Applications (VISAPP), pp. 1–8 (2014)

24. Herman, P.G.T.: Basic concepts of reconstruction algorithms. In: Fundamentals of Computerized Tomography, pp. 101–124. Springer, London (2009)

25. Duda, R.O., Hart, P.E., Stork, D.G.: Pattern Classification, 2nd edn. Wiley-Interscience, New York (2000)

26. Soleymani, M., Lichtenauer, J., Pun, T., Pantic, M.: A Multimodal Database for Affect Recognition and Implicit Tagging. IEEE Trans. Affect. Comput. 3(1), 42–55 (2012)

27. Li, X., Chen, J., Zhao, G., Pietikainen, M.: Remote heart rate measurement from face videos under realistic situations. In: IEEE Conference on Computer Vision and Pattern Recognition (CVPR), pp. 4321–4328 (2014)

28. Jain, P.A.K., Ross, D.A.A., Nandakumar, D.K.: Introduction. In: Introduction to Biometrics, pp. 1–49. Springer, US (2011)

29. Olson, D.L., Delen, D.: Performance evaluation for predictive modeling. In: Advanced Data Mining Techniques, pp. 137–147. Springer, Heidelberg (2008)

Consensus Clustering Using kNN Mode Seeking

Jonas Nordhaug Myhre[✉], Karl Øyvind Mikalsen, Sigurd Løkse,
and Robert Jenssen

Machine Learning @ UiT Lab,
UiT - The Arctic University of Norway, Tromsø, Norway
jonas.n.myhre@uit.no
http://site.uit.no/ml

Abstract. In this paper we present a novel clustering approach which combines two modern strategies, namely *consensus clustering*, and *two stage clustering* as represented by the *mean shift spectral clustering* algorithm. We introduce the recent kNN mode seeking algorithm in the consensus clustering framework, and the information theoretic kNN Cauchy Schwarz divergence as foundation for spectral clustering. In combining these frameworks, two well known problematic issues are directly bypassed; the kernel bandwidth choice of the kernel density based mean shift and the computational complexity of the mean shift iterations. We demonstrate experiments on both real and synthetic data as a proof of concept for our contributions.

1 Introduction

Clustering is one of the major areas of research in data analysis and related fields, including image analysis. For comprehensive reviews, see for example the textbooks [21], [7], [3].

One prominent methodology in nonparametric clustering, i.e. assuming no pre-defined parametric statistical models for the clusters to be found, is represented by the mean shift algorithm. Mean shift has experienced success in various applications, e.g. tracking [6], and is for example a component in Microsoft's Kinect® computer vision system [20]. It is an iterative nonparametric clustering approach introduced by Fukunaga and Hostetler [13], and is used for *seeking the modes* of a probability density function represented by a finite set of samples. The mean shift formulation is revisited by Cheng [4], which made its potential uses in clustering and global optimization more noticeable, and the mean shift algorithm furthermore gained popularity with the work of Comaniciu and Meer [5] and Georgescu et al. [14].

Particularly interesting developments in this line of research for the purpose of this paper, are recent attempts by Ozertem et al. [18] and by Agersborg and Jenssen [1] to couple the mean shift algorithm with spectral clustering [15,23]. The idea is to merge together the modes found by mean shift by a spectral clustering algorithm based on a matrix encoding similarities between every pair of modes. Results obtained were promising, however, several challenges were

© Springer International Publishing Switzerland 2015
R.R. Paulsen and K.S. Pedersen (Eds.): SCIA 2015, LNCS 9127, pp. 175–186, 2015.
DOI: 10.1007/978-3-319-19665-7_15

evident in both these methods: It is well-known that the mean shift algorithm is very sensitive to the particular size of the window employed for the underlying kernel density estimation procedure. Moreover, the procedure is slow and kernel density estimation in higher dimensions can be troublesome. In addition, the spectral clustering step also relies on a kernel density window size, which e.g. in Ozertem et al. [18] is chosen to equal the window size utilized in the mean shift.

This paper goes several steps further. First, we move away from kernel density estimation-based mean shift, utilizing instead the faster k-nearest neighbor (kNN) approach to mode seeking introduced very recently by Duin et al. [8]. Second, we lift the dependence on critical hyper parameters in the clustering procedure, by leveraging the full power of *evidence-based clustering*, also called *consensus clustering* [10]. This is achieved by running the mode seeking algorithm over a range of k-values. Each value of k is used to accumulate evidence about the clustering structure. There are many possible options, but in this work we limit the focus to two concrete approaches:

- In the first approach, what we will refer to as a *consensus matrix*, is computed. This entails simply counting for each k whether or not pairs of data points in the data set belong to the same basin of attraction (mode), for then to compute the average over all k. Based on the consensus matrix, a hierarchical clustering approach similar to that used in [9] and [10] is utilized in order to obtain the final clustering result.
- The second approach we investigate, is based on for each k to compute an information theoretic divergence measure between pairs of modes resulting in a similarity matrix between modes, for then to average over all k. Then, a spectral clustering procedure is executed on this matrix, similar to [1].

The proposed clustering method results in a fast mode seeking based clustering algorithm without the need to heuristically select the value of one critical hyper parameter (in our case the k), enabled by the consensus clustering ideas we adopt in this paper. We show that the resulting *consensus clustering using kNN mode seeking algorithm* obtains promising results.

The remainder of this paper is organized as follows: In section 2 we discuss and reveiw relevant background topics such as *clustering by mode seeking, two stage clustering* and *consensus clustering*. In section 3 the algorithms for the two proposed clusterings schemes are explained and specified. The algorithms are tested and compared on different data sets in section 4. concluded with a short conclusion and suggested improvements to be done in further work (see section 5).

2   Relevant Background Topics

2.1   Clustering by Mode Seeking

Mode seeking algorithms cluster data by assigning each data point to its closest local mode. It works by projecting each data point to the closest local mode of the kernel density estimate (KDE) using a gradient ascent approach. Using the standard KDE, $f(x) = \frac{1}{N}\sum_i k_h(\mathbf{x}, \mathbf{x}_i)$, the mean shift iterations for projecting a single $\mathbf{x}$ to its local mode is given as follows [5]:

$$\mathbf{x} \leftarrow \frac{\sum_{i=1}^{N} \mathbf{x}_i k_h(\mathbf{x}_i, \mathbf{x})}{\sum_{i=1}^{N} k_h(\mathbf{x}_i, \mathbf{x})} \qquad (1)$$

Looking beyond the available input points, any point within the basin of attraction of a local KDE mode will be in the cluster of that mode.

The kNN mode seeking algorithm, [8], represents a new generation of mode seeking algorithms, whereby the kernel density estimate is replaced by a kNN density estimate showing positive results, both in speed and accuracy. Also, notably different from mean shift, is the fact that projections are only done through the given input points, thus dramatically reducing computational complexity.

Given a kNN-density, where the density at a point $\mathbf{x}$ is simply inversely proportional to the distance to the k-th nearest neighbor, the algorithm can be stated as follows:

1. For each input point $\mathbf{x}_i$:
   – Define a pointer to the point within the k nearest neighbors with the highest kNN-density.
   – Repeat the process by following pointers from the initial pointer until a pointer that points to itself is found. This will be the local mode of $\mathbf{x}_i$.
2. Assign each $\mathbf{x}$ that converged to the same point to the same cluster.

This method is significantly faster and has comparable accuracy, despite only using input points for projections, compared to regular mean shift [8]. In addition, as opposed to k-means, [21], the method still retains the local properties of mean shift making it able to detect slightly non-linear cluster structures.

2.2   Two Stage Clustering

In [18], Ozertem et al. introduced a two step clustering scheme by first partitioning the input space into subsets using mean shift clustering, for then to utilize a variant of spectral clustering to do the final clustering. In the second stage of this process each data point is represented by its local mode as found by mean shift clustering, and the affinity matrix in the second step consists of (dis)similarities between the modes as opposed to the individual data points. From a computational perspective this significantly reduces the complexity as the spectral decomposition is reduced from $O(N^2)$ to $O(M^2)$, where N is the number of data points and M is the number of modes. In the original paper a heuristic approach was used as the final step [18]. Agersborg and Jenssen expanded the concepts and used true spectral clustering and proposed to use different choices of parameters in each step [1].

In addition to the computational advantages of two stage clustering is the fact that strongly nonlinear structures cannot in general be captured by a unimodal density. Thus, a single run of standard mean shift using a kernel density estimate cannot capture nonlinearities that goes beyond a slight bending or stretching of the local structure. A two stage clustering strategy could alleviate this by first decomposing nonlinear structure into subsections of the data represented by local modes, and then in the final stage merge the appropriate modes to obtain a global clustering.

2.3   Consensus Clustering

Consensus clustering is a relatively new methodology which has emerged over the last decade or so. One of the main motivations for introducing consensus clustering, is to acknowledge that there is no single clustering algorithm which will be appropriate for every dataset and different algorithms might produce different partitions for the same data set. This might make the interpretation of the clustering results a challenge. The idea of consensus clustering is to combine the results of several clustering trials to obtain a better partition than each individual trial. This is often done by constructing a similarity matrix, which we have called the *consensus matrix*, but is also referred to as the *co-association-* or *ensemble matrix* in the literature.

There are several proposed algorithms to combine clustering results. Fred and Jain [9–12] suggest to use the k-means clustering algorithm several times with random initial conditions. In each of the clustering trials, the number of clusters, k, is either fixed or chosen randomly in the range $k \in [k_{\min}, k_{\max}]$. The resulting partitions are then created in a voting process. A consensus matrix, $S = \{s_{ij}\}_{N \times N}$, is constructed by counting the number of times the points $\mathbf{x}_i$ and $\mathbf{x}_j$ are assigned to the same cluster in the M different partitions. Each time these data points are clustered together, it counts as one *vote*. This voting process is referred to as *evidence accumulation* [12]. The elements of S are then calculated by

$$s_{ij} = \frac{n_{ij}}{M}, \tag{2}$$

where n_{ij} is the number of times $\mathbf{x}_i$ and $\mathbf{x}_j$ has been assigned to the same cluster.

In the ideal case, we should have

$$s_{ij} = \begin{cases} 1 & \text{if } \mathbf{x}_i \text{ and } \mathbf{x}_j \text{ belong to the same cluster,} \\ 0 & \text{otherwise.} \end{cases} \tag{3}$$

This happens when $\mathbf{x}_i$ and $\mathbf{x}_j$ are clustered together in all of the k-means trials. We see that if the data points are ordered according to their final cluster assignment, the consensus matrix will be block diagonal.

The consensus matrix can be considered a similarity matrix. If two data points are clustered together in many of the different clustering solutions, they are considered more similar than two data points that are not clustered together as often. This similarity matrix can then be used to obtain a final partitioning/clustering.

3   The Proposed Clustering Scheme

In this section we present the new clustering scheme proposed in the Introduction. The approaches suggested both use the kNN mode seeking algorithm to build a consensus matrix over a range of k values, but the pairwise affinities in the matrix, as well as the last stage clustering schemes, will be different. This results in two algorithms which we will describe separately in the following subsections.

3.1   kNN Single Link (kNN-SL) Algorithm

In this algorithm, we build a consensus matrix by running the kNN mode seeking algorithm for a range of k values. In [10] Fred and Jain proposed to use several random initializations of the k-means algorithm to build a consensus matrix. The framework was later expanded to also vary the number of clusters in the k-means algorithm [12]. As opposed to k-means, there is no need for initialization in kNN mode seeking. Running the algorithm several times, in addition to adding computational complexity, does not present any variations and thus no benefits. For each iteration and for each pair of data points, $\mathbf{x}_i$ and $\mathbf{x}_j$, that are clustered together, the consensus matrix, S, is updated according to

$$S(i, j) = S(i, j) + \frac{1}{M}, \tag{4}$$

where M is the total number of clusterings.

In [10] a technique similar to single link clustering was introduced to detect consistent clusters within the consensus matrix. The idea is that for each pair of data points, their corresponding clusters are merged if $S(i, j) > t$, where t is a user-defined threshold. From now on we will refer to this as single link. In practice, this threshold has to be varied to obtain good results in different cases with different cluster structures. For simplicity we set the threshold manually in this work, assuming the number of clusters are known. A slightly modified version was introduced in [11] and [12]; instead of the threshold t, the dendrogram was used to find the clusters with the longest lifetime. We experienced that using these two alternatives sometimes resulted in one large cluster and one or more very small clusters[1]. To avoid this problem we propose to use a modified single link on the consensus matrix: For each pair (i, j) that does not belong to the same cluster and s.t. $S(i, j) > t$, we merge the clusters they belong to. After having performed this clustering we iterate through the data set once more and force small clusters (if present in the clustering results) to merge into a larger cluster. We do this for each data point, $\mathbf{x}_i$, that belongs to a cluster that is smaller than some threshold, e.g. $N/10$ datapoints, finding

$$j = \underset{l}{\operatorname{argmax}} \left\{ S(i, l) \right\}, \tag{5}$$

and merge the two clusters.

---

[1] By very small clusters we mean clusters that only contain a single or a few data points.

3.2   kNN Cauchy Schwarz (kNN-CS) Algorithm

In this algorithm the votes in the consensus matrix S, are replaced by kNN Cauchy Schwarz (CS) divergences [22]. The general CS divergence is an information theoretic similarity measure between two densities, [19]. In this work we use the *symmetric Cauchy Schwarz* measure which lets us use kNN density estimates in the measure. This was first introduced in [22]:

$$d_{CS}(p_1, p_2) = \frac{\frac{1}{2}\left(\int p_1(\mathbf{x})p_2(\mathbf{x})\mathrm{d}\mathbf{x}\int p_2(\mathbf{x})p_1(\mathbf{x})\mathrm{d}\mathbf{x}\right)}{\sqrt{\int p_1^2(\mathbf{x})\mathrm{d}\mathbf{x}\int p_2^2(\mathbf{x})\mathrm{d}\mathbf{x}}}. \tag{6}$$

The quantities $\int p_i(\mathbf{x})p_j(\mathbf{x})\mathrm{d}\mathbf{x}$ and $\int p_i^2(\mathbf{x})\mathrm{d}\mathbf{x}$ are calculated using kNN density estimates. The symmetry was introduced to avoid the effects of differences in expected values when using kNN densities, see [22] for further details and analysis. We calculate the Cauchy Schwarz divergences between each of the modes found by the kNN mode seeking algorithm. The CS divergence between each point is then represented as the CS divergence between the modes they belong to. The consensus matrix is built by, for each k, adding the pairwise divergences and finally averaging over all k. After building S, we do a spectral decomposition of the matrix, $S = E\Lambda E^T$ and, similar to [17], perform k-means clustering in the feature space represented by the eigenvectors in order to obtain the final clustering.

We note that this algorithm has in effect two parameters that need to be set, i.e. the number of clusters in the k-means algorithm and the number of eigenvectors to use in the spectral decomposition of the consensus matrix. In this work we assume for simplicity that we know the number of clusters and that, by convention, the same number of eigenvectors as clusters is a reasonable choice [23]. The choice of neighborhood size k is avoided in using the consensus strategy, thus only leaving an upper and lower bound to be set.

To summarize this section we include pseudocode for the two algorithms in Figure 1.

4   Experiments

In this section we present results illustrating the benefits and potential of the proposed methods. We have used both toy data and real datasets.

The first data set is a toy data set created to illustrate that the algorithms can handle nonlinear structure and clusters of different shape and geometry. The second data set is a subset of the 10K subset of the MNIST image data set and is used to illustrate that the algorithm can handle high dimensional data. The third experiment we include is the widely used Frey faces, to illustrate the potential of the algorithms in a completely unsupervised setting. We also include a small set of UCI benchmark datasets. In all experiments an initial range of k values where set to $k \in \{5, 6, \dots, 20\}$, and then manually tuned to obtain the best results.

If nothing is stated we assume that the number of clusters is known.

kNN-SL algorithm:

- **Input**: Data set X, range of k-values K and threshold t.
- Initialize S as $\mathbf{0}_{N \times N}$
- **Step 1**: For each $k \in K$:
  - Use kNN mode seeking to obtain a clustering of X.
  - For each pair of data points, (i,j), update S by $S(i,j) = S(i,j) + \frac{1}{|K|}$ if $\mathbf{x}_i$ and $\mathbf{x}_j$ belong to the same cluster.
- **Step 2**: Initially let each $\mathbf{x}_i$ be one individual cluster.
  - For each pair (i,j) that does not belong to the same cluster and s.t. $S(i,j) > t$, merge the clusters they belong to.
  - If datapoint $\mathbf{x}_i$ belongs to a "small" cluster, find $j = \underset{l}{\operatorname{argmax}}\{S(i,l)\}$ and merge the clusters that $\mathbf{x}_i$ and $\mathbf{x}_j$ belong to.

kNN-CS algorithm:

- **Input:** X, K and number of clusters K_c.
- Initialize S as $\mathbf{0}_{N \times N}$
- **Step 1**: For each $k \in K$:
  - Use kNN mode seeking to obtain a clustering of X.
  - For each pair of modes, (c_r, c_s), calculate the CS divergences $d_{rs} = d_{CS}(c_r, c_s)$ from (6).
  - For each pair of data points, (i,j), update S by adding the CS divergence between the two modes, $c_{i'}$ and $c_{j'}$, that represent the two data points; $S(i,j) = S(i,j) + \frac{d_{i'j'}}{|K|}$.
- **Step 2**: Calculate the eigendecomposition of S and perform k-means with input value K_c on the top K_c eigenvectors.

Fig. 1. The proposed algorithms

4.1 Toy Data: Two Moons and a Gaussian Blob

The first dataset is a two dimensional toy data set consisting of two moon shaped clusters with 400 data points in each and a spherical Gaussian cluster consisting of 200 data points. This is a clear example of a nonlinear dataset where standard methods like e.g. k-means perform poorly. Figure 2 shows 4 different clusterings of this dataset: k-means; a single run of the kNN mode seeking algorithm; and the two algorithms presented in this paper. We see that both k-means and the single run of the kNN mode seeking do not find the correct cluster structure. The kNN-SL gives a clustering that has no errors, whereas the kNN-CS gives a clustering with only a few errors in the moon shaped clusters.

4.2 MNIST Images

We chose a subset of the 10K MNIST image dataset, [16], containing the digits 3, 6 and 9. We used the vectorized images as features and used no feature selection methods, giving a 784×3024 input matrix for the clustering algorithm.

The clustering error percentages are presented in Table 1. We see that the two proposed algorithms give promising results; the error is 4.10% for both kNN-SL and kNN-CS, which is a notable improvement compared to a single run of

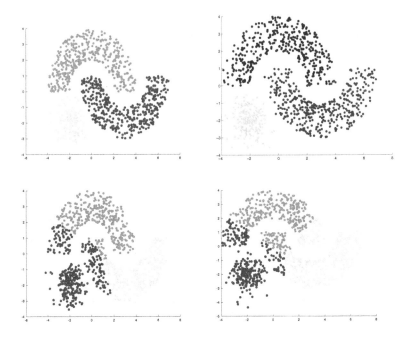

Fig. 2. Clustering of the two moon and Gaussian blob dataset. Upper left: kNN-SL. Upper right: kNN-CS. Lower left: Single run of mode seeking. Lower right: k-means.

the kNN mode seeking algorithm. We compare to the k-means algorithm which is considerably slower and has linear cluster boundaries, and a single run of the kNN mode seeking algorithm. As an example the kNN-SL algorithm took 0.4 seconds on the MNIST example, while a test run of the consensus framework with random initializations of k-means took 42 seconds.

Table 1. Clustering results for the MNIST images. Error in percentages.

Dataset	# features	# dim.	k	k-means (av.)	kNN mode seeking	kNN-SL	kNN-CS
MNIST	3024	784	3	5.79	9.39	4.10	4.10

We see a clear improvement over k-means, and note that the consensus stage is clearly relevant as the single run of kNN mode seeking gives poor results.

One of the benefits of using the kNN-CS method is that results can be visualized by plotting the eigenvectors of the Cauchy-Schwarz matrix. In Figure 3, a), we see the spectral decomposition consisting of the top three eigenvectors of the kNN CS matrix. The color coding corresponds to the results after running k-means on the eigenvectors. In b) we see the true labels. It is evident that the class structure is well represented by the eigenvectors. c) and d) shows the top three eigenvectors of the kNN CS matrix for two individual runs of the kNN mode seeking algorithm with color coding representing the true labels. The class structure is evident in both cases, but the separability is not as strong as in the consensus case where the structures are much more compact and distanced from each other.

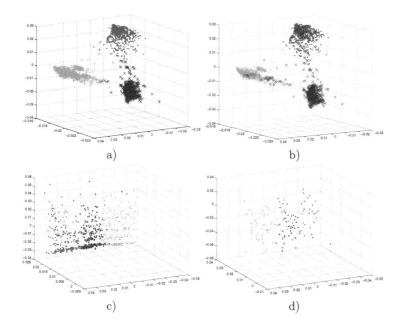

Fig. 3. a): Results from k-means on top three Cauchy-Schwarz concensus eigenvectors. b): True labels of MNIST data. c): Top three eigenvectors of CS matrix of a single run of kNN mode seeking with $k = 2$. d): Same as left, but $k = 5$.

Looking at the true labels we see that there is some overlap that an algorithm like k-means in the eigenvector feature space cannot capture. This is due to the fact that some of the images are overlapping in the input space, and our choice of not using any feature extractions.

4.3   Frey Faces

We tested both algorithms on the Frey faces with an arbitrary set of parameters to illustrate the algorithms in a setting where nothing is known in advance. Due to space limitations we only show the kNN-SL algorithm which, with the given parameters, gave a very clear partitioning of the face images. In Figure 4, 24 randomly selected images from each cluster found by the kNN-SL algorithm is shown in the top row. In the bottom row we show a k-means clustering with

Fig. 4. First row: 4 clusters obtained using the kNN-SL algorithm. Second row: a clustering obtained using k-means.

the same number of clusters as found by the kNN-SL algorithm. All in all, the kNN SL algorithm seems to give much more visually intuitive results, whilst the results of k-means does not give as much sense and is harder to interpret visually.

4.4   UCI Datasets

To conclude the experiments, we tested our algorithms on three datasets from the UCI repository [2]; Iris, Wine and Wisconsin breast cancer data. The performance of the different methods is presented in Table 2. We note that the results of our algorithms are combarable to that of k-means, indicating that the datasets are linearly separable, leaving the improvements by nonlinear considerations less notable. We also see that a single run of the kNN mode seeking algorithm does not give good results, indicating that the consensus stage is of clear benefit.

Table 2. Clustering results on a selection of UCI datasets. Error in percentages.

Dataset	# features	# dim.	k	k-means (av.)	kNN mode seek	kNN-SL	kNN-CS
Cancer	699	10	2	4.29	30.04	5.01	5.01
Iris	150	4	3	10.7	33.3	10.0	9.3
Wine	178	13	3	3.37	12.92	8.99	8.99

5   Conclusion

In this paper we have presented two new clustering algorithms that shows good potential in both strongly nonlinear and high dimensional data. We have investigated the kNN mode seeking algorithm in the consensus clustering framework.

In introducing the consensus clustering principles to the two-stage clustering scheme we see that critical parameter choices can be rendered unnecessary and greater robustness to scale and setting can in principle be achieved. To conclude this work we include a few critical points and possible directions of future research.

5.1 Future Work

- In principle any clustering algorithm can be used in the first stage, and algorithms such as quick-shift should be tested.
- The kNN mode seeking results in fewer number of clusters as the neighborhood parameter k increases, which if set too high will give large clusters that are not intuitive in the input space. So a theoretical threshold for the upper bound of k should be investigated.
- The kNN mode seeking algorithm is able to handle much larger data set sizes than traditional mean shift, so the algorithms should be investigated in a larger scale setting than this work.
- The individual steps in the kNN-CS algorithm leads to matrices of different size. In this work we simply expanded the matrix with all points in the same cluster having the same value compared to another cluster. A less memory intensive strategy should be investigated in addition to looking into eigenvector summation instead of matrix summation.
- The threshold parameter in the kNN-SL algorithm is not straight-forward to choose and needs to be investigated further.
- The speedup factor of the kNN mode seeking algorithm compared to regular mean shift and also k-means, which has been used extensively in consensus clustering, is considerable and should be investigated and presented further.

References

1. Agersborg, J., Jenssen, R.: Mean shift spectral clustering using kernel entropy component analysis. In: Proceedings of IEEE Workshop on Machine Learning for Signal Processing, Reims, France, September 21-24, 2014
2. Bache, K., Lichman, M.: UCI machine learning repository (2013). http://archive.ics.uci.edu/ml
3. Bishop, C.M.: Pattern Recognition and Machine Learning. Springer (2006)
4. Cheng, Y.: Mean shift, mode seeking, and clustering. IEEE Transactions on Pattern Analysis and Machine Intelligence 17(8), 790–799 (1995)
5. Comaniciu, D., Meer, P.: Mean shift: A robust approach toward feature space analysis. IEEE Transactions on Pattern Analysis and Machine Intelligence 24(5), 603–619 (2002)
6. Comaniciu, D., Ramesh, V., Meer, P.: Kernel-based object tracking. IEEE Transactions on Pattern Analysis and Machine Intelligence 25(5), 564–577 (2003)
7. Duda, R.O., Hart, P.E., Stork, D.G.: Pattern Classification, 2nd edn. John Wiley & Sons, New York (2001)

8. Duin, R.P.W., Fred, A.L.N., Loog, M., Pękalska, E.: Mode seeking clustering by knn and mean shift evaluated. In: Gimel'farb, G., Hancock, E., Imiya, A., Kuijper, A., Kudo, M., Omachi, S., Windeatt, T., Yamada, K. (eds.) SSPR & SPR 2012. LNCS, vol. 7626, pp. 51–59. Springer, Heidelberg (2012)
9. Fred, A.: Finding consistent clusters in data partitions. In: Kittler, J., Roli, F. (eds.) MCS 2001. LNCS, vol. 2096, pp. 309–318. Springer, Heidelberg (2001)
10. Fred, A.L.N., Jain, A.K.: Data clustering using evidence accumulation. In: Proceedings of the 16th International Conference on Pattern Recognition, vol. 4, pp. 276–280. IEEE (2002)
11. Fred, A., Jain, A.K.: Evidence accumulation clustering based on the k-means algorithm. In: Caelli, T., Amin, A., Duin, R.P.W., de Ridder, D., Kamel, M. (eds.) SSPR&SPR 2002. LNCS, vol. 2396, pp. 442–451. Springer, Heidelberg (2002)
12. Fred, A.L.N., Jain, A.K.: Combining multiple clusterings using evidence accumulation. IEEE Transactions on Pattern Analysis and Machine Intelligence 27(6), 835–850 (2005)
13. Fukunaga, K., Hostetler, L.: The estimation of the gradient of a density function, with applications in pattern recognition. IEEE Trans. Inf. Theor. 21(1), 32–40 (2006)
14. Georgescu, B., Shimshoni, I., Meer, P.: Mean shift based clustering in high dimensions: a texture classification example. In: Proceedings of the Ninth IEEE International Conference on Computer Vision, pp. 456–463. IEEE (2003)
15. Jenssen, R.: Kernel Entropy Component Analysis. IEEE Transactions on Pattern Analysis and Machine Intelligence 33(5), 847–860 (2010)
16. LeCun, Y., Bottou, L., Bengio, Y., Haffner, P.: Gradient-based learning applied to document recognition. Proceedings of the IEEE 86(11), 2278–2324 (1998)
17. Ng, A.Y., Jordan, M.I., Weiss, Y., et al.: On spectral clustering: Analysis and an algorithm. Advances in Neural Information Processing Systems 2, 849–856 (2002)
18. Ozertem, U., Erdogmus, D., Jenssen, R.: Mean shift spectral clustering. Pattern Recognition 41(6), 1924–1938 (2008)
19. Principe, J.C., Xu, D., Fisher, J.: Information theoretic learning. Unsupervised Adaptive Filtering 1, 265–319 (2000)
20. Shotton, J., Sharp, T., Kipman, A., Fitzgibbon, A., Finocchio, M., Blake, A., Cook, M., Moore, R.: Real-Time Human Pose Recognition in Parts from Single Depth Images. Communications of the ACM 56(1), 116–124 (2013)
21. Theodoridis, S., Koutroumbas, K.: Pattern Recognition, 4th edn. Academic Press, San Diego (2009)
22. Vikjord, V.V., Jenssen, R.: Information theoretic clustering using a k-nearest neighbors approach. Pattern Recognition 47(9), 3070–3081 (2014)
23. von Luxburg, U.: A Tutorial on Spectral Clustering. Statistics and Computing 17(4), 395–416 (2007)

Discriminating Yogurt Microstructure Using Diffuse Reflectance Images

Jacob Skytte[1]([✉]), Flemming Møller[2], Otto Abildgaard[1], Anders Dahl[1], and Rasmus Larsen[1]

[1] DTU Compute, Department of Applied Mathematics and
Computer Science, Technical University of Denmark,
Matematiktorvet B322, 2800 Kgs. Lyngby, Denmark
jlsk@dtu.dk
[2] DuPont Nutrition Biosciences ApS, Edwin Rahrs Vej 38,
8220 Aarhus, Denmark

Abstract. The protein microstructure of many dairy products is of great importance for the consumers' experience when eating the product. However, studies concerning discrimination between protein microstructures are limited. This paper presents preliminary results for discriminating different yogurt microstructures using hyperspectral (500-900nm) diffuse reflectance images (DRIs) – a technique potentially well suited for inline process control. Comparisons are made to quantified measures of the yogurt microstructure observed through confocal scanning laser microscopy (CSLM). The output signal from both modalities is evaluated on a 2^4 factorial design covering four common production parameters, which significantly change the chemistry and the microstructure of the yogurt. It is found that the DRIs can be as discriminative as the CSLM images in certain cases, however the performance is highly governed by the chemistry of the sample. Also, the DRIs shows better correlation to the CSLM images and are more discriminative when considering shorter wavelengths.

Keywords: Confocal scanning laser microscopy · Optical technique · Hyperspectral · Protein microstructure

1 Introduction

The quality perception and physical properties of fermented milk products are defined by the microstructure, formed through destabilisation and aggregation of the protein structures, during the milk fermentation process [1,2]. Confocal scanning laser microscopy (CSLM) is a popular microscopic technique for investigating the protein microstructure. This can be attributed the relatively easy sample preparation, which amounts to a fluorescent staining that is able to target the protein network directly, and produce highly detailed images of the protein microstucture [3].

However, while being practical, CSLM still requires sample extraction and preparation, which is not suitable for in-line process control during e.g. dairy

R.R. Paulsen and K.S. Pedersen (Eds.): SCIA 2015, LNCS 9127, pp. 187–198, 2015.
DOI: 10.1007/978-3-319-19665-7_16

production. In this regard, other optical techniques, which are non-invasive and non-contact, should be considered. Previously, transmittance and diffuse reflectance measurements have been used in great extent to monitor entire milk fermentations in relation to cheese making. Here, the initial structure formation is followed in order to predict the optimal cutting time, which results in a maximum cheese yield [4–6]. However, best to our knowledge little has been published in relation to discrimination of different protein microstructures. If possible, this potentially enables for detection of microstructural defects in dairy production, which can be beneficial for troubleshooting in the production line, and in general ensure a consistent product of high quality.

Thus, in the present work we seek to investigate the potential and limitations of using hyperspectral diffuse reflectance images (DRIs) for discriminating different yogurt microstructures. The DRIs are captured remotely, and are thereby non-contact, and requires no sample preparation – properties which are highly desirable when considering in-line applications. Previously, we have applied DRIs in relation to entire milk fermentations [7], and seen signals similar to those of transmittance and other diffuse reflectance techniques [5]. The discriminative properties of the DRIs in regard to microstructure, will be evaluated and discussed alongside CSLM images, quantified through image texture analysis. Both modalities are applied to a data set containing 16 unique yogurts created with different chemistry and microstructure, and has previously been used in [8]. Method evaluation is carried out by the means of classification and we furthermore attempts to correlate the signal output of the two modalities.

2   Materials and Methods

In this section, the experimental design is initially introduced, and hereafter the hyperspectral DRI technique is presented alongside the *decay parameter*, which is quantification of the DRIs into a single numerical value. Finally, a multidimensional CSLM image descriptor is briefly introduced alongside an approach to map this descriptor into a one-dimensional space, where it can be compared directly to the decay parameter.

2.1   Sample Design and Production

The samples were produced in a 2^4 factorial design spanning the four factors: *fat content, protein content, heat treatment temperature, and incubation temperature*. These factors are common process parameters that can be varied in yogurt production. The fat and protein content naturally affect the chemical composition of the yogurt, while the two latter factors define the amount of protein cross-linking that will be formed during the protein aggregation [3,9]. All factors were expected to affect the final microstructure. However, the heat-treatment and incubation temperature were only expected to result in subtle differences, as these factors only affect the amount of protein cross-linking.

The yogurt samples were produced by initially adjusting the fat- and protein content, and hereafter the milk was heat treated for 15 min at the target factor temperature level. After heat treatment, the milk was rapidly cooled in a cold-water bath. Finally, the milk was heated to the target incubation temperature, lactic acid bacteria were added to the milk, and the fermentation was initialised. The fermentation was continued until a pH of 4.6 was reached. Hereafter, the milk (now yogurt) was stirred and stored in a refrigerator for a week prior to measurements by DRI and CSLM. Three replicates of the experiment were performed on three consecutive days, resulting in a total of $3 \cdot 16 = 48$ yogurts. For each yogurt sample three DRI measurements were taken alongside 10 CSLM images.

The experimental design is summarised in Table 1, and Fig. 1 shows example CSLM images of the different microstructures for one of the replicates. For specific details on the experiment, and the data collection in relation to CSLM, please refer to [8].

Table 1. The 2^4 experimental design. Minus and plus denote low and high factor levels respectively. The actual factor level values are given in the left most column. The entire design is replicated across three days. The subsets, indicated in the first row, will be used during the method evaluation in Section 3.

	Subset 1				Subset 2				Subset 3				Subset 4			
	1	2	3	4	5	6	7	8	9	10	11	12	13	14	15	16
Fat content [1.5/3.5 g/100g]	-	-	-	-	-	-	-	-	+	+	+	+	+	+	+	+
Protein content [3.4/4.4 g/100g]	-	-	-	-	+	+	+	+	-	-	-	-	+	+	+	+
Heat treatment [75/90 °C/15min]	-	-	+	+	-	-	+	+	-	-	+	+	-	-	+	+
Incubation temp. [39/43 °C]	-	+	-	+	-	+	-	+	-	+	-	+	-	+	-	+

2.2 Diffuse Reflectance Imaging

We have recently introduced a hyperspectral DRI system [7, 10]. The system consists of a hyperspectral light delivery system made from a super continuum light source (*SuperK Extreme EXW-12, NKT Photonics, Birkerød, Denmark*) and an acousto-optic tuneable filter (*SuperK SELECT, NKT Photonics, Birkerød, Denmark*). The light delivery system produces a light beam (500-900 nm), which is focused on the sample surface, through a lens (focal length = 40 mm), at an oblique angle ($\approx 45°$). The spatial distribution of the resulting diffuse reflectance is captured using a CCD (*Grasshopper CCD, Point Grey Research, Richmond, Canada*). In front of the CCD a 6.5 cm spacer and an objective lens were installed (*23FM50L, Tamron Co. Ltd., Nagoya, Japan*), which produces an image of 1600×1200 pixels and a spatial resolution of 3.2 μm. A simplified schematic

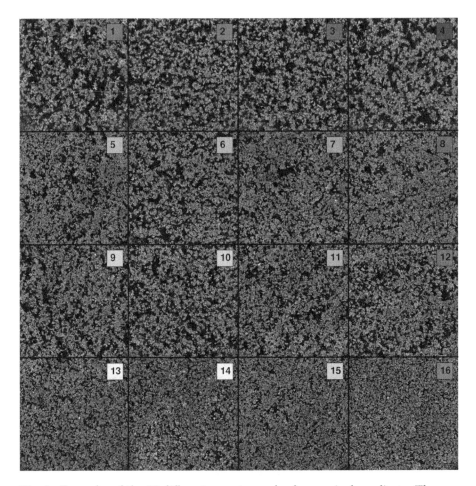

Fig. 1. Examples of the 16 different yogurt samples from a single replicate. The numbering corresponds to that of Table 1. Each image has a resolution of 1024×1024 pixels, and covers an area of 375×375 μm.

of the setup is shown in Fig. 2a, whereas Fig. 2b shows a captured image of semi-skimmed milk at 600 nm.

In order to quantify the DRIs we consider a light decay parameter [11], which quantifies the light intensity decay of the multiple scattered light, i.e. the light far away from the light incident point. The quantification scheme is illustrated in Fig. 2b and 2c. Here, the diffuse reflectance image is log-transformed twice and an intensity profile is extracted orthogonal to the direction of the incident light. A linear model is fitted to the outer part at both ends of the extracted profile, and the average slope of the two models (denoted the decay parameter from here on) describes the combined contribution of the absorption and scattering properties.

From light scattering theory it is well known that the main scatterer in milk and yogurt are the fat globules, due to their size [12,13]. However, the significantly smaller protein structures are also contributing to the overall scattering properties, and hereby the aggregation of the protein structures during fermentation can be observed by the scattering properties. This was verified in [14], where it was observed that the main optical difference between fermented and non-fermented milks is manifested in the scattering properties, while changes in the absorption properties are negligible. Thus, when considering dairy products, the decay parameter mainly reflects the scattering properties of the investigated sample.

2.3   CSLM Image Descriptor

The discriminative properties for a broad range of image descriptors have previously been covered for CSLM images similar to those presented in Fig. 1 [8]. From said study, we select the overall best performing CSLM image descriptor, and compare the discriminative properties to those of the decay parameter. The image descriptor employs the *bag-of-words* approach [15]. Here, small image patches are sampled from the data, and a k-means clustering is performed to obtain a finite *visual vocabulary*, in which the cluster centres comprises the *visual words*. An image can hereafter be described by densely sampling image patches, and mapping them to the most similar visual word in the vocabulary.

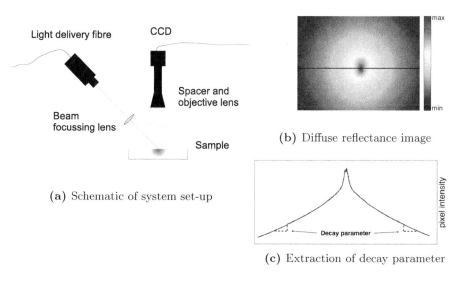

(a) Schematic of system set-up

(b) Diffuse reflectance image

(c) Extraction of decay parameter

Fig. 2. (a) Illustrates the core components of the system set-up and (b) shows an example of a double logarithmically transformed diffuse reflectance image. In (c) an intensity profile of the diffuse reflectance image (corresponding to the black line in (b)) is shown, and the extracted decay parameter is visualised.

Thus, the image is described as a frequency histogram of common image structures in the data set. Following previous work [8], we apply an image patch size of 7×7 pixels and use 128 entries in the visual vocabulary. The distance between two image descriptors can be expressed using the χ^2-distance [16].

2.4   Multidimensional Scaling

The CSLM image descriptor described in the previous section is of high dimensionality. Therefore, in order to compare it directly to the decay parameter, the observations are mapped to a one-dimensional space. This can be done through multidimensional scaling, where the observations are considered in a distance space. Thus, rather than representing N image descriptors in their original p-dimensional space, the descriptors are represented as the mutual distances between all pairs of observations. Thus, the observations can be described in an $N \times N$ dissimilarity matrix, $\mathbf{D}$.

Multidimensional scaling can hereafter be used to determine a low-dimensional representation of the data, where the mutual distances of $\mathbf{D}$ are approximately retained. This can be done by seeking the values $\mathbf{Z} = (\mathbf{z}_1, \mathbf{z}_2, \ldots, \mathbf{z}_N)^T \in \mathbb{R}^{N \times k}$ (where $k < p$) that minimise the stress function:

$$S_{\mathrm{SM}}(\mathbf{Z}) = \sum_{i=1}^{N} \sum_{j=1}^{N} \frac{(d_{ij} - ||\mathbf{z}_i - \mathbf{z}_j||)^2}{d_{ij}}, \tag{1}$$

where d_{ij} is an element of $\mathbf{D}$ and $|| \cdot ||$ is the Euclidean norm. The expression is a slightly modified version of the least squares formulation and denoted *Sammon mapping* [17], which puts more emphasis on preserving the small mutual distances. Sammon mapping was applied as some factors in the experimental design were only expected to make subtle changes to the microstructure.

2.5   Method Evaluation

To evaluate the discriminative properties of the decay parameter and the CSLM image descriptor, we apply the nearest-neighbour classification also used in [8]. This classification is performed on different partitions of the data set, in order to get an overview of the discriminative properties in relation to both chemical and microstructural composition of the yogurts. Additionally, we present the correlations between the one-dimensional representation of the CSLM image descriptor and the decay parameter extracted from the DRIs.

3   Results

3.1   Method Evaluation

Nearest Neighbour Classification Nearest neighbour classification was performed on the signal output from the decay parameter and CSLM image descriptor. For each class, a single observation was isolated (the test data), and the nearest neighbour classification model was built on the remaining data (the training data). The presented test classification rates are based on the average over 1000 random splits of the data set, and further averaged across the three replicates of the experimental design. Additionally, the classification results were calculated for different partitions of the data set, in order to highlight the specific capabilities of the two modalities. the following partitions were considered:

- **Entire data set (sixteen classes)**. The overall performance on the entire data set was evaluated.
- **Superset (four classes)**. Here, each of the subsets, defined in Table 1, constitutes a single class, and reflects how well different chemical compositions can be discriminated.
- **Subsets 1-4 (each subset has four classes)**. The subsets defined in Table 1 were used to evaluate how well the subtle microstructural changes are reflected in the measurements, as the chemical composition of the yogurt changes.

Classification results for all partitions are summarised in Fig. 3 while Fig. 4 provides the corresponding confusion matrices for the CSLM image descriptor and the decay parameter at two different wavelengths.

Looking at the classification rates for the *entire data set* and the *superset* (Fig. 3), the CSLM image descriptor appears to perform significantly better than the decay parameter. When considering the *entire data set*, the classification rates for the decay parameter tend to decrease as the wavelength increases, and for the shortest wavelengths there is even a slight overlap in performance with the CSLM descriptor. This corresponds well to the presented confusion matrices (Fig. 4).

The same tendency is not seen for the classification rates of the *superset*. Here the performance generally appears to be lower, with larger standard deviations, and virtually no wavelength dependency. We found this was due to the samples with a high level of fat (samples 9 through 16), in which the effect of protein content seemed to be obscured. This can also be seen in the confusion matrices. This confounding, combined with only four classes, is likely to cause the lower performance.

Moving on to *subsets* 1 and 2, it can be seen that the performance actually appears similar for CSLM and the decay parameter, especially at the lower wavelengths. Considering the *subsets* 3 and 4, which have a high fat content, the performance is a bit lower for the decay parameter and a wavelength dependency is only seen for *subset* 4, which has a high protein content. The results for the *subsets* also seem to correspond well to the confusion matrices.

Correlation Before the decay parameter and the CSLM image descriptor could be compared directly, multidimensional scaling (see Section 2.4) was performed on the CSLM image descriptors. The average approximation error for mapping the CSLM image descriptor into a one-dimensional space was found to be around 11% when using the Sammon mapping and around 17% when using the least

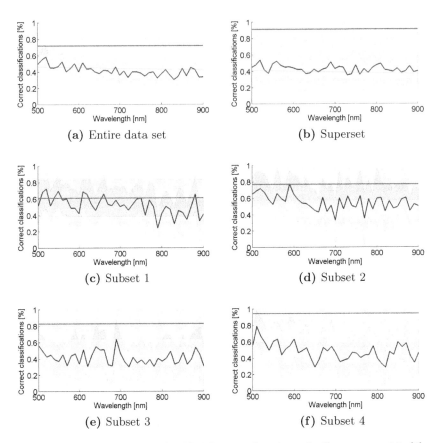

(a) Entire data set

(b) Superset

(c) Subset 1

(d) Subset 2

(e) Subset 3

(f) Subset 4

Fig. 3. Classification rates for the CSLM image descriptor (red) as reported in [8], and for the decay parameter (blue) for all considered wavelengths. The classification rates are provided for different partitions of the data set. The margins denote one standard deviation.

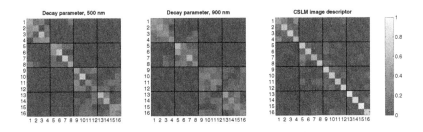

Fig. 4. Confusion matrices for the classification on the *entire data set*. The sample numbers corresponds to those of Table 1, and furthermore the grid highlights the four subsets defined in Table 1.

squares mapping. Hereby, the Sammon mapping was chosen for the multidimensional scaling. Hereafter, a correlation coefficient was calculated based on the average responses of the two modalities was, and further averages across the three replicates. The correlation coefficients are presented in Fig. 5a and again a wavelength dependency can be seen, and in this case it is even more prominent than for the classification rates.

The average responses, for a single replicate, are plotted in Fig. 5b against each other, at two different wavelengths. When comparing across wavelengths it quite clear how the signal at 500 nm is affected more by changes to protein content and the protein network microstructure compared to 900 nm. Especially for the samples with low fat content (sample 1 through 8) the effects of heat treatment and incubation temperature are pronounced. Contrary, at 900 nm there is a clear separation between low fat and high fat samples, while there is only a small effect from the protein content. Looking at the effects of heat treatment and incubation temperature they are more or less collapsed into a single point, making them hard to distinguish.

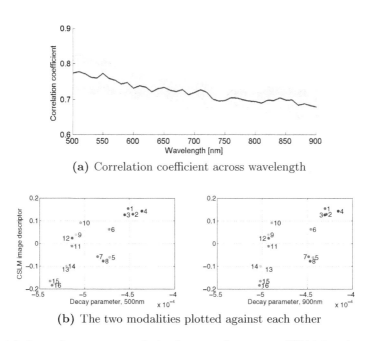

(a) Correlation coefficient across wavelength

(b) The two modalities plotted against each other

Fig. 5. (a) shows the average correlation between the average CSLM descriptor and the average decay parameter as a function of wavelength. The correlation is furthermore averaged across the three replicates and the margins denote one standard deviation. In (b) the average CSLM image descriptor and the average decay parameter plotted against each other at different wavelengths. The sample numbers and colours correspond to those of Table 1 and Fig. 1.

4 Discussion and Conclusion

We have assessed the discriminative properties of a single feature extracted from hyperspectral DRIs in regard to the protein microstructure of yogurts. Throughout the paper several observations can be made. The applied evaluation techniques generally showed a wavelength dependency, in which lower wavelengths correlated better to CSLM images of the microstructure and were better at discriminating between the different yogurt microstructures. However, when additional fat was added to the system, the microstructural effects from changing the protein content, heat treatment and incubation temperature diminished.

These findings correspond well to Mie theory [18] as the scattering efficiency of milk fat is known to be significantly larger than that of milk protein due to the difference in structure size; fat lies within the range 100-10000 nm while protein lies within 20-400 nm [12]. Additionally, the scattering contribution becomes smaller as the wavelength increases, when small structures (relative to the wavelength) are considered (Rayleigh scattering). For the applied wavelength interval (500-900 nm) this means that the scattering contribution from the fat structure remains fairly constant across the interval, whereas the contribution from the protein structures decays significantly across the interval. Thus, the effect of protein content and different protein microstructures should be more visible at lower wavelengths. This corresponds well to the observations of the evaluation techniques.

Comparing the classification performance between the two modalities, CSLM appeared to be more discriminative, however the classification performance was comparable in certain cases. This was especially clear for the samples 1 to 4 with low fat and protein content. Here, it should be noted that the CSLM have been captured at a single magnification level, and from Fig. 1 it can be seen that the less dense microstructure also appears more irregular. This suggests that the applied zoom level does not necessarily yield a representative view of the less dense microstructures and other zoom levels should be considered [8]. A similar, albeit inverted, problem was observed in relation to the decay parameter, where a high fat content seemingly confounded the scattering contribution from the other experimental factors. Here, a higher spatial resolution might be able to capture the appropriate dynamics in the depicted light diffusion. These observations highlight that the two applied modalities observe the samples at different scales.

Optical sensors have commonly been investigated in relation to the initial structure formation during cheese making. Claesson and Nitschmann [19] initially recommended near-infrared (NIR) light, as higher wavelengths showed a larger relative increase in the signal output, compared to lower wavelengths, during the structure formation. In the study by O'Callaghan et al. [20] commercially available sensors, for following the initial structure formation, are compared, and all investigated optical sensors are based on NIR light. In this regard the observations of this paper are remarkable, as they suggest that lower wavelengths should be favoured when the task is to discriminate between different yogurt microstructures. Thus, for this particular task, the results of this paper suggests that new optical sensors should be developed, rather than relying on the commercially available sensors used in cheese making.

In conclusion, we believe the results of this paper encourages further investigation of using short-wavelength DRIs as means of inline process control for detecting microstructural artefacts in dairy production, especially when low-fat dairy products are considered.

References

1. Muir, D.D., Hunter, E.A.: Sensory evaluation of fermented milks: vocabulary development and the relations between sensory properties and composition and between acceptability and sensory properties. International Journal of Dairy Technology **45**(3), 73–80 (1992)
2. Folkenberg, D., Dejmek, P., Skriver, A., Ipsen, R.: Relation between sensory texture properties and exopolysaccharide distribution in set and in stirred yoghurts produced with different starter cultures. Journal of Texture Studies **36**(2), 174–189 (2005)
3. Lee, W., Lucey, J.: Formation and physical properties of yogurt. Asian-Australasian Journal of Animal Sciences **23**(9), 1127–1136 (2010)
4. Lucey, J.: Formation and physical properties of milk protein gels. Journal of Dairy Science **85**(2), 281–294 (2002)
5. O'Callaghan, D.J., O'Donnell, C., Payne, F.: Review of systems for monitoring curd setting during cheesemaking. International Journal of Dairy Technology **55**(2), 65–74 (2002)
6. Castillo, M.: Cutting time prediction methods in cheese making. In: Encyclopedia of Agricultural, Food, and Biological Engineering, pp. 1–7 (2006)
7. Skytte, J.L., Nielsen, O.H.A., Andersen, U., Møller, F., Carstensen, J.M., Dahl, A.B., Larsen, R.: Monitoring optical changes during milk acidification using hyperspectral diffuse reflectance images. In revision (2014)
8. Skytte, J.L., Ghita, O., Whelan, P.F., Andersen, U., ller, F.M., Dahl, A.B., Larsen, R.: Evaluation of yogurt microstructure using confocal laser scanning microscopy and image analysis. Journal of Food Science (in press, 2015)
9. Lucey, J., Munro, P., Singh, H.: Effects of heat treatment and whey protein addition on the rheological properties and structure of acid skim milk gels. International Dairy Journal **9**(3), 275–279 (1999)
10. Nielsen, O.H.A., Dahl, A.L., Larsen, R., Møller, F., Nielsen, F.D., Thomsen, C.L., Aanæs, H., Carstensen, J.M.: Supercontinuum light sources for hyperspectral subsurface laser scattering. In: Heyden, A., Kahl, F. (eds.) SCIA 2011. LNCS, vol. 6688, pp. 327–337. Springer, Heidelberg (2011)
11. Carstensen, J.M., Møller, F., Frisvad, J.L.: Online monitoring of food processes using subsurface laser scattering. In: Advances in Process Analytics and Control Technologies, pp. 5–7 (2009)
12. Walstra, P., Walstra, P., Wouters, J.T., Geurts, T.J.: Dairy science and technology, 2nd edn. CRC Press (2010)
13. Martelli, F., Del Bianco, S., Ismaelli, A., Zaccanti, G.: Light propagation through biological tissue and other diffusive media: theory, solutions, and software. SPIE Press (2010)

14. Nielsen, O.H.A., Subash, A.A., Nielsen, F.D., Dahl, A.B., Skytte, J.L., Andersson-Engels, S., Khoptyar, D.: Spectral characterisation of dairy products using photon time-of-flight spectroscopy. Journal of Near Infrared Spectroscopy **21**(5), 375–383 (2013)
15. Prince, S.J.: Computer vision: models, learning, and inference. Cambridge University Press (2012)
16. Press, W.H., Teukolsky, S.A., Vetterling, W.T., Flannery, B.P.: Numerical recipes 3rd edition: The art of scientific computing. Cambridge University Press (2007)
17. Hastie, T., Tibshirani, R., Friedman, J., Hastie, T., Friedman, J., Tibshirani, R.: The elements of statistical learning, 2nd edn. Springer (2009)
18. Mie, G.: Contribution to the optical properties of turbid media, in particular of colloidal suspensions of metals. Ann. Phys. (Leipzig) **25**, 377–452 (1908)
19. Claesson, O., Nitschmann, H.: Optical investigation of the rennet clotting of milk. Acta Agriculturae Scandinavica **7**(4), 341–360 (1957)
20. O'Callaghan, D.J., O'Donnell, C., Payne, F.: A comparison of on-line techniques for determination of curd setting time using cheesemilks under different rates of coagulation. Journal of Food Engineering **41**(1), 43–54 (1999)

Biomedical Image Analysis

An Ensemble of 2D Convolutional Neural Networks for Tumor Segmentation

Mark Lyksborg$^{(\boxtimes)}$, Oula Puonti, Mikael Agn, and Rasmus Larsen

Department of Applied Mathematics and Computer Science,
Technical University of Denmark, Kgs. Lyngby, Denmark
{mlyk,oupu,miag,rlar}@dtu.dk

Abstract. Accurate tumor segmentation plays an important role in radiosurgery planning and the assessment of radiotherapy treatment efficacy. In this paper we propose a method combining an ensemble of 2D convolutional neural networks for doing a volumetric segmentation of magnetic resonance images. The segmentation is done in three steps; first the full tumor region, is segmented from the background by a voxel-wise merging of the decisions of three networks learned from three orthogonal planes, next the segmentation is refined using a cellular automaton-based seed growing method known as growcut. Finally, within-tumor sub-regions are segmented using an additional ensemble of networks trained for the task. We demonstrate the method on the MIC-CAI Brain Tumor Segmentation Challenge dataset of 2014, and show improved segmentation accuracy compared to an axially trained 2D network and an ensemble segmentation without growcut. We further obtain competitive Dice scores compared with the most recent tumor segmentation challenge.

Keywords: Tumor segmentation · Convolutional neural network · Ensemble classification · Cellular automaton

1 Introduction

Segmentation of brain tumors plays a role in radiosurgery, radiotherapy planning, and for monitoring tumor growth. Segmentation is challenging since tumor location and appearance vary greatly between patients.

Many successful method for doing voxel-based segmentation are based on the random forest (RF) classification scheme which predicts segmentation labels from user engineered image features. Tustison et al. [15] proposed a two-stage RF approach, with features derived from a Gaussian mixture model followed by a Markov random field segmentation smoothing. The RF was also used by Reza et al. [12] who designed features using textons and multifractional Brownian motion. Menze et al. [10] proposed a generative probabilistic atlas-based model which adapts to the intensity distribution of different subjects and later combined it with the RF classifier [9]. An example of a successfull method that does not use a RF classifier is the patch-based approach [2]. Here voxels are

© Springer International Publishing Switzerland 2015
R.R. Paulsen and K.S. Pedersen (Eds.): SCIA 2015, LNCS 9127, pp. 201–211, 2015.
DOI: 10.1007/978-3-319-19665-7_17

segmented by comparing image patches to a dictionary consisting of training patches where the corresponding expert labels are used for segmentation.

In recent years and due to advancements in computational power, deep neural networks have been revived. In the most recent Brain Tumor Segmentation Challenge 2014 (BraTS2014), this was reflected by a number of contributions using deep neural networks. The work by Davy et al. [3] presented a 2D convolutional network trained from an axial perspective. Two others presented 3D networks [16], [18], and while their implementations differed, the results indicated a benefit of using 3D information. An important property of a network is that it learns image features relevant for the specific segmentation problem. This alleviate researchers from having to engineer such features.

We revisit the idea of Davy et al. [3] but instead of using one 2D network to do voxel-based segmentations, we learn an ensemble of networks, one for each of the axial, sagittal and coronal planes and fuse their segmentations into a more accurate 3D informed segmentation. Unlike previous works using convolutional networks we do not segment the tumor and its sub-regions using a single multi-label classifier. Instead, we split the problem into two sequential segmentation problems. The first segmentation separates tumor from healthy tissue and refine the segmentation using a growcut algorithm [17]. The second segmentation performs the within-tumor sub-region segmentation using the tumor mask of the first segmentation to select voxels of interest.

The method (Fig. 1) is demonstrated on the BraTS2014 dataset. We were able to achieve improved ground truth segmentation accuracy compared to a 2D axially trained network [3] and Dice scores [4] just below the top methods of the challenge leaderboard (https://www.virtualskeleton.ch/BRATS/Start2014).

2   Data

Two datasets were downloaded from the BraTS2014 website (November, 2014).

The first dataset (data1) consisted of 106 high grade glioma (HGG) and 25 low grade glioma (LGG) subjects (no longitudinal repetitions), all with ground truth segmentations of the tumors. It was randomly split into a training set of 76 HGG/15 LGG subjects, and the rest (30 HGG/10 LGG) were used as test data. For each subject, we used a set of multimodal magnetic resonance imaging (MRI) volumes, consisting of two T2-weighted images (Fluid-attenuated inversion recovery (FLAIR) and (T2)) and a T1-weighted image with gadolinium contrast (T1c). The MRIs were skull stripped, rigidly oriented according to MNI space and re-sliced to 1 mm^3 as described in [6]. The ground truth segmentation consisted of five labels (background=0, necrosis=1, edema=2, non-enhancing=3, enhancing=4).

The second dataset (data2) consisted of 187 multi-modal MRI volumes from 88 different subjects with 99 longitudinal repetitions. Since only the BraTS2014 challenge organizers know the ground truth segmentations, it allowed for a blinded segmentation evaluation via the challenge website.

3   Method

The proposed method, outlined in Fig. 1, consists of four steps. First, the MRI volumes are bias corrected for scanner field inhomogeneity and standardized to similar cross subject intensities. Second, an ensemble of convolutional networks segments the tumor from healthy tissue. The third step (growcut) post processes the segmentation to improve the segmentation. The fourth step does the within-tumor segmentation using an additional ensemble of networks. The four steps of the method are detailed successively in section 3.1-3.4.

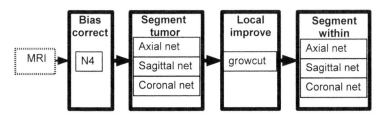

Fig. 1. Shows a schematic, outlining the pipeline of our method. The multi-modal MRI data is pushed through four successive stages of 1) bias correction, 2) whole tumor segmentation (tumor vs. none tumor), 3) localized post-processing of the segmentation and 4) a within-tumor segmentation stage.

3.1   Bias Correction and Standardization

MRI generally exhibits large intensity variations even within the same tissue type of a subject, largely due to field inhomogeneity of the scanner. To minimize this bias, the N4 method [14] was applied to each MRI.The N4 method works under the assumption that the bias field can be modeled by a smooth multiplicative model which is fitted iteratively to maximize the high frequency content of the MRI intensity distribution. To further standardize across different scanners, the maximum peak of each MRI intensity histogram was found, and the intensities scaled according to $I = I_c \cdot (I_b/I_p)$, where I_c is the N4 bias corrected image volume, I_p is the maximum peak intensity of I_c and I_b is a reference value which we fixed to $I_b = 200$. To achieve equal importance of the multi-modal MRI, their intensities were further standardised using a normal transformation applied to each of the different modalities.

3.2   Convolutional Network Ensemble: Whole Tumor

To segment tumor tissue, three convolutional neural networks were trained using a multi-modal image patch of dimension 46×46. Each 2D network learned to classify the same center voxel but viewed from an axial, sagittal and coronal perspective. Combining this ensemble of 2D networks enabled the segmentation method to become 3D aware.

The 2D networks are described by the architecture in Fig. 2. It shows a network consisting of 6 layers. Each perform an algebraic operation on the input data x and passes the result as input to the next layer. The process is repeated until reaching layer 6 which predicts the most probable classification label.

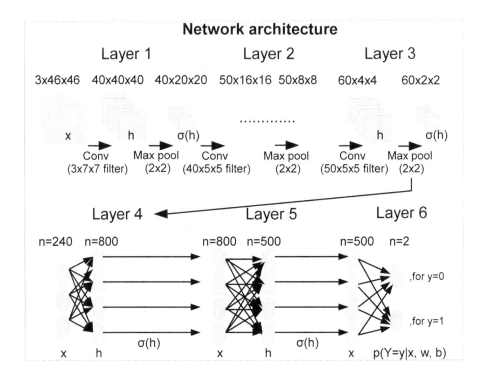

Fig. 2. Depicts a 2D deep neural network architecture consisting of six layers. The first three are convolutional layers, followed by two fully connected layers and a softmax layer where the arrows indicate the connections between layers. The squares illustrate the 2D nature of the input (x) and the intermediate representations (h) of the convolutional layers, where $x = [x_1...x_n]$ is a 3D matrix of n input patches and $h = [h_1...h_m]$, is the concatenation of m 2D filter response. The circles of the fully connected layers indicate its 1D nature with n being the number of neurons (=the circles), such that $x = [x_1...x_n]^T$ and $h = [h_1...h_n]^T$ are the 1D vector representations of the input and the neuronal activations.

Convolutional layers: The convolutional layers apply filtering and downsampling operations to image patches. The first layer uses a filter bank of size $40 \times 3 \times 7 \times 7$ which it applies to the $3 \times 46 \times 46$ image patch. This produces a feature map h of size $40 \times 40 \times 40$, where the first dimension indexes the feature maps, while the second and third dimensions indexes (row, column) coordinates. More specifically the jth map is calculated by $h_j = b_j + \sum_{i=1}^{n}(w_{ij} * x_i)$, where i

indexes the input channel and a trainable filter w_{ij}, the $*$ operator denotes 2D convolution and $n = 3$ is the number of input channels. Subsequently a 2×2 max pooling strategy is used to downsample h to size $40 \times 20 \times 20$ and the rectified linear unit function, $\sigma(h) = max(0, h)$ is applied. The remaining convolutional layers (two and three) perform the same type of operations but using filter banks of size $50 \times 40 \times 5 \times 5$ and $60 \times 50 \times 5 \times 5$ for the respective layers. The application of these filters and downsampling steps result in a number of the intermediate feature maps with the dimensionalities listed in the top part of Fig. 2.

Fully connected layers: Layer 4, 5 and 6 are fully connected layers meaning each neuron is exposed to the full input x of the previoues layer. Each of the 800 neurons in layer 4, evaluates the product $h_j = w_j^T x + b_j$ and applies the non-linear activation function $\sigma(h_j)$. Thereby transforming the 240 dimensional vector x into an 800 dimensional vector $\sigma(h)$ which is passed to layer 5. Layer 5 works similar to layer 4, but now generating a 500 dimensional feature vector $\sigma(h)$ which is propagated to layer 6. Layer 6 evaluates the softmax function

$$p(Y = y|x, w, b) = \frac{e^{w_y x + b_y}}{\sum_j e^{w_j x + b_j}}, \tag{1}$$

generating posterior probabilities for a number of classification labels, $y = \{0, 1\}$. Here w_j refer to a vector of linear parameters for the jth class, b_j is a bias weight and x is the 500 dimensional response vector from the previous layer.

Network Training Each of the 2D networks were trained by minimizing the following cost function

$$C(W, B) = \frac{1}{nd} \cdot \sum_{i=1}^{nd} -\ln(p(Y = y^i|x^i, W, B)) + \lambda \cdot \sum_{j=1}^{nw} W_j^2. \tag{2}$$

The first term of eq. (2) is the mean negative log-likelihood of the softmax probability and we have used capitalized (W, B) to indicate that it is a function of (w, b) parameters from different types of layers. Further, the training patches are denoted x^i, y^i, corresponding to the patch intensities and ground truth label of the ith training example. The second term of eq. (2) is a regularization term that adds robustness to the optimization problem by limiting the solution space to models with smaller parameter weights. It does so by penalizing the 2-norm of the parameters and through experimentation we found $\lambda = 0.0001$ to be suitable.

The cost function was minimized using a stochastic gradient descent (SGD) which relied on the back propagation algorithm to estimate gradients. The SGD performed iterative updates based on gradients estimated from mini-batches with a batch size of 200 where an update occurred after each mini-batch. Each gradient update was further augmented by a moment based learning rule [13] which updated the parameters as a weighted combination of the current gradients and the gradients of previous iteration update. We used a momentum coefficient of 0.9. Layer 4 and 5 were trained using the dropout learning [5] (dropout rate=0.5) which activates half the neurons for each training example. As a consequences the activations of these layers($\sigma(h)$) were divided by 2 when a network was applied to an unseen test image patch.

A GPU implementation for training the three 2D networks was achived using Theano [1].

Network Ensemble Merging Having learned the parameters of the three networks, their complementary decision information were merged. This was done using the posterior probablities of the last layer (layer 6). If the networks agreed on the same label we were highly confident in this classification and assigned the label of voxel x with probability $p(Y|x) = 1$. Otherwise a majority vote decided the class label and the probability was set to reflect this uncertainty by averaging the class probabilities of the three networks, $p(Y|x) = (1/3) \sum_{i=1}^{3} p_i(Y|x, w, b)$. The resulting label segmentations and their probabilities were then used as input for the growcut algorithm.

3.3   Cellular Automaton: Growcut

The growcut algorithm was initially proposed as a continuous state cellular automata method for automated segmentation based on user labeled seed voxels [17]. From these labels and a local intensity transition rule the algorithm decides whether voxels should be re-labelled.

We used the algorithmic formulation of [17] which we extended to 3D. The algorithm models each voxel as a cell with a state set $S(\Theta, l, C)$ consisting of a strength value $\Theta \in [0, 1]$, a label l and an intensity feature vector C. It is an iterative algorithm and for each iteration the strength and labels of the previous iteration remain fixed. During an iteration each image cell r is attacked by its neighboring cells $s \in N(r)$ where $N(r)$ denote the $3 \times 3 \times 3$ neighborhood of a volume and only if $g(C_r, C_s) \cdot \Theta_s > \Theta_r$, will Θ_r, and l_r be updated before the next iteration. The local transition rule is given by

$$g(C_1, C_2) = 1 - \frac{||C_1 - C_2||_2}{k} \tag{3}$$

Where we have normalized the intensities of C to be in the range $[0, 1]$ such that for $k = \sqrt{3}$, the value of $g(C_1, C_2) \in [0, 1]$. Since $g(C_1, C_2)$ can never exceed 1, any cells with strength $\Theta = 1$ will remain constant throughout the algorithm.

To use the growcut on the ensemble segmentations, the feature vector C was set to the multi-modal MRI intensities and the values of l, Θ were initialized with the labels and probability maps of the convolutional network ensemble. This initialization served as a strong prior for growcut segmentation, assuming that the segmentation was already near optimal.

Once growcut converged to a stable segmentation (100 iterations), a heuristic rule was used to identify the tumor. It was based on a connected components analysis to remove any spatially coherent clusters of voxels which were less than 80% of the biggest cluster.

3.4 Convolutional Network Ensemble: Within-Tumor

This ensemble of convolutional networks was used to segment the within-tumor sub-regions. The architecture of each network is similar to the previously described, but considers a smaller image patch and has only two convolutional layers, two fully connected dropout layers and softmax probability layer. The input patch size is $3 \times 34 \times 34$ and the first convolutional layer uses a filter bank of size $50 \times 3 \times 7 \times 7$ while the second one uses a filter bank of size $60 \times 50 \times 5 \times 5$. The justification of choosing a smaller patch size is that the within-tumor segmentation uses information on a smaller scale compared to the whole tumor segmentation. As with the previously described networks, the fully connected layers use 800 and 500 neurons respectively while the softmax layer, predicts one of four possible classification labels. The SGD optimization was again used to train the networks but for these specific networks we used $\lambda = 0.00005$.

Network Ensemble Merging The voxel-based decisions of the ensemble of axial, sagittal and coronal networks were either set to the label they all agree on, or according to the most probable average probability of the softmax probability.

4 Results

4.1 Test and Phenotype Performance

Testing our method on the 40 left out subjects (data1), resulted in the segmentation performances of Table 1. This table shows ground truth scores for three methods; A 2D convolutional network applied to the axial plane similar to [3], a method using only the ensemble part of our method (ensem) and our full method which is ensem in combination with growcut (ensem+grow). The scores of the table are given for pathologically relevant tumor regions. These are the whole tumor (labels: necrosis, edema, non-enhancing, enhancing), the enhanced tumor region and the tumor core (labels: necrosis, non-enhancing, enhancing). We see that using an ensemble improved the segmentation relative to a 2D network and achieved further improvement by including growcut post-processing. As a visual comparison example, two tumor segmentations based on our method and their

Table 1. Average segmentation performance scores of three convolutional neural network methods evaluated on 40 subjects of data1. The scores (Dice, positive predictive and sensitivity) were calculated for the different tumor regions.

Method	Dice scores			Positive predictive			Sensitivity		
	Whole	Core	Enh.	Whole	Core	Enh.	Whole	Core	Enh.
axial	0.744	0.642	0.629	0.732	0.624	0.642	0.811	0.746	0.707
ensem	0.786	0.686	0.676	0.786	0.707	0.693	0.825	0.743	0.717
ensem+grow	0.810	0.697	0.681	0.833	0.718	0.701	0.825	0.750	0.720

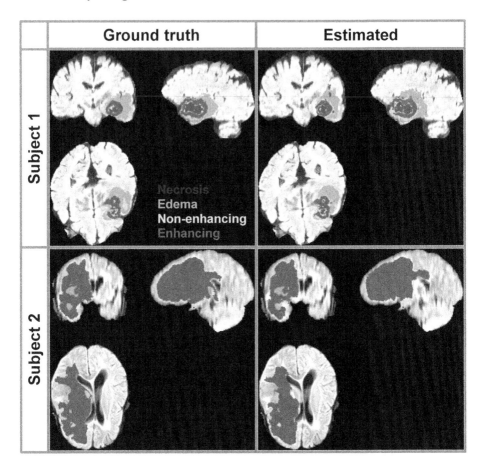

Fig. 3. This visual comparison shows both the proposed segmentation method and corresponding ground truth for two subjects. The Dice scores of subject 1 were 0.825 (whole), 0.795 (core) and 0.842 (enhanced) and for subject 2 they were, 0.892 (whole), 0.840 (core) and 0.854 (enhanced).

ground truth, are shown in Fig. 3. By dividing the test subjects based on tumor types (HGG/LGG), we evaluated their impact on method performance. This comparison (Fig. 4), reveals higher Dice scores with less variance for the HGGs, indicating a methodological bias towards the tumor type.

4.2 Blinded Challenge Performance

Testing our method on the blinded challenge dataset previously denoted data2 and performing an on-line evaluation of the segmentations, resulted in the average performance scores of Table 2. It lists the scores for the first time point of the 99 subjects (cross sectional) and the full challenge data (full data) where similar performances are achieved. It also includes the top 3 scores of the BraTS2014 challenge where our method is ranked amongst.

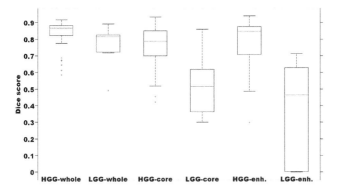

Fig. 4. Ground truth Dice scores performance for two different types of tumors (HGG and LGG). Red line indicate mean Dice score, blue boxes show the 25 and 75 percentiles of the scores while extreme observations are show with red dots.

Table 2. Shows the average segmentation performance scores of our method in grey (cross sectional and full data), for the BraTS2014 challenge data (data2). Also listed are the top three of the challenge (15/12-2014), ranked according to their whole tumor Dice scores. These are Urbag [16], Kleej [7], Dvorp [8].

Method	Dice scores			Positive predictive			Sensitivity		
	Whole	Core	Enh.	Whole	Core	Enh.	Whole	Core	Enh.
Cross sectional	0.801	0.637	0.586	0.803	0.682	0.554	0.857	0.715	0.745
Full data	0.799	0.631	0.625	0.783	0.629	0.580	0.861	0.736	0.776
Urbag	0.87	0.76	0.72	0.91	0.80	0.69	0.85	0.76	0.81
Kleej	0.87	0.76	0.73	0.90	0.73	0.66	0.85	0.83	0.87
Dvorp	0.60	0.30	0.29	0.86	0.58	0.56	0.53	0.27	0.28

5   Discussion

We have presented a method, combining an ensemble of 2D convolutional networks with the growcut method for making a 3D informed segmentation. It showed improved accuracy compared to a 2D network and an ensemble segmentation without growcut thereby validating the usefulness of the proposed method. The investigation of tumor type showed better performance for HGG, likely due to the imbalanced training data distribution (76 HGG/15 LGG). It could also indicate the presence of a measurable pathologic difference. If so, the training of a segmentation method for each type could lead to improved segmentations for both types. This would require knowing the tumor type in advance, information that was not readily available for the blinded challenge data. Our challenge results showed a nice performance although sub-par to the top two methods of the challenge but was superior to the remaining 11. It is noted that our methods performance is in the Dice score range that manual annotators can achieve according the results of [11]. They reported the Dice accuracy of annotators to be in the range of (0.74-0.85). This is comparable to the proposed method. A simple strategy for improving our work would be to extend the ensemble to use 3D network (computationally costly) or to investigate the inclusion of networks trained from more than orthogonal planes. In addition, the usage of using longitudinal information could also play a role towards improving segmentations.

References

1. Bergstra, J., et al.: Theano: a CPU and GPU math expression compiler. In: Python for Scientific Computing Conference (SciPy) (2010)
2. Cordier, N., Menze, B., Delingette, H., Ayache, N.: Patch-based segmentation of brain tissues. In: MICCAI-BraTS (Challenge on Multimodal Brain Tumor Segmentation), pp. 6–17 (2013)
3. Davy, A., Havaei, M., Warde-Farley, D., Biard, A., Tran, L., Jodoin, P.M., Courville, A., Larochelle, H., Pal, C., Bengio, Y.: Brain tumor segmentation with deep neural networks. In: MICCAI-BraTS, pp. 1–5 (2014)
4. Dice, L.R.: Measures of the amount of ecologic association between species. Ecology (1945)
5. Hinton, G.E., Srivastava, N., Krizhevsky, A., Sutskever, I., Salakhutdinov, R.: Improving neural networks by preventing co-adaptation of feature detectors. CoRR (2012)
6. Jakab, A.: Segmenting brain tumors with the slicer 3d software. Tech. rep., University of Debrecen / ETH Zürich (2012)
7. Kleesiek, J., Biller, A., Urban, G., Kothe, U., Bendszus, M., Hamprecht, F.: Ilastik for multi-modal brain tumor segmentation. In: MICCAI-BraTS, pp. 12–17 (2014)
8. Kwon, D., Akbari, H., Da, X., Gaonkar, B., Davatzikos, C.: Multimodal brain tumor image segmentation using glistr. In: MICCAI-BraTS, pp. 18–19 (2014)
9. Menze, B., Geremia, E., Ayache, N., Szekely, G.: Segmenting glioma in multimodal images using a generative-discriminative model for brain lesion segmentation. In: MICCAI-BraTS, pp. 56–63 (2012)
10. Menze, B., Leemput, K.V., Lashkar, D., Weber, M., Ayache, N., Golland, P.: Segmenting glioma in multi-modal images using a generative model for brain lesion segmentation, pp. 49–55 (2012)
11. Menze, B.H., et al.: The multimodal brain tumor image segmentation benchmark (brats). IEEE Transactions on Medical Imaging (2014)
12. Reza, S., Iftekharuddin, K.: Improved brain tumor tissue segmentation using texture features. In: MICCAI-BraTS, pp. 27–30 (2014)
13. Sutskever, I., Martens, J., Dahl, G.E., Hinton, G.E.: On the importance of initialization and momentum in deep learning. In: 30th International Conference on Machine Learning (ICML 2013), vol. 28, pp. 1139–1147, May 2013
14. Tustison, N.J., Avants, B.B., Cook, P.A., Zheng, Y., Egan, A., Yushkevich, P.A., Gee, J.C.: N4ITK: Improved N3 Bias Correction. IEEE Trans. Med. Imaging $29(6)$, 1310–1320 (2010)
15. Tustison, N., Wintermark, M., Durst, C., Avants, B.: Ants and arboles. In: MICCAI-BraTS, pp. 47–50 (2013)

16. Urban, G., Bendszus, M., Hamprecht, F.A., Kleesiek, J.: Multi-modal brain tumor segmentation using deep convolutional neural networks. In: MICCAI-BraTSs, pp. 31–35 (2014)
17. Vezhnevets, V., Konouchine, V.: GrowCut - interactive multi-label n-d image segmentation by cellular automata. In: Proceedings of Graphicon (2005)
18. Zikic, D., Ioannou, Y., Brown, M., Criminisi, A.: Segmentation of brain tumor tissues with convolutional neural networks. In: MICCAI-BraTS, pp. 36–39 (2014)

Anatomically Correct Surface Recovery: A Statistical Approach

Rasmus R. Jensen[✉], Jannik B. Nielsen,
Rasmus Larsen, and Rasmus R. Paulsen

DTU Compute, Technical University of Denmark, Richard Petersens Plads,
Building 324, 2800 Kgs. Lyngby, Denmark
{raje,jbol,rlar,rapa}@dtu.dk
http://www.compute.dtu.dk

Abstract. We present a method for 3D surface recovery in partial surface scans. The method is based on an Active Shape Model, which is used to predict missing data. The model is constructed using a bootstrap framework, where an initially small collection of hand-annotated samples is used to fit to and register unknown samples, resulting in an extensive statistical model. The statistical recovery uses a multivariate point prediction, where the distribution of the points is given by the Active Shape Model. We show how missing data in a partial scan, once point correspondence is achieved, can be predicted using the learned statistics. A quantitative evaluation is performed on a data set of 10 laser scans of ear canal impressions with minimal noise and artificial holes. We also present a qualitative evaluation on authentic partial scans from an actual direct in ear scanner prototype. Compared to a state-of-the-art surface reconstruction algorithm, the presented method gives matching prediction results for the synthetic evaluation samples and superior results for the direct scanner data.

Keywords: Surface recovery · Hole closing · Multivariate statistics · Shape modeling · In ear scanning · Active shape model

1 Introduction

Direct surface scanning of humans is an increasingly used modality where the applications include model creation in the entertainment industry, plastic surgery planning and evaluation, craniofacial syndrome evaluation [10,14], and in particular hearing aid production. In this paper, we are concerned with a particular surface shape namely that of the ear canal. Ear canal surface scans are used in custom hearing aid fitting. This is a very large industry that probably makes the ear the most scanned part of the human anatomy. A standard hearing aid producer generates more than a thousand scans per week. When producing custom in-the-ear devices like hearing aids and monitors, the standard routine is to inject silicone rubber into the patients ear and then laser scan this impression. While this technique normally creates complete surfaces, direct ear scanners are

© Springer International Publishing Switzerland 2015
R.R. Paulsen and K.S. Pedersen (Eds.): SCIA 2015, LNCS 9127, pp. 212–223, 2015.
DOI: 10.1007/978-3-319-19665-7_18

emerging and it is expected that probe scans with these devices will require handling of missing data due to occlusion in the complex anatomy of the human ear and the limited space for the scanner probe. In this paper we present a method for predicting missing data based on the information in the partial scan. Hole filling and missing data recovery is a well studied problem, in particular for 2D images. In 3D, data recovery is sometimes considered a by-product of the surface reconstruction algorithm. The algorithms used to generate triangulated surfaces from point clouds will usually try to cover missing areas using some mathematical or physical assumptions. One series of approaches uses Delaunay triangulation of border points [12]. Such methods are obviously susceptible to noise in the border points and will typically require some form of smoothing. An alternative strategy is to interpolate implicit (signed distance) functions locally or globally under various forms of regularisation [11,18]. Other methods, inspired from 2D inpainting approaches have also been investigated [6,7,20]. These are typically based on a variational definition of the behavior of the surface where the holes are.

In our method, we predict the missing points based on the existing points in the scan. Instead of using variational formulations or physical assumptions on the behaviour of the surface, we utilise population statistics of the given class of surfaces learned from an annotated and co-registered training set. We base our population statistics of the ear canal on an extensive statistical shape model of the ear canal constructed in a bootstrap framework. The method is general and is applicable to all surface scans, where a statistical shape distribution can be estimated. The 3D morphable models introduced for the analysis and synthesis of 3D faces [5] can also be used to recover missing data in surface scans [4]. In [5] a 3D statistical shape and texture model is built based on a set of registered training samples and from this a principal component analysis is performed giving a set of eigenvectors and values. To recover missing data the set of known points are found in a pre-processing step and the missing data points are found by computing the optimal linear combination of eigenvectors fitting the known data. This is combined with a ridge regression regularisation to avoid non-plausible shapes. The approach described in [5] is similar to our prediction step, but in contrast we also include the steps needed to identify the missing points in the described framework. Furthermore, we also weight the geodesic distance from the missing points to the known points in the prediction.

1.1 Data and Preprocessing

The data consists of 310 scanned left-ear impressions. The scans have been acquired from a traditional 3D scanner, resulting in meshes of arbitrary triangulation. From this collection, 12 representatives are chosen and from these point correspondence over the selected impressions is created using the method initially described in [17]. Furthermore, the Markov Random Field regularization of the correspondence field described in [16] was used to further optimize the dense correspondence. This small subset of impressions with point correspondence form the basis for the bootstrapping framework. This is used to encompass the entire collection of ear impressions, with the goal of constructing a statistical shape model as for example described in [8,17]. The method described in [17] requires manual annotation of anatomical landmarks which is non-trivial and therefore an automated method is preferred. A small collection of scans have been acquired by a prototype in-ear 3D scanner[1]. They are partial in the sense that some areas of the surface are missing due to noise and/or occlusion. Finally, a small set of scanned ear-impressions, not part of the original 310 samples, have had holes cut in them to mimic the nature of the partial scans. We denote these manually created partial scans as synthesized partial scans. This set is used for controlled evaluation of our method. In the following, some parameters have been assigned fixed values manually chosen for our data. These parameters should be validated for other uses of the framework.

2   Bootstrapped Active Shape Model

In order to accurately recover missing information in a partial scan we construct a statistical shape model [8]. For this, point correspondence is needed over the training set. Initially a small subset of samples is manually annotated and registered using the approach described in [16,17]. Using this subset, an Active Shape Model (ASM) is constructed as described in [8,17]. The statistical model is aligned and fitted to each unknown sample. This is done iteratively, allowing co-registration to and inclusion in the ASM, thereby expanding the model sample by sample. The ASM thus grows in size as the bootstrapping procedure processes unknown samples, allowing it to explain an increasing amount of shape variation from the dataset. Intuitively this leads to the expectation that the algorithm will become increasingly better at fitting to unknown shapes and that later samples are better registered than former, wherefore a revisit of early registrations may be chosen as a finalising step.

Assuming a collection of m aligned shapes, each consisting of p 3D points $\mathbf{v}_i = (x_1, y_1, z_1, \ldots, x_p, y_p, z_p)^T \in \mathbb{R}^n$. These shapes can be interpreted as being points in an $n = 3p$-dimensional space. The average shape is thus $\bar{\mathbf{v}} = \frac{1}{m} \sum_{i=1}^{m} \mathbf{v}_i$ and the shape deviation from mean $\mathbf{x}_i = \mathbf{v}_i - \bar{\mathbf{v}}$. In order to investigate the variation of the data, an observation matrix $\mathbf{X} = (\mathbf{x}_1, \ldots, \mathbf{x}_m) \in \mathbb{R}^{n \times m}$ can be constructed. The covariance matrix, $\mathbf{\Sigma}$, of $\mathbf{X}$ is found by

$$\mathbf{\Sigma} = \frac{1}{m} \mathbf{X} \mathbf{X}^T \in \mathbb{R}^{n \times n}. \tag{1}$$

Performing an Eigenvalue decomposition of this covariance matrix, thus provides insight in the primary modes of variation within the dataset $\mathbf{\Sigma} = \mathbf{P} \Lambda \mathbf{P}^T$, where $\mathbf{P} = (\mathbf{p}_1, \ldots, \mathbf{p}_m)$ is a matrix consisting of columns of Eigenvectors and $\Lambda = \mathrm{diag}(\lambda_1, \ldots, \lambda_m)$ is a diagonal matrix holding the Eigenvalues. These Eigenvalues corresponds to the variation expressed of the respective Eigenvector directions, i.e. $\lambda_i = \sigma_i^2$. In scenarios where $m < n$, only a subset of the Eigenvalues will be non-zero, the size of this subset will be denoted m'.

Given the collection of non-zero Eigenvalues and corresponding Eigenvectors described above, these can be used as a basis. Any shape $\tilde{\mathbf{v}}$ can then be synthesised by a linear combination of the Eigenvectors, weighted by their Eigenvalues:

$$\mathcal{M}(\mathbf{c}) = \tilde{\mathbf{v}} = \sum_{i}^{m'} c_i \lambda_i \mathbf{p}_i = \mathbf{P}\Lambda\mathbf{c}, \tag{2}$$

where $\mathbf{c} = (c_1, \ldots, c_{m'})$ is a vector of weights determining how much the individual Eigenvectors contributes in the synthesis. This constitutes the Active Shape Model and hereby the ASM can be interpreted as a function of the weights in $\mathbf{c}$, i.e. $\mathcal{M}(\mathbf{c})$.

The raw samples to be included in the ASM may not be positioned or oriented correctly relative to each other. Multiple approaches to automatic alignment of shapes exists, we have chosen to use 3D Shape Context Descriptors [9].

The descriptors describes a point on a 3D surface by a histogram of its local neighbourhood, indicating the local geometric distribution of points. Given a point $\mathbf{q}$ on a surface, any neighbouring point's relative position to $\mathbf{q}$ can be expressed in spherical coordinates (r, θ, φ). Here r is the radial distance between $\mathbf{q}$ and a neighbour $\mathbf{q}_n$. The inclination angle θ and the azimuthal angle φ requires a choice of reference-frame in order to be intercomparable between differently aligned samples. In this experiment, 3D data were acquired from a laser scanner using a rotating platform. The 3D representations of the ear impressions thus have a consistent vertical axis. This consistency can be utilised to construct a common frame of reference. In this frame of reference the third basis element is aligned with the normal of the point $\mathbf{q}$. This is formulated as $\mathbf{b}_3 = \mathbf{n_q} = (n_x, n_y, n_z)^T$. The first basis element is aligned with the vertical axis, with the restraint of being orthogonal to $\mathbf{b}_3$. Denoting a vector pointing along the fixed vertical axis $\mathbf{v} = (0, 1, 0)^T$, this is found by $\mathbf{b}_1 = \mathbf{v} - (\mathbf{v} \cdot \hat{\mathbf{b}}_3)\hat{\mathbf{b}}_3$, i.e. a vector rejection of $\mathbf{v}$ on $\mathbf{n_q}$, where $\hat{\mathbf{b}}$ denotes the normalised value of $\mathbf{b}$. As a result of orthogonal basis vectors in a right-handed coordinate-system, the second basis element is thus restrained to being $\mathbf{b}_2 = \mathbf{b}_3 \times \mathbf{b}_1$. From this basis, a rotation matrix, rotating to the local frame of reference can be constructed $\mathbf{R} = \begin{bmatrix} \hat{\mathbf{b}}_1 & \hat{\mathbf{b}}_2 & \hat{\mathbf{b}}_3 \end{bmatrix}$. Any neighbouring point, $\mathbf{q}_n$, can thus be described in $\mathbf{q}$'s local frame of reference by $\tilde{\mathbf{q}}_n = \mathbf{R}(\mathbf{q}_n - \mathbf{q})$. Within this frame of reference, the inclination angle and the azimuthal angle of the point is given by $\theta = \arccos(\tilde{q}_{n,z}/r)$ and $\varphi = \arctan(\tilde{q}_{n,y}/\tilde{q}_{n,x})$.

Based on the coordinates (r, θ, φ), points in the proximity of $\mathbf{q}$ can be grouped in a discrete set of bins. Hereby a histogram over the 3-dimensional distribution of points surrounding $\mathbf{q}$ can be constructed and used as a feature vector. In our experiment, (r, θ, φ) of points within a radius of 10 mm were divided into $(8, 13, 4)$ bins respectively, yielding a 416-dimensional feature vector or Shape Context Descriptor. The choice of utilising the vertical axis to construct a common frame of reference poses a constraint on the geometry as points having normals parallel to the vertical axis cannot be used. In practice this means that perfectly horizontal surfaces cannot be evaluated. Through the Hungarian method [13], point-descriptors are matched and based on this matching a corresponding transformation can be computed in a least squares sense. The standard χ^2 histogram distance is used as cost function [3]. An illustration is shown in Fig 1. The resulting set of matched points is used to compute the optimal translation and rotation in a least squares sense [9].

Using this method, unknown samples are aligned to the mean of the ASM, $\bar{\mathbf{v}}$, thus supplying a plausible pre-alignment. Failed pre-alignments are easily detected by evaluating the average Euclidean point to point distance between the mean shape and the aligned shape. In our dataset, alignments with average point-to-point distances above 5 mm are rejected.

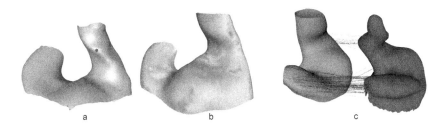

a   b   c

Fig. 1. The descriptor in the point marked by the red marker in a) is compared to the descriptors in all points of b). Colouring in b) corresponds to the χ^2 distance between the descriptors. c) Lines indicating the 100 most significant Shape Context matches between the two samples.

Given a roughly aligned unknown sample, $\mathbf{v}_a$, the alignment is refined and the ASM, $\mathcal{M}(\mathbf{c})$, is fitted. This is done in an iterative manner, where an Iterative Closest Point (ICP) [19] alignment of the sample is followed by an ASM-fitting of the model, and repeated upon until convergence is met. In our ICP implementation the points from the ASM surface are matched to their nearest surface neighbours on the new sample, with the constraint that points connected to a border should be ignored.

For the fitting, we seek to find a deformation of the Active Shape Model that minimises the error between the model and the unknown sample. An ASM constructed from the shape analysis of m samples, each consisting of n points, will be parametrised in an m'-dimensional space and thus have m' modes of variation.

Let $\mathbf{q}_i \in \mathbb{R}^3$ be a point belonging to the ASM, $\mathcal{M}(\mathbf{c})$, and let $\mathbf{q}'_i \in \mathbb{R}^3$ be the closest point on the target sample surface $\mathbf{v}_a$. We seek to find the set of weights $\mathbf{c}^*$ that minimises the sum of distances between $\mathbf{q}$ and $\mathbf{q}'$:

$$\arg\min_{\mathbf{c}} \|\mathcal{M}(\mathbf{c}) - \mathbf{v}_a\| = \arg\min_{\mathbf{c}} \frac{1}{m'} \sum_{i=1}^{m'} \|\mathbf{q}_i - \mathbf{q}'_i\| \tag{3}$$

We solve this optimisation problem by utilising an implementation of the Nelder-Mead method [15]. We reduced the number of parameters used to a number corresponding to 99% explained variance af the training data. As the model-fitting is basically a synthesisation from a k-dimensional (assumed) normal-distribution, a confidence level for an obtained set of parameters $\mathbf{c}^*$ can thus be computed by utilising the Mahalanobis distance M between the parameter set and the ASM distribution since $M^2 \sim \chi_n^2$. This allows validation of fittings by setting a reasonable confidence limit. In our implementation, a confidence level of 99.9% was used.

Having determined $\mathbf{c}^*$ for $\mathcal{M}$ and $\mathbf{v}_a$, the model mesh $\mathcal{M}(\mathbf{c}^*) = \tilde{\mathbf{v}}$ is propagated to the sample shape $\mathbf{v}_a$ in order to perform a point-wise registration using the procedure described in [16]. The result is a mesh of p points, following the shape of $\mathbf{v}_a$, all with correspondence to the model, $\mathcal{M}$. The quality of the registration is determined by computing the 20th percentile of the minimum angle in the projected triangles and rejecting registration where this is below $15°$. This measure is valid since the model mesh has been optimised and has near equilateral triangles. Secondly, the normals of the projection are compared to the normals of $\tilde{\mathbf{v}}$. Registrations having an average dot-product between the normals of $\tilde{\mathbf{v}}$ and the projection below 0.75 are rejected.

When an alignment and a registration is obtained using the iterative scheme above, they are both refined iteratively. During each iteration the registration-mesh is smoothed using simple meaning of the nearest neighbours. The surface normals of the smoothed mesh are found and regularised using local averaging of directions. A new set of correspondence points are found in the sample scan in the direction of the regularised normals and the alignment, $\mathbf{v}_a$, is adjusted accordingly. This process is repeated until convergence. As the sample input scan is expected to be more densely sampled than $\mathcal{M}(\mathbf{c}^*)$ the iterative update ensures a regular mesh with evenly distributed vertices. Each sample that is successfully fitted is added to the ASM. ASM is hereby improved to cover additional shape variation.

3   Surface Recovery on Partial Scans

As described, a crucial, and not easily solved, part of recovering missing data is to co-register a partial mesh with the ASM. This is required in order to obtain point-correspondence between model and surface, creating a partial scan with a mesh structure identical to that of the model. The process of co-registering an unknown scan to the ASM is basically addressed in section 2. In the case of reconstructing partial scans, however, the exact same approach may not suffice. This is mainly due to the fact that an automatic alignment between a partial scan and model may prove to be difficult for Shape Context features. The difficulties arise in scenarios where the key shape features of the model are not present on the scan or vice-versa. We limit ourselves to the already existing Shape Context alignment approach, and where this failed, manual alignment was used. The result of registering and fitting the ASM to a partial scan is that the ASM template mesh is deformed and propagated to the partial scans in areas where there are valid data. The template mesh vertices are marked as missing when the corresponding point or area in the partial scan is not present or valid. If an area is missing in the partial scan, the point projection will often result in that the project point is placed on a boundary in the partial scans, thus enabling detection of missing point correspondences. Given a registration, we aim to recover missing surface data in a partial scan such that the recovered data are anatomically correct. We approach this by using a statistical model and define the set of known and unknown data in a partial scan as follows:

$$\text{missing vertices: } \mathbf{s}_1^{\mathrm{T}} = (x_{11}, y_{11}, z_{11}, x_{12}, y_{12}, z_{12}, \ldots)$$
$$\text{known vertices: } \mathbf{s}_2^{\mathrm{T}} = (x_{21}, y_{21}, z_{21}, x_{22}, y_{22}, z_{22}, \ldots)$$

The correspondence allows for differentiation between known vertices and missing vertices in the partial scan. We will determine how the unknown data $\mathbf{s}_1$ are predicted from known vertices in $\mathbf{s}_2$. Without any prior knowledge of the distribution of data, we consider a shape $\mathbf{s}$ consisting of $\mathbf{s}_1$ and $\mathbf{s}_2$ as belonging to the normal distribution:

$$\mathbf{s} = \begin{bmatrix} \mathbf{s}_1 \\ \mathbf{s}_2 \end{bmatrix} \in N \left(\begin{bmatrix} \mu_1 \\ \mu_2 \end{bmatrix}, \begin{bmatrix} \boldsymbol{\Sigma}_{11} \; \boldsymbol{\Sigma}_{12} \\ \boldsymbol{\Sigma}_{21} \; \boldsymbol{\Sigma}_{22} \end{bmatrix} \right) \; , \; \boldsymbol{\Sigma}_{12}^{\mathrm{T}} = \boldsymbol{\Sigma}_{21} \tag{4}$$

The expected value of $\mathbf{s}_1$ given $\mathbf{s}_2$ is $\mathrm{E}\{\mathbf{s}_1|\mathbf{s}_2\} = \mu_1 + \boldsymbol{\Sigma}_{12}\boldsymbol{\Sigma}_{22}^{-1}(\mathbf{s}_2 - \mu_2)$. With the variance $\mathrm{V}\{\mathbf{s}_1|\mathbf{s}_2\} = \boldsymbol{\Sigma}_{11} - \boldsymbol{\Sigma}_{12}\boldsymbol{\Sigma}_{22}^{-1}\boldsymbol{\Sigma}_{21}$ From the ASM we get an aligned set of shapes. This training set is denoted $X_{aligned}$. From the training set the covariances $\boldsymbol{\Sigma}_{11}$ and $\boldsymbol{\Sigma}_{12}$ as well as the means (μ_1, μ_2) are learned. As there are far less shapes than points, $\boldsymbol{\Sigma}_{22}$ will be singular. Let $\boldsymbol{\Sigma}_{22} = \mathbf{P}\boldsymbol{\Lambda}\mathbf{P}^{\mathrm{T}}$ be the Eigenvalue decomposition. We restrict $\boldsymbol{\Sigma}_{22}$ to its affine support, i.e. the dimensions spanned by the Eigenvectors corresponding to the k positive Eigenvalues, such that $\boldsymbol{\Lambda}^* = \mathrm{diag}(\lambda_1, \lambda_2, \ldots, \lambda_k)$ and $\mathbf{P}^* = [\mathbf{p}_1 \; \mathbf{p}_2 \; \cdots \; \mathbf{p}_k]$. The projection of $\mathbf{s}_2$ using the k selected Eigenvectors $\mathbf{P}^*$: $\mathbf{y}_2 = \mathbf{P}^{*\mathrm{T}}\mathbf{s}_2$ has affine support for $\mathbf{s}_2$ and the variance:

$$\mathrm{V}\{\mathbf{y}_2\} = \mathrm{V}\{\mathbf{P}^*\mathbf{s}_2\} = \mathbf{P}^{*\mathrm{T}}\boldsymbol{\Sigma}_{22}\mathbf{P}^* = \boldsymbol{\Lambda}^* \tag{5}$$

The covariance of $\mathbf{s}_1$ and $\mathbf{y}_2$ is:

$$\mathrm{C}\{\mathbf{s}_1, \mathbf{y}_2\} = \mathrm{C}\{\mathbf{s}_1, \mathbf{P}^{*\mathrm{T}}\mathbf{s}_2\} = \mathrm{C}\{\mathbf{s}_1, \mathbf{s}_2\}\mathbf{P}^* = \boldsymbol{\Sigma}_{12}\mathbf{P}^* \tag{6}$$

Finally, the prediction of the unknown data $\mathbf{s}_1$ can be done using the projection $\mathbf{y}_2$:

$$\mathrm{E}\{\mathbf{s}_1|\mathbf{y}_2\} = \mu_1 + \boldsymbol{\Sigma}_{12}\mathbf{P}^*\boldsymbol{\Lambda}^{*-1}\mathbf{P}^{*\mathrm{T}}(\mathbf{s}_2 - \mu_2) \tag{7}$$

This expected value can be used for any unknown set of vertices $\mathbf{s}_1$ given a partial scan $\mathbf{s}_2$, be that a single missing vertex or all the missing data. If every unknown vertex is predicted according to the described method the known triangulation from the training set can be propagated to the predicted data set and will then constitute a full surface reconstruction. The method can also be used to filter data for noise if the known scan data are also recovered. By varying the number

k values of Eigenvectors used in the projection the fraction of described variance can be controlled.

Practically, the set of known vertices found during the registration of the partial scan is s_2 and the full scan as provided by the scanner is s_{scan}. Let s_1^* be the predicted missing data, s_2^* the prediction of the partial scan and s^* be the full reconstructed shape. The full average shape is denoted μ. With an initial registration the algorithm works as follows: We repeat the loop body with two

---

Algorithm 1. Anatomical surface recovery

1: **procedure** ANATOMICALSURFACERECOVERY$(X_{aligned}, s_2, s_{scan})$ ▷

2:    $s^* \leftarrow \begin{bmatrix} 0 \\ s_2 \end{bmatrix}$

3:    **repeat**

4:        Procrustes align s^* to μ and apply same transformation to s_{scan}

5:        Predict s_1^* using the described method   ▷ the described variance is increased in each iteration

6:        Predict s_2^* using the described method   ▷ the described variance is increased in each iteration

7:        $s^* \leftarrow \begin{bmatrix} s_1^* \\ s_2^* \end{bmatrix}$

8:        Find vertex correspondence between s^* and s_{scan}

9:        Update s_2 and s^* with the correspondence vertices from s_{scan}

10:    **until** convergence

11:    **return** s_1^* and s_2^* ▷

12: **end procedure**

---

different recovery approaches. First s_1^* and s_2^* are predicted all at once. In the last few loops the data are predicted vertex by vertex using only the nearest vertices in the prediction. The vertex distances are found as the geodesic distances on the mean shape, so these only have to be calculated once. The geodesic distances are used to ensure topological consistency when selecting a neighbourhood. Our shape model has 3096 vertices and in the local recovery we only use the 10 nearest of these. In the local prediction the recovered data is locally very true to the original scan. We restrict the Eigenvalues in the recovery to the ones describing 30% of the variance and then gradually raise this to 99.9%. Gradually raising the percentage of described variance helps the algorithm produce anatomically correct shapes and prevents the influence of bad correspondences in the initial iterations.

4   Results

Based on the method described in section 2, we were able to construct an extensive Active Shape Model of the left ear based on the available dataset. A total of 310 samples were processed and from these, 241 passed the automatic quality verification. As the Active Shape Model processes new samples, the complexity of the model increases and thus the fraction of variation explained per principal component must be expected to drop. The fraction of variation explained by the 10 first principal components were computed as the ASM grew in size and it was stabilising, indicating that the shape model eventually captures the true class variability. In the ASM 90% of all variance is contained within the first 37 modes of variation. We do, however, expect that the automatic registration procedure has induced an amount of false variation in form of vertex drifting along the sample surfaces. Such variation of course directly affects the compactness of the ASM in the form of low-variance principal components, assuming that the drifts are uncorrelated. The actual shape variation from the ear is therefore expected to be found within the first principal components. A final manual inspection of mesh distortions resulted in an additional 80 registrations being removed from the ASM. Effectively this resulted in the final ASM consisting of 161 shapes.

In order to compare our approach with existing methods for reconstruction, a collection of 10 scanned ear impressions, not included in the training data, was chosen and all scans had a reasonable sized hole cut in them. The holes were cut between first and second bend of the ear canal, in an area that is known to often be occluded when using experimental optical in-ear scanners. Hereby any reconstruction of these partial scans can be compared to the ground-truth, allowing for a quantitative comparison of methods.

For each mesh in the collection of *synthesised* partial scans the missing data was recovered. This was done using our method, both with and without smoothing, and the Markov Random Field (MRF) surface reconstruction approach [18]. The MRF approach has previously shown to reconstruct anatomical surfaces well. All reconstructions were then compared to the ground truth, by computing a signed distance (based on surface normals) between all reconstructed points and the original surface. In Fig. 2 the reconstructions of synthetic partial scans are shown, where the surface values denotes the signed distance between reconstruction and truth (in millimeters). The average signed point-distances between surface reconstructions can be seen in the table below:

#	MRF	Proposed	Proposed +local smoothing	#	MRF	Proposed	Proposed +local smoothing
1	-0.07	-0.17	-0.27	6	0.07	-0.05	-0.08
2	0.05	0.01	-0.01	7	0.08	-0.001	0
3	-0.04	0.02	0.001	8	0.01	-0.02	-0.03
4	-0.001	-0.015	-0.02	9	0.02	0.03	0.01
5	-0.07	-0.01	-0.013	10	-0.01	0.07	0.07

A significant outlier in the error is observed in sample #1. After inspection, this sample revealed an abnormal cavity in the skin of the ear-canal, explaining the higher error. It should be noted that no prior, neither statistical or physical, would be able to predict such errors. Although this comparison proves high performance of our method, it does not fully illustrate the strength of having a statistically based prior. The MRF approach predicts missing points based on the existing curvature of data in contrast to our method that predicts missing

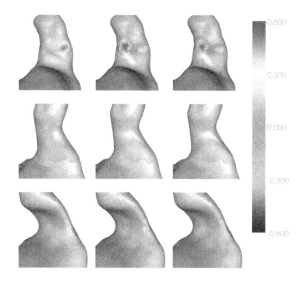

Fig. 2. Reconstruction of missing data for 3 different scans (rows), using Markov Random Field (MRF) reconstruction (column 1), our method (column 2) and the smoothed variant of our method (column 3). Surface values corresponds to the signed distance between reconstruction and ground truth.

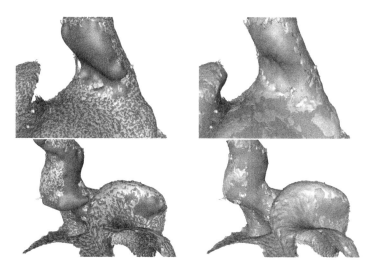

Fig. 3. Partial scans from a prototype direct ear scanner. Raw data is shown with grey. Surfaces reconstructed using the MRF method are red and the surfaces reconstructed using the proposed method are green.

points based on knowledge of the shape variation of an ear population. Effectively this means that where either noisy edges exists or data is sparse, the MRF approach has little chance of estimating the true surface. In this test each hole is surrounded by smooth noiseless surface areas providing an optimum setting for the MRF reconstruction. In the following, we will present a qualitative comparison based on authentic optical 3D scans of the ear, suffering from high noise and sparse point support.

We have tested our algorithm on 12 scans from a prototype direct in ear scanner [1]. In cases with a lot of noise, our strong prior enables our method to produce anatomically correct meshes that are also locally true to the covered areas. Qualitative inspection shows very good hole closing in the 12 scans. In addition all 12 scans were 3D printed as earplugs and tested by the respective test subjects with positive feedback. Fig 3 shows scans with a big part of the ear canal missing. The missing part has been recovered with both the MRF method and the proposed method. As can be seen, our proposed method produces what seems to be a much more plausible surface in the missing part.

5   Conclusion

We have shown that we can predict the missing parts of partial scans using a statistical model. The ability to predict missing data is comparable to state-of-the-art algorithms, when holes are relatively small and the data is fair without too much noise. On scans from a real in-ear scanner probe prototype, the qualitative results produced with the proposed method are much more plausible when visually inspected. The more extensive prior knowledge about the shape to be reconstructed makes the recovery much more robust, when recovering larger holes. The results also seem invariant to the presence of noise, and as such the method can also function as a noise filter. Surface reconstruction algorithms that only use the immediate vicinity in the reconstruction are very sensible to noise on the edges of the area to be recovered.

After using the proposed data recovery method on 12 scans they were 3D printed on a stereolithograpy (SLA) machine [2] and worn by the test subjects for a substantial time. They all proved to be well fitting in the subjects ears even though the hard material from the SLA machine makes the ear plugs very susceptible for non-accurate fitting. We have therefore demonstrated a complete pipeline from direct ear scanning to production of well fitting hearing devices.

Acknowledgments. This work was (in part) financed by the *Danish National Advanced Technology Foundation* (project no 019-2009-3). We thank Oticon A/S for supplying the scanned ear impression data.

References

1. 3Shape, Copenhagen. http://www.3Shape.com
2. Projet MP3000, 3Dsystems. http://www.3DSystems.com/

3. Belongie, S., Malik, J., Puzicha, J.: Shape matching and object recognition using shape contexts. IEEE Trans. on Pattern Analysis and Machine Intelligence **24**(4), 509–522 (2002)
4. Blanz, V., Mehl, A., Vetter, T., Seidel, H.P.: A statistical method for robust 3D surface reconstruction from sparse data. In: Proc. 3D Data Processing, Visualization and Transmission, pp. 293–300 (2004)
5. Blanz, V., Vetter, T.: A morphable model for the synthesis of 3D faces. In: Proc. 26th Annual Conference on Computer Graphics and Interactive Techniques, pp. 187–194 (1999)
6. Caselles, V., Haro, G., Sapiro, G., Verdera, J.: On geometric variational models for inpainting surface holes. Computer Vision and Image Understanding **111**(3), 351–373 (2008)
7. Clarenz, U., Diewald, U., Dziuk, G., Rumpf, M., Rusu, R.: A finite element method for surface restoration with smooth boundary conditions. Computer Aided Geometric Design **21**(5), 427–446 (2004)
8. Cootes, T., Taylor, C., Cooper, D., Graham, J.: Active shape models - their training and application. Computer Vision and Image Understanding **61**(1), 38–59 (1995)
9. Frome, A., Huber, D., Kolluri, R., Bülow, T., Malik, J.: Recognizing objects in range data using regional point descriptors. In: Pajdla, T., Matas, J.G. (eds.) ECCV 2004. LNCS, vol. 3023, pp. 224–237. Springer, Heidelberg (2004)
10. Hammond, P., Hutton, T., Allanson, J., Campbell, L., Hennekam, R., Holden, S., Patton, M., Shaw, A., Temple, I., Trotter, M., et al.: 3D analysis of facial morphology. American Journal of Medical Genetics Part A **126**(4), 339–348 (2004)
11. Kazhdan, M., Bolitho, M., Hoppe, H.: Poisson surface reconstruction. In: Proc. Eurographics Symposium on Geometry Processing, pp. 61–70 (2006)
12. Kolluri, R., Shewchuk, J., O'Brien, J.: Spectral surface reconstruction from noisy point clouds. In: Proc. Eurographics Symposium on Geometry Processing, pp. 11–21 (2004)
13. Kuhn, H.W.: The Hungarian method for the assignment problem. Naval Research Logistic Quarterly **2**, 83–97 (1955)
14. Lanche, S., et al.: A statistical model of head asymmetry in infants with deformational plagiocephaly. In: Ersbøll, B.K., Pedersen, K.S. (eds.) SCIA 2007. LNCS, vol. 4522, pp. 898–907. Springer, Heidelberg (2007)
15. Nelder, J.A., Mead, R.: A simplex method for function minimization. The Computer Journal **7**(4), 308–313 (1965)
16. Paulsen, R.R., Hilger, K.B.: Shape modelling using markov random field restoration of point correspondences. In: Taylor, C., Noble, J.A. (eds.) IPMI 2003. LNCS, vol. 2732, pp. 1–12. Springer, Heidelberg (2003)
17. Paulsen, R., Larsen, R., Nielsen, C., Laugesen, S., Ersbøll, B.: Building and testing a statistical shape model of the human ear canal. In: Dohi, T., Kikinis, R. (eds.) MICCAI 2002. LNCS, vol. 2489, pp. 373–380. Springer, Heidelberg (2002)
18. Paulsen, R., Bærentzen, J., Larsen, R.: Markov random field surface reconstruction. IEEE Trans. on Visualization and Computer Graphics **16**(4), 636–646 (2010)
19. Rusinkiewicz, S., Levoy, M.: Efficient variants of the icp algorithm. In: Proc. 3D Digital Imaging and Modeling, pp. 145–152 (2001)
20. Verdera, J., Caselles, V., Bertalmio, M., Sapiro, G.: Inpainting surface holes. In: Proc. of International Conference on Image Processing, vol. 2 (2003)

Boosting Small-Data Performance of LBP: A Case Study in Celiac Disease Diagnosis

Michael Gadermayr[1]([⊠]), Andreas Uhl[1], and Andreas Vécsei[2]

[1] Department of Computer Sciences, University of Salzburg, Salzburg, Austria
{mgadermayr,uhl}@cosy.sbg.ac.at
http://www.wavelab.at
[2] St. Anna Children's Hospital, Department of Pediatrics, Medical University,
Vienna, Vienna, Austria

Abstract. A major issue in computer aided celiac disease diagnosis is the prevalence of substantial intra-class and even intra-image variations. A method which splits the images into a set of smaller ones and finally applies a decision level fusion turned out to be a powerful technique to address these problems and to boost the classification accuracy. This is especially true if using Local Binary Patterns and derivatives. However, due to the sparsity and roughness of the final feature vectors, these methods are not optimal if being applied to such small images. Therefore, in this work two novel and two methods from literature are investigated to improve the performances of Local Binary Patterns. Experiments show that the overall classification accuracies can be improved, especially by means of a combination of the novel methods. The techniques presented in this work are not restricted to this certain problem definition. They rather can be applied in arbitrary scenarios with small sized image data.

1 Introduction

Celiac disease [14], which is commonly known as gluten intolerance, is a disorder that affects the small intestine after introduction of gluten containing food. The disease leads to an inflammatory reaction in the mucosa of the small bowel caused by a dysregulated immune response triggered by ingested gluten proteins of certain cereals. During the course of celiac disease, the mucosa loses its absorptive villi (see Fig. 1(b)) and hyperplasia of the enteric crypts occurs, leading to a strongly diminished ability to absorb any nutrients. According to a large study [6], the overall prevalence of the disease in the USA is 1:133. Figure 1 shows example images, captured during endoscopy.

Up to now, significant work has been done on computer aided celiac disease diagnosis [3,4,9,10]. Especially Local Binary Patterns (LBP) [15] and derivatives of this well known texture feature extraction method have been extensively investigated with respect to this problem definition [9–11] and turned out to be highly effective.

In recent work on computer aided celiac disease diagnosis [8], the authors have proposed an effective and efficient split and merge approach which splits a

© Springer International Publishing Switzerland 2015
R.R. Paulsen and K.S. Pedersen (Eds.): SCIA 2015, LNCS 9127, pp. 224–233, 2015.
DOI: 10.1007/978-3-319-19665-7_19

textured image into non-overlapping sub-images, classifies these sub-images and finally applies a decision level fusion. Especially with LBP (and derivatives), this method turned out to be highly appropriate for the problem definition. This is quite surprising, because the sub-images are very small (e.g. a sub-image size of 42×42 pixels turned out to be appropriate) and LBP is not designed to be applied to such small data. Applying the more sophisticated bag-of-visual words [19] technique the achieved accuracies are considerably lower. However, no matter if using LBP in combination with the split and merge approach, bag-of-visual words [19] or state-of-the art fisher vectors [16,17], the problem of small data is the same for all of these approaches:

A small sample size leads to a less precise estimation of the probability density of the LBP patterns which is given by the histogram. The generated histograms become potentially sparse as well as rough, depending on the chosen setup. Table 1 shows the average number of patterns per bin, for each number of center-pixel neighbors. It should be noticed that the distribution of LBP patterns is far away from being uniformly. We supposed that the sparsity of the histogram affects the classification performance in case a high number of neighbors (especially with twelve but also in case of ten and eight neighbors).

Table 1. Histogram bins and average number of patterns per bin in case of different setups having a 42×42 pixel image and an LBP radius of three pixels (i.e. $36 \times 36 = 1296$ patterns in total)

LBP Neighbors	Histogram bins	Mean patterns per bin	Sufficient patterns per bin? (assumption)
4	16	81.0	✓
6	64	20.3	✓
8	256	5.1	?
10	1024	1.3	?
12	4096	0.3	✗

To compute the original LBP [15] feature vector, first a binary vector for each pixel is generated by computing the sign of the differences between this pixel and a set of neighboring pixels. Each of these binary patterns can be interpreted as a number by multiplying the binary row vector with a column vector consisting of increasing powers of two $(1, 2, 4, 8, ...)$. The final feature vector consists of the global histogram computed over all of these numerical values in an image. In the

(a) Marsh 0: Healthy mucosa.   (b) Marsh 3: Villous atrophy.

Fig. 1. Example patches of healthy (a) and disease mucosa (b)

last decades several derivatives of LBP have been proposed including Extended Local Binary Patterns (ELBP) [13] and Local Ternary Patterns [18].

In this work, focus is on four independent techniques to increase the performance in case of small sized image data. The first one changes the general algorithm of LBP using soft histograms (Sect. 2.1), the second one concatenates specific low dimensional features (Sect. 2.2), the third one relies on image pre-processing (Sect. 2.3) and the last is based on feature post-processing (Sect. 2.4). Whereas the first two methods are existing approaches from literature [1,2], the second two techniques are newly introduced in this paper. In Sect. 3 experimental results are presented and discussed.

2   Boosting LBP's Performance

In this section, four independent methods are outlines to boost the performance of LBP (and derivatives) if being applied to small data.

2.1   Soft-Histogram (SH)

To increase robustness to noise and make its output continuous, Ahonen and Pietikäinen have proposed soft histograms for LBP [1]. Instead of assigning a pixel in an image to exactly one histogram bin, in this fuzzified approach one pixel contributes to a number of bins. The contribution of a pixel (x, y) to a bin i is given by

$$SLBP(x, y, i) = \prod_{p=0}^{P-1} [b_p(i) \cdot f_d(g_c - g_p) + (1 - b_p(i)) \cdot (1 - f_d(g_c - g_p))], \quad (1)$$

where P is the number of neighbors, $b_p(i)$ denotes the value of the p-th bit of i, g_c is the current center pixel and g_p is one of the neighboring pixels. f_d is the fuzzy membership function

$$f_d(z) = max(min(0.5 + 0.5\frac{z}{d}, 1), 0), \quad (2)$$

where d regulates the extent of fuzzification. For small d this method converges to the traditional LBP. Although this method is not dedicated to small image data, the soft assignment can be utilized to generate smoother histograms.

2.2   Multi-Neighborhood (MN)

In another recent work, Banerji et al. have proposed a method [2] to deal with small image data in a bag-of-words model. Instead of introducing a new methodology, the authors concatenate eight LBP histograms with varying small neighborhoods. The exact patterns are shown in Fig. 2. By concatenating feature vectors with few neighbors (four), each histogram only consists of 16 $(= 2^4)$ bins which should be advantageous in case of small data. By concatenating eight feature vectors with different neighborhoods, a higher distinctiveness is claimed to be achieved.

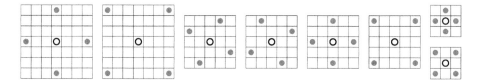

Fig. 2. The eight four-neighborhoods utlized by Banerji et al. [2]

2.3 Image-Enlargement (IE)

Whereas the methods mentioned so far change the feature extraction, we furthermore investigate the impact of an image enlargement, prior to the feature extraction stage. For this, the image is upscaled and missing points are bi-linearly interpolated. Thereby the number of pixels is increased by the square of the scaling factor which directly leads to substantially denser histograms. More sophisticated interpolation techniques (bi-cubic, spline) have also been tested, however, the obtained classification outcomes are highly similar with all methods.

2.4 Histogram-Smoothing (HS)

Finally we propose a histogram improvement technique which can be applied as a post processing method after LBP histogram generation. The main idea is to compensate the roughness of histograms by means of smoothing, which, to the best of our knowledge, has not been done before. One special motivation for this method is to achieve a similar behavior like Soft-Histogram LBP with a substantially lower computational expense.

The crucial thing is that an LBP histogram cannot be filtered by straight forward convolution with for example a Gaussian filter to obtain a smoother version. The problem is that neighboring histogram bins not necessarily exhibit a strong logical relationship. This issue is illustrated in Fig. 3.

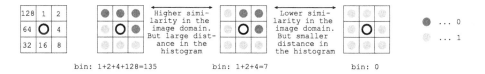

Fig. 3. Histogram smoothing

To cope with this issue, we construct a Matrix $M = m_{(i,j)}$ which defines the degree of similarity between all combinations of two binary patterns. This matrix is defined by means of the inverse hamming distance

$$m_{(s,t)} = \left(\frac{1}{P} \cdot \sum_{p=1}^{P} 1 - |b_p(s) - b_p(t)| \right)^k , \qquad (3)$$

where the positive value k adjusts the degree of smoothing by suppressing small values. A small k (e.g. $k = 1$) corresponds to extensive smoothing and vice versa.

Finally the smoothed histogram H^* is defined by

$$H^*(s) = \frac{1}{\sum_{t=1}^{2^P} m_{(s,t)}} \cdot \sum_{t=1}^{2^P} H(i) \cdot m_{(s,t)} . \tag{4}$$

This equation states that each bin contributes to each other bin in the histogram by the proportion specified by M. In the trivial case, where M is the identity matrix, smoothing is omitted and H^* is equal to H.

It should be mentioned that the matrix m could theoretically also be defined in a different way. However, we suppose that our definition based on the hamming distance poses a quite natural and plausible one.

2.5   Runtimes

Besides their high distinctiveness, LBP have become popular because of their low computational costs compared to more elaborated techniques. Therefore, we will briefly highlight the runtime[1] of the methods, presented in this section. Figure 4 shows the overall runtimes for computing the feature vector for one image (42×42 pixels), for different numbers of neighbors. Notice that the Multi-Neighbor LBP are only defined for a certain neighborhood and thereby cannot be configured, which results in a constant runtime in the figure. Whereas the Soft-Histogram approach corresponds to quite high computational costs, Histogram-Smoothing turned out to be distinctly faster. It should be noticed that the costs for the Soft-Histogram approach increase even more (linearly) with an increasing image size. The Histogram-Smoothing technique on opposite remains quite stable with an increasing image size, because the histogram creation is extremely fast (see costs of traditional LBP).

3   Experiments

3.1   Setup

The image testset used for the experiments contains images of the duodenal bulb and the pars descendens, which are parts of the small bowel, taken during duodenoscopies at the St. Anna Children's Hospital using pediatric gastroscopes (Olympus GIF N180 and Q165) (with a resolution of 768×576 and 528×522 pixels). Prior to processing, all images are converted to gray scale images because the additional use of color information did not lead to any substantial improvements. In a preprocessing step, texture patches with a fixed size of 128×128 pixels have been manually extracted. These patches are split into nine non-overlapping smaller sub-images with a size of 42×42 pixels. This splitting strategy, based on

---

[1] Tests are performed on an Intel(R) Core(TM) i5-2400 CPU @ 3.10GHz. The code has been implemented in C/MEX.

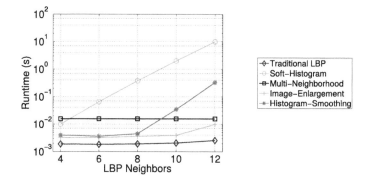

Fig. 4. Execution runtimes

splitting into 9 sub-images, turned out to be optimal in recent work on computer aided celiac disease diagnosis [8]. After splitting an image, feature extraction and classification is executed separately for each sub-image. Finally, the decisions are merged by means of majority voting. This strategy turned out to be more appropriate than a straight forward classification of the complete images. This is supposed to be due to the high intra-class and intra-image variations of the endoscopic images.

To get the ground truth for the texture patches, the condition of the mucosal areas covered by the images has been determined by histological examination of biopsies from corresponding regions. The severity of the villous atrophy has been classified according to the modified Marsh classification scheme [14]. Although it is possible to distinguish between different stages of the disease, we aim in distinguishing between images of patients with (Marsh-3) and without the disease (Marsh-0), as this two classes case is most relevant in practice. Our experiments are based on a data set containing 612 images (306 Marsh-0 and 306 Marsh-3 images) from 171 (131 Marsh-0 and 40 Marsh-3) individuals [12].

All overall accuracies computed are based on the mean accuracy of 32 random splits. One distinct split divides the data set into an approximately balanced training (50 %) and evaluation set (50 %), restricting images of one patient to be in the same set to avoid any bias.

Focus is on two different LBP versions which turned out to be suitable for celiac disease classification [7]:

- Local Binary Patterns (LBP) [15]: This is the most common LBP method based on a circular neighborhood and a certain number of sample points, which are equidistantly placed on the circle. Sample points which are in between pixel values are interpolated in a nearest neighbor sense. This is done, as previous work on computer aided celiac disease diagnosis [7] showed that the bi-linear interpolation, which is usually utilized, corresponds to a loss of accuracy.

- Extended Local Binary Patterns (ELBP) [13]: ELBP in this context consists of the LBP feature extraction based on the edge magnitude of the original image, computed by means of convolution with two orthogonal Sobel filters.

The value d in case of Soft-Histogram LBP is fixed to 12 and k in case of Histogram-Smoothing is fixed to 4, which turned out to be appropriate for all configurations. In case of Image-Enlargement, a resize factor of 2 turned out to be optimal. The restriction to (lower dimensional) uniform patterns did not lead to improvements as far as the classification accuracy is concerned. For feature discrimination, we deploy the linear support vector classifier [5] (SVM) which has been widely used in recent work.

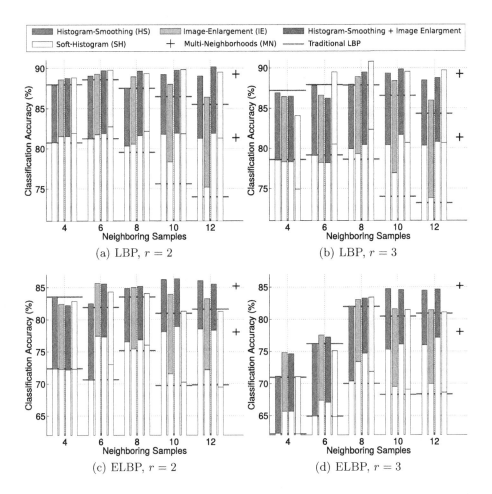

Fig. 5. Overall classification accuracies with different feature extraction methods and different configurations. For explanation see Sect. 3.2

3.2   Results and Discussion

In Fig. 5, the main results are shown. One subplot shows the overall classification accuracies for a certain feature, a certain neighborhood (two or three pixels), five numbers of neighbors and the investigated approaches. The top of the colored bars indicate the rates achieved if the nine sub-images of one complete image are fused, whereas the top of the white bars indicate the rates achieved without the decision level fusion. The solid lines indicate the accuracies achieved with traditional LBP based classification. In a similar manner, the top lines indicate the rates achieved with fusion and the bottom lines indicate the rates achieved without fusion. Similarly, the crosses (+) denote the rates obtained with the Multi-Neighborhood approach which has a fixed neighborhood. In the following, focus is on the fusion based (upper) accuracies that are more relevant in practice, however, there is a strong correlation between these values and the lower values without the decision level fusion.

Considering the LBP based feature extraction (solid lines) with a radius of one and two, the best accuracies are achieved in general with four, six or eight neighbors, which is not surprising if considering Table 1. With ten and especially with twelve neighbors, the classification accuracies decrease. A less distinct but still similar behavior is shown in case of ELBP. Regarding the Histogram-Smoothing method, it can be seen that the performance with ten and twelve neighbors can be improved consistently, whereas the fewer neighbored versions stay almost unchanged. In each case of the 10 to 12 neighbored versions, this approach is able to outperform the best traditional configuration. The less elaborated Image-Enlargement technique has a similar effect on the classification performance, however, the correlation between the number of neighbors and the improvement is less distinct and the improvements are weaker. The third bars (per bunch) indicate the accuracies obtained if combining Histogram-Smoothing with Image-Enlargement. Considering LBP versions with eight to twelve neighbors, this combination leads to even better accuracies. In case of ELBP, the image enlargement step obviously is less important as Histogram-Smoothing mostly cannot be outperformed by the combined method. Interestingly, the more computationally complex Soft-Histogram LBP on average corresponds to slightly lower rates. This method seems to be less appropriate for ELBP, however, in the special case of LBP with a radius of three pixels this technique generates the best overall results. This quite interesting behavior is supposed to be due to the larger differences between the pixels (in case of the larger radius), which can be directly exploited by the fuzzy histogram creation. Due to the binary quantization, the post-processing Histogram-Smoothing is (like traditional LBP) unable to exploit any additional information given by pixel differences. However, the major drawback of this method is the comparatively high computational effort (see Fig. 4). Therefore, we recommend to utilize the Histogram-Smoothing approach instead. Especially in case of larger images, the runtime of the Soft-Histogram method increases linearly with respect to the image pixels whereas the runtime of the Histogram-Smoothing is mainly related to the number of histogram bins. Although the Multi-Neighborhood LBP could be interpreted as a multi-resolution method (as thereby actually cannot be directly compared to the others) it is unable to outperform the best of the other configurations. Obviously the distinctiveness of high dimensional joint distribution cannot be achieved by a concatenation of lower dimensional joint distributions. Nevertheless, this feature is able to outperform the best classification rates obtained with traditional LBP.

4   Conclusion

We have proposed two novel and comparatively fast methods to improve the classification performances of Local Binary Patterns and derivatives, if being applied to small images. Especially if combining these techniques, reasonable improvements can be obtained, compared to traditional classification based on Local Binary Patterns and derivatives. The improvement techniques have been compared to two existing approaches from literature. One of them (Multi-Neighborhood LBP) turned out to be less appropriate. The other one (Soft-Histogram LBP) generates similarly accurate results, however, this feature is substantially more complex from computational point of view.

References

1. Ahonen, T., Pietikäinen, M.: Soft histograms for local binary patterns. In: Proceedings of the Finnish Signal Processing Symposium (FINSIG 2007), pp. 1–4 (2007)
2. Banerji, S., Sinha, A., Liu, C.: A new bag of words LBP (BoWL) descriptor for scene image classification. In: Wilson, R., Hancock, E., Bors, A., Smith, W. (eds.) CAIP 2013, Part I. LNCS, vol. 8047, pp. 490–497. Springer, Heidelberg (2013)
3. Ciaccio, E.J., Tennyson, C.A., Bhagat, G., Lewis, S.K., Green, P.H.R.: Classification of videocapsule endoscopy image patterns: comparative analysis between patients with celiac disease and normal individuals. BioMedical Engineering Online 9(1), 1–12 (2010)
4. Ciaccio, E.J., Tennyson, C.A., Lewis, S.K., Krishnareddy, S., Bhagat, G., Green, P.: Distinguishing patients with celiac disease by quantitative analysis of videocapsule endoscopy images. Computer Methods and Programs in Biomedicine 100(1), 39–48 (2010)
5. Fan, R.E., Chang, K.W., Hsieh, C.J., Wang, X.R., Lin, C.J.: LIBLINEAR: A library for large linear classification. Journal of Machine Learning Research 9, 1871–1874 (2008)
6. Fasano, A., Berti, I., Gerarduzzi, T., Not, T., Colletti, R.B., Drago, S., Elitsur, Y., Green, P.H.R., Guandalini, S., Hill, I.D., Pietzak, M., Ventura, A., Thorpe, M., Kryszak, D., Fornaroli, F., Wasserman, S.S., Murray, J.A., Horvath, K.: Prevalence of celiac disease in at-risk and not-at-risk groups in the united states: a large multicenter study. Archives of internal medicine 163, 286–292 (2003)
7. Gadermayr, M., Liedlgruber, M., Uhl, A., Vécsei, A.: Evaluation of different distortion correction methods and interpolation techniques for an automated classification of celiac disease. Computer Methods and Programs in Biomedicine 112(3), 694–712 (2013)

8. Gadermayr, M., Uhl, A., Vécsei, A.: Dealing with intra-class and intra-image variations in automatic celiac disease diagnosis. In: Proceedings of Bildverarbeitung für die Medizin 2015 (BVM 2015). Informatik aktuell, March 2015

9. Hegenbart, S., Uhl, A.: A scale-adaptive extension to methods based on LBP using scale-normalized laplacian of gaussian extrema in scale-space. In: Proceedings of the International Conference on Acoustics, Speech, and Signal Processing (ICASSP 2014), pp. 4352–4356 (2014)

10. Hegenbart, S., Uhl, A., Vécsei, A.: Impact of endoscopic image degradations on LBP based features using one-class SVM for classification of celiac disease. In: Proceedings of the 7th International Symposium on Image and Signal Processing and Analysis (ISPA 2011), Dubrovnik, Croatia, pp. 715–720, September 2011

11. Hegenbart, S., Uhl, A., Vécsei, A.: Impact of histogram subset selection on classification using multiscale LBP. In: Proceedings of Bildverarbeitung für die Medizin 2011 (BVM 2011), pp. 359–363. Informatik aktuell, March 2011

12. Hegenbart, S., Uhl, A., Vécsei, A., Wimmer, G.: Scale invariant texture descriptors for classifying celiac disease. Medical Image Analysis **17**(4), 458–474 (2013)

13. Huang, X., Li, S., Wang, Y.: Shape localization based on statistical method using extended local binary pattern. In: Proceedings of the 3rd International Conference on Image and Graphics (ICIG 2004), Hong Kong, China, pp. 1–4 (2004)

14. Oberhuber, G., Granditsch, G., Vogelsang, H.: The histopathology of coeliac disease: time for a standardized report scheme for pathologists. European Journal of Gastroenterology and Hepatology **11**, 1185–1194 (1999)

15. Ojala, T., Pietikäinen, M., Harwood, D.: A comparative study of texture measures with classification based on feature distributions. Pattern Recognition **29**(1), 51–59 (1996)

16. Perronnin, F., Dance, C.: Fisher kernels on visual vocabularies for image categorization. In: Proceedings of the IEEE Conference on Computer Vision and Pattern Recognition (CVPR 2007), pp. 1–8, June 2007

17. Perronnin, F., Liu, Y., Sanchez, J., Poirier, H.: Large-scale image retrieval with compressed fisher vectors. In: Proceedings of the IEEE Conference on Computer Vision and Pattern Recognition (CVPR 2010), pp. 3384–3391, June 2010

18. Tan, X., Triggs, B.: Enhanced local texture feature sets for face recognition under difficult lighting conditions. In: Zhou, S.K., Zhao, W., Tang, X., Gong, S. (eds.) AMFG 2007. LNCS, vol. 4778, pp. 168–182. Springer, Heidelberg (2007)

19. Varma, M., Zisserman, A.: Classifying images of materials: achieving viewpoint and illumination independence. In: Heyden, A., Sparr, G., Nielsen, M., Johansen, P. (eds.) ECCV 2002, Part III. LNCS, vol. 2352, pp. 255–271. Springer, Heidelberg (2002)

Image Registration of Cochlear μCT Data Using Heat Distribution Similarity

Hans Martin Kjer[1](✉), Sergio Vera[2,3], Jens Fagertun[1], Debora Gil[3],
Miguel Ángel González-Ballester[4,5], and Rasmus Paulsen[1]

[1] Department of Applied Mathmatics and Computer Science,
Technical University of Denmark, Copenhagen, Denmark
hmkj@dtu.dk
[2] Alma Medical Systems, Barcelona, Spain
[3] Computer Vision Center, Universitat Autònoma de Barcelona, Barcelona, Spain
[4] Department of Information and Communication Technologies,
Universitat Pompeu Fabra, Barcelona, Spain
[5] ICREA, Barcelona, Spain

Abstract. Better understanding of the anatomical variability of the human cochlear is important for the design and function of Cochlear Implants. Good non-rigid alignment of high-resolution cochlear μCT data is a challenging task.

In this paper we study the use of heat distribution similarity between samples as an anatomical registration prior. We set-up and present our heat distribution model for the cochlea and utilize it in a typical cubic B-spline registration model. Evaluation and comparison is done against a corresponding normal registration of binary segmentations.

1 Introduction

Image registration and finding data correspondence is a well known challenge in biomedical image analysis. The choice and performance of the registration model depends highly on the involved imaging modalities, the anatomy of the object, the desired end-goal, etc. [9]. Larger and more complex deformations make it more challenging to set-up the optimal registration procedure. It becomes more difficult for the optimization to avoid local minima as the amount of parameters in the transformation model increases. To efficiently solve the problem it is often required to include additional data pre-processing, prior knowledge, regularization or constraints.

In this study we work with registration of μCT images of the inner ear, which is the structure controlling hearing and balance. Establishing correspondences between samples is required to understand the anatomical/shape variability, which has uses in a range of interesting clinical applications regarding Cochlear Implants [13]. It can be in a patient-specific context, by advising recipients and surgeons to choose an electrode design suited for the anatomy of the user [12], and/or optimizing the CI-programming based on patient-specific physiological simulations [4]. Description of population-based anatomical variability further

© Springer International Publishing Switzerland 2015
R.R. Paulsen and K.S. Pedersen (Eds.): SCIA 2015, LNCS 9127, pp. 234–245, 2015.
DOI: 10.1007/978-3-319-19665-7_20

allow manufacturers to explore the general implant design. The inner ear is terminologically divided into two parts - the spiral formed cochlea (for hearing) and the vestibular system (for balance) consisting of three semi-circular canals in a close to perpendicular configuration (see Figure 1). We will focus mostly on the cochlea part in this study, as this to our experience is the more difficult part to register. The challenge is mainly due to the relatively large observable differences compared to the compactness of the spiral. The spiral outer dimensions approximates to 10x8x4 mm, and on average the cochlea winds 2.6 turns [5] but can approach up to three full turns. This corresponds to a difference in the order of 1-2 mm following the path of the spiral. The separation between the cochlear turns in the same region is typically one order of magnitude smaller. Further, the spiral lacks distinct features to identify corresponding locations. The whole spiral is a tube-like structure (see Figure 1) with a large degree of self-similarity in cross-sections.

Our aim is to set up an image registration procedure for cochlear data. Conventional practice is to start with a global alignment (rigid, affine etc.) followed by a non-rigid step consisting of very local deformations. The common global transformations cannot align cochlear shapes very well, as they cannot take into account the spiral nature of the data. This lack of global fit should be handled by the non-rigid registration instead. The desired non-rigid model should not just expand or reduce the apical part of the spiral to cope with variability in cochlea turning, but instead it should try to readjust the entire spiral. Essentially the model should be able to handle very local deformations while still adhering to a more global structure.

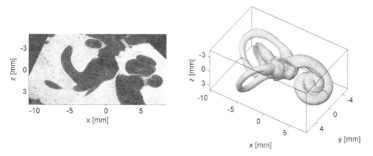

Fig. 1. Left: A slice from a μCT dataset showing the segmentation of the inner ear. Right: A surface model of the inner ear constructed from the segmentation of a μCT dataset.

There are different ways to modify the registration model to achieve this, and inclusion of prior-knowledge have been studied previously. An anatomical shape prior can be in form of a statistical shape model [2,6]. However, building shape models is in itself a labor intensive task rivaling if not surpassing the task of the registration, as the prerequisite for building the model is data that is already registered to have correspondences.

In the work of [1] an articulated skeleton model was pre-registered to intra-mouse data studies in order to recover large pose-differences between data acquisitions. Landmark correspondences of the skeleton model were then used to regularize the registration cost function. While in principle it is a useful approach to our case, corresponding landmarks are to our experience difficult to establish coherently and consistently for the cochlea.

It is also possible to do clever preprocessing of the data to obtain an image similarity measure more suited for the registration. In the work of [11] a selection of shape features were calculated from the objects and transformed into vector-valued 2D feature images, that were then registered using a classic image registration formulation. Skeletal features were used to provide the more global similarity between samples, while curvature and convexity features handles local similarity. The principle idea of processing the data to find a new similarity metric is sound and an approach that we follow. Instead of working from meshes and shape features we will work from the images and explore the use of a single image feature to improve our registrations - the heat distribution. Techniques for calculating volumetric maps of 3D heat distributions already exist, and have the potential to provide the required global context to the registration model. Since a heat map can be considered just another type of gray-scale image data, this approach would fit into already existing registration frameworks with little modification.

The purpose of this study is then to test and evaluate deformable registration using a B-spline transformation model on a series of inner ear/cochlear datasets with and without the use of heat distribution similarity in the registration model.

2   Materials and Methods

In this section we provide a more detailed description of the data and its processing, the set up and evaluation of registration models and the computation of heat distributions. In order to conceptualize and test the overall procedure we create and use some simple synthetic 2D images. This data is introduced in Section 2.1 and corresponding registration model described in Section 2.4. Details concerning the cochlear data and the initial processing are found in Section 2.2. The computation of the heat distribution in this data is described in Section 2.3. Finally, the registration models (for both data types) are detailed in Section 2.4 and their evaluation in Section 2.5.

2.1   2D Synthetic Data

Data Generation: Small synthetic 2D images are generated to demonstrate the concept of using maps of heat distributions in a registration model. Two binary 100x100 images, B_i, were created manually containing a foreground spiral region and a background. In order to create a classic gray-scale version of the images (I_i), random noise was added to each pixel. The noise models for both regions were Gaussian, $\mathcal{N}_j(\mu_j, \sigma_j)$. The corresponding volumetric heat distributions (H_i)

were generated simplistically; The apex of the spiral was manually selected as the source. Heat was propagated iteratively with a 4-neighborhood kernel. The heat spreads to previously untouched foreground voxels, and for each iteration the heat is decreased by 1. The synthetic data is presented in Figure 2.

I_1 H_1 I_2 H_2

Fig. 2. Synthetic 2D data with I_1 and I_2 showing the two gray-scale images, and H_1 and H_2 the corresponding heat map versions

Image Registration: In short, we initially calculate one rigid transformation that is applied to both of the moving images, i.e. I_2 and H_2. This is followed by non-rigid registrations between respectively the pair of grayscale and heat map images. The formulation and details on the images registrations are described in Section 2.4. The result of the deformations are visually compared and evaluated.

2.2   Cochlear Data

A collection of N=17 dried temporal bones from the University of Bern were prepared and scanned with a Scanco Medical μCT100 system. The data was reconstructed and processed to obtain image volumes of 48 micron isotropic voxel-sizes containing the inner ear (Figure 1, left).

Image Segmentation: The inner ear border was delineated semi-automatically to obtain a binary segmentation, B_i, of each dataset using ITK-SNAP [14].The images contain some openings and non-anatomical artifacts that had to be manually handled to obtain comparable segmentations across datasets. A surface model was generated for each dataset using Marching Cubes followed by a surface reconstruction [10] to obtain a well-formed triangular mesh (Figure 1, right).

Initial Rigid Alignment: Before proceeding further we choose to perform an initial registration of the data to bring it into a common space and orientation. We use a rigid transform to remove translational and rotational differences between the datasets while retaining variation in size or scaling.

The initial registration is done with principal component transformations calculated from the extracted surface models. One dataset was chosen as the reference, to which the others were aligned. In short, the mean vertex position, $\bar{p}_i$, of the i-th dataset is subtracted from all vertices translating the center of mass to position (0,0,0). Finding the eigenvectors of the 3-x-3 covariance matrix of the mesh vertex positions (after the translation) provides a rotation matrix to the principal axes. This essentially corresponds to fitting an ellipsoid to the point cloud of each dataset and aligning the ellipsoid axes, and it works consistently due to the asymmetry of the inner ear shape.

After the initial registration all images were cropped to contain only the cochlea region, since this is the structure of our focus. The first principal axis described above separates the cochlea from the vestibular region. Therefore, the cropping is accomplished easily by splitting each dataset at x = 0 (see Figure 1 and 3a).

2.3 Heat Distribution

The usage of heat distribution models for registration of complex anatomical shapes allows the generation of a global similarity between samples regardless of local differences in shape.

Calculating a heat map, H_i, for each dataset is done after the initial registration and is initiated by the placement of a source and sink. The source was manually set at the cochlear apex (see Figure 3a) and the sink was chosen as the inner ear center of mass (i.e. position (0,0,0)). The heat values at the two extremes were fixed. The heat distribution over time in a region is governed by the Partial Differential Equation (PDE)

$$\frac{\partial u}{\partial t} - \alpha \Delta u = 0 \tag{1}$$

which describes the distribution of heat, u, over time, t, in a medium with thermal conductivity α. With Δ being the Laplacian operator $\Delta u \equiv u_{xx} + u_{yy} + u_{zz}$. Assuming α to be one and $t \to \infty$ we obtain the thermal equilibrium state solution described by the Laplacian equation

$$\Delta u = 0 \tag{2}$$

Solving this PDE (Eq. 2) implies solving a boundary value problem with boundary conditions [3]. Careful assignment of the boundary values can be positive for the registration process. Assigning Dirichlet boundary conditions f to specific anatomical sites $\mathcal{A}$ such as the apex and the center of the cochlea creates a shape metric image that can be used for steering the registration process to an improved solution.

Discrete Laplacian on a Closed Domain: We want to solve

$$\Delta u = 0 \quad u_{|\mathcal{A}} = f \tag{3}$$

for $f = f(x, y, z)$ the boundary values defined at anatomical sites $\mathcal{A}$. All the foreground voxels of a binary image segmentation, B_i, will constitute the domain Ω where the heat diffusion will be applied. By applying the Laplace discrete operator to all image voxels, Equation 2 can be written in matrix form as $\mathbf{A}u = 0$. The matrix $\mathbf{A}$, called the graph Laplacian or adjacency matrix, encodes the

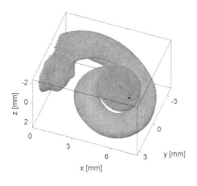
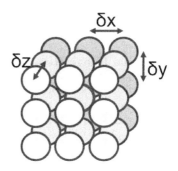

(a) Heat distribution at the surface of the cochlear. The source point in the apex is marked in black.

(b) Discrete voxel lattice. Central voxel highlighted in red. Neighbors in x, y and z axis are at distances $\delta x, \delta y, \delta z$ respectively.

Fig. 3. Heat distribution for 3D data

neighboring relations between voxels. This is because we in the voxel image lattice (see Figure 3b) can approximate the discrete Laplacian by computing the second order finite differences.

The solution to the Laplacian with Dirichlet anatomical conditions is obtained by solving the system of equations $\mathbf{A}u = \mathbf{b}$, with $\mathbf{b}$ being a row matrix encoding the boundary values at $\mathcal{A}$ given by:

$$f(x, y, z) = \begin{cases} 1, & \text{for } (x, y, z) \in \text{ cochlear apex (source)} \\ 0, & \text{for } (x, y, z) \in \text{ cochlea center of mass (sink)} \end{cases} \qquad (4)$$

Although $\mathbf{A}$ and $\mathbf{b}$ are sparse by definition, solving the system of equations with standard techniques might be unfeasible. Given that $\mathbf{A}$ is symmetric and positive definite we can use the Preconditioned Conjugate Gradient method using the Incomplete Cholesky Factorization of $\mathbf{A}$ as a pre-conditioner [7]. This allows solving the system iteratively in a short time and with a low memory footprint. For the generation of the map to be useful, the cochlea segmentation must ensure that the cochlear turns does not intersect each other in the segmentation.

Two Step Heat Map Generation: When solving the entire 3D domain using just a sink and a source voxel the decay of the heat function is very fast to our experience. We obtain a very small heat gradient throughout the cochlea and the resulting heat map is too flat to be used properly. We improve the heat map by applying a two step process for the generation of the map. First, we compute the heat map with a single voxel sink and source point, but using only the boundary voxels of the cochlea segmentation as the diffusion domain. This ensures that heat spreads over a reduced number of voxels, generating a boundary heat map with better gradient and slower heat decay. Second, the resulting boundary heat map is used as boundary condition for a second heat propagation over the entire cochlea segmentation domain.

2.4   Deformable Image Registration

The work-flow for non-rigid image registration is quite standard. The (N-1) moving datasets are registered to a chosen reference, following the formulation and framework of the `elastix` [8] toolbox.

The registration of the moving dataset, I_M, towards the fixed image, I_F, is formulated as a (parametric) transformation, T_μ, where the vector μ containing the p-parameters of the transformation model are found as an optimization of the cost function, $\mathcal{C}$.

$$\hat{\mu} = \arg\min_\mu \mathcal{C}(T_\mu, I_F, I_M) \tag{5}$$

The transformation model used in this paper is the cubic B-spline grid in a multi-resolution setting. The spacing between grid points follow a gradually decreasing schedule to start with a rough alignment that is slowly refined. The particular schedule used was (24, 16, 8) voxels.

Binary Set-up: We make a 'normal' registration between the segmentation volumes, to have something to compare our proposed usage of heat distributions against. The registration is done between the binary segmentation volumes, B_i, rather than the gray-scale volumes, I_i, for two reasons. First, the μCT data contain smaller artifacts and certain weakly contrasted edges, that were dealt with during the segmentation (Section 2.2). Secondly, the registration should not be influenced by the anatomical differences in the surrounding bone structure. The following cost-function was used for the registration:

$$\mathcal{C}_1 = \alpha \cdot \mathcal{S}_{\text{Sim}}(\mu, B_F, B_M) + (1-\alpha) \cdot \mathcal{P}_{\text{BE}}(\mu) \tag{6}$$

where α is a weight parameter in the interval [0,1], here chosen to 0.9 by means of experimentation. For the similarity term, $\mathcal{S}_{\text{Sim}}$, the sum of squared differences (SSD) is chosen. The term $\mathcal{P}_{\text{BE}}$ is the energy bending regularization used to penalize strong changes and foldings in the transformation.

Heat-map Set-up: In order to use the similarity of heat distributions in the registration, the cost function can essentially remain the same, simply replacing the underlying image data from the segmentations, B_i, to the heat maps, H_i. By experimentation we set $\alpha = 0.1$, while all other settings remains un-altered in order to provide a fair comparison between the two set-ups.

$$\mathcal{C}_2 = \alpha \cdot \mathcal{S}_{\text{Sim}}(\mu, H_F, H_M) + (1-\alpha) \cdot \mathcal{P}_{\text{BE}}(\mu) \tag{7}$$

Table 1. Statistics of registration evaluation metrics, reported as the mean $+/-$ 1 std. Model 1 and 2 refers respectively to Eq. 6 (binary) and Eq. 7 (heat).

Metric	Dice Score	Mean Err. [mm]	Max Err. [mm]	Apex Err. [mm]
Model 1	$0.96 \pm <0.01$	$0.07 \pm <0.01$	0.54 ± 0.13	0.97 ± 0.58
Model 2	$0.99 \pm <0.01$	$0.05 \pm <0.01$	0.43 ± 0.12	0.66 ± 0.58

Registration Model - 2D Synthetic Data: The two registrations models described above (Eq. 6 and Eq. 7) are also applied in the case of synthetic 2D data with some minor modifications. The cost function terms remains unaltered, i.e. the SSD was used for the similarity metric with added bending energy regularization. However, the weighting parameter was set to $\alpha = 0.7$ in both cases, and only a single resolution was used with no smoothing and a B-spline grid point spacing of 3 pixels.

2.5   Evaluation

We are interested in comparing the registration results, $\hat{\mu}_j$, from using either model 1 (Eq. 6) or model 2 (Eq. 7) with different metrics. For a voxel based score we calculate the Dice Coefficient between the deformed binary volume, $B_i(T_{\mu_j})$, and the reference, B_{Ref}. The ground truth mesh, M_i, can be compared to the deformed reference mesh, $M_{\mathrm{Ref}}(T_{\mu_j})$, from which we calculate the two-sided mean surface error and Hausdorff distance.

Since the above mentioned evaluation metrics are very generic and global we also use the apex error. A landmark is manually placed in the apex in all datasets, and we calculate the euclidean distance between the anatomical correspondence.

3   Results

2D Synthetic Data: The results with the synthetic data are shown in Figure 4. The 'normal' intensity registration (model 1), μ_I, was unable to fully capture

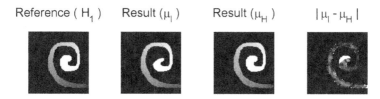

Reference (H_1)   Result (μ_I)   Result (μ_H) $|\mu_I - \mu_H|$

Fig. 4. Registration results on the synthetic 2D data. From left to right: The reference heat distribution H_1, The moving heat map, H_2, after transformation using the registration results, i.e. $H_2(T_{\mu_I})$ and $H_2(T_{\mu_H})$. Finally, the difference between the results, i.e. $|H_2(T_{\mu_I}) - H_2(T_{\mu_H})|$.

the full spiral with the given settings. When comparing the subtraction image of the two deformed heat maps, it should be noted that there is a difference throughout the entire spiral - suggesting that the registration based on the heat maps, μ_H, provides a more global twist of the spiral.

3D Cochlea Data: The quantitative evaluation is presented in Figure 5a and Table 1. The visual differences between the two registration models are illustrated in Figure 5b for a single case. In three cases the deformations resulted in an anatomically incorrect warping, where for instance the separation of the cochlea turns was not preserved. It is not apparent from the evaluation metrics, but very clear from a visual inspection of those samples.

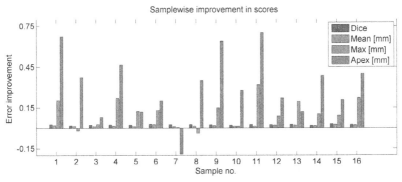

(a) Graph of the sample wise improvement between model 2 (heat) and model 1 (binary) in evaluation scores.

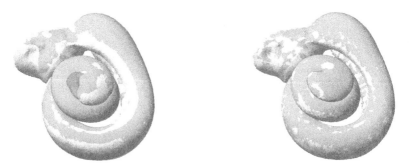

(b) Comparison of deformations. Left: Model 1 (binary) Right: Model 2 (heat). Blue transparent surface is ground truth and gray is the fitted surface.

Fig. 5. Results of the registration of 3D data

4   Discussion and Conclusion

The contribution of this study is a presentation and evaluation of using heat distribution similarity as a way of aiding image registration of cochlear samples. For now we have demonstrated its ability to add flexibility to the transformation and to improve registration accuracy. However, there are other important aspects to consider. Introducing additional pre-processing obviously adds more computations and processing time. It is likely to involve extra parameters to tune and it may contribute with noise and uncertainty to the registration. Our approach rely heavily upon a good segmentation of the data, which required a lot of manual labor. The additional processing time for calculating the heat-distributions were not a substantial issue considering the observed benefits. There are some factors that may affect the usage of the heat distributions. First, the manual placement of the source landmark inherently carries some uncertainty, but it is not immediately considered problematic. Secondly and more importantly, is the effect of the heat gradient throughout the cochlea. If the change in heat is too small, it might not have the desired guiding effect upon the registration, and too much change might force very strong deformations. Finding the right balance should be part of our future work. It is further important to note that the transformation model remains the same with this pre-processing strategy. The registration between the original images (segmentation or gray-scale) have the potential to find the same transformations as with the heat maps included. Without the heat distributions, the convergence rate may be slower and more levels of resolution and tweaking of registration parameters is required. The data pre-processing can have the added benefit of easing the registration set-up.

Our evaluation of the method is based mostly on global metrics. Their usefulness is limited, as they are hardly able to show whether a registration is successful or not. For that we need more anatomically meaningful evaluation metrics like the apex error. This error is very local, so it does not reveal if the desired deformation throughout the cochlea is achieved. The lack of consistent landmarks or uniquely identifiable locations on the cochlear makes it challenging to perform better quantitative evaluation of the registration. It would require setting up larger elaborate methods, exceeding the scope of this study. What we conclude from the results, is that heat distribution similarity adds flexibility to the registration, thereby allowing turning of the cochlea apex to be captured in a more anatomically correct manner.

Considerations can also be made to the chosen registration model. We work with the B-spline grid as the transformation model which has some limitations. Choosing a fluid- or optical flow-based model [9] could potentially be more suited for this kind of spiral anatomy.

Working on the binary data, better registrations were achieved with little regularization ($\alpha = 0.9$) in order to allow larger deformations. But since there is nothing to guide the transform to the anatomical correct place, then the method falls short. The maps of heat distributions provide global similarity to the otherwise locally defined B-spline transformation. It adds a lot of flexibility to the procedure - in fact too much. Strong regularization ($\alpha = 0.1$) was required to ensure reasonable deformations. Even though the results look very positive, our experience is that the procedure is not stable. It is likely to run into very large unreasonable deformations, that for instance goes across the separation of the cochlea turns. Essentially, we have a difficulty in applying enough and/or correct regularization. This is a problem to be addressed in future work. Additional regularization could for instance be forcing local rigidity in the bony structures surrounding the cochlea.

Of the 16 tested registrations, we observed three failed cases where deformations were unreasonable. These datasets are the cases least similar to chosen reference data. The issue is therefore not only lack of regularization, but part of the solution could also be by introducing coarser resolution levels in the registration. Further, this study was run on down-sampled data. The data is originally in a higher resolution, where the separation between cochlea turns is more clear. Using this data may help prevent the unreasonable deformations.

To conclude, we have presented a data pre-processing strategy for aiding non-rigid image registration using similarity of heat distributions. We have tested the idea on synthetic 2D data and on μCT of the cochlea, and demonstrated its ability to provide a global guidance and flexibility to the registration procedure.

Acknowledgments. The research leading to HEAR-EU results has received funding from the European Union Seventh Frame Programme (FP7/2007-2013) under grant agreement n°304857.

References

1. Baiker, M., Staring, M., Löwik, C.W.G.M., Reiber, J.H.C., Lelieveldt, B.P.F.: Automated registration of whole-body follow-up MicroCT data of mice. In: Fichtinger, G., Martel, A., Peters, T. (eds.) MICCAI 2011, Part II. LNCS, vol. 6892, pp. 516–523. Springer, Heidelberg (2011)
2. Berendsen, F.F., van der Heide, U.A., Langerak, T.R., Kotte, A.N.T.J., Pluim, J.P.W.: Free-form image registration regularized by a statistical shape model: application to organ segmentation in cervical MR. Computer Vision and Image Understanding **117**(9), 1119–1127 (2013)
3. Brechbuhler, C., Gerig, G., Kubler, O.: Parametrization of closed surfaces for 3-d shape-description. Computer Vision and Image Understanding **61**(2), 154–170 (1995)
4. Ceresa, M., Mangado Lopez, N., Dejea Velardo, H., Carranza Herrezuelo, N., Mistrik, P., Kjer, H.M., Vera, S., Paulsen, R.R., González Ballester, M.A.: Patient-specific simulation of implant placement and function for cochlear implantation surgery planning. In: Golland, P., Hata, N., Barillot, C., Hornegger, J., Howe, R. (eds.) MICCAI 2014, Part II. LNCS, vol. 8674, pp. 49–56. Springer, Heidelberg (2014)
5. Erixon, E., Högstorp, H., Wadin, K., Rask-Andersen, H.: Variational Anatomy of the Human Cochlea: Implications for Cochlear Implantation. Otology and Neurotology **30**(1), 14–22 (2009)
6. Heimann, T., Meinzer, H.P.: Statistical shape models for 3D medical image segmentation: A review. Medical Image Analysis **13**(4), 543–563 (2009)

7. Hestenes, M.R., Stiefel, E.: Methods of conjugate gradients for solving linear systems. Journal of Research of the National Bureau of Standards **49**(6), 409–436 (1952)
8. Klein, S., Staring, M., Murphy, K., Viergever, M.A., Pluim, J.P.: elastix: a toolbox for intensity-based medical image registration. IEEE Transactions on Medical Imaging **29**(1), 196–205 (2010)
9. Oliveira, F.P.M., Tavares, J.M.R.S.: Medical image registration: a review. Computer Methods in Biomechanics and Biomedical Engineering **17**(2), 73–93 (2014)
10. Paulsen, R., Baerentzen, J., Larsen, R.: Markov random field surface reconstruction. IEEE Transactions on Visualization and Computer Graphics **16**(4), 636–646 (2010)
11. Tang, L., Hamarneh, G.: SMRFI: shape matching via registration of vector-valued feature images. In: IEEE Conference on Computer Vision and Pattern Recognition (CVPR), pp. 1–8 (2008)
12. Vera, S., Perez, F., Balust, C., Trueba, R., Rubió, J., Calvo, R., Mazaira, X., Danasingh, A., Barazzetti, L., Reyes, M., Ceresa, M., Fagertum, J., Kjer, H.M., Paulsen, R., Ballester, M.Á.G.: Patient specific simulation for planning of cochlear implantation surgery. In: Linguraru, M.G., Laura, C.O., Shekhar, R., Wesarg, S., Ballester, M.Á.G., Drechsler, K., Sato, Y., Erdt, M. (eds.) CLIP 2014. LNCS, vol. 8680, pp. 101–108. Springer, Heidelberg (2014)
13. Wilson, B.S., Dorman, M.F.: Cochlear implants: A remarkable past and a brilliant future. Hearing Research **242**(1–2), 3–21 (2008)
14. Yushkevich, P.A., Piven, J., Hazlett, H.C., Smith, R.G., Ho, S., Gee, J.C., Gerig, G.: User-Guided 3D Active Contour Segmentation of Anatomical Structures: Significantly Improved Efficiency and Reliability. Neuroimage **31**(3), 1116–1128 (2006)

Pattern Recognition and Computational Imaging

Persistent Evidence of Local Image Properties in Generic ConvNets

Ali Sharif Razavian[✉], Hossein Azizpour, Atsuto Maki, Josephine Sullivan,
Carl Henrik Ek, and Stefan Carlsson

Computer Vision and Active Perception Lab (CVAP),
School of Computer Science and Communication (CSC),
Royal Institute of Technology (KTH), 100 44 Stockholm, Sweden
{razavian,azizpour,atsuto,sullivan,chek,stefanc}@csc.kth.se
http://www.csc.kth.se/cvap/

Abstract. Supervised training of a convolutional network for object classification should make explicit any information related to the class of objects and disregard any auxiliary information associated with the capture of the image or the variation within the object class. Does this happen in practice? Although this seems to pertain to the very final layers in the network, if we look at earlier layers we find that this is not the case. In fact, strong spatial information is implicit. This paper addresses this, in particular, exploiting the image representation at the first fully connected layer, i.e. the global image descriptor which has been recently shown to be most effective in a range of visual recognition tasks. We empirically demonstrate evidences for the finding in the contexts of four different tasks: 2d landmark detection, 2d object keypoints prediction, estimation of the RGB values of input image, and recovery of semantic label of each pixel. We base our investigation on a simple framework with ridge rigression commonly across these tasks, and show results which all support our insight. Such spatial information can be used for computing correspondence of landmarks to a good accuracy, but should potentially be useful for improving the training of the convolutional nets for classification purposes.

1 Introduction

There is at least one alchemy associated with deep convolutional networks (ConvNets). It occurs when ∼100,000 iterations of stochastic gradient descent (SGD), in tandem with ∼1 million labelled training images from ImageNet, transform the ∼60 million randomly initialized weights of a deep ConvNet into the best, by a huge margin, performing known visual image classifier [7,10,13,17,19,20]. Alongside this high-level alchemy is another related one w.r.t. the image representations learnt by the fully connected layers of a deep ConvNet [7,10,17,20]. These representations are explicitly trained to retain information relevant to semantic classes. But we show in this paper a striking fact, through various tasks, that these representations also retain *spatial* information, including the location of object parts and keypoints of object.

© Springer International Publishing Switzerland 2015
R.R. Paulsen and K.S. Pedersen (Eds.): SCIA 2015, LNCS 9127, pp. 249–262, 2015.
DOI: 10.1007/978-3-319-19665-7_21

Fig. 1. How many different local image properties can be predicted from a generic ConvNet representation using a *linear* model? In this figure, given the ConvNet representation of an image, we have estimated three different local properties. Namely, semantic segmentation for background (top left) and 20 object classes (bottom left) present in PASCAL VOC dataset, 194 facial landmarks (top right) and RGB reconstruction of the original image (bottom right). One can see that a generic ConvNet representation optimized for ImageNet semantic classification has embedded high level of local information.

The notion of predicting spatial information using a ConvNet itself is not new. Recent studies have introduced several approaches to extract spatial information from an image with deep ConvNet. Some have trained a specialized ConvNet to predict specific spatial information such as body parts and facial landmarks [8,21,24]. Others [9,15,19] have shown that it is possible to extract spatial correspondences using a generic ConvNet representation. But they consider representations from the ConvNet layers that only describe sub-patches of the whole image. Then in a similar manner to a sliding window approach they have an exhaustive spatial search, in tandem with their patch descriptor, to find the locations.

Unlike those works, we show that a global image representation extracted from the first fully connected layer of a *generic* ConvNet (*i.e.* trained for predicting the semantic classes of ImageNet) is capable of predicting spatial information *without doing an explicit search*. In particular, we show that one can learn a linear regression function (with results ranging from promising to good) from the representation to spatial properties: 2d facial landmarks, 2d object keypoints, RGB values and class labels of individual pixels, see figure 1. We chose these experiments to highlight the network's ability to reliably extract spatial information.

Why do we concentrate on the fully connected layers? Prior work has shown that these layers correspond to the most generic and compact image representation and produce the best results, when combined with a simple linear classifier, in a range of visual recognition tasks [2]. Therefore the starting point of this work was to examine what other information, besides visual semantic information, is encoded and easily accessible from these representations.

The results we achieve for the tasks we tackle indicate that the spatial information is implicitly encoded in the ConvNet representation we consider. Remember, the network has not been explicitly encouraged to learn spatial information during the training.

The contributions of the paper are:

- For the first time we systematically demonstrate that spatial information is persistently transferred to the representation in the first fully connected layer of a generic ConvNet (section 3).
- We show that one can learn a linear regression function from the ConvNet representation to both object parts and local image properties. In particular, we demonstrate that it is possible to estimate 2d facial landmarks (section 3.1), 2d object keypoints (section 3.1), RGB values (section 3.1) and pixel level segmentations (section 3.1).
- By using a simple *look-back* method we achieved accurate predictions of facial landmarks on a par with state of the art (section 3.1).
- We qualitatively show examples where semantically meaningful directions in the ConvNet representation space can be learned and exploited to accordingly alter the appearance of a face (section 4).

Before describing our experiments and results in the next section we explain why spatial information can be ever retained and so easily accessed in the first fully-connected layer of a generic ConvNet.

2   Flow of Information Through a ConvNet

A generic ConvNet representation extracted from the first fully-connected layer is explicitly trained to retain information relevant to semantic class. The semantic classes in the training data are independent of spatial information and therefore this information, as it is deemed unnecessary to perform the task, should be removed or at least structured in such a manner that it does not conflict with the task.

The weights of a ConvNet's convolutional layers encode a very large number of compositional patterns of appearance that occur in the training images. Thus, the multiple response maps output by a convolutional layer indicate which appearance patterns occur in different sub-patches (a.k.a. receptive fields) of a fixed size in the original image. The size of these sub-patches increases as we progress through the convolutional layers. When we come to the first fully-connected layer the network must compress the set of response maps ($13 \times 13 \times 256$ numbers assuming an `AlexNet` [13] ConvNet) produced by the final convolutional layer into a mere 4096 numbers. The compression performed seeks to optimize the ability of the network's classification layer (with potentially some more intermediary fully-connected layers) to produce semantic labels as defined by the ImageNet classification task.

The weights of the first fully connected layer are, in general, not particularly sparse. Therefore the *what* and *where* explicitly encoded in the convolutional layers are aggregated, merged and conflated into the output nodes of this first fully connected layer. At this stage it is impossible to backtrack from these responses to spatial locations in the image. Nevertheless, we show it is possible to predict from this global image descriptor, using linear regressors, the spatial locations of object parts and keypoints and also pixel level descriptors such as colour and semantic class.

3   Experiment

We study two families of tasks to explore which spatial information resides in the ConvNet representation:

- Estimate the (x, y) coordinate of an item in an image.
- Estimate the local property of an image at (x, y).

Given the ConvNet representation of an image for the first task, we *i*) estimate the coordinates of facial landmarks in three challenging datasets [3,14,18], and *ii*) predict the positions of object keypoints. We use the annotations [4] from the Pascal VOC 2011 dataset as our testbed. While for the second task, given a ConvNet representation, we *i*) predict the RGB values of every pixel in the original image (we use the ImageNet validation set as our test set), and *ii*) predict the semantic segmentation of each pixel in the original image (VOC 2012 Pascal dataset).

3.1   Experimental Setup

In all our experiments we use the same ConvNet. It has the `AlexNet` architecture [13] and is trained on ImageNet [1] using the reference implementation provided by `Caffe` [11]. Our image representation then corresponds to the responses of the first fully connected layer of this network because of its compactness and ability to solve a wide range of recognition tasks [2,7,10,17,20]. We will denote this representation by $\mathbf{f}$. Then the only post-processing we perform on $\mathbf{f}$ is to l_2 normalize it.

For every scalar quantity y we predict from $\mathbf{f}$, we do so with a linear regression model:

$$y \approx \mathbf{w}^T \mathbf{f} + w_0 \tag{1}$$

Table 1. Evaluation of facial landmark estimation on three standard face datasets and comparison with baslines and recent state of the art methods. The error measure is the average distance between the predicted location of a landmark and its ground truth location. Each error distance is normalized by the inter-occular distance.

	Helen [14]	LFPW [3]	IBUG [18]
Dataset Bias	0.501	0.242	0.352
RGB + ridge	0.096	0.074	0.160
STASM [16]	0.111	-	-
CompASM [14]	0.091	-	-
ConvNet + ridge	0.065	0.056	0.096
RCPR [5]	0.065	0.035	-
SDM [22]	0.059	0.035	0.075
ESR [6]	0.059	0.034	0.075
ETR [12]	0.049	0.038	0.064
ConvNet + *look-back*	0.058	0.049	0.074

We use a ridge regularised linear model because of its simplicity and for the following reason. All the class, pose and semantic information does exist in the original RGB image, as the human vision proves, but it is not easily accessible and especially not through linear models. However, we want to study if all this information is still encoded in the ConvNet representation, but in a much more accessible way and this is demonstrated by the use of a linear model compared to a much more capable prediction algorithm.

There are, of course, numerous ways we can estimate the coefficients $(\mathbf{w}, w_0)$ from labelled training. Assume that we have labelled training data $(y_1, \mathbf{f}_1), \ldots (y_n, \mathbf{f}_n)$ where each $y_i \in \mathbb{R}$ and $\mathbf{f} \in \mathbb{R}^d$ ($d = 4096$). The optimal values for $(\mathbf{w}, w_0)$ are then found solving this optimization problem

$$(\mathbf{w}^*, w_0^*) = \arg\min_{\mathbf{w}, w_0} \sum_{i=1}^{n} (y_i - \mathbf{w}^T \mathbf{f}_i - w_0) + \lambda \|\mathbf{w}\|^2 \qquad (2)$$

The closed form solution to this optimization problem is easily shown to be:

$$\mathbf{w}^* = \left(X^T X + \lambda I\right)^{-1} X^T \mathbf{y} \quad \text{and} \quad w_0^* = \frac{1}{n} \sum_{i=1}^{n} y_i \qquad (3)$$

where

$$X = \begin{pmatrix} \leftarrow \mathbf{f}_1^T \rightarrow \\ \leftarrow \mathbf{f}_2^T \rightarrow \\ \vdots \\ \leftarrow \mathbf{f}_n^T \rightarrow \end{pmatrix} \quad \text{and} \quad \mathbf{y} = \begin{pmatrix} y_1 \\ y_2 \\ \vdots \\ y_n \end{pmatrix} \qquad (4)$$

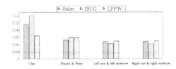

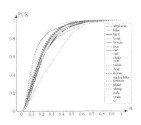

(a) Fig. 2(a) The normalized prediction error for different subsets of the landmarks after *look-back* (see the caption of table 1 for the error measure). The error is shown for three different face datasets. Since the bounding box around the chin is bigger than the bounding box around the other parts, the error for chin is higher than the rest of facial landmarks.

(b) Fig. 2(b) PCK evaluation for keypoint prediction of 20 classes of PASCAL VOC 2011

and it is assumed the columns of X have been centred. In all our experiments we set the regularization parameter λ with four-fold cross-validation.

Facial Landmarks. The first problem we address is the popular task of 2d facial landmark detection. Facial landmark detection is interesting since a large body of work has been applied to it. To train our landmark estimation model, for each landmark we estimate two separate linear regression functions, one for the x-coordinate of the landmark and one for the y-coordinate. Therefore we estimate the (x, y) coordinates of all the L landmarks from the image's ConvNet representation, $\mathbf{f}$, with

$$\hat{\mathbf{x}} = W_{\text{landmarks}}\mathbf{f} + \mathbf{w}_{\text{landmarks},0} \tag{5}$$

where $W_{\text{landmarks}} \in \mathbb{R}^{2L \times d}$ and $\mathbf{w}_{\text{landmarks},0} \in \mathbb{R}^{2L}$. Remember each row of $W_{\text{landmarks}}$ is learnt independently via the ridge regression solution of equation (3). For the rest of the tasks explored in this section we use a similar formulation to the one just described so we will not introduce new notation to describe them.

Table 2. Quantitative evaluation of our keypoint estimation for general objects on VOC11. The performance measure is the average PCK score with $\alpha = 0.1$.

	airplane	bike	bird	boat	bottle	bus	car	cat	chair	cow	table	dog	horse	mbike	person	plant	sheep	sofa	train	tv	**mean**
SIFT	17.9	16.5	15.3	15.6	25.7	21.7	22.0	12.6	11.3	7.6	6.5	12.5	18.3	15.1	15.9	21.3	14.7	15.1	9.2	19.9	15.7
SIFT+prior	33.5	36.9	22.7	23.1	44.0	42.6	39.3	22.1	18.5	23.5	11.2	20.6	32.2	33.9	26.7	30.6	25.7	26.5	21.9	32.4	28.4
ConvNet + ridge	21.3	25.1	22.7	16.4	47.3	27.2	29.9	25.4	19.7	26.3	22.0	27.1	25.5	21.8	33.8	41.0	28.2	23.0	23.9	47.3	27.8
Conv5 + sliding window [15]	38.5	37.6	29.6	25.3	54.5	52.1	28.6	31.5	8.9	30.5	24.1	23.7	35.8	29.9	39.3	38.2	30.5	24.5	41.5	42.0	33.3

Fig. 3. The landmarks predicted by our linear regressors for eight different images from the Helen Dataset. The leftmost image in each triplet shows the ground truth. The middle image shows the landmarks predicted by the linear regression functions from the ConvNet representation of the whole image to landmark coordinates. In the middle image the bounding boxes, defined by the initial predictions for the landmarks, used by *look-back* method are also shown. The rightmost image shows the final landmark predictions made by the *look-back* method.

Table 1 details the average errors, of our approaches and other methods, in the predicted location of the landmarks on three standard datasets: Helen [14], LFPW [3] and IBUG [18]. The reported errors are normalized by the distance between two eyes in the image according to the standard practice in the field [12]. The table reports the performance of both the baseline predictors of linear ridge regression from RGB and a random predictor and recent high performing systems [5,6,12,22] which generally involve learning a complicated non-linear function from RGB to the landmarks. Our predictor, ConvNet+ridge, produces a significantly better estimate than the baselines and its performance is comparable with state-of-the-art methods specifically designed to solve this problem. Our result indicates that the locations of landmarks can be reliablly extracted from the ConvNet representation.

ConvNet+ridge inherently loses around ± 10 pixel accuracy due to the pooling and strides in the first and second convolutional layers of the ConvNet. However, we can overcome this limitation in a simple manner which we term the *look-back trick*. We partition the landmarks into different subsets (such as

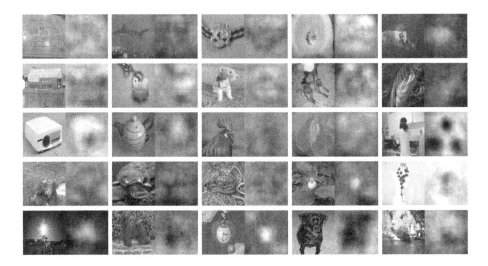

Fig. 4. RGB information linearly predicted from the ConvNet representation. For each pixel we train 3 independent linear regressors to predict the pixel's RGB value from the image's global ConvNet representation. We used the first 49K images from ImageNet's cross validation set for training and visualized the result for the last 1k images. Shown above are the results for 25 random images (left) taken from the test set and their reconstructions (right).

chin, left eye and left eyebrow, right eye and right eyebrow, and then mouth and nose), figure 3 shows some examples. We let the predicted position of each set of landmarks, using equation 5, define a square bounding box containing them with some margin based on the maximum prediction error for the landmarks in the training set. We then extract the ConvNet representation for this sub-image and use linear regression, as before, to estimate the coordinates of the landmarks in the bounding-box. This simple trick significantly boosts the accuracy of the predictions, and allows us to outperform all the s.o.a. methods except for the recent work of [12]. The more sets we have in the partition the better results we get. We used six sets for each dataset. See figure 3 for qualitative examples of the result of this method on sample images from the Helen dataset. Figure 2a also shows the prediction errors for different parts after look-up for three face datasets.

Object Keypoints. In our next task we predict the location of object keypoints. These keypoints exhibit more variation in their spatial location than facial landmarks. We use the keypoint annotations provided by [4] for 20 classes of PASCAL VOC 2011. We make our predictions using exactly the same basic approach as for facial landmarks. The classes of PASCAL task include many deformable objects (dog, cat, human, *etc.*) and objects which have high intra-class variation (bottle, plant, *etc.*) which makes the problem of key point

Table 3. Evaluation of Semantic Segmentation on the validation set of VOC12 measured in mean Average Precision (mAP)

	background	airplane	bike	bird	boat	bottle	bus	car	cat	chair	cow	table	dog	horse	mbike	person	plant	sheep	sofa	train	tv	**mean**
ConvNet	79.12	16.01	0.02	12.93	9.26	13.69	37.29	33.75	40.01	0.01	8.62	12.24	30.89	9.43	24.94	44.03	6.22	18.77	1.64	25.33	11.05	20.73

detection extremely difficult. In order to model these keypoints a separate set of regressors is learnt for each object.

Table 2 reports the accuracy of our results for keypoint prediction, together with those achieved by other methods [15]. The accuracy is measured using mean PCK [23]. A keypoint is considered to be correctly estimated if the prediction's Euclidean distance from the ground truth position is $\alpha \in [0, 1]$ times the maximum of the bounding box width and height. Our simple approach outperforms SIFT by a huge margin on localizing landmarks and is only slightly below the performance of SIFT+prior [15]. Figure 2b shows the plot of PCK vs α for 20 classes.

RGB Reconstruction. The results from the previous tasks show that our ConvNet representation does encode some levels of spatial information. The natural question is then *what does it actually remove?* To investigate this we try to evaluate if it is possible to invert the ConvNet mapping. First, we try to estimate the RGB values of the original input image from our ConvNet representation. For this, again, we simply learn $3 \times n_p$ linear regressors where n_p is the number of pixels in the image. In other words we learn an independent regressor for each pixel and each colour channel.

We use ImageNet as our testbed. We used the first 49k images from ImageNet's validation set for training and the last 1k images for testing. We resized each image to 46×46×3 and trained 6348 independent linear regressors. Some examples of the resulting RGB reconstruction are illustrated in figure 4. The mean absolute error of image reconstruction is 0.12. It is rather surprising that RGB values of an image can be extracted with this degree of accuracy from the ConvNet representation.

Semantic Segmentation. We applied the same framework which we employed for RGB reconstruction further to recover semantic labels of each pixel instead of its RGB values. The procedure is as follows: we resized each semantic segmentation map of VOC 2012 segmentation task down to a 30×30×21 image. We train a separate linear regressor to predict whether the pixel at position (x, y) belongs to class c or not encoded as 1 and 0. We have $x \in \{1, 2, \ldots, 30\}$ and similarly for y and $c \in \{1, 2, \ldots, 21\}$. Therefore a total of 18900 linear regressors are trained with ridge regression. Solving a classification problem via regression is not ideal. But the qualitative results shown in figure 5 are visually pleasing. They show the semantic segmentations produced by our approach for some images from the VOC12 validation set.

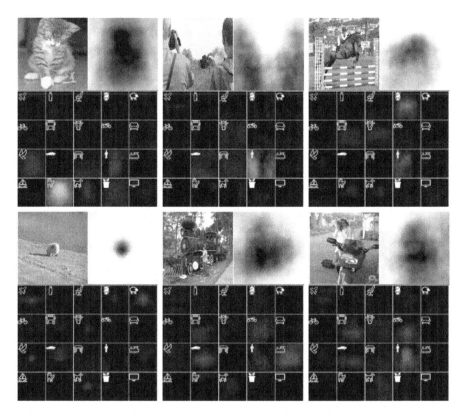

Fig. 5. Semantic segmentation results for images from PASCAL VOC. For each block of pictures, the top left hand picture is the original image and the one directly to its right is the *probability* map for the background class. The brighter the pixel the higher the probability. The bottom set of smaller images in the block display, in the same manner, the probabilities for the 20 classes of PASCAL VOC 2011. The probability masks are computed independently of one another though the scaling of the intensities in the displayed masks is consistent across all the masks. The learning is based on linear regression, the details of which are found in the main text.

After we apply the linear regressor for each class to each pixel, we get 21 responses. We then turn these responses into a single prediction using another linear model. We multiply the response vector by a matrix $M \in \mathbb{R}^{21 \times 21}$ and then choose the class which corresponds to the highest response in the output vector. Ideally M should model the relations between different class responses at a single pixel. We learn M, once again with ridge regression, and during training it tries to return a binary vector of length 21 with only one non-zero entry.

As our segmentation masks only have size 30×30 we resize the them back to their original size. We used the VOC12 training-set as the training data and augmented this set tenfold to get a better estimate and reported the result on the cross-validation set. Quantitative results for our segmentations are given in table 3. Although this result itself is not as good as s.o.a. on semantic segmentation task (mean average precision of 20.7 compared to 47.5 of s.o.a. method), it is intriguing to see that the global ConvNet representation contains this level of information. It is easy to envisage that such a segmentation could be incorporated into an object classifier or detector.

Fig. 6. Semantically altering a face using its generic ConvNet representation and semantically meaningful directions in the representation space. Given an image of a face and its ConvNet representation each row above shows the effect of altering the face's representation by moving in one direction of the representation space and then regressing from the resulting ConvNet representation back to its RGB representation. Each direction was learned from labeled training data and corresponds to a specific semantic concept: gender, glasses/no-glasses, head angle and head tilt. For gender we can see that the left-most image which corresponds to male has dark patches corresponding to a beard while the right-most image is clearly female. The glasses/no-glasses clearly alters the region around the eyes. The last two rows show variations caused by changes in head pose. Both the head angle and the tilt (last row) are clearly visible.

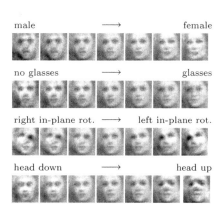

male $\longrightarrow$ female

no glasses $\longrightarrow$ glasses

right in-plane rot. $\longrightarrow$ left in-plane rot.

head down $\longrightarrow$ head up

4 Semantic Directions in Representation Space

The ConvNet is trained with one objective in mind, to learn a representation where every pair of classes is linearly separable. The representation space is thus carved into different volumes corresponding to the different classes. The results of the paper so far show each class volume retains significant intra-class variations. In this section we make a first step towards understanding how these variations are structured. To proceed we learn a separate linear regressor from the representation to each of the following variates for the LFW data-set *gender*, *have-glasses*, and *pose*. Each linear regressor specifies a direction in the representation space along which a semantic concept varies.

What happens with the images if we alter the representation along this direction? Can we change the gender or add glasses or continuously change the pose of the face in the image? We can achieve this if we extrapolate along an identified direction and then regress back to the RGB image as described in section 3.1. In more detail: the ConvNet representation, **f**, of a face can be written in terms of its projection onto a semantic direction, such as gender $\mathbf{w}_{\text{gender}}$, found via linear regression and its component orthogonal to $\mathbf{w}_{\text{gender}}$

$$\mathbf{f} = (\mathbf{w}_{\text{gender}}^{T}\mathbf{f})\,\mathbf{w}_{\text{gender}} + \tilde{\mathbf{f}} \qquad (6)$$

Then we can create a new ConvNet representation where the gender attribute of the face has been altered but not the other factors in the following simplistic manner.

$$\mathbf{f}' = \tilde{\mathbf{f}} + \lambda \mathbf{w}_{\text{gender}} \qquad (7)$$

with $\lambda \in [\lambda_{\min}, \lambda_{\max}]$. We then regress from $\mathbf{f}'$ back to the RGB image to visualize the result of the alteration, see figure 6 for some sample results.

What do the results of our small scale experiment convey? We can see that altering the pose direction in the representation does correspond well to the actual image transformation and that changing the gender corresponds to an altering of the face's color composition. Similarly glasses/no-glasses alters the appearance of the region around the eyes. However, it is easy to read too much into the experiments as it is severely limited by the linear structure of the regressors. And the fear of hallucinating experimental evidence for the elephant in the room - the concept of *disentanglement* - means we will leave our speculations to these comments. However, as such a simple approach is capable of finding some structures it would be interesting to investigate if the representation factorizes the variations according to semantic factors.

5   Conclusion

In this paper we have shown that a generic ConvNet representation from the first fully connected layer retains significant spatial information. We demonstrated this fact by solving four different tasks, that require local spatial information, using the simple common framework of linear regression from our ConvNet representation. These tasks are *i*) 2d facial landmark prediction, *ii*) 2d object keypoints prediction, *iii*) estimation of the RGB values of the original input image, and *iv*) semantic segmentation, *i.e.* recovering the semantic label of each pixel. The results demonstrated throughout all these tasks, using diverse datasets, show spatial information is implicitly encoded in the ConvNet representation and can be easily accessed. This result is surprising because the employed network was not explicitly trained to keep spatial information and also the first fully connected layer is a global image descriptor which aggregates and conflates appearance features, extracted from the convolutional layers, from all spatial locations in the image.

Acknowledgments. We would like to gratefully acknowledge the support of NVIDIA for the donation of multiple GPU cards for this research.

References

1. Imagenet large scale visual recognition challenge (2013). http://www.image-net. org/challenges/LSVRC/2013/
2. Azizpour, H., Sharif Razavian, A., Sullivan, J., Maki, A., Carlsson, S.: From generic to specific deep representations for visual recognition (2014). arXiv:1406.5774 [cs.CV]
3. Belhumeur, P.N., Jacobs, D.W., Kriegman, D.J., Kumar, N.: Localizing parts of faces using a consensus of exemplars. In: CVPR, pp. 545–552 (2011)
4. Bourdev, L., Malik, J.: Poselets: body part detectors trained using 3d human pose annotations. In: ICCV (2009)
5. Burgos-Artizzu, X.P., Perona, P., Dollár, P.: Robust face landmark estimation under occlusion. In: ICCV (2013)
6. Cao, X., Wei, Y., Wen, F., Sun, J.: Face alignment by explicit shape regression. In: CVPR, pp. 2887–2894 (2012)
7. Donahue, J., Jia, Y., Vinyals, O., Hoffman, J., Zhang, N., Tzeng, E., Darrell, T.: Decaf: a deep convolutional activation feature for generic visual recognition. In: ICML (2014)
8. Eigen, D., Puhrsch, C., Fergus, R.: Depth map prediction from a single image using a multi-scale deep network. In: NIPS (2014)
9. Fischer, P., Dosovitskiy, A., Brox, T.: Descriptor matching with convolutional neural networks: a comparison to sift (2014). arXiv:1405.5769v1 [cs.CV]
10. Girshick, R.B., Donahue, J., Darrell, T., Malik, J.: Rich feature hierarchies for accurate object detection and semantic segmentation. In: CVPR (2014)
11. Jia, Y., Shelhamer, E., Donahue, J., Karayev, S., Long, J., Girshick, R.B., Guadarrama, S., Darrell, T.: Caffe: Convolutional architecture for fast feature embedding (2014)
12. Kazemi, V., Sullivan, J.: One millisecond face alignment with an ensemble of regression trees. In: CVPR, pp. 1867–1874 (2014)
13. Krizhevsky, A., Sutskever, I., Hinton, G.E.: Imagenet classification with deep convolutional neural networks. In: NIPS (2012)
14. Le, V., Brandt, J., Lin, Z., Bourdev, L., Huang, T.S.: Interactive facial feature localization. In: Fitzgibbon, A., Lazebnik, S., Perona, P., Sato, Y., Schmid, C. (eds.) ECCV 2012, Part III. LNCS, vol. 7574, pp. 679–692. Springer, Heidelberg (2012)
15. Long, J., Zhang, N., Darrell, T.: Do convnets learn correspondence? (2014). arXiv:1411.1091 [cs.CV]
16. Milborrow, S., Nicolls, F.: Locating facial features with an extended active shape model. In: Forsyth, D., Torr, P., Zisserman, A. (eds.) ECCV 2008, Part IV. LNCS, vol. 5305, pp. 504–513. Springer, Heidelberg (2008)
17. Oquab, M., Bottou, L., Laptev, I., Sivic, J.: Learning and transferring mid-level image representations using convolutional neural networks. In: CVPR (2014)
18. Sagonas, C., Tzimiropoulos, G., Zafeiriou, S., Pantic, M.: A semi-automatic methodology for facial landmark annotation. In: CVPR Workshops, pp. 896–903 (2013)
19. Sermanet, P., Eigen, D., Zhang, X., Mathieu, M., Fergus, R., LeCun, Y.: Overfeat: integrated recognition, localization and detection using convolutional networks. In: ICLR (2014)
20. Sharif Razavian, A., Azizpour, H., Sullivan, J., Carlsson, S.: CNN features off-the-shelf: an astounding baseline for visual recognition. In: CVPR workshop of DeepVision (2014)

21. Toshev, A., Szegedy, C.: Deeppose: human pose estimation via deep neural networks. In: CVPR (2014)
22. Xiong, X., De la Torre, F.: Supervised descent method and its applications to face alignment. In: CVPR (2013)
23. Yang, Y., Ramanan, D.: Articulated human detection with flexible mixtures of parts. PAMI **35**(12), 2878–2890 (2013)
24. Zhang, N., Paluri, M., Ranzato, M., Darrell, T., Bourdev, L.: Panda: pose aligned networks for deep attribute modeling. In: CVPR (2014)

Wooden Knot Detection
Using ConvNet Transfer Learning

Rickard Norlander[1], Josef Grahn[2(✉)], and Atsuto Maki[1]

[1] Royal Institute of Technology (KTH), 100 44 Stockholm, Sweden
{norla,atsuto}@kth.se
[2] OptoNova AB, 171 54 Solna, Sweden
josef.grahn@gmail.com

Abstract. This paper presents a method of localizing wooden knots in images of oak boards using deep convolutional networks (ConvNets). In particular, we show that transfer learning from generic images works effectively with a limited amount of available data when training a classifier for this highly specialized problem domain. We compare our method with a previous commercially developed technique based on kernel SVM with local feature descriptors. Our method is found to improve the detection performance significantly: F_1 score 0.750 ± 0.018 vs 0.695. Furthermore, we report some observations regarding the behavior of KL-divergence on the test set which is counter-intuitive in its relation to the accuracy of classification.

Keywords: Detection · Wood · Knots · Convolutional networks · Deep learning · KL-divergence

1 Introduction

Automatic inspection of wooden surfaces is an increasingly important application in the manufacturing process of furniture and flooring[1]. In the forest industry, the most expensive part of running a saw mill is lumber, making up 75% of the cost [24]. The cost of misclassifying material gets greater as we go further in the processing chain since more value is added to the product in each stage. Thus, it is very important not to waste raw material by incorrectly classifying wood; small gains in classifier performance can translate into large cost savings. Detecting knots on wooden surfaces [18,20,22], which we are concerned with in this article, is a critical step in many processes and therefore the detection accuracy is of primary interest. One of the challenges is to cope with the large variation in knot appearances, and it can be difficult to gather sufficient amount of training data with noiseless labeling. Furthermore, the color range of knots completely overlaps with that of normal wood regarding oak material, which makes the task harder.

---

[1] Around 700,000 cubic meters of wooden boards are produced per year in Sweden alone [23].

© Springer International Publishing Switzerland 2015
R.R. Paulsen and K.S. Pedersen (Eds.): SCIA 2015, LNCS 9127, pp. 263–274, 2015.
DOI: 10.1007/978-3-319-19665-7_22

In the research area of image classification, Krizhesky et al. [14] outperformed the state-of-the-art with a large margin using a new architecture of deep convolutional network (ConvNet) trained with 1.2 millions images [1], and since then ConvNets have become popular and have been successfully applied to different tasks. The ability of deep ConvNets to learn representations has also been studied from various perspectives [4], including transfer learning [16]; the idea there is to learn an efficient generic visual representation by training a ConvNet on a large dataset from one problem domain, then using that network to perform a task in a different problem domain where the amount of labeled data might be smaller. A few authors have recently showed evidence supporting the efficacy of transfer learning in several visual recognition tasks [5,9,21,25].

In this paper, we apply ConvNet transfer learning to the problem of wooden knot detection, where the amount of available training data is limited, with the expectation that the network will yield a performance increase in comparison to the current state-of-the-art. The first contribution of the paper is thereby to show that the new detector based on a ConvNet indeed outperforms the pipeline based on HOG features combined with a kernel SVM classifier despite the limited availability of the training data. Secondly, we will discuss the behavior of Kullback Liebler-divergence (KL-divergence) on the test set when fine-tuning early layers in a network trained with transfer learning.

1.1 Related Work

Transfer learning: Transfer learning is a machine learning approach where data from one problem is used to increase performance in another problem. The approach has previously been used for neural networks and ConvNets, see [2,12,15,19] for a few examples. In [12], the authors trained a ConvNet, viewing it as consisting of two halves, an earlier half and a later half. Transfer of knowledge was achieved by keeping the early layers as-is, and training the later layers for a new task. In the framework of object detection with deep convolutional networks, it has been also shown [6,11] that fine-tuning the network for the target task can help the performance. Our approach is also motivated by the transferability studied in [3].

Knot detection: There have been many efforts described in the literature to find knots in images of wooden surfaces. Some of the previous approaches include [18,20,22]: In an early work on grading wooden board [18] first and second order partial derivatives are computed for each pixel, and used to assign a label such as *edgeeast*, *edgesouth* or *edgenorthwest*. Pixels are then merged into objects. In [22], small neural networks are employed taking gray levels from a 3x3x3 box from a CT-scan, and that box's distance to the center of the tree, as input. Another approach was to search for dark pixels in a photo, merge them into connected components, and remove small ones [20].

The reference method used in this study was developed by OptoNova, and employs HOG descriptor [8] features, which are classified with a soft margin kernel SVM [7]. To the authors knowledge, the system achieves the quality that is among the highest available in image-based commercial products in this domain.

2   Method

To detect and localize knots in an image of a wooden surface, we use a trained ConvNet to classify overlapping patches in a sliding window fashion at a fixed spatial scale as either *knot* or *wood*. The final layer of the network outputs a confidence value, that we use to signify how likely it is that each respective patch contains a wooden knot. The grid of confidence values can be seen as constituting a "confidence image" over the entire surface. Local maxima reaching above a set threshold in a smoothed version of the confidence image are considered detections.

Algorithm 1. Detection algorithm

1: **procedure** DETECT(image J)
2:   $I \leftarrow$ CROPBACKGROUND(J)
3:   **for all** positions (x, y) over I with stride n **do**
4:     $P_{x,y} \leftarrow$ EXTRACTPATCH(I, x, y)
5:     $c_{x,y} \leftarrow N(P_{x,y})$ ▷ The network N yields a confidence score
6:   **end for**
7:   $C' =$ GAUSSIANSMOOTH(C, σ)   ▷ Where $C = [c_{x,y}]$ is matrix
8:   $D \leftarrow \varnothing$
9:   **for all** $\boldsymbol{p} \in \{(x, y) : c'_{x,y} > t\}$ ordered by descending confidence **do**
10:     **if** $\forall \boldsymbol{q} \in D \; ||\boldsymbol{p} - \boldsymbol{q}|| > s$ **then**
11:       $D \leftarrow D \cup \{\boldsymbol{p}\}$
12:     **end if**
13:   **end for**
14:   **return** D
15: **end procedure**

The ConvNet is trained using extracted patches from annotated images. The annotations contain both positive and negative examples, to which additional randomly sampled negatives examples are added. We initialize the network using a network pre-trained on the ImageNet dataset. Before training, the top two layers of this network is replaced by three new layers with random weights.

Fig. 1. An ImageNet classifier is turned into a knot classifier by removing the m last layers and replacing them with n new layers. From left to right: image, convolutional layers, fully connected layers, newly added layers

Algorithm 2. Training algorithm

1: **procedure** TRAIN(images $\mathcal{J}$, annotations $\mathcal{A}$, pre-trained network M,
   number-to-remove m, layer-sizes ns)
2:     **for all** $J_i \in \mathcal{J}$ **do**
3:         $I_i \leftarrow$ CROPBACKGROUND(J_i)
4:         $\mathcal{S}_i \leftarrow \{(\text{EXTRACTPATCH}(I_i, x, y), label) : (J_i, x, y, label) \in \mathcal{A}\}$
5:         $\mathcal{R}_i \leftarrow \varnothing$
6:         **for** n_r random locations (x, y) in I_i **do**
7:             $P \leftarrow$ EXTRACTPATCH(I_i, x, y)
8:             **if** $\forall (Q, label) \in \mathcal{S}_i \ P \cap Q = \varnothing$ **then**
9:                 $\mathcal{R}_i \leftarrow \mathcal{R}_i \cup \{(P, \text{'negative'})\}$
10:            **end if**
11:        **end for**
12:    **end for**
13:    $\mathcal{S} \leftarrow \bigcup (\mathcal{S}_i \cup \mathcal{R}_i)$
14:    $N_0 \leftarrow$ REMOVETOPLAYERS(M, m)
15:    $N_1 \leftarrow [N_0 - \text{RELULAYERS}(ns) - \text{SOFTMAXLAYER}(\|\{label\}\|)]$
16:    $N_2 \leftarrow$ SGDTRAINTOPLAYERS(N_1, S)
17:    $N \leftarrow$ SGDTRAIN(N_2, S)
18:    **return** N
19: **end procedure**

2.1 Preprocessing: Cropping the Images

We preprocess the images $\{J_i\}$ by doing a background segmentation based on pixel brightness. Using this segmentation, a rectangular crop is applied such that only the wood surface remains. The resulting region is padded with a border of uniform gray, to enable extraction of patches partially outside the image, giving us images I_i.

Fig. 2. Picture of wooden board after cropping

2.2 Training

Creating training examples: From the cropped and padded images $\{I_i\}$, three sets of 300px × 300px patches $P_j \subset I_i$ are extracted: annotated knots $\mathcal{K}$, annotated hard negatives $\mathcal{H}$, and random negative patches $\mathcal{N}$. One class is used for each of these types, meaning that there are two negative classes and one positive class. The random patches are constrained not to overlap with patches from the two other categories.

Training the network: A trained classifier is obtained by taking the *Caffe Reference ImageNet Model*, a pre-trained ConvNet with architecture (showed in Figure 3) very similar to Krizhesky's[14], and fine-tuning it for detecting wooden knots. The transfer learning is done by taking the pre-trained network, removing the last 2 layers, and then adding 3 new layers with random weights at the end (see Figure 1): two ReLU layers with 256 hidden nodes followed by a softmax layer. The mean removal of the ImageNet model is replaced by a subtraction of 128 from all positions and channels[2].

The resulting network architecture has a mean removal layer first, followed by five convolutional layers, in turn followed by three ordinary fully connected hidden layers and then finally a fully connected softmax layer.

The network is trained by stochastic gradient descent with a minibatch size of 64 using the Caffe framework[13]. Random crops of size 227px × 227px are used. During the first 50,000 iterations the network is trained with the original layers frozen, and the remaining using a learning rate of 0.001, and a momentum of 0.9. Dropout is used after every fully connected hidden layer for regularization; the first layer with 50% probability to drop out, and the subsequent two 80%. A weight decay of 0.0005 is used for additional regularization.

The network is then *fine-tuned* by training all layers with a reduced learning rate (a factor 10 lower) and a reduced drop out rate (50% chance for all layers).

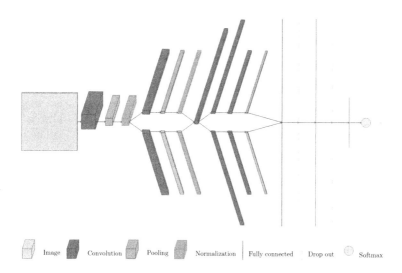

Fig. 3. Architecture of Caffe Reference ImageNet Model. Size of box represents size of data (width × height × channels) after that stage. The fully connected layers have been scaled down by a factor 1/5 to fit.

---

[2] Subtracting 128 was empirically found to be superior to both subtracting the mean of all patches in the dataset, and subtracting the mean (r,g,b) triplet over the dataset

2.3 Detection

Let I be an image containing an orthographically projected view of a flat wood surface, and let $P_{x,y} \subset I$ denote a 227px × 227px patch centered at coordinate (x, y) of I. We define the detection confidence $c_{x,y}$ at a coordinate (x, y) in I as $c_{x,y} = N(P_{x,y})$, where $N(P)$ is the output of our classifier N given P as input. This gives us a scalar field $C : (x, y) \mapsto c_{x,y}$, which we call the confidence image of the image I.

A smoothed confidence image is obtained by convolving C with a 2D Gaussian kernel G, yielding $C' = G * C$. Smoothing was done with $\sigma = 26.7$. The confidence image is thresholded to yield a list of detections. Duplicates are removed by going from the strongest to the weakest detection, removing any detection too close to an earlier one.

For run-time efficiency, we apply the classifier with a stride of n pixels in both directions. A stride of $n = 10$ pixels gave a good trade-off between run-time and detection performance according to some quick tests.

3 Experiments

3.1 Dataset

Our dataset consists of 2317 annotated RGB bitmaps of orthographically projected oak boards at a fixed distance, taken with evenly distributed diffuse lighting. Each image is approximately 2500 × 600 pixels (8 bits per channel), though the size varies somewhat by sample. The relevant oak surface of the boards are surrounded by the visible edges of supporting material and frames, and a dark background, giving us approximately 1800 × 500 pixels of oak surface per image.

The dataset has 3235 annotated knots and 918 annotated hard negatives. Most of the annotated knots fit within a 200 × 200 pixel window. The dataset is divided into two parts, a training set (60 %), and a test set (40 %). The test set is used to evaluate the detectors.

3.2 Experimental Design

The classifier was evaluated on the patches of the test set, and also as a detector on the images of the test set. To study the performance of the detector, the detector is applied to all test images. For each detection, an axis parallel square with side 120 px is imagined around it. If there is a knot inside that square, the detection is counted as a true positive, else as a false positive. An undetected knot is a false negative. The F_1 score as a function of threshold is computed, and the maximum F_1 score is used as the score of the detector.

$$score = \max_T F_1(T) = \max_T 2 \cdot \frac{precision(T) \cdot recall(T)}{precision(T) + recall(T)} \qquad (1)$$

3.3 Detector Performance

For the final detector, used to compare the ConvNet procedure to the HOG procedure, training was done using an increased amount of random negative patches (24470 patches instead of 2471 as used in other experiments). The best F_1 score for the final ConvNet was 0.750 and for the HOG 0.695. This difference is statistically significant. The precision-recall curves for the two detectors are shown overlaid in Figure 4. The detectors are about tied for lower recalls, with the ConvNet better at mid-high recalls, but being beat at the very highest recalls, and having a worse asymptotic. The precision at low recalls, meaning lower than about 0.2, was very sensitive to parameter choice; sometimes better than HOG, and sometimes worse.

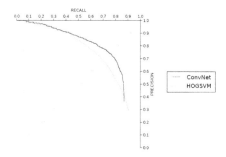

Fig. 4. Precision/recall for detectors shown with F_1-score isocurves

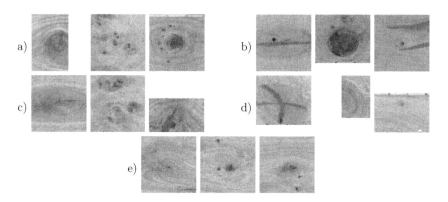

Fig. 5. a) Highest detection strength true positives - ConvNet   b) Lowest detection strength false negatives - ConvNet   c) Highest detection strength false positives - ConvNet   d) Lowest detection strength false negatives - HOG   e) Highest detection strength false positives - HOG

3.4   Effects of Transfer Learning

To determine to what degree transfer learning had helped, a classifier was trained without it. The network was trained for 120,000 iterations, after which learning rate and dropout rate was lowered. The network was trained for 40,000 iterations with these new parameters.

Accuracy vs iteration for the model trained from scratch, is displayed in Figure 6. Even after accuracy has converged, it is lower than the accuracy for the pre-trained network.

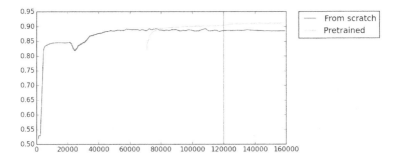

Fig. 6. Accuracy versus iteration for model trained from scratch and pre-trained model. The vertical line signifies start of fine-tuning. Smoothed with symmetric simple moving average of length 2000.

3.5   KL-Divergence During Fine-Tuning

Kullback Liebler-divergence of the training set was used as the optimization objective during training. Interestingly, when fine-tuning the network for our dataset, we observed a drastically worsening KL-divergence score on the test set, while the *classification* error on the test set continued to decrease (see Figure 7).

This means that while the classifier is getting better at *classifying*, it is also getting worse at assigning probabilities. As the probabilities for patches in the training set approach 0 and 1, it seems likely that the same happens on the test set, meaning that those examples it does get wrong, are penalized heavily.

The classifier was contrasted with one fine-tuned differently: learning rate and dropout rate were lowered during fine-tuning like for the normal classifier, but the early layers were not allowed to train. The KL-divergence increases very little. It seems that it is the training of the early layers that causes the issues.

3.6   Significance

In order to obtain a significance estimate of the F_1 score for a given, trained classifier, we employ statistical bootstrapping[10] on the test set. We do this by creating a new test result by sampling with replacement from all false negatives,

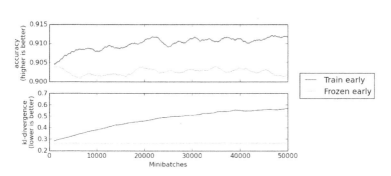

Fig. 7. All curves have been smoothed with symmetric simple moving average of length 2000. Train early: During the fine-tuning, the KL-divergence worsens as the accuracy improves. Frozen early: Lowered learning rate, dropout rate, but frozen early layers. Accuracy is worse, but KL-divergence is better.

false positives and true positives, yielding a new F_1 score, and repeat this process 1000 times. A centered 95 % confidence interval taken from the resulting data series gives a F_1 score uncertainty of ± 0.018.

4   Discussion

Dataset labels: It should be noted that the dataset used in the experiments has a certain degree of inconsistency in the labelings. This can partly be explained by the fuzziness of the underlying classes—knots can be arbitrarily small, and knots transition smoothly to wood when going radially through the trunk of the tree. There are also cases of presumed mislabeling present. This can be seen in the strongest false positive detection in Figure 5. Therefore, the performance measures are not very interesting in themselves but can still be used to compare and contrast across methods.

Transfer learning: Transfer learning from the ImageNet dataset yielded a higher accuracy than when training a network from scratch. In the latter case, training was done for an extended time after the accuracy had reached a stable value (see Figure 6). This indicates that the difference cannot simply be explained by a longer total training time of the pre-trained network. This supports the conclusion that transfer of knowledge does indeed occur, and that it enables features that couldn't otherwise have been learned for lack of data.

In this context, it is worth noting that the ImageNet dataset contains highly diverse data of many different objects in many different poses and configurations, whereas the problem we are transferring to is extremely specialized, and likely should require a much less diverse feature set to represent all possible inputs.

KL-divergence: One thing that was noted during the experiments was that when continuing training with a lower learning rate, the KL-divergence on test data worsened, even as the accuracy on the same data improved (see Figure 7). This was especially pronounced when the early layers were fine-tuned. The poor test KL-divergence means that it can be dangerous to interpret the output of the softmax as a probability. This situation could be corrected by applying probability calibration (see e.g. [17]) to the outputs.

On a more fundamental note, we find it curious that the optimization objective of the training algorithm (KL-divergence), which is meant to act as a proxy for the non-differentiable problem objective (labeling error), diverges on the test set as training progresses. In a sense, deliberately overfitting with regard to KL-divergence produces better test set accuracy for the labeling. This could suggest that there are proxy objectives that are better aligned with the problem of assigning labels than KL-divergence is, which could potentially yield a better classifier if employed during training.

5 Conclusions

We have shown that convolutional networks, and in particular when trained with transfer learning, can be effectively applied to the problem of detecting wooden knots in surfaces of oak wood. Our ConvNet detector, based on a network trained on the ImageNet dataset, outperformed a commercial detector based on conventional feature descriptors and kernel SVM by a statistically significant margin ($F_1 = 0.750 \pm 0.018$ vs 0.695).

By comparing with a network trained from scratch, we showed that transfer learning gives important improvements in this highly specialized problem domain. We also made observations regarding the KL-divergence on the test set during training, in particular that it exhibits a strong overfitting behavior even as the classification accuracy continues to improve.

Acknowledgments. The authors wish to thank Anders Boberg, Ali Sharif Razavian, and the Computer Vision Group of KTH for fruitful discussions. Anders Boberg and Christian Adåker of Optonova provided valuable comments on the paper. The support from the High Performance Computing team at KTH is also appreciated.

References

1. Imagenet large scale visual recognition challenge 2013 (ilsvrc2013). http://www.image-net.org/challenges/LSVRC/2013/
2. Argyriou, A., Evgeniou, T., Pontil, M.: Multi-task feature learning. In: NIPS, pp. 41–48 (2006)
3. Azizpour, H., Razavian, A.S., Sullivan, J., Maki, A., Carlsson, S.: From generic to specific deep representations for visual recognition (2014). arXiv:1406.5774 [cs.CV]
4. Bengio, Y., Courville, A.C., Vincent, P.: Representation learning: A review and new perspectives. IEEE Transactions on Pattern Analysis and Machine Intelligence **35**(8), 1798–1828 (2013)

5. Bottou, L., Laptev, I., Sivic, J.: Learning and transferring mid-level image representations using convolutional neural networks. In: CVPR (2014)
6. Chatfield, K., Simonyan, K., Vedaldi, A., Zisserman, A.: Return of the devil in the details: Delving deep into convolutional nets (2014). arxiv:1405.3531 [cs.CV]
7. Cortes, C., Vapnik, V.: Support-vector networks. Machine Learning **20**(3), 273–297 (1995)
8. Dalal, N., Triggs, B.: Histograms of oriented gradients for human detection. In: Schmid, C., Soatto, S., Tomasi, C. (eds.) International Conference on Computer Vision & Pattern Recognition, INRIA Rhône-Alpes, ZIRST-655, av. de l'Europe, Montbonnot-38334, vol. 2, pp. 886–893, June 2005
9. Donahue, J., Jia, Y., Vinyals, O., Hoffman, J., Zhang, N., Tzeng, E., Darrell, T.: Decaf: a deep convolutional activation feature for generic visual recognition. In: ICML (2014)
10. Efron, B.: Bootstrap methods: Another look at the jackknife. Ann. Statist. **7**(1), 1–26 (1979)
11. Girshick, R.B., Donahue, J., Darrell, T., Malik, J.: Rich feature hierarchies for accurate object detection and semantic segmentation. In: CVPR (2014)
12. Gutstein, S., Fuentes, O., Freudenthal, E.: Knowledge transfer in deep convolutional neural nets. IJAIT **17**(3), 555–567 (2008)
13. Jia, Y.: Caffe: An open source convolutional architecture for fast feature embedding (2013). http://caffe.berkeleyvision.org/
14. Krizhevsky, A., Sutskever, I., Hinton, G.E.: Imagenet classification with deep convolutional neural networks. In: Pereira, F., Burges, C.J.C., Bottou, L., Weinberger, K.Q. (eds.) Advances in Neural Information Processing Systems 25, pp. 1097–1105. Curran Associates Inc. (2012)
15. Li, L.-J., Su, H., Xing, E.P., Li, F.-F.: Object bank: a high-level image representation for scene classification & semantic feature sparsification. In: NIPS (2010)
16. Mesnil, G., Dauphin, Y., Glorot, X., Rifai, S., Bengio, Y., Goodfellow, I.J., Lavoie, E., Muller, X., Desjardins, G., Warde-Farley, D., Vincent, P., Courville, A.C., Bergstra, J.: Unsupervised and transfer learning challenge: a deep learning approach. In: JMLR Proceedings of the ICML Unsupervised and Transfer Learning, vol. 27, pp. 97–110 (2012)
17. Platt, J.C.: Probabilistic outputs for support vector machines and comparisons to regularized likelihood methods. In: Advances in Large Margin Classifiers, pp. 61–74. MIT Press (1999)
18. Pölzleitner, W., Schwingshakl, G.: Real-time surface grading of profiled wooden boards. Industrial Metrology **2**(3–4), 283–298 (1992). Machine Vision Technology in the Forest Products Industry
19. Pratt, L.Y.: Discriminability-based transfer between neural networks. In: NIPS (1992)
20. Qiu, Z.F.: A Simple Machine Vision System for Improving the Edging and Trimming Operations Performed in Hardwood Sawmills. Master's thesis, Virginia Polytechnic Institute and State University, Blacksburg, Virginia (1996)
21. Razavian, A.S., Azizpour, H., Sullivan, J., Carlsson, S.: Cnn features off-the-shelf: an astounding baseline for visual recognition. In: CVPR Workshop of DeepVision (2014)
22. Schmoldt, D.L., Li, P., Lynn Abbott, A.: Machine vision using artificial neural networks with local 3d neighborhoods. Computers and Electronics in Agriculture **16**(3), 255–271 (1997)

23. Skogsindustrierna. Skogsindustrin, en faktasamling, 2010 års branschstatistik, 26 11 2014. http://www.skogsindustrierna.org/MediaBinaryLoader.axd?Media Archive_FileID=62e53e92-510b-4134-a47e-08d6095b2a62&FileName=Faktasaml ing_Sv_2010.pdf
24. Image Systems. 2013 annual report (2013). http://mb.cision.com/Main/7480/ 9570148/233985.pdf
25. Zeiler, M.D., Fergus, R.: Visualizing and understanding convolutional networks. CoRR, abs/1311.2901 (2013)

Regularizing Image Intensity Transformations Using the Wasserstein Metric

Magnus Oskarsson[(✉)]

Centre for Mathematical Sciences, Lund University, Lund, Sweden
magnuso@maths.lth.se

Abstract. In this paper we direct our attention to the problem of discretization effects in intensity transformations of images. We propose to use the Wasserstein metric (also known as the Earth mover distance) to bootstrap the transformation process. The Wasserstein metric gives a mapping between gray levels that we use to direct our image mapping. In order to spatially regularize the image mapping we apply anisotropic filtering and use this to steer our mapping. We describe a general framework for intensity transformation, and investigate the application of our method on a number of special problems, namely histogram equalization, color transfer and bit depth expansion. We have tested our algorithms on real images, and we show that we get state-of-the-art results.

Keywords: Image enhancement · Discretization · Wasserstein metric

1 Introduction

Image intensity transformations are used in many applications. When we need to change the color space in some way we can do this by applying a transformation function from input colors to output colors. One problem that has to be handled is the discrete nature of the signal. As an example consider the classic problem of histogram equalization. This process is used to increase the contrast, in an optimal way. This is achieved by applying a gray level transformation such that when it is applied to the input image, the output image will get a completely flat gray level distribution. This can be done exactly if we work with continuous gray levels, but for a real image we will get discretization effects, which is illustrated in Figure 1. To the left a dark input image is shown, with its corresponding gray level distribution underneath. If we apply standard histogram equalization on the image, we get the middle image, with its corresponding gray level distribution below. One can see that the overall distribution is more spread out, but it is by no means flat. This is due to the discrete intensity gray values of the input image. We will in this paper show how we can enforce a special output gray value distribution using the so-called Wasserstein metric (or Vasershtein). To the right in Figure 1 one can see the result of applying our proposed method in the case of histogram equalization. Notice that we get less discretization effects in the image and that the corresponding output gray value distribution is completely flat.

© Springer International Publishing Switzerland 2015
R.R. Paulsen and K.S. Pedersen (Eds.): SCIA 2015, LNCS 9127, pp. 275–286, 2015.
DOI: 10.1007/978-3-319-19665-7_23

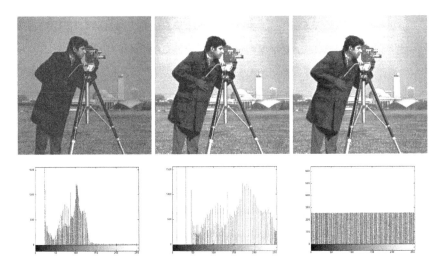

Fig. 1. Top row shows images, and bottom row shows the corresponding intensity distributions. To the left is a dark input image. The middle shows the result of standard histogram equalization. Due to the quantization of the input image, the distribution of the equalized won't be flat, and there will be gray levels that are not used. To the right is the result of applying our Wasserstein regularization using algorithm 1. The resulting distribution is flat, and we make use of all gray-level intensities. One can see that we get less discretization effects in the image, see e.g. the coat.

Histogram equalization is one example where one would like to enforce a special type of intensity value distribution, but there are numerous other applications, within e.g. HDR imaging [3] and within Chromatic adaptation and Color constancy [1,10]. We will in Section 5 give qualitative results on using our method for histogram equalization and for color transfer between images. For other methods on color transfer see e.g. [9].We will also in more detail study how we can use our proposed method for bit depth increase. For most of today's digital devices for capture and display of image data the bit depth varies, from e.g. 6 to 10 bits per color channel, due to technical limitations. When transferring image data between different modalities the need for changes in bit depth is apparent. Decreasing the bit depth is in many cases quite straightforward, but increasing it involves some form of interpolation. This problem is in general not well posed, and we need to regularize it in some way. One often assumes conditions on spatially nearby pixels, that they vary smoothly or piece-wise smoothly. There has been a number of previous work done in the area of bit depth increase. Let's assume a p-bit input image, I_{in}, with gray values in the range $[0, 2^p - 1]$ and a q-bit output image, I_{out}, with range $[0, 2^q - 1]$. We further assume that $p < q$. A basic idea is to just zero pad the input image, or in some other way spread out the dynamic range linearly so that $I_{out}(x, y) = I_{in}(x, y) \cdot 2^{q-p}$. Variations of these methods include multiplication with an ideal gain and then round to nearest integer in the output range, or making a non-linear transformation, e.g.

using gamma expansion. See [12] for details on these methods. Such methods all construct a one to one mapping that is based solely on the gray level at a given pixel, that for most problems leads to contouring artifacts along smooth gradients. To overcome such shortcomings some form of spatial filtering can be applied. We will in the experimental section compare our method to those of [14] (based on flooding) and [7] (based on minimum risk).

2   Problem Formulation and Motivation

We will in this section describe the general problem that we address in this paper. Assume that we have an input (gray value) image $I_{in}(x, y)$ with $(x, y) \in D \subset \mathbb{R}^2$, whose intensity values we would like to transform in some way. One way is to apply a function $f : \mathbb{R} \to \mathbb{R}$ so that $I_{out}(x, y) = f(I_{in}(x, y))$. As described in the introduction, this often introduces discretization effects due to the discrete values of I_{in}. In order to remove these effects one might apply some form of spatial regularization so that f is not only a function of the intensity value but also of the position in the image, i.e. $f : D \times \mathbb{R} \to \mathbb{R}$ and $I_{out}(x, y) = f(x, y, I_{in}(x, y))$. Often this function f is not explicitly given, instead the spatial regularization is done using some form of filtering. We will now look at the specific case where we have a priori information about the gray value distribution of the output image. We will look at the following problem.

Problem 1. Given an input image I_{in} and an output intensity distribution $h_{out}(t)$ find an output image I_{out} with gray value distribution equal to $h_{out}(t)$ and such that $||I_{in} - I_{out}||$ is small.

This is a quite general formulation and we will see in Section 5 that many different problems can be cast in this way. We will in this paper decribe a constructive non-iterative method that solves problem 1. We will use the Wasserstein metric to find a function that prescribes how we transfer the gray values in an optimal way in order to get a specific output intensity distribution. We will then use non-linear anisotropic smoothing of the input image to find the closest output image.

The paper is organized as follows. In Section 3 we present the Wasserstein metric and its application to our problem. In Section 4 we describe the basic outline of our method. The method applied to histogram equalization, color transfer and bit depth expansion is described in Section 5. Using our general method, we show results comparable to state-of-the-art methods.

Our method could be incorporated as a step in many existing image processing applications where one wants to avoid discretization effects. Our aim in this paper is not to present a novel method – for say bit depth expansion – but rather show that using a novel combination of standard components – not specifically tuned to a special application – we can achieve results that are very much comparable to state-of-the-art methods. One of the major strengths that we see with our proposed method is the hard regularization effect we get from using the Wasserstein metric. In many cases one could get good results by applying spatial regularization using anisotropic smoothing, but without the Wasserstein regularization, problems with parameter choices and over-smoothing become apparent.

3   The Wasserstein Metric

We will in this section describe how we use the Wasserstein metric. The general metric was introduced in [13] and the name was coined in [4]. In computer science it is known as the Earth mover's distance (EMD). Informally the metric measures the minimum work of transforming one distribution into another.

We will start by defining the metric. It can be defined on an arbitrary metric space for which every probability measure is a Radon measure, but we will use it in a more simple form. We use the metric space $\mathbb{R}$ with the normal Euclidean distance. Let $P(\mathbb{R})$ denote the collection of all probability measures μ on $\mathbb{R}$ with finite second moment: for some s_0 in $\mathbb{R}$,

$$\int_{\mathbb{R}} (s - s_0)^2 \, \mathrm{d}\mu(s) < +\infty. \tag{1}$$

Then the second Wasserstein distance between two probability measures μ and ν in $P(\mathbb{R})$ is defined as

$$W(\mu, \nu) := \left(\inf_{\gamma \in \Gamma(\mu, \nu)} \int_{\mathbb{R} \times \mathbb{R}} (s - t)^2 \, \mathrm{d}\gamma(s, t) \right)^{1/2}, \tag{2}$$

where $\Gamma(\mu, \nu)$ denotes the collection of all measures on $\mathbb{R} \times \mathbb{R}$ with marginals μ and ν on the first and second factors respectively. The function $\gamma(s, t)$ describes how this transformation is done. The minimizing γ is called *optimal transport*.

Here we will use the Wasserstein metric between the gray value distributions of two images. We will represent these distributions as discrete histograms. There are efficient algorithms for calculating the Wasserstein distance between two discrete distributions. We have used the fast method described in [8]. By estimating the distance we also get the optimal transport γ, which in this case is a matrix. The number $\gamma(s, t)$ tells how many pixels of gray value s in the input image that should be transformed to gray value t in the output image. As an illustration consider again the example in Figure 1. We have calculated the Wasserstein metric between the middle and the right histogram in Figure 1. Three rows of the corresponding optimal transport γ are shown in Figure 2. The estimated γ gives a number of constraints on the transformation that we apply on the input image. These constraints are in general not enough to give a unique output image, i.e. there are many output images that will yield the same output histogram. So we will need to add some more constraints to regularize our solution. This could be done in a number of ways, e.g. minimizing the difference between the input and output image or minimizing the gradients of the output image to get a smooth solution. This could of course also be application dependent, but one important point is that we can in many cases easily use the Wasserstein metric to ensure that the output image follows the desired gray value distribution. We will in the next section describe our proposed method based on anisotropic filtering.

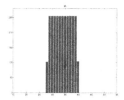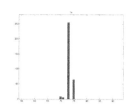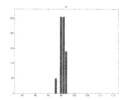

Fig. 2. Three rows of the transformation matrix γ between the middle histogram in Figure 1 and the histogram to the right in Figure 1. The bars depict from left to right $\gamma(35,:)$, $\gamma(74,:)$ and $\gamma(97,:)$. The sum of the bars equals the number of pixels with gray levels 35,74 and 97 in the input image in Figure 1.

4 Enforcing the Wasserstein Metric

We are now ready to describe how we can enforce the Wasserstein metric exactly. We will do this using a filtering approach, where we by smoothing the image steer our transformation.

We assume that we have calculated the optimal transport $\gamma(s,t)$ between the input and output gray levels. We then take the input image and smooth it anisotropically. You can use your favorite smoothing method; we will in Section 5 show results using three different smoothing methods, and the results are quite similar. The important thing is that we smooth enough to eliminate the discretization effects but so that not too much of the true edges in the image are lost. This means that some form of anisotropic filtering should be used. This will give us a smoothed version I_{sm} of the input image I_{in}. We can then for each pixel calculate the signed distance between the input image and the smooth image:

$$\Delta I(x,y) = I_{sm}(x,y) - I_{in}(x,y), \quad (x,y) \in D. \tag{3}$$

This gives a weighting for each pixel if it wants to decrease or increase its gray level. By sorting these distances for a certain input gray value, we get a priority list on the pixels of that color. We then use γ to transform the gray values in the order of this priority list. The method is summarized in algorithm 1.

Regarding color, we propose to use our method on each color channel separately. Since we specify the output distribution, the risk of color artifacts is small.

One crucial part of algorithm 1 is the construction of the smoothed version of the input image. This should be done by some form of edge preserving noise filtering. In our experiments we have tried three well performing noise reduction methods, namely Bilateral filtering [11], BM3D [2] and anisotropic filtering based on the structure tensor [6]. The results vary slightly, with BM3D giving the best PSNR values. However BM3D gives also in some cases some unwanted artifacts. More details can be found in the experimental evaluation.

Algorithm 1. Wasserstein regularized intensity transformation

---

1: Given I_{in} and a desired output intensity distribution $h_{out}(t)$.
2: Calculate the histogram $h_{in}(s)$ of I_{in}.
3: Estimate $\gamma(s,t)$ from the Wasserstein metric between $h_{in}(s)$ and $h_{out}(t)$
4: Estimate a smoothed version I_{sm} by anisotropically filtering I_{in} spatially.
5: Calculate the distance function $\Delta I(x,y) = I_{sm}(x,y) - I_{in}(x,y)$ $(x,y) \in D$.
6: **for** each gray level s **do**
7:    Sort the pixels with $I_{in} = s$ according to ΔI to get a priority list.
8:    Redistribute these pixels according to $\gamma(s,:)$ in the order of the priority list into the output image I_{out}.
9: **end for**

---

5   Applications

We will in this section describe how the method presented in the previous sections can be used in a number of applications. We give examples on histogram equalization, color transfer and bit-depth increase.

5.1   Histogram Equalization

We have already in the introduction seen an example of histogram equalization. We simply start by performing standard histogram equalization on the input image. We then run algorithm 1 with this image as input, and a flat target histogram h_{out}. Since histogram equalization normally is used to increase the intensity constrast, when running it on a color image one usually first transforms the image to a new colorspace (e.g. HSV) that separates color and intensity information. One then runs the algorithm on the intensity channel alone and transfers back to the original colorspace. The details are summarized in algorithm 2. In Figure 3 we show the result of running algorithm 2 on an over

---

Algorithm 2. Wasserstein regularized histogram equalization

1: Given an input image I_{in} convert the image to an HSV representation I_{HSV}.
2: Perform traditional histogram equalization on the V-channel I_V to get I_{Vhq}.
3: Estimate I_{Vhq2} using algorithm 1 with input I_{Vhq} and a flat h_{out}.
4: Convert I_{HSV2}, with V-channel equal I_{Vhq2}, to RGB to get I_{out}.

---

saturated image. To the left is the input image, in the middle is traditional histogram equalization and to the right is the result running our method. One can see that the discretization effects are much smaller.

5.2   Color Transfer

In this section we look into how we can use our method to transfer the color distribution of one image to another. One application where this can be used is

Fig. 3. The result of running algorithm 2 on an over saturated image. To the left is the input image, in the middle is the rersult of running traditional histogram equalization and to the right the result of our method. One can see that we get less quantization effect in the right hand image. The results are best viewed on screen.

the case when we have taken multiple images of the same scene with different illunination. An example where we have used our method is shown in Figure 4. To the left and in the middle two images of the same scene are depicted. To the left the image is taken without flash and in the middle with flash. In many cases one gets a more desirable illumination without flash but one also gets a more noisy image since the illumination is poor. There has been a number of previous work on how to combine two images taken with and without flash, see e.g. [9]. Here we just simply transfer the color distribution from the image with no flash to the image with flash. We do this by first calculating the distribution of the no flash image. Since we want to transfer color information we do this for each color channel separately. We then proceed in the same manner as we did for the histogram equalization, i.e. we start by applying a discrete histogram transformation on the flash image using the calculated color distribution from the no flash image. We do this by finding the tranformation $f(s)$ that minimizes

$$|| \int_0^s h_{in}(u)du - \int_0^{f(s)} h_{out}(u)du ||_2. \tag{4}$$

We have used the Matlab function `histeq` to do this. We then use $f(I_{in}(x, y))$ together with the desired distribution h_{out} as input to algorithm 1. The result can be seen to the right in Figure 4. One can see that we get an image without the noise from the no flash image but with the same color tone.

5.3 Bit Depth Increase

We will now show how our ideas can be used in bit depth expansion. We will base our method on the assumption that the high bit image should have the same gray level distribution as the low bit output image, but on a finer scale. In order to ensure this we start by estimating the high bit distribution from the low bit distribution. This is in many case a much better posed problem

Fig. 4. An example of color transfer using our proposed method. To the left is a noisy image taken without flash. In the middle is an image of the same scene taken with flash. To the right is the middle image where the colors have been transformed to match the distribution of left hand image.

than the actual bit expansion problem. We do this by interpolating the low bit distribution to a continuous distribution, and then resampling this distribution to the desired bit depth. From the low-bit input image we calculate the histogram, $h_{in}(s), s = 0, \ldots, (n-1)$, where $n = 2^p$. We assume that the input image is sampled from some ideal image with continuous probability distribution $h_0(u)$ so that

$$h_{in}(s) = \int_{s+0.5}^{s-0.5} h_0(u)du, \quad s = 0 \ldots (n-1). \tag{5}$$

In order to estimate h_0 from h_{in} we need to regularize the problem somewhat. We will use a spline-based approach. To this end we assume that h_0 can be approximated by a piece-wise polynomial of degree two,

$$h_0(u) = a_s + b_s u + c_s u^2, \quad (s - 0.5) \le u \le (s + 0.5). \tag{6}$$

Equation (5) together with the assumption that h_0 and its derivative are continuous, gives a linear system of equations in a_s, b_s and c_s. This in turn gives us an estimate of $h_0(u), -0.5 \le u \le n - 0.5$, from which we can discretize to get $h_{out}(t)$ with the desired output number of bins.

We now have all the components of our bit depth expansion. From a low bit input image we start by expanding it to the desired bit depth using ideal gain. From the gray value distribution of this image we can estimate the desired output gray value distribution using the method just described. We now are in the setting described in Section 4 and we can use algorithm 1 in order to estimate an output image that follows the desired gray value distribution. The steps in our bit expansion method are summarized in algorithm 3.

We have tested our algorithms on a number of real images. The originals were 8-bit color images, with gray values between 0 and 255. We then constructed low

Algorithm 3. Wasserstein regularized bit depth increase

1: Given an input image I_{in} with p bits.
2: Calculate the ideal gain q bit image I_g.
3: Calculate the gray value distribution $h_{in}(s)$ of I_g.
4: Estimate the output distribution $h_{out}(t)$ from $h_{in}(s)$ using a spline based interpolation.
5: Estimate I_{out} using algorithm 1 with input I_g and h_{out}.

Table 1. Peak Signal to Noise-ratio for a number of test images with different input bit-depth. See text for details.

Image	6 to 8 bit					4 to 8 bit				
	IG	MR	CA	BF	BM	IG	MR	CA	BF	BM
pepper	**47.06**	45.11	47.32	43.64	44.27	34.67	33.89	**37.31**	36.19	36.99
building	**47.14**	44.39	46.36	44.67	45.36	34.84	34.84	35.08	34.20	**35.27**
tree	**47.14**	44.49	46.14	44.59	45.05	34.89	34.94	35.57	34.89	**35.98**
flower	46.88	46.77	**49.64**	47.84	48.97	34.40	32.18	**37.37**	36.31	35.91
spider	47.10	41.19	**48.71**	46.70	47.80	34.86	34.47	**38.03**	38.08	37.43

bit versions by dividing the gray values by 2^k and rounding, to get an $(8-k)$-bit image. As a first example, the result from running algorithm 3 using bilateral filtering on the pepper image can be seen in Figure 5. The top row shows close ups of the ideal gain version of the input image. From left to right we have 5, 4 and 3 bit input images. The bottom row shows the output of our algorithm using bilateral filtering. In Figure 6 the resulting color distributions for 5 bit expansion is shown. It also shows the corresponding ground truth distributions in black. One can see that they follow each other very well. We have also conducted a test on a number of other real test images. These are taken from the database described in [5]. In this case the original images were 8-bit, that were converted to low bit images. We have also run two state-of-the-art bit expansion algorithms for comparison, namely the method of [7], based on minimum risk and the content adaptive bit-depth expansion algorithm of [14]. We have constructed 4-bit and 6-bit versions of the test images and run the algorithms to – in all cases – produce 8-bit results. The output images have then been compared to the ground truth 8-bit images. The results from this evaluation can be seen in table 1 where the peak signal to noise ratio is presented. We include results from ideal gain (IG), Mittal et al. (MR), Wan et al. (CA) and our approach using bilateral filtering (BF), BM3D (BM) and the structure tensor anisotropic filtering (ST). The corresponding results for the structure similarity index, SSIM [15] can be found in table 2. A number of observations can be made. We see that for small bit increase problems, the ideal gain actually performs very well. This is due to the fact that the error is always bounded by a small amount in this case. However when looking at the images one can see that the other algorithms output more pleasing results. This serves as a reminder that just looking at the PSNR values

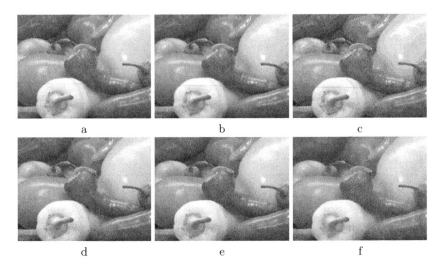

Fig. 5. Close-up results from running algorithm 3 on the pepper image, for a number of different bit depth inputs. In these examples bilateral filtering was used for the smoothing step. Top row shows, from left to right, five, four and three bit color input. Bottom row shows the resulting output images. The results are best viewed on screen.

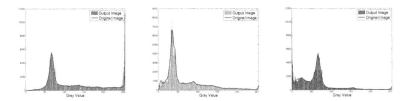

Fig. 6. The figure shows the result from running algorithm 3 using bilateral filtering. The resulting gray value distributions of the output image, for the red, green and blue channel respectively are shown. Also shown are the corresponding distributions for the ground truth 8-bit image. One can see that they follow each other well.

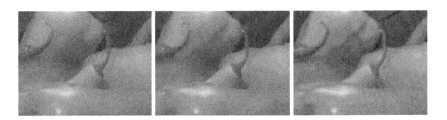

Fig. 7. Magnified results from running algorithm 3 using the three different filtering methods. From left to right it shows the result using the structure tensor adaptive filtering, using bilateral filtering and using BM3D. The results are best viewed on screen.

Table 2. SSIM for a number of test images with different input bit-depth. See text for details.

Image	6 to 8 bit						4 to 8 bit					
	IG	MR	CA	BF	BM	ST	IG	MR	CA	BF	BM	ST
pepper	0.99	0.98	0.99	0.98	0.98	0.99	0.87	0.89	**0.93**	**0.93**	0.91	**0.93**
building	0.99	0.99	0.99	0.99	0.99	0.99	0.93	0.93	**0.94**	0.93	0.92	**0.94**
tree	0.99	0.99	0.99	0.99	0.99	0.99	0.91	0.92	0.92	0.92	0.91	**0.93**
flower	0.97	0.99	0.98	0.98	0.98	0.98	0.84	**0.91**	0.90	**0.91**	0.90	0.87
spider	0.99	0.95	0.99	0.99	0.99	0.99	0.89	0.91	**0.96**	**0.96**	0.95	0.93

is not always a good way of evaluating the results. The SSIM measure gives a somewhat better way of comparing, but also suffers to some extent from the same problems. Setting this caveat aside one can see that our simple algorithm performs on par with the highly specialised state-of-the-art methods for 4-6 bit input.

In Figure 8 close ups for the results on the test images are shown for our method using bilateral filtering. From table 1 and 2 one can see that running our method using bilateral filtering or BM3D gives comparable results to each other. In Figure 7 a comparison for our method using the different filtering types is shown. One can see that we get some undesirable artifacts near edges using BM3D.

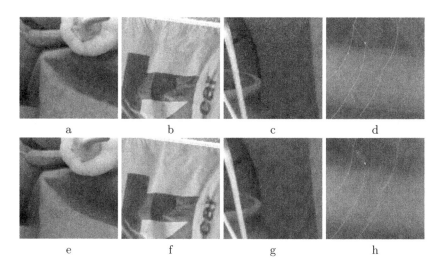

Fig. 8. Results from algorithm 3 for the test images from table 1. The top row (a-d) are close ups of parts of the four-bit input images. The optimal gain transformed images are shown. The bottom row (e-h) shows the resulting output 8-bit images, using algorithm 3 with bilateral filtering. The results are best viewed on screen.

6   Conclusion

We have in this paper introduced the notion of using the Wasserstein metric to regularize image intensity transformations. Using the optimal transport function γ and anisotropic filtering of the image we can steer the intensity transformation in a robust way and avoid discretization effects. We specifically tested our approach on the problem of bit depth expansion with state-of-the-art results.

Acknowledgments. This work was supported by ELLIIT and eSSENCE.

References

1. Brill, M.H.: The relation between the color of the illuminant and the color of the illuminated object. Color Research & Application **20**(1), 70–76 (1995)
2. Dabov, K., Foi, A., Katkovnik, V., Egiazarian, K.: Image denoising by sparse 3-d transform-domain collaborative filtering. IEEE Transactions on Image Processing **16**(8), 2080–2095 (2007)
3. Debevec, P.E., Malik, J.: Recovering high dynamic range radiance maps from photographs. In: ACM SIGGRAPH 2008 classes, p. 31. ACM (2008)
4. Dobrushin, R.L.: Prescribing a system of random variables by conditional distributions. Theory of Probability & Its Applications **15**(3), 458–486 (1970)
5. http://www.imagecompression.info/test_images/ (2013)
6. Malm, H., Oskarsson, M., Warrant, E., Clarberg, P., Hasselgren, J., Lejdfors, C.: Adaptive enhancement and noise reduction in very low light-level video. In: IEEE 11th International Conference on Computer Vision, ICCV 2007, pp. 1–8. IEEE (2007)
7. Mittal, G., Jakhetiya, V., Jaiswal, S.P., Au, O.C., Tiwari, A.K., Wei, D.: Bit-depth expansion using minimum risk based classification. In: VCIP, pp. 1–5 (2012)
8. Pele, O., Werman, M.: Fast and robust earth mover's distances. In: 2009 IEEE 12th International Conference on Computer Vision, pp. 460–467. IEEE (2009)
9. Petschnigg, G., Szeliski, R., Agrawala, M., Cohen, M., Hoppe, H., Toyama, K.: Digital photography with flash and no-flash image pairs. In: ACM Transactions on Graphics (TOG), vol. 23, pp. 664–672. ACM (2004)
10. Smithson, H.E.: Sensory, computational and cognitive components of human colour constancy. Philosophical Transactions of the Royal Society B: Biological Sciences **360**(1458), 1329–1346 (2005)
11. Tomasi, C., Manduchi, R.: Bilateral filtering for gray and color images. In: Sixth International Conference on Computer Vision, 1998, pp. 839–846. IEEE (1998)
12. Ulichney, R.A., Cheung, S.: Pixel bit-depth increase by bit replication. In: Photonics West 1998 Electronic Imaging, pp. 232–241. International Society for Optics and Photonics (1998)
13. Vasershtein, L.N.: Markov processes over denumerable products of spaces, describing large systems of automata. Problemy Peredachi Informatsii **5**(3), 64–72 (1969)
14. Wan, P., Au, O.C., Tang, K., Guo, Y., Fang, L.: From 2d extrapolation to 1d interpolation: Content adaptive image bit-depth expansion. In: 2012 IEEE International Conference on Multimedia and Expo (ICME), pp. 170–175. IEEE (2012)
15. Wang, Z., Bovik, A.C., Sheikh, H.R., Simoncelli, E.P.: Image quality assessment: from error visibility to structural similarity. IEEE Transactions on Image Processing **13**(4), 600–612 (2004)

3D Vision and Pattern Recognition

Categorisation of 3D Objects in Range Images Using Compositional Hierarchies of Parts Based on MDL and Entropy Selection Criteria

Vladislav Kramarev, Krzysztof Walas$^{(\boxtimes)}$, and Aleš Leonardis

Intelligent Robotics Laboratory, School of Computer Science, University of
Birmingham, Edgbaston, Birmingham B15 2TT, United Kingdom
{vvk201,walask,a.leonardis}@birmingham.ac.uk
http://www.cs.bham.ac.uk/research/groupings/robotics/

Abstract. This paper presents a new approach to object categorisation in range images using our novel hierarchical compositional representation of surfaces. The atomic elements at the bottom layer of the hierarchy encode quantized relative depth of pixels in a local neighbourhood. Subsequent layers are formed in the recursive manner, each higher layer is statistically learnt on the layer below via a growing receptive field. In this paper we mainly focus on the *part selection problem*, i.e. the choice of the optimisation criteria which provide the information on which parts should be promoted to the higher layer of the hierarchy. Namely, two methods based on *Minimum Description Length* and category based *entropy* are introduced.

The proposed approach was extensively tested on two widely-used datasets for object categorisation with results that are of the same quality as the best results achieved for those datasets.

Keywords: Range images · Object categorisation · Compositional hierarchies · Shape parts

1 Introduction

In recent years, the processing of range images has experienced a renaissance in the computer vision community. The topic was popular in the 1980s and early 1990s [3,5], but attention waned until the advent of affordable range cameras. This has led to two approaches: i) ideas from the 1990s have been re-tested using new hardware; ii) recent techniques for intensity images have been adapted to range images.

This work aims at improved representations of 3D shape for the purposes of categorisation. Based on the successful implementation of compositional hierarchies [6,16] and their use in categorisation tasks on intensity images, a proper hierarchical representation is sought for range data. However, this is not a trivial task as intensity and depth data are different in their properties. For example, the notion of scale variance for intensity images is associated with a projection

© Springer International Publishing Switzerland 2015
R.R. Paulsen and K.S. Pedersen (Eds.): SCIA 2015, LNCS 9127, pp. 289–301, 2015.
DOI: 10.1007/978-3-319-19665-7_24

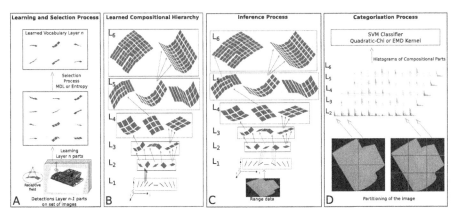

Fig. 1. Overview of the approach. Learning process (A) – a set of depth images is fed into the system. Detections of possible compositions for the next layer are found. Candidate parts undergo a selection process. A vocabulary for the selected layer is provided. Based on the learnt compositional hierarchy (B) an inference process is performed (C). The parts inferred for the specific object are fed into Histograms of Compositional Parts (D). Based on the discretised distribution of parts in partitioned images, categorisation of the object is performed.

from the 3D world onto a 2D image plane, whereas range images provide metric data and the notion of scale variance is thus associated with the support size – the area for which a descriptor is computed.

An overview of the information flow in the system is shown in Fig. 1. The approach presented in this paper is based on computing small depth differences at the bottom layer. These atomic parts are then combined, using statistical learning (Fig. 1B), to form compositions at the second layer of the hierarchy. The compositions at each subsequent layer of the hierarchy are learnt from the previous layer. This representation is inherently surface based. In the learning process (Fig. 1A) a set of depth images is fed into the system, then detections of possible compositions are found. The rich set of candidate parts goes through a selection process that provides a constrained vocabulary for the selected layer. The compositions are promoted to the next layer if they fulfil the selected optimisation criterion. This work studies two selection criteria and their influence on object categorisation. The Learnt Compositional Hierarchy inference process, where specific nodes of the hierarchy are activated, is performed for an example object (Fig. 1C). Subsequently the active compositions are fed into a Histogram of Compositional Parts (Fig. 1D). Based on the discretised distribution of parts in the partitioned images, the object is categorised.

The paper begins with a description of related work in the field of categorisation and detection using range images and compositional representations. In section 2, the proposed compositional hierarchy for range images is presented. Section 3 provides a study of the part selection process. The theoretical description is then followed in sections 4 and 5 by an evaluation based on two widely available datasets [7,13]. Finally, concluding remarks and plans for future work are given in section 6.

1.1   State of the Art

Most vision categorisation systems, either for intensity or depth images, are based on feature extraction and have three main sub-systems. i) keypoints (local extrema of a saliency measure) detector ; ii) keypoints descriptor; iii) feature matching algorithm, which performs the actual object recognition process. This survey examines all the aforementioned aspects of feature-based categorisation systems.

Keypoint Detection. An extensive survey of keypoint detection algorithms for depth data was presented in [9]. The authors divided these techniques into two categories: Fixed-Scale and Adaptive-Scale detectors. An evaluation of different keypoint detection algorithms was presented in [22], and results on the repeatability of keypoints (under slight object transformations) were reported.

Local Shape Descriptors. The detected keypoints should be equipped with a good descriptor, which maintains a high level of distinctiveness and separability between descriptors so as to make the matches between keypoints unique. A recent survey of local surface descriptors by Guo et al. [9] listed 38 different descriptor types and divided approaches into signature, histogram, and transform based methods.

Global Shape Descriptors. In contrast to local shape descriptors, global descriptors are designed to describe a whole object with a single descriptor – see [2] for a survey. The four main classes of descriptor are histogram, transform, 2D view and graph based. The latest approach reported in [20] used covariance descriptors. Another method is to use a Hough Transform for 3D shape recognition [24].

Compositional Hierarchies. Local shape descriptors are suitable for detection tasks as they are robust to clutter and viewpoint changes, whereas global shape descriptors are better for shape retrieval tasks – coping with intra-class variability. One concept to link these two worlds is that of compositional hierarchy.

Obtaining 3D object templates by hierarchical quantisation [15] is one way of building the compositional hierarchy for 3D data using a volumetric representation. An alternative approach is to use a Deep Neural Network that learns, in an unsupervised manner, the representation of the provided range data [18]. An approach using depth images and building the compositional representation from surface patches was described in our previous work [11]. In this paper we go beyond our previous results and provide a study of the mechanisms for establishing part importance, and hence how to obtain better classification performance.

Part Selection. This process is understood here as an optimisation technique for selecting appropriate parts which are then combined in the subsequent layer. It is strongly dependent on the actual task; e.g., for shape retrieval the parts ought to be generic, whereas for pose estimation the parts are required to be discriminative. The problem of part importance for 2D recognition and reconstruction task was considered in [8], as well as the more general problem of finding interesting, salient points [1] or ranking 3D features [23]. Additionally, the problem of how to learn to detect repeatable parts in depth data was addressed in [10]. In the context of 3D compositional hierarchies, our previous work [11] used a frequency-based part selection strategy, i.e. the probability of including a candidate part in the vocabulary depended on the frequency of observing that part in the training data.

Histogram Similarity Measures. In our approach, object categories are represented as stacked histograms of compositional parts (see Fig. 1D). Histograms have widely been used for image classification, as shown in study [26]. χ^2 and histogram intersection are very popular histogram similarity measures. However, these measures fail to take into account cross-bin similarities, which are very important for compositional hierarchical approaches, since different compositional parts may represent similar surface types.

Cross-bin relations are tackled with Earth Mover's Distance (EMD), defined as a minimal cost that must be paid to transform one histogram into the other. Zamolotskikh et al. [25] show three ways in which EMD kernels may be used with an SVM classifier. The Quadratic-Chi histogram distance measure [17] not only takes into account cross-bin relations, but also performs normalisation such that a difference between small bins becomes as important as a difference of large ones.

1.2 Contributions

The main contribution of this paper lies in a successful conception, design and implementation of a learnt compositional hierarchy of surface parts, which are used for 3D object categorisation. The representation optimises two different part selection criteria which results in state-of-the-art categorisation performance on two publicly available datasets. We also tested three different affinity measures to produce kernel functions for SVM classification.

2 Hierarchical Compositional Representation of Surfaces

This section outlines the compositional hierarchical representation for depth data using surface patches. The description is divided into two parts. First, the learning process is described; second, the inference procedure is specified.

The coordinate system for the remainder of this paper is as follows: the x and y axes span the image plane and the z-axis encodes depth information.

The general scheme of the proposed compositional hierarchy is shown in Fig. 2d. The representation is defined as a hierarchy of layers L_n where n denotes the layer number. The vocabulary of each layer L_n contains a set of parts representing surface patches with different geometrical properties.

The first layer L_1 consists of pre-defined parts. Following [11] we use quantized differences of depth between pixels at a fixed distance from each other (along the x-axis). An example of the vocabulary of the first layer parts is depicted in Fig. 2a, while an example of the surface, represented in terms of

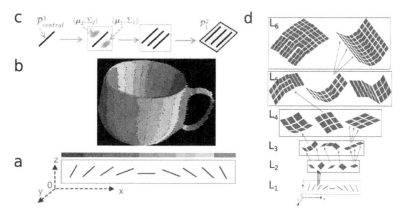

Fig. 2. Quantization of depth differences into nine bins (a). Realization of L_1 parts on the example object – colour coded depth differences (b). Three adjacent depth differences form a small oriented surface patch of layer L_2 (c). A scheme of the hierarchical shape vocabulary (d).

the first layer parts is shown in Fig. 2b. Each part P_i^n of the higher layers L_n, $\forall n > 1$ describes spatial configurations of the parts from the previous layer L_{n-1}:

$$P_i^n \equiv (P_{central}^{n-1}, \{P_j^{n-1}, \mu_j, \Sigma_j\}),\qquad(1)$$

where: $\mu_j = (x_j, y_j, z_j)$ is the mean relative position of the sub-part P_j^{n-1} w.r.t. the central sub-part $P_{central}^{n-1}$, and Σ_j is the covariance matrix representing variability of possible relative positions. These spatial configurations are described in a local neighborhood (termed *receptive field*) of the central sub-part $P_{central}^{n-1}$.

The process of constructing second layer parts is depicted in Fig. 2c. In the current implementation of our framework the design choice is to build parts of the odd layers describing relative positions of sub-parts adjacent in x-direction, while parts of even layers are formed by describing relative positions of sub-parts that are adjacent in y-direction.

2.1   Learning the Vocabulary of Parts

The hierarchical shape vocabulary for each layer L_n, $\forall n > 1$ is learnt using the procedure described in detail in our previous work [11]. In the current paper, only those steps of the algorithm that remained unchanged are outlined. Here the emphasis is on the proposed novel approaches to the part selection problem. The entire vocabulary learning procedure for the layer L_n, $\forall n > 1$ comprises the following steps:

1. Represent the given training range images in terms of parts of layer L_{n-1}. As a result we are given some instances (*part realizations*) of each vocabulary part of layer L_{n-1} that reside in certain locations in the training images. Let R_{ik}^n be the k-th part realization of part P_i^n of layer L_n. Usually each vocabulary part has many realizations in the training images.

2. In the local neighborhood of each part realization perform *local inhibition*, i.e. suppress strongly overlapped part realizations.
3. Build *statistical maps* characterizing the 3D spatial relations between part realizations of the layer L_{n-1} in training images.
4. Detect peaks in the statistical maps of occurrences of parts in a local neighbourhood. These peaks indicate the most frequently observed spatial configurations. Then we fit the area around each peak with 3-dimensional Gaussian, and establish its parameters μ_j and Σ_j.
5. Based on the peaks in statistical maps build *candidate parts* of the layer L_n as shown in Eq. (1) and insert these parts into $\mathcal{S}$, the set of candidate parts.
6. Perform a part selection procedure, i.e. select a subset $\mathcal{S}' \subseteq \mathcal{S}$ that satisfies some optimality criteria (*selection criteria*). The subset $\mathcal{S}'$ becomes a learnt vocabulary of the layer L_n. In this paper we propose, discuss and experimentally evaluate two novel part selection strategies, presented in section 3.

2.2   Inference

The main goal of the inference process is to detect vocabulary parts in input range image using a previously learnt hierarchical compositional shape vocabulary. Inference is sequentially performed for all layers starting from L_1. Since the parts of the layer L_1 represent quantized differences of depth measured in direction of the x axis, the inference process for this layer can be done as follows:

1. Convolve the range image with Gaussian-derivative filter (for x-derivative). The parameter σ can be chosen according to the image size and noise level. For our experiments we use $\sigma = 1.0$ for the SHREC07 dataset and $\sigma = 1.5$ for the Washington RGBD dataset.
2. Quantize the filter responses at each pixel and assign each of them to the bin that corresponds to the closest first layer part.

For each subsequent layer $L_n, \forall n > 1$ the inference process is done as follows:

1. Consider a local neighborhood (termed *receptive field*) around each part realization $R_{i_k}^{n-1}$. For this receptive field we call the part realization $R_{i_k}^{n-1}$ the *central part realization* and denote it as $R_{central}^{n-1}$.
2. Extract all other part realizations R_j^{n-1} present in this receptive field and their relative positions $\Delta X_j = [\Delta x_j, \Delta y_j, \Delta z_j]$ with respect to the the central part realization $R_{central}^{n-1}$.
3. Spatial configurations of $R_{central}^{n-1}$ and neighboring part realizations extracted from receptive field are then matched to vocabulary parts of the layer L_n. For instance, if we observe a spatial configuration: $R_i^n \equiv (R_{central}^{n-1}, P_j^{n-1}, \{\Delta X,\}_j)$
we have to match it to the vocabulary parts of layer L_n defined as shown in Eq. (1). If the match is found, we say that we detected a part realization of the layer L_n in the location of $R_{central}^{n-1}$.

As we proceed to higher layers of the hierarchy, the size of the receptive field increases. At the end of the whole procedure, the input depth image is described in terms of parts from the learnt vocabulary for each layer.

3 Part Selection Criteria

In our previous work [11] the part selection problem was described as follows. For the rich set of candidate parts $\mathcal{S} = \{P_i^n : i = 1..N\}$ for a given layer L_n, we want to obtain an efficient representation with a relatively small number of parts in the vocabulary. Additionally, to facilitate generalization using our representation, similar surfaces should be encoded by the same vocabulary element.

In order to fulfil these requirements we specify a procedure that selects a subset $\mathcal{S}' \subseteq \mathcal{S}$, solving the following optimization problem:

$$ E(\mathcal{S}') = \sum_{i=1}^{N} d(P_i, P'(P_i))\, \nu_i \; + \; \alpha\, |\mathcal{S}'| \qquad (2) $$

where ν_i is the frequency of occurrence of realizations of the i-th candidate part P_i^n in the training data, $d(\cdot, \cdot)$ is a distance function that quantifies the similarity between two parts (from the same layer), and $P'(P_i)$ is the part in $\mathcal{S}'$ that is closest to P_i^n. Finally $\alpha \in \mathbb{R}^+$ is a meta-parameter that regulates the trade-off between precision of the representation and the number of selected parts.

Two main disadvantages of this approach are: i) a selected vocabulary strongly depends on the frequency of parts' observation in the training images; e.g., three surface patches constituting a corner and surfaces of high curvature are usually observed less frequently than planar surfaces; ii) a vocabulary selected in this manner is not specifically designed for any particular task, i.e. a specific measure of part importance for solving different computer vision tasks is missing. Therefore, we introduce two different selection criteria.

Minimum Description Length. This part selection strategy finds the minimal subset of candidate parts which is required to represent most of the input range data in terms of the shape vocabulary. It is implemented as a greedy algorithm similar to the one used in [14]. Let us introduce two definitions first. The total coverage $Cover(P_i^n)$ of the part P_i^n is the sum of areas (expressed in the number of pixels) in training images where the part P_i is active.

The second measure is $Cover(P_i^n | \mathcal{S}')$, which is the *conditional coverage* of part P_i^n given that the subset $\mathcal{S}'$ is already included in the vocabulary. It measures the total area in the training images where the part P_i^n is detected, excluding those locations where realizations of parts from $\mathcal{S}'$ are detected. As part realizations may overlap with each other (in terms of area of images where they reside), conditional coverage is a non-increasing measure: As the subset $\mathcal{S}'$ grows, the conditional coverage of each non-selected part either remains unchanged or is lowered by the influence of an already selected part.

Consider learning a vocabulary for layer L_n. The part selection algorithm can be described as follows:

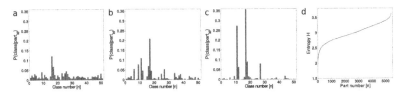

Fig. 3. Entropy based on the probability of the class given individual part $P(class|P_i^n)$. Histogram for part with: high entropy(a), mean entropy(b), low entropy(c). Sorted entropy values for the candidate parts at layer three (d).

1. Assume the set of selected parts $\mathcal{S}'$ is empty. All candidate parts are stored in the set $\mathcal{S}$.
2. Consider the part P_i^n in $\mathcal{S}$ which has the largest $Cover(P_i^n)$; remove this part from $\mathcal{S}$ and insert it into $\mathcal{S}'$. Candidate parts P_j^n which are similar to P_i^n (if $d(P_i^n, P_j^n) < Thresh)$) are also removed from the set $\mathcal{S}$.
3. Perform the following steps: in each iteration find in the set $\mathcal{S}$ the part P_k^n which has the largest $Cover(P_k^n|\mathcal{S}')$, remove this part from $\mathcal{S}$, and add it to the $\mathcal{S}'$; Parts that are similar to P_k^n, are also removed from $\mathcal{S}$.
4. Proceed until the largest value of $Cover(P_j^n|\mathcal{S}')$ becomes less than a pre-defined threshold value T.
5. The resulting vocabulary is $\mathcal{S}'$.

In contrast to the part selection criteria defined by the cost function in Eq. (2), this part selection algorithm allows selection of parts with high curvature as long as their total coverage is above the threshold value T.

Entropy-based part selection. In this part selection strategy we incorporate some discriminative information into the vocabulary learning procedure. The decision to include a candidate part to the vocabulary is based on the distribution of part realizations across object categories. If realizations of a candidate part P_i^n reside in objects of one category only, we consider this part quite category-specific, while if realizations of a candidate part appear in objects of many categories, we assume this part would be less helpful for categorization.

The category probability given a candidate part P_i^n $P(category|P_i^n)$ is approximated using histograms computed for all candidate parts throughout the whole training dataset. The entropy of each individual part is computed from the histogram using:

$$H = -\sum_{i=1}^{n} p_i log(p_i).$$ (3)

The $P(category|P_i^n)$ for the parts with high, mean and low entropy are shown in Fig. 3 a,b,c respectively. A graph presenting the sorted entropy H computed for all the the compositions detected at layer L_3 is shown in Fig. 3d. Our proposed strategy is to select a certain number of candidate parts with the highest entropy at each layer of the hierarchy.

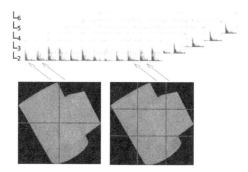

Fig. 4. A histogram of Compositional Parts – the histograms from all sub-regions and all layers detections are stacked together to form a category signature

4   Experiments

In order to test the performance of our hierarchical compositional representation two publicly available datasets were used. We focus our attention on the task of object categorization from range images. The RGB-D Washington Dataset [13] contains real world data registered with a Kinect-like device – 300 objects are split into 51 categories. We used only 20% of the images of each object instance (depth channel only). To partition the data into train and test sets, the exact list of object instances left out provided in [13] was used.

The second dataset used was SHREC07 [7], which contains 400 meshes representing objects that are split into 20 categories. We rotated these mesh models about the z-axis with a step of 18 degrees, thus producing $400{\times}20 = 8000$ depth images. We evaluated performance using leave-one-out cross-validation.

Learning of Hierarchical Shape Vocabulary. We learnt layers 2-6 of the compositional hierarchical shape vocabulary on each dataset separately. In our first experiment we learnt a compositional hierarchy using the MDL principle. In the second experiment we additionally included the most category-specific parts to the vocabulary of each layer (parts with low entropy). All the experiments were conducted in a way to avoid data snooping, i.e. we extracted category-specific parts from the training data only.

Classification. The procedure started with the inference of parts of layers 1-6 from range images. Then, following [11], we built stacked histograms of parts as shown in Fig. 4, i.e. we partitioned each object image into 14 sub-regions (1 for the whole object, plus $2{\times}2$ and $3{\times}3$ partitioning). The distribution of parts of layers 2-6 within each sub-region was represented as a histogram; histograms of each sub-region were then concatenated to form a HOCP (Histogram of Compositional Parts) surface descriptor. These descriptors were fed into an SVM classifier.

Experiments with kernels for SVM. Three different types of kernels for SVM were tested in our experiments. χ^2 kernels are implemented in standard packages for SVM. The EMD measure which does not produce a positive semi-definite kernel matrix was modified [25]. The following transformation: $K(S,Q) = exp(-EMD(S,Q))$, where S and Q are histograms, was applied. Additionally, a ground distance metric D_{ij} which denotes distance between bins i and j of the histogram was defined based on geometric similarity of parts. Note that we consider part similarities within each sub-region, and do not take into account cross sub-region relations. For Quadratic-Chi measure [17], it is required to define a bin-similarity matrix A_{ij}. We do it in the same way as in case of EMD kernels, i.e. only similarities of parts within each sub-region are taken into consideration. The Quadratic-Chi histogram distance is defined as:

$$QC_m^A(P,Q) = \sqrt{\sum_{ij} \left(\frac{(P_i - Q_i)}{(\sum_c (P_c + Q_c)A_{ci})^m} \right) \left(\frac{(P_j - Q_j)}{(\sum_c (P_c + Q_c)A_{cj})^m} \right) A_{ij}} \quad (4)$$

where: P and Q are two non-negative bounded histograms $P, Q \in [0, U]^N$; A is a non-negative symmetric bounded bin-similarity matrix; $A \in [0, U]^N \times [0, U]^N$ and $\forall_{i,j} \, A_{ii} \leq A_{ij}$.

5   Results and Discussion

The results achieved on the Washington dataset are shown in Fig. 5. Our experiments show that combined MDL and entropy-based selection performs better than MDL alone (see Fig. 5a), especially for higher layers where parts become more category-specific. Additionally, the comparison of performance of different kernels used in the classification procedure is shown in Fig. 5b. The best results were achieved for the Quadratic-Chi kernel, which takes into account cross-bin relations and performs normalisation as well, such that the difference between small bins becomes as important as the difference of large ones. This turns out to be a substantial property: all parts in the histograms are distributed non-uniformly and some non-frequent but discriminative parts may have a larger impact on category detection. This observation might also explain the poorer performance of the EMD kernel as pointed out in [17]. The comparison of our results with other approaches is given in Table 1, which shows that our approach is almost as good as the best results achieved for this dataset. Additionally we have also provided the results for the artificial data which are given in the dataset

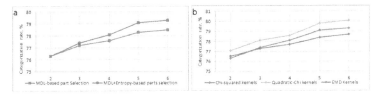

Fig. 5. Categorisation accuracy achieved on Washington RGBD dataset for: different part selection strategies – SVM with χ^2 kernel (a); different types of SVM kernels(b)

Table 1. Results for Washington RGB-D dataset [13] and SHREC'07 dataset [7]

Washington dateset		SHREC'07 dataset	
Method	Depth data only	Method	Depth data
Random Forest [13]	66.8±2.5	ISM 1-NN [19]	79.0
HCR [11]	75.6	BoW [21]	87.3
HMP3D [12]	76.5±2.2	HCR [11]	95.6
CNN-RNN [18]	78.9±3.8	ISM 2-NN [19]	100.0
SP+HMP [4]	81.2±2.3		
Ours	80,1±2.2	Ours	96.4

from the Shape Retrieval Contest SHREC07 [7]. Table 1 shows our approach is also almost reaching the top score.

6   Conclusion

The research presented in this paper is focused on the part selection problem and its influence on the performance of hierarchical compositional representations in the object categorisation task. The presented results show that an appropriate selection criterion can boost task performance. Compared to our previous approach, the gain for the RGB-D dataset is about 4%. Additional tests with the histogram similarity measure show that an additional one percent was added to the final result. The use of compositional hierarchies could not only improve performance, but being generative models, they can also furnish additional properties such as better scalability and robustness to partial occlusions. Moreover, they enable performing detection tasks without using sliding windows. A thorough investigation of all these aspects of compositional hierarchies is envisioned as future work.

Acknowledgments. We gratefully acknowledge the support of EU-FP7-IST grant 600918 (PaCMan). The authors would also like to thank Jeremy Wyatt and Sebastian Zurek for their helpful comments.

References

1. Aanæs, H., Dahl, A., Pedersen, K.S.: Interesting Interest Points. Int. J. of Computer Vision **97**(1), 18–35 (2012)
2. Akgul, C., Sankur, B., Yemez, Y., Schmitt, F.: 3D Model Retrieval Using Probability Density-Based Shape Descriptors. IEEE Trans. on Pattern Analysis and Machine Intell. **31**(6), 1117–1133 (2009)
3. Besl, P.J.: Surfaces in Range Image Understanding. Springer Series in Perception Engineering. Springer (1988)
4. Bo, L., Ren, X., Fox, D.: Unsupervised feature learning for RGB-D based object recognition. In: Desai, J.P., Dudek, G., Khatib, O., Kumar, V. (eds.) Experimental Robotics. STAR, vol. 88, pp. 387–402. Springer, Heidelberg (2013)

5. Faugeras, O.: Three-Dimensional Computer Vision. A geometric view point. MIT Press (1993)
6. Fidler, S., Leonardis, A.: Towards scalable representations of object categories: learning a hierarchy of parts. In: IEEE Conf. on Computer Vision and Pattern Recognition, CVPR 2007, pp. 1–8 (2007)
7. Giorgi, D., Biasotti, S., Paraboschi, L.: SHape REtrieval Contest 2007: Watertight Models Track
8. Guo, G., Wang, Y., Jiang, T., Yuille, A., Fang, F., Gao, W.: A Shape Reconstructability Measure of Object Part Importance with Applications to Object Detection and Localization. Int. J. of Computer Vision **108**(3), 241–258 (2014)
9. Guo, Y., Bennamoun, M., Sohel, F., Lu, M., Wan, J.: 3D Object Recognition in Cluttered Scenes with Local Surface Features: A Survey. IEEE Trans. on Pattern Analysis and Machine Intell. **36**(11), 2270–2287 (2014)
10. Holzer, S., Shotton, J., Kohli, P.: Learning to efficiently detect repeatable interest points in depth data. In: Fitzgibbon, A., Lazebnik, S., Perona, P., Sato, Y., Schmid, C. (eds.) ECCV 2012, Part I. LNCS, vol. 7572, pp. 200–213. Springer, Heidelberg (2012)
11. Kramarev, V., Zurek, S., Wyatt, J.L., Leonardis, A.: Object categorization from range images using a hierarchical compositional representation. In: 2014 22nd Int. Conf. on Pattern Recognition (ICPR) (2014)
12. Lai, K., Bo, L., Fox, D.: Unsupervised feature learning for 3D scene labeling. In: 2014 IEEE Int. Conf. on Robotics and Automation (ICRA), pp. 3050–3057 (2014)
13. Lai, K., Bo, L., Ren, X., Fox, D.: A large-scale hierarchical multi-view RGB-D object dataset. In: 2011 IEEE Int. Conf. on Robotics and Automation (ICRA), pp. 1817–1824 (2011)
14. Leonardis, A., Bischof, H., Maver, J.: Multiple eigenspaces. Pattern Recognition **35**(11), 2613–2627 (2002)
15. Li, B., Wu, T., Zhu, S.-C.: Integrating context and occlusion for car detection by hierarchical and-or model. In: Fleet, D., Pajdla, T., Schiele, B., Tuytelaars, T. (eds.) ECCV 2014, Part VI. LNCS, vol. 8694, pp. 652–667. Springer, Heidelberg (2014)
16. Ommer, B., Sauter, M., Buhmann, J.M.: Learning top-down grouping of compositional hierarchies for recognition. In: Proceedings of the 2006 Conf. on Computer Vision and Pattern Recognition Workshop, CVPRW 2006, pp. 194–211. IEEE Computer Society, Washington (2006)
17. Pele, O., Werman, M.: The quadratic-chi histogram distance family. In: Daniilidis, K., Maragos, P., Paragios, N. (eds.) ECCV 2010, Part II. LNCS, vol. 6312, pp. 749–762. Springer, Heidelberg (2010)
18. Socher, R., Huval, B., Bhat, B., Manning, C.D., Ng, A.Y.: Convolutional-Recursive Deep Learning for 3D Object Classification. In: Advances in Neural Information Processing Systems, vol. 25 (2012)
19. Salti, S., Tombari, F., Stefano, L.D.: On the use of implicit shape models for recognition of object categories in 3D data. In: Kimmel, R., Klette, R., Sugimoto, A. (eds.) ACCV 2010, Part III. LNCS, vol. 6494, pp. 653–666. Springer, Heidelberg (2011)
20. Tabia, H., Laga, H., Picard, D., Gosselin, P.H.: Covariance descriptors for 3D shape matching and retrieval. In: 2014 IEEE Conf. on Computer Vision and Pattern Recognition (CVPR), pp. 4185–4192 (2014)
21. Toldo, R., Castellani, U., Fusiello, A.: A bag of words approach for 3d object categorization. In: Computer Vision/Computer Graphics Collaboration Techniques, pp. 116–127. Springer (2009)

22. Tombari, F., Salti, S., Stefano, L.D.: Performance Evaluation of 3D Keypoint Detectors. Int. J. of Computer Vision **102**(1–3), 198–220 (2013)
23. Tuzel, O., Liu, M.-Y., Taguchi, Y., Raghunathan, A.: Learning to rank 3D features. In: Fleet, D., Pajdla, T., Schiele, B., Tuytelaars, T. (eds.) ECCV 2014, Part I. LNCS, vol. 8689, pp. 520–535. Springer, Heidelberg (2014)
24. Woodford, O., Pham, M.T., Maki, A., Perbet, F., Stenger, B.: Demisting the Hough Transform for 3D Shape Recognition and Registration. Int. J. of Computer Vision **106**(3), 332–341 (2014)
25. Zamolotskikh, A., Cunningham, P.: An assessment of alternative strategies for constructing EMD-based kernel functions for use in an SVM for image classification. In: Int. Workshop on Content-Based Multimedia Indexing, CBMI 2007, pp. 11–17 (2007)
26. Zhang, J., Marszalek, M., Lazebnik, S., Schmid, C.: Local Features and Kernels for Classification of Texture and Object Categories: A Comprehensive Study. Int. J. of Computer Vision **73**(2), 213–238 (2007)

Characterizing Digital Light Processing (DLP) 3D Printed Primitives

Emil Tyge[1], Jens J. Pallisgaard[2], Morten Lillethorup[2],
Nanna G. Hjaltalin[2], Mary K. Thompson[3], and Line H. Clemmensen[2](✉)

[1] Electrical Engineering, Technical University of Denmark, Lyngby, Denmark
[2] Applied Mathematics and Computer Science,
Technical University of Denmark, Lyngby, Denmark
lkhc@dtu.dk
[3] Mechanical Engineering, Technical University of Denmark, Lyngby, Denmark
mkath@mek.dtu.dk

Abstract. The resolution and repeatability of 3D printing processes depends on a number of factors including the software, hardware, and material used. When printing parts with features that are near or below the nominal printing resolution, it is important to understand how the printer works. For example, what is the smallest unit shape that can be produced? And what is the reproducibility of that process? This paper presents a method for automatically detecting and characterizing the height, width, and length of micro scale geometric primitives produced via a digital light processing (DLP) 3D printing process. An upper limit, lower limit, and best estimate for each dimension is reported for each primitive. Additionally, the roughness, rectangularity, and tilt of the top of each primitive is estimated. The uncertainty of the best estimate is indicated using standard deviations for a series of primitives. The method generalizes to unseen primitives, and the results illustrate that the dimension estimates converge as the size of the primitives increases. The primitives' rectangularity also increases as the size increases. Finally, the primitives specified with 5 to $68\mu m$ varying heights have been estimated to group into five different heights with fairly low variance of the best estimates of the heights. This reflects how the requested geometry is parsed and produced by the printer.

1 Introduction

Although the development of additive manufacturing technologies began in the mid-1980s [3], until recently they were limited mainly to models and prototypes. The direct manufacture of net shape parts is still relatively new and engineering applications that require high geometric precision and accuracy are still limited. This work is motivated by a desire to understand, improve, and control the resolution and repeatability of digital light processing (DLP) 3D printing to facilitate micro scale and precision production. DLP 3D printing uses light to solidify a liquid photopolymer. By changing the pattern of the light and incrementing the vertical position of the workpiece, the desired geometry is built up

© Springer International Publishing Switzerland 2015
R.R. Paulsen and K.S. Pedersen (Eds.): SCIA 2015, LNCS 9127, pp. 302–313, 2015.
DOI: 10.1007/978-3-319-19665-7_25

layer by layer. One of the advantages of the DLP technique is that the workpiece is suspended upside down from the build platform. This allows for better control of the process and thus better layer thickness and uniformity [6].

This work proposes a method for characterizing micro scale cuboid primitives that were produced via DLP 3D printing. This task is challenging because primitives are produced using the same process as the surrounding bulk material. Therefore, they share the same surface characteristics. In addition, the printing process produces features with rounded edges and tapered sidewalls. Thus, there are often no clear edges to detect or constant dimensions to identify, unlike data used for previously proposed imaging processing techniques to characterise engineered surfaces in e.g. [8]. Finally, the printed features were imaged using a focus variation microscope. This introduces noise, holes, and other artifacts into the data set.

The method presented in this work detects features on 3D printed samples, determines which features are primitives for future analysis, deletes erroneous values in the data set to be analyzed, and characterizes the dimensions of the detected primitives. To address the challenges associated with the production and measurement, an inner and outer boundary for each primitive is defined. From this, an upper and lower boundary and a best estimate of the desired characteristics (height, width, and length) of the primitives can be obtained. In addition, the primitives are characterized based on their centroid, roughness, rectangularity, and tilt. We illustrate the measures on an unseen sample and look at how they vary over the workpiece in general and for varying heights.

The paper is structured as follows. First, we introduce the experimental setup, the printed data, and the digitalized data (Section 2). Next, we introduce the method for detecting the primitives (Section 3) and define the measures of characterization (Section 4). This includes pre-processing and other data manipulation. Finally, we present the results of the method and conclusions (Sections 5 and 6).

2 Data

Three pairs of samples were produced in RCP30 (a pinkish peach photopolymer) using an EnvisionTEC Perfactory 3 Mini Multi Lens 3D printer. With the lens and settings used, the printing process has a nominal resolution of $32\mu m$ in x and y and a $15\mu m$ layer thickness. Each sample is a 10x10x5mm block with a 20x20 grid of features. The features on each sample have two fixed dimensions that are large relative to the nominal resolution of the machine and one variable dimension that is not (table 1). All features in a given row have the same specified dimensions. Thus, each sample should represent a total of 20 feature geometries, each replicated 20 times.

Each block was designed with a 0.5x0.5x0.75mm border to protect the features from damage during handling and small rectangular channels on the top left and bottom right corners of the border to indicate the orientation of the part (figure 1). The geometries were designed in SolidWorks and exported as

STL files. The digital masks for the DLP process were automatically generated from the STL files using EnvisionTEC's proprietary software Perfactory RP 2.6. This conversion means that the geometry requested in the STL file is known but the geometry specified by the masks is not. It is not guaranteed that all of the requested features were printed on any given part or that the features were printed with the specified dimensions.

Table 1. The printing specifications for the three pairs of workpieces

Pattern	Length (μm)	Width (μm)	Height (μm)
Tall and rectangular (X)	5-100	200	100
Tall and rectangular (Y)	200	5-100	100
Short and square (Z)	200	200	5-68

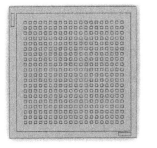

Fig. 1. CAD model for printing the primitives with changes in z (left) and an image of the printed primitives taken with a standard Leica camera (the Z_1 sample) (right). The heights of the primitives increase from top to bottom. Both images seen from the top. The workpiece is $1cm \times 1cm$.

The samples were imaged with an Alicona Infinite Focus microscope using a $5\times$ objective (x, y resolution: $1.75\mu m$). This microscope combines images taken at different vertical focus points to create a 3D height map, a color map, and a quality map. Like all optical metrology instruments, the Alicona is affected by the interaction of the light with the sample. Measurements are affected by the sample's material properties, its geometry, and any dirt or debris that might be present on its surface. As a result, data sets often contain spikes that do not represent true measurements (Figure 2) and have holes where the reflected light was unable to return to the sensor. The Alicona is unable to measure very steep slopes. Thus, the primitive sidewall data is often incomplete. The Alicona measures heights relative to its reference coordinate system. If the surface of the sample is not perfectly horizontal to the Alicona's system, a systematic planar tilt will be present in the data set. Finally, if the sample is rotated relative to the Alicona, the edges of the primitives will not be parallel to the measurement coordinate system.

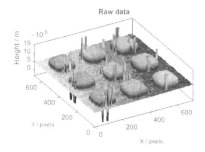

Fig. 2. Illustration of the surface of a 3D printed plate as captured by the Alicona

3   Methods

This section describes the pre-processing of the raw data, the detection of the primitives, and the definitions of their top, edge, and sidewalls. On this basis, the length, width, and height of the primitives is defined, as well as the centroid, the roughness, the rectangularity, and the tilt. In the next two sections, we concentrate on characterizing the first Z workpiece (Z_1).

3.1   Pre-processing

The pre-processing uses frequency filters to remove the optical artifacts created by the Alicona. This is done in two steps: a spike detection step and a frequency separation step. For the spike detection, we used a Gaussian high-pass filter as described in [4,5]. A series of different bandwidths were examined to determine a bandwidth adequate to identify the high-frequency noise patterns in the images (Table 2). Subsequently, a simple thresholding is performed to obtain the mask for the valid data (Figure 3).

In the second step, the data is split into regions of different frequency. This is done according to Whitehouse's guidelines for the identification and separation of surface features [9]. The idea is to separate the roughness of the surface (high-frequency noise), the waviness of the surface (medium frequency noise often associated with the manufacturing process), the primary profile of the surface (the printed surface of interest), and the orientation of the surface (low-frequency process or measurement noise). Waviness was not observed and therefore omitted. The cut-off frequencies were chosen manually from a series of Gaussian filters with varying bandwidths (Table 2). Previous work [1] using the same measurement instrument used cutoff values of $2.5\mu m$ and $500\mu m$ for identifying the roughness. In comparison, the values chosen in this work are more conservative. The orientation and the roughness are then removed as illustrated in Figure 4. The most critical parameter is the orientation cut-off frequency which separates the background from the foreground. Based on investigations on the samples presented here this is however also the parameter with largest span in which the results are robust.

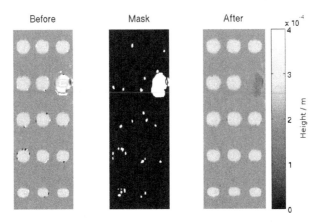

Fig. 3. The spike detection algorithm detects spikes using a high pass filter. This figure shows the data before reconstruction, the mask, and the data after the reconstruction. The mask includes data points that were marked as invalid by the Alicona.

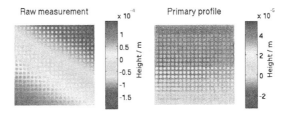

Fig. 4. The raw data are illustrated to the left. The data after removing spikes, roughness, and orientation are illustrated to the right. Note, the different scales on the colorbars.

3.2 Primitive Detection

The first step in the primitive detection involves an initial guess of where the primitives are by simple thresholding. To remove some of the false positives associated with debris and the roughness of the surface, the mask is opened with a 25px radius disk before labeling. This segmentation and the initial labeling yields some false positives, which are removed automatically from the set at a later time. The result is seen in Figure 5. Each primitive is labeled for separation using connected components labeling [2].

3.3 Tilt Correction

Once the primitives have been detected, a linear plane is fitted to the background. The tilt (likely due to manufacturing error) is estimated and removed for both the background as well as primitives. This was done locally for each primitive as the above orientation removal could be improved this way. The correction is illustrated in Figure 6.

Table 2. The chosen cut-off frequencies for the separations calculated from a defined cut-off frequency as a 3dB attenuation and the given standard deviations of the Gaussian filters. Included is the cut-off frequency used in the spike detection.

	Standard deviation σ	Cut-off at -3dB $[\mu m]$
Orientation	>100	>933
Primary profile	50-100	466-933
Roughness	<1	<9
Spike detection	<50	<466

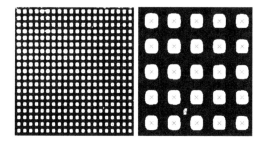

Fig. 5. The results from primitive detection after the morphological opening with the mask in black and the detected primitives in white. The centers of the primitives are marked with red crosses. Left: All primitives in the workpiece. Right: Detailed view of the lower right corner of the workpiece showing 25 detected primitives and one false positive.

3.4   Segmentation

For a given feature, the distributions of the heights (Figure 6, right) is generally bi-modal, with the larger lower peak coming from the surrounding surface and the smaller and higher peak belonging to the primitive. For generalisation purposes, a K-means algorithm is used to find the two cluster centers, and the midpoint between the two centers is used as a threshold on the height map. To ensure that there is only one object (the primitive) in the image, labeling is used and only the object with the largest area is kept for further analysis. Finally an erosion on the image is performed and subtracted from the original image to get the border of the object. Figure 7 illustrates the different steps in defining the boundary of the primitive.

After the border is found, each primitive is divided into four segments: the top, the sidewall, the floor, and invalid data. The invalid data is the part of the data where a spike has been detected. The sidewalls are defined as the parts of the primitive with an overall gradient. A normalised Sobel filter [7] is used to find the gradient row wise and column wise. The edges are found by using a threshold on the gradient image. In this case, everything with an angle greater than or equal to 30 degrees is classified as sidewall. To ensure that only pixels around the top pixels are used as sidewalls, morphological reconstruction is used [2], as illustrated in Figure 8. The top pixels and the floor are given from the detection of the primitives (Figure 5), combined with the sidewall (edge)

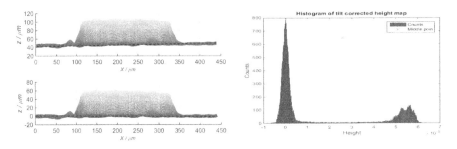

Fig. 6. Illustration of a primitive before and after the tilt correction (left). Histogram of tilt corrected height map (right).

Fig. 7. Illustration of the different steps used to find the border of the primitive

Fig. 8. Illustration of the effects of morphological reconstruction. Sidewalls are not always closed due to the pre-processing where invalid data are masked out.

detection and invalid data detection. Figure 9 (left) illustrates a primitive and its different segments.

4   Characterization

The definition of the top pixels together with the sidewalls of the primitives gives a starting point for characterizing the primitives. In the following subsections only valid data points are included in the estimations.

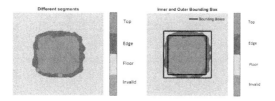

Fig. 9. Image of different segments (left). Different segments with bounding boxes (right).

4.1 Length and Width

We define the length (L) and width (W) as a best guess, an upper bound, and a lower bound. The upper and lower bound of the length and the width are determined by finding the smallest bounding box for the inner and outer boundary of the sidewalls. To account for the fact that the primitives may be rotated in the microscope, the primitive is rotated 90 degrees in steps of 2 degrees to find the smallest bounding box that encloses the pixels. The principle is shown in Figure 9 (right) with an angle of zero degrees.

The mean of the upper and lower bound is used as a measure of the best guess, i.e. $L_{best} = (L_{low} + L_{up})/2$ and $W_{best} = (W_{low} + W_{up})/2$. The upper and lower bound should not be considered uncertainties of the best guess, as we have no guarantee that the true estimate lies within our bounding boxes. The lower and upper bound can be interpreted as a measure of how broad the sidewalls are.

4.2 Height

The height (H) is defined as a best guess, an upper bound, and a lower bound. The median of all valid top pixels defines the best guess of the height ($H_{best} = median(z_i)$). The median is a robust measure in this context since it is not sensitive to local roughness or waviness of the primitive (see Figure 10). An

Fig. 10. Effects of calculating surface height as mean vs. median

upper and a lower bound are calculated as well, and the definition of these are the 2.5 percentile (lower bound, H_{low}) and the 97.5 percentile (upper bound, H_{up}) of pixels defined as top (example in Figure 11). There is still a chance that the true height is outside the upper and lower bound, but the 2.5 percentile and the 97.5 percentile are picked because of the possibility of noise in the data.

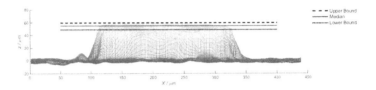

Fig. 11. Height estimates

4.3 Centroid

The centroid is calculated as the center of mass of the valid top pixels $[x_i, y_i]$ as $\mathbf{C}_{x,y} = \frac{1}{n} \sum_{i=1}^{n} [x_i, y_i]$, where n is the number of valid top pixels.

4.4 Roughness

The roughness measure indicates how rough the top of the primitive is. The roughness is defined as in [9] by $R_a = \frac{1}{n} \sum_{i=1}^{n} |z_i - \mu_z|$, where z_i is the height of the ith top point, and μ_z is the mean of all the top heights.

4.5 Rectangularity

Rectangularity measures how rectangular each primitive is. It is defined as the area of the primitive (number of top pixels) divided by the area of the smallest bounding box for the top pixels? which is the same as the lower bound of the length and width $S = \frac{n}{L_{low} \cdot W_{low}}$.

4.6 Tilt

The tilt of the top of the primitive characterizes the overall asymmetry in the printed primitive. For this, it is assumed that the top pixels can be described by a plane. The tilt is defined as the angle between a plane, P, fitted to the top pixels and the $(x - y)$-plane, O: $T = \angle(P, O)$.

5 Results

The sample Z_1 was used to calibrate the method and tune parameters (training), thus we will use sample Z_2 to test the performance of the proposed method (testing). Table 3 summarizes the number of detected primitives, together with the false and true negatives as compared to a manual detection by an expert. The results are similar in the training and in the testing sample after automatic post processing. We do not detect primitives that were not manually detected. And after post processing, we do not miss any of the primitives that were observed by visual inspection of the sample by an expert. The visual inspections found only 379 and 380 primitives in the samples as the smallest of the 20 rows was not visibly printed, and a single primitive in one row in the Z_1 sample was corrupted.

Table 3. Summary of the statistics on the detection of the primitives

Sample Type	Primitives detected manually	Detected in pre processing	False positives	After post processing	False positives
Sample Z_1	379	418	39	379	0
Sample Z_2	380	415	35	380	0

The characteristics of the primitives are summarized in Table 4 as means and standard deviations of all the primitives in the sample Z_2. The estimated heights are presented as a plot in Figure 12 as we expect the primitives to vary in height. There seem to be five different heights in the sample Z_2 although the specifications increased in height for each of the 20 rows in the sample. These indicate the true vertical step height used by the printer. Additionally, we note that the best estimates of primitives with similar heights are very close, and thus their uncertainty small, whereas the estimated lower and upper bounds for the estimate give a much wider span. The lower and upper bounds give a conservative boundary for the definition of our best estimate, whereas the standard deviation of the best estimates gives an uncertainty of our estimated best height.

Table 4. Summaries of the estimates for the measures characterizing the primitives. The mean and standard deviation (std.) of each measure for all the detected primitives in the sample Z_2 are given.

Measure	Width	Length	Rectangularity	Roughness	Top tilt
Mean	238.9 μm	247.5 μm	87.4 %	1.74μm	0.526°
Std.	20.89 μm	29.28 μm	4.98 %	0.359μm	0.269°

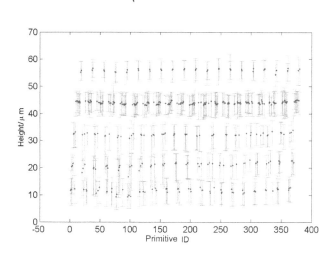

Fig. 12. Height chart of the sample Z_2

We use the five estimated levels of heights to illustrate how the length, width, and rectangularity vary as a function of height (Figure 13). It is apparent that as the height of the primitives increases, it is easier for the algorithm to segment them. Thus, the best estimates of width and length decrease and become more consistent. Furthermore, it shows that the top becomes gradually smaller and more rectangular as the height increases. The standard deviations of the best estimates give us an uncertainty estimate of the estimated best values, whereas the upper and lower bounds on the best estimate are related to the uncertainty of our definition of the estimate.

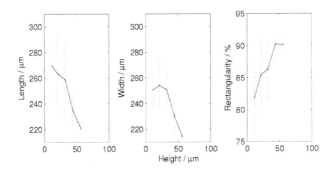

Fig. 13. Mean and standard deviations for the best estimates of the length, width, and rectangularity as a function of the grouped heights for sample Z_2

6   Conclusion

We presented a method for automatically detecting and characterizing the dimensions of micro scale geometric primitives produced via a digital light processing (DLP) 3D printing process. We proposed the best estimate of the height of a primitive to be the median of the top pixels as this is a more robust estimate than the mean. This robustness is also seen in the small standard deviations of the estimated heights for primitives of the same height. The length and width were defined using the top and the sidewalls to define lower and upper bounds for the primitives, and taking into account any rotations of the primitives that may occur. Finally, estimates of centroid, roughness, rectangularity and tilt of the top of a primitive were defined. Standard deviations for these estimates were also relatively small. The method was shown to have high precision (no false positives nor false negatives) when compared to a visual inspection by an expert.

The features for the samples presented in this work had a nominal size of $200\times 200\times 5-68\mu m$ in intervals of 1 or $5\mu m$ for a total of 20 different heights. However, it was shown that primitives were produced in only five heights. This could be due to the printer's parsing of the specifications, due to the thickness of the layers it is capable of printing, or due to a combination of the two. We observed that the lengths and widths of the primitives were consistently estimated when the primitives had a height of $50\mu m$ or more. Also the rectangularity of the primitives increased from 80% to 90% as the height increased. This is to be expected as the features were specified close to or below the minimum nominal resolution of the machine. We also showed that several characteristics of the printed primitives are worth taking into account, as they vary for primitives with varying size specifications.

In this work, we focused on the Z samples for clarity and because the Z primitives were generally better formed than the X and Y primitives. However, the method in this work was developed for and is applicable to cuboid primitives with variations in x, y, and z. Future work will include additional testing and tuning of the method for the more challenging variations in X and Y. It will also further address the repeatability and uncertainty of the defined characteristics. Alternative segmentation techniques using shape priors could also be of future interest both for more complex primitives as well as for implicit definitions of primitive characteristics.

References

1. Gasparin, S.: Verification of Tolerance Chains in Micro Manufacturing. Ph.D. thesis, Department of Production and Management, Technical University of Denmark (2012)
2. Gonzalez, R.C., Woods, R.E., Eddins, S.L.: Digital Image Processing using Matlab, 2 edn. Gatesmark Publishing (2009)
3. Huang, Y., Leu, M.C., Mazumder, J., Donmez, A.: Additive manufacturing: Current state, future potential, gaps and needs, and recommendations. Journal of Manufacturing Science and Engineering **137** (2015)
4. ISO-16610-21:2011: Geometrical product specifications (gps) - filtration - part 21: Linear profile filters: Gaussian filters (2011)
5. ISO-4287:199: Primary, waviness and roughness profiles (1997)
6. Jørgensen, A.R.: Design and Development of an Improved Direct Light Processing (DLP) Platform for Precision Additive Manufacturing. Master's thesis, DTU Mechanical Engineering, Technical University of Denmark (2015)
7. Sobel, I.: History and definition of the sobel operator (2014)
8. Verma, R., Raya, J.: Characterization of engineered surfaces. Journal of Physics: Conference Series **13**, 5–8 (2005)
9. Whitehouse, D.: 2 - identification and separation of surface features. In: Surfaces and Their Measurement, pp. 16–47. Kogan Page Science, Oxford (2002)

Joint Spatial-Depth Feature Pooling
for RGB-D Object Classification

Hong Pan[1,2(✉)], Søren Ingvor Olsen[1], and Yaping Zhu[1]

[1] Department of Computer Science, University of Copenhagen, 2100 København Ø, Denmark
{hong.pan,ingvor,yp.z}@di.ku.dk
[2] School of Automation, Southeast University, Nanjing 210096, China

Abstract. RGB-D camera can provide effective support with additional depth cue for many RGB-D perception tasks beyond traditional RGB information. However, current feature representations based on RGB-D camera utilize depth information only to extract local features, without considering it for the improvement of robustness and discriminability of the feature representation by merging depth cues into feature pooling. Spatial pyramid model (SPM) has become the standard protocol to split 2D image plane into sub-regions for feature pooling in RGB-D object classification. We argue that SPM may not be the optimal pooling scheme for RGB-D images, as it only pools features spatially and completely discards the depth topological information. Instead, we propose a novel joint spatial-depth pooling scheme (JSDP) which further partitions SPM using the depth cue and pools features simultaneously in 2D image plane and the depth direction. Embedding the JSDP with the standard feature extraction and feature encoding modules, we achieve superior performance to the state-of-the-art methods on benchmarks for RGB-D object classification and detection.

1 Introduction

Object classification using depth information have been explored for several decades. With the recent advances in depth acquisition techniques, such as the Kinect sensor, access of synchronized color and depth information has become available. The depth information facilitates characterization of the 3D structure of an object and provides effective support for the inference of objects beyond the traditional RGB information. Thus RGB-D cameras have been widely used in 3D reconstruction [1], scene labeling [2], object classification [3], detection [4] and segmentation [4].

Significant efforts have been made to exploit depth information in feature representation for depth images. Bo et al. [5] developed a set of kernel features on depth images that model size, 3D shape, and depth edges in a unified framework. These depth kernel features have been demonstrated to have much better performance than traditional 3D descriptors like spin images. Tang et al. [6] computed normal vector orientation of an object surface from the gradients of depth images. By concatenating the local histograms of azimuthal angle and zenith angle, they constructed the Histogram of Oriented Normal Vectors (HONV). Since HONV encodes the local distribution of the tangent plane orientation of an object surface, it can be used as a 3D geometric feature for object classification. The relational depth similarity features [7]

© Springer International Publishing Switzerland 2015
R.R. Paulsen and K.S. Pedersen (Eds.): SCIA 2015, LNCS 9127, pp. 314–326, 2015.
DOI: 10.1007/978-3-319-19665-7_26

calculate features derived from a similarity of depth histograms that represents the relationship between two local regions using the Bhattacharyya distance. In [8], a local point feature descriptor is initially evaluated to capture 2D and 3D gradient information and then aggregates the point-based information into local histograms to generate the final rotation and scale invariant object descriptor. Besides designing descriptors for depth images manually, unsupervised feature learning methods are also applied to learn discriminative features from depth images automatically. By adapting K-Means based feature learning to the RGB-D setting, Blum et al. [9] showed that it is possible to learn RGB-D descriptors from raw data that are competitive with state-of-the-art methods on the RGB-D object dataset. Bo et al. [10] trained visual feature dictionary and depth feature dictionary on image patches from RGB and depth channels respectively. By encoding and pooling RGB-D data over dictionaries using hierarchical matching pursuit, they learned image feature representations from raw RGB-D data in an unsupervised way. However, all these aforementioned methods only explore depth information for the feature extraction, without considering it for the feature pooling. To pool features extracted from depth images, most methods directly apply the standard spatial pooling [11] which pools depth features in the image plane. However, spatial pooling only summarizes 2D spatial distribution of depth features, completely discarding their depth distribution. Although the depth information captures the overall shape of an object, no extra performance gain is achieved during the feature pooling if spatial pooling is applied directly to depth images without any changes. In this sense, spatial pooling may not be a good choice of feature pooling for RGB-D based feature representation.

To take further advantage of the depth information, we propose a novel joint spatial-depth pooling (JSDP) scheme for feature pooling for depth images. In the JSDP scheme, we perform a spatial-depth partitioning on depth images and organize all image sub-regions based on the depth information. Multiple feature codewords within each cell are sequentially pooled for each depth layer in the spatial sub-region. Finally, concatenating pooled features from all cells in the spatial-depth space, we obtain the image-level feature representation for depth images. Both spatial and depth topological structures of depth images are effectively encoded in such a representation. We verify the performance of the proposed JSDP scheme for RGB-D object classification and detection. Evaluation results on RGB-D object dataset and our captured Kinect chicken dataset demonstrate that our JSDP scheme is more effective in learning discriminative depth feature representations than the standard spatial pooling.

Contributions of this work are twofold: 1). We propose the JSDP, a novel pooling scheme specially designed for RGB-D images, to merge the depth cue into the existing spatial pooling framework; 2). Integrating JSDP into the existing object classification pipeline, we significantly boost the feature discriminability for RGB-D images even with small codebook sizes.

2   Related Work

The standard object classification pipeline consists of four key components: feature extraction, codebook learning, feature encoding and feature pooling. Such a typical pipeline starts by extracting low-level local features like SIFT [12] or HOG [13] from local image patches. An overcomplete codebook (visual words) is then generated from these local features via clustering. This codebook thereafter is used to encode each local feature into a mid-level codeword by either hard assignment or soft assignment. After encoding, the image-level global representation is formed by spatially pooling mid-level codewords in each sub-region of the spatial pyramid. Such a global representation is then fed into a linear/nonlinear classifier.

Many feature extraction methods design handcrafted descriptors [12-16] to achieve a stable and robust object representation. In particular, orientation histogram descriptors like SIFT and HOG build a histogram of gradient orientations weighted by the gradient magnitudes within the feature point neighborhood. Histograms extracted from smaller spatial regions are normalized over larger regions. All histograms from smaller regions are stacked to form the final descriptor. Bo et al. [14] generated rich visual features by turning pixel-level attributes into patch-level features from a kernel's view, and developed a set of low-level descriptors called kernel descriptors (KDES). Wang et al. [15] merged the image label into the design of patch-level KDES and derived a variant KDES called supervised kernel descriptors. By adding the extra spatial co-occurrence constraints in the construction of KDES, Pan et al. [16] developed a set of improved KDES called context kernel descriptors which boost the robustness of KDES. To extract local features from depth images, some methods adapted 2D descriptors directly to depth images, deriving 3D descriptors such as 3D LBP [17] and histogram of depth [18]. Other methods [5-6] designed new descriptors that are tailored for depth images.

By decomposing input features onto the learned codebook, feature encoding transforms input features into codewords that have some desirable properties such as sparseness and statistical independence. The codeword is usually a vector with binary or continuous entries, depending on whether hard assignment or soft assignment is applied. In hard assignment methods like histogram encoding, only one visual word is assigned to each feature and the distance between input feature and the visual word is neglected. Whereas, in soft assignment methods multiple visual words may be assigned to a single feature, depending on the distance between the feature and the visual words.

In feature pooling, the whole image is first divided into several spatial sub-regions of interests in the image plane using some predefined structures (e.g. SPM). Codewords associated with local features are pooled over the image neighborhood. Distributions of the codewords within each sub-region are then summarized by a single "semi-local" feature vector such that some expected properties, like invariance to small image shift, compactness and better robustness to noise and clutter, are achieved. Most commonly used pooling approaches include *average* pooling, *sum* pooling and *max* pooling.

A predominant approach to define the spatial sub-regions for feature pooling comes from the idea of the SPM [11], where regular grids of increasing granularity are used to pool local features. The SPM provides a reasonable cover over the image plane with scale information, so it is widely used in most existing classification methods. Recently different variants of SPM have been exploited for object classification. To capture more spatial information, Wu and Rehg [19] supplemented overlapping spatial areas to the non-overlapped grid for the second and third levels of the SPM. Wang et al. [20] designed fan-shaped sub-regions to substitute the conventional rectangular-shaped sub-regions in SPM. Yan et al. [21] transplanted the sliding window technique into feature extraction for image classification. By changing the location, size and aspect ratio of a sliding window and computing the local features within the window, when it sequentially moves from left to right and from top to bottom in the image, they captured densely sampled window features with arbitrary locations, sizes and shapes of windows. Jia et al. [22] presented an alternative method to improve the SPM, by learning optimal pooling parameters for an over-complete set of receptive field candidates.

3   Our Methodology

We focus on the problem of object classification using RGB-D images, with an emphasis on the effective feature pooling that makes full use of both spatial and depth information. In more detail, depth images and RGB images are first generated by the RGB-D camera. For each image, we sample it spatially and obtain a set of feature points using a dense sampling grid. Local features are extracted from the image patches around each sampling point, and then encoded using the improved Fisher encoding [23]. For RGB images, we use the SPM to partition the image plane into sub-regions and *max* pool multiple codewords within each sub-region of the SPM. For depth images, we further split each sub-region into several cells along the depth direction, with each cell associated with a specific depth layer in the sub-region. Codewords from each cell are sequentially *max* pooled over the sub-region where the codewords belong to. Finally, pooled codewords from all sub-regions are concatenated together to derive the final image-level features which are fed into the classifier for classification. Fig.1 demonstrates the framework of our method for RGB-D object classification.

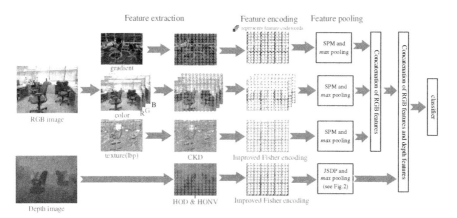

Fig. 1. The framework of our method for RGB-D object classification

3.1 Feature Extraction

For RGB images, we extract local features from image patches using our proposed context kernel descriptors (CKD) [16]. CKD is an improved version of KDES, which embeds context cue of image attributes into KDES and employs kernel entropy component analysis to reduce the feature dimensionality. The CKD derived using image attribute, a, can be formulated as

$$CKD_a(P) = \sum_{i=1}^{G}\sum_{j=1}^{L}u_{ij}\left\{\sum_{p\in P} w_p \boldsymbol{\kappa}_a(a_p,a_i)\boldsymbol{\kappa}_s(x_p,x_i)\boldsymbol{\kappa}_{con}[(x_p,a_p),(x_i,a_i)]\right\} \tag{1}$$

where P is an image patch, and $p\in P$ is the pixel in the image patch P. a_p is the normalized image attribute at the pixel p; x_p is the normalized 2D relative position of the pixel p in P. The items in the curly brackets of Eq.(1) define the context match kernel (CMK) of the CKD. Each attribute-based CMK consists of four terms: 1). The normalized linear kernel, w_p, weighting the contribution of each pixel to the CMK; 2). The attribute kernel, $\boldsymbol{\kappa}_a(a_p, a_q) = \exp(-\gamma_a\|a_p-a_q\|^2)= \varphi_a(a_p)^{\mathrm{T}}\varphi_a(a_q)$, evaluating the similarity of image attributes between pixel p and pixel q; 3). The spatial kernel, $\boldsymbol{\kappa}_s(x_p, x_q) = \exp(-\gamma_s\|x_p-x_q\|^2)=\varphi_s(x_p)^{\mathrm{T}}\varphi_s(x_q)$, measuring the relative distance of two pixels; 4) The context kernel, $\boldsymbol{\kappa}_{con}[(x_p,a_p),(x_q,a_q)] = 1/|N_k^p\|N_k^q| \sum_{x_u\in N_k^p}\sum_{x_v\in N_k^q}\boldsymbol{\kappa}_a(a_u,a_v) = \varphi_{con}(a_p)^{\mathrm{T}}\varphi_{con}(a_q)$,

comparing the spatial co-occurrence of image attributes at pixel p and pixel q. $\{a_i\}_{i=1}^{G}$ and $\{x_j\}_{j=1}^{L}$ are uniformly sampled from their support region, with G and L being the number of sampled basis vectors for the attribute kernel and spatial kernel, respectively. u_{ij} are the projection coefficients obtained by applying kernel entropy component analysis to the joint basis vector set: $\{\varphi_a(a_1)\otimes\varphi_s(x_1)\otimes\varphi_{con}(a_1),\ldots, \varphi_a(a_G)\otimes\varphi_s(x_L)\otimes\varphi_{con}(a_G)\}$, where $\otimes$ is the Kronecker product. If substituting image attribute a with the gradient, the RGB value or local binary patterns (*lbp*) operator [24] in Eq.(1), we can obtain the gradient CKD, the color CKD or the texture CKD, respectively. Details on the calculation of CKD can be found in [16].

To capture the local 3D shape and geometric features from the depth channel, we exploit histogram of oriented depths (HOD) [18], and histogram of oriented normal vectors (HONV) [6] on depth images. HOD is a variant HOG that is adapted to depth images. Similar to HOG, HOD divides a fixed window into cells, then computes local depth changes in each cell, and finally collects the oriented depth gradients into 1D histogram. In contrast, HONV characterizes the 3D geometric structure of an object as a local distribution of the normal vector orientation, because the object surface can be represented by its tangent plane orientation, i.e. the normal vector. For a point on the object surface, we calculate its azimuthal angle and zenith angle from the gradients of depth images. Then, the HONV descriptor for depth images is built by concatenating the local histograms of azimuthal angle and zenith angle.

3.2 Feature Encoding with Improved Fisher Encoding

After extracting local features from RGB-D images, we encode these features into codewords using improved Fisher encoding [23]. We generate codebooks separately for RGB images and depth images using Gaussian mixture model (GMM) clustering.

Given a set of D-dimensional local descriptors, $X = \{x_m\}_{m=1}^{M}$ $(x_m \in \mathbb{R}^D)$, extracted from images, in Fisher encoding, the generation processes of X is modelled with a GMM whose probability density $p(X|\theta)$ is given by

$$p(X \mid \theta) = \sum_{k=1}^{K} \lambda_k p(X \mid \mu_k, \Sigma_k), \quad p(X \mid \mu_k, \Sigma_k) = \frac{1}{\sqrt{(2\pi)^D |\Sigma_k|}} e^{-\frac{1}{2}(X-\mu_k)^T \Sigma_k^{-1}(X-\mu_k)} \quad (2)$$

where $\theta = (\lambda_1, \mu_1, \Sigma_1, \cdots, \lambda_K, \mu_K, \Sigma_K)$ is the parameter set of the GMM, containing the mixture weight λ_k, mean vector μ_k, and covariance matrix Σ_k of the Gaussian function. We assume that the covariance matrix Σ_k is diagonal and denote the variance vector as σ_k^2, so the GMM can be fully represented by $(2D+1)K$ parameters. The parameters are learned using the maximum likelihood (ML) criterion and the expectation maximization (EM) algorithm from a large number of local descriptors extracted from training images. After learning the parameter set, GMM assigns M descriptors to the K Gaussian components softly using Bayes formula

$$f_m(k) = \frac{\lambda_k p(x_m \mid \mu_k, \Sigma_k)}{\sum_{j=1}^{K} \lambda_j p(x_m \mid \mu_j, \Sigma_j)}, \quad m = 1, \ldots, M \quad (3)$$

For each $k=1, \cdots, K$, if we consider the D-dimensional gradient with respect to the mean vector μ_k and the standard deviation σ_k of the kth Gaussian function, it leads to

$$\alpha_{jk} = \frac{1}{M\sqrt{\lambda_k}} \sum_{m=1}^{M} f_m(k) \left(\frac{x_{jm} - \mu_{jk}}{\sigma_{jk}} \right), \; \beta_{jk} = \frac{1}{M\sqrt{2\lambda_k}} \sum_{m=1}^{M} f_m(k) \left[\frac{(x_{jm} - \mu_{jk})^2}{\sigma_{jk}^2} - 1 \right] \; (j=1, \cdots, D) \quad (4)$$

We define two vectors $\alpha_k = [\alpha_{1k}, \ldots, \alpha_{jk}, \ldots, \alpha_{Dk}]$ and $\beta_k = [\beta_{1k}, \ldots, \beta_{jk}, \ldots, \beta_{Dk}]$. The Fisher encoding [23] of the local descriptors is then formulated by the concatenation of α_k and β_k for all K Gaussian components, resulting the encoding codeword, $c = [\alpha_1, \beta_1, \cdots, \alpha_K, \beta_K]^T$, whose size is $2DK$. Since the relative displacements between the descriptors and each visual word of the codebook are kept in the codeword, Fisher encoding is able to retain some extra information lost in the quantization process. This explains why Fisher encoding outperforms other encoding schemes by a large margin on both Pascal VOC 2007 and Caltech-101 dataset. To boost the accuracy of feature encoding, we further improve the Fisher vectors α_k and β_k by applying power normalization and l_2 normalization to each Fisher vectors independently, as suggested in [23].

3.3   Feature Pooling for RGB Images

We employ a regular three-level SPM with 1×1, 2×2 and 4×4 grids to partition the whole RGB image into N ($N=1+4+16=21$) sub-regions of interests with increasingly fine resolutions in 2D image plane for feature pooling. In particular, each sub-region R_n ($n=1, \cdots, N$) is characterized by a set of codewords $c(\mathcal{L}_n^i)$ ($i=1, \cdots, |\mathcal{L}_n|$) at $|\mathcal{L}_n|$ locations identified by their indices $i=1, \cdots, |\mathcal{L}_n|$, with $\mathcal{L}_n$ denoting the set of locations within the sub-region R_n. Multiple codewords within R_n are *max* pooled using Eq.(5)

$$c(R_n) = max\left[c(\mathcal{L}_n^1), \cdots, c(\mathcal{L}_n^{|\mathcal{L}_n|})\right] \tag{5}$$

where $c(R_n)$ is the pooled feature within R_n. Note that the *max* function is conducted in a row-wise manner which results a vector with the same dimensionality of a single codeword. Finally, we concatenate pooled features from all sub-regions and normalize them using l_2 norm to generate the image-level RGB feature representation with a dimensionality of $2DKN$.

3.4   Feature Pooling for Depth Images

SPM [11] was introduced to take into account the rough geometry of an image. It repeatedly partitions an image into sub-regions and pools codewords of local features at increasingly fine resolutions. As a result, global feature is captured by the codewords with coarse grid and local spatial information is included in the codewords with finer grids. However, SPM only encodes 2D position in the image plane and the depth information is completely discarded during spatial pooling. It does not offer any extra performance boost during the feature pooling if SPM is directly applied to depth images without any changes.

To fully exploit the depth information, we develop a novel JSDP scheme which splits a 2D sub-region into cells with fine depth resolutions and pools sub-region's features along the depth direction. Similar to RGB images, we first apply a three-level SPM to divide the whole depth image into a total of N sub-regions with increasingly fine grids in 2D image plane. For each sub-region R_n, we further split it into H non-overlapped cells $(R_n^1, \ldots, R_n^H)$ with arbitrary shapes using K-means clustering on their depth values. Assuming H being the number of clusters and $h \in \{1,\ldots,H\}$ corresponding to the cluster center (depth layer), then each cell R_n^h consists of the pixels belonging to the hth depth layer within R_n and the combination of $\{R_n^1, \cdots R_n^H\}$ include pixels from all depth layers within R_n. Note that the number of clusters in different sub-regions may be varying, depending on the depth distribution in the sub-region. In this way, the JSDP offers finer decomposition on the spatial-depth space than the original SPM. We assign the codewords within the sub-region R_n to each cell. Codewords from each cell are then *max* pooled separately within R_n, which gives a set of H vectors $\left\{c\left(R_n^h\right)\right\}_{h=1}^H$ in R_n, with each vector $c(R_n^h)$ having a dimensionality of $2DK$. We concatenate pooled features from all cells within each sub-region, from the first sub-region to the last sub-region subsequently. By normalizing the concatenated feature vectors, we obtain the image-level representation, $F = \left[c'\left(R_1^1\right), \cdots, c'\left(R_1^H\right), \cdots, c'\left(R_N^1\right), \cdots, c'\left(R_N^H\right)\right]^T$, with a dimensionality of $2DKHN$ for depth images. Fig.2 shows the framework of the proposed JSDP scheme for feature pooling for depth images.

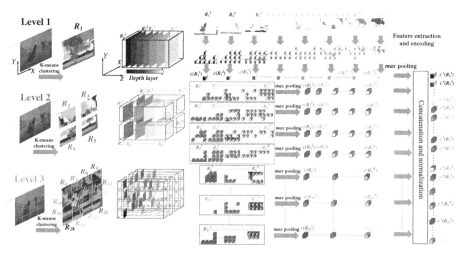

Fig. 2. The framework of the proposed JSDP scheme for feature pooling for depth images. This figure is best viewed in color

4   Experiments

To verify the advantage of the JSDP scheme, we evaluate the performance of our method on two RGB-D based applications: object classification and object detection.

We use the same parameter setting as in [16] for CKD calculation. Gradient CKD, color CKD and LBP CKD with 3-neighborhood are extracted on image patches of 16×16 pixels on RGB images with a sampling interval of 8 pixels. HOD and HONV are extracted on image patches of 8×8 pixels on depth images with a sampling interval of 4 pixels. We merge all three types of CKD to construct the combined CKD for RGB images. HOD and HONV are concatenated to provide the feature representation for depth images. We set the default codebook size to 1,000 for both RGB and depth images. The codebook is learned using K-means clustering on 400,000 RGB and depth descriptors from the training RGB-D images. We use a GMM with $K=256$ components to model the probability density of local descriptors for improved Fisher encoding. Linear SVM classifier is used through all experiments. The number of depth clusters H in each spatial sub-region is selected by cross-validation using the training set.

4.1   Object Classification on RGB-D Dataset

We test our method on the RGB-D dataset [25] to compare the classification performance of the JSDP and traditional SPM. The RGB-D dataset includes 250,000 segmented RGB-D images of 300 objects in 51 categories, with each object recorded from three viewing angles (30°, 45° and 60°). Two types of classification, i.e. category classification and instance classification, are considered. In category classification, several objects from each category are used to train the classifier, and the task is to determine the category name of a query object that has never been seen before. Whereas instance classification identifies whether the query object has been previously seen before.

Following the common leave-one-out protocol [3, 5, 25], for category classification, we randomly select one object from each category as the test sample and the remaining objects are used for training. For instance classification, we train the classifier using images captured from 30° and 60°, and test on the images capture from 45°. We conduct 10 random trials to obtain a reliable result. To justify that our method enables to take full advantage of both visual and depth information offered by the RGB-D camera, we evaluate the classification performance of our method using only RGB features, only depth features and combining both RGB and depth features. We choose SPM as the baseline method. For a fair comparison, we use the same feature setting, including local descriptors and improved Fisher encoding, in our method and the baseline SPM method, except for the different feature pooling schemes for depth images. The average classification accuracy and standard deviation of our method are reported in Table 1, compared with those of the baseline method and other state-of-the-art methods.

As observed in Table 1, except for category classification using only RGB features, our method outperforms all other methods for both category and instance classification. Thanks to the JSDP scheme, our method improves the classification accuracy of SPM by 4.4% and 4.2% respectively for category and instance classification using only depth features. We argue that the performance increase of our method comes from the benefit of the JSDP which samples low-level descriptor map more finely in 3D spatial-depth

Table 1. Comparison of classification performance (average accuracy% ± standard deviation) of our method, SPM and other state-of-the-art methods (DKD: depth kernel descriptors [5]; IDL: instance distance learning [26]; HMP-S: Hierarchical matching pursuit with sparse coding [10]; CKM: convolutional k-means descriptor [9]; R^2ICA: regularized reconstruction independent component analysis network [27])

Method	Category			Instance		
	RGB	depth	RGB-D	RGB	depth	RGB-D
our method	84.8±2.2	**92.9±2.6**	**94.7±3.4**	**93.1**	**58.1**	**95.6**
SPM	84.8±2.2	88.5±3.6	91.1±4.1	**93.1**	53.9	93.7
DKD	77.7±1.9	78.8±2.7	86.2±2.1	78.6	54.3	84.5
IDL	78.6±3.1	70.2±2.9	85.4±3.2	89.8	54.8	91.3
HONV	N/A	91.2±2.5	N/A	N/A	N/A	N/A
HMP-S	82.4±3.1	81.2±2.3	87.5±2.9	92.1	51.7	92.8
CKM	N/A	N/A	86.4±2.3	82.9	N/A	90.4
R^2ICA	**85.6±2.7**	83.9±2.8	89.6±3.8	92.43	55.69	93.23

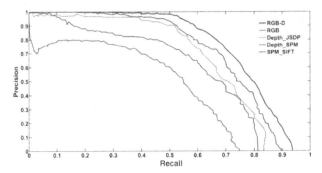

Fig. 3. Comparison of classification performance of our method and the baseline SPM with different codebook sizes

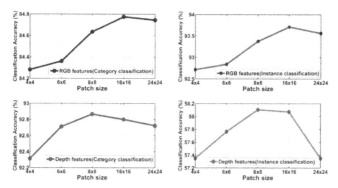

Fig. 4. Comparison of classification performance using RGB and depth features with different patch sizes

space, and represents neighboring descriptors jointly. Concurring with the observation in [5], we also notice that different feature types are suitable for different classification tasks. For example, shape features obtained from depth images are helpful to category classification because objects from the same category usually have stable shapes but vary significantly in appearances. In contrast, visual features obtained from RGB images are more effective for instance classification as a specific object instance has a relatively constant visual appearance under different viewing angles. The fact that integration of RGB and depth channels works much better than each single channel for both tasks justifies that our method can make full use of the RGB-D information.

To investigate the impact of codebook size on the classification performance, we train classifiers with different codebook sizes and compare the classification accuracy (using only depth features) of our method with that of the baseline SPM method in Fig.3. As expected, our method consistently outperforms SPM over all tested codebook sizes. It is interesting to note that the performance degradation of our method is very slight as codebook size becomes smaller. This means that restricting pools to features that are adjacent not only in 2D image plane but also along the depth direction boosts the classification performance even with relatively small codebooks. Additionally, classification accuracy increases as codebook size becomes larger and the performance is saturated when codebook size reaches around 4000. In Fig.4 we show the performance changes with varying image patch sizes for extraction of RGB and depth features in our method (codebook size is fixed to 1,000). Classification accuracy increases with the increase of patch size when patch size is smaller than 8×8. For RGB images, the optimal patch size is 16×16. However, due to the low resolution of depth images, the performance of depth features decreases when patch size exceeds 8×8.

4.2 Object Detection on the Kinect Chicken Dataset

We verify the performance of object detection on a Kinect chicken dataset captured by ourselves. The purpose of this application is to find and localize the chicken feet using both visual and depth information. This dataset is very challenging because chicken feet are tiny compared with other parts of the body and usually more than forty chickens are squeezed in a box. Multiple chicken feet may appear in one image, and in many cases feet are severely occluded. Finally the color of the feet is very similar to feather and chest. We followed the same setup in [16] to collect the training and test set.

Due to the occlusion and absence of texture, depth values of the points in the occluded or textureless regions are missing. Before extracting local features from depth images, we need to fill up the missing values in depth images. Since the missing values tend to be grouped together, we use a recursive median filter. Instead of considering all neighboring pixel values, we take the median of the non-missing values in a 5×5 grid centered on the current pixel. We apply this median filter recursively until all missing values are filled. Fig.5 shows an example of the color image, the original depth image (the pixel with blue color means its depth value is missing) and the filtered depth image.

To detect the object in a new image, we use the sliding window detector, where the detector evaluates a score function for all positions and scales in the image, and thresholds the scores to obtain object bounding boxes. Each detector window has a fixed size and we search across multi-scales on the image pyramid. We merge object bounding boxes detected at all scales and remove multiple overlapping detections using non-maximum suppression. To judge the correctness of detections, we adopt the protocol of the PASCAL Challenge criterion [28]. We compare the detection performance of the methods using our JSDP scheme (Depth_JSDP) and the standard SPM (Depth_SPM) for depth feature pooling. For the baseline method, we choose the SPM_SIFT method which applies the three-level SPM to spatially pool SIFT features extracted from RGB and depth images. Fig.6 plots the Precision-Recall (PR) curves of all methods. As shown in Fig.6, the method combining both RGB and depth information achieves higher detection performance than the methods using either set of cues alone. With proper preprocessing and JSDP scheme, our method using only depth cue (Depth_JSDP) even outperforms the SPM using SIFT features by a large margin.

| (a). color image | (b). original depth image | (c). filtered depth image |

Fig. 5. An example of the color image, the original depth image and the filtered depth image from the Kinect chicken dataset

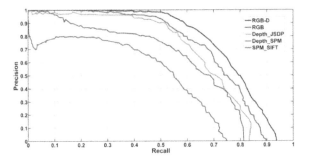

Fig. 6. PR curves of all methods evaluated on the Kinect chicken dataset

5   Conclusion

In this paper, we propose a novel JSDP scheme for RGB-D based feature representation. The proposed feature pooling strategy enables us to obtain a fine-grained partitioning in both image plane and along the depth direction. By combining feature extraction using CKD, HOD and HONV, improved Fisher encoding and joint spatial-depth feature pooling, we achieve state-of-the-art performance on RGB-D based object classification and detection. Currently, the partitioning of depth level is determined using K-mean clustering. However, the number of clusters in each spatial sub-region should be carefully tuned via cross-validation, which may not be optimal for depth images. Future work should consider the optimal partitioning of depth layer. One possible solution is to parameterize the number of clusters in each spatial sub-region and learn the optimal pooling parameters together with the parameters of SVM classifier.

Acknowledgements. This work is supported by The Danish Agency for Science, Technology and Innovation, project "Real-time controlled robots for the meat industry", and partly supported by NSF of Jiangsu Province, China under Grant BK20131296, and NSFC under Grant 61101165. The authors thank Lantmännen Danpo A/S for providing the chicken images.

References

1. Zhang, Q., et al.: When 3D reconstruction meets ubiquitous RGB-D images. In: CVPR, vol. 1, pp. 700–707 (2014)
2. Ren, X., et al.: RGB-(D) scene labeling: features and algorithms. In: CVPR (2012)
3. Lai, K., Bo, L., Ren, X., Fox, D.: RGB-D Object Recognition: Features, Algorithms, and a Large Scale Benchmark. Consumer Depth Cameras for Computer Vision, 167–192 (2013)
4. Gupta, S., Girshick, R., Arbeláez, P., Malik, J.: Learning rich features from RGB-D images for object detection and segmentation. In: Fleet, D., Pajdla, T., Schiele, B., Tuytelaars, T. (eds.) ECCV 2014, Part VII. LNCS, vol. 8695, pp. 345–360. Springer, Heidelberg (2014)
5. Bo, L., Ren, X., Fox, D.: Depth kernel descriptors for object recognition. In: International Conference on Intelligent Robots and Systems, vol. 1, pp. 821–826 (2011)
6. Tang, S., Wang, X., Lv, X., Han, T.X., Keller, J., He, Z., Skubic, M., Lao, S.: Histogram of oriented normal vectors for object recognition with a depth sensor. In: Lee, K.M., Matsushita, Y., Rehg, J.M., Hu, Z. (eds.) ACCV 2012, Part II. LNCS, vol. 7725, pp. 525–538. Springer, Heidelberg (2013)
7. Ikemura, S., Fujiyoshi, H.: Real-time human detection using relational depth similarity features. In: Kimmel, R., Klette, R., Sugimoto, A. (eds.) ACCV 2010, Part IV. LNCS, vol. 6495, pp. 25–38. Springer, Heidelberg (2011)
8. Fischer, J., Bormann, R., Arbeiter, G., Verl, A.: A feature descriptor for texture-less object representation using 2D and 3D cues from RGB-D data. In: ICRA, vol. 1, pp. 2112–2117 (2013)
9. Blum, M., Springenberg, J.T., Wulfing, J., Riedmiller, M.: A learned feature descriptor for object recognition in RGB-D data. In: ICRA, vol. 1, pp. 1298–1303 (2012)

10. Bo, L., Ren, X., Fox, D.: Unsupervised feature learning for RGB-D based object recognition. In: Desai, J.P., Dudek, G., Khatib, O., Kumar, V. (eds.) Experimental Robotics. STAR, vol. 88, pp. 387–402. Springer, Heidelberg (2013)
11. Lazebnik, S., Schmid, C., Ponce, J.: Beyond bags of features: spatial pyramid matching for recognizing natural scene categories. In: CVPR, vol. 2, pp. 2169–2178 (2006)
12. Lowe, D.: Distinctive image features from scale-invariant keypoints. IJCV **60**, 91–110 (2004)
13. Dalal, N., Triggs, B., Histograms of oriented gradients for human detection. In: CVPR, vol. 1, pp. 886–893 (2005)
14. Bo, L., Ren, X., Fox, D.: Kernel descriptors for visual recognition. In: NIPS (2010)
15. Wang, P., et al.: Supervised kernel descriptor for visual recognition. In: CVPR (2013)
16. Pan, H., Olsen, S.I., Zhu, Y.: Object classification and detection with context kernel descriptors. In: Bayro-Corrochano, E., Hancock, E. (eds.) CIARP 2014. LNCS, vol. 8827, pp. 827–835. Springer, Heidelberg (2014)
17. Banerjee, J., Moelker, A., Niessen, W.J., van Walsum, T.: 3D LBP-based rotationally invariant region description. In: Park, J.-I., Kim, J. (eds.) ACCV Workshops 2012, Part I. LNCS, vol. 7728, pp. 26–37. Springer, Heidelberg (2013)
18. Spinello, L., Arras, K.: People detection in RGB-D data. In: ICIRS, vol. 1, pp. 3838–3843 (2011)
19. Wu, J., Rehg, J.M.: Beyond the euclidean distance: creating effective visual codebooks using the histogram intersection kernel. In: ICCV, vol. 1, pp. 630–637 (2009)
20. Wang, X., Bai, X., Liu, W., Latecki, L.J.: Feature context for image classification and object detection. In: CVPR, vol. 1, pp. 961–968 (2011)
21. Yan, S., Xu, X., Xu, D., Lin, S., Li, X.: Beyond spatial pyramids: a new feature extraction framework with dense spatial sampling for image classification. In: Fitzgibbon, A., Lazebnik, S., Perona, P., Sato, Y., Schmid, C. (eds.) ECCV 2012, Part IV. LNCS, vol. 7575, pp. 473–487. Springer, Heidelberg (2012)
22. Jia, Y., Huang, C., Darrell, T.: Beyond spatial pyramids: receptive field learning for pooled image features. In: CVPR, vol. 1, pp. 3370–3377 (2012)
23. Perronnin, F., Sánchez, J., Mensink, T.: Improving the fisher kernel for large-scale image classification. In: Daniilidis, K., Maragos, P., Paragios, N. (eds.) ECCV 2010, Part IV. LNCS, vol. 6314, pp. 143–156. Springer, Heidelberg (2010)
24. Ojala, T., Pietikäinen, M., Mäenpää, T.: Multiresolution gray-scale and rotation invariant texture classification with local binary patterns. IEEE Trans. PAMI **24**(7), 971–987 (2002)
25. Lai, K., Bo, L., Ren, X., Fox, D.: A large-scale hierarchical multi-view RGB-D object dataset. In: ICRA, vol. 1, pp. 1817–1824 (2011)
26. Lai, K., Bo, L., Ren, X., Fox, D.: Sparse distance learning for object recognition combining RGB and depth information. In: ICRA, vol. 1, pp. 4007–4013 (2011)
27. Jhuo, I.-H., Gao, S., Zhuang, L., Lee, D.T., Ma, Y.: Unsupervised feature learning for RGB-D image classification. In: Cremers, D., Reid, I., Saito, H., Yang, M.-H. (eds.) ACCV 2014. LNCS, vol. 9003, pp. 276–289. Springer, Heidelberg (2015)
28. Everingham, M., et al.: The PASCAL visual object classes (VOC) challenge. IJCV **88**(2), 303–338 (2010)

Posters

Category-Sensitive Hashing and Bloom Filter Based Descriptors for Online Keypoint Recognition

Oscar Danielsson[✉]

CVAP/CSC, KTH, Teknikringen 14, 100 44 Stockholm, Sweden
osda02@csc.kth.se

Abstract. In this paper we propose a method for learning a category-sensitive hash function (i.e. a hash function that tends to map inputs from the same category to the same hash bucket) and a feature descriptor based on the Bloom filter. Category-sensitive hash functions are robust to intra-category variation. In this paper we use them to produce descriptors that are invariant to transformations caused by for example viewpoint changes, lighting variation and deformation. Since the descriptors are based on Bloom filters, they support a "union" operation. So descriptors of matched features can be aggregated by taking their union. We thus end up with one descriptor per keypoint instead of one descriptor per feature (By keypoint we refer to a world-space reference point and by feature we refer to an image-space interest point. Features are typically observations of keypoints and matched features are observations of the same keypoint). In short, the proposed descriptor has data-defined invariance properties due to the category-sensitive hashing and is aggregatable due to its Bloom filter inheritance. This is useful whenever we require custom invariance properties (e.g. tracking of deformable objects) and/or when we make multiple observations of each keypoint (e.g. tracking, multi-view stereo or visual SLAM).

Keywords: Keypoint recognition · Feature matching · Feature tracking · Hashing · Bloom filter

1 Introduction

The problem of finding corresponding points across sets of images is essential to many computer vision applications. Examples of such applications include 3D reconstruction from multiple views, visual SLAM, tracking, image alignment/registration and panorama stitching. Over the years, many successful detector/descriptor combinations have been proposed for matching features between image pairs [4,8–11,13]. These matching procedures are invariant to image plane translation and in some cases also to scaling, rotation and full affine transformation.

In some cases the desired invariance properties of the detector/descriptor cannot be explicitly modeled. In such cases authors have employed various machine

© Springer International Publishing Switzerland 2015
R.R. Paulsen and K.S. Pedersen (Eds.): SCIA 2015, LNCS 9127, pp. 329–340, 2015.
DOI: 10.1007/978-3-319-19665-7_27

learning techniques to produce descriptors with custom invariance properties defined by data [1–3]. We will mention some examples of descriptor learning in the following section.

In cases where each keypoint is tracked across several images it is desirable to exploit the fact that we accumulate many observations of each keypoint to extend/improve the keypoint appearance model. This is typically referred to as keypoint recognition [7,12,16]. In keypoint recognition the matching problem is reformulated as a classification problem. Each tracked keypoint is treated as a separate class and classifiers can be trained and used to match features in new images to known keypoints. We will mention some more examples of keypoint recognition in the next section.

In this paper we combine ideas from descriptor learning and keypoint recognition. The first part of our method, category-sensitive hashing, is inspired by descriptor learning (see figure 1(a)). We use a training set of images with known feature-to-keypoint correspondences to learn hash functions that map features corresponding to the same keypoint to the same hash bucket. In practice, this achieves robustness, but not full invariance to the transformations present in the training set.

The second part of our method, Bloom filter based descriptors, is inspired by keypoint recognition methods. Each keypoint is represented by a binary array (see figure 1(b)). A set of category-sensitive hash functions are used to set some of the elements in this array to 1. If two keypoints are matched, their descriptors can be combined by or-ing them together. Combining descriptors is a way of modeling the remaining appearance variation not handled by the category-sensitive hash functions.

The main contributions of this paper are (1) to propose a method for learning a category-sensitive hash function and (2) to propose a feature descriptor based on the Bloom filter. The main advantage of this descriptor is that it can be aggregated, so that a keypoint has a single descriptor instead of one separate descriptor for each observation (feature). The rest of the paper is structured as follows. In the next section we mention some related work on descriptor learning and keypoint recognition. In section 3 we describe our category-sensitive hashing and in section 4 we describe the Bloom filter descriptor. The experimental evaluation is in section 5 and we conclude in section 6.

2   Related Work

2.1   Descriptor Learning

The goal of descriptor learning is to learn a feature descriptor that minimizes some matching error on a data set with known correspondences. Brown et al. divide the descriptor computation process into a set of blocks, each parameterized by a set of parameters and settings, which are optimized on correspondences extracted from a large multi-view stereo dataset [1].

Calonder et al. let each keypoint in a training set represent one class and train randomized trees to map from feature to keypoint [2,3]. The training set

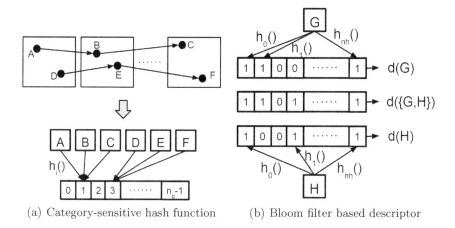

(a) Category-sensitive hash function   (b) Bloom filter based descriptor

Fig. 1. Overview of our method. a) Given a training set of images with known feature correspondences ($\{A, B, C\}$ and $\{D, E, F\}$), we learn a hash function $h_i()$ that maps corresponding features to the same bucket (and non-corresponding features to different buckets). b) A feature descriptor ($d(G)$ and $d(H)$) is constructed by repeatedly hashing the feature using category-sensitive hash functions and setting the corresponding bits of a binary array to 1. The descriptor for a set of (matching) features ($d(\{G, H\})$) is computed by or-ing together the descriptors of each feature in the set.

contained several observations (features) corresponding to each keypoint. Given a new feature, the randomized tree outputs a probability distribution over the keypoints seen during training. This distribution (after some post-processing) is taken to be the descriptor of the feature. So a feature is described in terms of its similarity to the keypoints seen during training.

Our category-sensitive hashing is similar in spirit to the work of Calonder et al. in the sense that we also describe features in terms of their similarity to keypoints seen during training (although we do it implicitly). But while Calonder et al. use a system of offline and online trees to adapt their descriptor at runtime, we adapt to runtime input by aggregating the Bloom filter descriptors of matched features.

2.2 Keypoint Recognition

Works on keypoint recognition reformulate the matching problem as a classification problem. It is typically assumed that a model of the target object or scene is available for offline training. Lepetit et al. train a random forest to map input features to a fixed set of keypoints on a known object [7]. An advantage of this approach is that the invariance properties of the matching can be controlled explicitly through the training data and the choice of which image measurements to use can be handled by the learner. It is demonstrated that a high computational performance can be achieved. Shotton et al. take one step further and train a random forest regressor to map directly from any pixel in an input rgb-d image to a 3D point in the scene [14], removing the need for a feature detector.

All of the above mentioned methods require a model of the object or scene to be available for offline training. In contrast, Williams et al. use fixed (non-data dependent) sets of n_s randomly chosen binary image measurements to hash features into n_h different hash tables [16]. Each of the $n_b = 2^{n_s}$ hash buckets stores a binary string with one bit for each of the n_p current keypoints, indicating which keypoints have observations that hash to that bin. The storage required is $n_b \cdot n_p \cdot n_h$ bits, which limits the number of keypoints that can be maintained (since not only n_p but also n_s has to be large to allow discrimination between many keypoints). Williams et al. report experiments with only 80 keypoints. Klein et al. report using this method with a few thousand keypoints [6]. Ozuysal et al. present a method that is similar in spirit to Williams et al. and coin the term random ferns [12].

Our Bloom filter based descriptor is quite similar to [16] and we devote a paragraph in section 4 to illustrate the main differences. In short we let all n_h hash functions index the same table, allowing us to use much higher values of n_s, n_p and n_h.

3   Category-Sensitive Hashing

The goal of category-sensitive hashing is to learn a hash function $h(\bullet)$ such that $h(A) = h(B)$ iff A and B have the same category. In our experiments categories correspond to keypoints, but the method presented in this section is of course not limited to this application.

Evaluating the hash function In the following, we describe how the hash function is evaluated on feature A, at location (x_A, y_A) in image I. The hash function is implemented using a binary decision tree (see figure 2(a)). The internal nodes of the decision tree contain a weak classifier, defined in equation 1. The binary classifier first computes a response r by subtracting the image intensities at two locations, $(x_A + x_0, y_A + y_0)$ and $(x_A + x_1, y_A + y_1)$, and then thresholds the difference at $-d_{min}$. The offsets (x_0, y_0) and (x_1, y_1) are parameters of the weak classifier. The threshold d_{min} is a constant and is set to a small positive value (typically 5). The purpose of setting $d_{min} \neq 0$ is to avoid noisy classifications in constant image regions [16]. If the weak classifier returns -1, the feature continues to the left child, otherwise it continues to the right child. Each leaf node stores a hash bucket index, which is returned.

$$
\begin{aligned}
r(x_A, y_A; x_0, y_0, x_1, y_1) &= I\,(x_A + x_0, y_A + y_0) \\
&\quad - I\,(x_A + x_1, y_A + y_1) \\
g(x_A, y_A; x_0, y_0, x_1, y_1) &= \begin{cases} -1 & \text{if } r(x_A, y_A; x_0, y_0, x_1, y_1) \leq -d_{min} \\ 1 & \text{if } r(x_A, y_A; x_0, y_0, x_1, y_1) > -d_{min} \end{cases}
\end{aligned}
\tag{1}
$$

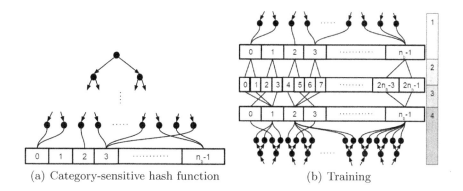

(a) Category-sensitive hash function   (b) Training

Fig. 2. a) The category-sensitive hash function is implemented using a binary decision tree. Each leaf node is linked to one hash bucket. Interior nodes classify features based on image intensities. b) One round of hash-function training: (1) Leaf nodes and hash buckets before training, (2) Split, (3) Merge, (4) Leaf nodes and hash buckets after training (upside-down). See text for details.

Training the hash function The training of the hash function much resembles breadth-first training of decision trees (as described in chapter 21.2.2 of [5]). The main difference is that we find one split for each hash bucket instead of one split for each current leaf node. Figure 2(b) illustrates one iteration of training.

Step 1 shows the state of the hash function before training starts. Each current leaf node of the underlying decision tree is linked to one hash bucket.

In *step 2*, each hash bucket is split by a weak classifier. We sample a number n_c of candidate weak classifiers for each hash bucket and initialize left and right histogram accumulators for each candidate weak classifier (each histogram accumulator is a histogram over category labels). So we have $n_b \cdot n_c$ candidate weak classifiers and $n_b \cdot n_c \cdot 2$ histogram accumulators in total. We then iterate over each labeled feature (A, y) in the training set. The current hash bucket of A is computed by applying the current hash function, then all n_c candidate weak classifiers for that bucket is applied to A and the corresponding left/right histogram accumulators are updated by adding one to the counter for label y. The histogram accumulators are then used to compute the information gain of each candidate weak classifier and the best weak classifier is selected. A new level is added to the underlying decision tree and each previous leaf node is set to store the weak classifier that was selected for its linked bucket.

In *step 3* the $2 \cdot n_b$ "temporary" hash buckets resulting from the split in step 2 are merged greedily until only n_b buckets remain. Let E be the entropy computed over all current buckets (see equation 2, where S_k is the number of training features and E_k is the label entropy in bucket k). For each pair of buckets (i, j), we compute the increase $\epsilon(i, j)$ in the entropy E resulting from merging buckets i and j (E_{i+j} is the entropy computed from all features in both buckets i and j) and merge the pair that results in the smallest entropy increase.

$$E = \frac{\sum_{k=0}^{2 \cdot n_b - 1} S_k \cdot E_k}{\sum_{k=0}^{2 \cdot n_b - 1} S_k} \tag{2}$$

$$\epsilon(i, j) = (S_i + S_j) \cdot E_{i+j} - (S_i \cdot E_i + S_j \cdot E_j)$$

Finally *step 4* shows the state of the hash function after training. A new level has been added to the underlying decision tree. Let new leaf node l be the left (or right) child of previous leaf node p. Then the linked bucket of l can be found as follows: start at p in step 1, then go left (or right) to the "temporary" bucket in step 2, then follow the line form the "temporary" bucket to the bucket it was merged into in step 4, this is the linked bucket of l.

4   Bloom Filter Based Descriptor

A Bloom filter $\mathcal{V}$ is defined by an array of n_b bits and a set of n_h hash functions, $h_1, \ldots, h_{n_h}$, each with range $\{0, \ldots, n_b - 1\}$. Initially all n_b bits in the array are set to 0. As illustrated in figure 1(b), a feature G is added to the filter by hashing it with each of the n_h hash functions and setting the corresponding bits to 1. To check if a feature is in the set we similarly hash it with each of the n_h hash functions and check if the corresponding bits are *all* set to 1. False positives are possible, but false negatives are not.

Theoretical properties The Bloom filter has a number of relevant theoretical properties. Firstly the probability of false positives can be computed based on the number, n_f, of *independent* features that have been added to the filter:

$$p_{fpp} = \left(1 - \left(1 - \frac{1}{n_b}\right)^{n_h \cdot n_f}\right)^{n_h} \approx \left(1 - e^{-n_h \cdot n_f / n_b}\right)^{n_h} \tag{3}$$

Minimizing equation 3 with respect to n_h gives us the optimal number of hash functions:

$$n_h = \frac{n_b}{n_f} \cdot \ln 2 \tag{4}$$

One great property of the Bloom filter is that the internal array does not change if we add a feature that is already in the filter. In our case we will typically add many similar features from neighbouring images. Since we are using *category-sensitive* hashing functions (which have been trained to be robust to our inter-image transformations) each new feature will only toggle very few new bits to 1. Therefore the effective number of *independent* features stored in the filter will be much less than the number of features we have actually inserted. We observe that we can compute the probability of false positives in terms of the number, n_z, of zeros in the internal array:

$$p_{fpp} = \left(1 - \frac{n_z}{n_b}\right)^{n_h} \tag{5}$$

Equating eqation 3 with equation 5 and solving for n_f gives us the number of *independent* features in the filter as a function of the number of zeros in the filter array [15]:

$$n_f = -\frac{n_b \cdot \ln(n_z/n_b)}{n_h} \tag{6}$$

Comparing descriptors Since the Bloom filter descriptors essentially represent sets of features, a reasonable similarity measure is the intersection over union. Let $\mathbf{d}$ and $\mathbf{d}'$ be two descriptors. We can estimate the number of *independent* features, n_f and n'_f, using equation 6. We can also estimate the number, $n_f^{\cup}$, of independent features in the union of $\mathbf{d}$ and $\mathbf{d}'$ by letting $n_z^{\cup}$ (see equation 6) be the number of bits that are zero in *both* $\mathbf{d}$ *and* $\mathbf{d}'$. Then we can compute the intersection over union similarity s:

$$s = \frac{n_f + n'_f - n_f^{\cup}}{n_f^{\cup}} = \frac{\ln(n_z) + \ln(n'_z) - \ln(n_z^{\cup}) - \ln(n_b)}{\ln(n_z^{\cup}) - \ln(n_b)} \tag{7}$$

Comparison to the method of Williams et al. [16] As mentioned in the introduction, our method is quite similar to the method of Williams et al. [16]. In figure 3 we illustrate the main difference. For each keypoint we store a single bit array and all hash functions index into that array. Williams et al. store a separate array for each hash function. While this eliminates the risk of collision between hash functions, it increases the memory footprint by a factor of n_h. Using a single array for all hash functions enables us to use much larger n_h and n_b, i.e. we can use more and finer partitionings of our feature space. In addition, we use trained category-sensitive hash functions instead of random locality sensitive hash functions and we also use a different similarity measure.

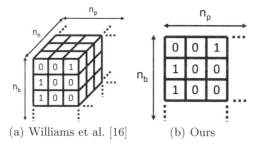

(a) Williams et al. [16]   (b) Ours

Fig. 3. Memory layout for a set of n_p keypoints. (a) Williams et al. [16] use a $n_b \times n_h$ bit array to store their binary scores for each keypoint. (b) We let all hash functions work on the same array and use only a n_b bit array.

5   Experiments

5.1   Experiment 1

The main purpose of this experiment is to evaluate the recognition rate of the Bloom filter descriptor as a function of the number of hash functions used and the number of observations of each test keypoint. We generate 20 training sets and one test set by applying random affine warps to the images in figure 4 (the right-most image generated the test set). The training sets are used to train 20 category-sensitive hash functions, which are then used to compute Bloom filter descriptors. The test set is used for performance evaluation.

The affine warps are of the form $R_\theta R_{-\phi} diag(\lambda_1, \lambda_2) R_\phi$, where $diag(\lambda_1, \lambda_2)$ is a diagonal 2 x 2 matrix and R_γ is rotation by γ radians. Both for training and test θ, λ_1, λ_2 and ϕ were sampled uniformly in the ranges $[-\pi/2, \pi/2]$, $[0.6, 1.5]$, $[0.6, 1.5]$ and $[0, 2\pi]$, respectively. For hash function training we generated 1500 warps of each training image. For test we generated 50 warps of the test image. In addition, we generated 1000 extra warps of the test image to plot the performance as a function of the number of observations.

Features were extracted using the Harris corner detector and ground truth correspondences were computed from the known warping parameters.

We use recognition rate to measure performance. For each feature in a warped version of the test image we find the most similar descriptor in the original test image and call it a match. The recognition rate is the number of correct matches divided by the total number of matches (i.e. the number of features extracted from the warped test image). The recognition rate is averaged over all 50 warps of the test image.

Fig. 4. Source images for generating training sets (left) and test set (right) using random affine warps

Figure 5 shows the results of this experiment. Figure 5(a) shows the entropy (see equation 2) as a function of number of training rounds/tree levels for each of the 20 hash functions. Figure 5(b) shows the recognition rate as a function of the number of hash functions used to compute the descriptor. Figure 5(c) shows the recognition rate as a function of the number of observations of each keypoint (using 20 hash functions). For reference, the recognition rate achieved by using a single BRIEF descriptor [4] is 0.16. Finally figure 5(d) shows the average estimated number of *independent* features in each descriptor as a function of the actual number of observations. This measures the ability of the category-sensitive hash function to absorb intra-category variation and ideally the number of independent features should be constant at 1.

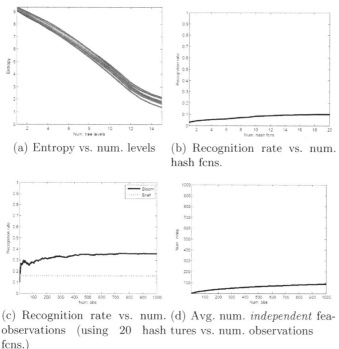

(a) Entropy vs. num. levels   (b) Recognition rate vs. num. hash fcns.

(c) Recognition rate vs. num. observations (using 20 hash fcns.)   (d) Avg. num. *independent* features vs. num. observations

Fig. 5. Experiment 1 results. See text for details.

5.2 Experiment 2

The purpose of this experiment is to test the method on a structure from motion application. The input images are shown in figure 6. These images are added sequentially to the structure-from-motion pipeline. When a new image is added, we first extract Harris corner features and Bloom descriptors and perform a putative matching to the existing keypoints in the map [1]. Given those putative matches we extract a small set of similar images by retrieving images that contain observations of the matched keypoints. We thus have a set of putative image matches. We then do robust matching with respect to a fundamental matrix using RANSAC for all putatively matched images. Keypoint matches

---

[1] Note that we can match directly to keypoints and not to features since we maintain an aggregated Bloom filter descriptor for each keypoint.

Fig. 6. Experiment 2 input images

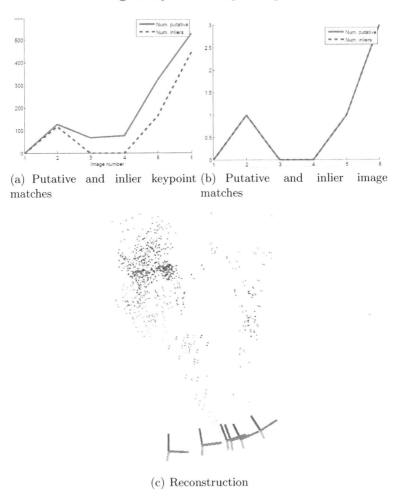

(a) Putative and inlier keypoint (b) Putative and inlier image
matches   matches

(c) Reconstruction

Fig. 7. Experiment 2 results. See text for details.

that are inliers with respect to all relevant fundamental matrices are inlier keypoint matches. Images that contain a sufficient number of inlier keypoint matches
are inlier image matches. Figures 7(a) and 7(b) plot the number of putative and
inlier keypoint and image matches for each added image. The average inlier ratio
is 46% for keypoints and 100% for images. Figure 7(c) shows the final reconstruction; the colored dots in the figure are reconstructed keypoints and the red, green

and blue line segments represent the x, y and z axes of the camera coordinate systems of each input image.

6   Conclusion

In this paper we proposed a method for online keypoint recognition. In an offline step, we first train category-sensitive hash functions to build invariance to inter-image transformations. We then use aggregatable Bloom filter descriptors to learn the remaining appearance variation of each keypoint online. The main benefit of the Bloom filter descriptor is that it can be aggregated, so two descriptors that have been robustly matched and thus correspond to the same keypoint can be aggregated into a single new descriptor, describing the complete appearance variation of the keypoint. We can thus maintain one descriptor per keypoint instead of one descriptor per feature.

We first evaluated the matching performance of the method on a synthetic dataset generated from applying a sequence of affine warps to one source image. We then demonstrated that the method is useful in practice by employing it in an incremental structure from motion application.

We believe that category-sensitive hashing and Bloom filter descriptors can be useful in other applications as well. Most closely related are other applications of tracking, where we might first train category-sensitive hash functions to build invariance to the class of transformations that we expect our target objects to exhibit and then use the Bloom filter descriptor to represent the "growing" appearance model of the tracked object.

References

1. Brown, M., Hua, G., Winder, S.: Discriminant learning of local image descriptors. IEEE Transactions on Pattern Analysis and Machine Intelligence 1, 43–57 (2011)
2. Calonder, M., Lepetit, V., Fua, P.: Keypoint signatures for fast learning and recognition. In: Proceedings of the European Conference on Computer Vision (2008)
3. Calonder, M., Lepetit, V., Fua, P.l., Konolige, K., Bowman, J., Mihelich, P.: Compact signatures for high-speed interest point description and matching. In: Proceedings of the International Conference on Computer Vision (2009)
4. Calonder, M., Lepetit, V., Strecha, C., Fua, P.: Brief: Binary robust independent elementary features. In: Proceedings of the European Conference on Computer Vision (2010)
5. Criminisi, A., Shotton, J.: Decision Forests for Computer Vision and Medical Image Analysis. Springer Publishing Company (2013)
6. Klein, G., Murray, D.: Parallel tracking and mapping for small ar workspaces. In: Proc. International Symposium on Mixed and Augmented Reality (2007)
7. Lepetit, V., Fua, P.: Keypoint recognition using randomized trees. IEEE Transactions on Pattern Analysis and Machine Intelligence 28(9), 1465–1479 (2006)
8. Lowe, D.: Distinctive image features from scale-invariant keypoints. International Journal of Computer Vision 60, 91–110 (2004)

9. Matas, J., Chum, O., Urban, M., Pajdla, T.: Robust wide baseline stereo from maximally stable extremal regions. In: Proceedings of British Machine Vision Conference (2002)

10. Mikolajczyk, K., Schmid, C.: A performance evaluation of local descriptors. IEEE Transactions on Pattern Analysis and Machine Intelligence **27**(10), 1615–1630 (2005)

11. Mikolajczyk, K., Tuytelaars, T., Schmid, C., Zisserman, A., Matas, J., Schaffalitzky, F., Kadir, T., Van Gool, L.: A comparison of affine region detectors. International Journal of Computer Vision **65**(1–2), 43–72 (2005)

12. Ozuysal, M., Calonder, M., Lepetit, V., Fual, P.: Fast keypoint recognition using random ferns. IEEE Transactions on Pattern Analysis and Machine Intelligence **32**(3), 448–461 (2010)

13. Rosten, E., Drummond, T.: Machine learning for high-speed corner detection. In: Proceedings of the European Conference on Computer Vision (2006)

14. Shotton, J., Glocker, B., Zach, C., Izadi, S., Criminisi, A., Fitzgibbon, A.: Scene coordinate regression forests for camera relocalization in rgb-d images. In: Proceedings of the Conference on Computer Vision and Pattern Recognition (2013)

15. Swamidass, S.J., Baldi, P.: Mathematical correction for fingerprint similarity measures to improve chemical retrieval. Journal of chemical information and modeling **47**(3), 952–964 (2007)

16. Williams, B., Klein, G., Reid, I.: Real-time slam relocalisation. In: Proceedings of the International Conference on Computer Vision (2007)

Deep Semantic Pyramids for Human Attributes and Action Recognition

Fahad Shahbaz Khan[1]([✉]), Rao Muhammad Anwer[2], Joost van de Weijer[3],
Michael Felsberg[1], and Jorma Laaksonen[2]

[1] Computer Vision Laboratory, Linköping University, Linköping, Sweden
fahad.khan@liu.se
[2] Department of Information and Computer Science,
Aalto University School of Science, Aalto, Finland
[3] Computer Vision Center, CS Department, Universitat Autonoma de Barcelona,
Barcelona, Spain

Abstract. Describing persons and their actions is a challenging problem due to variations in pose, scale and viewpoint in real-world images. Recently, semantic pyramids approach [1] for pose normalization has shown to provide excellent results for gender and action recognition. The performance of semantic pyramids approach relies on robust image description and is therefore limited due to the use of shallow local features. In the context of object recognition [2] and object detection [3], convolutional neural networks (CNNs) or deep features have shown to improve the performance over the conventional shallow features.

We propose deep semantic pyramids for human attributes and action recognition. The method works by constructing spatial pyramids based on CNNs of different part locations. These pyramids are then combined to obtain a single semantic representation. We validate our approach on the Berkeley and 27 Human Attributes datasets for attributes classification. For action recognition, we perform experiments on two challenging datasets: Willow and PASCAL VOC 2010. The proposed deep semantic pyramids provide a significant gain of 17.2 %, 13.9 %, 24.3 % and 22.6 % compared to the standard shallow semantic pyramids on Berkeley, 27 Human Attributes, Willow and PASCAL VOC 2010 datasets respectively. Our results also show that deep semantic pyramids outperform conventional CNNs based on the full bounding box of the person. Finally, we compare our approach with state-of-the-art methods and show a gain in performance compared to best methods in literature.

Keywords: Action recognition · Human attributes · Semantic pyramids

1 Introduction

Human attributes description such as gender, hair style, and clothing style and action category recognition such as playing music, riding bike, and taking photo are two of the most challenging problems in semantic computer vision. The two

© Springer International Publishing Switzerland 2015
R.R. Paulsen and K.S. Pedersen (Eds.): SCIA 2015, LNCS 9127, pp. 341–353, 2015.
DOI: 10.1007/978-3-319-19665-7_28

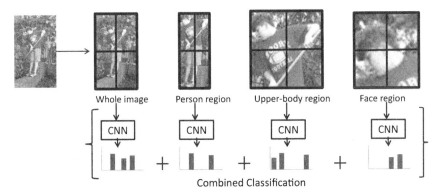

Fig. 1. Overview of deep semantic pyramids approach. We use whole image, full-body, upper-body and face regions for feature extraction. The upper-body and face regions are automatically localized using pre-trained state-of-the-art body part detectors. Each region is then used to construct a spatial pyramid representation of deep features. Finally, representations from all regions are concatenated into a single feature vector for classification. It is worth to mention that same pipeline is used for both human attributes classification and action recognition.

tasks are difficult since scale, viewpoint and pose varies significantly in real-world scenarios. Furthermore, images can appear in different illumination conditions, in low resolution and with back-facing people. These factors make the task of robust pose normalization and image description extremely challenging. In this paper, we focus on two problems namely: human attributes recognition and action category recognition.

Most state-of-the-art approaches rely on part-based representations [4–6] to counter the problem of pose normalization for human attributes classification. These approaches either use the deformable part models [7] or poselets [8] to obtain part locations. The part locations are then used to construct pose-normalized representations for classification. In the context of action recognition, conventional approaches either employ the bag-of-words framework [18,22,24] or focus on finding human-object interactions [15,20,21] to obtain improved performance. The bag-of-words based methods make use of local features such as shape, texture and color to represent local patches. On the other hand, approaches based on finding human-object interactions also use local features for patch description.

Recently, Khan et al. [1] have proposed an approach, semantic pyramids, for pose normalization. The method aims at fusing information from the full-body, upper-body and face regions of a person in an image. The parts of a person are automatically localized using state-of-the-art face and upper-body detectors. This ensures that no additional part annotations are required neither at training nor at test time. Spatial pyramid based image representations are then constructed for each part location. Consequently, the final image representation is obtained by combining the full-body, upper-body and face pyramids for each instance of a person. In this work, we also use pose-normalized semantic pyramids representation for human attributes and action recognition.

The performance of semantic pyramids approach heavily relies on the choice of the feature descriptors used to describe each part location in an image. Conventionally, local feature descriptors, also known as *shallow* features, have been employed for body part description [1]. Recently, convolutional neural networks (CNNs) [9], also known as *deep* features, have shown to provide excellent performance on large scale image classification tasks [10]. Deep features have also been applied successfully to many other applications such as object detection [3], pose estimation [11], and attributes classification [6]. However, substantial amount of training data is required for learning these robust networks. The work of [12] shows that off-the-shelf CNNs features, trained on ImageNet dataset, are generic and can be applied to any standard image classification dataset. Here, we investigate to what extent off-the-shelf CNNs features fare when used within the semantic pyramids method for the tasks of human attributes classification and action recognition.

Contributions: In this paper, we propose to augment semantic pyramids with deep features for attributes classification and action recognition. The approach combines information from the whole image, full-body, upper-body and face regions. Similar to [1], we employ state-of-the-art body part detectors to automatically localize face and upper-body regions. In this way, no extra annotations for body parts are required either at training or test time. The best candidate bounding boxes are selected for each part location for feature extraction. Instead of shallow features used in [1], we employ pre-trained deep features learned from the ImageNet dataset for each region description. Each body region is divided geometrically in various blocks to obtain a spatial pyramid representation. The deep features are then computed for each region block providing a rough spatial description. Finally, the deep spatial pyramid representations from the whole image, full-body, upper-body and face are combined into a single feature vector for classification. Figure 1 shows an overview of deep semantic pyramids approach.

For human attributes classification, we validate our approach on the Berkeley and 27 Human Attributes benchmark datasets. For action recognition, we perform experiments on two challenging datasets: Willow and PASCAL VOC 2010. Our results show that significant improvements are obtained by deep semantic pyramids over standard semantic pyramids for both attributes and action recognition. Furthermore, deep semantic pyramids approach improve the performance compared to conventional CNNs trained on the full bounding box of the person alone. Finally, we show deep semantic pyramids outperform state-of-the-art methods for both human attributes and action recognition tasks.

2   Our Approach

Our approach combines the advantages of semantic pyramids and deep features in a single framework for attributes classification and action recognition. We start by providing a brief introduction to conventional semantic pyramids followed by our proposed deep semantic pyramids.

2.1 Semantic Pyramids

The semantic pyramids approach has been recently introduced by Khan et al. [1] for pose normalization. Instead of relying on single body part, semantic pyramids approach aims at combining information from different part locations for gender and action recognition. In the work of [1], information is combined from full-body, upper-body and face regions of a person. The approach employs pre-trained state-of-the-art upper-body and face detectors to automatically extract semantic information. The use of pre-trained detectors ensures that no extra overhead to annotate part regions is required for each person instance. The method assumes that the bounding box information of a person is available. To obtain the upper-body part of a person, a pre-trained upper-body detector[1] based on part-based detection framework [7] is employed. To extract the face region of a person, a pre-trained face detector [13] built on top of part-based framework [7] is used. The face detector is trained using positive instances from the MultiPIE dataset and negative samples taken from the popular INRIA person dataset.

Fusing body part detector outputs: Each body part detector provides a set of hypotheses by firing at multiple locations. In the work of [1], a simple method is proposed to select the optimal part locations. The method works by defining the task of finding the optimal part location as an energy minimization problem. It was shown to provide improved results compared to the baseline approach of selecting the part location with the highest scoring confidence. Finally, the full-body, upper-body and face bounding boxes are combined to obtain a semantic representation.

Image representations: For gender recognition, multiple feature descriptors (HOG, WLD and CLBP) are extracted in a spatial pyramid manner for each of the body parts. The different pyramid representations are then combined in a single feature vector for classification. Similarly, for action recognition, the bag-of-words framework with multiple visual features (SIFT, Color names, Color-SIFT) is employed to construct semantic pyramids.

2.2 Deep Semantic Pyramids

We combine part-based semantic pyramids and deep features to obtain a robust pose-normalized deep representation. To this end, our objective is to use CNNs for learning powerful features and the simplicity of semantic pyramids to obtain robust pose-normalized representation. We use deep features [14] pre-trained on the ImageNet dataset while demonstrating best performance on ImageNET 2014 challenge. The network takes fixed size 224x224 RGB image as input. The depth of the network varies from 11 (8 convolution and 3 FC) weight layers to 19 weight layers (16 convolution and 3 FC). Inside these two deep networks, the number of channels start from 64 in the first layer and increased by a factor of 2 after each max-pooling layer.

---

[1] The upper-body detector is available at: http://groups.inf.ed.ac.uk/calvin/calvin_upperbody_detector/

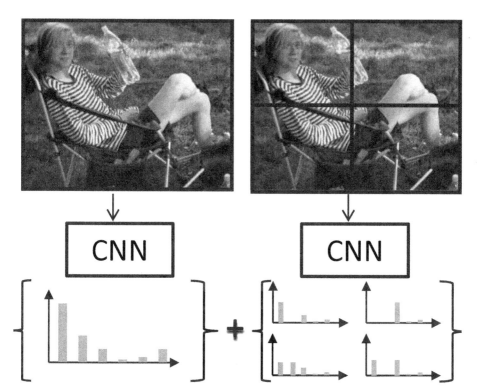

Fig. 2. Overview of deep spatial pyramid representation used for attributes classification and action recognition. We apply a two-level pyramid scheme where deep features are extracted separately for each image partition. The final representation is obtained by concatenating deep features from all the region partitions.

Unlike previous network architectures which employed large receptive fields in the first layers, the deep networks [14] employ small 3x3 receptive fields throughout the entire network. The respective fields are convolved with every pixel input with a stride of 1. The use of small receptive fields enables the incorporation of three non-linear rectification layers instead of a single one. This helps to obtain a more discriminative decision function. In our work, we use the fully connected layers from both 11 and 19 weight layer networks for image description. This provides us with a feature vector of size 4096x2. It is worth to mention that the dimensionality of deep features is significantly lower than the shallow representations commonly employed in the bag-of-words framework. For more details, we refer to [14].

In this work, we use whole image, full-body, upper-body and face regions. The full bounding box information for each person instance is provided both at training and test time with all the datasets. As discussed earlier, the bounding boxes of upper-body and face regions are automatically extracted using the approach presented by [1]. We construct a spatial pyramid representation using deep features for each region as illustrated in Figure 1. A spatial pyramid upto

Fig. 3. Example images from the datasets used in our experiments. Top row: images from the Berkeley Attributes dataset used for attributes classification task. Bottom row: images from the Willow action dataset used for action recognition task.

level 2 is used in our work. Figure 2 shows an overview of our deep spatial pyramid representation approach applied for each of the body parts.

Since the deep network takes a fixed-size input, we crop each image partition and resize it to 224x224 pixels. Each partition is then represented by a 4096 dimensional feature vector. The final representation is obtained by concatenating all the feature vectors from each image partition resulting in a 5x4096 dimensional feature vector. The spatial pyramids of the whole image, full-body, upper-body and face regions are normalized and concatenated, resulting in a 4x5x4096 size feature vector which is then input to the classifier for classification. The same procedure is applied for both deep networks described above. We employ non-linear SVM with intersection kernel for classification.

3 Attributes Classification

We start with an introduction of the datasets used in our experiments followed by our experimental results. Finally, we compare deep semantic pyramids with state-of-the-art methods in literature.

3.1 Dataset

We perform experiments on the Berkeley and 27 Human Attributes benchmark datasets. The Berkeley dataset consists of 4013 training and 4022 test instances. The images are collected from PASCAL and H3D datasets. The dataset consists of nine attributes: *male, long hair, glasses, hat, tshirt, longsleeves, shorts, jeans and long pants.*[2] The images in the dataset are very challenging since persons appear in different poses, viewpoints and scales with only 60% of the persons in

---

[2] The Berkeley dataset is available at: http://www.cs.berkeley.edu/~lbourdev/poselets/

the photos have both eyes visible. The 27 Human Attributes (HAT) dataset consists of 9344 images of 27 different human attributes such as *crouching, casual jacket, wedding dress, young and female*.[3] Figure 3 (top row) shows some example images from the Berkeley dataset.

3.2 Experimental Results

We first compare the performance of deep semantic pyramids with the standard shallow semantic pyramids. Afterwards, we provide a comparison with state-of-the-art approaches. For attributes classification, the performance is represented by average precision as the area under the precision-recall curve.

Deep vs Shallow Semantic Pyramids Here, we validate deep semantic pyramids approach with the conventional shallow semantic pyramids. In all cases, we use spatial pyramid representations for attributes classification. We use 2 level spatial pyramid: level 1 corresponds to standard image-level representation and level 2 comprises of 2x2 partitioning of an image. In case of level 2, feature representation from the previous level is also concatenated.

Table 1(a) shows a comparison between deep pyramids and shallow pyramids using different regions of an image for attributes classification. In case of the whole image (WI), using deep semantic pyramids improve the performance by 22.3% and 11.2% in mean AP on Berkeley and 27 Human Attributes (HAT) datasets respectively. Overall, deep semantic pyramids provide a performance boost of 17.2% and 13.9% in mean AP over the conventional shallow pyramids on the to datasets respectively.

The results clearly suggest that combining deep pyramids based on different body part regions improve the performance compared to using only the full bounding box of a person. Moreover, deep semantic pyramids significantly improve the performance over standard semantic pyramids for attributes classification. It is worth to mention that the deep features used in the semantic pyramids are generic and not trained for the task of attributes classification.

State-of-the-art Comparison: We compare deep semantic pyramids with state-of-the-art approaches in literature. Table 2 shows a comparison of state-of-the-art approaches with deep semantic pyramids on the Berkeley Attributes dataset. The conventional poselets approach [4] provides a mean AP of 65.2% on this dataset. The DLPoselets approach which employs the same poselets to train an attribute classifier provides a mean AP of 69.2%. The only difference between poselets and DLPoselets is that the latter uses deep features which improves the performance by 4.0% over the traditional poselets.

The approach of [6] provides a mean AP of 78.9% on this dataset. The method employs poselets to obtain part locations and train a poselet-level deep network on an additional large dataset of human attributes. Moreover, the method uses

---

[3] The 27 Human Attributes dataset is available at: https://sharma.users.greyc.fr/hatdb/

Table 1. Classification performance of deep semantic pyramids (DP) compared to standard shallow pyramids (SP) for attributes classification and action recognition tasks. The results are shown for whole image (WI), full-body (FB), upper-body (UB), face (FC) and combined representations. The deep pyramids approach significantly outperforms the standard shallow pyramids on all datasets.

(a) Attributes Classification

	WI	FB	UB	FC	Combine
Berkeley (SP)	51.6	57.2	53.7	55.0	62.1
Berkeley (DP)	73.9	75.2	68.6	65.6	**79.3**
27 HAT (SP)	44.3	46.2	43.0	38.4	57.6
27 HAT (DP)	55.5	66.8	59.1	55.9	**71.5**

(b) Action Recognition

	WI	FB	UB	FC	Combine
Willow (SP)	62.4	63.7	51.1	52.7	66.7
Willow (DP)	87.9	88.6	57.8	56.0	**91.0**
PASCAL (SP)	51.6	52.8	47.8	48.6	55.8
PASCAL (DP)	71.9	81.2	59.8	58.8	**85.3**

Table 2. Comparison of deep semantic pyramids approach with state-of-the-art on the Berkeley dataset. Deep semantic pyramids, despite their simplicity, achieve the best performance on 5 out of 9 categories while providing competitive performance compared to state-of-the-art methods.

	male	long hair	glasses	hat	tshirt	longsleeves	shorts	jeans	long pants	mean AP
Poselets [4]	82.4	72.5	55.6	60.1	51.2	74.2	45.5	54.7	90.3	65.2
DLPoselets [4]	92.1	82.3	76.3	65.6	44.8	77.3	43.7	52.5	87.8	69.2
DPD [5]	83.7	70.0	38.1	73.4	49.8	78.1	64.1	78.1	93.5	69.9
RAD [16]	88.0	80.1	56.0	75.4	53.5	75.2	47.6	69.3	91.1	70.7
PANDA [6]	**91.7**	**82.7**	**70.0**	74.2	49.8	86.0	79.1	**81.0**	96.4	79.0
This Paper	88.8	79.8	47.6	**84.2**	**66.4**	**88.0**	**83.3**	79.1	**96.5**	**79.3**

pre-trained deep features trained on the ImageNet to describe the full body of a person. In this way, the classifier exploits the complementarity in the deep features of parts and holistic regions since they are trained on different image data. Different to [6], our approach, while only using off-the-shelf deep features trained on the ImageNet, provides comparable performance to the previous best method.

Table 3 shows a comparison of state-of-the-art approaches with deep semantic pyramids on 27 Human Attributes (HAT) dataset. The approach of [15] based on expanded part based models (EPM) obtain a mean AP of 58.7%. The rich appearance part dictionary of humans approach (RAD) by [16] achieves a mean AP of 59.3%. The standard semantic pyramids approach (SP) provides a mean AP of 57.6%. Deep semantic pyramids outperform best reported results in literature by achieving a mean AP of 71.5% on this dataset.

4   Action Recognition

Here, we evaluate the performance of deep semantic pyramids for the task of action recognition in still images. In case of action recognition, the bounding box of each person instance is provided both at training and test time. The task is to recognize the action category label associated with the bounding box. We use the same pipeline as was used for the task of attributes recognition earlier. For action recognition, the performance is again represented by average precision as area under the precision-recall curve.

Table 3. Comparison of deep semantic pyramids approach with state-of-the-art on 27 Human Attributes (HAT) dataset. Deep semantic pyramids obtain the best performance on 22 out of 27 categories compared to state-of-the-art methods.

	female	frontalpose	profilepose	turnedback	upperbody	standing	runwalk	crouching	sitting	armsbent	elderly	middleaged	young	teen
EPM [15]	85.9	93.6	67.3	77.2	**97.9**	98.0	74.6	24.0	62.7	94.0	38.9	68.9	64.2	36.2
RAD [16]	91.4	**96.8**	77.2	**89.8**	96.3	97.7	63.5	12.3	59.3	**95.4**	32.1	70.0	65.6	33.5
SP [1]	86.1	92.2	60.5	64.8	94.0	96.6	76.8	23.2	63.7	92.8	37.7	69.4	67.7	36.4
This Paper	**93.7**	95.6	67.0	85.2	96.0	**98.4**	83.6	32.1	86.6	95.1	55.1	76.6	75.3	44.8

	kid	baby	tanktop	tshirt	casualjacket	mensuit	longskirt	shortskirt	smallshorts	lowcuttop	swimsuit	weddingdress	bermudashorts	mean AP
EPM [15]	49.7	24.3	37.7	61.6	40.0	57.1	44.8	39.0	46.8	61.3	32.2	64.2	43.7	58.7
RAD [16]	53.5	16.3	37.0	67.1	42.6	64.8	42.0	30.1	49.6	66.0	46.7	62.1	42.0	59.3
SP [1]	55.9	18.3	40.6	65.6	40.6	57.4	33.3	38.9	44.0	67.7	46.7	46.3	38.6	57.6
This Paper	**74.9**	**39.8**	**55.9**	**81.5**	**62.2**	**74.1**	**59.7**	**53.1**	**62.4**	**85.8**	**63.0**	**75.7**	**58.3**	**71.5**

4.1 Datasets

To validate deep semantic pyramids, we use two challenging action recognition datasets: Willow and PASCAL VOC 2010. The willow dataset comprises of seven action classes: *interacting with computer, photographing, playing music, riding bike, riding horse, running and walking*.[4] We also validate our approach on the PASCAL VOC 2010 dataset. The PASCAL VOC dataset consists of nine action classes: *phoning, playing instrument, reading, riding bike, riding horse, running, taking photo, using computer and walking*.[5] Both these datasets are extremely challenging due to significant amount of scale, illumination, pose and viewpoint variations. Figure 3 (bottom row) shows some example images from these datasets.

4.2 Deep vs Shallow Semantic Pyramids

Here, we compare deep semantic pyramids with conventional semantic pyramids for the task of action recognition. In the work of [1], the bag-of-words framework with multiple features have been employed for each part location in an image. As a baseline, we use the bag-of-words framework with SIFT features to construct shallow semantic pyramids. Table 1(b) shows a comparison between deep pyramids and shallow pyramids on the two action recognition datasets. On the Willow action dataset, deep semantic pyramids improve the overall performance by 24.3% in mean AP. Similarly, on the PASCAL VOC 2010 validation set the conventional shallow pyramids provide a mean AP of 55.8%. Deep semantic pyramids improve the classification performance by providing a mean AP of 85.3%. The results obtained on both action datasets clearly suggest that deep semantic pyramids significantly improve the performance compared to standard semantic pyramids for action classification.

Figure 4 shows top correct (top-row) and incorrect predictions (bottom-row) for the phoning class from the PASCAL VOC 2010 dataset. Three out of four

---

[4] The Willow dataset is available at: http://www.di.ens.fr/willow/research/stillactions/

[5] PASCAL 2010 is available at: http://www.pascal-network.org/challenges/VOC/voc2010/

Fig. 4. Images from the PASCAL VOC 2010 dataset. Top row: top correct predictions for phoning class. Bottom row: top incorrect predictions for phoning class.

misclassified examples are from taking photo category which has certain degree of visual similarity with the phoning class.

State-of-the-art Comparison: we compare deep semantic pyramids with state-of-the-art methods in literature. Table 4 shows a comparison with state-of-the-art methods on the Willow dataset. Our approach provides the best performance on 6 out of 7 action categories on this dataset. Deep semantic pyramids approach obtains a mean AP of 91.0%, which is the best results reported on this dataset [1,17,18,22–24]. The work of [17] based on using manually labeled data for enhancing the efficiency of the pre-training and fine-tuning stages of the deep feature training obtains a mean AP of 80.4%. Khan et al. [18] propose to fuse color and shape features and obtain 70.1% mean AP. The work of [1] based on multi-cue semantic pyramids obtains a mean AP of 72.1%. Our approach which augments the semantic pyramids with deep features significantly improves the performance from 72.1% to 91.0% mean AP.

Table 5 shows a comparison with state-of-the-art methods on the PASCAL VOC 2010 test set. The method of [19] based on poselets vectors achieves a mean AP of 59.7%. The color and shape fusion approach by [18] provides a mean AP of 62.4%. The work of [20] based on localizing humans and human-object relationships achieves a recognition performance of 62.0%. Learning a sparse basis of attributes and parts framework by [21] obtains a mean AP of 65.1%. The multi-cue semantic pyramids approach [1] provides a mean AP of 63.5%. On this dataset, deep semantic pyramids achieve a mean AP of 86.1%, which is the best results reported on this dataset [1,18–21]. It is worthy to mention that deep semantic pyramids method does not take into account the human-object interactions. Such approaches [20,21] are complementary and could be combined with the proposed method to further improve the results.

Table 4. Comparison of deep semantic pyramids approach with state-of-the-art results on the Willow dataset. Deep semantic pyramids provide the best results on 6 out of 7 action classes on this dataset.

	int. computer	photographing	playingmusic	ridingbike	ridinghorse	running	walking	mean AP
BOW-DPM [22]	58.2	35.4	73.2	82.4	69.6	44.5	54.2	59.6
POI [23]	56.6	37.5	72.0	90.4	75.0	59.7	57.6	64.1
DS [24]	59.7	42.6	74.6	87.8	84.2	56.1	56.5	65.9
CF [18]	61.9	48.2	76.5	90.3	84.3	64.7	64.6	70.1
EPM [15]	64.5	40.9	75.0	91.0	87.6	55.0	59.2	67.6
SC [25]	67.2	43.9	76.1	87.2	77.2	63.7	60.6	68.0
SM-SP [1]	66.8	48.0	77.5	93.8	87.9	67.2	63.3	72.1
EDM [17]	86.6	**90.5**	89.9	98.2	92.7	46.2	58.9	80.4
Our approach	**96.6**	87.0	**99.4**	**99.7**	**99.6**	**79.4**	**75.0**	**91.0**

Table 5. Comparison of deep semantic pyramids approach with state-of-the-art methods on the PASCAL VOC 2010 test set.

	phoning	playingmusic	reading	ridingbike	ridinghorse	running	takingphoto	usingcomputer	walking	mean AP
Poselets [19]	49.6	43.2	27.7	83.7	89.4	85.6	31.0	59.1	67.9	59.7
IaC [26]	45.5	54.5	31.7	75.2	88.1	76.9	32.9	64.1	62.0	59.0
POI [23]	48.6	53.1	28.6	80.1	90.7	85.8	33.5	56.1	69.6	60.7
LAP [21]	42.8	60.8	41.5	80.2	90.6	87.8	41.4	66.1	74.4	65.1
WPOI [20]	55.0	81.0	69.0	71.0	90.0	59.0	36.0	50.0	44.0	62.0
CF [18]	52.1	52.0	34.1	81.5	90.3	88.1	37.3	59.9	66.5	62.4
SM-SP [1]	52.2	55.3	35.4	81.4	91.2	89.3	38.6	59.6	68.7	63.5
Our approach	**65.1**	**94.0**	**71.9**	**97.6**	**97.7**	**93.8**	**83.3**	**93.4**	**77.2**	**86.1**

5 Conclusion

This paper combines pose-normalized semantic pyramids and deep features representation. Semantic pyramids combine information from the whole image, full-body, upper-body and face regions. We employ pre-trained body part detectors that automatically localize upper-body and face regions in an image. The use of pre-trained detectors ensures that no extra annotations are required either at training or test times. We propose to use a spatial pyramid based deep feature representation to describe each of these image regions. The final representation is obtained by combining the pyramidal feature vectors from al regions. The proposed approach is evaluated on two challenging tasks: human attributes classification and action recognition, demonstrating promising performance compared to state-of-the-art methods in literature.

Currently our approach employs pre-trained deep features from ImageNet. Future work involves learning deep features on large attributes and action datasets with a more careful optimization of network topology, choice of activation and pooling functions.

Acknowledgments. This work has been supported by SSF through a grant for the project CUAS, by VR through a grant for the projects ETT, by EU's Horizon 2020 Program through a grant for the project CENTAURO, through the Strategic Area for ICT research ELLIIT, and CADICS, project TIN2013-41751 of Spanish Ministry of Science and the Catalan project 2014 SGR 221, grants 255745 and 251170 of the Academy of Finland and *Data to Intelligence (D2I)* DIGILE SHOK project. The calculations were

352   F.S. Khan et al.

performed using computer resources within the Aalto University School of Science "Science-IT" project.

References

1. Khan, F.S., van de Weijer, J., Anwer, R.M., Felsberg, M., Gatta, C.: Semantic pyramids for gender and action recognition. TIP **23**(8), 3633–3645 (2014)
2. Oquab, M., Bottou, L., Laptev, I., Sivic, J.: Learning and transferring mid-level image representations using convolutional neural networks. In: CVPR (2014)
3. Girshick, R., Donahue, J., Darrell, T., Malik, J.: Rich feature hierarchies for accurate object detection and semantic segmentation. In: CVPR (2014)
4. Bourdev, L., Maji, S., Malik, J.: Describing people: A poselet-based approach to attribute classification. In: ICCV (2011)
5. Zhang, N., Farrell, R., Iandola, F., Darrell, T.: Deformable part descriptors for fine-grained recognition and attribute prediction. In: ICCV (2013)
6. Zhang, N., Paluri, M., Ranzato, M., Darrell, T., Bourdev, L.: Panda: Pose aligned networks for deep attribute modeling. In: CVPR (2014)
7. Felzenszwalb, P., Girshick, R., McAllester, D., Ramanan, D.: Object detection with discriminatively trained part-based models. PAMI **32**(9), 1627–1645 (2010)
8. Bourdev, L., Malik, J.: Poselets: Body part detectors trained using 3d human pose annotations. In: ICCV (2009)
9. LeCun, Y., Boser, B., Denker, J., Henderson, D., Howard, R., Hubbard, W., Jackel, L.: Handwritten digit recognition with a back-propagation network. In: NIPS (1989)
10. Krizhevsky, A., Sutskever, I., Hinton, G.: Imagenet classification with deep convolutional neural networks. In: NIPS (2012)
11. Toshev, A., Szegedy, C.: Deeppose: Human pose estimation via deep neural networks. In: CVPR (2014)
12. Azizpour, H., Sullivan, J., Carlsson, S.: Cnn features off-the-shelf: an astounding baseline for recognition. In: CVPRW (2014)
13. Zhu, X., Ramanan, D.: Face detection, pose estimation, and landmark localization in the wild. In: CVPR (2012)
14. Simonyan, K., Zisserman, A.: Very deep convolutional networks for large-scale image recognition (2014). arXiv preprint arXiv:1409.1556
15. Sharma, G., Jurie, F., Schmid, C.: Expanded parts model for human attribute and action recognition in still images. In: CVPR (2013)
16. Joo, J., Wang, S., Zhu, S.C.: Human attribute recognition by rich appearance dictionary. In: ICCV (2013)
17. Liang, Z., Wang, X., Huang, R., Lin, L.: An expressive deep model for human action parsing from a single image. In: ICME (2014)
18. Khan, F.S., Anwer, R.M., van de Weijer, J., Bagdanov, A., Lopez, A., Felsberg, M.: Coloring action recognition in still images. IJCV **105**(3), 205–221 (2013)
19. Maji, S., Bourdev, L.D., Malik, J.: Action recognition from a distributed representation of pose and appearance. In: CVPR (2011)
20. Prest, A., Schmid, C., Ferrari, V.: Weakly supervised learning of interactions between humans and objects. PAMI **34**(3), 601–614 (2012)
21. Yao, B., Jiang, X., Khosla, A., Lin, A.L., Guibas, L.J., Li, F.F.: Human action recognition by learning bases of action attributes and parts. In: ICCV (2011)
22. Delaitre, V., Laptev, I., Sivic, J.: Recognizing human actions in still images: a study of bag-of-features and part-based representations. In: BMVC (2010)

23. Delaitre, V., Sivic, J., Laptev, I.: Learning person-object interactions for action recognition in still images. In: NIPS (2011)
24. Sharma, G., Jurie, F., Schmid, C.: Discriminative spatial saliency for image classification. In: CVPR (2012)
25. Khan, F.S., van de Weijer, J., Bagdanov, A., Felsberg, M.: Scale coding bag-of-words for action recognition. In: ICPR (2014)
26. Shapovalova, N., Gong, W., Pedersoli, M., Roca, F.X., Gonzàlez, J.: On importance of interactions and context in human action recognition. In: Vitrià, J., Sanches, J.M., Hernández, M. (eds.) IbPRIA 2011. LNCS, vol. 6669, pp. 58–66. Springer, Heidelberg (2011)

Democratic Tone Mapping Using Optimal K-means Clustering

Magnus Oskarsson[(✉)]

Centre for Mathematical Sciences, Lund University, Lund, Sweden
magnuso@maths.lth.se

Abstract. The field of high dynamic range imaging addresses the problem of capturing and displaying the large range of luminance levels found in the world, using devices with limited dynamic range. In this paper we present a novel tone mapping algorithm that is based on K-means clustering. Using dynamic programming we are able to, not only solve the clustering problem efficiently, but also find the global optimum. Our algorithm runs in $O(N^2K)$ for an image with N luminance levels and K output levels. We show that our algorithm gives comparable result to state-of-the-art tone mapping algorithms, but with the additional large benefit of a total lack of parameters. We test our algorithm on a number of standard high dynamic range images, and give qualitative comparisons to a number of state-of-the-art tone mapping algorithms.

Keywords: Image processing · Tone mapping · K-means clustering

1 Introduction

The human visual system can handle massively different levels in input brightness. This is necessary to cope with the large range of luminance levels that appear around us – for us to be able to navigate and operate in dim night light as well as in bright sun light. The field of high dynamic range (HDR) imaging tries to address the problem of capturing and displaying these large ranges using devices (cameras and displays) with limited dynamic range. During the last years the HDR field has grown and today many camera devices have built in functionality for acquiring HDR images. This can be done in hardware using sensors with pixels that can capture very large differences in dynamic range. It can also be done by taking several low dynamic range (LDR) images at different exposures and then combining them using software, [5,8,21]. One important part when working with HDR images is the ability to visualize them on LDR displays. The process of transferring an HDR image to an LDR image is known as tone mapping. Depending on the application the role of the tone mapping function can be different, but in most applications the ability to capture both detail in darker areas and very bright ones is important. Tone mapping can also be an important component in image enhancement for e.g. images taken under poor lighting [16,28]. We will in this paper present a new framework for doing

© Springer International Publishing Switzerland 2015
R.R. Paulsen and K.S. Pedersen (Eds.): SCIA 2015, LNCS 9127, pp. 354–365, 2015.
DOI: 10.1007/978-3-319-19665-7_29

automatic tone mapping without the need for manual parameter tuning. We will look at the tone mapping problem as a clustering problem. If we are given an input image with large dynamic range, i.e. with a large range of intensity values, we want to map these intensity values to a much smaller range. We can describe this problem as a clustering of the input intensity levels into a smaller set of output levels. In our setting we are looking at an HDR input with a very large input discretization and doing the clustering in three dimensions is not tractable. Iterative local algorithms will inevitably lead to local minima. Instead we work with only the luminance channel, and we show how we can find the global optimum using dynamic programming. This leads to a very efficient and stable tone mapping algorithm. We call our algorithm democratic tone mapping since all input pixels get to vote on which output levels we should use. An example of the output of our algorithm can be seen in Figure 1.

Fig. 1. The result of running our tone mapping algorithm on an HDR input image. We get a clear image, with details preserved and with lighting intact. There are no parameters that need to be set. HDR radiance map courtesy of P. Debevec [19].

1.1   Related Work

A large number of tone mapping algorithms have been proposed over the years. Some of the first work include [25,27]. One can divide the tone mapping algorithms into global algorithms, that apply a global transformation on the pixel intensities, and local algorithms, where the transformation also depends on the spatial structure in the image. For a discussion on the differences see [29]. The global algorithms include simply applying some fixed function such as a logarithm or a power function. In [6] the authors present a method that adapts a logarithmic function to mimic the human visual system's response to HDR input. In [11] the image histogram is used and a variant of histogram equalization is applied but with additional properties based on ideas from human perception. Using histogram equalization will often lead to not efficiently using the colorspace, due to discretization effects.

The local algorithms usually apply some form of local filtering to be able to increase contrast locally. This often comes at the cost of higher computational complexity and can lead to strange artifacts. In [7] the authors use bilateral filtering to steer the local tone mapping. In [18] a perceptual model is used to steer the contrast mapping, which is performed in the gradient domain. In [17] the authors address the problem of designing display-dependent tone mappings. In [20] the authors propose an automatic version of the zone system developed by Ansel Adams for conventional photographic printing. The method also includes local filtering based on the photographic procedure of dodging and burning. The global part of their method is in spirit similar to our approach. In [12] they use K-means to cluster the image into regions and then apply individual gamma correction to each segment.

We address the problem of tone mapping as a clustering problem. This is not an entirely new idea in the realm of quantization of images. The idea of clustering color values was popular during the 1980's and 1990's, when the displays had very low dynamic range, and the object was to take an ordinary 24-bit color image and map it to a smaller palette of colors that could be displayed on the screen. In this case there have been a number of algorithms that use variants of K-means clustering, see [3,22,23]. Here the clustering was done on three dimensional input, i.e. color values. The algorithms used variants of the standard K-means [13] to avoid local minima. The number of input points was quite small and the number of output classes i.e. the palette, was relatively small so these methods worked well, but as shown in Section 5.1 they are prone to get stuck in local minima, when the size of the problem increases.

2   Problem Formulation

Let's consider the following problem. We are given an input gray value image, $I(x, y)$, with a large number, N, intensity levels. We would like to find an approximate image $\hat{I}(x, y)$ with a smaller amount, K, intensity levels, i.e. we would like to solve

$$\min_{c_1, c_2, \ldots, c_K} ||I - \hat{I}||_2, \tag{1}$$

where $I(x, y) \in \{u_1, u_2, \ldots, u_N\}$ and $\hat{I}(x, y) \in \{c_1, c_2, \ldots, c_K\}$. If we calculate the histogram corresponding to the input image's distribution we can reformulate the problem as:

Problem 1 (K-means clustering tone mapping). Given $K \in \mathbb{Z}^+$ and a number of gray values $u_i \in \mathbb{R}$ with a corresponding distribution histogram $h(i)$,

$i = 1, \ldots, N$, the K-means tone mapping problem is finding the K points $c_l \in \mathbb{R}$ that solve:

$$D(N, K) = \min_{c_1, c_2, \ldots, c_K} \sum_{i=0}^{N} h(i) d(u_i, c_1, \ldots, c_K)^2, \tag{2}$$

where

$$d(u_i, c_1, \ldots, c_K) = \min_l |u_i - c_l|. \tag{3}$$

This is a weighted K-means clustering problem. One usually solves it using some form of iterative scheme that converges to a local minimum. A classic way of solving it, is alternating between estimating the cluster centers c_l and the assignment of points u_i to clusters. If we have assigned n points u_i to a cluster l then the best estimate of c_l is the weighted mean

$$c_{\{1,\ldots,n\}} = \frac{\sum_{i=1}^{n} h(i) u_i}{\sum_{i=1}^{n} h(i)}. \tag{4}$$

For ease of notation we will henceforth use the notation c_l for cluster number l or $c_{\{1,\ldots,n\}}$ for the cluster corresponding to points $\{u_1, \ldots, u_n\}$. The contribution of this cluster to the error function (2) is then equal to:

$$f(u_1, \ldots, u_n) = \sum_{i=1}^{n} h(i)(u_i - c_{\{1,\ldots,n\}})^2. \tag{5}$$

The assignment that minimizes (2) given the cluster centers c_l is simply taking the nearest c_l for each point u_i. One can keep on iteratively alternating between assigning points to clusters and updating the cluster centers according to (4). It can easily be shown that this alternating scheme converges to a local minimum, but there are no guarantees that this is a global minimum. In fact for most problems it is highly dependent on the initialization. There are numerous ways of initializing. See [24] for an extensive review of K-means clustering methods.

The K-means clustering problem is in general NP-hard, for most dimensions, sizes of input and number of clusters, see [1, 4, 15, 26] for details. However, since the points we are working with are one-dimensional i.e. $u_i \in \mathbb{R}$, we can actually find the global minimum of problem 1 using dynamic programming. This is what makes our method tractable. In the next section we will describe the details of our approach. We will in Section 4 describe how we use our solver to construct a tone mapping method for color images.

3   A Dynamic Programming Scheme

Problem 1 is a weighted K-means clustering problem, with data points in $\mathbb{R}$. We will now show how we can devise a dynamic programming scheme that accurately and fast gives the minimum solution to our problem. For details on dynamic programming see e.g. [10].

We use an approach similar to [2, 26] and modify it to fit our weighted K-means problem. Since our data points are one-dimensional we can sort them in ascending order. Assume that we have obtained a solution $D(n, k)$ to (2) and let u_i be the smallest point that belongs to cluster k. Then it is clear that $D(i-1, k-1)$ is the optimal solution for the first $i-1$ points clustered into $k-1$ sets. This gives us the following recurrence relation for our problem:

$$D(n, k) = \min_{k \le i \le n} (D(i-1, k-1) + f(u_i, \ldots, u_n)). \tag{6}$$

Equation (6) defines the Bellman equation for our dynamic programming scheme. and gives us our tools to solve problem 1. We iteratively solve $D(n, k)$ using (6) and store the results in an $N \times K$ matrix. The initial values for $n = 1$ or $k = 1$ are given by the trivial solutions. We can read out the optimal solution to our original problem at position (N, K) in the matrix. The clustering and the cluster centers of the optimal solution are then found by backtracking.

Algorithm 1. K-means clustering using dynamic programming

1: Given input points $\{u_1, \ldots, u_N\}$, a distribution $h(i), i = 1, \ldots, N$ and K.
2: Iteratively solve $D(n, k)$ using (6) and (10) for $n = 2, \ldots, N$ and $k = 2, \ldots, K$.
3: Find the centers $c_l, l = 1, \ldots, K$ and the clustering by backtracking from the optimal solution $D(N, K)$.

In order to efficiently calculate $D(n, k)$ we need to be able to iteratively update the function f from (5). We do this in the following manner. We start by calculating the cumulative distribution $H(i)$ of $h(i)$, given by

$$H(i) = \sum_{j=1}^{i} h(j), \quad i = 1, \ldots, N. \tag{7}$$

We can then update the weighted mean of a point set $\{u_1, \ldots, u_n\}$ by:

$$c_{\{1, \ldots, n\}} = \frac{h(n)u_n + H(n-1) \cdot c_{\{1, \ldots, n-1\}}}{H(n)}. \tag{8}$$

Using this update we can also formulate an update to the error contribution of those points by:

$$f(u_1, \ldots, u_n) = \sum_{i=1}^{n} h(i)(u_i - c_{\{1, \ldots, n\}})^2 = \tag{9}$$

$$= \sum_{i=1}^{n-1} h(i)(u_i - c_{\{1, \ldots, n-1\}})^2 + \frac{H(n-1)}{H(n)}(u_n - c_{\{1, \ldots, n-1\}})^2 \cdot h(n). \tag{10}$$

To show this we can, without loss of generality, assume that we have transformed the coordinates so that $c_{\{1, \ldots, n-1\}} = 0$ and hence $\sum_{i=1}^{n-1} h(i)u_i = 0$. This gives according to (8):

$$c_{\{1, \ldots, n\}} = h(n)u_n/H(n). \tag{11}$$

Then

$$\sum_{i=1}^{n} h(i)(u_i - c_{\{1,\dots,n\}})^2 = \sum_{i=1}^{n} h(i)(u_i - \frac{h(n)u_n}{H(n)})^2 = \quad (12)$$

$$= \sum_{i=1}^{n-1} h(i)(u_i - \frac{h(n)u_n}{H(n)})^2 + h(n)(u_n - \frac{h(n)u_n}{H(n)})^2 = \quad (13)$$

$$= \sum_{i=1}^{n-1} h(i)(u_i - \frac{h(n)u_n}{H(n)})^2 + h(n)u_n^2 \frac{H(n-1)^2}{H(n)^2} = \quad (14)$$

$$= \sum_{i=1}^{n-1} h(i)(u_i^2 - 2u_i \frac{h(n)u_n}{H(n)} + \frac{h(n)^2 u_n^2}{H(n)^2}) + h(n)u_n^2 \frac{H(n-1)^2}{H(n)^2} = \quad (15)$$

$$= \sum_{i=1}^{n-1} h(i)u_i^2 + \frac{H(n-1)h(n)^2 u_n^2}{H(n)^2} + h(n)u_n^2 \frac{H(n-1)^2}{H(n)^2} = \quad (16)$$

$$= \sum_{i=1}^{n-1} h(i)u_i^2 + \frac{H(n-1)h(n)u_n^2}{H(n)} \frac{(h(n) + H(n-1))}{H(n)} = \quad (17)$$

$$= \sum_{i=1}^{n-1} h(i)u_i^2 + \frac{H(n-1)h(n)u_n^2}{H(n)}. \quad (18)$$

Without using (10) each entry $D(n, k)$ would take n^2 iterations to calculate, and the total complexity would become $N \cdot K \cdot N^2 = N^3 K$. However using (10) we can compute $f(u_1, \dots, u_n)$ in constant time, and this gives a total complexity of $N^2 K$.

4   Tone Mapping of Color Images

The discussion in the previous section was concerned with gray scale images. In this section we will describe the whole algorithm for an HDR color input image. We assume an RGB input image. Algorithm 1 is based on that the input points u_i are one-dimensional. There are a number of ways in which one could apply the clustering on a color image. One could run algorithm 1 on the R-,G- and B-channel independently or transfer the image into another color space such as HSV and do the processing on the V-channel. In order to have a fast, efficient and color-preserving method we have opted to run the algorithm on the luminance channel. We start by doing a preprocessing step by taking the logarithm of the RGB image, giving us I_{log}. We then estimate the luminance channel I_{gr} from I_{log}, using a standard weighted average. We can then run algorithm 1. When we have clustered the luminance channel into the desired K levels, we calculate our transfer function $F(s) : \{u_1, \dots, u_N\} \rightarrow \{1, \dots, K\}$ by finding the nearest neighbour of each input level s:

$$F(s) = \arg\min_{l} ||c_l - s||_2. \quad (19)$$

The output image is then constructed by applying the function F on the whole RGB-image pixel-wise. The different steps are sumarized in algorithm 2.

Algorithm 2. Democratic Tone Mapping (DTM)

1: Given a high bit color input image: I_{in}
2: Take the log to get $I_{log} = \log I_{in}$
3: Calculate the intensity channel I_{gr} of I_{log} .
4: Calculate the histogram $h(s)$ of I_{gr}.
5: Find the centers c_l using algorithm 1.
6: Estimate $F(s) : u_i \rightarrow c_l$ using nearest neighbours.
7: $I_{out} = F(I_{log})$.

---

5   Results

We have implemented our tone mapping algorithm and conducted a number of tests. In Section 5.1 we study the time complexity of our algorithm and then in Section 5.2 we show results on a set of standard HDR images and compare with a number of different tone mapping algorithms. We have consistently used $K = 256$ in our experiments, corresponding to 8-bit output, but this could be set to any output quantization you like.

5.1   Algorithm Complexity and Stability

A standard iterative K-means algorithm will converge to a local minimum. Algorithm 1 will converge to the global minimum, but one may ask how often the iterative scheme gets stuck in a local minimum, and how far this is from the global optimum. In order to investigate this we did a simple qualitative experiment where we ran our algorithm on an input image (with 2000 gray levels) and $K = 256$. We then ran the standard iterative K-means clustering and compared the resulting solution to the global optimum. We repeated this for a large number of runs with random initialization. In Figure 2a the results are shown. It shows a histogram over the L_2 differences between the local solution for the cluster centers and the true solution. The center points were of course sorted before the norm was taken. The figure clearly shows that in this case there was a large difference between the local solutions and the true solution, and in no case was the true optimum found using the local iterative method. Next we wanted to check if the total algorithm followed the expected complexity. In order to do this we ran algorithm 2 on an input image and varied the image size, the number of input gray levels N and the number of output gray levels K. Our implementation was done in Matlab, with the most time consuming step, i.e. the dynamic programming part, done using compiled mex-functions. The tests were conducted on a Mac mini with an 2.5 Ghz Intel core i5 processor. The results are shown in Figure 2. In (b) we plot the total running time of algorithm 2 for different sizes of input images. One can see that the graph has a clear affine shape. This is in accordance with what would be expected. The dynamic programming part is independent of the image size, given that the number of input gray levels is fixed. The linear part comes from steps 2-4 and 7 of algorithm 2. In (c) and (d) the respective dependences on K and N are shown. The most time consuming part of the algorithm is the dynamic programming step, and this is linear in K and quadratic in N which is validated in the graph.

5.2   Results on HDR Images

We have tested our method on a number of HDR input images and compared with a number of standard tone mapping algorithms. The images were collected from [9, 19]. We used the HDR image tool *Luminance HDR* [14] to do the processing. It contains implementations of a number of tone mapping algorithms.

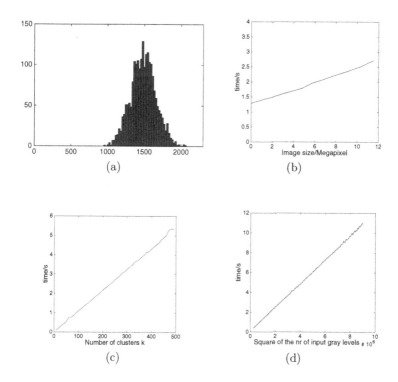

Fig. 2. (a) Histogram over the L_2-norms of the differences between the global optimum and local optimums after local optimization using random initialization. (b-d) Execution time for running the complete algorithm 2 as a function of (b) image size, (c) the output discretization K and (c) the square of the input discretization N. All plots follow the predicted behavior of the algorithm.

MANTIUK [17]   REINHARD [20]   Proposed algorithm 2

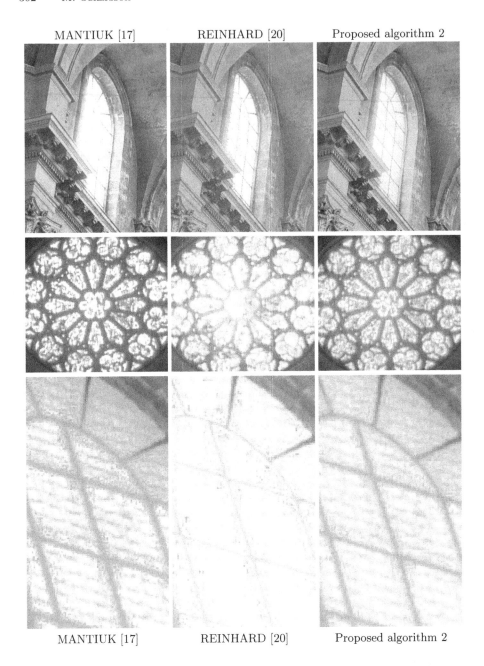

MANTIUK [17]   REINHARD [20]   Proposed algorithm 2

Fig. 3. The figure shows cutouts from the results on (top to bottom) NancyChurch3, Rosette and NancyChurch1. HDR radiance maps courtesy of R. Mantiuk [9] and P. Debevec [19]. The figure shows from left to right [17], [20] and our method. One can see that the compared methods suffer from over-saturation, color artifacts and loss of detail. The results are best viewed on screen.

Fig. 4. The result of running our algorithm 2 on a number of HDR images No parameters need to be set to produce the output. The results are best viewed on screen. HDR radiance maps courtesy of P. Debevec [19] and R. Mantiuk [9].

We have throughout our tests only used the default parameter settings as supplied by *Luminance HDR*. It is probably so that in some cases better results can be found by tweaking the parameters manually, but since our method doesn't contain any parameters and the goal for us was to have an automatic system we opted for the default parameters. We have compared our method to the methods of Drago et al [6], Mantiuk et al [17,18], Reinhard et al [20] and Durand et al [7]. Of these we found that [17] and [20] gave significantly better results over the set of test images. Our method gave very similar results to these two methods.

In Figure 3 we show magnified cutouts from three example images. Here we can see that the two compared methods (on the left) exhibit problems with over-saturation, loss of detail resolution and color artifacts.

6 Conclusion

We have in this paper presented a novel tone mapping algorithm that is based on K-means clustering, using a dynamic programming approach. This enables us to not only solve the clustering problem efficiently but also find the global optimum. Our algorithm runs in $O(N^2K)$ for an image with N input luminance levels and K output levels, with comparable result to state-of-the-art tone mapping algorithms. One large benefit of our algorithm is its total lack of parameters. Some of the compared local methods can be tuned to get better effect in local color and contrast, but in many cases a totally automatic procedure is highly desirable. Our approach would also be quite straightforward to extend to HDR video, by working on a spatiotemporal block. Since the algorithm is linear in the number of pixels this would be very efficient.

Acknowledgments. This work was supported by ELLIIT and eSSENCE.

References

1. Aloise, D., Deshpande, A., Hansen, P., Popat, P.: Np-hardness of euclidean sum-of-squares clustering. Machine Learning **75**(2), 245–248 (2009)
2. Bellman, R.: A note on cluster analysis and dynamic programming. Mathematical Biosciences **18**(3), 311–312 (1973)
3. Celenk, M.: A color clustering technique for image segmentation. Computer Vision, Graphics, and Image Processing **52**(2), 145–170 (1990)
4. Dasgupta, S., Freund, Y.: Random projection trees for vector quantization. IEEE Transactions on Information Theory **55**(7), 3229–3242 (2009)
5. Debevec, P.E., Malik, J.: Recovering high dynamic range radiance maps from photographs. In: Proceedings of the 24th Annual Conference on Computer Graphics and Interactive Techniques, SIGGRAPH 1997, pp. 369–378. ACM (2007)
6. Drago, F., Myszkowski, K., Annen, T., Chiba, N.: Adaptive logarithmic mapping for displaying high contrast scenes. Computer Graphics Forum **22**(3), 419–426 (2003)
7. Durand, F., Dorsey, J.: Fast bilateral filtering for the display of high-dynamic-range images. ACM Transactions on Graphics (TOG) **21**(3), 257–266 (2002)

8. Grossberg, M.D., Nayar, S.K.: High dynamic range from multiple images: Which exposures to combine. In: Proc. ICCV Workshop on Color and Photometric Methods in Computer Vision (CPMCV), Nice, France (2003)
9. http://pfstools.sourceforge.net/hdr_gallery.html (Accessed 2014-09-01)
10. Kleinberg, J., Tardos, É.: Algorithm design. Addison-Wesley (2005)
11. Larson, G.W., Rushmeier, H., Piatko, C.: A visibility matching tone reproduction operator for high dynamic range scenes. IEEE Transactions on Visualization and Computer Graphics 3(4), 291–306 (1997)
12. Lee, J.W., Park, R.H., Chang, S.: Local tone mapping using the k-means algorithm and automatic gamma setting. IEEE Transactions on Consumer Electronics 57(1), 209–217 (2011)
13. Lloyd, S.: Least squares quantization in pcm. IEEE Transactions on Information Theory 28(2), 129–137 (1982)
14. http://qtpfsgui.sourceforge.net (Accessed: 2014-09-01)
15. Mahajan, M., Nimbhorkar, P., Varadarajan, K.: The planar k-means problem is NP-hard. In: Das, S., Uehara, R. (eds.) WALCOM 2009. LNCS, vol. 5431, pp. 274–285. Springer, Heidelberg (2009)
16. Malm, H., Oskarsson, M., Warrant, E., Clarberg, P., Hasselgren, J., Lejdfors, C.: Adaptive enhancement and noise reduction in very low light-level video. In: IEEE 11th International Conference on Computer Vision, 2007. ICCV 2007, pp. 1–8. IEEE (2007)
17. Mantiuk, R., Daly, S., Kerofsky, L.: Display adaptive tone mapping. ACM Transactions on Graphics (TOG) 27(3), 68:1–68:10 (2008)
18. Mantiuk, R., Myszkowski, K., Seidel, H.P.: A perceptual framework for contrast processing of high dynamic range images. ACM Transactions on Applied Perception (TAP) 3(3), 286–308 (2006)
19. http://www.pauldebevec.com/Research/HDR (Accessed: 2014-10-01)
20. Reinhard, E., Stark, M., Shirley, P., Ferwerda, J.: Photographic tone reproduction for digital images. ACM Transactions on Graphics (TOG) 21(3), 267–276 (2002)
21. Robertson, M.A., Borman, S., Stevenson, R.L.: Dynamic range improvement through multiple exposures. In: Proceedings International Conference on Image Processing, ICIP 99, Kobe, Japan. vol. 3, pp. 159–163. IEEE (1999)
22. Scheunders, P.: A comparison of clustering algorithms applied to color image quantization. Pattern Recognition Letters 18(11), 1379–1384 (1997)
23. Scheunders, P.: A genetic c-means clustering algorithm applied to color image quantization. Pattern Recognition 30(6), 859–866 (1997)
24. Steinley, D.: K-means clustering: a half-century synthesis. British Journal of Mathematical and Statistical Psychology 59(1), 1–34 (2006)
25. Tumblin, J., Rushmeier, H.: Tone reproduction for realistic images. Computer Graphics and Applications, IEEE 13(6), 42–48 (1993)
26. Wang, H., Song, M.: Ckmeans. 1d. dp: optimal k-means clustering in one dimension by dynamic programming. The R Journal 3(2), 29–33 (2011)
27. Ward, G.: A contrast-based scalefactor for luminance display. Graphics gems IV, pp. 415–421 (1994)
28. Warrant, E., Oskarsson, M., Malm, H.: The remarkable visual abilities of nocturnal insects: Neural principles and bioinspired night-vision algorithms. Proceedings of the IEEE 102(10), 1411–1426 (2014)
29. Wilkie, K., Devlin, A., Chalmers, A., Purgathofer, W.: Tone reproduction and physically based spectral rendering. Eurographics 2002: State of the Art Reports, pp. 101–123 (2002)

Analysis of Thermal Video for Coarse to Fine Particle Tracking in Volcanic Explosion Plumes

Maxime Bombrun[1,2,3,4](✉), Vincent Barra[1,2], and Andrew Harris[3,4]

[1] Clermont-Université, Université Blaise Pascal, LIMOS, BP 10448,
63000 Clermont-Ferrand, France
[2] CNRS, UMR 6158, LIMOS, 63173 Aubiere, France
[3] Clermont-Université, Université Blaise Pascal, LMV, BP 10448,
63000 Clermont-Ferrand, France
[4] CNRS, UMR 6524, LMV, 63038 Clermont-Ferrand, France
bombrun@isima.fr

Abstract. This paper presents two algorithms for feature extraction and segmentation. The first algorithm is applied to detect tens of thousands of ballistic targets moving at high velocities (100's m/s) and with different sizes, velocities, shapes and directions. Upon detection, we compute statistics for each of these parameters for each particle, without any assumption or a-priori information. The second algorithm was developed to detect a slow moving convective cloud. The challenge was to follow the evolution of the cloud contours which comprised a heterogeneous element in front of a homogeneous, but moving (trees in wind), background. These algorithms were applied to images acquired with thermal cameras with different settings (frame rate, frame size, focal length, instantaneous field of view). A case study is presented using images of volcanic and made-man explosive events.

Keywords: Segmentation · Feature extraction · Contours · Thermal imagery

Introduction

The first high-temporal-resolution (operating at 20 Hz) ground-based infrared imaging system, was produced in 1965. However, the first hand-held system came with the introduction of high-spatial resolution focal plane arrays in 1993, with the first uncooled micro-bolometer-based system being produced in 1997. These developments, coupled with advances in high-speed digital electronics that allowed imagery to be stored on small memory disks "revolutionized the commercialization of thermal imaging systems" [1]. From that point onwards, infrared imaging science expanded rapidly in many domains [2]. Thermal imaging cameras (TIC) produce a thermal image of a scene that provides information regarding both its radiative and dynamic properties, a capability which makes TIC useful for a multitude of hot spot tracking roles.

© Springer International Publishing Switzerland 2015
R.R. Paulsen and K.S. Pedersen (Eds.): SCIA 2015, LNCS 9127, pp. 366–376, 2015.
DOI: 10.1007/978-3-319-19665-7_30

Infrared Search and Track (IRST) systems were first developed for air defence applications [3], as well as for military applications. Today, they are also used in civil applications, such as surveillance on land, at sea and in the air and to provide warning of intruder ingress [4], as well as to survey areas where structural failure and disasters may occur. Thermal emission of gears operating on tanks or helicopters can, for example, be used to detect, track and lock-on to the target, so that many automatic target recognition (ATR) algorithms have been proposed to this end [5]. These algorithms segment and recognize vehicles, ships and aircraft [6]. TIC civilian applications include fire control [7], monitoring of buildings [2], medicine [8], computer-aided diagnosis systems [9] and volcanology [10].

One of the first field-based thermal measurement campaigns at an active volcano was completed by Thomas A. Jaggar [11,12]. He illustrated the benefits of remote thermal measurements against the common contact measurements, describing problems associated with contact-based measurement which included equipment and personnel safety as well as the limited measurement time available for a contact measurement imposed by the radiated heat from a lava lake. The first attempt to run a radiometer continuously at a volcanic target was completed for a persistently degassing vent by Tazieff [13] and during an explosive volcanic eruption by Shimozuru [14]. Between 1965 and the end of 2007, at least 60 studies reported results obtained using ground-based broad-band radiometers for explosions, fumaroles and geothermally heated surfaces as well as lava flow, lakes and domes [10]. Applications to volcanological science by thermal cameras were clustered in five main groups by Spampinato [15], these being studies of hydrothermal areas and fumarole fields; lava bodies; explosive activity and volcanic plumes; pyroclastic flow deposits; fracturing and cracking. The most popular of these applications has been analysis of explosive activity, which accounted for 48 % of the studies published between 2001 and 2011. In fact, some of the first publications involving the application of thermal camera data in the domain of volcanology focused on the dynamics of explosive eruption plumes [16]. The key advance in generating this popularity in volcanic studies has been the ability to collect thermal video with spatial resolutions of a few centimeters and sampling frequencies of up to 120 Hz, with the operator being free to choose and modify the dynamic range, sampling rate, field of view, and targeted area, as well as acquisition start and stop times.

Here, we thus focus on the application of thermal video data to explosive emissions where we aim to segment two major components of an explosive volcanic emission (plume) using the thermal data. First, we focus on all coarse particles as they exit the vent to gather parameters such as size, shape, velocity and mass for the solid (particulate) fraction of the plume, this being the contribution of particles with a diameter between 1 cm and 5 cm (lapilli-size) and between 6.5 cm to 35 cm (bombs-sized). We next analyze the plume of gas and fine particles whose ascent will be buoyancy driven [17] and which can rise to over 25 000 meters above the vent.

1   Particle Study (cm-sized analysis)

1.1   Methodology

The thermal camera used in this study was a forward looking infrared (FLIR) FLIR Systems SC655 equipped with a 3.6× magnification lens and recording at 200 frames per second. The focal length was 88.9 mm and the IFOV was 0.19 mrad. We note that our frames are usually 600 × 480 pixels in size, but this is automatically truncated to allow recording at rates greater than 30 Hz. For example, at 200 Hz, the image size is 600 × 120 pixels. This resizing is automatically performed by the acquisition software and the resized frame is centered on the same pixel as the full frame and the spatial resolution does not change. The pixel dimension (L_p) will depend on the detector instantaneous field of view (IFOV). This is defined by a cone opening at angle β_{IFOV} and the distance to the target (D), so that the pixel diameter is given (for a paraxial approximation defined for a small IFOV), by $L_p = 2[Dtan(\beta_{IFOV}/2)] = D \times \beta_{IFOV}$.

Given the large number of particles involved in a volcanic explosion and the quantity of data recorded by the thermal camera (two hundred 640 × 120 pixel images per second = 150 kB of data every second or 1.8 GB per minute), we opted for a simple, yet-effective algorithm to extract particle parameters. A first step is to remove the static objects of the image. This is the static background, i.e. a set of components defined using the image prior to the event. The static background can usually be removed by pre-processing approaches [18]. Given the time of the event onset ($t = 0$), the easiest way to remove the static background is to consider the difference between the current frame I_t and a reference frame acquired before the event, termed the "background image" ($I_{t<0}$ or I_{Ref}). Now, we can detect the position of each particles in each image by subtracting the previous frame I_{t-1} from the current frame I_t. However, all moving elements are detected by this process, including slow targets we do not want to detect (e.g., birds, meteorological clouds). This is termed the "dynamic background". Finally, we removed both the static and the dynamic background by generating a first derivative image at time t (T_t):

$$T_t = I_t - \frac{\alpha I_{t-1} + \gamma I_{Ref}}{\alpha + \gamma} \ \forall t \in \{1, n\} \tag{1}$$

where α and γ are weights derived empirically and which change according to the predominance of the static versus dynamic background. After this step only particles and a low intensity hint of the background persist. Because we only want to detect components among the brightest features, we process $F_t = T_t \cdot \mathbf{1}_{\{I_t - I_0 \geq th\}}$ using a New White Top-Hat transform [19]:

$$MNWTH(F_t) = F_t - min(((F_t \oplus \Delta B) \ominus B_b), F_t) \tag{2}$$

where $\oplus$ is the binary dilation operator and $\ominus$ the binary erosion operator. Parameters ΔB and B_b are respectively an empty and a full square-shaped structuring elements. We apply a 21 pixel diameter box with, following Bai and Zhou [19], a three-pixel wide perimeter for ΔB. That is, while pixels in the central 15-pixel-wide box have values of zero, those in the three-pixel-wide perimeter have values of one.

The second part of the algorithm tracks each particle through time. This allows us to compute the velocity of each particle, but also cleans up false detections which may have occurred during the segmentation process. We chose the maximum intensity pixel of the target as the initial position with subpixel accuracy obtained following Shindler et al. [20]. Now, $\omega_{i,t} = (x_{i,t}, y_{i,t})$ is the subpixel-position of particle i at time t. We defined the velocity of the particle in the image plane from the pixel distance traveled by the particle between two consecutive frames (Δt):

$$U_{i,t} = \frac{\|\omega_{i,t+1} - \omega_{i,t}\|}{\Delta t} \tag{3}$$

The next position of particle i can now be estimated following several conditions (spatial, intensity, trajectory). We then estimated the velocity in meters per second based on the frame rate and assuming a planar projection. Thus, dimensions in pixel (X_{pix}, where X may be a velocity or the pixel width or height) are converted in millimeters (X_{mm}) by

$$X_{mm} = \frac{RD}{f\,sin(90 - \phi)} X_{pix} \tag{4}$$

in which R is the spatial resolution of the camera, D is the distance and ϕ is the tilt angle of the camera. Here, we are not interested in trajectories, instead our aim is to compute particle parameters as soon as they exit the vent. Consequently, we calculated our parameters using the closest usable frame to the vent. We used the radius of the particle short axis r_S and long axis r_L to compute the characteristic width of the particle i from the average radius, $r = \frac{r_S + r_L}{2}$. Particle volume (V_i) is then computed assuming a prolate spheroid, so that $V_i = (4/3)\pi r_S^2 r_L$. Finally, given an appropriate density (ρ_i), particle volume can be converted to mass ($m_i = \rho_i V_i$). This algorithm was tested and validated on an artificial experiment [21], a summary of which is given here.

1.2   Natural Case

The algorithm was tested on videos containing high velocity particles imaged at Stromboli volcano (Aeolian Islands, Italy). In 2012, we completed eight hours of recording spread over four days spanning 27 September-5 October during which time we recorded 13 eruptions. In 2014, we recorded for eight hours on 17 and 18 May, capturing a further 18 events. We set up our high speed camera at Pizzo Sopra la Fossa, a natural platform which overlooks Stromboli's active craters from a distance of 280 m, with the camera being tilted downwards at an angle of -23 degrees. With this geometry, we can detect particles down to 5.5 cm. Emission durations ranged from 5 s to 50 s, with an average of 14 s. The number of particles detected during single events ranged from 610 to 5 320, with

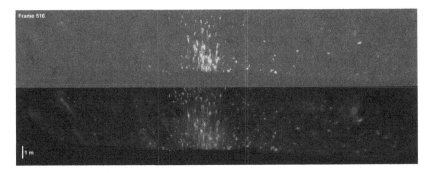

Fig. 1. Particles detected (bottom, in red) from the original image (top). Particles on the sides are static deposit from a previous eruption.

an average of 2 685. A total of 83 220 particles were detected for all 31 eruptions (Fig. 1). The particle size distribution (Fig. 2, top) revealed that the majority of the particles (67 %) were between the detection lower limit, 5.5 cm, and 10 cm; with the mean particle width being 10 cm on which there was a standard deviation of 5.6 cm. In Fig. 3, we assessed particle shape in terms of a normalized shape index: $(r_L-r_S)/(r_L+r_S)$. Following this index, a perfectly oblate shape will have a value of -1/3, whereas a perfectly prolate shape will have a value of +1/3; a perfect sphere will have a value of 0. We found that only 17 % of our particles approximated a spherical shape. Of the remaining 83 %, 29 % were oblate and 54 % were prolate. The dominance of the prolate shape is consistent with particle deformation in the direction of motion. We used the density of samples, from lapilli to bomb sized particles as collected during sample-collection campaigns to Stromboli in 2008 [22,23], 2010 [24] and 2011 [25] to compute the mass of each particle and the total mass ejected during each eruption. Derivations for erupted masses ranged between 1 270 kg and 11 820 kg, with a mean of 4 585 kg. The particle mass distribution (Fig. 2, middle) revealed that most particles had a relatively low mass, with 46 310 (or 56 %) of all of detected particles having masses of less than 4 kg. This population accounted for 10 220 kg or 4.6 % of the total mass. However, the 2 524 particles greater than 25 cm (3 % of the total detected particles) accounted for 44 % of the total mass.

The velocity distribution (Fig. 2, bottom) had a mode between 20 m/s and 30 m/s, with an average velocity of 45 m/s on which the standard deviation was 36 m/s. Particle velocities at Stromboli are generally less than 100 m/s [26,27]. In our study, 91 % of all of particles measured had velocities of less than 100 m/s. However, 7 330 particles (8.8 %) had velocities greater than 100 m/s and up to 240 m/s. This approaches the higher velocities recently found for normal explosion at Stromboli by Taddeucci et al. [28], Delle Donne and Ripepe [29] and Harris et al. [30]. Finally, considering the large number of particles detected (83 220), the impact of outliers is vanishingly small. We concluded that our dataset is statistically robust. Full data sets and overview statistics are given in Bombrun et al. [31].

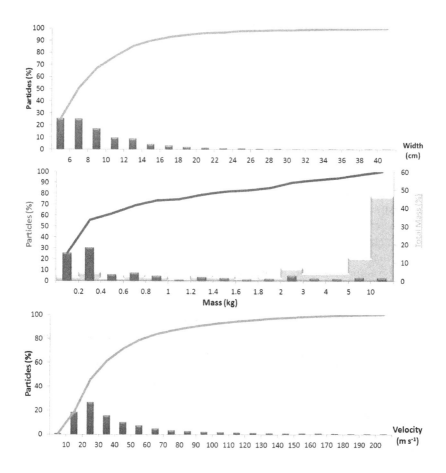

Fig. 2. Particle size (top), mass (middle) and velocity distribution (bottom). Curves represent the cumulative number of particles. The mass histogram also shows in light gray the impact of the heavy particles on the total mass.

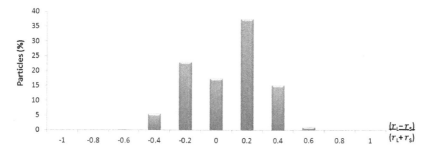

Fig. 3. Particle shape distribution. Positive values represent particle with a prolate shape while negative values are particle with oblate shape.

2   Plume Study (meter-sized analysis)

2.1   Target

Our primary objective was to develop an operational algorithm capable of detecting a moving plume and parametrizing its dynamics through time. A volcanic plume is a mixture of particles, gases, and entrained atmospheric air [32]. Such volcanic plumes are slow moving targets which may be dispersed on both local and global scales so that frame rates of 1 Hz are more than adequate. Consequently we recorded using a FLIR Systems SC660 saving at 3 second intervals onto an internal memory card. The focal length was 38 mm and the IFOV was 0.65 mrad

The first step of the algorithm was to consider the differentiation $(D_{t,t-step})$ between the current frame (I_t) and the previous frame (I_{t-step}) to highlight the dynamic background. We applied a single level discrete 2-D wavelet transformation, using a Daubechies wavelet (db1), on the absolute value of $D_{t,t-1}$ to compute the approximation coefficient matrix. The approximation coefficients are the high-scale, low-frequency components thus they contain much less noise than the original image and enhance the constrast but are slightly more than half the size of the original image. We next performed a direct reconstruction from the 2-D wavelet coefficient to obtain a reconstructed approximation image. From the absolute value of the reconstructed image, we computed a single threshold for the image using Otsu's method [33] to obtain a partial mask of the plume. We cleaned this mask by applying a morphological opening transformation with a 1 pixel radius disk and removing detected elements of less than 5 pixels in area. We completed this mask by performing the same process with another differentiation, $D_{t,Ref}$, this being the difference between the current frame (I_t) and a reference frame recorded before the event (I_{Ref}). We summed the two masks to obtain the final differentiated mask. However, because the wavelet transformation produced an approximation image, in the next step, we performed a morphological reconstruction, i.e., we applied a repeated dilatation process to the mask until its contour fitted the original image, I_t. Each successive dilation was constrained to lie underneath I_t. We cleaned the final image by removing outliers to finally compute the plume exterior contour using a Canny edge detector.

2.2   Applications

We first tested the algorithm on thermal video for the ascent of a volcanic ash plume at Santiaguito volcano, Guatemala. This video was recorded in 2005 and the emission was 170 s (5 100 frames) in duration. The background was composed of a homogeneous sky with low-intensity meteorological clouds, with the ground contrasting well with the plume (Fig. 4(a)). A low-intensity lava flow was apparent on the left-hand side of the vent. Unfortunately the algorithm was too efficient in considering low contrast image elements so that some (moving) meterological clouds were detected as a part of the plume. We thus removed clouds on the basis of their being not pixel-connected to the plume. This was achieved by considering the largest component and improved the contrast by using wavelets on the differentiated image as a pre-processing step.

The second video was recorded at Stromboli volcano, Italy on May the 28, 2012. The camera was set up at Pizzo Sopra la Fossa and pointed at the North-East crater over a line of sight distance of 300 m so that the image covered a height of 94 m. Plume emission lasted 67 s (i.e. 2 000 frames). The background was a homogeneous sky and cold ground around the vent, although another vent to the left of the active vent produced unwanted detections (Fig. 4(b)). In addition, the distance between the camera and the vent was shorter than at Santiaguito, thus the impact of heat radiated by the crater was more problematic. During plume ascent, overturn convection thermally renewed the plume surface so as to continually bring hot spots to the surface of the plume to create a random intensity to the plume images, thus making intensity tracking difficult.

The third video was recorded at an experimental facility near Buffalo, USA. During June 2014, the University at Buffalo completed experiments that used small chemical explosive charges buried in layered aggregates to simulate the effects of subsurface hydrothermal and phreatomagmatic explosions [34]. At the same time, three more powerful blasts were performed. These released a plume of fine sand particles. The blast used to test our algorithm was that of Pad 5, Blast 4. The energy produced by the explosion was 2.30×10^6 J and the depth below the surface was 0.5 m. The camera was set up 74 m from the source so that the

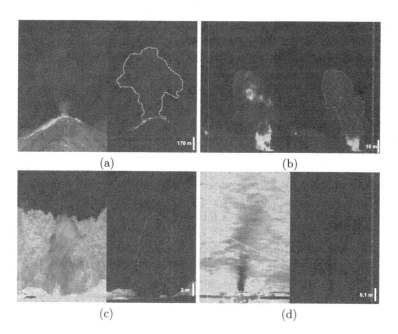

(a)   (b)

(c)   (d)

Fig. 4. Performance of the plume segmentation algorithm applied to videos from Santiaguito volcano (a), Stromboli volcano (b), Buffalo (c) and Munich experiments (d)

field of view was 23 m height. The ambient background was composed of trees at ambiant temperature, moving in the wind to create a moving background. The top of the video comprised sky that had a huge contrast with the trees. This video was the most difficult to process due to the numerous and contrasting features in the video (Fig. 4(c)).

The last video was recorded at an experimental facility near Munich, Germany, where the Ludwig-Maximilians University completed large-scale ash settling experiments in June 2014. Natural basaltic ash (0 – 500 m) was released with different controlled volumetric flow rates in a shock tube system. The experiment used to test our algorithm was that of experiment #33. The sample came from Monte Rossi Scoria (Italy); it was water saturated, the sample porosity was 30 %, its volume was 29.44 cm^3 and the pressure of the decompression was 15 Mpa. The camera was set up horizontally at a distance of 4 m so that the field of view was 1.2 m height. The algorithm succeeded in performing plume detection despite the fact that the sample was colder than the background (Fig. 4(d)).

Conclusion

We present, here, new approaches to deal with segmentation and feature extraction in thermal video obtained for explosively-generated plumes. The first algorithm detects, tracks and parameterizes small dim, but relatively large (ballistic) targets in high-speed IR videos. Based on a mathematical morphology transformation hybridized with refinement by thresholding, this method allowed us to obtain a statistically robust database of 83 000 particles emitted during explosions at Stromboli volcano. Statistically, most of the particles have sizes between 5 and 15 cm, and the majority of individual particle masses are below 0.5 kg. The particle velocity distribution is positively skewed with a mode between 20 and 30 m/s. The second algorithm detect and track fine particles in plumes ascending under buoyancy. The detection method applied to this case is based on a background subtraction by Daubechies wavelet transformation with a refinement by image reconstruction. It was tested on several cases with different levels of difficulties. Even so, this algorithm proved to be robust enough to detect plumes despite of complex image background scenarios. These two algorithms are designed to provide necessary information to allow improved understanding and modeling of dynamics for all ejected components during volcanic explosions. Statistically robust databases for vent-leaving particle dynamics remain scarce.

The ability to measure the dynamics of volcanic emissions as they exit the vent and the computation of particle parameters, for all particle sizes - from fine (ash) to coarse (lapilli-bombs) - is an excellent way to understand the dynamics related to the fragmentation and particle emission processes that lead to the volcanic plume and cloud. In this regard, using algorithm output to compute plume parameters such as height, front velocity and spreading angle will be used to constrain models that describe the source geometry and height of volcanic jets.

Acknowledgments. This research was financed by the French Government Laboratory of Excellence initiative n?ANR-10-LABX-0006, the Région Auvergne and the European Regional Development Fund.This is Laboratory of Excellence ClerVolc contribution number 157.

References

1. Holst, G.C.: Common Sense Approach to Thermal Imaging, p. 377p. JCD Publishing, Winter Park (FL) (2000)
2. Kylili, A., Fokaides, P.A., Christou, P., Kalogirou, S.A.: Infrared thermography (IRT) applications for building diagnostics: A review. Appl. Energy **134**, 531–549 (2014)
3. de Jong, A.N.: IRST and its perspective, SPIE's 1995 International Symposium on Optical Science, Engineering, and Instrumentation. International Society for Optics and Photonics, pp. 206–213, September 1995
4. Fernández-Caballero, A., Castillo, J.C., Serrano-Cuerda, J., Maldonado-Bascón, S.: Real-time human segmentation in infrared videos. Expert Syst. Appl. **38**(3), 2577–2584 (2011)
5. Li, B., Chellappa, R., Zheng, Q., Der, S., Nasrabadi, N., Chan, L., Wang, L.: Experimental evaluation of FLIR ATR approaches - A comparative study. Comput. Vision Image Understanding **84**(1), 5–24 (2001)
6. Yilmaz, A., Shafique, K., Shah, M.: Target tracking in airborne forward looking infrared imagery. Image Vision Comput. **21**(7), 623–635 (2003)
7. Amon, F., Pearson, C.: Thermal Imaging in Firefighting and Thermography Applications. Radiometric Temperature Measurements: II. Applications **43**, 279–331 (2009)
8. Arora, N., Martins, D., Ruggerio, D., Tousimis, E., Swistel, A.J., Osborne, M.P., Simmons, R.M.: Effectiveness of a noninvasive digital infrared thermal imaging system in the detection of breast cancer. The American Journal of Surgery **196**(4), 523–526 (2008)
9. Faust, O., Acharya, U.R., Ng, E.Y.K., Hong, T.J., Yu, W.: Application of infrared thermography in computer aided diagnosis. Infrared Phys. Technol. **66**, 160–175 (2014)
10. Harris, A.: Thermal Remote Sensing of Active Volcanoes: A User's Manual. Cambridge University Press, Cambridge (2013)
11. Jaggar, T.A.: Volcanologic investigations at Kilauea. Am. J. Sci. **44**, 161–221 (1917a)
12. Jaggar, T.A.: Thermal gradient of Kilauea lava lake. Journal of the Washington Academy of Sciences **7**(3), 397–405 (1917b)
13. Tazieff, H.: New investigations on eruptive gases. Bull. Volcanol. **34**(2), 421–438 (1970)
14. Shimozuru, D.: Observation of volcanic eruption by an infrared radiation meter. Nature **234**, 457–459 (1971)
15. Spampinato, L., Calvari, S., Oppenheimer, C., Boschi, E.: Volcano surveillance using infrared cameras. Earth Sci. Rev. **106**(1), 63–91 (2011)
16. Dehn, J., Harris, A., Ripepe, M.: Infrared Imaging of Strombolian Eruptions. AGU Fall Meeting Abstracts **1**, C1 (2001)
17. Turner, J.S.: The starting plume in neutral surroundings. J. Fluid Mech. **13**(3), 356–368 (1962)

18. Brutzer, S., Hoferlin, B., Heidemann, G.: Evaluation of background subtraction techniques for video surveillance. In: 2011 IEEE Conference on Computer Vision and Pattern Recognition (CVPR), pp. 1937–1944 (2011)
19. Bai, X., Zhou, F.: Analysis of new top-hat transformation and the application for infrared dim small target detection. Pattern Recognit. **43**(6), 2145–2156 (2010)
20. Shindler, L., Moroni, M., Cenedese, A.: Spatialtemporal improvements of a two-frame particle-tracking algorithm. Meas. Sci. Technol. **21**(11), 115401 (2010)
21. Bombrun, M., Barra, V., Harris, A.: Algorithm for particle detection and parameterization in high-frame-rate thermal video. J. Appl. Remote Sens. **8**(1), 083549–083549 (2014)
22. Coló, L.: Study of vesiculation in basalt magma through volcanological, textural and geophysical analyses: The case study of Stromboli, PhD dissertation, Department of Earth Sciences, Univ. Firenze, Florence, Italy
23. Gurioli, L., Coló, L., Bollasina, A., Harris, A.J., Whittington, A., Ripepe, M.: Dynamics of Strombolian explosions: Inferences from field and laboratory studies of erupted bombs from Stromboli volcano. J. Geophys. Res. **119**(1), 319–345 (2014)
24. Gurioli, L., Harris, A.J., Coló, L., Bernard, J., Favalli, M., Ripepe, M., Andronico, D.: Classification, landing distribution, and associated flight parameters for a bomb field emplaced during a single major explosion at Stromboli, Italy. Geology **41**(5), 559–562 (2013)
25. Leduc, L., Gurioli, L., Harris, A., Coló, L., Rose-Koga, E.F.: Types and mechanisms of strombolian explosions: characterization of a gas-dominated explosion at Stromboli, Bull. Volcanol. (2014)
26. Chouet, B., Hamisevicz, N., McGetchin, T.R.: Photoballistics of volcanic jet activity at Stromboli. J. Geophys. Res. **79**(32), 4961–4976 (1974)
27. Patrick, M.R., Harris, A.J., Ripepe, M., Dehn, J., Rothery, D.A., Calvari, S.: Strombolian explosive styles and source conditions: insights from thermal (FLIR) video. Bull. Volcanol. **69**(7), 769–784 (2007)
28. Taddeucci, J., Scarlato, P., Capponi, A., Del Bello, E., Cimarelli, C., Palladino, D., Kueppers, U.: High-speed imaging of Strombolian explosions: The ejection velocity of pyroclasts. Geophys. Res. Lett. **39**(2) (2012)
29. Delle Donne, D., Ripepe M.: High-frame rate thermal imagery of Strombolian explosions: Implications for explosive and infrasonic source dynamics. J. Geophys. Res. **117**(B9) (2012)
30. Harris, A.J., Ripepe, M., Hughes, E.A.: Detailed analysis of particle launch velocities, size distributions and gas densities during normal explosions at Stromboli. J. Volcanol. Geotherm. Res. **231**, 109–131 (2012)
31. Bombrun, M., Harris, A., Barra, V., Gurioli, L., Battaglia, J., Ripepe, M.: Anatomy of a strombolian eruption: inferences from particle data recorded with thermal video. J. Geophys. Res. (in Preparation)
32. Carey, S., Bursik., M.: Volcanic plumes, pp. 527–544. Encyclopedia of volcanoes. Academic Press, San Diego (2000)
33. Otsu, N.: A Threshold Selection Method from Gray-Level Histograms. IEEE Transactions on Systems, Man and Cybernetics **9**(1), 62–66 (1979)
34. Valentine, G., Graettinger, A.H., Macorps, E., Ross, P., White, J.D.L., Döhring, E., Sonder, I.: Experiments with vertically- and laterally-migrating subsurface explosions with applications to the geology of phreatomagmatic and hydrothermal explosion craters and diatremes. Bull. Volcanol. (in Preparation)
35. Jessop, D.E., Jellinek, A.M.: Effects of particle mixtures and nozzle geometry on entrainment into volcanic jets. Geophys. Res. Lett. **41**(11), 3858–3863 (2014)

Change Point Geometry for Change Detection in Surveillance Video

Brandon A. Mayer[(✉)] and Joseph L. Mundy

Brown University, 182 Hope Street, Provdence, RI 02903, USA
brandon_mayer@brown.edu, mundy@lems.brown.edu

Abstract. A change detection algorithm is proposed based on geometric descriptors of space-time appearance discontinuities in fixed camera video. At each pixel in a video frame, intensity subsequences with similar appearance are segmented using a Hidden Semi-Markov Model (HSMM). The start of each per-pixel homogeneous subsequence, referred to as change point vertices, are then clustered across pixel locations using an efficient graph based segmentation algorithm to construct a change point hull. The geometry of the change point hull provides a discriminating feature for distinguishing coherent movement from random or stochastic appearance changes and is simultaneously a rich descriptor for reasoning about object velocity and direction. State of the art results are shown in change detection, a fundamental computer vision problem for identifying regions of video that exhibit meaningful variations as defined by the application context.

Keywords: Change detection · Video processing · Automated surveillance

1 Introduction

Change detection for fixed camera video sequences is a fundamental problem in computer vision which refers to a class of algorithms for detecting space-time regions in which a scene changes in a meaningful way. Change detection may be an end unto itself, e.g. as a monitoring tool in surveillance systems, or as a pre-processing step for further reasoning about regions identified as meaningful change. While change detection algorithms abound, these methods admit a simple three class taxonomy based on the semantic level of the underlying features of the approach: Pixel (low), Region (mid), and Object (high) level change detection algorithms.

Pixel or low level change detection algorithms attempt to classify meaningful changes on a per-pixel basis by distinguishing rare from common intensity sequences. While these algorithms tend to be computationally efficient, easy to parallelize and effective at identifying temporal discontinuities, they lack knowledge of the typical spatial structure of appearance variations and as such fail to reliably describe and distinguish between meaningful and irrelevant scene dynamics. Pixel level methods tend to trade simplicity for a shallow vocabulary

© Springer International Publishing Switzerland 2015
R.R. Paulsen and K.S. Pedersen (Eds.): SCIA 2015, LNCS 9127, pp. 377–387, 2015.
DOI: 10.1007/978-3-319-19665-7_31

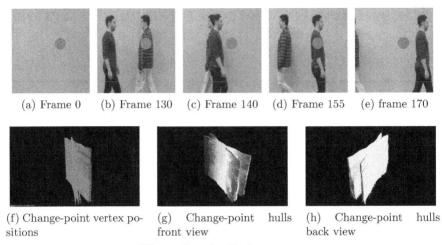

(a) Frame 0   (b) Frame 130   (c) Frame 140   (d) Frame 155   (e) frame 170

(f) Change-point vertex po-   (g) Change-point hulls   (h) Change-point hulls
sitions   front view   back view

Fig. 1. Crossing Paths sequence

with which to describe coherent action or behaviors, requiring significant ad-hoc
post-processing that is typically algorithm specific and fragile.

Object (high) level change detection algorithms operate on the opposite end
of the semantic spectrum, first attempting to recognize object categories present
in a scene prior to reasoning about their behavior. While in theory this approach
offers the most direct and rich vocabulary for describing scene dynamics, these
systems suffer from severe practical limitations, requiring enormous amounts
of training data per object category. For example, a generic object class such
as a human may exhibit significant appearance variations under different lighting, camera resolutions or perspectives. Additionally, normalizing for interclass
variability restricts the algorithms ability to transfer object models to different
applications and scenes. Further compounding the problem, it is impossible to
define *apriori* all object classes which may be observed in a video sequence, let
alone learning or building an accurate object model for each class.

Region (mid) level change detection algorithms identify space-time features
that are correlated with object behavior without explicitly localizing and classifying all object classes in a scene. The proposed region or mid level method
is a compromise between the efficient low-level and descriptive but impractical
high-level approaches which uses the geometry of space-time discontinuities to
localize and quantify coherent actions in video sequences.

First, a Hidden Semi-Markov Model (HSMM) is used to segment per-pixel
observations into temporal regions with similar appearance and duration. At
each pixel, the start of a segmented intensity subsequence, a 3D point in 2D
space-time known as a change-point vertex, marks the beginning of an approximately homogeneous intensity sequence which differs significantly from the previous segment [10]. An efficient graph-based clustering algorithm [4] is used to
group neighboring change-point vertices based on the expected appearance of
the temporal segment to form a change-point hull. The change-point hull could

be thought of as space-time "super-voxel" of discontinuities, demarcating regions of dissimilar appearance. The initial segmentation retains the efficiency of pixel level algorithms while the clustering step builds a rich, data-driven space-time descriptor with minimal computational overhead. The shape of the change-point hulls (clusters) provide a discriminating vocabulary for describing coherent motion in video sequences.

As a motivating example, consider the "Crossing Paths" sequence of fig. 1. In this video, a camera has been observing an indoor area when two people walk into the scene, crossing paths approximately at the frame center, and continue past the camera view. First, the per-pixel algorithm groups similar appearances into segments along the temporal axis as visualized in fig. 4a which shows a single pixel intensity sequence stacked as a vertical column. The initial temporal segmentation corresponding to the pixel location at the center of the pink circle would produce temporal groups that would be correlated with the semantic class sequence: (wall appearance, person one appearance, wall appearance, person two appearance, wall appearance). The beginning of each temporal segment defines a point in 3D (2D space-time) called a change point vertex. Figure 4b visualizes change point vertices, the image space-time location of temporal appearance discontinuities, as black spheres. The edges that are constructed between neighboring change point vertices in a later step are visualized as dotted lines. Figure 1f shows the location of all change point vertices recovered after the pixel independent segmentation for the "Crossing Paths" video as points in video frame space-time.

Weighted edges are constructed between neighboring change vertices and clustered using a graph based segmentation algorithm [4] where each cluster of change point vertices are referred to as change point hulls. Figures 1g and 1h show the recovered change-point hulls visualized as points in space time where color denotes hull membership. While there may be appearance variations within a single object class (the person walking from right to left has a multi-colored shirt, beige pants and dark hair), the change point hulls exhibit a coherent planar shape. Figure 1f shows the change point vertices as the people occlude the wall. The wall appearance is so uniform that in figure 1h the transition from each person back to the wall is all assigned to the same change hull (yellow).

As shown in the "Crossing Paths" experiment, coherent object motion induces planar geometries with respect to the change point hulls while the velocity of object motion is correlated with the normal direction of the change-point hull with respect to the principle axis of the camera. Furthermore, by observing the relative positions in space and time of change point hulls, it is possible to reason about object trajectory, velocity and occlusion while further experiments reveal image noise, random and incoherent motion induce elliptical or spherical change-point surfaces.

An example of a more complex change hull geometry generated by periodic motion is shown in fig. 2c. The wind turbine moves in a periodic circular motion which pixel-level change detection algorithms struggle to model as background motion [10]. However, the recovered change point hulls exhibit a coherent structure with a global helical shape that can be approximated locally with connected planes.

The singular values of a 3D spatial covariance matrix composed of the location of change point vertices within the same change point hull (cluster) is used to quantify the "planarity" of the space-time discontinuity for identifying coherent motion and recognizing meaningful scene changes.

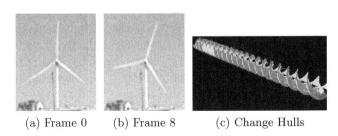

(a) Frame 0   (b) Frame 8   (c) Change Hulls

Fig. 2. Fields Point Turbine

2   Related Work

Pixel level methods are the most common class of algorithms for change detection [1,2,6–8,12,14]. Gaussian Mixture Models [7,14] are a standard parametric per-pixel intensity model where each pixel location in video is modeled using a mixture of Gaussians distribution. Many heuristics have been proposed for associating certain modes of the mixture distribution with the background or foreground of a scene [14], removing shadows and increasing parametric learning accuracy and speed [7], and incorporating multiple models of slowly occurring or fast intensity changes as well as other region-level edge statistics [2]. However, each of these methods suffer from the same problems in that a GMM can only model typical pixel intensities, the order and duration of a pixel appearance has no effect on the probability of the observed pixel intensity sequence.

Low-level change detection methods also include non-parametric models such as [1,6] which explicitly store a history of observed intensities at each pixel. Both algorithms specify routines where per-pixel background models "forget" about unlikely past observations and update the history with more common intensities by randomly resampling the memory buffer. Again these models suffer from permutation invariance; shuffling frames of video does not produce significantly different background models. Additionally, the amount of memory assigned to each pixel's memory buffer implicitly defines an upper bound for modeling periodic phenomena such as the turbine of fig. 2.

The method described in [12] transforms a windowed history of intensity observations to the frequency domain to associate common Fourier coefficients with background at each pixel in a video sequence and a meaningful change as a significant deviation from an average of previously computed frequency coefficients. While this method does indirectly model intensity sequences, the parameter governing the window length implicitly sets a fixed scale on the type of temporal patterns the algorithm can reliably model and, like other low level methods, must define algorithm specific heuristics to account for spatially coherent motion and behaviors.

The duration dependent codebook proposed in [10] models intensity sequences at every pixel location in a frame of video using a Duration Dependent Markov Model (DDHMM). During a training phase, a codebook is constructed based on local state assignments, mappings between per-pixel intensity subsequences and DDHMM state-duration pairs that summarize the appearance and temporal statistics of each intensity segment. State-duration assignments that occur during new video of the same scene that are uncommon relative to the training codebook are labeled as significant change. While the proposed method uses the same per-pixel DDHMM model and learning algorithm proposed in [10], this research investigates the plausibility of analyzing the geometry of clustered per-pixel discontinuities for visual reasoning and change detection. The novel contributions of this work relative to [10] include the introduction of change point vertices, the position of a state label transition in space-time representing a pixel-independent discontinuity. Change point vertices are clustered to form change point hulls that represent local patches of appearance discontinuities that transition to similar intensities. Finally, a novel classifier based on shape descriptors of change point hulls, derived via spectral analysis of scatter matrices composed of the space-time positions of vertices associated with each change point hull is used to detect changes in video.

The Spatial-Temporal Local Binary Pattern change detection algorithm [15] (STLBP) uses a local gradient descriptor for identifying common textures in video. While the STLBP descriptor is the most similar feature of the reviewed algorithms to the proposed method of analyzing spatial-temporal discontinuities there are major differences. First, the STLBP algorithm defines a fixed local neighborhood for computing the gradient around each pixel while the proposed algorithm uses a data driven approach to directly model the natural scale of homogeneous sequences and their corresponding discontinuities. Secondly, STLBP describes local texture using a gradient histogram, taking a bag-of-words approach. The shape of the appearance discontinuities is therefore lost, and with it the ability to reason about higher level motion or behaviors occurring in target videos. The proposed method however, uses the shape of appearance discontinuities as a fundamental feature for local scene description and change detection.

The work of [11] attempts to detect the presence of predefined activities in video such as "watching TV" or "making tea" using object recognition. This high level algorithm required assembling a dataset of over 1 million frames of video for learning only 18 activities. The authors acknowledge inter-class appearance variability as a source of significant difficulties, citing the example that a refrigerator looks very different when it is closed compared to when it is opened. Standard unsolved object recognition challenges and benchmarks such as the

PASCAL challenge [3] consist of almost 12,000 images for training and evaluating classification of 20 object categories while the ambitious ImageNet [13] consists of over 14 million annotated images and 10,000 object classes. These datasets and challenges underscore the difficulty in modeling the appearance variability of even a small number of pre-defined object classes even in an era of ubiquitous computing and big-data. Because robust object detection is still an unsolved computer vision task, it is necessary for performant, state of the art change detection algorithms to operate within the low or medium levels of the change detection semantic taxonomy, at least for the foreseeable future.

3   Algorithm

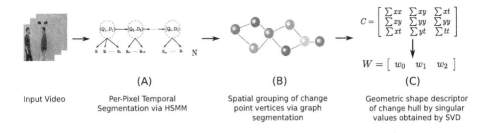

(A)	(B)	(C)
Input Video	Per-Pixel Temporal Segmentation via HSMM	Spatial grouping of change point vertices via graph segmentation	Geometric shape descriptor of change hull by singular values obtained by SVD

Fig. 3. Visualization of proposed algorithm. Each pixel of an input video is segmented into intensity subsequences with similar appearance and duration using a Hidden Semi-Markov Model. The beginning of each subsequence, a 3D point in 2D space-time and known as a change point vertex, are clustered into groups with similar appearance using a graph segmentation algorithm to form a change point hull. The vertices within a change point hull are used to construct a spatial covariance matrix which is decomposed via Singular Value Decomposition (SVD) to obtain the eigenvector and eigenvalues of the changepoint hull. The eigenvalues are then used as a descriptor for coherent motion and detecting meaningful appearance aberrations.

An outline of the proposed method is shown graphically in fig. 3. The intensity time series associated with each pixel location of fixed camera video is modeled using a class of Hidden Semi-Markov Models [5,9] known as a Duration Dependent Markov Model (DDHMM). The learning algorithm outlined in [10] is applied to each pixel location independently to produce an initial per-pixel segmentation of approximately homogeneous appearance subsequences. Temporal appearance discontinuities are then clustered using the graph-based segmentation algorithm described in [4] to group similar neighboring appearance discontinuities. The eigenvalues of the spatial covariance matrix composed of the locations of appearance discontinuities within the same cluster are used as a shape descriptor for identifying coherent motion and detecting meaningful changes.

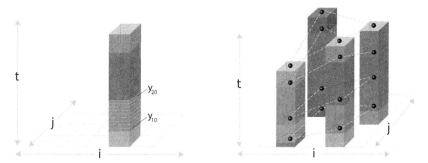

(a) Initial pixel independent temporal appearance segmentation.

(b) Clustering per-pixel change vertices via graph segmentation

Fig. 4. Figure 4a shows the independent per-pixel temporal segmentation of intensity subsequences into homogeneous groups with similar appearance and duration. The beginning of each sequence, known change point vertices, are visualized in figure 4b as black spherical points in 3D (2D image space and time). Each change point vertex is connected to its four nearest neighbors and assigned an edge weight which is used for segmenting the change hull.

3.1 Per-Pixel Intensity Sequence Model

An input video sequence is decomposed into a collection of per-pixel intensity time series: $Y(i,j) = (y_1, \ldots, y_T)$, one for each pixel location (i,j) for a video sequence with T frames. Denoting a random variable with a capital letter and specific instantiations of the corresponding variable with the matching lower case, a DDHMM models the sequence of observations using a sequence of latent state pairs: $(S_1, D_1), (S_2, D_2), \ldots, (S_l, D_l))$ where S_i is a state label and D_i is a random variable that represents the time spent in state S_i [10].

The DDHMM joint probability of a per-pixel intensity sequence and state-duration sequences is computed according to

$$p(y_1, \ldots, y_T, s_1, d_1, \ldots, s_L, d_L) = p(s_1)p(d_1 \mid s_1) \underbrace{\prod_{i=1}^{d_1} p(y_i \mid s_1)}_{\text{Initial state-duration}} \cdots$$

$$\underbrace{\prod_{l=2}^{L-1} p(d_l \mid s_l)p(s_l \mid s_{l-1}) \prod_{j=1}^{d_l} p(y_{r_i+j} \mid s_l)}_{\text{Internal state-durations, transitions and emission}} \underbrace{p(D_L \geq d_L)p(s_L \mid s_{(L-1)}) \prod_{z=1}^{d_L} p(y_{r_{(L-1)}+z} \mid s_L)}_{\text{right-censor term}}$$

$$(1)$$

Where $p(D_i = d_i \mid S_i = s_i)$, $p(S_i = s_i \mid S_{i-1} = s_{i-1})$ and $p(y_t \mid S_i = s_i)$ are the duration, state transition and emission distributions respectively, $r_i = \sum_{m=1}^{i} d_m$ and $p(s_1)$ is an initial distribution of state labels. The term $p(D_l \geq d_l \mid s_l)$ is called the state survival distribution and is included in the computation to account for the fact that the end of an observation sequence may not coincide with the end of a homogeneous subsequence and may just be a consequence of missing data [5]. The duration and transition distributions were chosen to be multinomial with zero self-transition probability while the emission distributions are univariate Gaussian. A graphical representation of the likelihood function is shown in standard graph-plate notation in step (A) of fig. 3 and indicates there is one HSMM for each of the N pixels in each frame of video.

3.2   Temporal Appearance Discontinuities

The computationally efficient algorithm developed in [10] is employed for learning the parameters and complexity of the per-pixel DDHMM model. The algorithm processes each intensity observation y_t in order, testing three hypothesis by comparing the current observation with the existing state conditional distributions: Extend the current state-duration label (s_l, d_l) by associating observation y_t with the current segment, associating y_t with an already existing state, or creating a new state label. Model complexity is regularized using a modified AIC criteria and the reader is referred to [10] for the remaining details.

The output of the per-pixel learning algorithm are the parameters of the emission, transition and duration distributions and assignments of pixel observations $(y_1, \ldots, y_t)$ to state-duration segments: $((s_1, d_1), \ldots, (s_l, d_l))$.

3.3   Clustering Change Point Vertices

The state duration pair assignments $((s_1, d_1), \ldots, (s_l, d_l))$ run-length encode temporal appearance discontinuities within an observation sequence. For any given pixel location (i, j), the temporal location of the kth discontinuity can be computed as $t_k = \sum_{m=1}^{k-1} d_m$, recovering a vertex in three dimensions representing a local temporal appearance discontinuity at video frame location (i, j, t_k).

Each local temporal discontinuity (change point vertex) is connected to its four nearest neighbors as shown in fig. 4b. Figure 4b visualizes per-pixel intensity sequences from video as vertical columns. The beginning of semi-homogeneous temporal subsegments, the change point vertices, are shown as black spheres. Edges are created that connect a given change point vertex to its closest neighbor in each of its four nearest columns (pixel sequences). Each edge is weighted by the absolute difference in expected value of the state conditional emission distribution for the state assigned to the respective change vertex by the learning algorithm in 3.2. The graph-based clustering algorithm described in [4] is used to spatially group per-pixel temporal discontinuities based on similar appearance. While any spatially aware clustering method could be used, the algorithm in [4] is not only extremely fast in practice, easily scaling to millions of change point vertices, but has favorable theoretical complexity guarantees and is a standard tool in the computer vision community. The graph segmentation algorithm defines a spatial scale parameter which is set to 300 in all experiments.

4   Detecting Change

A background model is created by first dividing the image plane into a non-overlapping grid of cells. During a training phase, each change point hull is assigned to a grid cell according to the majority membership of its vertices. First, a threshold is applied to the smallest eigenvalue of the change point hull. If the smallest eignvalue is greater than τ_w, it is assumed the hull does not fit a planar model and thus does not represent coherent motion and is discarded. For all remaining change point hulls, the angle of the normal direction of the hull is computed with respect to the reference by projecting the smallest eigenvector of the data covariance matrix decomposition onto the image plane. For each cell of the grid, a 2d histogram of normal directions and absolute value of the smallest eigenvalue, a measure of how well a planar model fits the change point hull, is maintained as a background model.

During testing, the eigenvalue threshold τ_w is again applied to each change hull, discarding hulls which do not fit a planar model. The remaining change hulls are assigned to grid cells and compared with the background histogram. Deviations,from the background model are determined by thresholding the joint probability of a change hull's normal direction and smallest singular value with respect to the background model by a constant τ_h. All vertices that comprise a hull deemed to be abnormal are labeled as change. In all experiments, the grid cell size was set to 20×20 pixels, $\tau_w = 0.3$ and $\tau_h = 0.2$ and empirically determined.

5   Empirical Results and Discussion

Figures 5 and 6 visualize the results of the proposed change detection system. In figure 5, a person walks into the scene from right to left, and most of the person is detected as change. However, his pants are a very similar color to the hallway rendering it difficult to detect appearance discontinuities between the pants and the background resulting in false negatives on the pedestrians legs.

Figure 6 shows a different pedestrian walking into view, stopping in the center before continuing off frame. Again, most pixels associated with the pedestrian are

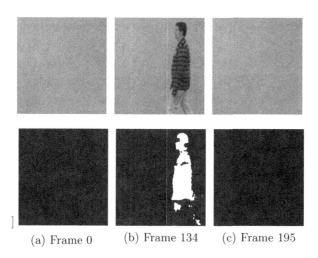

    (a) Frame 0   (b) Frame 134   (c) Frame 195

Fig. 5. Detecting changes in a scene monitoring a hallway. The top row are the original frames of video, the bottom visualizes changes detected by the algorithm as white pixels and black as background.

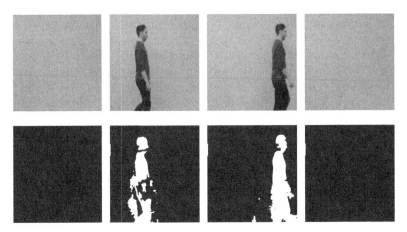

Fig. 6. Change detection results for person walking into a scene, stopping, then continuing forward. The top row are the original frames and the bottom visualizes detected changes as white and background is colored black.

detected, however there are a few errors owing to the similar color of the background to the pedestrians skin color and shadows.

The proposed change point vertices and hulls show promise as effective features for change detection. Future work will focus on coupling the planar model and change point hull clustering algorithm for directly segmenting locally planar spatio-temporal appearance discontinuities rather than the bottom up approach presented. Modules for detecting and removing shadows will also be incorporated to recover a more refined segmentation. Additionally, it is desirable that future work relax the fixed camera assumptions in order to extend the applicability of the described approach as more ego-centric and multi-view datasets have become commonplace.

References

1. Barnich, O., Van Droogenbroeck, M.: Vibe: A universal background subtraction algorithm for video sequences. IEEE Transactions on Image Processing **20**(6), 1709–1724 (2011). doi:10.1109/TIP.2010.2101613
2. Evangelio, R.H., Paetzold, M., Keller, I., Sikora, T.: Adaptively splitted gmm with feedback improvement for the task of background subtraction. IEEE TRANSACTIONS on Information Forensics and Security (accepted for publication)
3. Everingham, M., Van Gool, L., Williams, C., Winn, J., Zisserman, A.: The pascal visual object classes (voc) challenge. International Journal of Computer Vision **88**(2), 303–338 (2010). doi:10.1007/s11263-009-0275-4. http://dx.doi.org/10.1007/s11263-009-0275-4
4. Felzenszwalb, P.F., Huttenlocher, D.P.: Efficient graph-based image segmentation. International Journal of Computer Vision **59** (2004)
5. Guédon, Y.: Estimating hidden semi-markov chains from discrete sequences. Journal of Computational and Graphical Statistics **12**(3), 604–639 (2003). http://www.jstor.org/stable/1391041

6. Hofmann, M., Tiefenbacher, P., Rigoll, G.: Background segmentation with feedback: the pixel-based adaptive segmenter. In: 2012 IEEE Computer Society Conference on Computer Vision and Pattern Recognition Workshops, CVPRW, pp. 38–43 (2012). doi:10.1109/CVPRW.2012.6238925

7. Kaewtrakulpong, P., Bowden, R.: An improved adaptive background mixture model for real-time tracking with shadow detection. In: Proceedings of 2nd European Workshop on Advanced Video Based Surveillance Systems, vol. 5308 (2001)

8. Kim, K., Chalidabhongse, T.H., Harwood, D., Davis, L.S.: Real-time foreground-background segmentation using codebook model. Real-time Imaging **11**, 172–185 (2005). doi:10.1016/j.rti.2004.12.004

9. Levinson, S.: Continuously variable duration hidden markov models for automatic speech recognition. Computer Speech & Language **1**(1), 29–45 (1986). doi:10.1016/S0885-2308(86)80009-2. http://www.sciencedirect.com/science/article/pii/S0885230886800092

10. Mayer, B.A., Mundy, J.L.: Duration dependent codebooks for change detection. In: Proceedings of the British Machine Vision Conference, BMVC (2014)

11. Pirsiavash, H., Ramanan, D.: Detecting activities of daily living in first-person camera views. In: 2012 IEEE Conference on Computer Vision and Pattern Recognition (CVPR). IEEE (2012)

12. Porikli, F., Wren, C.: Change detection by frequency decomposition: wave-back. In: Proc. of Workshop on Image Analysis for Multimedia Interactive Services (2005)

13. Russakovsky, O., Deng, J., Su, H., Krause, J., Satheesh, S., Ma, S., Huang, Z., Karpathy, A., Khosla, A., Bernstein, M., Berg, A.C., Fei-Fei, L.: ImageNet Large Scale Visual Recognition Challenge (2014). arXiv:1409.0575

14. Stauffer, C., Grimson, W.E.L.: Adaptive background mixture modelsfor real-time tracking. In: IEEE Computer Society Conference on Computer Vision and Pattern Recognition, vol. 2, p. 252 (1999). doi:10.1109/CVPR.1999.784637

15. Zhang, S., Yao, H., Liu, S.: Dynamic background modeling and subtraction using spatio-temporal local binary patterns. In: 15th IEEE International Conference on Image Processing, ICIP 2008, pp. 1556–1559 (2008). doi:10.1109/ICIP.2008.4712065

Progressive Visual Object Detection
with Positive Training Examples Only

Ekaterina Riabchenko[1]([✉]), Ke Chen[2], and Joni-Kristian Kämäräinen[2]

[1] Department of Mathematics and Physics, Lappeenranta University of Technology,
Lappeenranta, Finland
`ekaterina.riabchenko@lut.fi`
[2] Department of Signal Processing, Tampere University of Technology,
Tampere, Finland

Abstract. Density-aware generative algorithms learning from positive examples have verified high recall for visual object detection, but such generative methods suffer from excessive false positives which leads to low precision. Inspired by the recent success of detection-recognition pipeline with deep neural networks, this paper proposes a two-step framework by training a generative detector with positive samples first and then utilising a discriminative model to get rid of false positives in those detected bounding box candidates by the generative detector. Evidently, the discriminative model can be viewed as a post-processing step which improves the robustness by distinguishing true positives from false positives that confuse the generative detector. We exemplify the proposed approach on public ImageNet classes to demonstrate the significant improvement on precision while using only positive examples in training.

Keywords: Object detection · Generative learning · Discriminative learning · Gabor features · Histogram of oriented gradients (HOG)

1 Introduction

The problem of visual object class detection has been actively investigated in the vision community for more than ten years. With the development of datasets (increasing the dataset size and introducing the challenging images largely varying in pose, scale, lighting conditions, etc.), a number of algorithms have been proposed to cope with such a problem. The first generation datasets, e.g., UIUC car dataset [1] or Caltech-4 [11], contained only a few classes with hundreds of examples, and almost perfect results were obtained with generative part-based models [6,11]. These generative models were part-based describing appearance of local parts and tolerating their spatial distortion, but the most popular approaches were based on visual Bag-of-Words (BoW) [25], which omitted spatial structure of object parts and described the classes via their local part histograms. With the help of strong discriminative learning methods, the BoW approach

© Springer International Publishing Switzerland 2015
R.R. Paulsen and K.S. Pedersen (Eds.): SCIA 2015, LNCS 9127, pp. 388–399, 2015.
DOI: 10.1007/978-3-319-19665-7_32

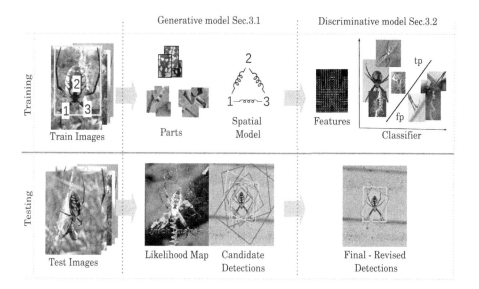

Fig. 1. Workflow of our proposed approach for visual object detection. To train a generative model, only positive instances of each object class with annotated bounding boxes and semantic object parts are employed. The true positive and false positive detections, obtained from generative model with training images, are used as positive and negative input examples of a discriminative model, which learns to discover their dissimilarities. During testing candidate object detections of the generative method are re-scored with the discriminative method, leading to the reduction of false positives and therefore the increase in precision. Here *tp* denotes true positives and *fp* - false positives.

obtained the top accuracy [4] on the second generation datasets, e.g., Caltech-101 [9]. However, discriminative approaches with BoW features failed when they were applied to objects with severe view point changes and occlusion, so the concept of explicit local parts to describe objects were resurrected. The Deformable Part Model (DPM) is the state-of-the-art discriminative part-based approach being constantly within the top performers in the third generation datasets, e.g., the annual Pascal VOC challenge [8]. Recently, the fourth generation datasets, such as ImageNet [24] and COCO [20], appear with thousands of classes and examples within them. The DPM model is clearly below the state-of-the-art [13,29], but other discriminative model still dominate the field. In particular, the deep neural networks [13,16] which have shown to implicitly learn a local part detector layers [14]. However, the complementary property of generative learning is that learning requires only positive examples. This leads to a large number of false positives which can be avoided by modelling the "no-class" (background) distribution to compute posterior probabilities for detection [9]. Detection fails if an ad hoc modelled background model or selected examples are poor.

To overcome the main limitation of the generative approach and still learn from positive examples only, this paper proposes a progressive generative-discriminative pipeline for object detection. The pipeline exploits the complementary properties of the two approaches: i) generative models first capturing the appearance distribution of a class and producing compact intra-class variance and ii) discriminative models learning the decision boundary between correct and false positives producing large inter-class variance. By separating these stages as compared to the existing monolithic systems, we can establish a generative-discriminative model for visual class detection (Fig. 1). Similar mechanism was introduced in Regions with Convolutional Neural Networks (RCNN) [13], which utilises a general objectness detector [2] to generate a large number of bounding box candidates and then applies the CNN classifier to obtain true positives in the images. Our system differs from their approach rather strongly in the sense that 1) our generative model produces much less candidates (i.e., two orders of magnitude reduction) and 2) requires only positive examples. Intuitively, our proposed framework can be viewed as a progressive coarse-to-fine pipeline: first localise the candidate locations with a generative object detector and then find true objects among those candidates with discriminative model. We exemplify our hypothesis using the recent bio-inspired fully probabilistic Generative Object Detector (GOD) [22,23] and the state-of-the-art discriminative DPM model [10]. We demonstrate that superior precision-recall with challenging ImageNet classes can be achieved for the proposed two-stage pipeline.

2   Related Work

Visual Object Detection – The problem of object detection, which is to localise and classify objects appearing in still images, is a hot topic in computer vision. Due to challenges posed by variations in scale, pose, appearance, and lighting conditions, the problem attracts wide attention and a number of algorithms have been proposed. Existing object detection algorithms can be divided into two categories: model-free methods [3,4,13,25,29] and model-based methods [1,6,10,11,22,23]. Specifically, the difference between model-free methods and model-based methods lie on the usage of the explicit object models with constraints between object parts. In the stream of model-free methods, the discrimination of feature representation plays a dominating role mitigating large variations of pose, scale and appearance, thus spatial pyramids of Bag-of-Words [17] and more recent deep features [13,29] were adopted. On the other hand, with introducing the object models, both the appearance of local object parts and geometric correlation between object parts can be simultaneously learned in a unique framework. In earlier work of generative part-based constellation algorithms [11], location of parts was limited and only a sparse set of candidates, selected by a saliency detector, was considered. In [6], the proposed pictorial structure model can tolerate the changes of pose and geometric deformation of object, but label annotation for each object part was required. Alternatively, Riabchenko et al [22,23] employed the bio-inspired Gabor features and Gaussian Mixture Models to capture both local appearance of parts and inter-part spatial correlation. Compared to the generative object detectors, the discriminative frameworks have also been proposed and achieved the superior detection performance. In discriminative multi-instance learning [10], the positive instances with weak labels (i.e., only the bounding boxes for the whole object and no annotated labels for parts) and negative instances are used to localise both the object and also its parts with latent SVM.

Generative-Discriminative Approaches – Presented in [26] and described in the Sec. 1 advantages and disadvantages of discriminative and generative approaches in object recognition inspire researchers to develop a hybrid system to take the best of both paradigms. Specifically, hybrid generative-discriminative approaches have been widely proposed in different applications of computer vision such as scene classification [5], tracking [19] and image classification [18]. The hybrid approaches for visual object recognition can be divided into two categories: feature encoding based [18,21] and learning based [12,15,28]. On one hand, in [21], generative part is used to encode a multi-level representation, which is then fed into a discriminative classifier for object recognition. On the other hand, most of the existing hybrid approaches [15,28] incorporated discriminative classifier into a generative framework to improve the discrimination of the model. Framework in [12] shares similar structure as the proposed algorithm, but in our framework generative and discriminative stages are based on different and more generic features (Gabors and HOGs), while in [12] the same codebook representation is used by both stages of the hybrid system.

Contributions – The novelties and contributions of this paper are three-fold:
- The principle of the proposed generative-discriminative framework is a genetic paradigm for visual object detection, which generative and discriminative parts in our algorithm can be replaced readily by any detector.
- The observation that discriminative model can be utilised to improve the precision of generative detector is exploited in a coarse-to-fine manner.
- The experiments with the recent benchmarking ImageNet dataset verify the effectiveness of the proposed algorithm[1].

3   Methodology

As shown in Fig. 1, the pipeline of the proposed framework can be divided into generative part (see Sec. 3.1) and discriminative part (see Sec. 3.2). Sec. 3.3 presents the specifics of the generative-discriminative hybrid formulation.

3.1   Generative Object Detector (GOD)

The generative object detection, e.g., constellation model [11], is employed for object detection because of its capability of handling complex compositionality (large intra-class variations) [26]. In this section, we investigate the pipeline

---

[1] https://bitbucket.org/EkaterinaRiabchenko/gabor_object_detector_code/

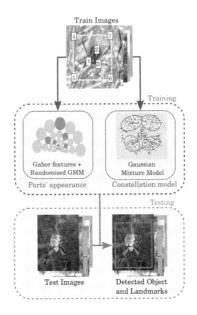

Train Images

Training

Gabor features +
Randomised GMM

Gaussian
Mixture Model

Parts' appearance   Constellation model

Testing

Test Images   Detected Object
and Landmarks

Fig. 2. The Generative Object Detector (GOD) framework for detecting visual classes.

of Generative Object Detector (GOD) [22], which general structure is shown in Fig. 2. In generative part-based object detection algorithm, both bounding boxes containing the whole object and manually-labelled object parts are used to train the model. Therefore, the suggested part-based GOD employs both local discriminative appearance of parts and also informative inter-part spatial arrangement.

To exclude the effect of geometric distortions on the object appearance model, all train images are aligned together prior to feature extraction. Images are aligned using homography transformation matching their parts' locations. In this aligned space object's structure becomes evident and is modelled along with the relative locations of the bounding box corners by the Gaussian mixture model. Each location is described with 2D Gaussian as illustrated in Fig. 2 (Constellation model). Object parts are modelled with the biologically inspired Gabor features, which have been successfully used in many vision applications. In order to reduce dimensionality of the features and provide a specifically optimised descriptor for each object part the concept of Randomised Gaussian Mixture Model is employed forming an appearance model [23].

During testing appearance model produces likelihood maps, which is then sampled for candidate locations of object parts with consecutive suppression procedure. The final step is the search for feasible object hypothesis (the required number of hypothesis can be predetermined), when candidate locations are pruned using constellation model and prior information about data statistics (Fig. 1 - Testing). Nevertheless, pruning still keeps a lot of false positive detections what results in relatively low precision in the presence of the high recall.

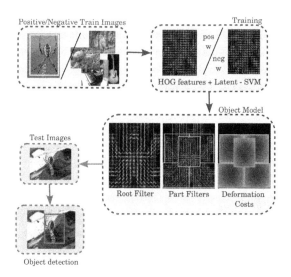

Fig. 3. The Discriminative Object Detector (DOD), e.g., deformable part-based model (DPM), for learning and detecting visual categories. Note that in our final system the negative training examples are produced by the GOD detector.

This observation and the fact that GOD scores are likelihoods - not posterior probabilities of object vs. non-object detection encourage us to add a discriminative part to solve the problem.

3.2 Discriminative Object Detector (DOD)

The discriminative models of visual class detection can be divided to scanning window and part-based models. A successful and popular example of the scanning window is the Viola-Jones detector [27]. The strength of the scanning window approach is conceptual simplicity, but the drawback is difficulty to capture distortions by view point change, occlusion and background clutter. Moreover, an effective scanning window method requires a large number of training examples.

Robustness to the distortions can be improved by dividing the window to sub-window bins and computing a histogram feature where the histogram dimensions represent the spatial structure as binned features [17]. This approach is adopted in the Histogram of Oriented Gradients (HOG) [7]. Local parts of objects are typically sufficiently rigid and therefore HOGs can capture them well. HOGs and HOG based deformable part-based model (DPM) [10] are used in our experiments as discriminative stage. The DPM has only a few tunable parameters, owing it to the fact that selection of the parts, learning their descriptors and learning the discriminative function for detection are all embedded in the latent support vector machine framework (see Fig. 3). Intuitively, DPM model is to alternatingly optimise the learning weights and the relative locations of deformable part filters in order to achieve high response in foreground and low response in background. With the learned DPM model, the part learned filters are used to scan the whole feature pyramid map to find regions with high response, which can finally determine locations of the object.

3.3   Hybrid Generative-Discriminative Pipeline

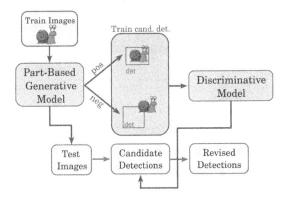

Fig. 4. Generative-discriminative hybrid approach.

The limitations of using either generative or discriminative approaches solely encourages us to develop a hybrid detector to overcome the limitations. In related work (Sec. 2) state-of-the-art hybrid approaches were described, encouraging us to adopt a two-stage pipeline of a discriminative object detector to improve the detection performance of a generative one. In this pipeline the discriminative object detector can be viewed as a post-processing stage of the generative object detector. Fig. 4 illustrates the pipeline of the proposed hybrid method.

The generative method is trained by positive examples of the query image category with annotated object parts and bounding boxes. Discriminative method, on the other hand, uses the training stage outputs of the generative method as its inputs. Candidate detections of the generative method are transformed to the aligned space using the detected part locations. After alignment detections are scaled to the size 64×64 pixels and subsequently fed to the discriminative part for re-scoring. Generative output candidates having bounding box overlap ratio $A > 0.7$ with the ground truth are used as positive examples in discriminative training and the outputs with $A < 0.2$ as the negatives. This representation of positive and negative data allows the discriminative method to learn, exploit and emphasise the difference in appearance of the true positives and false positives that the generative part produces but is blind itself [13]. During testing the discriminative re-scoring procedure is applied to all detection candidates produced by generative method on the test data. These re-scored detections of the discriminative stage are further processed by non-maximum suppression which removes spatially overlapping candidates. Non-maximum suppression removes candidates hyp_i with lower scores if their overlap ratio is greater than 0.5:

$$\frac{B_{hyp1} \cap B_{hyp2}}{B_{hyp1} \cup B_{hyp2}} \geq 0.5 \ . \tag{1}$$

4 Experiments

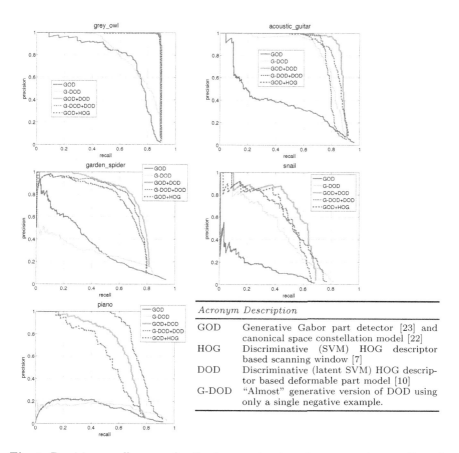

Fig. 5. Precision-recall curves for the Imagenet categories *grey owl*, *acoustic guitar*, *garden spider*, *snail* and *piano*. All methods use generative and use only positive examples in training.

4.1   Settings

Five challenging categories from the ImageNet database were used in our experiments: acoustic guitar, piano, snail, garden spider and grey owl. Categories are represented with objects appearing in different scales, orientations, lighting conditions, with limited 3D pose changes and moderate intra-class variation and were randomly divided into training and testing groups of approximately the same size.

4.2   Performance Metrics

A widely accepted measure for the object detection accuracy, overlap ratio, is used in our work. Overlap ratio A reflects precision of bounding box based object localisation. Object is considered to be located correctly if $A > 0.5$, where A is equal to intersection/union ratio of the ground truth and candidate (hypothesis) detection:

$$A = \frac{B_{gt} \cap B_{hyp}}{B_{gt} \cup B_{hyp}} \ . \tag{2}$$

In general, a generative method can produce a large number of hypotheses to guarantee that at least one passes the test in (2). That would result high recall, but poor precision which is the problem of generative methods. The discriminative part of the proposed pipeline aims to reduce the number of *false positives* (fp) by keeping the number of *true positives* (tp) high. Therefore it is meaningful to compute precision and recall values in the following way:

$$Precision = \frac{tp}{tp + fp}, \quad Recall = \frac{tp}{\text{Total number of positives}}.$$

4.3   Results

The results of various implementations of the proposed pipeline are shown in Fig. 5. The implementations are based on the publicly available code: Gabor object detector (GOD) by the authors [22,23], scanning window based detector (HOG) by Dalal and Triggs [7], and the state-of-the-art discriminative part-based model (DOD) by Felzenszwalb et. al. [10]. In addition to the standard DOD we constructed a generative version of it (G-DOD) by allowing only a single negative example. From the results in Fig. 5 it is obvious that the plain generative methods (GOD, G-DOD) achieve high recall but poor precision - they detect the correct class, but are also triggered by many other things. The tested progressive generative-discriminative combinations (GOD+DOD, G-DOD+DOD, GOD+HOG) achieve almost the same recall as the generative, but with significantly better precision. The two strongest combinations are GOD+DOD and G-DOD+DOD indicating the superiority of the part-based approaches.

5 Conclusions

This paper proposes a hybrid generative-discriminative learning paradigm for visual class detection - a paradigm where the generative part generates detection candidates and the discriminative part learns to separate true and false positives. In the experiments, the paradigm significantly improved performance of generative detectors which is explained by the two-stage system where the discriminative stage mitigates the presence of excessive false positives. Our results indicate that despite the huge popularity of the discriminative learning in visual class detection, also the generative approach without ad hoc background modelling can be adopted, but needs to be paired with the discriminative true positive classifier. Our results show that this can be achieved without sacrificing the main properties of generative learning: training with positive examples only and presence of other classes does not affect the trained detector. We believe that the proposed framework can be facilitated in large scale visual problems where the best part-based discriminative methods (e.g., [10]) fail due to ambiguity between fine-grained class differences [29].

Acknowledgments. This work is funded by Academy of Finland under the grant no. 267581.

References

1. Agarwal, S., Roth, D.: Learning a sparse representation for object detection. In: Heyden, A., Sparr, G., Nielsen, M., Johansen, P. (eds.) ECCV 2002, Part IV. LNCS, vol. 2353, pp. 113–127. Springer, Heidelberg (2002)
2. Alexe, B., Deselaers, T., Ferrari, V.: Measuring the objectness of image windows. IEEE Transactions on Pattern Analysis and Machine Intelligence **34**(11), 2189–2202 (2012)
3. Blaschko, M.B., Lampert, C.H.: Learning to localize objects with structured output regression. In: Forsyth, D., Torr, P., Zisserman, A. (eds.) ECCV 2008, Part I. LNCS, vol. 5302, pp. 2–15. Springer, Heidelberg (2008)
4. Bosch, A., Zisserman, A., Munoz, X.: Image classification using random forests and ferns. In: IEEE International Conference on Computer Vision, ICCV 2007, pp. 1–8 (2007)
5. Bosch, A., Zisserman, A., Muoz, X.: Scene classification using a hybrid generative/discriminative approach. IEEE Transactions on Pattern Analysis and Machine Intelligence **30**(4), 712–727 (2008)
6. Crandall, D., Felzenszwalb, P., Huttenlocher, D.: Spatial priors for part-based recognition using statistical models. In: IEEE Computer Society Conference on Computer Vision and Pattern Recognition, CVPR 2005, vol. 1, pp. 10–17 (2005)
7. Dalal, N., Triggs, B.: Histograms of oriented gradients for human detection. In: IEEE Computer Society Conference on Computer Vision and Pattern Recognition, CVPR 2005, vol. 1, pp. 886–893 (2005)
8. Everingham, M., Van Gool, L., Williams, C.K.I., Winn, J., Zisserman, A.: The PASCAL Visual Object Classes Challenge 2012 (VOC2012) Results (2012). http://www.pascal-network.org/challenges/VOC/voc2012/workshop/index.html

9. Fei-Fei, L., Fergus, R., Perona, P.: Learning generative visual models from few training examples: an incremental bayesian approach tested on 101 object categories. Computer Vision and Image Understanding **106**(1), 59–70 (2007)

10. Felzenszwalb, P.F., Girshick, R.B., McAllester, D., Ramanan, D.: Object detection with discriminatively trained part-based models. IEEE Transactions on Pattern Analysis and Machine Intelligence **32**(9), 1627–1645 (2010)

11. Fergus, R., Perona, P., Zisserman, A.: Object class recognition by unsupervised scale-invariant learning. In: IEEE Computer Society Conference on Computer Vision and Pattern Recognition, CVPR 2003, vol. 2, pp. 264–271 (2003)

12. Fritz, M., Leibe, B., Caputo, B., Schiele, B.: Integrating representative and discriminant models for object category detection. In: IEEE International Conference on Computer Vision, ICCV 2005, vol. 2, pp. 1363–1370 (2005)

13. Girshick, R., Donahue, J., Darrell, T., Malik, J.: Rich feature hierarchies for accurate object detection and semantic segmentation. In: Computing Research Repository arXiv.org, CoRR. vol. abs/1311.2524 (2013)

14. Girshick, R.B., Iandola, F.N., Darrell, T., Malik, J.: Deformable part models are convolutional neural networks. CoRR abs/1409.5403 (2014). http://arxiv.org/abs/1409.5403

15. Kapoor, A., Winn, J.M.: Located hidden random fields: learning discriminative parts for object detection. In: Leonardis, A., Bischof, H., Pinz, A. (eds.) ECCV 2006. LNCS, vol. 3953, pp. 302–315. Springer, Heidelberg (2006)

16. Krizhevsky, A., Sutskever, I., Hinton, G.: Imagenet classification with deep convolutional neural networks. In: NIPS (2012)

17. Lazebnik, S., Schmid, C., Ponce, J.: Beyond bags of features: spatial pyramid matching for recognizing natural scene categories. In: IEEE Computer Society Conference on Computer Vision and Pattern Recognition, CVPR 2006, vol. 2, pp. 2169–2178 (2006)

18. Li, Y., Shapiro, L.G., Bilmes, J.A.: A generative/discriminative learning algorithm for image classification. In: IEEE International Conference on Computer Vision, ICCV 2005, vol. 2, pp. 1605–1612 (2005)

19. Lin, R.S., Ross, D., Lim, J., Yang, M.H.: Adaptive discriminative generative model and its applications. In: Advances in neural information processing systems, NIPS 2004, pp. 801–808. The MIT Press (2004)

20. Lin, T.-Y., Maire, M., Belongie, S., Hays, J., Perona, P., Ramanan, D., Dollár, P., Zitnick, C.L.: Microsoft COCO: common objects in context. In: Fleet, D., Pajdla, T., Schiele, B., Tuytelaars, T. (eds.) ECCV 2014, Part V. LNCS, vol. 8693, pp. 740–755. Springer, Heidelberg (2014)

21. Perina, A., Cristani, M., Castellani, U., Murino, V., Jojic, N.: A hybrid generative/discriminative classification framework based on free-energy terms. In: IEEE International Conference on Computer Vision, ICCV 2009, pp. 2058–2065 (2009)

22. Riabchenko, E., Kämäräinen, J.K., Chen, K.: Density-aware part-based object detection with positive examples. In: International Conference on Pattern Recognition, ICPR 2014. IEEE (2014)

23. Riabchenko, E., Kämäräinen, J.K., Chen, K.: Learning generative models of object parts from a few positive examples. In: International Conference on Pattern Recognition, ICPR 2014. IEEE (2014)

24. Russakovsky, O., Deng, J., Huang, Z., Berg, A.C., Fei-Fei, L.: Detecting avocados to zucchinis: what have we done, and where are we going? In: IEEE International Conference on Computer Vision, ICCV 2013, pp. 2064–2071 (2013)

25. Sivic, J., Zisserman, A.: Video google: A text retrieval approach to object matching in videos. In: IEEE International Conference on Computer Vision, ICCV 2003, pp. 1470–1477 (2003)
26. Ulusoy, I., Bishop, C.M.: Generative versus discriminative methods for object recognition. In: IEEE Computer Society Conference on Computer Vision and Pattern Recognition, CVPR 2005, vol. 2, pp. 258–265 (2005)
27. Viola, P., Jones, M.: Robust real-time face detection. International journal of computer vision **57**(2), 137–154 (2004)
28. Zhang, D.Q., Chang, S.F.: A generative-discriminative hybrid method for multi-view object detection. In: IEEE Computer Society Conference on Computer Vision and Pattern Recognition, CVPR 2006, vol. 2, pp. 2017–2024 (2006)
29. Zhang, N., Donahue, J., Girshick, R., Darrell, T.: Part-based R-CNNs for fine-grained category detection. In: Fleet, D., Pajdla, T., Schiele, B., Tuytelaars, T. (eds.) ECCV 2014, Part I. LNCS, vol. 8689, pp. 834–849. Springer, Heidelberg (2014)

RSD-HoG: A New Image Descriptor

Darshan Venkatrayappa[(✉)], Philippe Montesinos, Daniel Diep,
and Baptiste Magnier

Ecole des Mines D'Ales, LGI2P, Parc Scientifique Georges Besses,
30035 Nimes, France
{darshan.venkatrayappa,philippe.montesinos,daniel.diep,
baptiste.magnier}@mines-ales.fr

Abstract. In this paper we propose a novel local image descriptor called RSD-HoG. For each pixel in a given support region around a key-point, we extract the rotation signal descriptor(RSD) by spinning a filter made of oriented anisotropic half-gaussian derivative convolution kernel. The obtained signal has extremums at different orientations of the filter. These characteristics are combined with a HoG technique, to obtain a novel descriptor RSD-HoG. The obtained descriptor has rich, discriminative set of local information related to the curvature of the image surface. With these rich set of features, our descriptor finds applications in various branches of computer vision. For evaluation, we have used the standard Oxford data set which has rotation, brightness, illumination, compression and viewpoint changes. Extensive experiments on these images demonstrates that our approach performs better than many state of the art descriptors such as SIFT, GLOH, DAISY and PCA-SIFT.

Keywords: Image descriptor · Half gaussian kernel · Feature matching · Rotation signal descriptor · HoG

1 Introduction

In computer vision, problems related to object matching, tracking, panorama generation, image classification, structure and motion estimation are effectively addressed by the popular approach of image representation by a set of local image descriptors. The main purpose of local image descriptor is to capture the geometry of a support region around a key-point. In addition to this, the image descriptor should be invariant to certain image transformations such as rotation, brightness, blurring and scale changes. Scanning through the computer vision literature, one can come across the term image matching pipeline. The image matching pipeline has four stages. In the first stage, key-points or regions are selected using the popular detectors such as LoG[2], DoG [3] or Harris Affine [4]. This is followed by the extraction of features or feature description from the support region around the key-point. Next, various post processing steps such as normalization[3], quantization[5] and dimensionality reduction[1] is

© Springer International Publishing Switzerland 2015
R.R. Paulsen and K.S. Pedersen (Eds.): SCIA 2015, LNCS 9127, pp. 400–409, 2015.
DOI: 10.1007/978-3-319-19665-7_33

applied. The final block involves matching the descriptor using different distance measures such as euclidean distance[3], hamming distance[6], Earth Mover's Distance(EMD)[7].

We are mainly interested in the second stage of the above described pipeline. The popular approach to extract features from a support region is to use the Histogram of Gradients(HoG)[8]. SIFT[3] effectively makes use of HoG to generate a descriptor. In PCA-SIFT[1] the dimension of the SIFT descriptor is reduced by applying the PCA technique. GLOH[9] and DAISY[10] use radial and daisy binning strategies respectively to improve on the existing SIFT descriptor. The standard version of SURF[11] achieves speed-up over SIFT by using Haar wavelets. MROGH[12] and MRRID[12] improve on the rotational invariance aspect by pooling local features based on their intensity orders in multiple support regions. In RIFF[13], radial and tangential components are extracted from the support region to form the descriptor. CSLBP[14] and MRRID[12] use local binary patterns to encode the image structure in the support region. A detailed evaluation of these descriptors can be found in[25].

There is a line of research oriented towards object recognition and image matching on camera-enabled mobile devices (e.g. phones and tablets). Limited computational power and storage space on these devices has enabled the emergence of binary descriptors. The main idea behind binary descriptor is that each bit is independent and Hamming distance can be used as similarity measure. Some of the most popular binary descriptors are BRIEF[6], ORB[15], BRISK[16] and FREAK[17]. A detailed evaluation of these descriptors can be found in[18].

Filter responses has been used in abundance for image description. Schmid and Mohr[19] use differential invariant responses to compute new local image descriptors. Differential invariant responses are obtained from a combination of Gaussian derivatives of different orders, which are invariant to 2-dimensional rigid transformations. Larsen et al.[20] follow a new approach for the construction of an image descriptor based on local k-jet, which uses filter bank responses for feature description. Palomares et al.[21] have come up with a local image descriptor issued from a filtering stage made of oriented anisotropic half-gaussian smoothing convolution kernels. In their work the authors use euclidean invariance is achieved by FFT correlation between the two signatures/descriptors. Moderate deformation invariance is achieved using Dynamic Time Warping (DTW).

The contributions of this paper include a new approach for descriptor generation. We embed the response of an anisotropic half Gaussian kernel in a HoG framework. For each pixel in the support region a rotation signal descriptor(RSD) is extracted by spinning a filter made of oriented anisotropic half-Gaussian derivative convolution kernel. We select two orientations at which a global maxima and a global minima occurs. Thus, for each pixel in the support region we have two orientations and a magnitude. These orientations are binned by weighing them with the magnitude.

2   Methodology

2.1   Image-Processing

Isotropic Gaussian filters Fig.1(a), Fig.1(b) are widely used for smoothing images. But, it is well known that this type of filters blur the image features. Gaussian anisotropic filtering overcome this by preserving the features along a particular direction. Compared to isotropic filters, anisotropic filters are elongated along one of the directions. Fig.1(c) and Fig.1(d) shows smoothing and derivative anisotropic filters respectively. We use a filter made of anisotropic half Gaussian derivative kernel as in [22] [23]. An anisotropic half-Gaussian derivative filter 1(f) is designed with a Gaussian half-smoothing filter in Y direction and a derivative Gaussian filter in X direction. The filtering in the Y direction acts as a causal integration, as the filtering in X direction is a full derivative. Then, rotating the filter around pixels generates a description around the pixels. Applying such filters on an edge point will produce a minima and a maxima in two directions. On a straight line edge these two direction are exactly opposite (180°), but generally the difference of angles reflects the curvature at edge points.

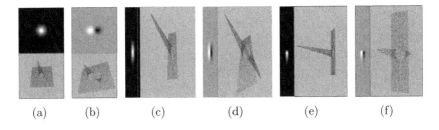

(a)   (b)   (c)   (d)   (e)   (f)

Fig. 1. (a) Isotropic smoothing filter. (b) Isotropic derivative filter. (c) Anisotropic smoothing filter. (d) Anisotropic derivative filter. (e) Half anisotropic smoothing filter. (f) Half anisotropic derivative filter.

As shown in Fig 2(a). at pixel (x, y), a derivative kernel is applied to obtain a derivative information $\varphi(x, y, \theta)$ in a function of orientation $\theta \in [0; 360°[$:

$$\varphi(x, y, \theta) = I_\theta * C \cdot H(-y) \cdot x \cdot e^{-\left(\frac{x^2}{2\lambda^2} + \frac{y^2}{2\mu^2}\right)} \tag{1}$$

Where I_θ corresponds to a rotated image of orientation θ, C is a normalization coefficient, (x, y) are pixel coordinates, and (μ, λ) the standard deviation of the anisotropic Gaussian kernel. Only the causal part of this filter along the Y axis is used. This is obtained by cutting the kernel in the middle, in an operation that corresponds to the Heaviside function H. As in [23] we have chosen to rotate the image instead of the filter, there by reducing the algorithmic complexity by making use of a recursive Gaussian filter [24].

2.2   Rotational Signal Descriptor(RSD)

RSD is obtained by rotating the above described filter around a key-point. Fig. 2(c) shows a sample RSD obtained by applying the Gaussian derivative half filter at the the pixel location (x_p, y_p) in steps of $2°$. We compute the gradient $\|\nabla I\|$ and the two angles for the key-point/pixel at location (x_p, y_p) by considering the global extrema of the function $\mathcal{Q}(x_p, y_p, \theta)$. The two angles θ_1 and θ_2 define a curve crossing the pixel(an incoming and outgoing direction). Two of these global extrema are combined to maximize $\|\nabla I\|$, i.e :

$$
\begin{cases}
\|\nabla I\| = \max_{\theta \in [0,360°[} \mathcal{Q}(x_p, y_p, \theta) - \min_{\theta \in [0,360°[} \mathcal{Q}(x_p, y_p, \theta) \\
\theta_1 = \arg\max_{\theta \in [0,360°[} \left(\mathcal{Q}(x_p, y_p, \theta)\right) \\
\theta_2 = \arg\min_{\theta \in [0,360°[} \left(\mathcal{Q}(x_p, y_p, \theta)\right)
\end{cases}
\tag{2}
$$

We can spin an anisotropic half Gaussian derivative kernel at a key-point and the resulting response(RSD) can be considered as a descriptor. But, RSD alone gives a weak description, as it fails to capture the geometry around the key-point. This is the main motivation for combining the HoG technique with RSD.

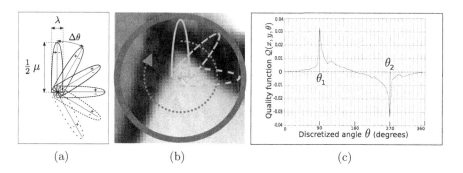

(a)   (b)   (c)

Fig. 2. (a) A thin rotating Gaussian derivative half-filter. (b) Half Gaussian kernel applied to a keypoint x_p, y_p. (c) Extrema of a function $\mathcal{Q}(x_p, y_p, \theta)$. $\mu = 10$, $\lambda = 1$ and $\Delta\theta = 2°$. Note that the initial orientation of the filter is vertical, upwardly directed and steerable clockwise.

2.3   Pre-Processing

Prior to feature extraction, the image is smoothed with a Gaussian filter. Then, key-points(regions) need to be localized. We have used Harris affine feature detector. It can also be noted that any of the existing feature detector can be used for this step. As in Fig. 3, we first extract image patches surrounding the key-points. Then, depending on the key-point attributes such as scale and orientations, we rotate the patch by its orientation. This is followed by scale normalizing the oriented patch to a fixed size of 41x41. More details about the process for patch extraction and normalization can be found in [4].

2.4 RSD-HoG Construction

The framework of the RSD-HOG extraction is illustrated in Fig. 3. On each pixel of the normalized patch, we apply the rotating semi Gaussian filter to obtain the RSD. From this RSD, we extract two angles and a magnitude for each pixel as explained above. Then we bin the two angles separately as in Eq.3 and Eq.4. The image patch is divided in to 16 blocks. Since the image patch is of size 41x41, most of the blocks are of size 10x10 (blocks on the extreme right and extreme bottom are of size 11x11). Each of these block contributes 8 bins to the final descriptor. We fuse the two intermediate descriptors to form the final descriptor as in Eq.5. The intermediate descriptors in Eq.3 and Eq.4 alone can be used as descriptors. But, fusing these two descriptors as in Eq.5 results in a more robust description. The performance of two intermediate descriptor and the final descriptor for the boat dataset(Rotation changes) can be seen in the first row of Fig.4.

$$RSD - HoG - Theta1 = \{\theta_{1_{bin1}}, \theta_{1_{bin2}}, \theta_{1_{bin3}}, \theta_{1_{bin4}} ..... \theta_{1_{bin128}}\} \qquad (3)$$

$$RSD - HoG - Theta2 = \{\theta_{2_{bin1}}, \theta_{2_{bin2}}, \theta_{2_{bin3}}, \theta_{2_{bin4}} ..... \theta_{2_{bin128}}\} \qquad (4)$$

$$RSD - HoG = \{\theta_{1_{bin1}}, \theta_{1_{bin2}}, ... \theta_{1_{bin128}}, \theta_{2_{bin1}}, \theta_{2_{bin2}}, ... \theta_{2_{bin128}}\} \qquad (5)$$

3 Experiments, Discussions and Results

3.1 Dataset and Evaluation

We evaluate and compare the performance of our descriptor against the state of the art descriptors on the standard dataset using the standard protocol provided

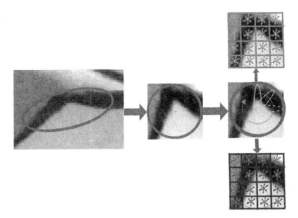

Fig. 3. Affine region is normalized to a square of size 41x41. On each pixel of the patch, RSD is generated and the two angles θ_1 and θ_2 are extracted. These angles are binned separately.

by Oxford group. The binaries and dataset are obtained from website linked to [25] (http://www.robots.ox.ac.uk/~vgg/research/affine/) . The dataset used in our experiments has different geometric and photometric transformations such as change of scale, image rotation, viewpoint change, image blur, JPEG compression and illumination change. For each type of image transformation there is a set of six images with established ground truth homographies.

Recall versus precision curves as proposed by [25] are used to evaluate our descriptor. This is based on the number of correspondences, correct matches and false matches obtained for an image pair. Number of correspondences is defined as the number of pairs of features whose euclidean distance is below a certain threshold. We vary the threshold in steps to obtain the recall vs precision curves. A correct match is recorded when the pair of features with the smallest euclidean distance coincides with the pair of points/regions matched by the ground-truth. As in Eq.6, recall is defined as the total number of correctly matched regions over the number of corresponding regions between two images of the same scene. From Eq.7, 1-precision is represented by the number of false matches relative to the total number of matches.

$$\text{recall} = \frac{\text{Total number of correct matches}}{\text{Number of correspondences}} \qquad (6)$$

$$1\text{-precision} = \frac{\text{Number of false matches}}{\text{Number of correct matches} + \text{Number of false matches}} \qquad (7)$$

3.2 Parameter Selection

Our descriptor has 4 different parameters that are tabulated in the table 1. The rotation step of the filter is fixed to 5°. Increasing the rotation step results in loss of information. We have fixed the number of bins to 8 per block, resulting in a $8*16 = 128$ bins for 16 blocks. Increasing the number of bins results in the same performance but, increases the dimensionality of the descriptor. All the parameters are chosen empirically.

Table 1. Parameters

filter Height (μ)	filter Width (λ)	Rotation step ($\Delta\theta$)	No of BINS
6	1	5°	8

3.3 Descriptor Performance

The performance of RSD-HoG is compared against SIFT-OXFORD, SIFT-PATCH, GLOH, DAISY and PCA-SIFT. For SIFT-OXFORD, PCA-SIFT and GLOH the descriptors are extracted from the binaries provided by Oxford group (http://www.robots.ox.ac.uk/~vgg/research/affine/)[25]. DAISY descriptor is

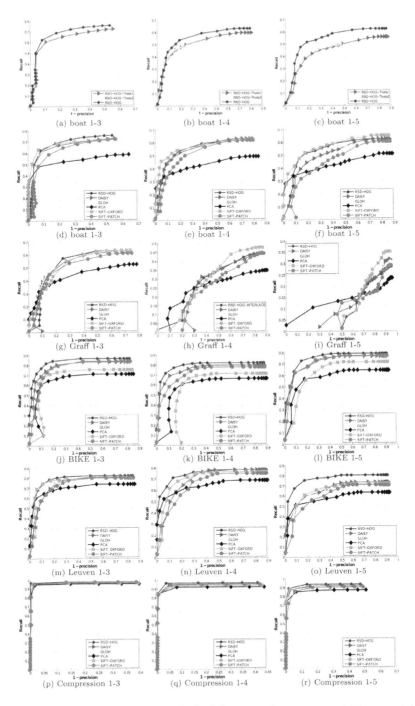

(a) boat 1-3

(b) boat 1-4

(c) boat 1-5

(d) boat 1-3

(e) boat 1-4

(f) boat 1-5

(g) Graff 1-3

(h) Graff 1-4

(i) Graff 1-5

(j) BIKE 1-3

(k) BIKE 1-4

(l) BIKE 1-5

(m) Leuven 1-3

(n) Leuven 1-4

(o) Leuven 1-5

(p) Compression 1-3

(q) Compression 1-4

(r) Compression 1-5

Fig. 4. Recall vs Precision curves for Oxford dataset using nearest neighbour matching method

extracted from the code provided by [10]. SIFT-PATCH is the SIFT descriptor applied on a patch using the VLFEAT library [26]. Due to lack of space we restrict ourself to image pairs(1-3),(1-4) and (1-5).

1. Rotation changes.
   First, we compare the performance of $RSD - HoG$ (Eq.5) with the intermediate descriptors $RSD - HOG - Theta1$ (Eq.3)and $RSD - HOG - Theta2$ (Eq.4). From the graphs in the first row of Fig.4 it is clear that $RSD - HoG$ performs better than the two intermediate descriptors. This is same for all the images with different transformations. Due to lack of space we restrict ourselves to graphs for rotational changes. When $RSD - HOG$ is compared with other descriptors it can be seen that our descriptor performs better than other descriptors. This can be seen in the 2nd row of Fig.4.

2. Viewpoint and Blur changes.
   Graphs in the third row of Fig.4 represent Recall vs Precision curves for the Viewpoint changes. It can be seen that for the first 2 cases (1-2),(1-3)and (1-4) $RSD - HoG$ performs similar to other descriptors. For the final case the performance of $RSD - HoG$ deteriorates. This is a challenging sequence and all the other descriptors perform badly. Graphs in the fourth row of Fig.4 represent Recall vs Precision curves for the Blur changes. From the graphs it is clear that $RSD - HoG$ outperforms other descriptors.

3. Brightness and Compression changes.
   Based on graphs in the fifth row of Fig.4, we conclude that the performance of $RSD - HoG$ is superior to the performance of other descriptors when it comes to handling Brightness variations. Similarly, graphs in the last row of Fig.4 illustrate the dominance of our descriptor for compression variations.

4 Conclusion

This paper proposes a new image descriptor called RSD-HoG. It also proposes a new approach to construct the descriptor by interlacing the bins of the two intermediate descriptors. On the standard dataset provided by the Oxford group, RSD-HoG outperforms other state of the art descriptors. Currently, high complexity and the dimension of the descriptor are a major drawback. In the future we would like to reduce both the complexity and dimension of our descriptor. Here, we have used a fixed set of parameters for the anisotropic half Gaussian kernel. In the future, we would like to experiment with other variations of the anisotropic half Gaussian kernel. We would also like to focus on the real time implementation of our descriptor using parallel programming techniques. Another direction of our future work would be to test our approach on tasks related to object detection, writer classification and shape retrieval.

References

1. Ke, Y., Sukthankar, R.: PCA-SIFT: A more distinctive representation for local image descriptors. In: Computer Vision and Pattern Recognition(CVPR), pp. 506–513. IEEE Computer Society (2004)

2. Lindeberg, T.: Feature Detection with Automatic Scale Selection. International Journal of Computer Vision(IJCV) **30**, 79–116 (1998)
3. Lowe, D.G.: Distinctive Image Features from Scale-Invariant Keypoints. International Journal of Computer Vision(IJCV) **60**, 91–110 (2004)
4. Mikolajczyk, K., Schmid, C.: Scale & Affine Invariant Interest Point Detectors. International Journal of Computer Vision(IJCV) **60**, 63–86 (2004)
5. Chandrasekhar, V., Takacs, G., Chen, D.M., Tsai, S.S., Reznik, Y.A., Grzeszczuk, R., Girod, R.: Compressed Histogram of Gradients: A Low-Bitrate Descriptor. International Journal of Computer Vision(IJCV) **96**, 384–399 (2012)
6. Calonder, M., Lepetit, V., Özuysal, M., Trzcinski, T., Strecha, C., Fua, P.: BRIEF: Computing a Local Binary Descriptor Very Fast. IEEE Trans. Pattern Anal. Mach. Intell.(PAMI) **34**, 1281–1298 (2012)
7. Lazebnik, S., Schmid, C., Ponce, J.: A Sparse Texture Representation Using Local Affine Regions. IEEE Trans. Pattern Anal. Mach. Intell.(PAMI) **27**, 1256–1278 (2005)
8. Dalal, N., Triggs, T.: Histograms of oriented gradients for human detection. In: Computer Vision and Pattern Recognition(CVPR), pp. 886–893 (2005)
9. Mikolajczyk, M., Schmid, C.: A performance evaluation of local descriptors. IEEE Trans. Pattern Anal. Mach. Intell.(PAMI) **27**, 1615–1630 (2005)
10. Tola, E., Lepetit, V., Fua, P.: DAISY: An Efficient Dense Descriptor Applied to Wide Baseline Stereo. IEEE Trans. Pattern Anal. Mach. Intell.(PAMI) **32**, 815–830 (2010)
11. Bay, H., Ess, A., Tuytelaars, T., Van Gool, L.J.: Speeded-Up Robust Features (SURF). Computer Vision and Image Understanding **110**, 346–359 (2008)
12. Fan, B., Wu, F., Hu, Z.: Rotationally Invariant Descriptors Using Intensity Order Pooling. IEEE Trans. Pattern Anal. Mach. Intell.(PAMI) **34**, 2031–2045 (2012)
13. Takacs, G., Chandrasekhar, V., Tsai, S.S., Chen, D.M., Grzeszczuk, R., Girod, B.: Rotation-invariant fast features for large-scale recognition and real-time tracking. Sig. Proc.: Image Comm. **34**, 334–344 (2013)
14. Heikkilä, M., Pietikäinen, M., Schmid, C.: Description of interest regions with local binary patterns. Pattern Recognition **42**, 425–436 (2009)
15. Rublee, E., Rabaud, V., Konolige, K., Bradski, G.R.: ORB: An efficient alternative to SIFT or SURF. In: IEEE International Conference on Computer Vision, ICCV, pp. 2564–2571 (2009)
16. Leutenegger, S., Chli, M., Siegwart, R.: BRISK: binary robust invariant scalable keypoints. In: IEEE International Conference on Computer Vision, ICCV, pp. 2548–2555 (2011)
17. Alahi, A., Ortiz, R., Vandergheynst, P.: FREAK: fast retina keypoint. In: IEEE Conference on Computer Vision and Pattern Recognition, ICCV, pp. 510–517 (2012)
18. Figat, J., Kornuta, T., Kasprzak, W.: Performance evaluation of binary descriptors of local features. In: Chmielewski, L.J., Kozera, R., Shin, B.-S., Wojciechowski, K. (eds.) ICCVG 2014. LNCS, vol. 8671, pp. 187–194. Springer, Heidelberg (2014)
19. Schmid, C., Mohr, R.: Local grayvalue invariants for image retrieval. IEEE Transactions on Pattern Analysis and Machine Intelligence, 530–535 (1997)
20. Larsen, A.B.L., Darkner, S., Dahl, A.L., Pedersen, K.S.: Jet-based local image descriptors. In: Fitzgibbon, A., Lazebnik, S., Perona, P., Sato, Y., Schmid, C. (eds.) ECCV 2012, Part III. LNCS, vol. 7574, pp. 638–650. Springer, Heidelberg (2012)
21. Palomares, J.L., Montesinos, P., Diep, D.: A new affine invariant method for image matching. In: 3DIP Image Processing and Applications, vol. 8290 (2012)

22. Magnier, B., Montesinos, P.: Evolution of image regularization with PDEs toward a new anisotropic smoothing based on half kernels. In: SPIE, Image Processing: Algorithms and Systems XI (2013)
23. Montesinos, P., Magnier, B.: A new perceptual edge detector in color images. In: Blanc-Talon, J., Bone, D., Philips, W., Popescu, D., Scheunders, P. (eds.) ACIVS 2010, Part I. LNCS, vol. 6474, pp. 209–220. Springer, Heidelberg (2010)
24. Deriche, R.: Recursively implementing the gaussian and its derivatives. In: ICIP, pp. 263–267 (1992)
25. Mikolajczyk, K., Schmid, C.: A Performance Evaluation of Local Descriptors. IEEE Trans. Pattern Anal. Mach. Intell., 1615–1630 (2005)
26. Vedaldi, A., Fulkerson, B.: VLFeat: An Open and Portable Library of Computer Vision Algorithms (2008)

Using Motion Tracking to Detect Spontaneous Movements in Infants

Mikkel D. Olsen[✉], Anna Herskind, Jens Bo Nielsen,
and Rasmus R. Paulsen

Department of Applied Mathematics and Computer Science,
Technical University of Denmark, Richard Petersens Plads,
Building 324, 2800 Kgs. Lyngby, Denmark
mdol@dtu.dk

Abstract. We study the characteristics of infants' spontaneous movements, based on data obtained from a markerless motion tracking system. From the pose data, the set of features are generated from the raw joint-angles of the infants and different classifiers are trained and evaluated using annotated data. Furthermore, we look at the importance of different features and outline the most significant features for detecting spontaneous movements of infants. Using these findings for further analysis of infants' movements, this might be used to identify infants in risk of cerebral palsy.

Keywords: Motion analysis · Motion tracking · Movement classification · Motion features

1 Introduction

In the last decades, motion tracking has become more and more popular. Whether it is marker-based or markerless, vision-based or sensor-based, the common goal is to estimate the pose and movement of people. Since the introduction of the Microsoft Kinect depth sensor in 2010, motion tracking has become a relative easy problem to solve. Without much effort, the underlying pose and motion parameters can be obtained and the next step is thus to utilize these parameters. In relation to the initial purpose of the Kinect sensor, the extracted pose parameters was used as input to the Microsoft XBox console, to control the character within a computer game. However, the list of applications is far more comprehensive. In [1,2] the pose estimation is used to extract features such as speed and step length. Features like these can be used for recognizing people, based on their gait, as shown in [3]. Other studies do not focus on recognizing a specific person, but instead recognizing different actions, such as walking, running, boxing, jumping, etc. [4]. However, common for most studies is that they focus on recognizing movements, that are easy to differentiate from each other, such as walking/jumping/punching/etc. Recently, new studies and challenges consider the concept of looking at more similar actions, such as recognizing sign language gestures, where two gestures can seem very similar to

© Springer International Publishing Switzerland 2015
R.R. Paulsen and K.S. Pedersen (Eds.): SCIA 2015, LNCS 9127, pp. 410–417, 2015.
DOI: 10.1007/978-3-319-19665-7_34

the untrained observer [5]. In this study, we focus on movements of infants. It is known that infants in the age of 3-5 months have special movements called fidgety movements [6]. Among high-risk infants such as infants born preterm, absent or abnormal fidgity movements is a strong indicator for the motor disorder cerebral palsy. Doctors are thus able to identify a high risk of cerebral palsy, in the early months after birth, based on assessing these special movements. Small movements in the trunk, neck and limbs characterize these special movements. The movements are easiest to detect when the infant is lying on its back, unstimulated [7]. However, kicking and crying influences the infants' movements and the fidgety movements will be obscured by these larger movements. Moreover, a pacifier can completely dampen the strength of the fidgety movements. In order to be able to recognize the fidgety movements, one approach is to first detect and remove the sequences where the fidgety movements do not appear and secondly to classify the remaining movements. In this paper, we focus on the first step, where we classify sequences of motion data of awake infants, with the goal of segmenting the sequence into segments of spontaneous/non-spontaneous movements. The classification is based on features obtained from a vision based and markerless motion tracking approach. A number of previous studies focus on quantifying these spontaneous movements. In [8] the authors quantify spontaneous kicks by tethering the legs to a mobile stand. When the infant kicks, the mobile moves and this information is used for further analysis. In [9], a similar mobile system is combined with a 2D based motion tracking system. Using both the mobile-observations as well as the motion tracking results, the kicking frequency can be obtained. In this study, the goal is to;

1. Test different classifiers for segmenting spontaneous movements, based on data extracted from a markerless motion tracking system.
2. Examine the importance of different movement based features in order to classify spontaneous movements.

2   Methods

2.1   Motion Data

The data used in this study are temporal RGB-D data obtained with the Microsoft Kinect sensor. The recorded data contains both color and depth information of infants in the age of 1-6 months (corrected with respect to term). During the recording-session, the infant was positioned on a mat, while the RGB-D camera was positioned above the infant. No equipment was attached to the infant and the infant was thus able to move freely and unaffected. However, it was required that the infant only wore a short-sleeved bodystocking, in order to see the joints of the over- and under-extremities. Furthermore, the infant was in a good mood and unstimulated during the recording. The infant's parents were informed about the procedure beforehand and at any time; the parents could choose to stop the session. Unless the session was interrupted, the recording was done for minimum 5 minutes.

2.2   Motion Tracking

The pose estimation and motion tracking of the infants are obtained using a previously developed system [10,11]. To summarize, the system fits an articulated 3D model to the 3D data obtained from the depth sensor. The model is structured from a set of relative simple 3D structures, namely cylinders, spheres and superellipsoids. A set of parameters define the shape and orientation of these structures, which are length, radius and angle/direction with respect to their relative parent structure. The stomach/torso defines the root structure and all other structures are connected either directly or indirectly to this structure. The fitting process is done by adjusting the orientation parameters, while minimizing the error-metric between the 3D data and the 3D model. The error-metric is simply based on the Euclidean distance between the model and the data. Figure 1 illustrates an example for the resulting pose estimation.

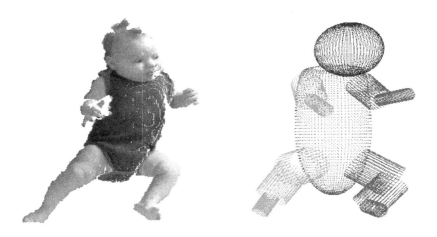

Fig. 1. Left: Colored point cloud obtained from the depth sensor. Right: 3D model fitted to the observed data.

2.3   Classification

The result from the motion tracking is a set of joint parameters, describing the pose of the recorded infant for each timestamp. The features used in this study are based on angular velocities and accelerations of the joints. For each frame, we calculate the angular velocities and accelerations, based on the joint angles in the current frame and the two previous frames. However, instead of using the raw data from a single frame, we transform the data using a sliding window approach, where we both generate mean- and median-filtered joint features. The transformations used for this approach are average, median, variance and the

Frobenius norm. Furthermore, we take the max/min values of the filtered velocities/accelerations, as we are interested in detecting frames where the infant is lying still vs. frames where the infant is doing an extreme movement with any part of the body. For classification methods we use *K-Nearest Neighbors (KNN)*, *Support Vector Machine (SVM)* and *Decision Tree*. For *KNN* we use two parameters for k, namely $k = 1$ and $k = 5$. In order to evaluate the different classifiers' performance, parts of the data have been annotated manually. The movements have been annotated either as spontaneous or calm.

3   Results

The dataset used in this study consists of 50k labelled frames taken from data recordings of 11 infants. For each frame, the frame was either labelled as being spontaneous or not. This labelling was done by one of the authors. Based on the four classification methods used in this study we examine how the training/test size influences the results. In Figure 2, the accuracy is shown, for different sizes of the training set. The test-set is simply the remaining data, when the training set has been extracted. For all four classification methods, the methods give good results, even with a small training set/large test set.

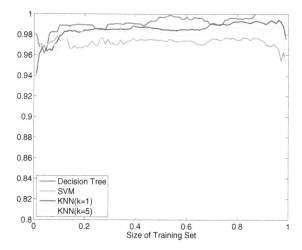

Fig. 2. The achieved accuracies for the four classifiers are illustrated, as a function of increasing size of the training set. The size is with respect to the total size of the data.

However, the classifiers are trained and tested without taking into account, that data trained from one infant is used to classify data from the same infant. We therefore train the classifiers on data from one infant, while the testing is done on data from the remaining infants. This is considered the worst case, as one could increase the size of the training set, by using more than one infant for training. In Figure 3, the result can be seen, where cross-validation is used in order to consider training with all infants. Again, the size of the training set is varied, but in this case, the size of the total data set is related to the particular infant. This new choice of training/test sets yields an overall decrease in accuracy, as expected, but we are still able to obtain satisfactory results.

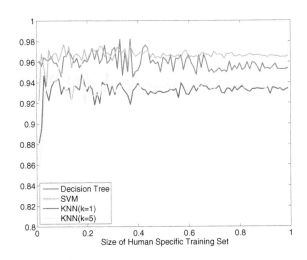

Fig. 3. For a more fair result, the training set is only based on data from one infant and the test set is based on data not belonging to the same infant. Cross-validation is used to train the classifiers on each infant.

Using a leave-one-out approach, we train a decision tree (the classifier that obtained the best results above) on data from all but one infant and segment the data from the leaved-out infant. The segmentation can be seen in Figure 4 where the ground truth segmentation can be compared with the estimated segmentation. Doing this for all infants, i.e. training the model on all but one infant and test the model on the leaved out infant, we are able to estimate the mean and standard deviation of the accuracy, which shows how good the methods are to generalize to an unknown infant. This has been done for all four methods and the results can be seen in Figure 5. We observe that we are still able to obtain good results for all four methods.

3.1   Parameter Importance

In order to point out the most important features used for detecting spontaneous movements, we use a leave-one-out approach. By removing one feature and training the classifiers, we compare the accuracy with the result obtained with the full set of features. This is done using 10-fold cross-validation. Figure 6 shows the results for the four types of classifiers. It should be noted that the importance-quantity has been normalized. It can be seen that the most important features

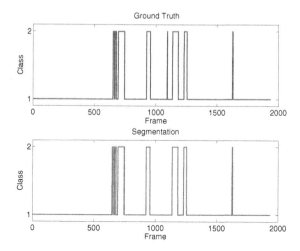

Fig. 4. Comparison between ground truth and estimated segmentation. Class 1 is spontaneous movements and Class 2 is non-spontaneous movements. Top: The ground truth segmentation of one infant's spontaneous movements. Bottom: The estimated segmentation of the infant's spontaneous movements.

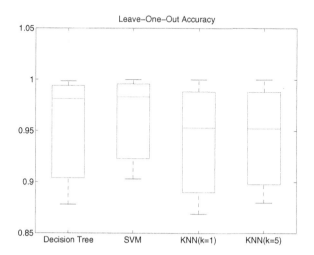

Fig. 5. Results for doing leave-one-infant-out experiment.

are based on velocities and that the maximum and summed velocity in a time windows significantly characterizes the spontaneous movements.

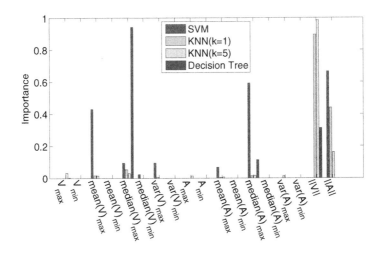

Fig. 6. The importance of the different parameters are illustrated for the four classifiers, based on the leave-one-out approach

4   Conclusion

Using annotated motion tracking data of moving infants in the age of 1-6 months, we have been able to segment sequences of spontaneous movements in infants. This was done using four different classifiers, which all proved to obtain similar results, ranging from $92-98\%$ accuracy, based on different classifiers and different sizes of the training/test data. In addition, we evaluated the importance of the different features used in this study, where the maximum velocity and summed velocity over time are important features for the spontaneous movements.

Acknowledgments. The authors would like to thank the Helene Elsass Center and the Ludvig and Sara Elsass Foundation for funding the project as well as all of the infants and their families for participating in this study.

References

1. Jensen, R.R., Paulsen, R.R., Larsen, R.: Analysis of gait using a treadmill and a time-of-flight camera. In: Kolb, A., Koch, R. (eds.) Dyn3D 2009. LNCS, vol. 5742, pp. 154–166. Springer, Heidelberg (2009)
2. Gabel, M., Renshaw, E., Schuster, A., Gilad-Bachrach, R.: Full body gait analysis with kinect. In: Proceedings of EMBC 2012 (2012)
3. Little, J., Boyd, J.: Recognizing People by Their Gait: The Shape of Motion (1996)

4. Zhou, F., De la Torre, F., Hodgins, J.K.: Hierarchical Aligned Cluster Analysis for Temporal Clustering of Human Motion. IEEE Transactions on Pattern Analysis and Machine Intelligence (PAMI) (2013)
5. Agarwal, A., Thakur, M. K.: Sign language recognition using Microsoft Kinect (2013)
6. Einspieler, C., Prechtl, H.F.: Prechtl's assessment of general movements: a diagnostic tool for the functional assessment of the young nervous system. Mental Retardation and Developmental Disabilities Research Reviews (2005)
7. Einspieler, C., Prechtl, H.F.R., Bos, A.F., Ferrari, F., Cioni, G.: Prechtl's Method on the Qualitative Assessment of General Movements in Preterm. Term and Yong Infants (2005)
8. Heathcock, J.C., Bhat, A.N., Lobo, M.A., Galloway, J.C.: The relative kicking frequency of infants born full-term and preterm during learning and short-term and long-term memory periods of the mobile paradigm. Physical Therapy (2005)
9. Landgraf, J.F., Tudella, E.: Effects of external load on spontaneous kicking by one and two-month-old infants. Brazilian Journal of Physical Therapy (2008)
10. Olsen, M.D., Herskind, A., Nielsen, J.B., Paulsen, R.R.: Body-part tracking of infants. In: 22nd International Conference on Pattern Recognition (2014)
11. Olsen, M.D., Herskind, A., Nielsen, J.B., Paulsen, R.R.: Model-based motion tracking of infants. In: Agapito, L., Bronstein, M.M., Rother, C. (eds.) ECCV 2014 Workshops. LNCS, vol. 8927, pp. 673–685. Springer, Heidelberg (2015)

OMEG: Oulu Multi-Pose Eye Gaze Dataset

Qiuhai He[1(✉)], Xiaopeng Hong[1], Xiujuan Chai[2], Jukka Holappa[1],
Guoying Zhao[1], Xilin Chen[1,2], and Matti Pietikäinen[1]

[1] Department of Computer Science and Engineering, University of Oulu, Oulu, Finland
{qhe,xhong,jukkaho,gyzhao,mkp}@ee.oulu.fi
[2] Key Lab of Intelligent Information Processing of the Chinese Academy of Sciences,
The Institute of Computing Technology of the Chinese Academy of Sciences,
Beijing, People's Republic of China
{chaixiujuan,xlchen}@ict.ac.cn

Abstract. Data is in a very important position for pattern recognition tasks including eye gaze estimation. In the literature, most researchers used normal face datasets, which are not specifically designed for eye gaze estimation. As a result, it is difficult to obtain fine labeled eye gaze direction. Therefore large datasets with well-defined gaze directions are desired.

To facilitate related researches, we collect and establish the Oulu Multi-pose Eye Gaze Dataset. Inspired by the psychological observation that gaze direction is intrinsically linked with the head orientation, we are devoted to a new data set of eye gaze images captured under multiple head poses. It finally results in a dataset containing over 40K images from 50 subjects, who were asked to fixate on 10 special points on screen under different poses respectively. We investigate a new eye gaze estimation approach by using the IGO based description, and compare it with other popular eye gaze estimation approaches to provide the baseline results on our dataset.

Keywords: Eye gaze · Head pose · Dataset

1   Introduction

Data is in a significant position for computer vision tasks including eye gaze estimation [4, 5, 6, 7, 15, 17, 18, 27]. In the literature, most researchers used normal face datasets, which are not specifically designed for eye gaze estimation. Several datasets such as the Ulm [30] and the HPEG [26] datasets are presented more recently. However, in HPEG datasets [26], only three coarse gaze directions ('straight forward', 'extreme left' and 'extreme right') are available. Although the Ulm dataset [30] owns multiple gaze and head directions, it only contains 20 subjects. As a result, large datasets with well-defined gaze directions are desired.

Many psychological studies [18, 23, 28] indicate that gaze direction and head orientation are intrinsically linked with each other. Head pose is a coarse indication of gaze, especially when the eyes of human beings are not visible, such as under remote CCTV camera or with sunglasses. Links of head pose and eye gaze also indicate the social attention transfer. More importantly, as indicated by [19, 20], judging where

© Springer International Publishing Switzerland 2015
R.R. Paulsen and K.S. Pedersen (Eds.): SCIA 2015, LNCS 9127, pp. 418–427, 2015.
DOI: 10.1007/978-3-319-19665-7_35

other people are looking comes from a combination of both eye gaze directions and head orientations [9, 24]. A graphic example of the famous 'Wollaston illusion' [14] shows that though the eyes are identical between the two face images, because of the difference of head pose, the appearances of gaze direction are different. To our best knowledge, only the newly published Columbia Gaze Data Set [2] takes the intrinsic connection between eye gaze and head poses into account. The datasets for multiple-pose eye gaze estimation are still intensely expected.

To facilitate the researches in eye gaze estimation, we designed and collected the Oulu Multi-pose Eye Gaze (OMEG) dataset. It includes 200 image sequences from 50 subjects (For each subject it includes four image sequences). Each sequence consists of 225 frames captured when people are fixating on 10 targeting points on the screen. The first three sequences of each subject are captured under three fixed head poses, namely 0 (the frontal) and ±30 degree respectively. The last sequence is in a free pose style. Table 1 compares our gaze dataset with other existing ones [2].The image sequences as well as the calibrated eye gazes, 'ground truth', will be made publicly available.

Moreover, we provide baseline results on our dataset by evaluating the popular approaches on eye gaze estimation [2]. Especially, we investigate a new eye gaze estimation approach by using the image gradient orientation (IGO) based description [11], which shows good robustness to illumination variations and outliers in the tasks of image registration [1,12], face recognition [11, 29], and pose estimation [31].

The remaining parts of this paper are organized as follows. Section 2 describes the hardware system setup used during the collection and recording procedure. We provide the calculation of ground truth in Section 3 and the baseline results in Section 4. Section 5 discusses the influence of different head poses in gaze estimation.

Table 1. Gaze dataset comparison

	HPEG	Ulm	Columbia	Ours (OMEG)
#Subjects:	10	20	56	**50**
#Gaze:	3	2-9	21	**10**
#Fixed Head Poses:	2	19	5	**3**
#Free Head Poses:	w/	w/o	w/o	**w/**
#Total image:	~5,500	2,220	5,880	**44,827**

2   Data Collection

This section describes the design of our dataset (Section 2.1), the sensor used to provide accurate location data in real world (Section 2.2), the environment setup (Section 2.3), and the data collection procedure (Section 2.4).

2.1   Basic Design

The directions of eye gaze are defined as the angles between the visual axis and the optical axis of the camera, as shown in Figure 1(a). Moreover, we assume that the human's face is a virtual plane and use the normal direction of the facial plane to represent the head pose. To fix the visual focus, a large screen is used to display 10 red crosses (Figure 1(c)) as the viewpoints. We employ an industry tracker with high accuracy to acquire the positions of eye's center, viewpoints and the direction of facial plane.

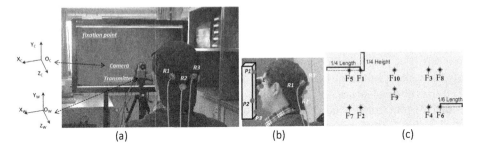

Fig. 1. Configuration for data collection. (a) Environment setting. The coordinates according to the transmitter and the camera are considered as the World Coordinate System and the Camera Coordinate System respectively; (b) $R1$ to $R3$ are three receivers fixed on a hat; $P1$ to $P3$ are three points sampled from the rectangle plane which is an approximation of the face direction; 'E' is the center of the human eyes; (c) The distribution of the fixation points.

2.2 High-accuracy Tracker System

We use the FASTRAK 3D tracker [8] to acquire the 3D position data. It consists of three units, including a system electronic unit, a transmitter, and several receivers. In the workflow, the transmitter is set as the origin of the World Coordinate System and the reference for the position and orientation measurements of the receivers. The receivers detect the magnetic fields emitted by the transmitter. The static accuracy of the receivers is claimed to be 0.08 cm root mean square (RMS) for positions, and $0.15°$ RMS for orientations.

2.3 Environment Setup

The environment for data collection is shown in Figure 1. A sequence of red crosses is displayed on large screen as the fixation point. A uEye 1540-c industry camera with a 1/2" CMOS image sensor and a resolution of 1280 (H) x 1024 (V) pixel is mounted in near front of the subject to capture the image sequences. The transmitter is mounted in a fixed position just under the camera. Both the camera and the screen with all the fixation points are calibrated before data collection as shown in Figure 1(a).

As can be seen from Figure 1, the subjects will wear a hat with three receivers during data collection procedure. For each subject, we assume the angle between the facial plane and the virtual plane constituted by these three receivers is constant. As a result, the virtual facial plane at any time point can be recovered by using the corresponding 3D positions of these three receivers.

2.4   Data Collection Procedure

Under our data collection design, the subjects need to fixate on the points displayed on screen. Ten fixation points are distributed as Figure 1(c) illustrates. These points are displayed continuously by every two seconds. The sequence of fixation points is displayed for five times. Therefore, the time to capture a whole loop in one pose is 100 seconds. For the fixed pose situation, the subject was asked to focus on the points only by eyes, but keep his/her head stable. During the data collection procedure, the three receivers on hat will record the transformation data of position all the time.

To represent the variations from different poses, a four-step collection is carried out. In the first three steps, the subject is asked to position in three fixed poses, namely the frontal pose, 30° to the left, and 30° to the right, respectively. The subject is asked to keep his/her head stable. In the final step, the subject is allowed to move his/her head freely. We collected samples from 50 subjects, in which 10 out of 50 are female. Some example images are illustrated in Figure 2.

(a)   (b)

Fig. 2. Example image of the data collection: (a) Subjects in the frontal poses; (b) one subject focusing on the same fixation points in the three different poses.

3   Ground Truth Annotation

As introduced in Section 2.3, according to the spatial relationship between the facial plane and the hat plane, the direction of the facial plane can be recovered by using the 3D position of the three receivers on hat, as well as the position of the eyes' center. This section describes the details of acquiring the eye gaze direction.

3.1   Gaze Definition

A geometrical model for gaze estimation is illustrated by Figure 3. In HCI scenario, eye gaze refers to the pointer from the viewer's two eyes to an object. Note that the gaze orientation θ in 3D space has three rotational degrees of freedom, namely the azimuth (or yaw), elevation (or pitch), and roll, as illustrated in Figure 3(b). In our research, we take the 'yaw' and 'pitch' into consideration. Thus we define the direction of eye gaze as $\theta = \langle \alpha, \beta \rangle$, where α and β are rotations around the vertical and horizontal axis respectively as Figure 3(c).

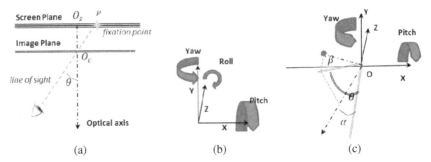

Fig. 3. Geometrical model of eye gaze. (a) the 2D projection of geometrical model; (b) three rotation degrees of freedom (DOF) of a 3D angular; (c) an example to represent the gaze angle into two of the three DOFs, namely Yaw and Pitch.

3.2   Eye Gaze Direction

Before the data collection procedure, we record the initial positions of the three points $(P1^{(0)}, P2^{(0)}, P3^{(0)})$ on the facial plane and the three points $(R1^{(0)}, R2^{(0)}, R3^{(0)})$ on hat, through which we can compute the initial normal vector $V_P^{(0)}$ of facial plane by Eq. (1) , as well as the normal vector of hat plane $V_R^{(0)}$. More specifically,

$$V_P^{(0)} = \left(P2^{(0)} - P1^{(0)}\right) \times \left(P3^{(0)} - P1^{(0)}\right) . \tag{1}$$

Therefore, the angle θ between $V_P^{(0)}$ and $V_R^{(0)}$ can be computed by Eq. (2).

$$\theta = \cos^{-1}(V_P^{(0)} \cdot V_R^{(0)}) \tag{2}$$

During data collection, we record the position data of $R1^{(t)}, R2^{(t)} \ R3^{(t)}$ at time t, $t = 1,...,T$. Then we compute the unit normal vector $\mathcal{U}_R^{(t)}(x_R^{(t)}, y_R^{(t)}, z_R^{(t)})$ of $V_R^{(0)}$ and $V_R^{(t)}$. As the angle θ is constant, according to [13], the rotation matrix $\mathcal{R}$ is

$$\mathcal{R} = \cos\theta \cdot \mathbf{I} + \sin\theta \cdot \left[\mathcal{U}_R^{(t)}\right]_X + (1 - \cos\theta) \cdot \mathcal{U}_R^{(t)} \otimes \mathcal{U}_R^{(t)}, \tag{3}$$

where $\mathbf{I}$ is the identity matrix, $\left[\mathcal{U}_R^{(t)}\right]_X$ is the cross product matrix of $\mathcal{U}_R^{(t)}$, and $\mathcal{U}_R^{(t)} \otimes \mathcal{U}_R^{(t)}$ is the tensor product matrix, which are presented by Eqs. (4) and (5), respectively.

$$\left[\mathcal{U}_R^{(t)}\right]_X = \begin{bmatrix} 0 & -z_R^{(t)} & y_R^{(t)} \\ z_R^{(t)} & 0 & -x_R^{(t)} \\ -y_R^{(t)} & x_R^{(t)} & 0 \end{bmatrix} \tag{4}$$

$$\mathcal{U}_R^{(t)} \otimes \mathcal{U}_R^{(t)} = \begin{bmatrix} x_R^{(t)^2} & x_R^{(t)} y_R^{(t)} & x_R^{(t)} z_R^{(t)} \\ z_R^{(t)} x_R^{(t)} & y_R^{(t)^2} & y_R^{(t)} z_R^{(t)} \\ x_R^{(t)} z_R^{(t)} & y_R^{(t)} z_R^{(t)} & z_R^{(t)^2} \end{bmatrix} \tag{5}$$

In light of the initial positions of eyes' center ($E^{(0)}$) and those three points ($R1^{(0)}$, $R2^{(0)}$, $R3^{(0)}$) on hat collected, their pairwise relation is determined. Given any of the three points on hat at time t, we are able to deduce the corresponding position of the eyes' center ($E^{(t)}$). To minimize the mean square error, we average the predicted positions deduced via the following equation:

$$E^{(t)} = \frac{1}{3}\left[\sum_{i=1}^{3}\left(R_i^{(t)} - \mathcal{R}\cdot(R_i^{(0)} - E^{(0)})\right)\right] \tag{6}$$

Therefore, according to the definition above, the eye gaze direction is the visual axis relative to the Camera Coordinate System (C_u, C_l), and the visual axis is the vector from eyes center to the fixation points (F_1, F_2, $\cdots$, F_j, $\cdots$, F_{10}). We then obtain the visual axis $V_E^{(j)}$ by Eq. (7).

$$V_E^{(j)} = P_j - E^{(t)} \tag{7}$$

As a consequence, we compute the pitch angle α and the yaw angle β of the eye gaze by Eq. (8).

$$\alpha = \cos^{-1}(V_E^{(j)}\cdot C_u),\ \beta = \cos^{-1}(V_E^{(j)}\cdot C_l) \tag{8}$$

4   Baseline Results

In this section, we show the landmark labelling and pre-processing procedure for eyes images (Section 4.1), and describe the methods of feature extraction (Section 4.2). Section 4.3 presents the experimental results of eye gaze estimation on OMEG.

4.1   Landmark Labelling and Pre-processing

Landmarks localization is a key step in nearly all face analysis tasks. We employed the state-of-the-art Bayesian based landmark detector [32] to obtain five landmarks including two eye centers, the nose tip and two mouth corners. It takes into account both the local and global constraints. Some example of landmark detection results on the images from the collected datasets are illustrated in Figure 4(a). It can be observed that the detector successfully detects the landmarks even with non-frontal views, non-neutral expressions or occlusions caused by glasses or beards. Despite this, to ensure the accuracy of the locations, we check the landmarks image by image and revise the ones with large errors manually.

(a)   (b)

Fig. 4. Examples of normalization. (a) Landmarks detected by the approach [32]; (b) Normalized average face of all subjects in each pose.

We align and crop all the face images by three steps. The first step is to rescale each image such that the ratio of the upper facial height to the cropped image height is 96:256. The upper facial height is the distance between the center of two eyes and the mouth center. Then the nose tip is set to be the center of each image. Finally, we crop the face images by the resolution of 256 × 256 pixels. Figure 4(b) shows the average face of all subjects in each fixed pose respectively.

For all experiments, we crop the eyes image from the normalized face images. In specific, we align the eyes center as the eyes image center, then crop the eyes image in the resolution of 30 × 150 pixels. Figure 5 shows examples for 10 eye gaze images from the 3 head poses respectively.

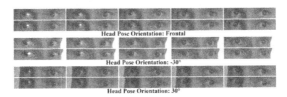

Fig. 5. Sample of eye images.

4.2   Feature Extraction

In [2], PCA [21] and multiple discriminant analysis (MDA) [22] based subspaces were used as the feature vectors and the support vector machine are used to learn the mapping from feature vector to the gaze locking labels. It is shown that this simple approach still achieves promising results. In analogue to [2], we report the results of baseline experiments with PCA and MDA subspaces.

Moreover, fueled by the success of IGO based facial descriptors [11, 31], we propose to use them for eye gaze estimation. More specifically, we characterize each image pixel by its gradient orientation. The IGO is expressed by a complex number, where both the real and imaginary parts are taken into account. Then we encode the IGO images via dimensionality reduction including 2D discrete cosine transform (DCT2), PCA and MDA. All feature vectors are of the same dimension for fair comparisons.

4.3   Recognition Procedure

Instead of treating the eye gaze estimation as a classification problem [2], we regard it as a regression problem. The reason is that the distribution of the yaw and pitch on the whole dataset are continuous in -38° to 36°and -10° to 29° respectively, as shown in Figure 6.We use off-the-shelf nonlinear regression models, support vector regression (SVR) [3], to learn the mapping from the feature space to the continuous gaze label. For those representations in angle, cosine kernel is used. For others, the RBF kernel is used unless otherwise noted. The optimal parameter settings are reached via grid search.

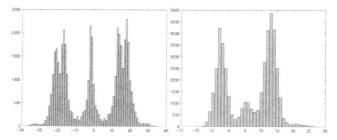

Fig. 6. The distribution of the yaw and pitch on the whole dataset.

We evaluate the eye gaze direction via leave-one-out cross validation. In specific, for each round, eyes' images in four sequences of 49 subjects are used for training while the images of the remaining subject are for testing. The average Mean Absolute Error (MAE) and average Pearson product-moment Correlation Coefficient (PCC) between the predicted gaze angle and the ground truth are used for performance measurement. Table 2 provides the performance of both the pixel intensity and IGO in DCT2, PCA and MDA subspaces, where d is the dimensionality of the extracted feature. As the experimental results suggest, the IGO eye gaze descriptor performs comparably or better than the pixel intensity. One exception is for yaw estimation. The intensity-PCA shows the best result. The reason is that the luminance distribution, which is lost in the IGO based representations, is crucial to the gaze perception for yaw changes [25]. Moreover, MDA, which is usually used for classification tasks, does not work as well as PCA and DCT2, as the eye gaze estimation is regarded as a regression problem in this paper.

Table 2. Baseline results ($d = 90$)

	IGO-DCT2	IGO-PCA	IGO-MDA	Intensity-DCT2	Intensity-PCA	Intensity-MDA
MAE(Yaw)	9.05	8.69	18.08	9.33	7.1	14.04
PCC(Yaw)	0.81	0.75	-0.02	0.75	0.86	0.16
MAE(Pitch)	5.96	5.77	7.02	6.08	7.32	6.91
PCC(Pitch)	0.65	0.56	0.01	0.56	0.68	-0.02

5   Discussion

To discuss the influence of different head poses in gaze estimation, we designed a set of experiments, which randomly pick fifty percent of subjects in one pose as the training set and the left subjects in other poses as the testing set. The data in three fixed discrete yaws, are chosen for these experiments. In terms of accuracy in Table 2 we employ the intensity-PCA as an example to extract features. As listed in Table 3, the performance under the same pose is much higher than the one under different poses. It means the eye gazes are distinctively different when head poses vary. Therefore, multi-pose gaze estimation is highly challenging. Fortunately, our dataset provides an opportunity of in-depth investigation in this issue.

Table 3. The pose influence in gaze estimation. Pose-(number) reflects the frontal, -30° and 30° head poses respectively.

(MAE/PCC)	Train Pose-1	Train Pose-2	Train Pose-3
Test Pose-1	**5.31/0.90**	11.54/0.57	11.66/0.64
Test Pose-2	13.85/0.25	**8.73/0.73**	15.44/0.18
Test Pose-3	13.70/0.37	18.64/0.22	**9.22/0.71**

6   Conclusions

In this paper we introduced the Oulu Multi-pose Eye Gaze Dataset. Unlike most existing gaze datasets, we collected the eye gaze data under multiple poses. We provided five landmark labels and the eye gaze angles as the ground truth. Lastly, to evaluate the effectiveness of our dataset, we reported baseline results of using IGO based description and the intensity via three dimensionality reduction techniques. The experimental results suggest that multi-pose gaze estimation is highly challenging. In spite of this, our dataset enables in-depth investigations in this topic. In future, we will evaluate other commonly used approaches such as [10, 16, 24, 25, 33], and publish the OMEG dataset with the ground truth.

Acknowledgements. This work was supported by the Academy of Finland and Infotech Oulu, and partially supported by the FiDiPro program of Tekes. Xilin Chen was partially supported by the Natural Science Foundation of China under contract No. 61390511.

Refferences

1. Fitch, A., Kadyrov, A., Christmas, W., Kittler, J.: Orientation correlation. In: Proc. BMVC. Citeseer, pp. 1–10 (2002)
2. Smith, B., Yin, Q., Nayar, S.: Gaze locking: passive eye contact detection for human-object interaction. In: Proc. UIST., pp. 271–280. ACM (2013)
3. Chang, C., Lin, C.: LIBSVM: a library for support vector machines. ACM Trans. Intelligent Systems and Technology, **2**(27) (2011)
4. Morimoto, C., Amir, A., Flickner, M.: Detecting eye position and gaze from a single camera and 2 light sources. In: Proc. ICPR., pp. 314–317. IEEE (2002)
5. Beymer, D., Flickner, M.: Eye gaze tracking using an active stereo head. In: Proc. CVPR. IEEE (2003)
6. Hansen, D., Pece, A.: Eye tracking in the wild. Comput. Vis. Image Und. **98**(1), 155–181 (2005)
7. Hansen, D., Ji, Q.: In the eye of the beholder: A survey of models for eyes and gaze. IEEE Trans. Pattern Anal. Mach. Intell. **32**(3), 478–500 (2010)
8. FASTRAK 3D tracker. http://www.cortechsolutions.com/Products/EL/EL-FP/EL-FP-FT
9. Lu, F., Okabe, T., Sugano, Y., Sato, Y.: Learning gaze biases with head motion for head pose-free gaze estimation. Image and Vision Computing **32**(3), 169–179 (2014)
10. Lu, F., Sugano, Y., Okabe, T., Sato, Y.: Adaptive Linear Regression for Appearance-Based Gaze Estimation. IEEE Trans. Pattern Anal. Mach. Intell., PrePrints (2014)

11. Tzimiropoulos, G., Zafeiriou, S., Pantic, M.: Subspace learning from image gradient orientations. IEEE Trans. Pattern Anal. Mach. Intell. **34**(12), 2454–2466 (2012)
12. Tzimiropoulos, G., Argyriou, V., Zafeiriou, S., Stathaki, T.: Robust fft-based scale-invariant image registration with image gradients. IEEE Trans Pattern Anal. Mach. Intell. **32**(10), 1899–1906 (2010)
13. Bar-Itzhack, I.: New method for extracting the quaternion from a rotation matrix. Journal of Guidance, Control, and Dynamics **23**(6), 1085–1087 (2000)
14. Illusion of face 9. http://www.psy.ritsumei.ac.jp/~akitaoka/kao9e.html
15. Wang, J., Sung, E.: Study on eye gaze estimation. IEEE Trans. Systems, Man, and Cybernetics, Part B: Cybernetics **32**(3), 332–350 (2002)
16. Kim, K., Ramakrishna, R.: Vision-based eye-gaze tracking for human computer interface. In: Proc. SMC, pp. 324–329. IEEE (1999)
17. Tan, K., Kriegman, D., Ahuja, N.: Appearance-based eye gaze estimation. In: Proc. WACV, pp. 191–195. IEEE (2002)
18. Symons, L., Lee, K., Cedrone, C., Nishimura, M.: What are you looking at? acuity for triadic eye gaze. J. Gen. Psychol. **131**(4), 451–469 (2004)
19. Cline, M.: The perception of where a person is looking. Am. J. Psychol. **80**(1), 41–50 (1967)
20. Gamer, M., Hecht, H.: Are you looking at me? Measuring the cone of gaze. J. Exp. Psychol. [Hum Percept.]. **33**(3), 705–715 (2007)
21. Turk, M., Pentland, A.: Eigenfaces for recognition. Journal of Cognitive Neuroscience **3**(1), 71–86 (1991)
22. Duda, R., Hart, P., Stork, D.: Pattern classification. John Willey & Sons **2**, 114–124 (2001)
23. Jenkins, R.: The lighter side of gaze perception. Perception **36**, 1266–1268 (2007)
24. Valenti, R., Sebe, N., Gevers, T.: Combining Head Pose and Eye Location Information for Gaze Estimation. IEEE Trans. Image Process **21**(2), 802–815 (2012)
25. Ando, S.: Luminance-induced shift in the apparent direction of gaze. Perception **31**, 657–674 (2002)
26. Asteriadis, S., Soufleros, D., Karpouzis, K., Kollias, S.: A natural head pose and eye gaze dataset. In: Proc. AFFINE Workshop (2009)
27. Baluja, S., Pomerleau, D.: Non-intrusive gaze tracking using artificial neural networks. Tech. rep., Department of Computer Science, Carnegie Mellon University (1994)
28. Langton, S., Honeyman, H., Tessler, E.: The influence of head contour and nose angle on the perception of eye-gaze direction. Perception & Psychophysics **66**(5), 752–771 (2004)
29. Zhang, T., Tang, Y.Y., Fang, B., Shang, Z., Liu, X.: Face recognition under varying illumination using gradientfaces. IEEE Trans. Image Process. **18**(11), 2599–2606 (2009)
30. Weidenbacher, U., Layher, G., Strauss, P., Neumann, H.: A comprehensive head pose and gaze database. In: Proc. IET (2007)
31. Hong, X., Zhao, G., Pietikainen, M.: Pose Estimation via Complex-Frequency Domain Analysis of Image Gradient Orientations. In: Proc. ICPR. IEEE (2014)
32. Zhao, X., Shan, S., Chai, X., Chen, X.: Cascaded Shape Space Pruning for Robust Facial Landmark Detection. In: Proc. ICCV. IEEE (2013)
33. Sugano, Y., Matsushita, Y., Sato, Y.: Appearance-Based Gaze Estimation Using Visual Saliency. IEEE Trans. Pattern Anal. Mach. Intell. **35**(2), 329–341 (2013)

Image Alignment for Panorama Stitching in Sparsely Structured Environments

Giulia Meneghetti$^{(\boxtimes)}$, Martin Danelljan, Michael Felsberg, and Klas Nordberg

Computer Vision Laboratory, Linköping University, 581 83 Linköping, Sweden
{giulia.meneghetti,martin.danelljan,michael.felsberg,
klas.nordberg}@liu.se

Abstract. Panorama stitching of sparsely structured scenes is an open research problem. In this setting, feature-based image alignment methods often fail due to shortage of distinct image features. Instead, direct image alignment methods, such as those based on phase correlation, can be applied. In this paper we investigate correlation-based image alignment techniques for panorama stitching of sparsely structured scenes. We propose a novel image alignment approach based on discriminative correlation filters (DCF), which has recently been successfully applied to visual tracking. Two versions of the proposed DCF-based approach are evaluated on two real and one synthetic panorama dataset of sparsely structured indoor environments. All three datasets consist of images taken on a tripod rotating 360 degrees around the vertical axis through the optical center. We show that the proposed DCF-based methods outperform phase correlation-based approaches on these datasets.

Keywords: Image alignment · Panorama stitching · Image registration · Phase correlation · Discriminative correlation filters

1 Introduction

Image stitching is the problem of constructing a single high resolution image from a set of images taken from the same scene. We consider panorama stitching, merging images taken by a camera on a tripod that rotates about its vertical axis through the optical center, Fig. 1 Left. A panorama stitching pipeline usually contains three major steps: *Camera calibration*, estimation of the camera parameters; *Image alignment*, computation of the geometric transformation between the images; *Image stitching and blending*, transformation of all the images to a new coordinate system and their blending to eliminate visual artefacts.

Mobile applications and desktop software for panorama images are usually designed to produce visually good results, focussing on the third step. However, accurate estimation of the transformation is required in increasingly many fields, including computer graphics (image-based rendering), computer vision (surveillance applications, automatic quality control, vehicular systems applications) and medical imaging (multi-modal MRI merging). In this paper, we therefore investigate the problem of image alignment for panorama stitching.

© Springer International Publishing Switzerland 2015
R.R. Paulsen and K.S. Pedersen (Eds.): SCIA 2015, LNCS 9127, pp. 428–439, 2015.
DOI: 10.1007/978-3-319-19665-7_36

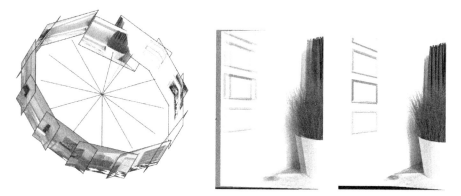

Fig. 1. Left: Visualization of an incorrect image alignment. The blue lines represents the optical axis for each image and the green line represents the vertical axis around which the camera is rotating. The top-most image is misaligned with respect to the others, this will greatly reduce the visual quality of the panorama and generate errors in the estimated transformation. **Middle:** Resulting image alignment using phase correlation for an image pair in our *Synthetic dataset*. In this case the images are clearly misaligned. **Right:** Image alignment result of the same image pair using the proposed method. In this case, the alignment is correct.

Image alignment methods can be divided into two categories: *feature-based* methods and *direct* (or *global*) methods [4,20,25]. Feature-based methods first extract descriptors from a set of image features (e.g. points or edges). These descriptors are then matched between pairs of images to estimate the relative transformation. Direct methods instead estimate the transformation between an image pair by directly comparing the whole images. Feature-based methods often provide excellent performance in cases when there are sufficient reliable features in the scene. However, these methods often fail in sparsely structured scenes, when not enough distinct features can be detected. We find such cases, for example, in indoors scenarios, where uniform walls, floors and ceilings are common, or in outdoor panoramas, where sky and sea can dominate. In this work, we tackle the problem of image alignment for panorama stitching in sparsely structured scenes, and therefore turn to the direct image alignment methods. Since our camera is rotating by small angles the transformation between two consecutive images can be approximated as a translation in the image plane. Given this assumption we restrict our investigation to phase correlation approaches [12,18].

Recently, Discriminative Correlation Filter (DCF) [3,8–10,15] based approaches have successfully been applied to visual tracking. These methods have shown robustness to many types of distortions and changes in the target appearance, including illumination variations, in-plane rotations, scale changes and out-of-plane rotations [9,10,15]. The multi-channel DCF approaches also provide a consistent method based on several image features, instead of just relying on grayscale values. We therefore investigate to what extent DCF-based methods can be used for the image alignment problem in panorama stitching.

1.1   Contributions

In this paper, we investigate the image alignment problem for panorama stitching in sparsely structured scenes. For this application, we evaluate four different correlation-based techniques in an image alignment pipeline. Among phase correlation approaches, we evaluate the standard phase correlation approach (POC) method and a regularized version of phase correlation (RPOC) developed for surveillance systems [12].

Inspired by the success of discriminative correlation filter based visual trackers, we propose an image alignment approach based on DCF. Two versions are evaluated: the standard grayscale DCF [3] and a multi-channel extension using color names (DCF-CN) for image representation , as suggested in [10]. Image alignment results for these four methods are presented on three panorama stitching datasets taken in sparsely structured indoors environments. We provide quantitative and qualitative comparisons on one synthetic and two real datasets. Our results clearly suggest that both the proposed DCF-based image alignment methods outperform the POC-based methods.

2   Background

Image alignment is a well-studied problem with applications in many fields. Image stitching, target localization, automatic quality control, super-resolution images and multi-modal MRI merging are some of many applications that use registration between images. Many techniques have been proposed [4,20,25], and they can be divided in two major categories.

2.1   Feature-Based Methods

The feature-based methods mostly differ in the way of extracting and matching the features in an image pair. After the corresponding features have been found, a process of outlier removal is used to improve robustness to false matching. The estimation of the geometric transformation is usually computed from the corresponding features using Direct Linear Transformation and then refined using bundle adjustment techniques. A classical example of a feature-based registration approach is Autostitch [5,6], a panorama stitching software.

Feature-based methods often fail to perform accurate image alignment in sparsely structured scenarios or when the detected features are unevenly distributed. In such cases, direct methods are preferable since they utilize a global similarity metric and do not depend on local features.

2.2   Direct Methods

Direct methods can be divided into intensity-based and correlation-based approaches, depending on the kind of similarity measure (or error function). The sum of square difference and the sum of absolute differences between the intensity values of the pixels of two images, are two intensity-based similarity metrics. Normalized cross correlation, that computes the scalar product of two image windows and divides it by the product of their norms, is instead a correlation-based similarity metric. Given the error (or score) function, various techniques can be applied to find the optimum, such as, exhaustive search of all possible alignments, which is prohibitively slow, hierarchical coarse-to-fine techniques based on image pyramids, which suffer from the fact that image structures need not be on the same scale as the displacement, and Fourier transform-based techniques. The latter techniques are based on the shift theorem of the Fourier transform. If two images, are related by a translation, standard *phase correlation* (or *phase-only correlation*, POC) estimates the shift between them by looking for the peak in the inverse Fourier transform of the normalized cross-power spectrum. The normalization is introduced, since, it significantly improves the peak estimation compare to using the cross-power spectrum [16]. For image alignment, this latter technique is preferable, since it uses all the information available in the image. Given two images that differ by a translation, phase correlation is a simple and robust technique for retrieving the displacement between them. Therefore, we consider this class of techniques to formulate a novel approach to image alignment based on the MOSSE [3] tracker and its color names extension [10].

2.3 Related Work

Phase correlation is a frequency domain technique usually applied in various applications, since it is very accurate, simple and robust to illumination variation and noise in the images. Many versions have been proposed during the years [4,20,25]. Phase correlation for image alignment was first introduced by Kuglin and Hines [18], who compute the displacement as the maximum of the inverse Fourier transform of the normalized cross-power spectrum between two images. Subpixel precision techniques, were later introduced for improving the peak estimation, using fitting functions [13,21], or finding approximate zeros of the gradient of the inverse Fourier transform of the normalized cross-power spectrum [1], which is more robust against border effect and multiple motions. Foorosh [13] suggested to prefilter the phase difference matrix to remove aliased components (generally at high spatial frequencies), but filtering must be adjusted to each image and sensor. Phase correlation can also be used to estimate other image transformations than pure translation, such as in-plane rotation and scale between two images [11]. Other techniques are based on the Log-polar transformation, since it maps rotation and scaling to translation. Used in combination with correlation, it can robustly estimate scale and in-plane rotations [23]. Chen *et al.* [7] propose a solution for rotated and translated images that computes Fourier-Mellin invariant descriptors. Eisenbach *et al.* [12] proposed a phase correlation regularization based on the noise of the image.

Phase correlation does not lose the efficiency depending on the baseline between the images (if they consistently overlap), moreover it is robust against sparsely structured images where feature-based methods fail to detect features. Among all the available phase correlation techniques, we choose the original

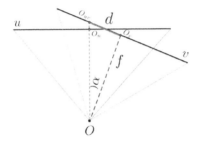

Fig. 2. Representation of the geometrical relation between the angle α and the displacement d.

phase correlation algorithm (POC) [18] and the regularized phase correlation (RPOC) [12].

Recently, discriminative correlation filter based methods [3,8–10,15] have successfully been applied to related field of visual tracking and have shown to provide excellent results on benchmark datasets [17,24]. These methods work by learning an optimal correlation filter from a set of training samples of the target. Bolme et al. proposed the MOSSE tracker [3]. Like standard POC, it only employs grayscale images to estimate the displacement of the target. This method has however been extended to multi-channel features (e.g. RGB) [9, 10,15]. Danelljan et al. [10] performed an extensive evaluation of several color representations for visual tracking in the DCF-based Adaptive Color Tracker. In their evaluation it was shown that the Color Names (CN) representation [22] provided the best performance. In this work, we therefore investigate two DCF-based methods for the problem of image alignment. First, we evaluate the standard grayscale DCF method (MOSSE) and second, we employ the color name representation used in the adaptive color tracker.

3   Method

In this section we present the the evaluation pipeline for the image alignment and the methods investigated. The images are assumed to have been taken from a camera fixed on a tripod. Between each subsequent image, the camera is assumed to have been rotated around the vertical axis through the optical center. The rotations are further assumed to be small enough such that two subsequent images have a significantly overlapping view of the scene, at least 50%. We also assume known camera calibration and we, therefore, work on rectified images to compensate for any lens distortion.

3.1   Image Alignment Pipeline

Our image alignment pipeline contains three basic steps that are performed in an iterative scheme. Given a pair of subsequent images u and v, the following procedure is used:

1. Estimate the displacement d between the images u and v using an image alignment method.
2. Using the displacement d, estimate the 3×3 homography matrix H, that maps the image plane of v to the image plane of u.
3. Warp image v to the image plane of u using the homography H.
4. Iterate from 1. using the warped image as v.

Fig. 2 shows a geometrical illustration of the displacement estimation d. O is the common optical center of images u and v, which is projected, respectively, in O_u and O_v. O_{uv} consists in the intersection of the optical axis of u with the image v. The translation between the images is identified as the distance between O_{uv} and O_v. The evaluated image alignment methods used to estimate this displacement, are described in Section 3.2 and 3.3. Given an estimate of the displacement d between the image pair, we can calculate a homography transformation H between the images using the geometry of the problem. Since the camera rotates about the vertical axis through the optical center, the angle α of rotation can be computed as:

$$\alpha = \tan^{-1}\left(\frac{d}{f}\right). \tag{1}$$

Here, f is the focal length of the camera. The homography H between the two images can then be computed as

$$H = K R_\alpha K^{-1}. \tag{2}$$

Here, K is the intrinsic parameter matrix and R_α is the rotation matrix corresponding to the rotation α about the vertical axis

$$R_\alpha = \begin{pmatrix} \cos(\alpha) & 0 & -\sin(\alpha) \\ 0 & 1 & 0 \\ \sin(\alpha) & 0 & \cos(\alpha) \end{pmatrix}. \tag{3}$$

The presented iteration scheme is employed for two reasons. First, it is known that correlation-based methods are biased towards smaller translations due to the fact that a windowing operation and circular correlation is performed. Second, the initial estimate of the displacement is affected by the perspective distortions, since the correlation-based methods assume a pure translation transformation between the image pair. However, as the iterations converge, the translation model will be increasingly correct since the image v is warped according to the current estimate of the displacement. Hence, the estimation of the rotation angle is refined with each iteration. In practice, we noticed that the methods converge already after two iterations in most cases. We therefore restrict the maximum number of iterations to three.

3.2   Phase-Only Correlation

The phase correlation is a frequency domain technique used to estimate the delay or shift between two copies of the same signal. This technique is based on the shift properties of the Fourier transform and determines the location of the peak of the inverse Fourier transform of the normalized cross-power spectrum. Consider two images u and v such that v is translated with a displacement $[x_0, y_0]$ relative to u:

$$v(x, y) = u(x + x_0, y + y_0) \tag{4}$$

Given their corresponding Fourier transforms U and V, the shift theorem of the Fourier transform states that U and V differ only by a linear phase factor

$$U(\omega_x, \omega_y) = V(\omega_x, \omega_y) \cdot e^{i(\omega_x x_0 + \omega_y y_0)} \tag{5}$$

where ω_x and ω_y are the frequency component of the columns and the row of the image. The correlation response s of the normalized cross-power spectrum of U and V is computed from its inverse Fourier transform:

$$s = \mathscr{F}^{-1} \left\{ \frac{U^* \cdot V}{|U^* \cdot V|} \right\} \tag{6}$$

where U^* represents the complex conjugate of U and $\cdot$ denotes the point-wise multiplication. The displacement is then computed as the maximum of the response function. In the ideal case, the inverse Fourier transform of the normalized cross-power spectrum is a delta function centered at the displacement between the two images. A regularized phase correlation version can be found in Eisenbach et al. [12], where the response is computed by regularizing the phase correlation using a constant λ. This parameter should be in the order of magnitude of the noise variance in the individual components of the cross spectrum $V \cdot U^*$:

$$s = \mathscr{F}^{-1} \left\{ \frac{U^* \cdot V}{|U^* \cdot V| + \lambda} \right\} \tag{7}$$

3.3   Discriminative Correlation Filters

Recently, Discriminative Correlation Filters (DCF) based approaches have successfully been applied to visual tracking and have obtained state-of-the-art performance on benchmark datasets [15,17]. The idea is to learn an optimal correlation filter given a number of training samples of the target appearance. The target is then localized in a new frame by maximizing the correlation response of the learned filter. By considering circular correlation, the learning and detection tasks can be performed efficiently using the Fast Fourier transform (FFT). The tracker implemented by Bolme et al. [3], called MOSSE, uses grayscale patches for learning and detection, and thus only considers luminance information. This approach has been generalized to multidimensional feature maps (e.g. RGB) [2,14], where the learned filter contains one set of coefficients for every feature dimension.

In the application of image alignment, we are only interested in finding the translation between a pair of images. The first image is set as the reference training image used for learning the correlation filter. We consider the D-dimensional feature map with components u_j, $j \in \{1, \ldots, D\}$. The goal is to learn an optimal correlation filter f_j per feature dimension that minimizes the following cost:

$$\varepsilon = \left\| \sum_{j=1}^{D} f_j \star u_j - g \right\|^2 + \lambda \sum_{j=1}^{D} \|f_j\|^2. \tag{8}$$

Here, the star $\star$ denotes circular correlation. The first term is the L^2-error of the actual correlation output on the training image compared to the desired correlation output g. In this case, g is a Gaussian function with the peak on the displacement. The second term is a regularization with a weight λ. The considered signals f_j, u_j and g are all of the same size, corresponding to the image size in our case. The filter that minimizes the cost (8) is given by

$$F_j = \frac{G^* \cdot U_j}{\sum_{k=1}^{D} U_k^* \cdot U_k + \lambda}. \tag{9}$$

Here, capital letters denote the discrete Fourier transform (DFT) of the corresponding signals.

To estimate the displacement, the correlation filter is applied to the feature map v extracted from the second image. The correlation response is computed in the Fourier domain as:

$$s = \mathscr{F}^{-1} \left\{ \sum_{j=1}^{D} F_j^* \cdot V_j \right\} = \mathscr{F}^{-1} \left\{ G \cdot \frac{\sum_{j=1}^{D} U_j^* \cdot V_j}{\sum_{j=1}^{D} U_j^* \cdot U_j + \lambda} \right\} \tag{10}$$

The displacement can then be found by maximizing s.

The multi-channel DCF provides a general framework for incorporating any kind of pixel-dense features. Danelljan et al. [10] recently performed an evaluation of several color features in a DCF-based framework for visual tracking. In their work it was shown that the Color Names (CN) [22] representation concatenated with the grayscale channel provides the best result compared to several other color features. We therefore evaluate this feature combination in the presented DCF approach. We refer to this method as DCF-CN.

Eq. 10 resembles the procedure (6) used for computing the POC response. However, two major distinctions exist. First, DCF employs the desired correlation output g, which is usually set to a Gaussian function with a narrow and centered peak. In standard POC the desired response is implicitly considered to be the Dirac function. In the DCF approach g acts as a lowpass filter, providing a smoother correlation response. The second difference is that the cross-correlation is divided by the cross power spectrum in the POC approach. In the DCF method, the cross-correlation is instead divided by the power spectrum of the reference image. For this reason, DCF is not symmetric but depends on which image that is considered the reference.

Fig. 3. Left: Sample image from the *Synthetic dataset.* **Middle:** Sample images from the *Lunch Room Blue* dataset. **Right:** Sample image from the *Lunch Room* dataset.

4 Experiments

In this section we present the datasets and the evaluation methodology for the image alignment methods.

4.1 Datasets

To the best of our knowledge, no dataset with sparsely structured scenes were publicly available, before we acquired and published the following three datasets[1]. **Synthetic dataset**: consists of 72 images of a room rendered with Blender[2] with a resolution of 1280×1920 px. Intrinsic parameters were retrieved from Blender and the camera is rotating by 5 degrees between consecutive images. This dataset depicts a sparsely structured scene.
Lunch Room Blue: consists of 72 images acquired with a Canon DS50 and perspective lenses with a resolution of 1280×1920 px at poor light condition.
Lunch Room: consists of 72 images acquired with a Canon DS70 and wide angle lenses Samyang 2.8/10mm (about 105 degree of field of view), with a resolution of 5740×3780 px.
For the image acquisition of the real datasets, a panorama head was used to approximate a fixed rotation of 5 degrees around the vertical axis about the optical center of the camera. These datasets were acquired in the same room with different light conditions. They naturally contain more structure than the synthetic images. We have tested all methods on rectified images to remove lense distortion effects. Fig. 3 shows sample images for the three datasets.

---

[1] http://www.cvl.isy.liu.se/research/datasets/passta/
[2] http://www.blender.org/

4.2   Results and Discussion

We compare four different correlation-based methods: phase correlation (POC) [18], regularized phase correlation (RPOC) [12] and discriminative correlation filter (DCF-CN) with and without (DCF) the color names [3,10]. For reference, a state-of-the-art feature-based approach for panoramic image stitching has been included [19].

The results are shown using three different evaluation metrics. Table 1 (I) shows the standard deviation of the estimated angles compared to the reference angle of 5 degrees. Table 1 (II) shows the success rate of the four methods on the three datasets. An estimated angle is considered to be an inlier (and therefore a success) if the error is smaller than a threshold. The value for the threshold has been computed as the 95th percentile of the absolute error on each dataset for all four methods, or 2 degrees, whether is lower. Finally, Table 1 (III) shows the average estimated angle in the three datasets when only considering the successful estimates (inliers).

Table 1. Results of each method for all three datasets. **I**: Standard Deviation of the estimated angles from the reference angle (degrees). **II**: Inlier rate for the four methods (threshold set at 95 percentile). **III**: Average inter-frame rotation in degrees (successful cases).

	Synthetic			Lunch Room Blue			Lunch Room		
	I	II	III	I	II	III	I	II	III
Feature-based	0.95	98.63%	4.97	4.68	84.93%	5.04	0.86	94.52%	4.70
POC	2.52	31.94%	5.20	1.41	90.41%	5.41	0.56	97.22%	5.29
RPOC	2.47	41.67%	4.98	1.44	91.78%	5.19	1.57	87.50%	5.08
DCF	**0.06**	**100.00%**	**5.00**	**0.62**	**98.63%**	**5.18**	**0.51**	**97.22%**	**4.97**
DCF-CN	**0.07**	**100.00%**	**4.99**	**0.61**	**98.63%**	**5.17**	**0.50**	**97.22%**	**4.98**

We observe that the proposed DCF-based methods outperform the POC methods in all three datasets. The achieved success rates, (Table 1 (II)), in the synthetic dataset clearly demonstrate that POC-based methods fail on the majority of cases. In the same scenario, both DCF-based methods provide a 100% inlier rate and below 0.07 degrees in standard deviation. Among the successful estimates on the synthetic dataset, the DCF-based approaches still outperform the evaluated POC methods. The average angle, (Table 1 (III)), is correct within 0.01 degrees for the DCF methods. For the Lunch Room Blue dataset DCF and DCF-CN achieve significantly lower standard deviations of 0.61 and 0.62 degrees respectively compared to 1.41 for POC and 1.44 degrees for RPOC. Similarly, there is a clear difference in the inlier rate. On the Lunch Room dataset, the standard DCF and DCF-CN achieve a slight improvement over normal POC, while RPOC provides inferior results. Table 1 (II) shows that the DCF-based methods provide the same inlier rate as POC. However, they perform better in terms of accuracy both in standard deviation, (Table 1 (I)), and mean angle estimation, (Table 1 (III)). Table 1 (II) and (III) show that the feature-based method performs well when it is able to retrieve reliable features. Nevertheless, we notice that it is inferior to both the DCF-based methods.

The success of the DCF-based approaches is likely due to their robustness to geometric distortions, which has previously been demonstrated in the application of visual tracking. This property is largely attributed to the desired correlation output g, which regularizes the correlation response as discussed in Section 3.3. Moreover, our results indicate an improvement in precision and robustness when using the color names representation instead of only grayscale images in our DCF-based framework. Fig. 1 Middle and Right show a comparison between the standard POC and the DCF using color names representation on an image pair.

5   Conclusions

In this paper, we tackle the problem of image alignment for panorama stitching in sparsely structured scenes. We propose an image alignment pipeline based on discriminative correlation filters. Two DCF-based versions are evaluated on three panorama datasets of sparsely structured indoor environments. We show that the proposed methods are able to perform robust and accurate image alignment in this scenario. Additionally, both DCF-based methods are shown to outperform the standard and the regularized phase-correlation approaches.

Future work will consider extending our evaluation with other panorama datasets of even more challenging scenarios. We will also look into generalizing our image alignment pipeline for more general image mosaicking problems.

Acknowledgments. The authors thank Andreas Robinson for providing the synthetic dataset. This research has received funding from the Swedish Foundation for Strategic Research through the grant VPS and from Swedish Research Council through grants for the projects energy models for computational cameras (EMC^2). This work was also supported by the EC's Horizon 2020 R&I Programme, grant agreement No 644839 .

References

1. Alba, A., Aguilar-Ponce, R.M., Vigueras-Gómez, J.F., Arce-Santana, E.: Phase correlation based image alignment with subpixel accuracy. In: Batyrshin, I., González Mendoza, M. (eds.) MICAI 2012, Part I. LNCS, vol. 7629, pp. 171–182. Springer, Heidelberg (2013)
2. Boddeti, V.N., Kanade, T., Kumar, B.V.K.V.: Correlation filters for object alignment. In: CVPR (2013)
3. Bolme, D.S., Beveridge, J.R., Draper, B.A., Lui, Y.M.: Visual object tracking using adaptive correlation filters. In: CVPR (2010)

4. Brown, L.G.: A survey of image registration techniques. ACM Computing Surveys **24**, 325–376 (1992)
5. Brown, M., Lowe, D.: Recognising panoramas. In: IJCV, Nice, vol. 2, pp. 1218–1225, October 2003
6. Brown, M., Lowe, D.G.: Automatic panoramic image stitching using invariant features. IJCV **74**(1), 59–73 (2007)
7. Chen, Q., Defrise, M., Deconinck, F.: Symmetric phase-only matched filtering of Fourier-Mellin transforms for image registration and recognition. TPAMI **16**(12), 1156–1168 (1994)
8. Danelljan, M., Häger, G., Khan, F.S., Felsberg, M.: Coloring channel representations for visual tracking. In: SCIA (2015)
9. Danelljan, M., Häger, G., Shahbaz Khan, F., Felsberg, M.: Accurate scale estimation for robust visual tracking. In: BMVC (2014)
10. Danelljan, M., Shahbaz Khan, F., Felsberg, M., van de Weijer, J.: Adaptive color attributes for real-time visual tracking. In: CVPR (2014)
11. De Castro, E., Morandi, C.: Registration of translated and rotated images using finite fourier transforms. TPAMI **9**(5), 700–703 (1987)
12. Eisenbach, J., Mertz, M., Conrad, C., Mester, R.: Reducing camera vibrations and photometric changes in surveillance video. In: AVSS, pp. 69–74, August 2013
13. Foroosh, H., Zerubia, J., Berthod, M.: Extension of phase correlation to subpixel registration. IEEE Transactions on Image Processing **11**(3), 188–200 (2002)
14. Galoogahi, H., Sim, T., Lucey, S.: Multi-channel correlation filters. In: ICCV (2013)
15. Henriques, J.F., Caseiro, R., Martins, P., Batista, J.: High-speed tracking with kernelized correlation filters. CoRR abs/1404.7584 (2014)
16. Horner, J.L., Gianino, P.D.: Phase-only matched filtering. Applied Optics **23**(6), 812–816 (1984)
17. Kristan, M., et al.: The visual object tracking vot2014 challenge results. In: Agapito, L., Bronstein, M.M., Rother, C. (eds.) ECCV 2014 Workshops. LNCS, vol. 8926, pp. 191–217. Springer, Heidelberg (2015)
18. Kuglin C.D., Hines, D.C.: The phase correlation image alignment method. In: 1975 International Conference on Cybernetics and Society (1975)
19. MATLAB: Computer Vision Toolbox - version 8.4.0 (R2014b). The MathWorks Inc., Natick, Massachusetts (2015)
20. Szeliski, R.: Image alignment and stitching: A tutorial. Found. Trends. Comput. Graph. Vis. **2**(1), 1–104 (2006)
21. Takita, K.: High-accuracy subpixel image registration based on phase-only correlation. IEICE Transactions on Fundamentals of Electronics, Communications and Computer **86**(8), 1925–1934 (2003)
22. van de Weijer, J., Schmid, C., Verbeek, J.J., Larlus, D.: Learning color names for real-world applications. TIP **18**(7), 1512–1524 (2009)
23. Wolberg, G., Zokai, S.: Robust image registration using log-polar transform. In: ICIP (2000)
24. Wu, Y., Lim, J., Yang, M.H.: Online object tracking: a benchmark. In: CVPR (2013)
25. Zitov, B., Flusser, J.: Image registration methods: a survey. Image and Vision Computing **21**, 977–1000 (2003)

Microscopy Image Enhancement for Cost-Effective Cervical Cancer Screening

Joakim Lindblad[1]([✉]), Ewert Bengtsson[2], and Nataša Sladoje[2,3]

[1] Faculty of Technical Sciences, University of Novi Sad, Novi Sad, Serbia
joakim@cb.uu.se
[2] Centre for Image Analysis, Department of Information Technology,
Uppsala University, Uppsala, Sweden
ewert@cb.uu.se
[3] Mathematical Institute, Serbian Academy of Sciences and Arts, Belgrade, Serbia
natasa.sladoje@it.uu.se

Abstract. We propose a simple and fast method for microscopy image enhancement and quantitatively evaluate its performance on a database containing cell images obtained from microscope setups of several levels of quality. The method utilizes an efficiently and accurately estimated relative modulation transfer function to generate images of higher quality, starting from those of lower quality, by filtering in the Fourier domain. We evaluate the method visually and based on correlation coefficient and normalized mutual information. We conclude that enhanced images exhibit high similarity, both visually and in terms of information content, with acquired high quality images. This is an important result for the development of a cost-effective screening system for cervical cancer.

1 Introduction

In microscopy, very high quality optical systems are considerably more expensive than those of a standard quality; significant reduction in overall system cost can be achieved if cheaper optics can be utilized without sacrificing too much of performance. Similarly, when facing large scale imaging tasks, there is also a trade of regarding the number of pixels to utilize and the reached processing speed. Decreasing the pixel size by a factor two, in order to increase the amount of image detail, leads to an increase in the number of pixels to process by a factor of four. This often translates to a corresponding increase in operational costs of the system.

We are working on a project to design a cost-effective screening system for cervical cancer, based on the detection of subtle malignancy associated changes (MAC) in the chromatin structure of cell nuclei, imaged using bright-field microscopy [7]. An example of our image material is shown in Fig. 1. For a successful differentiation of chromatin distribution seen as nuclear texture properties of the observed samples, it is essential to work with images of a quality sufficient to resolve the details needed for the analysis. On the other hand, to enable efficient processing of the acquired data, where the number of images to

R.R. Paulsen and K.S. Pedersen (Eds.): SCIA 2015, LNCS 9127, pp. 440–451, 2015.
DOI: 10.1007/978-3-319-19665-7_37

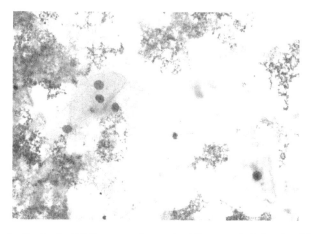

Fig. 1. Part of a PAP-smear, imaged with extended depth of focus

analyse is typically very high, the size of images, in terms of number of pixels, must be reasonable.

To keep costs at a reasonable level, a good balance between the quality of data and the cost of its processing is a necessity. In the cervical cancer screening study we work on, we have observed a satisfactory performance when utilizing images acquired using a high quality setup with a top of the line lens at 40×. The system would become significantly more cost-effective if we could, e.g., instead use a more standard lens at 20×. The secondary magnification, which determines final pixel size, also has to be optimized. The quality of the acquired images is affected by several different parameters of the imaging system and the overall performance optimization is a rather challenging task. An example showing one cell nucleus, extracted from images acquired by seven different microscopy configurations is shown in Fig 2.

To maximize the performance of the analysis, two approaches can be followed: (i) To develop feature extraction methods with increased precision and robustness, and make them suited for efficient analysis of lower quality images; (ii) To enhance image quality (to reduce noise and effects of limited resolution) by utilizing appropriate image processing methods, so that application of classical feature extraction methods provides satisfactory results.

We proposed in [6] a method for generating images at lower optical resolution, starting from higher quality ones, based on an efficient estimation of the relative modulation transfer function (RMTF). This facilitates evaluation of feature estimation methods in terms of robustness w.r.t. change of image quality and resolution. The method has shown to work very well; features estimated from synthesized images closely resemble those of real images acquired at the (low) goal resolution.

In this paper we follow the second track, that is, we aim to enhance the quality of acquired images and by that enable better subsequent analysis by classical image analysis methods. We use the same idea as in [6], but now we utilize the

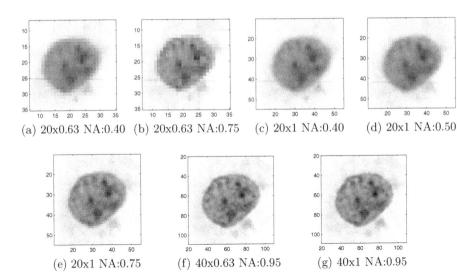

Fig. 2. Examples of one extracted cell nucleus from images acquired by the seven used microscopy configurations. For display purposes the images are magnified to the same size; the actual image matrices vary significantly in size.

estimated RMTFs to enhance low quality images, rather than degrade high quality ones. This is of course a much more challenging task; it is well known that the image deconvolution problem is, in the presence of noise, numerically unstable, often leading to severe problems with exploding noise levels. Image deconvolution and denoising are therefore typically done by iterative procedures and utilizing some a priori knowledge of the system. Approaches based on sparse regularized energy minimization are numerous and very popular [5, 9, 10]. However, they are also relatively complex and computationally demanding. The approach that we propose in this paper is based on direct multiplication in the Fourier domain. It is fast and simple, and offers an appealing balance between performance and cost. Explicit usage of the transfer functions of individual optical systems is avoided. Instead, the method relies on the estimated relative transfer functions between microscope setups, which limits the noise magnification and provides excellent results for our task. This is confirmed by the conducted quantitative evaluation.

2   Background and Previous Work

The point spread function (PSF) is the spatial response of an imaging system to a point light source; knowledge of the PSF reveals how sharp details can be reproduced by the imaging system. The (complex valued) system optical transfer function (OTF), is the Fourier transform of the system PSF. The modulation transfer function (MTF) is the modulus of the OTF, and is the most fundamental descriptor of the performance of an optical system. In this work we observe the

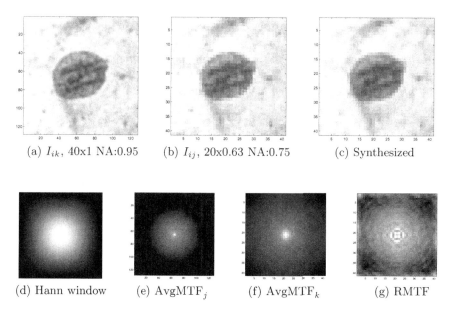

(a) I_{ik}, 40x1 NA:0.95   (b) I_{ij}, 20x0.63 NA:0.75   (c) Synthesized

(d) Hann window   (e) AvgMTF$_j$ (f) AvgMTF$_k$ (g) RMTF

Fig. 3. (a) Initial (sensed) high resolution image I_{ik} acquired using a high quality 40×
lens. (b) Reference image at desired goal quality I_{ij} acquired with a cheaper 20× lens
and a lower sampling rate. (c) Synthesized reduced quality image $\tilde{I}_{ij}$ according to (5).
(d) Used spatial weighting function, a 2D Hann window. (e,f) Average MTF of setups
j and k. (h) Estimated RMTF H_{kj} according to (4).

ratio of the MTFs between different imaging systems, which we refer to as the
relative modulation transfer function (RMTF).

An intuitive approach to take, in order to generate images simulating different image acquisition conditions, is to first estimate the PSF of each optical setup
and then to utilize them to deconvolve an initial image by the source PSF and
then convolve with the destination PSF. Accurate estimation of the PSF, however, is for a number of reasons, a very challenging tasks. We have found method
relying on edge model assumptions and/or regularized energy minimization both
difficult to use in practice and often providing results of not high enough quality [4,12]. We have proposed a parameter free method to directly estimate the
difference in performance between different setups, instead of trying to extract
an absolute characteristics of each optical setup separately, [6]. By this, we avoid
a number of difficulties and approximations leading to imprecision. In the following we briefly recall the details of the RMTF estimation.

2.1 Relative Modulation Transfer Function Estimation and Generation of Reduced Quality Images

Following [6], we denote by I_{ij} an image of a specimen i, captured with an optical setup j. The acquired image I_{ij} is a result of a convolution of the intensity

function of the imaged scene/specimen S_i with the PSF P_j of the used imaging device, $I_{ij} = S_i * P_j$. The same relation expressed in the frequency domain is given by a pointwise multiplication, $F_{ij} = S_i \cdot O_j$, where F_{ij} is the Fourier transform of the image I_{ij}, $F_{ij} = \mathcal{F}(I_{ij})$, S_i is the spectral representation (Fourier transform) of the scene S_i, and O_j is the OTF of the device (setup) j. Given F_{ik}, originating from an image of the same scene S_i, but acquired using a different optical configuration k, the spectral representation F_{ij} can be expressed as

$$F_{ij} = S_i O_j = S_i O_k \frac{O_j}{O_k} = F_{ik} \frac{O_j}{O_k}. \tag{1}$$

The *relative OTF*, describing what differentiates two imaging systems, can be estimated from the collection of values F_{ij}, without explicit knowledge of the scenes S_i. Assuming that we have acquired images of one same scene S_i by optical setups j and k, we can compute

$$\frac{O_j}{O_k} = \frac{F_{ij}S_i}{F_{ik}S_i} = \frac{F_{ij}}{F_{ik}}. \tag{2}$$

To reduce edge effects and sensitivity to displacements of the scenes, we first multiply each image in the spatial domain with a 2D Hann window. We further reduce translation sensitivity by ignoring the phase component of the system. Thus, observing the magnitude of the spectra, we obtain the formula for the relative modulation transfer function H_{kj}:

$$H_{kj} = \frac{|O_j|}{|O_k|} = \frac{|F_{ij}|}{|F_{ik}|}. \tag{3}$$

To ensure numerical stability and reduce noise sensitivity, we use the fact that the MTFs of the different setups are spatially invariant and do not depend on the imaged specimen, which allows averaging over several images. By summing magnitude spectra, we also ensure that values do not cancel each other.

A simple, robust and effective formula for estimating the relative transfer function is given in [6] as

$$H_{kj} = \frac{\sum_{i=1}^{m} |F_{ij}|}{\sum_{i=1}^{m} |F_{ik}|}, \tag{4}$$

where m is the number of different specimen imaged by each of the different setups.

To generate synthetic images at optics quality j, starting from images acquired by a setup k, it is sufficient to filter the Fourier transform of the initial image by the appropriate relative transfer function, and compute the inverse Fourier transform ($\mathcal{F}^{-1}$) of the result:

$$\tilde{I}_{ij} = \mathcal{F}^{-1}(\mathcal{F}(I_{ik}) \cdot H_{kj}). \tag{5}$$

An example of generating an image of a lower quality starting from a high quality one by utilizing the estimated RMTF and Eq. (5) is illustrated in Fig. 3.

3 Algorithm for Enhancement of Microscopy Images Acquired with Different Setups

The objective of this publication is different from that of [6]; our aim now is image enhancement, i.e., we wish to synthesize a higher quality image starting from a lower quality one. This is an ill-posed problem that we address by utilizing efficiently estimated RMTF, as described in the previous section. The enhanced image is determined as

$$\tilde{I}_{ij} = \mathcal{F}^{-1}(\mathcal{F}(I_{ik}) \cdot H_{kj} \cdot BW_{jk}). \tag{6}$$

where $\mathcal{F}^{-1}$ is the inverse Fourier transform and BW_{jk} is a 7-th order Butterworth filter with a cutoff frequency at 0.95 times the Nyquist frequency of the smaller of the two images j and k. The included Butterworth filter reduces the slight ringing effect and limits noise enhancement. We also tested Wiener deconvolution in combination with the estimated RMFT, but the above expression turned out to be both simpler and on average better performing. The Wiener filter approach could possibly become more useful with a detailed analysis of the spectral properties of the image noise.

The complete procedure for RMTF estimation for each pair of n available optical setups utilizing images of m specimen and for generation of synthetic images of a goal quality comparable with that of setup j utilizing initial images acquired with a setup k is as follows:

Algorithm:

1. For each specimen S_i, $i = 1 \ldots m$, acquire one image I_{ij} for each optical setup j, $j = 1 \ldots n$.
2. For each image compute the modulus of its Fourier transform, $|F_{ij}| = |\mathcal{F}(I_{ij})|$. For each optical setup j, sum spectra for the m specimen images: $\sum_{i=1}^{m} |F_{ij}|$.
3. For each pair of n optical setups, form the ratio H_{kj} according to (4). Utilized values are the n sums computed in the previous step.
4. Generate images of a desired goal quality of setup j, starting from real images acquired with a setup k, according to equation (6).

4 Experiments

We evaluate the method on Papanicolaou (Pap) stained microscopy images of cervical cells. Biological material was supplied by the Regional Cancer Center (RCC) in Thiruvananthapuram, Kerala, India. Image acquisition of 13 Pap-smear specimen was performed using an Olympus BX51 bright-field microscope equipped with a Hamamatsu ORCA-05G 1.4 Mpx monochrome camera. The microscope light path was filtered using a 570 nm bandpass filter (20 nm pass-band). The microscope was fitted with an E-662 Piezo server controller and actuator (Physik Instrumente GmbH & Co. KG, Karlsruhe, Germany). This allowed Z-axis step control with a 0.1 μm resolution during image acquisition.

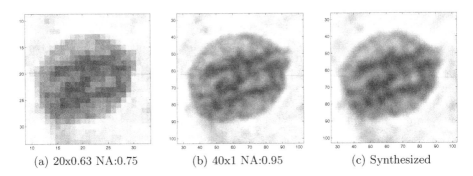

(a) 20x0.63 NA:0.75   (b) 40x1 NA:0.95   (c) Synthesized

Fig. 4. (a) Initial (sensed) low resolution image I_{ik}. (b) Reference image at desired goal quality I_{ij}. (c) Enhanced image $\tilde{I}_{ij}$ according to (6).

Each field of view was imaged at seven different resolutions, achieved through combinations between four objectives (20×, 0.40 NA; 20×, 0.50 NA; 20×, 0.75 NA; 40×, 0.95 NA) and two camera adapters (0.63×, 1.00×). The chosen combinations are listed in Table 1. Fields of view were imaged at 21 focus levels, spaced at a 0.2 μm offset, for each resolution. This assured that in-focus information is available over the entire image field. In total, 55 fields of view were acquired from the 13 specimen. A seeded watershed algorithm was applied to an extended depth of focus [2] image, generated from each focus stack, to segment manually marked nuclei, a part of such an image is shown in Fig. 1. Nuclei were then registered between resolution levels so that the same nucleus could be identified at all different resolutions. Fig. 2 shows one cell nucleus as it appears in the seven different microscopy configurations. The dataset is freely available and is documented in [8]. Cells close to the image borders were removed, leaving a total of 350 × 7 images. The data set is split in two halves, s.t. one part is used for

Table 1. List of objective and adapter combinations used to acquire images for the multi-resolution dataset and the resulting effective pixel size

Objective magnification	Objective NA	Camera adapter magnification	Effective pixel size (μm)
20	0.40	0.63	0.50
20	0.75	0.63	0.50
20	0.40	1.00	0.32
20	0.50	1.00	0.32
20	0.75	1.00	0.32
40	0.95	0.63	0.25
40	0.95	1.00	0.16

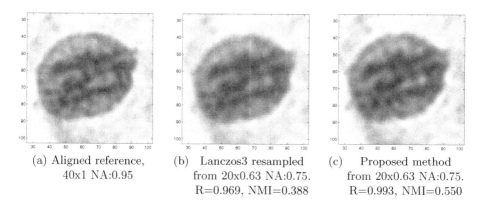

(a) Aligned reference,
40x1 NA:0.95

(b)   Lanczos3 resampled
from 20x0.63 NA:0.75.
R=0.969, NMI=0.388

(c)   Proposed method
from 20x0.63 NA:0.75.
R=0.993, NMI=0.550

Fig. 5. (a) Aligned reference image. (b) Lanczos resampled image. (c) Resampled image according to (6).

training (i.e. estimation of RMTFs) and the other part is used for performance evaluation.

RMTFs are computed as described in Section 3. We notice that for higher frequencies, which are essentially blocked by both of the involved optics, the RMTF approaches 1.0, seen as brighter corners in Fig. 3. As long as high frequent sensor noise is moderate, this does not lead to any problems; there is no large amplification of any frequency. Application of the Butterworth filter, as written in Eq (6), is therefore the only additional processing step we include.

5   Quantitaive Evaluation

Instead of relying on secondary estimated features, we perform a more direct evaluation by pixel-wise comparison of enhanced images with accurately registered images acquired at the goal resolution. For such an approach accurate registration is of utmost importance. We have used a combination of phase based registration followed by a simplex search to minimize weighted cross correlation in the spatial domain.

Our focus is on the highly textured chromatin pattern within the cell nuclei. That region is a small part of each image; to not bias the evaluation by the surrounding less textured cytoplasm background, we find important to use an appropriate weighting mask. For that purpose, we use the same 2D Hann window as when computing the RMFT functions (Sect. 2.1). By this weighting, we also reduce edge effects and further improve the precision of the registration.

The overall mean intensity and contrast values are not very informative for comparison of the type of images we work with. Since image intensities are not absolute quantitative for light microscopy images, standard pixel-wise distance measures such as mean squared error (MSE) and peak signal to noise ratio (PSNR) are not directly applicable. For image intensities normalized to zero mean and unit variance, the MSE is equivalent to the Pearson correlation coefficient R, with a simple relation between them, MSE $= 2(1 - R)$. The correlation coefficient also corresponds to the structure component of the structural similarity index (SSIM), [13], (the other two components of SSIM are irrelevant for normalized images). These observations lead us to select the Pearson correlation coefficient as our first measure of similarity.

Another commonly used pixel-wise image similarity measure, which is insensitive to intensity and contrast changes, is normalized mutual information (NMI). NMI is a measure of the statistical dependence between two random variables. It can be qualitatively considered as a measure of how well one image explains the other. We use NMI as our second similarity measure, where the joint histogram of two images is computed using 64×64 bins, which gives a suitable quantization of the intensity scale.

5.1 Image Registration with Subpixel Precision

For useful pixel-wise comparison, the two images need to be perfectly registered. We apply a sub-pixel registration method proposed in [11] and further improved in [3]. This method operates in the Fourier domain and uses a refined DFT computation to estimate the peak in the cross correlation image with sub-pixel accuracy. The use of a log-polar transformation enables determination of rotation and scaling as well. Combined with a 2D Hann window, this method gives a fast and reasonably accurate image alignment. However, the used similarity measures are very sensitive to even the slightest misalignment and we observe that the log-polar phase correlation, due to near rotational symmetry of many of the nuclei, does not always provide high enough quality alignment for our purposes. We therefore perform a final sub-pixel refinement in the spatial domain, facilitated by a bounded Simplex optimization, which provides us the precision required.

5.2 Baseline Reference

To better appreciate the enhancement result, we evaluate how the two selected performance measures rank the similarity of repeated acquisition of the same cell, if the specimen is taken out of the microscope and put back, and then registered in the same way as our enhanced images. We consider a performed image enhancement successful if we reach a similarity with the target image which is not less that the lowest observed similarity by such repeated acquisitions of the same cell nucleus. Averaged results for 108 repeated acquisition are shown in Figures 6 and 7, for cross-correlation and NMI respectively, as semi-transparent surfaces intersecting the bar-plots. We expect that realistic variations due to imaging conditions are significantly larger than for repeated acquisition of the same microscope slide which does not involve variations in staining and operating conditions. We therefore find this selected baseline reference as sufficiently representative/demanding.

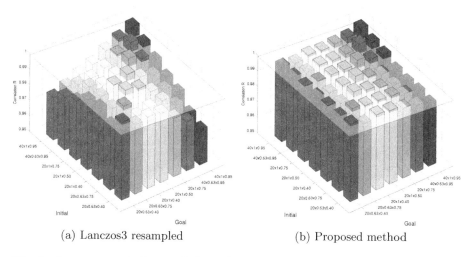

(a) Lanczos3 resampled   (b) Proposed method

Fig. 6. Average correlation coefficients R between generated images and registered (ground truth) reference images, for all pairs of available initial and goal setups (qualities). (a) Lanczos resampled images. (b) Images generated according to (6). The semi-transparent plane corresponds the to lowest observed correlation between registered images of the same specimen, when repeatedly imaged without changing the optical setup.

5.3   Results

As an alternative to our proposed enhancement method, we observe resampling from one image resolution to the other using a Lanczos-3 interpolation. According to [1], the Lanczos kernel (with a = 3) keeps low frequencies and rejects high frequencies better than any other (achievable) filter seen so far. We find Lanczos interpolation comparable in terms of speed and complexity to the enhancement method we propose. We present and compare the computed weighted cross correlation and weighted NMI for both methods.

Results for the 175×7 images in our test set are presented in Fig 6 (correlation coefficients R) and in Fig 7 (NMI). Both measures lead to almost identical conclusion regarding achievable levels of image enhancement, by both observed methods Each bar in the presented bar-plots indicates similarity (correlation or NMI) between the enhanced initial image and the registered reference (goal) image for one particular combination of microscope setups. The enhancement method is successful (better than at least one repeated acquisition) if the transparent plane intersects the bar; in other words, all the bars with tops above the plain correspond to goal setups whose image quality can be reached by the corresponding enhanced initial setup. Clearly, the proposed method significantly outperforms Lanczos interpolation. The proposed fast and simple method provides a number of options for optimization in image acquisition and enables considerable reduction of image data (changing optics from 40×1 to 20×0.63

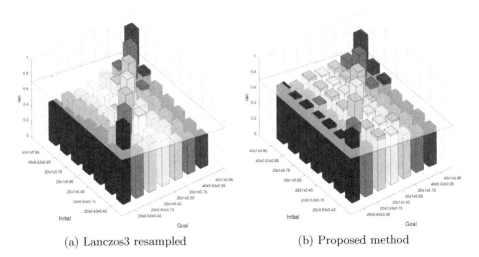

(a) Lanczos3 resampled   (b) Proposed method

Fig. 7. Normalized mutual information (NMI) between generated and reference images, for all pairs of available initial and goal setups. (a) Lanczos resampled images. (b) Image generated according to (6). The plane corresponds to lowest observed correlation for repeated images of the same specimen.

results in more than a tenfold reduction of the image data), without sacrificing too much of relevant information.

6   Conclusions and Future Work

We have presented a method for microscopy image deconvolution, based on efficiently and accurately estimated relative modulation transfer function (RMTF). This simple and fast enhancement method enables generating images of higher quality, starting from those of lower quality, by a multiplication in the Fourier domain. We have evaluated the proposed method on a database containing cell images acquired by microscope setups of several levels of quality. We have performed pixel-wise comparison of the initial image, enhanced to the goal quality, with the registered image acquired by the setup having that goal quality, by observing correlation coefficients and normalized mutual information as measures of similarity. The tests show that the proposed method significantly outperforms the enhancement based on Lanczos interpolation and enables cost-effective image acquisition, since the desired quality of images can be achieved by the proposed subsequent processing at a high speed and low cost.

Acknowledgments. We are grateful to Dr K. Sujathan at the Regional Cancer Centre in Kerala, India for providing the cellular samples and to Dr Patrik Malm for making the used data set publicly available. J. Lindblad and N. Sladoje are supported by the Ministry of Science of the Republic of Serbia through Projects ON174008 and

III44006 of the Mathematical Institute of the Serbian Academy of Sciences and Arts. N. Sladoje is supported by the Swedish Governmental Agency for Innovation Systems (VINNOVA).

References

1. Blinn, J.: Jim Blinn's Corner: Dirty Pixels. Morgan Kaufmann Publishers Inc. (1998)
2. Forster, B., Van de Ville, D., Berent, J., Sage, D., Unser, M.: Extended depth-of-focus for multi-channel microscopy images: A complex wavelet approach. In: IEEE Int. Symp. Biomed. Imaging: Macro to Nano, vols. 1 and 2, pp. 660–663 (2004)
3. Guizar-Sicairos, M., Thurman, S.T., Fienup, J.R.: Efficient subpixel image registration algorithms. Optics Letters **33**(2), 156–158 (2008)
4. Joshi, N., Szeliski, R., Kriegman, D.: PSF estimation using sharp edge prediction. In: IEEE Conference on Computer Vision and Pattern Recognition, CVPR 2008, pp. 1–8. IEEE (2008)
5. Khare, A., Tiwary, U.S., Jeon, M.: Daubechies complex wavelet transform based multilevel shrinkage for deblurring of medical images in presence of noise. International Journal of Wavelets, Multiresolution and Information Processing **7**(05), 587–604 (2009)
6. Lindblad, J., Sladoje, N., Malm, P., Bengtsson, E., Moshavegh, R., Mehnert, A.: Optimizing optics and imaging for pattern recognition based screening tasks. In: Proc. Int. Conf. on Pattern Recogn., Stockholm, Sweden, pp. 3333–3338, August 2014
7. Malm, P.: Image Analysis in Support of Computer-Assisted Cervical Cancer Screening. Ph.D. thesis, Uppsala University, Department of Information Technology (2013)
8. Malm, P.: Multi-resolution cervical cell dataset. Tech. Rep. 37. Uppsala University, Division of Visual Information and Interaction (2013)
9. Oliveira, J.P., Bioucas-Dias, J.M., Figueiredo, M.A.: Adaptive total variation image deblurring: a majorization-minimization approach. Signal Processing **89**(9), 1683–1693 (2009)
10. Osher, S., Burger, M., Goldfarb, D., Xu, J., Yin, W.: An iterative regularization method for total variation-based image restoration. Multiscale Modeling & Simulation **4**(2), 460–489 (2005)
11. Reddy, B., Chatterji, B.N.: An FFT-based technique for translation, rotation, and scale-invariant image registration. IEEE Transactions on Image Processing **5**(8), 1266–1271 (1996)
12. Smith, E.H.B.: PSF estimation by gradient descent fit to the ESF. In: Electronic Imaging 2006, pp. 60590E–60590E. International Society for Optics and Photonics (2006)
13. Wang, Z., Bovik, A.C., Sheikh, H.R., Simoncelli, E.P.: Image quality assessment: From error visibility to structural similarity. IEEE Transactions on Image Processing **13**(4), 600–612 (2004)

Quantification of Brain Access of Exendin-4 in the C57BL Mouse Model by SPIM Fluorescence Imaging and the Allen Mouse Brain Reference Model

Casper Bo Jensen[1]([✉]), Anna Secher[2], Jacob Hecksher-Sørensen[2], Knut Conradsen[1], and Rasmus Larsen[1]

[1] Department of Applied Mathematics and Computer Science,
Technical University of Denmark, Kgs. Lyngby, Denmark
{cboa,knco,rl}@dtu.dk
[2] Novo Nordisk, Global Research, Måløv, Denmark
{aasc,jhes}@novonordisk.com

Abstract. With the recent advance in 3D microscopy such as Single Plane Illumination Microscopy (SPIM) it is possible to obtain high resolution image volumes of the entire mouse brain. These data can be used to study the access of several peptides such as the glucagon-like peptide-1 (GLP-1) analogue Exendin-4, into the brain with the aim of developing medication for obesity. To investigate mode of action of the medication it is important to identify the specific anatomical brain nuclei that are targeted by the compound. Such segmentations can be obtained using an annotated digital brain atlas. We construct a SPIM brain atlas based on the Allen mouse brain 3D reference model and use it to analyze the access of peripherally injected Exendin-4 into the brain compared to a negative control group. The constructed atlas consists of an average SPIM volume obtained from eight C57BL mouse brains using group-wise registration. A cross-modality registration is performed between the constructed average volume and the Allen mouse brain reference model to allow propagation of annotations to the SPIM average brain. Finally, manual corrections of the annotations are performed and validated by visual inspection. The study shows that Exendin-4 have access to brain regions such as the arcuate hypothalamic nucleus and the nucleus of the solitary tract, which are areas involved in regulating food intake.

Keywords: Mouse brain · Allen mouse brain 3D reference model · Digital atlas · Atlas segmentation · Image registration

1 Introduction

Obesity is a disease, which has become a worldwide epidemic growing at an alarming rate. For the individual the consequence of obesity is an increased risk of acquiring metabolic disorders like type 2 diabetes and cardiovascular diseases.

© Springer International Publishing Switzerland 2015
R.R. Paulsen and K.S. Pedersen (Eds.): SCIA 2015, LNCS 9127, pp. 452–461, 2015.
DOI: 10.1007/978-3-319-19665-7_38

Glucagon-like peptide-1 (GLP-1) analogues such as Exendin-4 have shown a positive effect on weight loss and thus belongs to a class of peptides which might be used for tomorrow's obesity medication. A way to study the distribution of GLP-1 analogues in the brain after administration is using histology, [3]. Due to the numerous histological slides that need to be produced, these types of studies are expensive and time consuming. Additionally, it is difficult to compare results across studies due to the difficulty of precisely denoting anatomical structures in the data.

One technique that might overcome these limitations is the new imaging modality Single Plane Illumination Microscopy (SPIM), which is a non-destructive method to produce well-registered optical sections suitable for 3D reconstruction [7]. SPIM is a type of fluorescence microscopy with the ability to produce 3D data of macroscopic objects in cellular resolution, e.g. of the mouse brain [5].

A popular segmentation strategy in neuro-imaging is the use of computational atlases, used in various imaging modalities both in human and animal models [4]. An atlas typically consists of a reference volume with accompanied annotations. The reference volume can be produced by computation of averages of ensembles of segmented images after image registration, [2]. A new image can then be segmented by image registration to the atlas volume and superimposition of the segmented structures from the atlas. For common imaging modalities some computational atlases of the mouse brain are available, e.g. [6], [9]. To the authors' knowledge no SPIM brain atlases have been published.

We construct a SPIM atlas by group-wise registration of recorded mouse brains. A good initial guess of the annotations are obtained by cross-modality registration to an existing atlas, and finally manual corrections are performed to complete the atlas. The Allen mouse brain reference model, [9], is used as the source of the annotations due to the model's high quality and detailed annotations.

We use the constructed atlas to investigate the access of peripherally injected Exendin-4 into the C57BL mouse brain based on quantification inside the segmented brain structures.

2   Method

2.1   Allen Mouse Brain Reference Model

A 3-D reference model, [9], is available for download using the API of the Allen Brain Atlas Data Portal [1]. The model is based on 132 annotated coronal plates of the adult mouse brain. Annotations are transferred from this reference model onto the constructed SPIM brain atlas.

Reference Volume. The Allen 3-D brain volume was reconstructed from annotated plates using a combination of high frequency section-to-section histology registration with low-frequency histology to (ex-cranio) MRI registration. The reference volume was constructed in 2006, [15], and later updated in 2011. The volume is based on Nissl stains that highlights brain regions of high nuclei concentration. The volume is available for download in 25 μm isotropic resolution. Prior to usage a smoothing of the reference volume and removal of the outer part of the olfactory bulb were performed.

Reference Annotations. The full Allen atlas consists of 1204 symmetric 3-D structures, which are more than needed in this study. For the study of GLP-1 analogues 56 structures were chosen, with the highest concentration of structures in regions relevant for appetite control and obesity such as the hypothalamus. Each structure is color-coded to visually show the hierarchical position in the brain.

2.2   SPIM Brains

In total 16 mice brains were recorded using SPIM. Eight brains were used for atlas construction and eight brains were used to quantify the access of Exendin-4 into the brain.

Tissue Preparation and Data Recording. The conditions of housing and care of the animals as well as performance of the experiments are in agreement with the Danish law of animal experimentation. After sedation the mice were euthanized by cardiac perfusion with heparinized saline followed by neutral buffered formalin. The brains were removed and cleared for SPIM by a stepwise dehydration and clearing process using tetra hydro-flurane and di-benzyl-ether (DBE), respectively.

Data were recorded with a dual side illumination Lavision system utilizing a SuperK white light laser, a 620-nm emission filter, a 700-nm excitation filter, an Olympus microscope, and an Andor Neo sCMOS camera. The brain samples were immersed in a DBE bath during recording to minimize the difference in refractive index. The recordings were performed in 5.16 μm isotropic resolution.

2.3   Atlas Construction

The constructed atlas contains 56 brain structures. Using the naming convention of the Allen reference model, [9], the structures are: Isocortex, AOB, AON, MOB, HPF, CA1, CA2, CA3, DG, BLA, ACB, CEA, CP, LSc, LSr, LSv, MS, SF, SH, TH, PVH, PVHd, ARH, SO, Pvi, PVa, Pvpo, OV, SFO, DMH, SCH, PVp, PH, VMH, LHA, ZI, ME, CLI, DR, IF, SNc, SNr, IPN, RL, VTA, PBl, PBm, AP, NTS, CB, ts, VL, AQ, c, V3, and V4. Two additional annotations are included consisting of other tissue and background, respectively.

Pre-processing. Following an initial cropping, the brain volumes were down sampled to 15 μm isotropic resolution and the axes were reordered to match the orientation of the Allen reference model with the first axis being dorsal-ventral, the second axis being lateral-medial, and the third axis being rostral-caudal. The data recording process deformed the structure of the olfactory bulb. Therefore this structure was cropped from the data along with the medulla oblongata, which is not part of the Allen reference model. The background voxels were set to zero and additional zero-padding was performed to center the brain inside the volume. Data obtained with the SPIM modality contains a bias field due to continuos attenuation of the laser sheet by the tissue sample, as well as a non-uniform intensity profile in the generated laser sheet depending on the microscope construction. Bias field correction was applied using a toolbox developed in [8]. Outliers originating from air bubbles trapped in the ventricular system during the tissue preparation process were removed.

After the individual pre-processing of the brains, intensity normalization was performed based on matching the median value of the brains. This was done to avoid creating an average volume biased towards scans with higher intensities caused by different microscope settings rather than on real biological differences.

Creation of SPIM Atlas. Creation of the SPIM atlas was based on image registration between recorded SPIM data and the Allen reference model. The main registrations used in this work are based on a hierarchical transformation model, introduced in [11], which captures the global and local deformations of the tissue,

$$\mathbf{T}(x,y,z) = \mathbf{T}_{global}(x,y,z) + \mathbf{T}_{local}(x,y,z) \tag{1}$$

where the global transformation is a standard affine transformation. The local transformation model, a Free Form Deformation (FFD), is in 3D defined by an $n_x \times n_y \times n_z$ mesh of control points $\mathbf{\Phi}$ with spacing $(\delta_x, \delta_y, \delta_z)$. The underlying image is then deformed by manipulating the mesh of control points based on B-splines.

A fast way to regularize the deformation is to apply multi-level B-splines [12]; i.e. given control point resolutions $\Phi_1...\Phi_H$, at levels $1, ..., H$, the final local transformation is the sum of the transformations at each level,

$$T_{local} = \sum_{h=1}^{H} T_{local}^h \tag{2}$$

All transformations were calculated and applied using the Image Registration Toolkit, which was used under Licence from Ixico Ltd. [11], [12], [14].

The constructed SPIM atlas, based on the eight recorded SPIM scans, was created based on the following algorithm,

Algorithm 1. SPIM atlas construction

1: Register (rigid) all mouse brains to Allen reference model
2: Template = Intensity average of all registered mouse brains
3: **Repeat**
4:     Register (FFD) all mouse brains to template
5:     Template = Intensity average of all registered mouse brains
6: **Until** template stops changing
7: Register (FFD) Allen reference model (volume data + annotation data) to SPIM template

In line 1, using normalized mutual information, all scans were linearly (3 degrees of freedom for rotations, 3 degrees of freedom for translations) registered towards a pre-existing atlas, namely the Allen reference model. All scans were then averaged to create the first population atlas, representing the average anatomy of the study samples. An iterative 3 generation multi scale non-linear alignment procedure was then begun, registering each mouse towards the atlas of the previous non-linear generation using cross correlation as similarity measure. In line 6, the root-mean-square error between the voxel intensities of the current atlas and the previous atlas was calculated and an appropriate threshold value chosen to define the state where the atlas stopped changing. In line 7, the FFD transformation was calculated again based on the volume data of the Allen reference model. The calculated transformation was then applied to the annotation data of the model to bring these into alignment with the SPIM atlas volume. The last step in completing the SPIM atlas was manual correction of the computed annotations.

2.4   Exendin-4 Study

A concentration of 240 nmol/kg Exendin-4 was fluorescently labelled with Vivo-Tag-S 750 (Perkin Elmer) and injected into 6-8 weeks old male C57BL mice (Taconic) two hours prior to euthanization.

A two channel SPIM scan was performed of the brains with one channel recording the auto-fluorescence of the tissue, and the other channel recording the specific signal of the labelled Exendin-4. Similarly, four negative control brains were scanned following vehicle injection using the same data recording protocol. Segmentations of the brains were obtained by non-linear registration to the constructed atlas and propagation of the annotations. Detection of signal in the statistical analysis was performed by observing the 95th percentile inside each segmented brain area after removal of any bleed-through signal from the auto-fluorescence channel. The 95th percentile was used to eliminate outliers caused by small air bubbles typically situated on the surface of the tissue.

3   Results

3.1   Overview of Constructed Atlas

A mid-coronal (a-b), mid-transverse (c-d), and mid-sagtial (e-f) view of the constructed SPIM atlas is seen in Figure 1. The left column of images shows the reference volume, and the right column shows the annotations overlaid onto the reference volume.

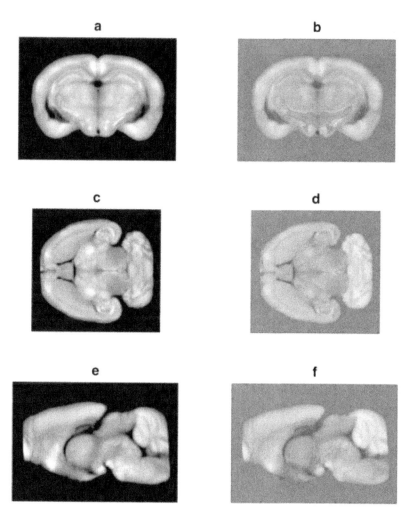

Fig. 1. Overview of constructed atlas. Left column (a,c,e) shows the atlas volume and the right column (b,d,f) shows the atlas with overlaid annotations. Green denotes the isocortex, red colors are part of the hypothalamus and thalamus, yellow is the cerebellum, blue structures belong to cerebral nuclei, and purple denotes midbrain structures.

3.2 Segmentation Example

An example of an automatic segmentation performed using the constructed atlas is seen in Figure 2. The left image shows an example of an auto-fluorescence channel recorded as part of the Exendin-4 study, and the right image shows the corresponding specific channel overlaid with calculated annotations. Strong signals are seen ventrally in the hypothalamic structures and caudally near the hindbrain structures.

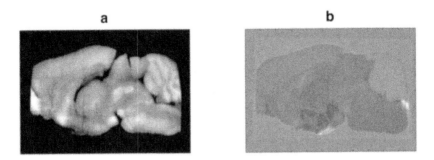

Fig. 2. Example of segmentation of a mouse brain following injection of fluorescent labelled Exendin-4. (a): Auto-fluorescence channel of the recording. (b): Specific fluorescence channel overlaid with calculated segmentaiton. High intensity (white) corresponds to a high fluorescence signal. Green denotes the isocortex, red colors are part of the hypothalamus and thalamus, yellow is the cerebellum, blue structures belong to cerebral nuclei, and purple denotes midbrain structures.

3.3 Quantification Results

Quantification results inside segmented brain regions for the Exendin-4 study are seen in Figure 3. The bar height for each structure corresponds to the mean value of the 95th percentile detected inside that structure in the four mouse brains. The error bars show the standard deviation. Signal is detected inside Nucleus of the solitary tract (NTS), Area postrema (AP), Median eminence (ME), Periventricular hypothalamic nucleus - posterior part (PVp), Vascular organ of the lamina terminalis (OV), Periventricular hypothalamic nucleus - anterior part (PVa), Arcuate hypothalamic nucleus (ARH), Septofimbrial nucleus (SF), Lateral septal nucleus, caudal part (LSc). Signal is defined as a p-value less than 0.05 when performing a two sample t-test between the Exendin-4 group and the negative control group, with the null hypothesis of equal means in the groups, and the alternative hypothesis being the Exendin-4 group having a larger mean value than the negative control group. The sample size is four mice in each group. The scale of the x-axis on the plot is in arbitrary unit.

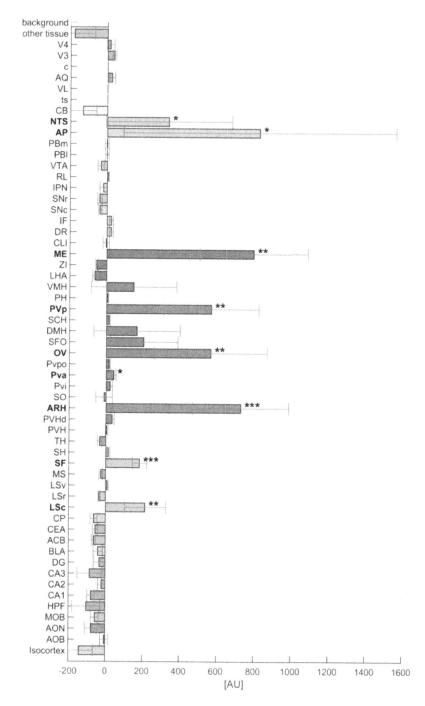

Fig. 3. Signal detection inside the automatically segmented brain regions following injection of Exendin-4. *p<0.05; **p<0.01; ***p<0.001 in a right tailed two sample t-test between the Exendin-4 group and the negative control group. Colors and acronyms follow the convention of the Allen 3D reference model.

4   Discussion

Access of Exendin-4 is seen in circumventricular structures such as ME, OV, and AP, which are brain areas not protected by the blood-brain-barrier and therefore expected to show a signal if any GLP-1 receptors are present. Access is also observed in other areas known to contain GLP-1 receptors such as the ARH and NTS. These areas have previously been identified as being part of the complex system that regulates food intake [13].

Observing the quantitative results in Figure 3, it is seen that some bars have a negative value. This is not expected in a scan setup where the value zero corresponds to no measured signal. The negative values appear due to the method of subtracting bleed-through signal of the auto-fluorescence channel. In future studies this can be avoided by using a better algorithm to remove the bleed-through signal. Although 58 t-test were made, no correction for multiple comparisons has been applied since the nature of the study was explorative.

Due to the lack of a ground truth a measure such as the Dice score can not be computed to evaluate the quality of the atlas, but by visually comparing the constructed atlas to other resources such as [10] the annotations of the structures appear to be correct. Basing a new atlas on a well established resource such as the Allen reference model has shown to reduce the dependency on neuro-anatomical expertise in order to construct the atlas. This is useful when working with a new image modality such as the SPIM system, and a similar approach can also be useful for constructing atlases for tomorrow's imaging systems.

Required manual corrections, and the overall quality of the atlas, is heavily influenced by the registration between the Allen reference model and the constructed SPIM average brain. The registration is challenging since it is both cross-modality and cross-subject. We have obtained a satisfactory result by varying registration parameters, but improvements can be obtained by manually adding landmarks. This could especially be useful around the ventricular system where the largest differences are observed between the reference model and the SPIM scans.

5   Conclusion

Access of Exendin-4 in brain structures known to regulate food intake is successfully demonstrated. Based on visual inspection the constructed brain atlas contains correct annotations of the included structures. Evaluating brain access of GLP-1 analogues, such as Exendin-4, will be important to investigate mode of action of the analogues with hope of developing future obesity medication. Since the constructed atlas is based on the Allen mouse brain reference model additional brain structures can easily be added if found relevant for study of other substances than GLP-1-analogues.

References

1. Allen institute for brain science. allen brain atlas [internet]. http://www.brain-map.org
2. Balci, S.K., Golland, P., Shenton, M., Wells, W.M.: Free-form b-spline deformation model for groupwise registration. In: MICCAI... International Conference on Medical Image Computing and Computer-Assisted Intervention, vol. 10, p. 23. NIH Public Access (2007)
3. Balland, E., Dam, J., Langlet, F., Caron, E., Steculorum, S., Messina, A., Rasika, S., Falluel-Morel, A., Anouar, Y., Dehouck, B., et al.: Hypothalamic tanycytes are an erk-gated conduit for leptin into the brain. Cell Metabolism **19**(2), 293–301 (2014)
4. Castro-González, C., Ledesma-Carbayo, M.J., Peyriéras, N., Santos, A.: Assembling models of embryo development: Image analysis and the construction of digital atlases. Birth Defects Research Part C: Embryo Today **96**(2), 109–120 (2012)
5. Dodt, H.U., Leischner, U., Schierloh, A., Jährling, N., Mauch, C.P., Deininger, K., Deussing, J.M., Eder, M., Zieglgänsberger, W., Becker, K.: Ultramicroscopy: three-dimensional visualization of neuronal networks in the whole mouse brain. Nature Methods **4**(4), 331–336 (2007)
6. Dorr, A., Lerch, J.P., Spring, S., Kabani, N., Henkelman, R.M.: High resolution three-dimensional brain atlas using an average magnetic resonance image of 40 adult c57bl/6j mice. Neuroimage **42**(1), 60–69 (2008)
7. Greger, K., Swoger, J., Stelzer, E.: Basic building units and properties of a fluorescence single plane illumination microscope. Review of Scientific Instruments **78**(2), 023705 (2007)
8. Larsen, C.T., Iglesias, J.E., Van Leemput, K.: N3 bias field correction explained as a bayesian modeling method. In: Cardoso, M.J., Simpson, I., Arbel, T., Precup, D., Ribbens, A. (eds.) BAMBI 2014. LNCS, vol. 8677, pp. 1–12. Springer, Heidelberg (2014)
9. Lein, E.S., et al.: Genome-wide atlas of gene expression in the adult mouse brain. Nature **445**(7124), 168–176 (2006)
10. Paxinos, G., Watson, C.: The rat brain in stereotaxic coordinates: hard cover edition. Academic press (2006)
11. Rueckert, D., Sonoda, L.I., Hayes, C., Hill, D.L.G., Leach, M.O., Hawkes, D.J.: Non-rigid registration using free-form deformations: Application to breast mr images. IEEE Transactions on Medical Imaging **18**, 712–721 (1999)
12. Schnabel, J.A., et al.: A generic framework for non-rigid registration based on non-uniform multi-level free-form deformations. In: Niessen, W.J., Viergever, M.A. (eds.) MICCAI 2001. LNCS, vol. 2208, pp. 573–581. Springer, Heidelberg (2001)
13. Secher, A., et al.: The arcuate nucleus mediates glp-1 receptor agonist liraglutide-dependent weight loss. The Journal of Clinical Investigation **124**(10), 4473 (2014)
14. Studholme, C., Hill, D.L., Hawkes, D.J.: An overlap invariant entropy measure of 3d medical image alignment. Pattern Recognition **32**(1), 71–86 (1999)
15. Yushkevich, P.A., Avants, B.B., Ng, L., Hawrylycz, M., Burstein, P.D., Zhang, H., Gee, J.C.: 3D mouse brain reconstruction from histology using a coarse-to-fine approach. In: Pluim, J.P.W., Likar, B., Gerritsen, F.A. (eds.) WBIR 2006. LNCS, vol. 4057, pp. 230–237. Springer, Heidelberg (2006)

Measuring the Radius of Meniscus Ring During the Growth of Silicon Rods

Rihards Fuksis[1], Mihails Pudzs[1]([✉]), Alexey Kravtsov[2], and Anatoly Kravtsov[2]

[1] Institute of Electronics and Computer Science, 14 Dzerbenes Str., Riga, Latvia
{Rihards.Fuksis,Mihails.Pudzs}@edi.lv
[2] SIA "KEPP EU", 5 Carnikavas Str., Riga, Latvia
{info,doc}@keppeu.lv

Abstract. In this paper we describe an image processing algorithm for measuring the meniscus radius of ingots when pulling silicon rods from the melt, which is heated by electron beams. We describe the image processing steps that are performed for segmentation of meniscus region — line filtering in complex domain and radius estimation that is based on the bisectors of chords algorithm by incorporating angular information. We test 3 radius measurement methods of meniscus region and analyze the stability on synthetic images as well as on video from the growth process. We also performed an experiment where silicon rod was grown using the developed image processing and control algorithm. We obtained the final result of 2 mm radius stability on the silicon rod.

1 Introduction

There is a high demand for high efficiency crystalline silicon solar cells. Float zone (FZ) grown silicon can be used in cell manufacturing and possibly lead to an increase in their efficiency because of lower defect content in its crystalline structure thanks to growth method. However, raw material for FZ feedstock — silicon rods, originally produced by slow vapor deposition in the Siemens-process, have significantly higher costs compared to feedstock used in other methods of silicon crystal growth. The paper [6] describes growing and testing of silicon rods with growth by FZ method, and mentions the scaling of the process for industrial application. Growing of the rod is performed by dipping a seed crystal into the melt and slowly pulling up and rotating. The melt is heated using electron beams, emitted from two electron guns. Focal spots of the heat, produced by electron beams, are moving along the two opposite half circle arcs with specified radii. The radii of the arcs, along with the amount of power that is transferred to the melt by the electrons, form a temperature conditions of the process. In the current stage of our research, it is assumed that the power and position of electron beams remain constant during the process. However, the rods, grown in

This work was supported by the Project "Competence centre of Latvian electric and optical equipment production" co financed by the European Union (agreement no. L-KC-11-0006).

© Springer International Publishing Switzerland 2015
R.R. Paulsen and K.S. Pedersen (Eds.): SCIA 2015, LNCS 9127, pp. 462–471, 2015.
DOI: 10.1007/978-3-319-19665-7_39

the early experimental stages, had varying diameters [6]. The goal is to grow a cylindrical rod that meets the desired diameter, therefore less material has to be cut off after growth. Given the constant power and position of electron beams, a factor that influences the diameter of grown rod is its pulling speed.

There are two general methods for measuring the diameter of growing ingots employed by well known Czochralski crystal growth method: weight control and optical control. Analogously, we use the optical control method — the device is equipped with a video camera, providing a video representation of the process. We measure the diameter of the bright arc around the growing rod. This arc is an optical phenomenon formed by the light reflected from meniscus [9]. In our closed-loop system, the measured value of diameter is then used to control the pulling speed. We should mention that in order to control trajectory and power of the electron beams, the same imaging sensor can be used, which is reserved for future development.

2   Image Segmentation

To perform the measurements on the meniscus region and obtain its radius, we first have to extract the meniscus region from the image. Growth method, where the melt is heated by using two electron beams that run on a circular trajectory, rises additional challenge to measure the radius of meniscus. Because of the bright spots left behind the electron beams, we first apply several enhancement and segmentation steps.

The camera that captures images of the growing process is mounted above the crucible, so it sees a meniscus region and rod from the above at a slight angle. It should be considered that the level of melt decreases during the process. Therefore, the meniscus ring is observed only partially and in perspective under the non-constant angle (e.g. Fig. 2, left). Most of the circle detection methods that are mentioned further, experience performance degradation if the observed shape deviates from a perfect circle (i.e. it is stretched or forms an ellipse). Additionally, if radius is measured using only a part of circle pixels (arc), then if circle is deformed, the determined value will be dependent on which part of the arc was used in the measurement.

We use affine transformations on the input image to correct the perspective distortions. Because camera is fixed during the growth procedure, we use a checkerboard pattern to obtain calibration matrix before the growing process has started. After corners of the square checkerboard are detected, the coordinate transformation matrix can be calculated. This matrix transforms coordinates from within the plane of the calibration checkerboard to equivalent screen coordinates and can be used to remap pixels of the input image. During the growth process, every frame is mapped using this transformation matrix before processing. Thus, we ensure that the processed meniscus shape is as close to a circular arc as possible.

While enhancement procedure is necessary to improve the quality of the processed image (i.e. the shape of the meniscus), the segmentation step is performed to select only the pixels that belong to the meniscus. The segmentation is crucial for some of the circle detection methods.

Meniscus region of interest (ROI) is obtained by following steps shown in block diagram in Fig. 1. After the input image is obtained from the camera, we

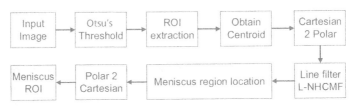

Fig. 1. Meniscus ROI segmentation block diagram

need to select the main ROI in which all of the image processing will be performed. For this task, we first perform clustering-based image thresholding by using Otsu's method. After thresholding, the largest non-zero region that represents the melt area is selected. To include in the ROI also the part of the melt covered by the rod, we perform convex hull operation on the obtained region. The resulting ROI includes melt, meniscus and rod. The input image from the camera during the silicon growth process, image after perspective correction and obtained main ROI are shown in the Fig. 2. We then find the centroid of the main ROI and use it as a center for conversion of the image into polar coordinate system. Since calculated centroid is guaranteed to be close to the middle of the circular meniscus ring, the polar coordinate system is a natural choice for detection of meniscus ROI which is of a circular shape. After converting

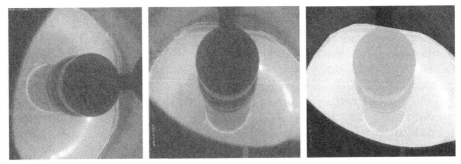

Fig. 2. Left: Input image, where silicon rod is being pulled from the melt, **middle:** input image after perspective correction, **right:** obtained main ROI.

the image into polar coordinate system, we apply line filter, called Line Non Halo Complex Matched Filter (L-NH-CMF), to extract only line like objects [8]. Next we search for the brightest points in every column and then classify them by intensity and distance from the polar coordinate center. Points representing meniscus region are the brightest and nearest pixels to the center of polar coordinate system. Image converted to polar coordinate system, image filtered with L-NH-CMF and obtained meniscus ROI are shown in Fig. 3. After obtaining points representing meniscus region we convert them back to Cartesian coordinate system and by performing morphological dilation we slightly enlarge the meniscus region.

After we have obtained the meniscus region, we apply circle detection and radius measurement algorithms on all non-zero pixels within meniscus region.

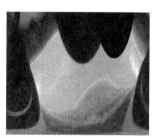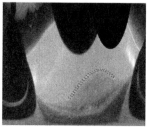

Fig. 3. Left: Image in polar coordinate system, **middle:** image after L-NH-CMF, **right:** obtained meniscus region points.

3   Circle Detection

3.1   Analysis of State of the Art Methods

Circle detection includes the determination of its center and radius. There are several circle detection methods presented previously, however, not every method can be used when dealing with a half circle or an arc, as in the case of meniscus of the growing rod. Most widely used method for circle detection is Hough Transform (HT), introduced in [3]. HT is a raster voting approach, which means that during the analysis of the image, possible candidates for the circle centers are accumulated in 3D spatial array of votes, called accumulator. Although many modifications of HT exist [10], [2], which can reduce the size of the required accumulator memory, the performance of the method is still dependent upon the size of the chosen accumulator. Also other non-HT methods could be of interest to the reader of this paper, such as [4], [1]. Less complex circle detection methods are vectorized, i.e. work with geometrical primitives, such as points and lines, to calculate and accumulate votes. They are also more sensitive to the distortions of the input data — it must be provided that most of the processed edges come from the same circle. In our setup, this is ensured by the segmentation procedure.

A few simple and effective vectorized circle detection methods were introduced by Li-qin et.al. — edge normals [5] and perpendicular bisector of chords [7]. First method relies on the fact that two normals to the circle edges intersect in the center of the circle.

Given N edge points, a total of $N \cdot \frac{N-1}{2}$ pairs of edge points can be analyzed. However, to reduce the complexity of algorithm, fewer pairs of edge points can be selected at random. For each analyzed pair of edge points $\{(A_x, A_y), (B_x, B_y)\}_i$, center candidate $(a, b)_i$ can be calculated as follows:

$$
\begin{cases}
a = A_x - \frac{A_x \cdot (B_y \cdot (A_x - B_x) - B_x \cdot (A_y - B_y))}{A_x \cdot B_y - A_y \cdot B_x} \\
b = A_y - \frac{A_y \cdot (B_y \cdot (A_x - B_x) - B_x \cdot (A_y - B_y))}{A_x \cdot B_y - A_y \cdot B_x},
\end{cases}
\tag{1}
$$

where $\mathbf{A} \equiv (\mathbf{A_x, A_y})$ and $\mathbf{B} \equiv (\mathbf{B_x, B_y})$ are unit normal vectors for edges in points A and B. Radius candidate r_i is then estimated as the mean distance between edge points A_i, B_i and the center candidate $(a, b)_i$. Circle center and radius are obtained statistically from an array of candidate values.

Despite the simplicity of this method, its performance is limited by the algorithm for estimation of edge direction. Imprecise edge detection results in the skewed normals and incorrect intersection points (center and radii candidates). A quick analysis of the error propagation can demonstrate this and provide some useful conclusions. In general, given some measured values $x_0, ...x_n$ with known uncertainties (standard deviations) $\sigma_{x_0}, ...\sigma_{x_n}$, and an expression $y = f(x_0, ...x_n)$ to calculate new value — y, we can use the method of partial derivatives to calculate the propagated error — σ_y. Assuming small errors $\sigma_{x_0}, ...\sigma_{x_n}$, the value σ_y can be estimated as follows:

$$
\sigma_y = \sqrt{\left(\frac{\partial y}{\partial x_0}\right)^2 \cdot \sigma_{x_0}^2 + \left(\frac{\partial y}{\partial x_1}\right)^2 \cdot \sigma_{x_1}^2 + \left(\frac{\partial y}{\partial x_2}\right)^2 \cdot \sigma_{x_2}^2 ...}
\tag{2}
$$

By comparing the values of summands under the square root, it is possible to conclude which of the parameters $x_0, ...x_n$ influence the error of y, and in what proportion.

In our case, we try to analyze the uncertainty of values a, b, using coordinates of points A, B, vectors $\mathbf{A, B}$, and the expression (1). Since $\mathbf{A_x} \equiv \cos(\angle A)$, $\mathbf{A_y} \equiv \sin(\angle A)$, and similarly for point B, the expression (1) can be rewritten in terms of point coordinates (A_x, A_y), (B_x, B_y) and the angles of edge normals — $\angle A, \angle B$. Because results for both coordinates a and b are similar, only first one is shown in details:

$$
a = A_x - \frac{\cos(\angle A) \cdot (\cos(\angle B) \cdot (A_y - B_y) - \sin(\angle B) \cdot (A_x - B_x))}{\sin(\angle A - \angle B)}
\tag{3}
$$

$$
\frac{\partial a}{\partial A_x} = \frac{\cos(\angle A) \cdot \sin(\angle B)}{\sin(\angle A - \angle B)} + 1 \qquad \propto \frac{1}{\sin(\angle A - \angle B)}
\tag{4}
$$

$$
\frac{\partial a}{\partial B_x} = -\frac{\cos(\angle A) \cdot \sin(\angle B)}{\sin(\angle A - \angle B)} \qquad \propto \frac{1}{\sin(\angle A - \angle B)}
\tag{5}
$$

$$
\frac{\partial a}{\partial A_y} = -\frac{\cos(\angle A) \cdot \cos(\angle B)}{\sin(\angle A - \angle B)} \qquad \propto \frac{1}{\sin(\angle A - \angle B)}
\tag{6}
$$

$$
\frac{\partial a}{\partial B_y} = \frac{\cos(\angle A) \cdot \cos(\angle B)}{\sin(\angle A - \angle B)} \qquad \propto \frac{1}{\sin(\angle A - \angle B)}
\tag{7}
$$

$$\frac{\partial a}{\partial \angle A} = \frac{\cos(\angle B)^2 \cdot (A_y - B_y) - \cos(\angle B) \cdot sin(\angle B) \cdot (A_x - B_x)}{\sin(\angle A - \angle B)^2} \tag{8}$$

$$\frac{\partial a}{\partial \angle B} = \frac{\cos(\angle A)^2 \cdot (A_y - B_y) - \cos(\angle A) \cdot sin(\angle A) \cdot (A_x - B_x)}{\sin(\angle A - \angle B)^2} \tag{9}$$

By analyzing the calculated derivatives, we can conclude that the most important factors that influence the precision of center estimation are:

1. difference of edge angles ($\angle A - \angle B$) (perpendicular edges provide the most precise center estimation, because of the high value of squared $sin(\angle A - \angle B)$),
2. angles $\angle A$ and $\angle B$ (it can be shown that the propagated angular error (8)-(9) can be significantly larger than the propagated coordinate error (4)-(7) due to presence of point coordinates A_x, A_y, B_x, B_y in the numerator).

Other approach, called perpendicular bisector of chords [7] improves the observed drawback. This method uses pairs of perpendicular bisectors of each two chords in the circle. For example, in Fig. 4 two chords $A'A''$ and $B'B''$ and their respective perpendicular bisectors are shown — it can be seen that these bisectors intersect at the center of the circle (a, b). Given N edge points, a total of $\frac{3 \cdot N!}{(N-4)! \cdot 4!}$

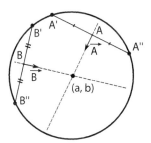

Fig. 4. Chords $A'A''$ and $B'B''$ and their respective perpendicular bisectors

combinations of chords can be analyzed, which is significantly more than for the previous approach. However, similarly as in the previous example, we can randomly select fewer quadruples of points $\{A', A'', B', B''\}_i$ and for each group to calculate the center candidate (intersection point of bisectors) $(a, b)_i$, and radius candidate (mean distance from edge points A', A'', B', B'' to the center candidate (a, b)).

To analyze the precision of this algorithm we consider following argument: suppose a chord is given by two pairs of coordinates, i.e. (A'_x, A'_y) and (A''_x, A''_y). Then, the coordinates of the chord midpoint can be calculated as: $A_x = \frac{(A'_x + A''_x)}{2}$ and $A_y = \frac{(A'_y + A''_y)}{2}$. Provided equal standard deviation σ' for the detected endpoints and the independence, the error of calculated center is smaller — $\sigma = \frac{\sigma'}{\sqrt{2}}$. Moreover, the tangent unit vector of chord bisector can be calculated as:

$$A_x = \frac{A'_y - A''_y}{l_A}, \qquad\qquad A_y = -\frac{A'_x - A''_x}{l_A}, \tag{10}$$

where l_A is the length of the chord $A'A''$. The partial derivatives show that the angular error is dependent of the length of the chords, i.e:

$$\frac{\partial \boldsymbol{A}_x}{\partial A'_x} = -\frac{(A''_y - A'_y) \cdot (A''_x - A'_x)}{l_A^3} \qquad \in O\left(\frac{1}{l_A}\right) \qquad (11)$$

$$\frac{\partial \boldsymbol{A}_x}{\partial A'_y} = \frac{1}{l_A} - \frac{(A''_y - A'_y)^2}{l_A^3} \qquad \in O\left(\frac{1}{l_A}\right), \qquad (12)$$

and etc. The longer are the observed chords, the more precise are directions of their respective bisectors. Further analysis of error propagation, given the chord centers A, B and direction vectors $\boldsymbol{A}, \boldsymbol{B}$ is identical to one, carried for edge normal method. With a proper selection of analyzed chords, subpixel precision can be achieved. We summarize our derivations by mentioning two conditions that are checked during the random analysis of chords:

- length criteria – the chords are analyzed only if their respective lengths are at least 5 pixels. Thus, we ensure that the impact of the coordinate error on the calculated bisectors is suitable;
- angle criteria – the chords are analyzed only if the angle between their appropriate bisectors is in interval of $\left[\frac{\pi}{6}, \frac{5\pi}{6}\right]$. Thus, we ensure that the influence of bisector angle error is suitable.

3.2   Proposed Method

Since edges, obtained by L-NH-CMF are multiple pixels in width, in order to increase the precision of the method further, we propose a modified approach for selection of the chord endings. A vector, obtained by the L-NH-CMF filter, points the direction of extracted edge line. This information might be used effectively: pixel values that are read (using bilinear interpolation) perpendicularly to this vector, form a certain function $f(t)$, which we call as "cross section". An example of typical cross section is given in Fig. 5. For any discrete non-zero starting point (x, y), $(x, y \in \mathbb{Z})$, the cross section can be used to estimate the position of detected line more precisely. In our experiments, we found the median approach to be most robust, i. e. line center t_{center} is calculated using:

$$\int_{-\infty}^{t_{center}} f(t)dt = 0.5 \cdot \int_t f(t)dt. \qquad (13)$$

It must be noted, however, that this operation takes additional time to calculate, compared to the standard chord bisector approach, and is prone to systematic errors if image filtering is not accurate enough. Figure 6 demonstrates introduced improvement — each positioned vector in this image begins from a non-zero pixel (detected by the filter) and shows the coordinate correction, applied using the proposed method. The dashed line demonstrates real position of the circle edge used to generate this synthetic image. After the coordinate correction, circle parameters are calculated in the same way as described in section 3.1.

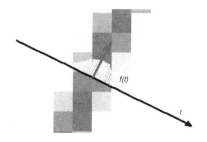
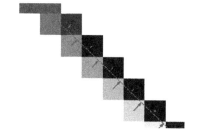

Fig. 5. Line and it's cross-section values; red arrow shows calculated line center and direction

Fig. 6. Estimation of the line center for each non-zero pixel that is acquired after filtering with L-NH-CMF

4   Experiments

We compare three methods: Hough transform, perpendicular bisector of chords, and proposed modified perpendicular bisector of chords that uses vector information obtained from L-NH-CMF. We analyze computation time, precision and accuracy. A quantitative evaluation of the observed approaches is difficult because of the absence of the ground truth data for the meniscus radii. Even though the radius of the grown rod can be thoroughly measured after the process, it doesn't represent the meniscus radius exactly [9]. Therefore, we perform two different experiments. First experiment is carried on a series of synthetic arc images with known radii. Because of the presence of ground truth data, we can evaluate accuracy of the observed circle detection methods. Our second experiment is carried on a series of real growth process images (from a video). The aim of this experiment is to evaluate the consistency of data, i.e. its precision in the real world conditions.

4.1   Radius Measurement of Arcs with Various Central Angles

It is important that the method used for the radius measurement of meniscus detects radius of a circular arc with central angle of pi or even less. Therefore our first experiment consists of generating synthetic images of circular arcs with various central angles ranging from $[\frac{\pi}{4} : 2\pi]$ and measuring the radius stability with each of the previously decribed algorithms. The radius was set to 400 pixels. Results from this experiment are shown in Fig. 7, left. As it can be seen form the Fig. 7, left, our proposed method is most stable, also when the radius of arc with central angle of $\frac{\pi}{4}$ has to be detected. It is noticable that HT tends to converge to $R + 1pix$ value. This can be because HT measures the outside part of the arc.

4.2   Radius Mesurement of Meniscus

We have recorded a video of silicon rod growth and processed 500 frames to evaluate precision of radius measurement. Each circle detection method measures

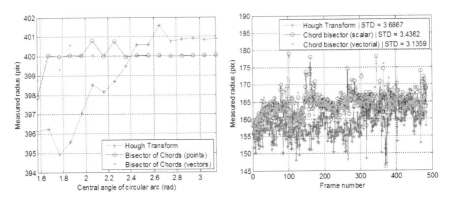

Fig. 7. Left: Radius measurement of arcs with different central angles, **right:** radius measurement of meniscus from the silicon growth video.

the value $r_{measured} \equiv r_{true} + \Delta r$, which differs from the true radius value r_{true} by some Δr. If we assume the independence between r_{true} and error Δr, the standard deviation:

$$STD(r_{measured}) = \sqrt{Var(r_{true}) + Var(\Delta r)}, \tag{14}$$

can be used to compare the precision of each method $\sqrt{Var(\Delta r)}$, because the value of $Var(r_{true})$ is identical for all compared methods. Obtained results are shown on the right side of the Fig. 7. The ratio of processing times for HT, scalar and vectorial bisector of chords is 27 : 1 : 13. In 3.4% of the frames segmentation fails to extract an arc of at least $\frac{\pi}{4}$ central angle, therefore, these frames are ommited from the final evaluation. In a system, a sliding buffer of last 30 measured radius values is used to calculate the median value. In this way we eliminate segmentation errors and obtain less varying estimated radius value. Using PID controller the estimated radius is used to calculate the pulling speed of the rod. Control of the rod growth is performed similarly as described in [9]. For reference, images of rod grown in manual mode and in automatic mode are shown in the Fig. 8.

Fig. 8. Left: Manually grown rod, **right:** rod grown with proposed method.

5   Conclusions

In this paper we have described algorithms for automatic control of rod growth process. In particular, we first examined the enhancement and segmentation of the input image to obtain the pixels of the meniscus. Next, the circular shape of the meniscus was analyzed using three circle detection methods: raster — HT, and vectorial — original and modified perpendicular bisectors of chords. We compared these methods in terms of accuracy (on synthetic images), precision and processing time (on rod growth video). HT (phase coding implementation) is the slowest approach with least performance, the original bisectors of chords is the fastest approach, but its performance can be further improved by additional analysis of the information of L-NH-CMF vectors, at the expense of the processing time. To guide proper implementation of the vectorial circle detection methods, we also analyzed the conditions that cause degradation of the precision. We provided the visual comparison of the rods, grown in manual mode and in automatic mode, using described approach.

References

1. Davies, E.: Radial histograms as an aid in the inspection of circular objects. Control Theory and Applications, IEE Proceedings D **132**(4), 158–163 (1985)
2. Davies, E.: A modified hough scheme for general circle location. Pattern Recognition Letters **7**(1), 37–43 (1988)
3. Duda, R.O., Hart, P.E.: Use of the hough transformation to detect lines and curves in pictures. Commun. ACM **15**(1), 11–15 (1972)
4. Jia, L.Q., Liu, H.M., Wang, Z.H., Chen, H.: An effective non-ht circle detection for centers and radii. In: 2011 International Conference on Machine Learning and Cybernetics (ICMLC), vol. 2, pp. 814–818, July 2011
5. Jia, L.Q., Peng, C.Z., Liu, H.M., Wang, Z.H.: A fast randomized circle detection algorithm. In: 2011 4th International Congress on Image and Signal Processing (CISP), vol. 2, pp. 820–823, October 2011
6. Kravtsov, A.: Ingots pulled with electron beam heating from skull - a new feedstock for fz crystals applicable for solar cells. In: 2014 IEEE 40th Photovoltaic Specialist Conference (PVSC), pp. 2991–2993, June 2014
7. Luo, L., Xu, D., Zhang, Z., Zhang, J., Qu, W.: A fast and robust circle detection method using perpendicular bisector of chords. In: 2013 25th Chinese Control and Decision Conference (CCDC), pp. 2856–2860, May 2013
8. Pudzs, M., Greitans, M., Fuksis, R.: Complex 2d matched filtering without halo artifacts. In: 2011 18th International Conference on Systems, Signals and Image Processing (IWSSIP), pp. 1–4, June 2011
9. Winkler, J., Neubert, M., Rudolph, J.: A review of the automation of the czochralski crystal growth process. Acta Physica Polonica A **124**(2), 181–192 (2013)
10. Yuen, H.K., Princen, J., Illingworth, J., Kittler, J.: Comparative study of hough transform methods for circle finding. Image Vision Comput. **8**(1), 71–77 (1990)

Accuracy in Robot Generated Image Data Sets

Henrik Aanæs[(✉)] and Anders Dahl

Department of Applied Mathematics and Computer Science,
Technical University of Denmark, Kgs. Lyngby, Denmark
aanes@dtu.dk
http://roboimagedata.compute.dtu.dk/

Abstract. In this paper we present a practical innovation concerning how to achieve high accuracy of camera positioning, when using a 6 axis industrial robots to generate high quality data sets for computer vision. This innovation is based on the realization that to a very large extent the robots positioning error is deterministic, and can as such be calibrated away. We have successfully used this innovation in our efforts for creating data sets for computer vision. Since the use of this innovation has a significant effect on the data set quality, we here present it in some detail, to better aid others in using robots for image data set generation.

Keywords: Image data set · Performance evaluations robotics for imaging

1 Introduction

Computer vision has undergone a tremendous development over the last couple of decades, and from being mainly a pure research topic, it has now found it's way into numerous commercial products. Hereby it reflects the large increase in our abilities to address the issues considered. It could, however, be argued that the empirical evaluation has not quite kept up. As noted by the group associated with the PASCAL visual object challenge [4], in relation to this; "A question often overlooked by the computer vision community when comparing results on a given data set is whether the difference in performance of two methods is statistically significant.". To achieve such significance in empirical investigations, sufficiently large data sets of good quality are needed, which we assume is also a motivation for the said PASCAL challenge.

To facilitate such empirical evaluation for other aspects of computer vision, other data sets have also been compiled e.g. [5,8,9]. In many cases robots are a great enabler in making such much needed data sets, as done in e.g. [1,2,6,7,10], where the robot is used to move the camera around an object, whereby a large number images are taken with well defined and repeatable camera positions.

An issue in using robots in this way is that there is typically a relatively large error between the position the robot places the camera at, and the position it is requested to place the camera at. This error is large enough to have practical influence on the data set quality. In order to address this issue, *we here present an*

© Springer International Publishing Switzerland 2015
R.R. Paulsen and K.S. Pedersen (Eds.): SCIA 2015, LNCS 9127, pp. 472–479, 2015.
DOI: 10.1007/978-3-319-19665-7_40

innovation on how to address this, and thus increasing the accuracy of the camera positioning. This is a small, but nonetheless very important, detail that makes a substantial difference in the produced data set quality. As such we used this innovation in our previous work on robot generated image data sets, [1,2,6,7], but would here like to take the opportunity to describe it in some detail, such that other can better reproduce it, as well as describing the experiments that validates this approach.

The positioning error of the robot has a deterministic and a stochastic part (the deterministic part is often also referred to as a bias). The innovation presented here is based on the observation that the stochastic part is very small, and that the error is almost entirely deterministic. To put it a bit more plainly, if you run a given positioning script for the robot, you do not get the camera positions you ask for, but you get the same sequence of positions every time you run the script. Our validation of this finding is given in Section 4, on our setup described in Section 2.

Based on this observation, we thus design and run a positioning script in front of a calibration plate, and find the camera positioning via the Camera Calibration Toolbox Matlab[1] by Jean-Yves Bouguet. The procedure is detailed in Section 3, and effectively removes the deterministic part of the positioning error.

2   Our Robot Setup

Even though the innovation of this paper generalize, it is made in a specific context, which is also the context of the experimental evaluation. For completeness we thus present our robotic setup here, which is the one we also used in [2,6,7].

Our robotic setup includes an industrial 6 axis ABB robot placed in a light shielded enclosure, and the robot and the interior of the enclosure are painted black to minimize reflections from the environment. On the robot arm we have placed a stereo camera setup with structured light for 3D scene reconstruction. We employ individually controlled LED point light sources to ensure precise scene illumination. This setup gives a very high flexibility in moving the cameras to a given position and viewing direction for acquiring images under varying illumination together with a 3D surface reconstruction from precisely that viewing direction. The setup is shown in Figure 1.

By using point light sources for illumination and acquiring images with one light source turned on at the time, we can artificially relight the scene by linear combining acquired images [3]. Hereby a continuum of illuminations can be obtained.

This setup enables very accurate data sets of real objects where we know the exact camera positioning, scene or object surface, and we know the exact geometry of the light sources. Such data is essential for empirically evaluating computer vision based on a solid statistical foundation.

---

[1] http://www.vision.caltech.edu/bouguetj/calib_doc/

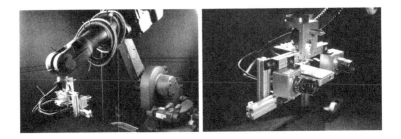

Fig. 1. The robotic setup. Left shows the full industrial robot and right is a closeup of the stereo cameras and light projector for structured light scanning.

Fig. 2. An example image of a calibration plate used for camera position calibration

3   Robot Positioning Procedeure

For completeness we here describe the procedure we apply to get high accuracy camera positions from the system described in Section 2 is as follows:

1. Design a robot positioning script In making a data set we almost always want an identically repeating camera movement (composed of discreet camera positions) over a sequence of different scenes, i.e. different objects depicted. This camera movement is designed via a positioning script.
2. This script is run with a scene consisting of a calibration plate, c.f. Figure 2.

Fig. 3. An image of placing the robot positioning tool at the origo of the calibration plate

3. The discreet positions of the camera movement are found via camera calibration, in our case via the Camera Calibration Toolbox Matlab[2] by Jean-Yves Bouguet.
4. The camera positions estimated in point 3. are used as camera positions for the data set generation, where the calibration plate is substituted with the scene or objects for a given data set.

Is noted, that the information of the requested camera positions of the script is not directly propagated to the positions used for evaluation. Also even though these camera positions might be generated by a mathematical equation, e.g. located on a sphere, this is not exactly where the cameras are positioned.

4   Experiential Results

To validate the proposed approach as outlined in Section 3, we first validated that there was a significant error between the camera positions requested and the camera positions achieved. We did this by placing a calibration sheet flat in the robot cage and aligning the robots coordinate system to that calibration plate, c.f. Figure 3. The result is that any camera calibration made from this calibration plate would be in the same global coordinate system as the robot.

---

[2] http://www.vision.caltech.edu/bouguetj/calib_doc/

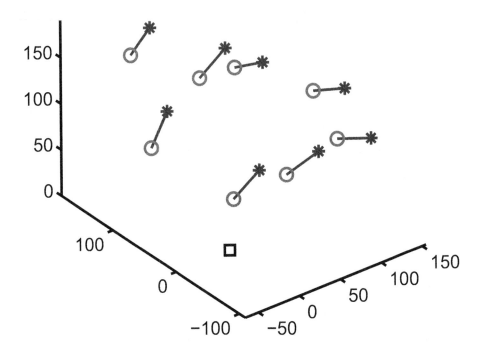

Fig. 4. Difference between requested positions, red circles, and achieved positions, blue stars. Note that the difference can not be made up from a rigid transformation. The black square denotes the origo.

This was verified by having the robot go back to various places on the calibration plate. We then requested the robot to go to eight different positions, where the camera took images of the calibration plate. These images were subsequently used to estimate the camera positions via camera calibration. The result and the discrepancy between the requested and the achieved camera positions is shown in Figure 4. Initially we performed this experiment to calibrate the *rigid transformation* between the robot tool and the camera, but the was not possible with sufficient accuracy as seen from Figure 4. This was the empirical data that made us realize, that we needed an alternative method of determining accurate camera positions, whereby we came of with the innovation presented in this paper.

Next we wanted to validate the low stochastic element of this error, and thus the applicability of our innovation presented here. A property of the robot indicated in its specification. To do this we made a script for the robot to take the image of Figure 5, move well away and go back to the same position. The result was that we got almost identical images as illustrated in Figure 6, where

Fig. 5. Image of a calibration plate that was taken by the robot, for the robot to move well away and the move back and repeat the image. The red line is drawn in, to indicate the positions of the two scan lines of Figure 6.

it is seen that the stochastic positioning error is small compared to the image noise. In this regard it should be noticed, that it is having an camera model that describes the relative movement between camera that matter, as such if the positioning error is small compared to the imaging noise a success is achieved.

To further validate that the camera positions were highly repeatable, also over the one to two months it took to record a complete data set, we performed regular recalibrations of the camera positions in the two data sets of [2,6]. As an example in [6], this resulted in "Over the two months of data acquisition period we performed 10 calibrations, and the average standard deviation of the camera positions were 0.0031 mm. The reprojection error here was 0.067 pixels." Most of this drift could be explained by temperature variations, and resulting changing of the robot arms dimensions. Thus also this aspect of the described approach was validated.

5 Discussion and Conclusion

In this paper we have presented the method we have used to achieve high camera positioning accuracy when using robots for generating large image data sets for

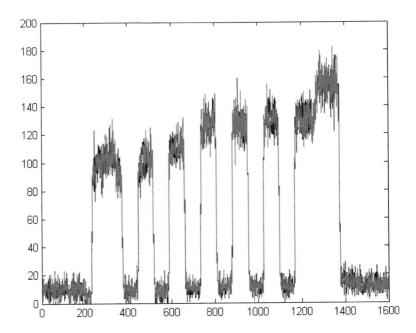

Fig. 6. The pixel intensities of the scan line denoted in red in Figure 5. One for each of the two images. Here it is seen that the transition between black and white happens at the exact same place, given the accuracy achievable due to image noise. (this is a scan line from a checker board, so ideally the curves should have straight top and bottom parts.)

computer vision. This method is based on the observation that the robots positing error is almost entirely deterministic, why it can be corrected by calibration.

This innovation has very important practical implications and provide a solution to a problem when compiling data sets. A problem we have struggled somewhat with, and are aware that others have too. As computer vision mature we believe through empirical evaluations will play a more significant role, and as such that many other will want to use robotics for this endeavor. As such we believe it relevant to share this practical innovation here with sufficient detail that it is easy to reproduce.

References

1. Aanæs, H., Dahl, A.L., Pedersen, K.S.: On recall rate of interest point detectors. In: 3DPVT 2010: Fifth International Symposium on 3D Data Processing, Visualization and Transmission (2010)
2. Aanæs, H., Dahl, A.L., Pedersen, K.S.: Interesting interest points. International Journal of Computer Vision **97**, 18–35 (2012)

3. Einarsson, P., Chabert, C.-F., Jones, A., Ma, W.-C., Lamond, B., Hawkins, T., Bolas, M.T., Sylwan, S., Debevec, P.E.: Relighting human locomotion with flowed reflectance fields. In: Rendering Techniques, pp. 183–194 (2006)
4. Everingham, M., Gool, L., Williams, C.K., Winn, J., Zisserman, A.: The pascal visual object classes (voc) challenge. Int. J. Comput. Vision **88**(2) (2010)
5. Geusebroek, J.-M., Burghouts, G.J., Smeulders, A.W.M.: The amsterdam library of object images. Int. J. Comput. Vision **61**(1) (2005)
6. Jensen, R., Dahl, A., Vogiatzis, G., Tola, E., Aanaes, H.: Large scale multi-view stereopsis evaluation. In: Proceedings of the IEEE Conference on Computer Vision and Pattern Recognition, pp. 406–413 (2014)
7. Kim, S., Kim, S.D., Dahl, A., Conradsen, K., Jensen, R.R., Aanæs, H.: Multiple view stereo by reflectance modeling. In: 2011 International Conference on 3D Imaging, Modeling, Processing, Visualization and Transmission (2012)
8. Mikolajczyk, K., Tuytelaars, T., Schmid, C., Zisserman, A., Matas, J., Schaffalitzky, F., Kadir, T., Van Gool, L.: A comparison of affine region detectors. Int. J. Comput. Vision **65** (2005)
9. Moreels, P., Perona, P.: Evaluation of features detectors and descriptors based on 3d objects. Int. J. Comput. Vision **73**(3) (2007)
10. Seitz, S.M., Curless, B., Diebel, J., Scharstein, D., Szeliski, R.: A comparison and evaluation of multi-view stereo reconstruction algorithms. In: CVPR, vol. 1, pp. 519–528 (2006)

Face Verification Based on Gabor Region Covariance Matrices

Zinelabidine Boulkenafet[1,2]([✉]), Elhocine Boutellaa[2], Messaoud Bengherabi[2], and Abdenour Hadid[1]

[1] Center for Machine Vision Research, University of Oulu, Oulu, Finland
zboulken@ee.oulu.fi
http://www.cse.oulu.fi/CMV
[2] Center for Development of Advanced Technologies CDTA, Baba Hassen, Algeria
http://www.cdta.dz

Abstract. This paper introduces a novel face verification approach using the Gabor Region Covariance Matrices (GRCM). First, we represent the face images with d dimensional Gabor images. Then, we divide these images into overlapping regions. From each region, we compute a $d \times d$ covariance matrix. Inspired by the GMM-UBM speaker verification framework, we propose a new decision rule based on the Riemannian mean of the Gabor region covariance matrices computed from background faces. Finally, score normalization techniques are incorporated in the proposed framework to enhance the verification performance. Extensive experiments on two benchmark databases, namely Banca and SCface showed very interesting results which compare favorably against many state-of-the-art methods.

1 Introduction

Because of its natural and non-intrusive interaction, identity verification and recognition using facial information is among the most active and challenging areas in computer vision research [13]. Despite the great deal of progress during the recent years, face biometrics is still a major area of research. Wide range of viewpoints, occlusions, aging of subjects and complex outdoor lighting are challenges in face recognition. Face recognition methods can generally be divided into two classes: global matching methods and local or component matching methods. The global methods represent the whole face image with a single feature vector which can be used as an input to a classifier. Among the several classifiers proposed in the literature we can cite: the minimum distance classification applied in the eigenspace [21], the Fisher discriminant analysis [3], the neural network [6], the Support Vector Machine, SVM [4] . In term of performance, the global methods give good results in classifying near frontal faces. However, their robustness degrades against pose changes since the global feature vectors are sensitive to rotation and translation. By dividing the face images into components and allowing certain geometrical flexibility between these components during the classification stage, the local matching methods have shown good performances compared with the global methods [10].

© Springer International Publishing Switzerland 2015
R.R. Paulsen and K.S. Pedersen (Eds.): SCIA 2015, LNCS 9127, pp. 480–491, 2015.
DOI: 10.1007/978-3-319-19665-7_41

For both global and local methods, feature extraction and representation is a crucial step. It is widely believed that the features extracted with a spatial-frequency analysis are more robust to pose and illumination changes [26]. As wavelet transformations are localized in both time and frequency domains, it can be a good choice for representing the face images [17]. Among the various wavelet techniques proposed in the literature, the Gabor functions provide the optimal resolution in both spatial and frequency domains [5]. The application of the Gabor wavelet in face recognition was pioneered by Lades et al. in 1993 [12], when they proposed a face recognition system (Dynamic Link Architecture, DLA) based on the Gabor jets extracted from the nodes of a rectangular grid. Later on, Wiskott et al. extended the DLA methods and proposed the Elastic Base Graph Matching method (EBGM) [24], where the rectangular grid was replaced by a number of facial landmarks. Since then, a large number of face recognition systems were proposed based on this Gabor wavelet transformation [20].

In 2006, Tuzel et al. [22] proposed a new object detection and classification method called Region Covariance Matrices (RCMs). This method is based on the analysis of the feature covariance matrices computed inside a region of interest. As the covariance matrices do not encode information regarding the ordering and the number of points, the RCMs method inherits certain robustness against small rotation and scaling. Furthermore, the subtraction of the mean during the covariance computation can reduce the effect of the global illumination changes. In the original RCMs method [22], the covariance matrices were computed from a set of features including pixels coordinates, color values and the norm of the first and second order gradient. Although these features yield in good results in detecting and tracking objects, their application to the face recognition problem [15] did not show promising performance. To enhance this performance, Pang et al. [15] proposed a face recognition system using Gabor Region Covariance Matrices (GRCMs), where the pixel location and the Gabor features were used to construct the region covariance matrices. Their experimental results have demonstrated the effectiveness of GRCM compared to the original RCM method.

In the present work, we adopt the idea behind the use of the Universal Background Model in the GMM-UBM speaker verification system [18], and propose a new face verification approach based on the Gabor Region Covariance Matrices (GRCM) [15]. After constructing symmetric definite positive GRCM from a background set of human faces, we use the Riemannian mean function to compute a Universal Background Gabor Region Covariance Matrices (UBGRCM). These matrices are used later on, in the classification stage to estimate the similarity between the GRCM extracted from the query and the target images. Furthermore, we have studied the effect of the normalization methods on the resulting scores. The experimental results on two challenging databases (Banca and SCface) showed the efficiency of our proposed method compared to many state-of-the-art methods.

The reminder of this paper is organized as follows. In Section 2, we describe the Gabor wavelet transformation. In Section 3 and Section 4, we present the GRCMs and our proposed approach, respectively. Section 5 presents the experimental setup whereas Section 6 discusses the obtained results. Finally, Section **??** concludes this paper.

2   Gabor Based Face Representation

Since the discovery of crystalline organization of the primary visual cortex in mammalian brains by Hubel and Wiesel [11], an enormous amount of research has been concentrated in understanding this area and the proprieties of its cells. As these research works found that the simple cells in human visual cortex are selectively tuned to orientation as well as spatial frequency, Daugman proposed in [5] to approximate the response of these cells by the Gabor function:

$$\varphi_{u,v}(z) = \frac{\|K_{u,v}\|}{\sigma^2} e^{(-\|K_{u,v}\|^2 \|z\|^2 / 2\sigma^2)} [e^{(izk_{u,v})} - e^{-\sigma^2/2}] \tag{1}$$

Where $z = (x, y)$ is the pixel coordinate, $\|.\|$ denotes the norm operator, σ is the standard deviation of a Gaussian envelope and $K_{u,v}$ is a wave vector defined by:

$$K_{u,v} = K_v e^{i\phi_u} \tag{2}$$

Where, $K_v = k_{max}/f_v$ and $\phi_u = \frac{\pi u}{8}$. k_{max} is the maximum frequency and f_v is the spacing factor. v and u represent respectively the scale and the orientation of the wave vector. This Gabor function is similar to enhancing the edge contours as well as the valleys and the ridge contours of an image. In the case of face images, this corresponds to enhancing eyes, mouth and nose which are the main discriminating points in human faces.

Some previous works [14] [25] showed that the use of the Gabor kernels computed in 5 scales ($v \in \{0\ldots4\}$) and 8 orientations ($u \in \{0\ldots7\}$) with $k_{max} = \pi/2$, $f_v = \sqrt{2}^v$ and $\sigma = 2\pi$ give a good representation for the face images. The real parts of these kernels are presented in Figure 1.

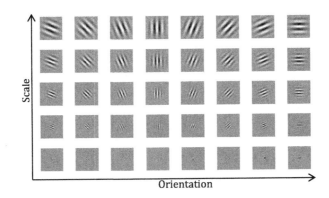

Fig. 1. The real parts of the Gabor Kernels computed in 5 scales and 8 orientations

Finally, The Gabor representation of a face image I can be obtained by convolving this image with the Gabor filters as follows:

$$G_{u,v}(z) = |I(z) * \varphi_{u,v}(z)| \tag{3}$$

Where $z = (x, y)$, $*$ denote the convolution operator and $|.|$ is the magnitude operator.

3 Gabor Region Covariance Matrices

Let I be a face image and let $G_{u,v}\{u = 0...7, v = 0...4\}$ its 2-D Gabor transformation. Each pixel p_i of the original image I will be represented by a row pixel:

$$w_i = [x, y, G_{0,0}(x, y), G_{1,0}(x, y), ..., G_{7,4}(x, y)]$$

Where x and y are the location of the pixel p_i.

The Covariance Matrix of a region R (Figure 2) is a matrix C_R with diagonal entries correspond to the variance of the features and the non-diagonal entries correspond to their correlation.

$$C_R = \frac{1}{n-1} \sum_{i=1}^{n} (w_i - \mu_R)(w_i - \mu_R)^t \tag{4}$$

In equation 4, n represents the number of the row pixels inside the region R and μ_R is their corresponding mean:

$$\mu_R = 1/n \sum_{i=1}^{n} w_i \tag{5}$$

Although the variance of the coordinates x and y is the same for all the regions of the same size, they are still important since their correlations with the other features are used as the non-diagonal entries of the matrix. Therefore, the constructed GRCMs capture both spatial and statistical properties.

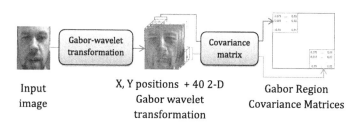

Input image — Gabor-wavelet transformation — X, Y positions + 40 2-D Gabor wavelet transformation — Covariance matrix — Gabor Region Covariance Matrices

Fig. 2. Computation of the Gabor Region Covariance Matrices (GRCMs)

In [22], the authors used the integral images of each feature and the multiplication of any two features to compute the covariance matrix of any region with only few access memory. For more detail about this technique reader is refered to [22].

The main advantages of using the covariance matrices to represent the face images are 1) The covariance matrices provide a natural way to fuse multiple features without the need of any normalization methods. 2) They are basically invariant to scaling and rotation of the images, as the order and the number of the points are not represented by the covariance matrices. 3) They are robust to global illumination changes, since the mean is subtracted during the covariance computation.

4   Proposed Approach

In this work, we assume that the region covariance matrices representing the face images contain two types of information: discriminating information specific to each user and common information shared between the human faces. Thus, to enhance the discrimination of the GRCMs method it is worth to reduce the effect of the common information. Inspired by the use of the Universal Background Model (UBM) in Gaussian Mixtures Model-Universal Background Model (GMM-UBM) speaker verification framework [18], we propose to model the common information by a Universal Background Gabor Region Covariance Matrices (UBGRCMs), and use these matrices in the scoring stage to estimate the similarity between the test and the enrollment GRCMs. The UBGRCMs are the mean of the GRCMs extracted from a background set of human faces (Figure 3). As the covariance matrices are symmetric definite positive and lie in the Riemannian manifold, the Riemannian mean is used instead of the Euclidean mean.

4.1   Riemannian Mean

Let $\{C_1, C_2, \ldots\ldots, C_P\}$ a set of P covariance matrices. The Riemannian mean [16] of these matrices is the matrix C which minimizes the sum of the squared distances.

$$C = \underset{C}{\mathrm{argmin}} \sum_{i=1}^{P} \rho^2(C_i, C) \tag{6}$$

Where $\rho(C_i, C)$ is the distance between the two covariance matrices C and C_i (see Section 4.2). As C is defined through a minimization procedure, we approximate it by the intrinsic Newton gradient descent method. In the following (Algorithm 1), we describe the algorithm computing the mean Riemannian of a P covariance matrices.

In this algorithm, $ln(M)$ and $exp(M)$ were computed as:

$$ln(M) = U ln(D) U^t$$
$$exp(M) = U exp(D) U^t$$

Algorithm 1. Computation of the mean Riemannian covariance matrix

---

Data: Covariance Matrices $\{C_1, C_2, \ldots\ldots, C_P\}$
Result: Mean Covariance Matrix C
$C = C_t$ $(t \in \{1..P\})$;
nb_iterations=5;
it=1;
while $it<=nb\_iterations$ **do**
  $\quad$ M=zeros(size(C));
  $\quad$ **for** $i=1$:P **do**
    $\quad\quad$ $\lfloor$ $M = M + C^{1/2}ln(C^{-1/2}C_iC^{-1/2})C^{1/2}$
  $\quad$ M=M/P;
  $\quad$ $C = C^{1/2}exp(C^{-1/2}MC^{-1/2})C^{1/2}$;
  $\quad$ it=it+1;

Where U is an orthogonal matrix and D is the diagonal matrix of the eigen-values $(M = UDU^t)$.

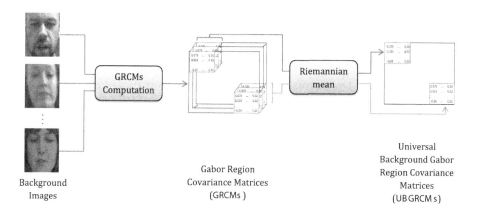

Fig. 3. Computation of the Universal Background Gabor Region Covariance Matrices (UBGRCMs)

4.2 Distance Measure

To compare two covariance matrices (C_1 and C_2), the eigenvalue based distance [7] is adopted. This distance is calculated as follows:

$$\rho(C_1, C_2) = \sqrt{\sum_{i=1}^{n} ln^2\lambda_i(C_1, C_2)} \qquad (8)$$

Where $\{\lambda_i(C_1, C_2)\}_{i=1...n}$ are the generalized eigenvalues of the two covariance matrices C_1 and C_2.

Now, let $X = \{C_x^1, C_x^2, ...C_x^N\}$, $Y = \{C_y^1, C_y^2, ...C_y^N\}$, $U = \{C_u^1, C_u^2, ...C_u^N\}$ be three sets of GRCMs corresponding respectively to the reference image r, the test image t and the UBGRCMs of a background set images u.

In the first step, the similarity (D_1) between the test and the reference Gabor region covariance matrices is computed as follows:

$$D_1(Y, X) = \sum_{i=1}^{N} \rho(C_y^i, C_x^i) \tag{9}$$

In the second step and in order to reduce the effect of the common information, the similarity between the test and the reference GRCM (D_2) is computed using the Log-Likelihood Ratio test.

$$D_2(Y, X, U) = \log(p(Y|X)) - \log(p(Y|U)) \tag{10}$$

As the similarity between two sets of GRCM $(X_1$ and $X_2)$ is given by the Eigen-value based distance (equation 9), we use the following approximation to transform this distance into probability:

$$p(X_1|X_2) = \exp(-\alpha D_1(X_1, X_2)) \tag{11}$$

Where α is a positive constant. By substituting (11) into (10) we obtain:

$$\begin{aligned} D_2(Y, X, U) &= \log(\exp(-\alpha D_1(Y, X))) - \log(\exp(-\alpha D_1(Y, U))) \\ &= -\alpha(D_1(Y, X) - D_1(Y, U)) \end{aligned} \tag{12}$$

Because α is a positive constant, we consider only the difference between the two distances $D_1(Y, X)$ and $D_1(Y, U)$ as a final score. Figure 4 illustrates the computation of the two similarity measures D_1 and D_2.

5 Experimental Data and Setup

We tested our approach on two benchmark databases: Banca [2] and SCface [8]. Following, we describe these databases and their corresponding parameters.

SCface database: The Surveillance Cameras face database (SCface) [8] is a very challenging database. It was acquired in a real-life scenario using commercially surveillance equipments. In the DayTime authentication protocol used in this study, the clients of the database were divided according to their ID numbers into three subsets. The clients with ID numbers between 1-43 were used to construct the training subset, used to learn the background parameters such as the background models and the subspace matrices. In our work, we use the high quality migshot images of this subset to compute the UBGRCMs. The development and the test subsets are constructed respectively by the clients

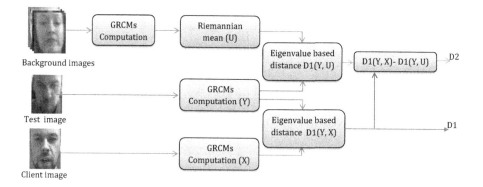

Fig. 4. Computation of the two distances D_1 and D_2

with ID numbers between 44-87 and 88-130. In both these subsets, the mugshot images were used to construct the clients models, while the test images were taken from 5 surveillance cameras at 3 different distances: close (1 m), medium (2.60 m) and far (4.20 m). Because of the low quality of the SCface images, the face images were cropped with dimension of 112×96 and histogram equalization is applied to each cropped image. Finally, the GRCMs were computed from 16×16 pixels regions with 8 pixels step.

BANCA database: The multi-modal BANCA database [2] contains video recordings of 52 subjects (26 male and 26 female). These recordings were captured over 12 different sessions spanning on three months. Sessions 1-4 contain recordings under controlled scenario, while sessions 5-8 and 9-12 contain degraded and adverse scenarios, respectively. Five pre-selected still face images were taken from each video. The 52 subjects were divided into 2 equal groups: G1 and G2 (13 male and 13 female each) which represent respectively the development and the evaluation sets.

From the 7 authentication protocols proposed for BANCA database, our experiments were done only on the pooled (P) protocol as it is the most challenging protocol. In this protocol, the client models of the two groups were created using only 5 images from the controlled scenario, while the test images were taken from the three scenarios (controlled, degraded and adverse). The GRCMs are computed from 8×8 pixel regions with 4 pixels step. Before computing the GRCM, the Banca face images were cropped and resized to 88×68 and Tan & Triggs pre-processing was applied on each image. The GRCMs extracted from the background set images are used to compute the UBGRCM.

In both Banca and SCface databases, the scores generated on the development set were used to compute the Equal Error Rate (EER) which represent the point where the False Acceptance Rate (FAR) and the False Rejection Rate (FRR) are equal. The threshold θ corresponding to this point was then applied to the evaluation scores to obtain the Half Total Error Rate (HTER), which is the mean of the FAR and FRR at that threshold.

Table 1. The performance of the GRCM method on BANCA and SCface databases

Method	BANCA		SCface	
	EER%	HTER%	EER%	HTER%
GRCM $+D_1$	18.8	19.8	31.3	34.7
GRCM $+D_2$	9.1	10.7	16.9	19.8
GRCM $+D_2+$ Z-NORM	9.8	8.9	15.0	16.2
GRCM $+D_2+$ T-NORM	6.2	9.3	16.5	24.6
GRCM $+D_2+$ ZT-NORM	**6.2**	**6.0**	**13.6**	**15.7**

Table 2. Comparison of the proposed approach with state-of-the-art methods on Banca and SCface databases

Method	BANCA		SCface	
	EER%	HTER%	EER%	HTER%
MRH [19]	14.3	13.8	42.6	42.5
GMM [23]	11.9	12.8	30.3	29.8
LBP	15.2	15.4	41.1	42.8
LGBPHS [9]	13.2	16.1	-	-
Gabor Graphs [9]	11.7	12.4	-	-
GRCM $+D_2$	**9.1**	**10.7**	**16.9**	**19.8**
MRH+ZT-Norm [19]	9.3	8.4	28.3	30.3
GMM+ZT-Norm [23]	8.3	7.0	23.3	22.7
LBP+ZT-Norm	6.7	**5.0**	17.4	19.0
GRCM $+D_2+$ZT-Norm	**6.2**	6.0	**13.6**	**15.7**

In this work, we have also studied the effect of the score normalization techniques on the performance of our system. Three normalization methods [1] have been tested: Zero-Normalization (Z-Norm), Test-Normalization (T-Norm) and ZT-Norm which is a combination of the two previous methods. The Z-Norm method aims to characterize the response of each client model to a variety of (impostor) test images, while the T-Norm is used to compensate the variations of the testing image. As in both Banca and SCface databases the development and the evaluation sets are independent, the normalization statistics of the development set were estimated using the evaluation set data and vice versa.

6   Results and Discussion

In this section, we report the performance of the proposed approach on the aforementioned databases. First, a comparison between the performance of the two decision rules (D_1 and D_2) is presented. From Table 1, we can clearly see that the D_2 method provides performance improvement for both databases compared to the D_1 method. Specifically, the HTER is reduced with 42.93% and 45.95 % on Banca and SCface databases, respectively.

To further improve these performances, we applied normalization on the obtained scores. Although these methods were proposed for speaker recognition, their application to the face modality showed significant performance improvements [23]. The results also show that the ZT-Norm method improves the performance with 20,70% and 43,92%, on SCface and Banca databases, respectively.

Tables 2 compares the performance of the proposed method against some state-of-the-art face verification methods. From this table, we can observe that without the ZT-Norm normalization our proposed approach outperforms the Local Binary Pattern (LBP), the Multi-Region probabilistic Histograms (MRH) and the Gaussian Mixture models (GMM) methods on both Banca and SCface databases. Our method gives better results than the Local Gabor Binary Pattern Histogram Sequence (LGBPHS) and the Gabor graph methods on Banca database. With the ZT-Norm normalization, our approach still gives the best performance compared to LBP, GMM and MRH methods, except on the development set of Banca database where the LBP method outperforms our approach.

7 Conclusion

In this work, we investigated the use of the Gabor Region Covariance Matrices (GRCMs) in the face verification problem. First, we represented the face images with $W \times H \times d$ dimensional feature matrices which are divided into many overlapping regions. For each region, we computed a $d \times d$ covariance matrix. The direct use of the eigenvalue-based distance between the covariance matrices extracted from the test and the enrollment images did not yield in reliable performances. To overcome these limitations, we proposed a new decision rule using UBGRCMs computed from a background set of human faces. The UBGRCMs theoretically represent the common information of different human faces which should be ignored when comparing two faces. The conducted experiments showed that the proposed decision rule improved the performance of our system on two challenging databases: Banca and SCface. In addition, we have further improved the obtained results by applying different scores normalization methods. Finally, a comparison with some state-of-the-art methods showed the efficiency of our proposed method.

Acknowledgments. The financial support of the Academy of Finland is fully acknowledged.

References

1. Auckenthaler, R., Carey, M., Lloyd-Thomas, H.: Score normalization for text-independent speaker verification systems. Digital Signal Processing **10**(13), 42–54 (2000). http://www.sciencedirect.com/science/article/pii/S1051200499903603
2. Bailly-Baillire, E., Bengio, S., Bimbot, F., Hamouz, M., Kittler, J., Marithoz, J., Matas, J., Messer, K., Popovici, V., Pore, F., Ruiz, B., Thiran, J.P.: The banca database and evaluation protocol. In: Kittler, J., Nixon, M. (eds.) Audio- and Video-Based Biometric Person Authentication. Lecture Notes in Computer Science, vol. 2688, pp. 625–638. Springer, Heidelberg (2003)

3. Belhumeur, P.N., Hespanha, J.P., Kriegman, D.J.: Eigenfaces vs fisherfaces: recognition using class specific linear projection. IEEE Trans. Pattern Analysis and machine intelligence **19**(7), 711–720 (1997)
4. Cortes, C., Vapnik, V.: Support-vector networks. Machine Learning **20**(3), 273–297 (1995). http://dx.doi.org/10.1023/A:1022627411411
5. Daugman, D.G.: Two dimensional spectral analysis of cortical receptive field profile. Vision Research **20**, 847–856 (1980)
6. Fleming, M., Cottrell, G.: Categorization of faces using unsupervised feature extraction. Int Joint Conf. on Neural Networks **2**, 65–70 (1990)
7. Frstner, W., Moonen, B.: A metric for covariance matrices. In: Grafarend, E., Krumm, F., Schwarze, V. (eds.) Geodesy-The Challenge of the 3rd Millennium, pp. 299–309. Springer, Berlin Heidelberg (2003). doi:10.1007/978-3-662-05296-9_31
8. Grgic, M., Delac, K., Grgic, S.: Scface- surveillance cameras face database. Multimedia Tools Application. **51**(3), 863–879 (2011)
9. Günther, M., Wallace, R., Marcel, S.: An open source framework for standardized comparisons of face recognition algorithms. In: Proceedings of the 12th International Conference on Computer Vision - Volume Part III, ECCV 2012, pp. 547–556. (2012)
10. Heisele, B., Ho, P., Wu, J., Poggio, T.: Face recognition: component-based versus global approaches. Computer Vision and Image Understanding **91**(12), 6–21 (2003). http://www.sciencedirect.com/science/article/pii/S1077314203000730, special Issue on Face Recognition
11. Hubel, D.H., Wiesel, T.N.: Ferrier lecture: Functional architecture of macaque monkey visual cortex. Proceedings of the Royal Society of London. Series B, Biological Sciences **198**, 1–59 (1977)
12. Lades, M., Vorbruggen, J., Buhmann, J., Lange, J., von der Malsburg, C., Wurtz, R., Konen, W.: Distortion invariant object recognition in the dynamic link architecture. IEEE Transactions on Computers **42**(3), 300–311 (1993)
13. Li, S.Z., Jain, A.K. (eds.): Handbook of Face Recognition, 2nd edn. Springer (2011)
14. Li, Y., Ou, Z., Wang, G.: Face recognition using gabor features and support vector machines. In: Wang, L., Chen, K., S. Ong, Y. (eds.) ICNC 2005. LNCS, vol. 3611, pp. 119–122. Springer, Heidelberg (2005)
15. Pang, Y., Yuan, Y., Li, X.: Gabor-based region covariance matrices for face recognition. IEEE Transactions on Circuits and Systems for Video Technology **18**(7), 989–993 (2008)
16. Pennec, X., Fillard, P., Ayache, N.: A riemannian framework for tensor computing. International Journal of Computer Vision **66**, 41–66 (2006)
17. Qian, S., Chen, D.: Joint Time-frequency Analysis: Methods and Applications. PTR Prentice Hall (1996). http://books.google.fr/books?id=DggfAQAAIAAJ
18. Reynolds, D.A., Quatieri, T.F., Dunn, R.B.: Speaker verification using adapted gaussian mixture models. Digital Signal Processing **10**, 19–41 (2000)
19. Sanderson, C., Lovell, B.C.: Multi-region probabilistic histograms for robust and scalable identity inference. In: International Conference on Advances in Biometrics. pp. 199–208 (2009)
20. Shen, L., Bai, L.: A review on gabor wavelets for face recognition. Pattern Analysis and Applications **9**(2–3), 273–292 (2006). doi:10.1007/s10044-006-0033-y
21. Turk, M.A., Pentland, A.P.: Face recognition using eigenfaces. In: IEEE Conf. on Computer Vision and Pattern Recognition, CVPR 1991, pp. 586–591 (1991)

22. Tuzel, O., Porikli, F., Meer, P.: Region covariance: a fast descriptor for detection and classification. In: Proc. 9th European Conf on Computer Vision, pp. 589–600 (2006)

23. Wallace, R., McLaren, M., McCool, C., Marcel, S.: Cross-pollination of normalization techniques from speaker to face authentication using gaussian mixture models. IEEE Transactions on Information Forensics and Security **7**(2), 553–562 (2012)

24. Wiskott, L., Fellous, J.M., Kruger, N., von der Malsburg, C.: Face recognition by elastic bunch graph matching. In: Proceedings International Conference on Image Processing, 1997, vol. 1, pp. 129–132, Oct 1997

25. Wiskott, L., Fellous, J.M., Kuiger, N., Von der Malsburg, C.: Face recognition by elastic bunch graph matching. IEEE Transactions on Pattern Analysis and Machine Intelligence **19**(7), 775–779 (1997)

26. Zhao, W., Chellappa, R., Phillips, P.J., Rosenfeld, A.: Face recognition: A literature survey. ACM Comput. Surv. **35**(4), 399–458 (2003). http://doi.acm.org/10.1145/954339.954342

Detecting Rails and Obstacles
Using a Train-Mounted Thermal Camera

Amanda Berg[1,2(✉)], Kristoffer Öfjäll[1],
Jörgen Ahlberg[1,2], and Michael Felsberg[1]

[1] Computer Vision Laboratory, Department of Electrical Engineering,
Linköping University, 581 83 Linköping, Sweden
{amanda.berg,kristoffer.ofjall,jorgen.ahlberg,michael.felsberg}@liu.se
https://www.cvl.isy.liu.se
[2] Termisk Systemteknik AB, Diskettgatan 11 B, 583 35 Linköping, Sweden
{amanda.,jorgen.ahl}berg@termisk.se
https://www.termisk.se

Abstract. We propose a method for detecting obstacles on the railway
in front of a moving train using a monocular thermal camera. The problem is motivated by the large number of collisions between trains and
various obstacles, resulting in reduced safety and high costs. The proposed method includes a novel way of detecting the rails in the imagery,
as well as a way to detect anomalies on the railway. While the problem at
a first glance looks similar to road and lane detection, which in the past
has been a popular research topic, a closer look reveals that the problem
at hand is previously unaddressed. As a consequence, relevant datasets
are missing as well, and thus our contribution is two-fold: We propose
an approach to the novel problem of obstacle detection on railways and
we describe the acquisition of a novel data set.

Keywords: Thermal imaging · Computer vision · Train safety · Railway
detection · Anomaly detection · Obstacle detection

1 Introduction

Every year, there is a large number of collisions between trains and objects inap-
propriately and unexpectedly located on or close to the railway. Such unexpected
objects are, for example, animals (moose, deer, reindeer), humans, vehicles, and
trees. Collisions with such objects affect the safety of the train passengers, most
likely kills the animal or human being located on or near the rail track, cause
delays in the train traffic, and also results in costs for repairing the train after
the collision.

A train driving at normal speed has a stopping distance of at least one
kilometre and, hence, it is often far too late to brake the train to a full stop
when the engine-driver detects an undesirable object in front of the train. Under
impaired visibility such as bad weather conditions (rain, fog, or snow fall), or

R.R. Paulsen and K.S. Pedersen (Eds.): SCIA 2015, LNCS 9127, pp. 492–503, 2015.
DOI: 10.1007/978-3-319-19665-7_42

when driving in dusk/dawn or in the dark, the situation is even worse. The chances that the engine-driver detects an unexpected object in front of the train and manages to reduce the speed of the train before a collision, are virtually non-existent. Note also that even if a train needs one kilometre to reach a full stop, the capability to detect certain obstacles also at shorter distances is valuable. For example, a collision with a moose at 50 km/h instead of 200 km/h will still kill the moose, but the repair costs for the train will be significantly lower.

In this paper, we describe a system using a thermal camera to detect obstacles on or near the rails in front of the train. The reason to use a thermal camera is its independence of illumination and its ability to see in complete darkness. The images will, however, be of lower resolution than those of a modern visual camera, which also means that we will need to carefully assess the compromise between pixel footprint size and field of view.

In order to detect obstacles, we first need to localize the rails in the incoming stream of thermal images. Secondly, we need to find possible obstacles. Since we do not know the type of obstacles to find in advance, we have chosen to develop an anomaly detector, i.e., we try to detect objects that do not look like rails where rails are expected to be.

1.1   Railway vs. Road Detection

At a first glance, the problem addressed here might look similar to that of road detection, which is a popular research topic since it is a prerequisite for applications in intelligent cars (safety systems as well autonomous driving). However, at a closer look, the two problems are quite different. Roads are typically structure-less, but with defined borders such as lines, curbs, or railings. In urban areas and on highways, visual road detection is carried out by detection of lane markers. A common approach is to reproject the image onto the ground plane followed by line detection in the resampled image [1,6,7]. Using other sensors such as LIDAR, similar lane detection approaches are used [5]. Sometimes, the detection of driveable areas, i.e., flat areas without 3D elevation, is the crucial component.

For railways, we have a different situation. The railway has a defined structure; two rails at a specified distance from each other and perpendicular sleepers. On the other hand, there are no defined borders or lane markers. We thus need a different strategy than for roads and lanes, and we have developed a new method for detecting railways. Nonetheless, some ideas from lane detection are transferable to this new domain; for example, resampling the image in a ground plane grid is advantageous compared to line detection directly in the camera image [4]. Unfortunately, this resampling destroys information close to the vehicle where the road is densely sampled in the original image, while much effort is spent representing far areas where little information is available. Our proposed method attain the advantages of a ground plane projection without resampling each frame. Thus, our contributions are:

- We have collected a dataset of thermal video recorded from a train.
- We propose a method for detecting the railway in such video.
- We propose a method for detecting possible obstacles on the railway.

1.2   Outline

In the remaining of the paper, we will first describe the acquisition of test data (Section 2) and then the proposed rail and obstacle detection algorithms (Section 3). Experimental results are presented in Section 4, and finally our conclusion and an outlook can be found in Section 5.

2   Data Collection

In order to collect relevant image data, we mounted a thermal camera and a mirror into a custom camera house – basically a metal box, see Fig. 1a. The purpose of the arrangement with the mirror is to lower the risk of the (expensive) thermal camera to break due to collision with small objects. In a final system, a smoother housing with a protective window will be used. The used camera is a FLIR SC655 acquiring images in the long-wave (thermal) infrared band, *i.e.*, in the wavelengths 8–12 μm. It has a resolution of 640×480 pixels and acquires 50 frames per second. Two different optics were used, with horizontal fields of view of 7 and 25 degrees respectively. The 7 degree optics give a good resolution at large distances (more than one kilometre), however, when the railway is curved, it often is outside the field of view. The 25 degree optics almost always keeps the railway within the field of view, but the detection distance is much lower. The prioritization will in the end be made by the customer, and might be different for different trains (the two extremes, 7 and 25 degrees, are both quite unlikely). In the following, for the sake of presentation, images acquired using the 25 degree optics are shown.

The camera house was mounted to a train as shown in Fig. 1b. Obviously, this is an exposed placement, not to be copied to the final system. A recording computer was installed inside the train, with a display visible to the driver (Fig. 1c). In addition, a forward-looking video camera was placed inside the train. Note that the thermal camera cannot be placed there, since the glass in the windshield is intransparent to long-wave infrared radiation.

    (a)   (b)   (c)

Fig. 1. The camera installation for data collection. (a) The camera house with a 45 degree mirror. (b) The camera house mounted on the front of a train. (c) The display at the driver's panel.

3 Proposed Method

3.1 System Overview

The system includes a thermal camera in a temperature-controlled housing (currently under development) connected to a computer and a display with a graphical user interface. The computer runs software for acquiring thermal images, computing the scene geometry, detecting the railway, detecting and tracking possible obstacles, and giving alarms to the driver conditioned on certain critera. This process is illustrated in Fig. 2.

Since the extrinsic and intrinsic parameters of the camera can be assumed to be known, the scene geometry is computed first. This includes the homography from pixel to ground coordinates (relative to the train) and possible rail locations. The geometry is computed once, and used, in each frame, for a rough estimation of the rail location as described in Section 3.2. Next, this estimate is refined using an adaptive correlation filter, which is also used for anomaly detection, *i.e.*, finding obstacles on the rails, see Section 3.3.

Moreover, a foreground-background segmentation algorithm is used for finding moving objects near the railway, and detected foreground objects as well as anomalies are kept track of using a multi-target tracker. Finally, the output of the tracking is subject to a filtering, where only detected obstacles fulfilling certain alarm criteria will be reported to the operator. This paper focuses on the three first steps, *i.e.*, the blocks with solid borders in Fig. 2.

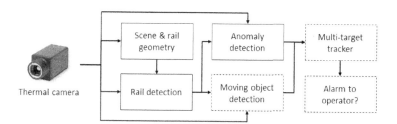

Fig. 2. The system for rail and obstacle detection. The components with solid contours are in the focus of this paper.

3.2 Scene Geometry and Rail Detection

Assuming a flat ground, which is appropriate in a railway setting with limited gradients, there is a one to one mapping from pixels to points in a ground coordinate system fixed to the train, commonly referred to as the inverse perspective mapping (IPM), a homography determined from the known camera parameters. Further, the train has a fixed position and orientation relative to the railway during all normal modes of operation. Assuming a locally constant curvature of the railway, the curvature is the only free parameter determining the position of the rails in the image. This is exploited to obtain fast and reliable rail detections. These assumptions allow us to obtain the advantages of rail detection in the reprojected ground plane image without the need of explicitly reprojecting each frame, thus avoiding the drawbacks of sampling.

Rail Geometry. Given the design of a railway engine, it is apparent that the rails will be parallel to the engine at a point midway between the fore and aft bogies, see Fig. 3a, later referred to as the *parallel point*. The orthogonal offset at this point, λ in Fig. 3a, the signed distance between the center of the railway and the center of the engine, is determined by the local curvature, $Q = 1/R$, and the wheel base, c. It is given by the width of a circle segment

$$\lambda = \frac{1}{Q} - \sqrt{\frac{1}{Q^2} - \frac{c^2}{4}} \approx \frac{Qc^2}{8}, \tag{1}$$

where the approximation for small curvatures is linear in Q. Together with the length-wise camera mount offset t and camera parameters, this determines the position of the rails in the image for each possible curvature.

The deviation, d in Fig. 3b, of a rail from the parallel point can be derived from geometric relations and is given by

$$d = h \cot \left(\frac{\pi - \sin^{-1}(hQ)}{2} f \right) \tag{2}$$

with the inverse

$$Q = \frac{1}{R} = \frac{1}{h} \sin \left(\pi - 2 \cot^{-1} \frac{d}{h} \right). \tag{3}$$

The geometry and parameters are illustrated in Fig. 3b.

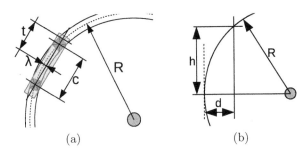

(a)   (b)

Fig. 3. Illustration of railway geometry. (a) Geometry of a railway engine on a railway with constant curvature $1/R$. (b) Geometry of a constant curvature rail.

Histogram Bin Mapping. Given (1), (3) and the camera parameters, the corresponding curvature of the left and right rail, if passing through a given pixel, can be determined for each pixel below the horizon. Placing bins in the one dimensional curvature space, look-up images are generated, mapping each pixel to a curvature bin for the left and right rail respectively. Such mappings are shown in Fig. 4, where a suitable range of curvature is discretized into 100 bins. In automotive applications, the lateral position of the car on the road is not fixed, thus requiring at least a two dimensional histogram. Pre-calculation of bin mapppings is thus not plausible in an automotive setting.

Further, the expected orientation of each rail in the image, if passing through a given pixel, can be determined. This is shown in Fig. 5, where 0 is vertical and $\pm\pi/2$ is horizontal.

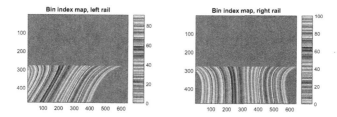

Fig. 4. Images illustrating the mapping from pixel positions to the corresponding curvature histogram bin indexes, for left and right rail respectively.

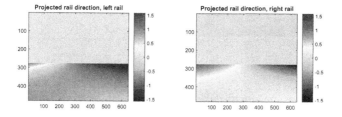

Fig. 5. Expected rail direction in image, left and right rail respectively

Curvature Estimation. The curvature histogram mappings and the expected orientation are calculated in advance for rails close to the camera where the flatness and constant curvature assumptions hold. For detecting rails further ahead, a different approach is used, where lines in the original image are traced, starting from the histogram based detection. The detected lines are projected onto the ground plane, whereafter a spline-based curvature rail model is fitted to the projected detections. By this, the model can be fitted in the ground plane while only the detected lines are projected, not the full image. However, the histogram based detection is the focus of this paper.

For each frame, Gaussain derivative filters are applied, estimating edge strength and orientation. For each pixel (x, y) and rail, the edge strength $A_m(x, y)$ is modulated depending on the difference between the estimated orientation $P_m(x, y)$ and the expected orientation $P_e(x, y)$, Fig. 5, according to

$$A_m(x, y) \exp\left(-\frac{(P_m(x, y) - P_e(x, y))^2}{\sigma_P^2}\right),\qquad(4)$$

where the parameter σ_P determines the orientation error tolerance. The modulated value is added to the curvature bin determined by the bin look-up image, Fig. 4. Assuming limited rail curvature and camera view, the modular nature of the orientation does not require any special attention.

Finally, the peak of the curvature histogram is extracted. The result is illustrated in Fig. 6, where an image is shown with the areas corresponding to the histogram peak overlaid. The histogram is also shown, together with the corresponding histogram obtained without orientation modulation. Using orientation weighting, false curvature responses are significantly reduced, resulting in a stronger peak to noise ratio in the histogram.

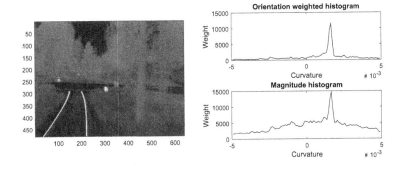

Fig. 6. Left: Camera image with areas mapping to the peak histogram bin overlaid. Top right: Curvature histogram generated from the image using orientation dependent weighting of edge magnitudes (4). Bottom right: Histogram generated from the same image without orientation weighting.

3.3   Combined Correction and Anomaly Detection

A rail mask which does not follow the rail properly will cause false detections to appear. This will happen, for example, when the assumption above about constant curvature does not hold. Therefore, the rail mask needs to be corrected before anomaly detection can be applied. Correction as well as anomaly detection is performed row-wise using an adaptive correlation filter, similar to the one used in the MOSSE tracker [2]. The original image as well as the binary mask from the rail detection serves as input. In each frame, for each row of the original image, all pixels within the rail mask are rescaled. Rescaling is performed using cubic interpolation and an example of an image with rescaled masked rows can be seen in Fig. 7. As opposed to [2], the correlation filter is one-dimensional, similar to the scale filter in [3], and applied row-wise.

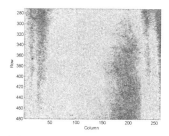

(a) Original image with rail mask overlay in dark blue.
(b) Masked and rescaled image rows.

Fig. 7. (a) The original image and the binary rail mask serves as input to the rail mask correction and anomaly detector. (b) All pixels within the rail mask are rescaled row-wise in order for the masked rows to have the same width.

Rail Mask Correction. Rail mask correction is an iterative procedure. The correlation filter is trained to give a Gaussian distribution, $\mathcal{N}(w/2, w/2)$, where w is the filter width, in response when applied to one-row image patches of rails. If the mask does not follow the rail properly, the filter responses will have a similar offset since the filter is trained to give a Gaussian with its mean in the center of the rails. By adjusting the horizontal positions of the rail mask rows based on the filter response information, the rail mask can be corrected. In Fig. 8, an example of an erroneous rail mask and its filter responses before and after correction can be seen.

Correction is performed bottom-up using the filter responses, starting with the response at the bottom row. All filter response rows are correlated with different displacements to the bottom row, one by one, and the displacement with the highest correlation is considered the final displacement for that row. In order to enforce smoothness in the correction displacement, each row is only allowed to have a displacement of ± 1 pixel relative to the previous row. Detections from the previous frame are used during the correction phase in order not to introduce errors in the corrected mask. That is, rows which had a detection in the previous frame are not corrected and their displacements are set to the one of the previous row without a detection.

A correction like the one described above is performed in each iteration of the correction phase. In each iteration, a new rescaled image and new responses are calculated. If the mean correlation over all rows of the current iteration to the mean response of all previous non-detected rows is lower than the mean correlation of the previous iteration, the iteration is stopped and the correction of the previous iteration is accepted as the final one. Approximately three iterations are needed to correct the rail mask if it has a moderate offset.

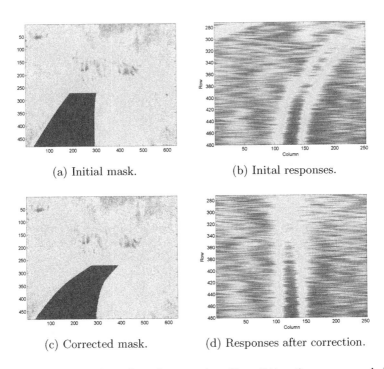

(a) Initial mask.   (b) Inital responses.

(c) Corrected mask.   (d) Responses after correction.

Fig. 8. Example of a rail mask correction. Here, 3 iterations were needed.

Detection of Anomalous Rows. When the rail mask has been corrected, the resulting resized image is analyzed for anomalous rows. In this step, the filter responses from the final, corrected rail mask are used. Given a filter response $y_{t,j}$ at time t and row j, a correlation coefficient $c_{t,j}$ is calculated between $y_{t,j}$ and the median of $y_{t,j}$, $j \in S_{t-1}$. S_{t-1} is the set of rows without a detection in the previous frame. The median is used in order to reduce the influence of outliers. The ℓ^1-norm $b_{t,j} = |c_{t,j} - m_{t-1,j}|$ is then thresholded to find detections.

$$d_{t,j} = \{0\ b_{t,j} < \gamma 1\ b_{t,j} \geq \gamma \tag{5}$$

where $d_{t,j}$ indicates whether the row is anomalous or not and $\gamma \in [0,1]$ is a constant. $m_{t-1,j}$ is the weighted mean of all previous correlation coefficients of row j, updated as $m_{t,j} = \beta c_{t,j} + (1 - \beta)m_{t-1,j}$, with an update factor $\beta \in [0,1]$.

Instead of using the median filter response, the filter responses could be correlated to the Gaussian used for training. However, due to contrast variations and other distortions, a normalisation would be needed. Using the median response vector has proven to be the best method for this application.

Correlation Filter Update. All filter operations are performed in the Fourier domain using the Fast Fourier Transform in order to reduce computation time. The correlation filter is trained as

$$H = \frac{\sum_{j \in S} \overline{G} F_j}{\sum_{j \in S} \overline{F_j} F_j} \qquad (6)$$

where S is the set of image rows of the rescaled image that are to be used for training. F_j is a Fourier transformed pixel row and G is the Fourier transform of the ideal filter response. In this case the ideal filter response is a Gaussian with its peak centered between the two rails. The bar denotes complex conjugation and the product $\overline{F_j} F_j$ is point-wise. The derivation of (6) is given in [2]. The filter response $y_{t,j}$ at time t and row j of image row z, is found as

$$y_{t,j} = \mathcal{F}^{-1}\{\overline{H_t} Z\}. \qquad (7)$$

In each new frame, the filter is adaptively updated using a weighted average as

$$H_t = \alpha \left(\frac{\sum_{j \in S_t} \overline{G} F_j}{\sum_{j \in S_t} \overline{F_j} F_j} \right) + (1 - \alpha) H_{t-1} \qquad (8)$$

where S_t is the set of rows at time t that have qualified for filter update and $\alpha \in [0, 1]$ is the update factor. The rows used for filter update are randomly chosen among the rows that did not have a detection.

4   Experimental Results

The test sequence that was used to evaluate the performance of the system consists of 386 frames. When the sequence was recorded, the train was driving at about 200 km/h on a railway which slightly bends to the right.

Three simulated objects are introduced on the rail during the sequence. Objects are assumed not to suddenly appear and to increase in size as the train approaches. The first object is a square and the second object is a rectangle simulating a pipe lying over the rails. The third object is an upright rectangle simulating a standing object, human or animal. The temperature of the objects are set to $T_b + \Delta T$ where T_b is the surrounding background temperature and ΔT is a temperature difference. Furthermore, the edges of the objects are smoothed using an averaging filter. Two example frames from the test sequence where the simulated objects are present can be seen in Fig. 9.

In each frame, 100 randomly selected rows are used to train the adaptive correlation filter. The update factor of the filter, α, was set to 0.025 and the update factor of the correlation coefficients, β, was set to 0.1.

The detection and performance evaluation is performed row-wise. Two parameters were varied during the evaluation: The detection threshold γ and the temperature difference ΔT. In each frame, the height of the rail mask was

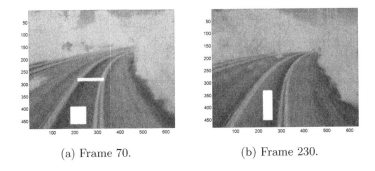

(a) Frame 70.   (b) Frame 230.

Fig. 9. The simulated objects (a) 1, 2, and (b) 3 in the test sequence.

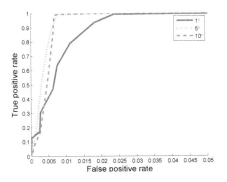

Fig. 10. ROC-curves of the true positive and false positive rates for three different values of ΔT.

set to 209 rows which yields 80674 rows for evaluation. A plot containing ROC-curves for $\Delta T = 1°C$, $5°C$ and $10°C$ can be found in Fig. 10.

As expected, the results improve when the temperature difference increases. The results for $\Delta T = 5°$ and $\Delta T = 10°$ can be considered to be equal. A significant improvement can, however, be noted between $\Delta T = 1°$ and $\Delta T = 5°$. In order for the method to be useful, a true positive rate of at least 90% and a false positive rate of at maximum $1 - 2\%$ are needed. Occasional false detections can be handled and as long as the true positive rate of an object is larger than the true positive rate per row, missed detections can be handled as well. In the case of $\Delta T \geq 5°$, these criteria are fulfilled.

5   Conclusion

The conclusion is that the rail detection method works satisfactory, but, as expected, can only be used at a limited range due to its assumption of constant curvature. The combined correction and anomaly detection method successfully compensates for model errors, and also gives detection results useful in the practical application. Future and ongoing work will include further development of both these algorithms. There are also several special cases that will need to be addressed, such as heated railroad switches and connecting railroads, that currently result in detections. In addition to that, detection of foreground objects and/or moving objects near (not on) the rails will be added to the system.

The next step is to install the system on one or more test trains and perform extensive testing and data collection at different speeds, weather conditions, and environments. These tests will be performed during 2015, and will most likely result in the discovery of additional special cases and circumstances that will need to be addressed.

Acknowledgments. This work was financed by Rindi Solutions AB. The research was funded by the The Swedish Research Council through framework grants for projects Energy Minimization for Computational Cameras (2014-6227) and Extended Target Tracking. The development of the multi-target tracker was supported by the European Community Framework Programme 7, Privacy Preserving Perimeter Protection Project (P5), grant agreement no. 312784. We also gratefully acknowledge the train company Tågkompaniet for using their train.

References

1. Aly, M.: Real time detection of lane markers in urban streets. In: IEEE Intelligent Vehicles Symp. (2008)
2. Bolme, D.S., Beveridge, J., Ross, D., Bruce, A., Lui, Y.M.: Visual object tracking using adaptive correlation filters. In: Proc. of IEEE Conf. on Computer Vision and Pattern Recognition (2010)
3. Danelljan, M., Häger, G., Khan, F., Felsberg, M.: Accurate scale estimation for robust visual tracking. In: Proc. of the British Machine Vision Conf. (2014)
4. Borkar, A., Hayes, M., Smith, M.: Robust lane detection and tracking with ransac and kalman filter. In: IEEE International Conf. on Image Processing (2009)
5. Kammel, S., Pitzer, B.: Lidar-based lane marker detection and mapping. In: IEEE Intelligent Vehicles Symp. (2008)
6. Kreucher, C., Lakshmanan, S.: LANA: A Lane Extraction Algorithm that Uses Frequency Domain Features. IEEE Trans. on Robotics and Automation **15**(2) (1999)
7. Otsuka, Y., Muramatsu, S., Takenaga, H., Kobayashi, Y., Monji, T.: Multitype lane markers recognition using local edge direction. In: IEEE Intelligent Vehicles Symp. (2002)

Dictionary Based Segmentation in Volumes

Monica Jane Emerson[1]([✉]), Kristine Munk Jespersen[2],
Peter Stanley Jørgensen[3], Rasmus Larsen[1], and Anders Bjorholm Dahl[1]

[1] DTU Compute, Lyngby, Denmark
{monj,rlar,abda}@dtu.dk
[2] DTU Wind Energy, Roskilde, Denmark
kmun@dtu.dk
[3] DTU Energy, Roskilde, Denmark
psjq@dtu.dk

Abstract. We present a method for supervised volumetric segmentation based on a dictionary of small cubes composed of pairs of intensity and label cubes. Intensity cubes are small image volumes where each voxel contains an image intensity. Label cubes are volumes with voxel-wise probabilities for a given label. The segmentation process is done by matching a cube from the volume, of the same size as the dictionary intensity cubes, to the most similar intensity dictionary cube, and from the associated label cube we get voxel-wise label probabilities. Probabilities from overlapping cubes are averaged and hereby we obtain a robust label probability encoding. The dictionary is computed from labeled volumetric image data based on weighted clustering. We experimentally demonstrate our method using two data sets from material science – a phantom data set of a solid oxide fuel cell simulation for detecting three phases and their interfaces, and a tomogram of a glass fiber composite used in wind turbine blades for detecting individual glass fibers.

Keywords: Volume segmentation · Materials images · X-ray tomography · Learning dictionaries · Glass fiber segmentation

1 Introduction

High resolution volumetric scanning has become a widely used technique in areas like material science and medicine, and automated quantification methods are necessary in order to obtain size and shape measures from these data. We present a method for supervised segmentation of volumetric data. The method is trained from manual annotations, and these annotations make the method very flexible, which we demonstrate in our experiments.

Our method infers label information locally by matching the pattern in a neighborhood around a voxel to a dictionary, and hereby accounts for the volume texture. Texture segmentation has been widely addressed in 2D [4,8,19], whereas volumetric texture segmentation has received less attention [1]. This fact could be due to the extra computational effort introduced in 3D. However, 3D texture segmentation is highly appropriate for quantifying size and shape in 3D data. Applications in this paper are from energy material science.

© Springer International Publishing Switzerland 2015
R.R. Paulsen and K.S. Pedersen (Eds.): SCIA 2015, LNCS 9127, pp. 504–515, 2015.
DOI: 10.1007/978-3-319-19665-7_43

Denmark is pursuing to obtain 100% of the energy from renewable resources by 2050 [6]. For this reason, it is important to develop renewable energy technologies, which involves investigating material properties to ensure efficiency and lifetime. Imaging the 3D micro-structure can be essential in characterizing and understanding such properties, e.g. the geometric configuration of a solid oxide fuel cell or the fiber geometry in a wind turbine blade material, which are the applications we investigate here.

Our applications contain three spatial dimensions, but data could also be two spatial dimensions and time as the third. If it were to be the latter, the evolution of the material's micro-structure under certain conditions (e.g. temperature or tension) could be investigated. Moreover, the flow of different elements (e.g. gas or liquid) through porous materials can be investigated [17]. Other applications are segmentation of anatomical structures in medical imaging [1,16], seismic facies analysis [14] or crystallography [15]. Many of the volumetric texture segmentation algorithms are extensions of common 2D techniques [2] or 2D segmentation propagation approaches for segmenting 3D materials [18].

Wind turbines blades commonly use glass fiber composites for the load carrying parts of the blades, for which the fatigue damage mechanisms are not well understood. Wind turbine blades have long expected lifespans where they experience a high number of load cycles, which gives rise to fatigue damage evolution. In addition, the blade lengths are being increased because the power output of a wind turbine is proportional to the blade length squared. As fatigue is one of the main limiting factors of designing longer blades, improving the understanding of fatigue damage evolution in glass fiber composites is important [7,13]. Here microstructure analysis using imaging is an important tool, both for material characterization and modeling.

Solid oxide fuel cells (SOFC) operate by oxidizing a fuel to produce electricity and heat. The electrodes of an SOFC are typically two-phase porous systems. The two solid phases are responsible for electron and ion conduction and the pores allow transport of gaseous reactants and products to and from the electrochemically active sites at the triple phase boundaries (TPB). The chemical reactions can only take place at the TPBs where there is access for electrons, ions and gases through the corresponding three phases. The performance of an SOFC is thus strongly dependent on the density of TPBs in the electrodes and on how easily, electrons ions and gases can be transported to and from the TPBs [10]. The microstructure of an SOFC can only be indirectly controlled through a complicated interaction between powder particle sizes, casting methods and sintering temperatures. 3D characterization of the micro-structure is thus becoming an increasingly important tool to correlate the characteristics of the micro-structure to the cell performance and the production recipes.

In this paper we extend the 2D segmentation algorithm in [5] to 3D. The method is based on a dictionary of image patches and corresponding label patches. Here we replace the image patches with volume cubes and investigate the effects on the segmentation. We see an improved performance in some of our experiments by extending to 3D, but at the expense of longer computation times. However, we obtain close to perfect segmentation of individual glass fibers in wind turbine blades, and also high performance in segmenting solid oxide fuel cell data.

The paper is organized as follows. In Section 2, we provide a description of the algorithm. Section 3 explains the data sets and materials which are utilized for the comparative study. In Section 4, the focus is on the results, where three methods (method from literature, 2D dictionary and 3D dictionary) are compared for each data set. Finally, Section 5 draws some conclusions.

2   Method

In the process of extending [5] to 3D, we have however changed some parts and therefore we include a description of the entire method despite the overlap with [5]. The method is based on a dictionary of small intensity cubes coupled with label cubes, and the dictionary is learned using weighted clustering. First we describe the dictionary, then we explain the problem we are optimizing, and finally we describe an algorithm to compute the dictionary and the method for inferring label information to an unlabeled volume.

The dictionary is based on annotated training data, where the annotation assigns each voxel in the training volume to one class label. Given a volume $V_I : \Omega \rightarrow \mathbb{R}$ where $\Omega \subset \mathbb{R}^3$ and an annotation of that volume $V_L : \Omega \rightarrow \mathbb{N}$ with labels $l = 1, \ldots, k$, we want to build a dictionary $\mathbf{D} = (\mathbf{D}_I, \mathbf{D}_L)$ consisting of the intensity dictionary $\mathbf{D}_I \in \mathbb{R}^{m \times n}$ and the associated label dictionary $\mathbf{D}_L \in \mathbb{R}^{km \times n}$. Each column in $\mathbf{D}_I$ contains a vector representation of small intensity cubes of side length M where $m = M^3$, and n is the number of dictionary elements. The columns of $\mathbf{D}_L$ contain vectorized label cubes represented as probabilities of labels. Therefore, each label vector contains km elements, where the first m elements are the probabilities of label 1, the next m elements are for label 2, etc. We get

$$\sum_{l=0}^{k-1} \mathbf{d}_{Li}(lm + \tau) = 1 \text{ for all } \tau \in \{1, \ldots, m\},$$

where $\mathbf{d}_{Li}$ is column i in $\mathbf{D}_L$.

An ideal dictionary would be

$$\hat{\mathbf{D}} = \arg\min_{\mathbf{D}} \sum_{\eta=1}^{o} \left(\hat{\lambda} \|\mathbf{d}_{Li(\eta)} - \mathbf{v}_{L\eta}\|_2^2 + \|\mathbf{d}_{Ii(\eta)} - \mathbf{v}_{I\eta}\|_2^2 \right), \quad (1)$$

where $\mathbf{v}_{I\eta}$ and $\mathbf{v}_{L\eta}$ are the η'th intensity cube and label cube from V_I, V_L respectively with $\eta = 1, \ldots, o$ where o is the number of intensity cubes in V_I and $\hat{\lambda}$ is a scaling factor. $i(\eta)$ is the index of the nearest intensity dictionary element

$$i(\eta) = \arg\min_i \|\mathbf{d}_{Ii} - \mathbf{v}_{I\eta}\|_2^2. \quad (2)$$

The first norm in (1) $\|\mathbf{d}_{Li(\eta)} - \mathbf{v}_{L\eta}\|_2^2$ measures the Euclidean distance between the label dictionary element, and label cube and the second norm in (1)

$\|\mathbf{d}_{Ii(\eta)} - \mathbf{v}_{I\eta}\|_2^2$ is the Euclidean distance between the intensity dictionary element and intensity cube. Our aim is to minimize both simultaneously because we hereby obtain a discriminative dictionary and good clustering properties. We will later show that this is advantageous when using the dictionary for segmenting an unlabeled image.

Finding a solution to (1) is a hard problem. Without the first norm concerning the labels it is a k-means clustering problem, which is NP-hard, and we have not found a solution with the addition of the label information. So, based on (1) we suggest a heuristic clustering algorithm which has given good performance in our experiments. The basic idea is to estimate a weight from the label information and use that in a weighted k-means clustering approach.

The algorithm for building the dictionary is based on iteratively updating a set of dictionary elements. Initially a random set of ξ associated intensity and label cubes are selected as $\hat{\mathbf{v}}_j = (\hat{\mathbf{v}}_{Ij}, \hat{\mathbf{v}}_{Lj})$ from the annotated training volume and vectorized, where $j = 1, \ldots, \xi$. A subset of n patches are randomly selected as the initial dictionary $\mathbf{D}^0$, where $n < \xi$. New dictionary elements are now estimated iteratively as

$$\mathbf{d}_{Ii}^{t+1} = \frac{1}{v_i} \sum_{\kappa \in S_i} (1 - \lambda \|\mathbf{d}_{Li}^t - \hat{\mathbf{v}}_{L\kappa}\|_2) \hat{\mathbf{v}}_{I\kappa}, \tag{3}$$

where $\mathbf{d}_{Ii}^{t+1}$ is the intensity dictionary element at iteration number $t + 1$. S_i is the set of indices with intensity cubes closest to dictionary element i

$$\kappa \in S_i \text{ s.t. } \kappa = \arg\min_{j} \|\mathbf{d}_{Ii} - \mathbf{v}_{Ij}\|_2^2.$$

The normalization factor is estimated as

$$v_i = \sum_{\kappa \in S_i} (1 - \lambda \|\mathbf{d}_{Li} - \hat{\mathbf{v}}_{L\kappa}\|_2). \tag{4}$$

This approach gives high weight to training samples with labels similar to the dictionary element and low weight to dissimilar samples. The label dictionary elements are estimated as average labels for the cluster as

$$\mathbf{d}_{Li}^{t+1} = \frac{1}{|S_i|_0} \sum_{\kappa \in S_i} \hat{\mathbf{v}}_{L\kappa}, \tag{5}$$

where $|S_i|_0$ is the cardinality of S_i. In our experiments we have seen a satisfactory result with little change in the dictionary after approximately 10 iterations.

The dictionary is used for segmenting a volume by building a label probability volume. This is done by matching the intensity dictionary elements to the volume we want to segment, and adding the associated label dictionary elements to an empty label probability volume.

Given a volume $U_I : \Omega \to \mathbb{R}$ that we want to segment with $U_I \in \mathbb{R}^{x \times y \times z}$ we compute a label probability volume $U_L : \Omega \to \mathbb{R}$ with $U_L \in \mathbb{R}^{x \times y \times z \times k}$. Initially we set U_L to having all elements zeros. We can extract vectorized intensity cubes

$\mathbf{u}_{Ih}$ of the same spatial size as the dictionary elements, where $h = 1,\dots,\rho$ is the number of possible cubes with side length M, so e.g. for an odd M we get $\rho = (x - M + 1)(y - M + 1)(z - M + 1)$, which is a little less than the number of voxels due to the volume boundaries. Each $\mathbf{u}_{Ih}$ is matched to the nearest intensity dictionary element using Euclidian distance. For a given intensity vector $\mathbf{u}_{Ih}$ we get the nearest dictionary element

$$i(h) = \arg\min_i \|\mathbf{d}_{Ii} - \mathbf{u}_{Ih}\|_2^2. \tag{6}$$

From this we take the corresponding label dictionary element $\mathbf{d}_{Li(h)}$ and add it to the label volume U_L at the coordinates of h'th cube extracted from U_I for each of the k labels. When the probabilities are added we weigh them using a Gaussian weight function with standard deviation σ centered at the cube. After adding the probabilities in U_L up, we simply normalize by dividing the sum over label probabilities for each voxel to make the probabilities sum to one over all k labels.

Some smoothing at boundaries occurs which especially affects small features. In order to account for that, we estimate label-wise weights on an annotated validation set where we minimize the difference between the obtained probability volume and the annotation. We are given an annotated volume Q_L and the computed label probability volume P_L using a trained dictionary. Then we rearrange these volumes to $\mathbf{Q}_L$ and $\mathbf{P}_L$ such that each row contains the voxel-wise probabilities and each column represents the labels with each row summing to 1, i.e. $\mathbf{Q}_L(r,l) \in \{0,1\}$, $\mathbf{P}_L(r,l) \in [0,1]$ and $\sum_{c=1}^{k} \mathbf{Q}_L(r,l) = \sum_{c=1}^{k} \mathbf{P}_L(r,l) = 1$, where $\mathbf{Q}_L(r,l)$ and $\mathbf{P}_L(r,l)$ are elements from $\mathbf{Q}_L$ and $\mathbf{P}_L$ at row r and column l respectively. We want to find the weight matrix $\mathbf{W} \in \mathbb{R}^{k \times k}$ that minimizes

$$\mathbf{W} = \arg\min_{\mathbf{W}} \|\mathbf{Q}_L - \mathbf{P}_L\mathbf{W}\|_2^2,$$

where the solution is found as

$$\mathbf{W} = (\mathbf{P}_L^T\mathbf{P}_L)^{-1}\mathbf{P}_L^T\mathbf{Q}_L.$$

The voxel-wise probability of the final segmentation is obtained as

$$\tilde{\mathbf{u}}_L(\mathbf{x}) = \mathbf{u}_L(\mathbf{x})\mathbf{W}, \tag{7}$$

where $\mathbf{u}_L(\mathbf{x}) \in \mathbb{R}^k$ is a vector of label probabilities of the voxel from the spatial position $\mathbf{x} = (x,y,z)^T$ in the intensity volume U_I.

3   Materials

Two data sets are employed for the comparative study including:

1. Real data from glass fiber used for wind turbine blades.
2. Phantom data of solid oxide fuel cells.

3.1   Glass Fiber

The data set was obtained through 3D X-ray computed tomography imaging. The scanned sample is a cut-out of a fatigue test specimen and the dimensions of approximately $5 \times 5 \times 10$ mm. The material considered is a uni-directional (UD) glass fiber/polyester composite used in the load carrying beam of a wind turbine blade. Uni-directional in this case means that the fibers are aligned in one main direction, making the composite strong in one direction, and weak in other directions. In order to hold the UD fiber bundles in place during manufacturing, they are stitched to a thin layer of transverse backing fiber bundles. As the backing only contributes lightly to the mechanical properties of the material, the main focus in this study is on segmenting the UD fibers.

In Figure 1, we see one of the training slices and its corresponding annotated labeling where three different classes are defined: centers, fibers and matrix.

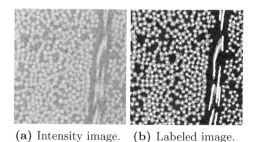

(a) Intensity image.   (b) Labeled image.

Fig. 1. One slice of the fiber training data. In *white*: centers, *gray*: fibers and *black*: matrix.

3.2   Solid Oxide Fuel Cell Phantom

We simulated a 3D SOFC phantom using a random process employing a simple curvature minimization scheme. Here the target phase fractions of 0.24, 0.38 and 0.38 where used for the pore, ion conducting and electron conducting phases respectively. This phantom creation scheme greatly simplifies many aspects of the evolution of a real micro-structure during sintering and as such the created micro-structure is not suited for comparison of higher order properties to a real SOFC. However, the scheme provides 3D micro-structure data that qualitatively matches the structure observed in real SOFC data sets [9]. The scheme is thus well suited as ground truth for segmentation. After the phantom creation of the artificial 3D micro-structure data the X-ray projections and reconstruction were simulated using slice wise radon and inverse radon transform using AIR tools[1]. 3% Gaussian noise was added to the radon transformed data before reconstructing it.

In Figure 2, we can see one of the training slices and its corresponding annotated labeling, where three classes have been defined, corresponding to each of the three phases.

---

[1] http://www2.compute.dtu.dk/~pcha/AIRtools/

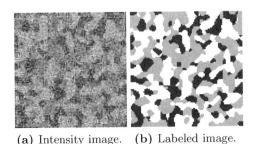

(a) Intensity image.   (b) Labeled image.

Fig. 2. One slice of the fuel cell training data. In *white*: phase one, *gray*: phase two and *black*: phase three.

4   Results

In this section we provide the results from our algorithm and compare it to well established image analysis methods. Glass fiber detection is compared to 2D scale space blob detection [12] and SOFC segmentation is compared to Markov random field (MRF) segmentation solved using graph cuts with alpha expansion [3,11]. For both methods we chose parameters that minimized the segmentation error. It should be noted that the parameters for the MRF are not learned, i. e. they are known.

For the dictionary algorithms, several parameters need to be set. It is known that the segmentation is most sensitive to the change in atom size M, i.e. the side length of the cubes, and number of dictionary elements n, so segmentation errors will be calculated for different parameter settings so as to select the optimal.

4.1   Glass Fiber

For the glass fiber, the dictionaries have been trained with 9 slices of size 200×200 pixels, the validation set also contains 9 slices of the same size. The performance is calculated over only one test slice of size 500×500 pixels.

The performance measure is computed object-wise over the center class, and represents the true positive rate and false positive rate. We segment the center part of the fibers, and the individual fibers are found as the center of mass using connected component analysis on the center segments. Comparison to the manual marked ground truth is done by counting the number of true matches, which are found as points that have each other as nearest neighbors as well as a distance of less than 4 voxels. The 4 voxels are chosen because the average radius of the glass fibers is around 4 voxels. Results are shown in Table 1. The computational time, defined as the time to train, validate and classify the one test slice, has also been calculated.

The computational time (C_{time}) grows as the number of elements in the dictionary increases (n) or the size of the volume cube (M) becomes bigger. The average C_{time} is 100.3 seconds for 3D, whereas it is 3.2 seconds for the 2D dictionary.

Table 1. Performance measure dictionaries with different parameters

M	n	TPR^{2D}	FPR^{2D}	TPR^{3D}	FPR^{3D}
3	50	0.8563	0.1674	0.9099	0.1202
3	250	0.9082	0.1678	0.9511	0.1520
3	1000	0.9350	0.1721	0.9561	0.1165
5	50	0.9468	0.0399	0.9926	0.0177
5	250	0.9762	0.0248	0.9977	0.0104
5	1000	0.9799	0.0208	0.9963	0.0121
7	50	0.9866	0.0104	0.9896	0.0104
7	250	0.9873	0.0117	0.9973	**0.0080**
7	1000	0.9910	0.0144	**0.9980**	0.0087
9	50	0.9484	0.0171	0.9461	0.0107
9	250	0.9930	0.0100	0.9940	0.0104
9	1000	**0.9953**	**0.0097**	0.9977	0.0100

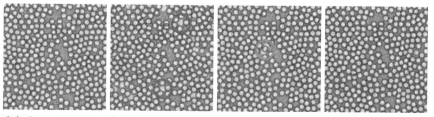

(a) Ground truth. (b) Blob detection. (c) 2D dictionary. (d) 3D dictionary.

Fig. 3. Ground truth and circles around detected fiber centers

In Figure 3, we see a zoomed image of fibers with circles around each of the detected centers for each of the three methods (blob detection, 2D dictionary and 3D dictionary) and the ground truth image. Circles are plotted with radius 4 for illustration purposes. As can be seen qualitatively from the images, the performance of the dictionary methods is substantially better than the one obtained through blob detection. The centers in the blob detection are found less accurately compared to those in the ground truth and some centers are not found (e.g. red circles in Figure 3). The displacement of the centers in the 2D and 3D dictionary with respect to the ground truth is very small. Moreover, the 3D dictionary performs slightly better than the 2D dictionary, as it finds all the centers, whereas in the 2D method results there are two centers which have been detected as one only center (blue circle Figure 3). This is because there are some pixels connecting these two centers.

Quantitatively the three methods can be compared using the performance measures TPR and FPR.

1. **Blob detection**: TPR = 0.8339 and FPR = 0.0737.
2. **2D dictionary** ($M = 9$, $n = 1000$): TPR = 0.9953 and FPR = 0.0097.
3. **3D dictionary** ($M = 7$, $n = 1000$): TPR = 0.9980 and FPR = 0.0087.

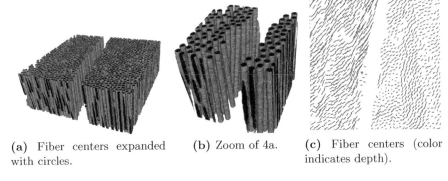

(a) Fiber centers expanded with circles.

(b) Zoom of 4a.

(c) Fiber centers (color indicates depth).

Fig. 4. Segmentation over a stack of 100 slices

In Figure 4, a stack of 100 slices of 300×300 pixels was segmented using the 3D dictionary ($M = 7$, $n = 1000$). In these images we present the results in 3D, where the fiber orientation can be visualized (straight fibers appear as points in 4c). Note how accurate the fiber orientation can be visualized using this approach.

4.2 Solid Oxide Fuel Cell Phantom

For the fuel cell data, the measure used to evaluate the performance is defined as the percentage of pixels which are classified correctly over all three classes. Results are shown in Table 2. The dictionaries are trained with a volume of $50 \times 100 \times 100$ pixels, validated with another volume of $50 \times 100 \times 100$ and the performance is measured over a volume of $100 \times 100 \times 100$ voxels.

As for the glass fiber, the computational time is two orders greater when using the 3D dictionary. In Figure 5, we see one segmented slice from the test set for each of the three methods (MRF, 2D dictionary and 3D dictionary) compared

Table 2. Performance measure dictionaries with different parameters

M	n	Performance^{2D}	Performance^{3D}
3	50	0.8864	0.9115
3	250	0.8917	**0.9197**
3	1000	0.8913	0.9192
5	50	0.9029	0.8886
5	250	0.9103	0.9034
5	1000	**0.9119**	0.9060
7	50	0.8819	0.8227
7	250	0.8995	0.8453
7	1000	0.9069	0.8512
9	50	0.8407	0.7455
9	250	0.8743	0.7786
9	1000	0.8886	0.7803

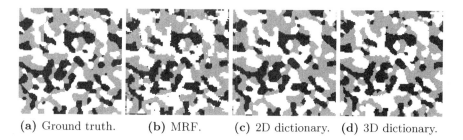

(a) Ground truth.   (b) MRF.   (c) 2D dictionary.   (d) 3D dictionary.

Fig. 5. Ground truth and segmentations of fuel cell phantoms

to the ground truth image. In this case, the benefit from the 3D expansion of the dictionary method is not significant due to the excessive smoothing introduced by the 3D dictionary. However, the dictionary methods do slightly outperform the MRF technique, as we can see from in the following quantitative results:

1. **MRF**: Performance = 0.9078.
2. **2D dictionary** ($M = 5$, $n = 1000$): Performance = 0.9119.
3. **3D dictionary** ($M = 3$, $n = 250$): Performance = 0.9197.

5   Conclusions

In this paper, we have presented a highly flexible and accurate method for 3D segmentation of complex image structures. The method is an extension of a 2D segmentation method and we have investigated if adding a new spatial dimension improved the segmentation performance, as this third dimension provides extra contextual information. We have conducted an investigation to demonstrate the flexibility of the proposed method. Our investigation included experiments for segmenting individual glass fibers in X-ray computed tomography data and for segmenting three phases in phantom data of solid oxide fuel cell data. With the glass fiber data we obtained close to perfect segmentation of the fiber centers. For the fuel cell phantoms we almost see no improvement going from 2D to 3D, which might be due to the excessive smoothing introduce by the 3D algorithm. The fiber detection was compared to scale space blob detection and the solid oxide fuel cell data was compared to Markov random field segmentation using alpha expansion. In both cases both the 2D and 3D methods outperformed these standard methods.

In the current implementation the computational cost is high, but the method has not been optimized for speed. Especially the 3D version is computational expensive with two orders of magnitude higher computation time and our plan to optimize the method for computational speed in our future work. With the ease of training and very high performance, we believe that the proposed methods can be a very useful tool in quantifying structures in complex volumetric data like tomograms of material samples.

References

1. Aldasoro, C.C.R., Bhalerao, A.: Volumetric texture segmentation by discriminant feature selection and multiresolution classification. IEEE TMI **26**(1), 1–14 (2007)
2. Blot, L., Zwiggelaar, R.: Synthesis and analysis of solid texture: application in medical imaging, pp. 9–12 (2002)
3. Boykov, Y., Veksler, O., Zabih, R.: Fast approximate energy minimization via graph cuts. IEEE Transactions on Pattern Analysis and Machine Intelligence **23**(11), 1222–1239 (2001)
4. Cremers, D., Rousson, M., Deriche, R.: A review of statistical approaches to level set segmentation: integrating color, texture, motion and shape. International Journal of Computer Vision **72**(2), 195–215 (2007)
5. Dahl, A.L., Larsen, R.: Learning dictionaries of discriminative image patches. In: 22nd BMVC (2011)
6. Government, T.D.: The danish climate policy plan - towards a low carbon society. Technical report, Dahish Energy Agency (2013)
7. Hansen, J.Z., Brøndsted, P., Jacobsen, T.K.: The effects of fibre architecture on fatigue life-time of composite materials. Ph.D. thesis, Technical University of Denmark, Risø National Laboratory for Sustainable Energy (2013)
8. Ilea, D.E., Whelan, P.F.: Image segmentation based on the integration of colourtexture descriptorsa review. Pattern Recognition **44**(10), 2479–2501 (2011)
9. Jørgensen, P.S., Yakal-Kremski, K., Wilson, J., Bowen, J.R., Barnett, S.: On the accuracy of triple phase boundary lengths calculated from tomographic image data. Journal of Power Sources **261**, 198–205 (2014)
10. Jørgensen, P., Ebbehøj, S., Hauch, A.: Triple phase boundary specific pathway analysis for quantitative characterization of solid oxide cell electrode microstructure. Journal of Power Sources **279**, 686–693 (2015)
11. Kolmogorov, V., Zabin, R.: What energy functions can be minimized via graph cuts? IEEE Transactions on Pattern Analysis and Machine Intelligence **26**(2), 147–159 (2004)
12. Lindeberg, T.: Feature detection with automatic scale selection. International Journal of Computer Vision **30**(2), 79–116 (1998)
13. Nijssen, R.P.L.: Fatigue life prediction and strength degradation of wind turbine rotor blade composites. Contractor Report SAND2006-7810P, Sandia National Laboratories, Albuquerque, NM (2006)
14. Randen, T., Monsen, E., Signer, C., Abrahamsen, A., Hansen, J.O., Sæter, T., Schlaf, J., Sønneland, L., et al.: Three-dimensional texture attributes for seismic data analysis. In: 70th Annual International Meeting, Society of Exploration Geophysics Expanded Abstracts, pp. 668–671 (2000)
15. Tai, C., Baba-Kishi, K.: Microtexture studies of pst and pzt ceramics and pzt thin film by electron backscatter diffraction patterns. Textures and Microstructures **35**(2), 71–86 (2002)
16. Tu, Z., Zhou, X.S., Comaniciu, D., Bogoni, L.: A learning based approach for 3D segmentation and colon detagging. In: Leonardis, A., Bischof, H., Pinz, A. (eds.) ECCV 2006. LNCS, vol. 3953, pp. 436–448. Springer, Heidelberg (2006)

17. Ushizima, D., Parkinson, D., Nico, P., Ajo-Franklin, J., MacDowell, A., Kocar, B., Bethel, W., Sethian, J.: Statistical segmentation and porosity quantification of 3d x-ray microtomography. In: SPIE Optical Engineering Applications, pp. 813502–813502. International Society for Optics and Photonics (2011)
18. Waggoner, J., Zhou, Y., Simmons, J., De Graef, M., Wang, S.: 3d materials image segmentation by 2d propagation: a graph-cut approach considering homomorphism. IEEE TIP **22**(12), 5282–5293 (2013)
19. Zhang, J., Tan, T.: Brief review of invariant texture analysis methods. Pattern Recognition **35**(3), 735–747 (2002)

Face Recognition Using Smoothed High-Dimensional Representation

Juha Ylioinas[✉], Juho Kannala, Abdenour Hadid, and Matti Pietikäinen

Center for Machine Vision Research,
University of Oulu, P.O. Box 4500, 90014 Oulu, Finland
juyl@ee.oulu.fi

Abstract. Recent studies have underlined the significance of high-dimensional features and their compression for face recognition. Partly motivated by these findings, we propose a novel method for building unsupervised face representations based on binarized descriptors and efficient compression by soft assignment and unsupervised dimensionality reduction. For binarized descriptors, we consider Binarized Statistical Image Features (BSIF) which is a learning based descriptor computing a binary code for each pixel by thresholding the outputs of a linear projection between a local image patch and a set of independent basis vectors estimated from a training data set using independent component analysis. In this work, we propose application specific learning to train a separate BSIF descriptor for each of the local face regions. Then, our method constructs a high-dimensional representation from an input face by collecting histograms of BSIF codes in a blockwise manner. Before dropping the dimension to get a more compressed representation, an important step in the pipeline of our method is soft feature assignment where the region histograms of the binarized codes are smoothed using kernel density estimation achieved by a simple and fast matrix-vector product. In detail, we provide a thorough evaluation on FERET and LFW benchmarks comparing our face representation method to the state-of-the-art in face recognition showing enhanced performance on FERET and promising results on LFW.

1 Introduction

Automatic face recognition from images is a major research area in computer vision. The high societal impact and practical significance of face recognition technologies is evident given the ever-increasing digital image databases and wide availability of cameras in various consumer devices (e.g. smart phones, Google Glasses). Thus, face recognition has many applications in several areas, including, for example, content-based image retrieval, security and surveillance (e.g. passport control), web search and services (e.g. automatic face naming in services like Facebook) and human computer interaction.

The first studies on automatic face recognition emerged already in 1970's and since then various methods have been developed resulting in continuous improvements in performance. Examples of well known early techniques include

© Springer International Publishing Switzerland 2015
R.R. Paulsen and K.S. Pedersen (Eds.): SCIA 2015, LNCS 9127, pp. 516–529, 2015.
DOI: 10.1007/978-3-319-19665-7_44

the *Eigenfaces* and *Fisherfaces* methods [1,2]. A comprehensive review of the field from its early days until the beginning of 2000's is presented in [3]. However, despite decades of research and all the developments and efforts, there is still a clear gap in accuracy and robustness between the automatic face recognition systems and human level of performance. In fact, the problem of automatic face recognition is still a very active research topic and there are plenty of recent developments [4–13]. Important driving forces behind the recent progress are public datasets and benchmarks that are used for comparing and evaluating different methods. Examples of well known and widely used benchmarks are the Facial Recognition Technology (FERET) database [14] and the Labeled Faces in the Wild (LFW) database [15].

A typical face recognition system consists of detection, alignment, representation, and classification steps. In this paper, along with many other recent studies, our focus is on face representation. Usually, face representation is composed of two distinct steps where (i) a certain kind of face representation is first generated from a normalized input face image and then (ii) subspace analysis is performed to produce a significantly lower dimensional representation [16]. The step (i) can be performed by common signal processing techniques, such as Gabor wavelets and Discrete Fourier Transform, whereas the step (ii) by applying Principal Component Analysis (PCA) or Linear Discriminant Analysis (LDA). The way the input face is processed divides the face representation methods further into holistic and so called local methods. Especially, the use of methods based on local image descriptors has resulted in a great success, the notable ones including gradient based Scale Invariant Feature Transform (SIFT), Histograms of Oriented Gradients (HOG), and Local Binary Patterns (LBP). Especially binarized local image descriptors, like LBP, have gained a great favour in a wide spectrum of face analysis studies. An essential part of local face description methods is the use of statistical histograms over a discrete vocabulary of the resulting local descriptor features.

In this paper, we propose a novel *unsupervised* face representation method which builds on the recently proposed local image description method called Binarized Statistical Image Features (BSIF) [17]. BSIF is a learning based method which computes a binary code for each pixel by thresholding the inner products between a vectorized local image patch outputs of a linear projection between a local image patch and a set of basis vectors which are learnt via Independent Component Analysis (ICA) from training image patches. The BSIF method is inspired by LBP and its derivatives, but in contrast to many of them, BSIF does not use a manually predefined set of filters but learns them by utilizing the statistics of images under interest. In particular, in this paper we show that it is beneficial to learn separate sets of linear filters for different face regions by utilizing training image patches from face images. Thus, the binary codes for pixels of a certain face region are obtained by using the corresponding filters, specifically learnt to describe patches in that region. This is in contrast to [17] which uses the same filters for all pixels and learns them from natural images (but not specifically from face images). The face regions are finally represented by histograms of the resulting binary codes and the final face descriptor is obtained by concatenating the histograms of different regions, as in [18] and [17]. As an important step of our representation, before compressing the histogram based face representation to a lower dimensional subspace using Whitening PCA (WPCA), we propose to smooth each region histogram using a kernel method suitable for n-dimensional binary data. Most importantly, we show that the smoothing can be accomplished by a simple matrix-vector product. Unlike other recent learning based descriptors, our approach does not need hand-crafted local pixel patterns and vector quantization, for example, using k-means during learning and, most importantly, it avoids cumbersome large look-up tables at test time. Our contributions include: (i) we advance descriptor based methods; (ii) we provide insights to benefits of unsupervised application specific descriptor learning; (iii) we introduce a practical method for local descriptor soft-assigments; and (iv) we show the importance of soft-assigment as a predecessor for dimensionality reduction.

Based on our evaluations, by using the face representation method proposed herein one is able to gain the state-of-the-art performance on the widely used FERET dataset. We also validate our proposal on more challenging conditions using the popular LFW dataset showing promising results.

2   Related Work

There is a lot of previous research on different aspects of automatic face recognition systems [19]. Some studies focus on the first stages of the pipeline, i.e. face detection and alignment [20], whereas others focus on learning classifiers or similarity metrics for chosen face representations [10]. However, this paper concentrates on the representation problem as it has been shown to be a crucial component for robust performance in challenging real-world scenarios [13,15]. We next review some recent works that we consider to be the most closely related to our work.

High-dimensional features have been found very potential in designing representations in object recognition. For example in [21], it was shown that together with the chosen feature itself, equally important is to consider how many of them to use and how dense or in how many scales they are extracted. Indeed, these are the key elements that are acknowledged in many studies for obtaining an informative representation. The only setback is that a method which embodies all of these elements usually outputs a very high-dimensional representation. To compress the representation for a more practical usage, efficient dimension reduction methods are needed as noted in [7].

In [7], Chen et al. discussed about benefits of a high-dimensional face representation and practically showed that the increase in dimensionality has a positive impact on the accuracy while applied to face verification. Their method was based on face landmark detection following encodings of the detected key-points (such as eyes, nose, and mouth corners). They compared several local descriptors which all ended up to improved recognition accuracy while the feature dimension was increased by varying landmark numbers and sampling scales. In [11], a high-dimensional representation was constructed concatenating LBP histograms computed from the whole face area using overlapping blocks and different kinds of LBP parameter configurations. However, the authors argued that the added accuracy in high-dimensional face representation can be revealed only after dimensionality reduction, which they showed using whitening PCA among other methods.

Although the claimed pivotal role of high-dimensionality, there are some clear hints that the underlying feature extraction method has its own impact and should be taken into careful consideration. To this end, learning encoders for hand-crafted descriptors has lately been shown to yield outperforming results compared to completely hand-crafted ones. For example, the best performing descriptor in [22], an LBP-based descriptor combined with unsupervised codebook learning via *k-means* outperformed such descriptors as the conventional LBP and HOG, in all given settings. In turn, a quite recent supervised descriptor, proposed in [8], is based on first fixing the LBP-like sampling strategy and then learning discriminative filters and so-called soft-sampling using a formulation similar to two-dimensional Linear Discriminant Analysis. Finally, the method was shown to outperform many of the existing LBP-based, completely hand-crafted descriptors.

Our approach connects all aspects of the methods discussed above for producing a discriminative face representation. The desired high-dimensionality [7] is reached at the descriptor level, using a local binary descriptor called BSIF [17]. In our method, we basically learn descriptors that produce higher dimensional histograms but, unlike LBP, in a more justified manner without sacrificing further loss of information during the encoding of pixel neighborhoods. Like in [8], we learn the descriptors in a blockwise manner from aligned face images, but apart from that, our approach does not need hand-crafted local pixel patterns and vector quantization using large look-up tables. We use overlapping blocks, like in [11], but before compression we further propose to smooth each region based histogram using kernel density estimation. Finally, an efficient compression is achieved by projecting the whole representation into a lower dimension using the whitening PCA method.

3   Our Method

In this section, we review the most important steps of our face representation method. We first introduce the BSIF descriptor and then present the utilized soft-assignment method suitable for binary descriptors. Finally, we introduce the WPCA dimensionality reduction method and provide some discussion about the used face matching methods together with other related details.

Binarized Statistical Image Features. Binarized Statistical Image Features (BSIF) is a data-driven local image description method which is widely inspired by LBP and its derivatives. In BSIF, a predefined number of linear filters are learnt using a set of training image patches using a criterion which aims to maximize the statistical independence between the responses of the convolutions of each individual filter and the given image patches [17]. Evidently, by maximising the statistical independence one is able to learn the most optimal set of filters with respect to the following independent quantization of the response vector coordinates, which is the fundamental part of all local binary descriptor methods. Moreover, the maximization of the statistical independence results in entropy growth between the coordinates leading to an effective description process in overall. This is also the main difference to the LBP method where the derivative pixel neighborhood tests are usually set without taking any criterion into consideration. This discussion above should justify the reason why we call BSIF as an optimal binarized descriptor. If a binarized descriptor is used to produce a high-dimensional representation, it is highly important to take the full advantage of the descriptor's encoding capability.

One BSIF operation is a linear matrix vector product, $\mathbf{s} = \mathbf{W}\mathbf{x}$, where $\mathbf{x}$ is a vector containing all the pixels of a local image patch of a size $w \times w$ (i.e. $\mathbf{x} \in \mathbb{R}^{w \times w}$), and $\mathbf{W}$ is a matrix of a size $n \times w^2$ containing the n linear filters which are stacked row by row. The output, vector $\mathbf{s} \in \mathbb{R}^n$, is then binarized by thresholding each of its elements s_i at zero finally yielding an n-bit long binary string treated as a codeword characterising the contents of the local neighborhood area on a certain location in the image.

For learning the linear filters, one needs to sample a training set consisting of image patches of the same size than the window of the desired descriptor. In the original paper [17], the training set was sampled from natural images, but the images can also be sampled from application-specific images, like it is done in this study. In the very beginning, the mean luminance is removed from each patch. Then, the linear filters are learnt so that the matrix $\mathbf{W}$ is first decomposed into two parts by $\mathbf{W} = \mathbf{U}\mathbf{V}$, where $\mathbf{V}$ is a whitening transformation matrix learnt from the same training image patches and $\mathbf{U}$ is then finally estimated using Independent Component Analysis (ICA). The whitening transformation, usually accomplished via PCA, may also contain the reduction of dimensionality which in general lightens our computations but also reduces the effects caused by different image artefacts in image patches which are usually recorded by the last principal components. Here, we reduce the dimension of our training vectors to the length equal to the desired number of filters. Finally, to accomplish ICA we applied FastICA [23].

Soft-assigned BSIF Descriptors. Originally, the idea of descriptor-space soft assignment was to tackle the problems caused by hard assignment of descriptors to discrete visual codewords. In this procedure, also known as the bag-of-visual-words representation, two image feature descriptors are treated identical if they are assigned to the same visual codeword of the visual vocabulary generated by some clustering algorithm, such as k-means. As noted in [24], such a hard quantization leads to errors as even a small variation in the feature value may cause totally different assignments. In soft-assignment the objective is to describe an image patch by a weighted combination of visual words. In general, soft-assignment has been investigated in both with using visual vocabularies generated by some clustering algorithm [24] and with binarized local descriptors [25]. The soft-assignment method we are using is based on kernel density estimation. The normal kernel, proposed by [26], is given by

$$K_\lambda(l|l') = \lambda^{n-d(l,l')}(1 - \lambda)^{d(l,l')}, \tag{1}$$

where l and l' are both n-dimensional binary codewords, $d(l, l')$ is the Hamming distance between the codewords, and $\lambda \in [\frac{1}{2}, 1)$ is the bandwidth (smoothing) parameter.

The smoothing operation is put into action by first constructing a kernel matrix $\mathbf{S}$ so that

$$\mathbf{S}_\lambda = \begin{bmatrix} K_\lambda(0|0) & \cdots & K_\lambda(0|2^n - 1) \\ \vdots & \ddots & \vdots \\ K_\lambda(2^n - 1|0) & \cdots & K_\lambda(2^n - 1|2^n - 1) \end{bmatrix}. \tag{2}$$

Descriptor space soft-assignment is then accomplished by introducing a matrix-vector product $\mathbf{S}_\lambda \mathbf{h} \in \mathbb{R}_+^{2^n}$ where $\mathbf{h}$ is a histogram (in column format) of binary codewords on a certain image area and n is the number of filters.

The amount of weighting among the codewords is controlled by the smoothing parameter λ. Letting $\lambda = 1$ coincides with the naive estimator, i.e. the basic histogram of codewords. In that case the kernel matrix $\mathbf{S}_\lambda$ equals the identity matrix. On the contrary, by setting $\lambda = 1/2$ all codewords are given the same weight 2^{-n} which finally yields to evenly distributed codewords. It is noteworthy that the kernel in (1) is analogous with the well-known Gaussian kernel that operates in continuous domain. Although soft assignment with binarized descriptors is quite well-known, we show its efficiency while combined with dimensionality reduction which, to the best of our knowledge, was not considered in previous studies.

Whitening PCA. To compress the high-dimensional representation we use Whitening Principal Component Analysis (WPCA). WPCA has proven to provide extra boost to the face recognition performance in many studies [6,8,11,27]. The first benefit of using WPCA is the resulting reduced dimension of the final representation. In our algorithm, for example, it turns out useful as the length of the descriptor histogram is 2^n, where n is the number of filters. If the input face is divided into 7×7 blocks the final representation yields $2^n \times 7 \times 7$ which can finally prove too large in certain circumstances. The second benefit comes from the whitening part where the features projected along the principal components are divided by their standard deviations. It has been shown that the whitening part is important in order to equalize the influence of the principal components to the matching process which is often performed using the Cosine similarity. The PCA part is accomplished using the Turk-Pentland strategy where instead of calculating the covariance matrix $\mathbf{A}\mathbf{A}^\mathrm{T}$, where $\mathbf{A} = [\mathbf{a}_1\mathbf{a}_2\ldots\mathbf{a}_M]$ collects mean-subracted feature vectors in column format, we calculate $\mathbf{A}^\mathrm{T}\mathbf{A}$ which is a matrix of a much smaller size. The eigenvectors of $\mathbf{A}\mathbf{A}^\mathrm{T}$ are then $\mathbf{u}_i = \mathbf{A}\mathbf{v}_i/\|\mathbf{A}\mathbf{v}_i\|_2$, where $\mathbf{v}_i$ are the eigenvectors of $\mathbf{A}^\mathrm{T}\mathbf{A}$ [1].

In general, PCA may suffer with sparse and high-dimensional data leading to the overfitting problem [28]. One reason of this problem in our case is that while using BSIF with increasing number of filters the resulting histograms of descriptor labels will become larger and sparser since the number of descriptor label occurrences is always constrained according to the block size. The result is that applying PCA most likely overfits as the correlation between the possible pairs of coordinates is most probably represented by only a few samples in the data. Based on our results, it seems that the overfitting problem can be most likely alleviated by introducing the smoothing operation which ensures that there are much less non-zero elements in the concatenated representation than in the non-smoothed one.

Matching Faces. For matching faces, we used the Hellinger distance. According to [29], this distance can be calculated as

$$d(\mathbf{x}, \mathbf{y})^2 = \|\mathbf{x}\|_2^2 + \|\mathbf{y}\|_2^2 - 2\mathbf{x}^\top \mathbf{y} = 2 - 2\mathbf{x}^\top \mathbf{y}, \tag{3}$$

where both $\mathbf{x}$ and $\mathbf{y}$ are properly preprocessed face representations. If we used the $L2$ normalized representations of $\mathbf{x}$ and $\mathbf{y}$, we would be measuring the Euclidean distance between them. To measure the distance based on the Hellinger kernel, before applying (3), we first (i) $L1$-normalize both representations and then (ii) replace all coordinate values by their square roots (see the detailed reasoning in [29]). Following the majority of previous face recognition studies, for the WPCA projected representation we use the Cosine distance. To accomplish this, we further $L2$-normalize the WPCA compressed representation and apply (3), which can be easily shown to be equal as measuring the Cosine distance between the input representations.

In our FERET evaluation, we straightly calculate the distance between two input representations using the steps given above. However, in the LFW evaluation, we use an additional step which has been used in some recent studies to gain some additional boost in performance. In detail, we use the *flip-free* strategy described in [30]. That means, instead of direct distance calculations of two input representations we horizontally flip all images before feature extraction and calculate the average of the distances between all possible four combinations of the representations stemming from the original and horizontally flipped images.

4   Experiments

We use the Face Recognition Technology (FERET) [14] and the Labeled Faces in the Wild (LFW) [15] datasets. To better understand the possible benefits of using application-specific images in learning the descriptor for high-dimensional representation, we compare the face-based BSIF descriptor to the one which was learnt using natural images. Our baseline is the popular LBP descriptor with different bit lengths and several different radii. Finally, we compare our proposal to the state-of-the-art methods which were reported using the given two datasets.

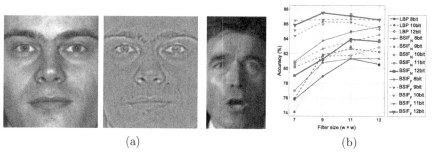

(a)   (b)

Fig. 1. (a) An example of a cropped and preprocessed face used in the FERET experiments, and a crop used in the LFW experiment. (b) The effect of the descriptor's length (in bits) and the support area. The curves are for raw representations each having a length of $7 \times 7 \times 2^n$, where n is the number of bits of the descriptor $dup2$.

For LFW experiments, we evaluate our method barely in the unsupervised evaluation category using the recently updated protocol [15].

Setup. FERET [14] is a standard dataset for benchmarking face recognition methods in constrained imaging conditions. FERET is composed of several different subsets with varying pose, expression, and illumination. We are interested in the frontal profile images of it, which are divided into five sets known as fa, fb, fc, $dup1$, and $dup2$. For gallery, we use fa containing 1,196 images of 1,196 subjects. For probes, we use the rest four subsets, where fb contains 1,195 images covering varied expressions, fc contains 194 images with varied illumination conditions, $dup1$ contains 722 images taken later in time, and $dup2$, which contains 234 images taken at least one year after the corresponding gallery images. LFW [15], regarded as *de-facto* evaluation benchmark for face verification in unconstrained conditions, consists of 13,233 images of 5,749 subjects. LFW is organized in to two disjoint subsets called View 1 and 2. View 1 is a development set containing 2,200 face image pairs for training and 1,000 pairs for testing. View 2, which is meant to be used in reporting the final performance, is a 10-fold cross-validation set of 6,000 face pairs. Herein we use the LFW aligned (LFW-a) [31] version where all the original LFW images are aligned using a commercial face alignment system.

As it will be seen, we evaluate the proposed method on two face recognition modes, namely in identification and verification. For the former we use the FERET dataset whereas for the latter we use the LFW dataset. In this paper, the major part of the parameters used in the LFW evaluation is set based on the results of the preceding FERET evaluation. We are also trying to utilize as much as possible the existing knowledge on different LFW experiments found from the literature to minimise parameter tuning.

Face Identification on FERET. We first align all face images based on the provided eye coordinates and rescale them to the size of 150×130 pixels. We further preprocess all face images by applying the method proposed in [32] (see Fig. 1 (a)). Then, we divide the face into 7×7 blocks which are of 30×28 pixels using a vertical and horizontal overlap of 10 and 11 pixels, respectively. Finally we apply the given local binary descriptor, record the frequencies of the resulting codewords in the given block, and store them to separate histograms. After processing the whole face area, the resulting block-based histograms are concatenated to form the final representation of the face. While the soft-assignment of the codewords is applied, it is done separately for each block-based histogram before they are concatenated.

To see whether application-specific learning is beneficial for constructing local binary descriptors for describing faces, we form a specific training set and perform descriptor learning locally for each separate block resulting in a bank of descriptors, each of them specialized in describing some particular facial region. Indeed, it has been shown many times that different face regions provide different contributions to face recognition [8,18]. In practice, we use a standard training set, which contains altogether 762 faces, provided by the CSU package [33]. Using the desired descriptor window size we then randomly sample each separate face region by evenly taking 50,000 image patches from the given 762 images and perform the descriptor learning. As we use the method given in [32], the training images are preprocessed accordingly. We compare the resulting descriptors with the corresponding ones learnt from 13 natural images [17]. For the baseline, we use the circular 8, 10 and 12 bit LBP descriptors with several different radii. To compare all these representations we use the nearest neighbor classifier applying the Hellinger distance. To take a stand on the issue of the fast growth in the representation based on local binary descriptors, we reduce the length of the final representation to 1,195 via WPCA and finally report the results using the Cosine distance. For computing the WPCA transform, we use all faces in the gallery.

The parameters we must tune are the window size of the descriptor and its dimension. For LBP, the dimension equals to the number of neighborhood pixels used in the feature calculation. For BSIF, the dimension is the number of filters, or statistically independent basis vectors. To see the influence of the window size and the dimension, we show the mean accuracy of *dup1* and *dup2* in Fig. 1 (b). The results indicate that BSIF clearly outperforms LBP and that the same window size 11×11 performs consistently well for all tested descriptors. The best dimension, however, seems to differ as for the BSIF descriptor based on natural image patches ($BSIF_N$) it seems to be 10, and for the BSIF based on face image patches ($BSIF_F$), all four starting from 9 to 12 bits, seem to perform well. From now on, we fix the number of filters as 11, for both $BSIF_N$ and $BSIF_F$ descriptors.

For comprehensiveness, we report the results on all subsets using 11-bit BSIF descriptors. We also attest the usefulness of soft-assignment, setting λ as 0.9, before compressing (WPCA and Cosine distance) the representation. Based on the results in Table 1, using face image patches in descriptor learning clearly benefits. One also observes that the result of compression is remarkable. Moreover, the utilized soft-assignment method further boosts up the performance while combined with compression. In general, we noticed that by using BSIF_F combined with soft-assignments and compression, the performance was better in 16 out of 20 test cases (from 8 to 12 bits and from 7×7 to 13×13 size of filters) compared with its compressed non-smoothed version. The mean accuracies over all parameter combinations and over all subsets for the smoothed and non-smoothed BSIF_F were 96.1% and 95.5%, respectively.

Table 1. Comparative results on FERET using 11-bit and 11×11 size of descriptors. The first two columns are for raw features with the Hellinger distance metric, and *sa* refers to soft-assignment.

	BSIF_N	BSIF_F	BSIF_F + WPCA	BSIF_F^{sa} + WPCA
fb	97.9	99.0	99.7	99.7
fc	100	100	100	100
dup1	84.3	88.2	93.9	95.2
dup2	82.9	85.0	91.9	94.4
mean	91.3	93.1	96.4	97.3

Comparing our best result to the state-of-the-art, shown in Table 2, we can observe that the accuracy of our method is the best one. It must be noted that the earlier best methods, the DFD and LGXP descriptors, are based on supervised learning. Moreover, at least POEM, I-LQP, and G-LQP uses horizontal image flipping to further boost the performance, whereas our method does not use any flipping strategies in this experiment. Finally, according to [6], G-LQP is based on fusion on decision level, which has also shown to provide some gain in performance compared to using descriptors separately.

Face Verification on LFW. In this experiment, after geometrical alignment we rescale all faces to the size of 150×81 using a slightly different cropping than in the previous experiment, see Fig. 1 (a). This time the face is divided into 14×8 blocks which are of 20×18 pixels using a horizontal and vertical overlap of 10 and 9, respectively. These selections are made largely based on the results provided by [34]. Based on the FERET experiment, we use 11-bit coding for both the BSIF_N and BSIF_F descriptors. For BSIF_F, we learn the descriptors locally for each block this time resulting in 112 specialized face descriptors. Soft-assignment is performed like previously but for the compression the final dimension is fixed to 2000, like in [6]. Unlike in the previous experiment, we do not apply preprocessing as it did not seem to provide any improvement based on the evaluations on View 1.

Table 2. Comparison to the state-of-the-art on FERET. The first value is for raw features and the second (after slash mark) is for compressed features. All but LGXP uses WPCA for compression. LGXP uses supervised Fisher Linear Discriminant (FLD) approach.

	POEM [27]	DFD [8]	LGOP [35]	LGXP [16]	I-LQP [6]	G-LQP [6]	Ours
fb	97.6 / 99.6	99.2 / 99.4	98.8 / 99.2	98.0 / 99.0	99.2 / 99.8	99.5 / 99.9	99.0 / 99.7
fc	95.0 / 99.5	98.5 / 100	99.0 / 99.5	100 / 100	69.6 / 94.3	99.5 / 100	100 / 100
dup1	77.6 / 88.8	85.0 / 91.8	83.5 / 89.5	82.0 / 92.0	65.8 / 85.5	81.2 / 93.2	88.2 / 95.2
dup2	76.5 / 85.0	82.9 / 92.3	83.8 / 88.5	83.0 / 91.0	48.3 / 78.6	79.9 / 91.1	85.0 / 94.4
mean	86.7 / 93.2	91.4 / 95.9	91.3 / 94.2	90.8 / 95.5	70.7 / 89.6	90.0 / 96.0	93.1 / 97.3

The setting of the LFW protocol forces us to learn the descriptor bank 10 times, separately for each fold. For learning a BSIF bank for one fold under evaluation, we randomly picked a set of 1800 face images from the rest nine folds. This procedure confirms that we do not learn from those persons that appear in the testing set. Also, for computing the WPCA transform we used only those images that belong to the nine training folds. According to the updated protocol for evaluating methods under unsupervised paradigm, we report the performances in terms of ROC curves and by measuring the area under these curves (AUC).

The results, shown in Fig. 2 and in Table 3, indicate that our method is comparable with other methods reported in the literature. If we compared only raw features (without compression) our method would actually produce the highest AUC value. However, comparing our proposed approach to the top-performers, Pose-adaptive filtering (with WPCA according to [36]) and MRF-Fusion-CSKDA [37], it should be noticed that these methods use different kind of pose correction and therefore the results are not directly comparable in terms of image features. Moreover, it should be noted that among all of those methods using the aligned version of the LFW dataset (LFW-a), our proposed representation yields the best result.

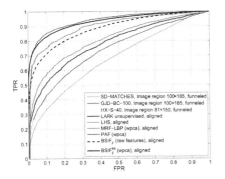

Table 3. Comparison to the state-of-the-art methods on LFW in the unsupervised evaluation category.

method	AUC
SD-MATCHES, 125×125, funneled [34]	0.5407
GJD-BC-100, 122×225, funneled [34]	0.7392
H-XS-40, 81×150, funneled [34]	0.7547
LARK unsupervised, aligned [38]	0.7830
LHS, aligned [39]	0.8107
MRF-LBP (WPCA) [40], aligned	0.8994
Pose Adaptive Filtering (WPCA) [36]	0.9405
MRF-Fusion-CSKDA (WPCA) [37]	0.9894
$BSIF_N$, aligned	0.8026
$BSIF_F$, aligned	0.8843
$BSIF_F^{a}$ (WPCA), aligned	0.9318

Fig. 2. ROC curves averaged over 10 folds of View 2 under *unsupervised* evaluation category

5   Conclusions

Recent studies have pointed out the importance of high-dimensional features for improving the accuracy of face recognition. In this paper, we contributed to this aspect by presenting an optimal way of learning local image descriptors that we applied in building unsupervised face representations. The descriptor, which our face representation builds on, is based on the recent Binarized Statistical Image Features (BSIF). We showed that by learning the BSIF descriptors regionally from distinct face parts results in a very discriminative representation. In boosting up the recognition performance, we empirically approved the remarkable role of the whitening PCA (WPCA) transformation. To boost up it even further, before applying WPCA, we proposed a preprocessing step that we named histogram smoothing. We showed the histogram smoothing operation is accomplishable via a simple matrix-vector product.

Our proposed face representation yielded outperforming results compared with the current state-of-the-art on the widely known FERET benchmark. This was achieved without any kind of feature fusion or image flipping strategies that are used by most of the earlier best methods. To complement this, after slight modifications, the face representation proved highly competitive in more demanding face recognition scenarios. As for these scenarios, the method was inspected following the guidelines of the unsupervised evaluation category of the updated LFW benchmark protocol yielding promising results.

References

1. Turk, M., Pentland, A.P.: Face recognition using eigenfaces. In: CVPR, pp. 586–591 (1991)
2. Belhumeur, P.N., Hespanha, J.P., Kriegman, D.: Eigenfaces vs. fisherfaces: Recognition using class specific linear projection. IEEE TPAMI **19**(7), 711–720 (1997)
3. Zhao, W., Chellappa, R., Phillips, P.J., Rosenfeld, A.: Face recognition: A literature survey. ACM Comput. Surveys **35**(4), 399–458 (2000)
4. Huang, G.B., Lee, H., Learned-Miller, E.: Learning hierarchical representations for face verification with convolutional deep belief networks. In: CVPR (2012)
5. Chen, D., Cao, X., Wang, L., Wen, F., Sun, J.: Bayesian face revisited: a joint formulation. In: Fitzgibbon, A., Lazebnik, S., Perona, P., Sato, Y., Schmid, C. (eds.) ECCV 2012, Part III. LNCS, vol. 7574, pp. 566–579. Springer, Heidelberg (2012)
6. Hussain, S.u., Napoleon, T., Jurie, F.: Face recognition using local quantized patterns. In: BMVC (2012)
7. Chen, D., Cao, X., Wen, F., Sun, J.: Blessing of dimensionality: High-dimensional feature and its efficient compression for face verification. In: CVPR, pp. 3025–3032 (2013)
8. Lei, Z., Pietikäinen, M., Li, S.Z.: Learning discriminant face descriptor. IEEE TPAMI **36**(2), 289–302 (2014)
9. Sun, Y., Wang, X., Tang, X.: Hybrid deep learning for face verification. In: ICCV, pp. 1489–1496 (2013)
10. Cao, X., Wipf, D., Wen, F., Duan, G.: A practical transfer learning algorithm for face verification. In: ICCV, pp. 3208–3215 (2013)
11. Barkan, O., Weill, J., Wolf, L., Aronowitz, H.: Fast high dimensional vector multiplication for face recognition. In: ICCV, pp. 1960–1967 (2013)
12. Parkhi, O.M., Simonyan, K., Vedaldi, A., Zisserman, A.: A compact and discriminative face track descriptor. In: CVPR (2014)
13. Taigman, Y., Yang, M., Ranzato, M.A., Wolf, L.: Deepface: Closing the gap to human-level performance in face verification. In: CVPR (2014)
14. Phillips, P., Wechsler, H., Huang, J., Rauss, P.J.: The FERET database and evaluation procedure for face recognition algorithms. IVC **16**(5), 295–306 (1998)
15. Huang, G.B., Learned-Miller, E.: Labeled faces in the wild: Updates and new reporting procedures: Technical report UM-CS-2014-003. University of Massachusetts, Amherst (2014)

16. Xie, S., Shan, S., Chen, X., Chen, J.: Fusing local patterns of Gabor magnitude and phase for face recognition. IEEE TIP **19**(5), 1349–1361 (2010)
17. Kannala, J., Rahtu, E.: BSIF: Binarized statistical image features. In: ICPR, pp. 1364–1366 (2012)
18. Ahonen, T., Hadid, A., Pietikäinen, M.: Face description with local binary patterns: Application to face recognition. IEEE TPAMI **28**(12), 2037–2041 (2006)
19. Li, S.Z., Jain, A.K. (eds.): Handbook of Face Recognition, 2nd Edition. Springer (2011)
20. Huang, G.B., Mattar, M., Lee, H., Learned-Miller, E.: Learning to align from scratch. In: NIPS, pp. 773–781 (2012)
21. Coates, A., Lee, H., Ng, A.: An analysis of single-layer networks un unsupervised feature learning. Ann Arbor **1001**, 48109 (2010)
22. Cao, Z., Yin, Q., Tang, X., Sun, J.: Face recognition with learning-based descriptor. In: CVPR, pp. 2707–2714 (2010)
23. Hyvärinen, A.: Fast and robust fixed-point algorithms for independent component analysis. IEEE TNN **10**(3), 626–634 (1999)
24. Philbin, J., Chum, O., Isard, M., Sivic, J., Zisserman, A.: Lost in quantization: improving particular object retrieval in large scale image databases. In: CVPR, pp. 1–8 (2008)
25. Ylioinas, J., Hadid, A., Hong, X., Pietikäinen, M.: Age estimation using local binary pattern kernel density estimate. In: Petrosino, A. (ed.) ICIAP 2013, Part I. LNCS, vol. 8156, pp. 141–150. Springer, Heidelberg (2013)
26. Aitchison, J., Aitken, C.: Multivariate binary discrimination by the kernel method. Biometrika **63**(3), 413–420 (1976)
27. Vu, N.S., Caplier, A.: Enhanced patterns of oriented edge magnitudes for face recognition and image matching. IEEE TIP **21**(3), 1352–1365 (2012)
28. Raiko, T., Ilin, A., Karhunen, J.: Principal component analysis for large scale problems with lots of missing values. In: Kok, J.N., Koronacki, J., Lopez de Mantaras, R., Matwin, S., Mladenič, D., Skowron, A. (eds.) ECML 2007. LNCS (LNAI), vol. 4701, pp. 691–698. Springer, Heidelberg (2007)
29. Arandjelović, R., Zisserman, A.: Three things everyone should know to improve object retrieval. In: CVPR (2012)
30. Huang, C., Zhu, S., Yu, K.: Large scale strongly supervised ensemble metric learning, with applications to face verification and retrieval TR115 (2007)
31. Wolf, L., Hassner, T., Taigman, Y.: Effective unconstrained face recognition by combining multiple descriptors and learned background statistics. IEEE TPAMI **33**(10), 1978–1990 (2011)
32. Tan, X., Triggs, B.: Enhanced local texture feature sets for face recognition under difficult lighting conditions. IEEE TIP **19**(6), 1635–1650 (2010)
33. Bolme, D.S., Beveridge, J.R., Teixeira, M., Draper, B.A.: The CSU face identification evaluation system: its purpose, features, and structure. In: Crowley, J.L., Piater, J.H., Vincze, M., Paletta, L. (eds.) ICVS 2003. LNCS, vol. 2626, pp. 304–313. Springer, Heidelberg (2003)
34. Ruiz-del Solar, J., Verschae, R., Correa, M.: Recognition of faces in unconstrained environments: A comparative study. EURASIP Journal on Advances in Signal Processing (2009)
35. Lei, Z., Yi, D., Li, S.Z.: Local gradient order pattern for face representation and recognition. In: ICPR (2014)
36. Yi, D., Lei, Z., Li, S.Z.: Towards pose robust face recognition. In: CVPR (2013)
37. Arashloo, S., Kittler, J.: Class-specific kernel fusion of multiple descriptors for face verification using multiscale binarised statistical image features. IEEE TFS (2014)

38. Seo, H.J., Milanfar, P.: Face verification using the lark representation. IEEE TIFS **6**(4), 1275–1286 (2011)
39. Sharma, G., ul Hussain, S., Jurie, F.: Local higher-order statistics (LHS) for texture categorization and facial analysis. In: Fitzgibbon, A., Lazebnik, S., Perona, P., Sato, Y., Schmid, C. (eds.) ECCV 2012, Part VII. LNCS, vol. 7578, pp. 1–12. Springer, Heidelberg (2012)
40. Arashloo, S.R., Kittler, J.: Efficient processing of mrfs for unconstrained-pose face recognition. In: BTAS (2013)

Gender Classification by LUT Based Boosting of Overlapping Block Patterns

Rakesh Mehta[1]([✉]), Manuel Günther[2], and Sébastien Marcel[2]

[1] Tampere University of Technology, Tampere, Finland
rakesh.mehta@tut.fi
[2] Idiap Research Institute, Martigny, Switzerland
{manuel.guenther,marcel}@idiap.ch

Abstract. The paper addresses the problem of gender classification from face images. For feature extraction, we propose discrete Overlapping Block Patterns (OBP), which capture the characteristic structure from the image at various scales. Using integral images, these features can be computed in constant time. The feature extraction at multiple scales results in a high dimensionality and feature redundancy. Therefore, we apply a boosting algorithm for feature selection and classification. Look-Up Tables (LUT) are utilized as weak classifiers, which are appropriate to the discrete nature of the OBP features. The experiments are performed on two publicly available data sets, Labeled Faces in the Wild (LFW) and MOBIO. The results demonstrate that Local Binary Pattern (LBP) features with LUT boosting outperform the commonly used block-histogram-based LBP approaches and that OBP features gain over Multi-Block LBP (MB-LBP) features.

1 Introduction

Gender classification is an important task that finds its applications in a number of areas such as security, surveillance, criminology, multimedia, etc. A number of biometric cues have been used for this purpose, such as face images [1], person gait [2], fingerprints [4], speech or the combination of face and fingerprints [3]. In this paper, we focus on gender classification from face images, as these can be easily captured and does not require special devices, but only an ordinary camera.

A number of approaches have been proposed for gender classification from the face images. The classification pipeline from images consists of two main steps: feature extraction and classification. A variety of features have been used for gender classification, such as Haar [5], SIFT [6], Local Binary Patterns (LBP) [7], Shape Context [6], Local Directional Patterns (LDP) [9], Interlaced Derivative Pattern (IDP) [8], or Local Circular Patterns (LCP) [10]. Some approaches have also used a combination of these features to capture discriminative information from the images [6,7]. Originally, LBP is a local texture descriptor. However, because of its high discriminative power and computational simplicity, it has been applied in face processing tasks such as face detection [19], face recognition

© Springer International Publishing Switzerland 2015
R.R. Paulsen and K.S. Pedersen (Eds.): SCIA 2015, LNCS 9127, pp. 530–542, 2015.
DOI: 10.1007/978-3-319-19665-7_45

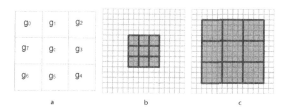

Fig. 1. (a) The notation used for LBP (b) The MB-LBP blocks for block size 2×2 (c) MB-LBP blocks for block size 4×4

[16], emotion recognition [18], and also for gender classification LBP and its variants have shown promising results.

For classification, Linear Discriminant Analysis (LDA), Nearest Neighbor (NN), Radial Basis Function network and Support Vector Machines (SVM) were studied [11]. The results show that SVM outperforms the other algorithms only by a small margin. On the other hand, when the number of features are high, boosting has shown good performance [5], [26]. The advantage of boosting compared to the other classifiers is that it makes the classification process faster, as only a relatively small number of discriminative features are required during the testing phase. For a comparative study of different approaches, we refer the readers to [17].

LBP features are computed by taking the difference of the pixels in a restricted neighborhood and, therefore, they are not able to capture information at different scales. To incorporate information at higher scales, Multi-Block LBP (MB-LBP) was proposed [15], which takes difference of block sums instead of pixels. However, as the block size increases, the distance between the adjacent blocks becomes too large to capture the relation with respect to its neighborhood. Thus, to efficiently include the relation from the surrounding even at larger scales, in this paper we propose Overlapping Block Patterns (OBP), which capture local image gradient information at different scales from the image. Using integral images, these features can be computed in constant time.

To select only a relatively small number of discriminative features, we apply boosting. We use Taylor Boosting [12], which is a generalized algorithm that supports a family of loss functions and first and second order optimization. Taylor Boosting has been combined with Look-Up Tables (LUT) as weak classifiers [20] to design classification algorithms specifically for non-metric and discrete features such as OBP. The experiments on two challenging face image databases demonstrate that the proposed OBP features outperform not only LBP, but also MB-LBP features. The proposed algorithm also has the advantage of low complexity, as the features are computed in constant time and the classification using boosting is only linearly dependent on the number of weak classifiers.

The remaining of this paper is organized as follows: In Section 2, we start with discussing LBP and MB-LBP features, then we present the novel OBP features. Finally, gender classification using LUT based boosting is discussed. The experiments are performed on two public data sets following their standard protocols and the results are reported in Section 3. Finally, Section 4 concludes the paper.

2   OBP based Gender Classification

In this section we first discuss the LBP features and its extension MB-LBP. Then, we propose the novel OBP features that capture discriminative information of blocks from the immediate neighborhood. Finally, we present the LUT based boosting algorithm, which can be used with discrete features like LBP, MB-LBP and OBP.

2.1   LBP and MB-LBP

The original LBP operator captures the relation of a pixel with its neighboring 3×3 pixels. It is computed by taking the difference of a pixel around it neighbors as:

$$F(g_c) = \sum_{i=0}^{7} s(g_i - g_c) \cdot 2^i \tag{1}$$

with:

$$s(x) = \begin{cases} 1 : x \geq 0 \\ 0 : x < 0 \end{cases} \tag{2}$$

where g_c denotes the central pixel, for which the LBP feature is computed, and g_i are the neighboring pixels. Fig. 1(a) shows the notation used for the position of the pixels for LBP. If an LBP feature is to be computed at location (x, y) in image I, the parameters of (1) and (2) are given as $g_c = I(x, y)$, $g_0 = I(x - 1, y - 1)$, $g_1 = I(x, y-1) \ldots g_7 = I(x-1, y)$. Although fast to compute and discriminative, these features are sensitive to noise as they are computed by taking the difference of the individual pixels. Another limitation of these features is their inability to capture the information at variable scale size.

To overcome these limitations, MB-LBP features have been proposed which use rectangular blocks, instead of the pixel values. The relation between the adjacent blocks is given by (1) and (2), however, in this case the parameters g_c and g_i represent the sum of the blocks instead of individual pixel intensity. The sum of the pixels intensities for a block of size $L \times L$ is represented as:

$$S_L(x, y) = \sum_{i=0}^{L-1} \sum_{j=0}^{L-1} I(x + i, y + j), \tag{3}$$

where (x, y) represent the upper left corner of the block and it is used to denote its position. Thus, for MB-LBP the parameters of (1) are defined as: $g_c = S_L(x, y)$, $g_0 = S_L(x - L, y - L)$, $g_1 = S_L(x, y - L)$, $\ldots g_7 = S_L(x - L, y)$. The blocks for MB-LBP feature for different block sizes $(L = 2, 4)$ are shown in Fig. 1.

The key idea behind LBP based features is to compute the first order derivative of the central values along the eight different neighboring directions and encode the sign of these derivatives. Without loss of generality, in the following we consider the derivative along a single direction for LBP and MB-LBP features at a position (x, y) in image I, but the same discussion applies for all other directions as well. The derivative is considered along the direction of g_0, thus it is given as $g_c - g_0$, which corresponds to the first bit during the computation of the LBP or MB-LBP feature value. For LBP feature computation, derivative along the direction of g_0 pixel can be represented as:

$$g_c - g_0 = I(x, y) - I(x - 1, y - 1). \tag{4}$$

Hence, only the variations in the immediate neighborhood around the point (x, y) are observed.

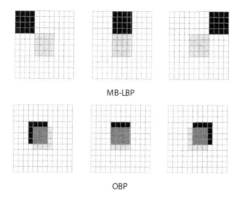

MB-LBP

OBP

Fig. 2. Difference in block positioning between MB-LBP and OBP

In case of MB-LBP feature computation, the derivative along g_0 is given as:

$$g_c - g_0 = S_L(x, y) - S_L(x - L, y - L). \tag{5}$$

Comparing (4) and (5) it can be observed that both take the difference of function at a point with its neighbor. However, in (5) the difference of the function is taken at step size L. Although the direction of the derivative in MB-LBP is similar to LBP, it is not taken from the immediate neighborhood like in case of LBP. For larger block size this step increases substantially and it does not provide the accurate estimate of the derivative at that point any longer.

2.2 OBP

The proposed OBP features capture the relation of the block with respect to its immediate neighborhood. Similar to the LBP and MB-LBP features, the derivative is computed along eight directions corresponding to the adjacent neighboring blocks and the sign of the derivative is encoded by multiplying with unique

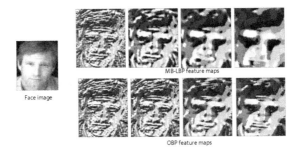

Fig. 3. The face image and the feature maps generated from this image using OBP and MB-LBP features at scales $L = 1, 3, 5, 7$ (left to right)

weight. However, unlike the MB-LBP features the derivative is taken at finer rate, which captures the details around the block in a more efficient manner.

To compute the OBP feature at coordinate (x, y) in image I, the parameters g_c and g_i of (1) are defined as $g_c = S_L(x, y)$, $g_0 = S_L(x - 1, y - 1)$, $g_1 = S_L(x, y - 1)$, $\ldots$ $g_7 = S_L(x - 1, y)$. It should be noted that the only difference in the definition of these parameters between MB-LBP and OBP is the step size of L for MB-LBP and 1 for OBP. To further illustrate this difference, the blocks and their positions are explained in Fig. 2 for block of size 4×4. It can be observed that the neighboring blocks overlap with the center block in case of OBP. The light gray color represents the central blocks, black indicates the neighboring block and the dark gray represents the overlapping area. For block size L the overlap is $L - 1$, which is the maximum possible overlap between two blocks in any direction. This overlap helps in capturing the subtle difference from the neighborhood of the blocks and was empirically found to obtain the best classification performance.

Fig. 3 shows the face image and the MB-LBP and OBP feature images for different block sizes $L = 1, 3, 5$ and 7. It can be observed that for small sizes, both the MB-LBP and OBP capture the fine details and the feature images are similar. In fact, for block size $L = 1$, LBP, MB-LBP and OBP are identical. However, as the block size increases, more differences between the feature images can be observed. The OBP feature images at higher scales show finer details when compared to the MB-LBP images. Furthermore, at higher scales the border pruning effect in case of the MB-LBP features is evident. The resulting feature image for MB-LBP features is always $3L - 1$ pixels shorter in each dimension because features cannot be computed for the first L and last $2L - 1$ pixels in each dimension. In opposition, for OBP only $L + 1$ features are removed at the border, the difference can best be seen in the feature image at scale 7 in Fig. 3.

In order to capture the micro-structure at different scales, we extract OBP features at various block sizes. We restrict the features to square shape because we empirically observed that they are sufficient to capture the block based information. However, the features can easily be generalized to rectangular shape, which results in a substantial increase in the number of features and, therewith, in the time required for training – without any significant improvement of the classification performance.

2.3 LUT based Taylor Boosting

For gender classification, features are extracted at multiple block sizes from the face images. This results in a large number of features even for small images. Most of these features are redundant and correlated. In order to select a small number of highly discriminative features, we apply boosting using the Taylor Boosting algorithm [12]. The main characteristics of the applied boosting algorithms are: 1) Taylor Boosting has shown to perform better than the more commonly used AdaBoost algorithm, 2) Look-Up Tables (LUT) are used as the weak classifier, which is appropriate to the proposed discrete OBP features, 3) the algorithm is very general and support different kind of loss functions and optimization strategies

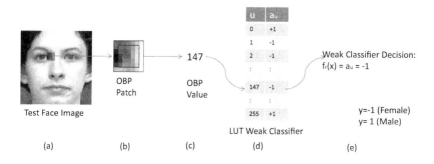

Fig. 4. Decision of a single weak LUT classifier using OBP features: (a) Test image with the feature position (b) the extracted block and its immediate neighborhood (c) the OBP feature value computed for this feature (d) the LUT of the weak classifier (e) the weak decision for the weak classifier

Let the labeled training samples be represented as $\{(\mathbf{x_n}, y_n)_{n=1:N}\}$, where $y_n \in \{-1, 1\}$ denotes the class of the samples $\mathbf{x_n}$. The goal of the boosting algorithm is to build a strong classifier F as a weighted linear combination of R weak classifiers f_r:

$$F(\mathbf{x}) = \sum_{r=1}^{R} \alpha_r f_r(\mathbf{x}) \tag{6}$$

by minimizing some loss function $L(F) = \sum_n l(y_n, F(\mathbf{x_n}))$. Boosting can be interpreted as gradient descent in the functional space, where at each iteration a weak classifier is added to minimize the local loss. Taylor Boosting was proposed as a generalized boosting algorithm that can support first and second order optimization and a variety of loss functions. In this paper, we use Taylor Boosting

Data: Training samples, weak classifier f_i, loss $L(F)$
Result: Strong classifier F
initialization F = 0
for $r = 1$ to $r \leq R$ **do**
    Select the weak classifier $f_r = f(\mathbf{x}; d, a)$
    $d^* = \arg \min\limits_{d} - \sum\limits_{u} \left| \sum\limits_{n, \mathbf{x_n} = u} L'_n(F) \right|$
    $a_u = - \sum\limits_{n, \mathbf{x_n}, d^* = u} L'_n(F)$
    Compute weight using line search: $\alpha_r = \arg \min\limits_{\alpha} L(F + \alpha f_r)$
    Update strong classifier: $F \leftarrow F + \alpha_r f_r$
end
return F

Algorithm 1. Taylor Boosting using LUT as weak classifier.

with Look-Up Table as weak classifiers and logistic loss to optimize expectation loss formulation [20].

An important contribution of the paper is to introduce Look-Up Tables (LUT) as the weak classifier with the Taylor Boosting algorithm for gender classification. Commonly, the decision stump is used as the weak classifier in boosting [22]. Decision stump is parametrized by a threshold and assumes that the features are metric in nature. However, the proposed LBP based features are non-metric because each LBP value represents a distinct pattern that is discrete and bounded, feature values lie in the range of $[0, 255]$. Therefore, a stump classifier cannot be used as weak classifier for those features. Instead, we use a LUT as a weak classifier $f_r(\mathbf{x})$, which selects a single feature and uses it for predicting the class of the test sample. The weak classifier $f_r(\mathbf{x})$ is parametrized by a feature index d and a look-up table a. Therefore, the parametrized form of the weak classifier is represented as $f_r(\mathbf{x}; d, a)$, and on each round of boosting the parameters d, a and the weight α_r of the weak classifier are determined. The feature index represents size L of the OBP feature and its position (x, y) in the image, while the LUT has 256 entries and each entry a_u corresponds to a specific discrete value of the feature. The value a_u gives the weak classification decision for a sample based only on the feature index d. The training algorithm for the binary classification problem, e. g., gender classification is given in Algorithm 1. For more detailed analysis of the boosting algorithm please refer to [20].

Fig. 4 shows the classification using LUT for a single weak classifier during testing. The specific feature corresponding to the classifier is extracted from the image and the feature value is computed. This feature value is looked up in the LUT to make the decision for the current weak classifier. The final decision incorporates a linear combination of these individual decisions (Eq. (6)) and compares the result with a certain threshold.

3 Experiments

Experiments are conducted on two publicly available large face data sets: MOBIO [23] and Labeled Faces in Wild (LFW) [24]. In this section, we first provide brief information about the data sets and the protocols used for testing. Afterwards, the experimental setup is specified and, finally, the results are presented.

3.1 Data set and Protocol

To evaluate the performance in the uncontrolled setting, we use the data sets Labeled Faces in the Wild (LFW) and MOBIO.

LFW consists of 13,233 images of celebrities acquired in uncontrolled environments leading to high variability in terms of pose, illumination and facial expressions. Experiments are conducted using the BeFIT protocol,[1] in which the images are randomly divided into five subsets and leave-one-out cross validation is performed. Thus, in each split, four subsets of images are used for training and the fifth is used for testing. The final performance is reported as the average accuracy over the five rounds.

The MOBIO data set consists of 61 hours of audio-visual data of 150 people captured within 12 different sessions. This data set is challenging as the images are captured using mobile device and, therefore, the samples are noisy. Here, we use only facial images that have been extracted from these videos [23]. The total number of images is above 27,000, evenly divided into subsets for training, development and testing. The training samples are used for learning the strong classifier, the development set is used to determine the threshold to minimize the error and the final unbiased accuracy is reported on the test set.

The evaluation metrics used in our work are classification accuracy, true positive rate (TPR) and true negative rate (TNR) defined as [17]:

$$TPR = \frac{TP}{P}, \quad TNR = \frac{TN}{N}, \quad \text{Accuracy} = \frac{TP+TN}{P+N}, \tag{7}$$

where TP and TN are the number of samples correctly classified as positive (i. e. male) or negative (i. e. female), respectively, and P and N are the total numbers of positive and negative samples. Furthermore, we used a variant of the receiver operating characteristic (ROC) curve that plots the fraction of males classified correctly over the fraction of females classified incorrectly.

3.2 Experimental Setup

The images from both data sets are cropped, rotated and geometrically normalized based on the eye locations, which are hand-labeled[2] for the MOBIO

---

[1] http://fipa.cs.kit.edu/431.php
[2] http://www.idiap.ch/resource/biometric

database and automatically detected[3] for LFW. The size of the images is set to 36×36 in all the experiments, based on the results from [17], where the best accuracy was reported for this size. The inter-ocular distance is set to half of the images width, having eye positions located at 14 pixels from top, see Fig. 4(a) for an example. After obtaining the normalized face images, a photometric normalization [21] is performed.

In our experiments on gender classification, the results are reported using four different algorithms:

- PCA + LDA: Principle Component Analysis (PCA) is applied on the raw image pixels to retain 98% of the variance and Linear Discriminant Analysis (LDA) is used as classifier. Although it seems a naive approach, it has shown promising results for gender classification [13].
- LBPHS + LDA: Each face image is divided into 6×6 blocks each of size 6×6 pixels. The uniform LBP features are computed for each block and histograms are obtained. The histograms are concatenated to form the feature vector, whose dimensionality is reduced with PCA as explained above. Again, LDA is used as the classifier.
- MB-LBP + Boosting: Multi-Block LBP features are extracted from the face images using square blocks of sizes 1×1 to 7×7. Strong LUT classifiers are obtained after 800 rounds of boosting.
- OBP + Boosting: Overlapping Binary Pattern features are extracted from the face images using square blocks of sizes 1×1 to 7×7. Strong LUT classifiers after 800 rounds of boosting are used.

The development of the algorithms for this paper is done using the open source machine learning toolbox Bob [25]. The code to reproduce the results of the paper is publicly available[4].

3.3   Results

The results for both data sets and all tested algorithms are presented in Tables 1 and 2. They show the accuracies of the different approaches along with the TPR and TNR. For MOBIO it can be observed that the PCA + LDA achieves an accuracy of 80.04%, which is outperformed by the 81.58% of LBPHS + LDA. Clearly, LBP features work better than simple pixel values as used by PCA. Further, the MB-LBP features along with LUT based boosting achieves an accuracy of 83.24%, which is significantly higher than both the PCA and LBPHS features with LDA. The gain in performance can be attributed to the fact that the features are extracted at different scales and only discriminative features are utilized during classification. The OBP features further gain 2.11% compared to the MB-LBP features. Here, we would like to point out that the accuracy is not the mean of TPR and TNR because the number of male and female samples are different (see (7)).

---

[3] http://lear.inrialpes.fr/people/guillaumin/data.php

[4] The source code is available at https://pypi.python.org/pypi/bob.paper.SCIA2015.

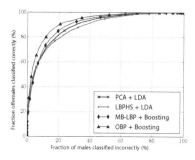 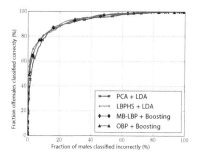

Fig. 5. ROC curves of all methods on the MOBIO and LFW test set

Table 1. Classification Results on the MOBIO test set

Method	Accuracy	TPR	TNR
PCA + LDA	80.04 %	78.02 %	83.95 %
LBPHS + LDA	81.58 %	**86.56 %**	71.89 %
MB-LBP + Boosting	83.24 %	85.82 %	78.21 %
OBP + Boosting	**85.35 %**	86.42 %	**83.28 %**

Table 2. Average classification Results on LFW

Method	Accuracy	TPR	TNR
PCA + LDA	85.92 %	86.08 %	85.39 %
LBPHS + LDA	88.06 %	88.73 %	**85.76 %**
MB-LBP + Boosting	90.42 %	97.12 %	67.32 %
OBP + Boosting	**90.81 %**	**97.49 %**	67.79%

The performance on LFW is in general higher than on MOBIO, most probably because the LFW protocol includes more training data. Additionally, the samples are less noisy and the illumination is not as adverse as in MOBIO. Nevertheless, a similar trend can be observed in the performances of the algorithms. The PCA and LBPHS features perform inferior to the MB-LBP and OBP features. The best overall performance is again achieved by OBP + Boosting, it gains more 5% and 2% over PCA + LDA and LBPHS + LDA, respectively. The OBP features outperform MB-LBP features by a small margin, which indicates that overlapping of features helps in capturing more discriminative information at higher scales.

To visualize the results on different operating points, the ROC curves for all the approaches are plotted and shown in Figures 5. From the ROC curves it can be observed that there is a substantial performance improvement by the LUT based approaches over the LDA based approaches. Further, among the LUT boosting methods, OBP features constantly outperform MB-LBP.

The testing using the proposed algorithm can be performed in real time because evaluating the strong classifier for a sample simply involves a weighted sum of the responses of the weak classifiers. Thus, the classification of a sample using R rounds of boosting involves R feature computations, evaluation of the weak classifier response for each feature and, finally, summation of these responses. As discussed earlier, the feature computation using integral images can be implemented at constant time. Evaluation of R weak classifiers involves R elementary LUT indexing operations and summations. Therefore, both the feature extraction and classification times are linear in the number of weak classifiers R. Note that the number of features involved in boosting are much less than LBPHS based approaches. For instance, in our experiments the boosting based approaches involves 800 feature computation, whereas the feature vector length for the LBPHS is 2124 $(= 6 \times 6 \times 59)$.

4   Conclusion

A new method for gender classification from face images is presented. Novel steps are introduced at both the feature extraction and the classification stage. Discrete Overlapping Block Features (OBP) features are proposed to overcome the limitation of LBP and MB-LBP features. These features are fast to compute, discriminative in nature and can capture information at variable size. OBP are combined with Look-Up Tables based Taylor Boosting. Experiments are performed on two large publicly available data sets using their standardized protocols. The results demonstrate that OBP features consistently outperform the MB-LBP features and the combination of these features with boosting outperforms LBP histogram based approaches. The proposed algorithm can be used in real time as the complexity is linear in the number of weak classifiers, which makes it fast and efficient.

Acknowledgments. The research leading to this paper has received funding from the Swiss National Science Foundation under the National Center of Competence in Research IM2 (www.im2.ch) and the FP7 European project BEAT (www.beat-eu.org).

References

1. Gao, W., Ai, H.: Face gender classification on consumer images in a multiethnic environment. In: Tistarelli, M., Nixon, M.S. (eds.) ICB 2009. LNCS, vol. 5558, pp. 169–178. Springer, Heidelberg (2009)
2. Li, X., Maybank, S.J., Yan, S., Tao, D., Xu, D.: Gait Components and their Application to Gender Recognition. IEEE Transactions on Systems, Man, and Cyber. 145–155 (2008)
3. Jain, A.K., Nandakumar, K., Lu, X., Park, U.: Integrating faces, fingerprints, and soft biometric traits for user recognition. In: Maltoni, D., Jain, A.K. (eds.) BioAW 2004. LNCS, vol. 3087, pp. 259–269. Springer, Heidelberg (2004)

4. Badawi, A., Mahfouz, M., Tadross, R., Jantz, R.: Fingerprint-based gender classification. In: International Conference on Image Processing, Computer Vision, and Pattern Recognition, pp. 41–46 (2006)
5. Shakhnarovich, G., Viola, P.A., Moghaddam, B.: A Unified Learning Framework for Real Time Face Detection and Classification. IEEE Int. Conf. on FG (2002)
6. Wang, J.-G., et al.: Boosting dense SIFT descriptors and shape contexts of face images for gender recognition. In: CVPRW (2010)
7. Yang, Z., Ai, H.: Demographic classification with local binary patterns. In: Lee, S.-W., Li, S.Z. (eds.) ICB 2007. LNCS, vol. 4642, pp. 464–473. Springer, Heidelberg (2007)
8. Shobeirinejad, A., Gao, Y.: Gender classification using interlaced derivative patterns. In: IEEE International Conference on Pattern Recognition (2010)
9. Jabid, T., Kabir, M.H., Chae, O.: Gender classification using local directional pattern (LDP). In: IEEE International Conference on Pattern Recognition (2010)
10. Wang, C., Huang, D., Wang, Y., Zhang, G.: Facial image-based gender classification using local circular patterns. In: IEEE ICPR, pp. 2432–2435 (2012)
11. Moghaddam, B., Yang, M.-H.: Learning Gender with Support Faces. IEEE Transactions on PAMI, 707–711 (2002)
12. Saberian, M.J., Masnadi-Shirazi, H., Vasconcelos, N.: Taylorboost: first and second-order boosting algorithms with explicit margin control. In: CVPR (2011)
13. Bekios-Calfa, J., Buenaposada, J.M., Baumela, L.: Revisiting Linear Discriminant Techniques in Gender Recognition. IEEE Transactions on PAMI, 858–864 (2011)
14. Trefný, J., Matas, J.: Extended set of Local Binary Patterns for Rapid Object Detection. Computer Vision Winter Workshop (2010)
15. Liao, S.C., Zhu, X.X., Lei, Z., Zhang, L., Li, S.Z.: Learning multi-scale block local binary patterns for face recognition. In: Lee, S.-W., Li, S.Z. (eds.) ICB 2007. LNCS, vol. 4642, pp. 828–837. Springer, Heidelberg (2007)
16. Ahonen, T., Hadid, A., Pietikinen, M.: Face recognition with local binary patterns. In: Computer Vision, pp. 469–481. Springer (2004)
17. Mäkinen, E., Raisamo, R.: Evaluation of Gender Classification Methods with Automatically Detected and Aligned Faces. IEEE Transactions on Pattern Analysis and Machine Intelligence, 541–547 (2008)
18. Zhao, G., Pietikainen, M.: Dynamic Texture Recognition using Local Binary Patterns with an Application to Facial Expressions. IEEE TPAMI (2007)
19. Jin, H., Liu, Q., Lu, H., Tong, X.: Face detection using improved LBP under bayesian framework. In: IEEE ICIG, pp. 306–309 (2004)
20. Atanasoaei, C.: Multivariate Boosting with Look-up-Tables for Face Processing. Ph.d thesis, EPFL (2012)
21. Tan, X., Triggs, B.: Enhanced local texture feature sets for face recognition under difficult lighting conditions. In: Zhou, S.K., Zhao, W., Tang, X., Gong, S. (eds.) AMFG 2007. LNCS, vol. 4778, pp. 168–182. Springer, Heidelberg (2007)
22. Viola, P., Jones, M.J.: Robust Real-time Face Detection. International Journal of Computer Vision, 137–154 (2004)
23. McCool, C., Marcel, S., Hadid, A., et al.: Bi-modal Person Recognition on a Mobile Phone: Using Mobile Phone Data. IEEE ICME Workshop on Hot Topics in Mobile Multimedia (2012)
24. Huang, G.B., Ramesh, M., Berg, T., Learned-Miller, E.: Labeled Faces in the Wild: A Database for Studying Face Recognition in Unconstrained Environments. Technical Report. University of Massachusetts, Amherst (2007)

25. Anjos, A., El Shafey, L., Wallace, R., Günther, M., McCool, C., Marcel, S.: Bob: a free Signal Processing and Machine Learning Toolbox for Researchers. In: ACM Multimedia, pp. 1449–1452 (2012)
26. Wu, B., Haizhou, A., Huang, C.: LUT-based adaboost for gender classification. In: Audio and Video Based Biometric Person Authentication. Springer, Berlin Heidelberg (2003)

Author Index

Printed in the United States
By Bookmasters